# HIGHER EDUCATION:
## Handbook of Theory and Research

### Volume XII

# HIGHER EDUCATION:

## Handbook of Theory and Research

### Volume XII

Edited by

**John C. Smart**

*University of Memphis*

Published under the sponsorship of
The Association for Institutional Research (AIR)
and
The Association for the Study of Higher Education (ASHE)

**AGATHON PRESS**
**New York**

© 1997 by Agathon Press
5648 Riverdale Avenue
Bronx, NY 10471-2106

ISBN: 0-87586-118-0 (paper)
ISBN: 0-87586-119-9 (cloth)
ISSN: 0882-4126

Library of Congress Catalog Card Number: 86-642109

Printed in the United States

# Contents

# The Contributors

BOB BOICE is professor of psychology at the State University of New York at Stony Brook and former head (for 16 years) of faculty development centers at that campus and others. He has won honors for teaching courses such as the history of psychology but he is far prouder of the teaching awards won by the students and junior faculty he has mentored.

JOHN M. BRAXTON is Associate Professor in the Department of Educational Leadership at Peabody College, Vanderbilt University. His research interests include the college student experience with an emphasis on student college choice and student departure. His research on these topics has been published in the *Journal of College Student Development, Research in Higher Education, The Review of Higher Education*, and other volumes of *Higher Education: Handbook of Theory and Research.*

CORINNA A. ETHINGTON is a professor of educational research in the Department of Counseling, Educational Psychology and Research at the University of Memphis where she teaches statistics and research methods. Her research interests are within the broad domain of gender differences at all educational levels, with a decided focus on performance, persistence, and achievement in mathematics and scientific fields.

IRWIN FELLER is Director of the Graduate School of Public Policy and Administration and Professor of Economics at the Pennsylvania State University, where he has been on the faculty since 1963. His current research interests include the evaluation of federal aqnd state technology programs, the economicsd of acadmic research, and the university's role in technology-based economic development. He is the author of one book (*Universities and State Governments*) and more than 75 refereed journal articles, book chapters, and research reports, as well as of numerous papers presented to academic, progessional, and policy audiences. His research is supported by grants from the National Science Foundation and several other governmental and independent funding sources. He has also been a consultant to the President's Office of Science and Technology, the Ford Foundation, and the National Institute of Standards and Technology and many other organizations.

PHILO HUTCHESON is assistant professor of higher education at Georgia State University, College of Education, Educational Policy Studies Department. He earned his Ph.D. at The University of Chicago, and his research interests include the role of professors in institutional governance, the history of higher education, and public policy concerning higher education. Prior to becoming a professor, Dr. Hutcheson spent nearly twenty years in college administration. Most recently he was an assistant academic dean at Hamline University in Minnesota, with responsibility for liaison between the academic administration and students.

ROBERT M. JOHNSON, JR. is currently the Director of Institutional Research at Belmont University, Nashville, Tennessee. He is a doctoral candidate in the Higher Education Administration Program at Peabody College, Vanderbvilt University. He earned his first doctorate in Hebrew Bible studies, focusing on linguistics. His combined research interests include discourse analysis, both textual and conversational, and ideological criticism.

JEFFERY E. OLSON, an associate professor of education at St. Joh's University, New York, focusesw his research on the economics of doctoral universities, particularly on questions of cost and productivity. He is a member of the editorial board of *Research in Higher Education* and has taught at Stanford University and the University of Utah. His terminal degrees include a Ph.D. in Administration and Policy Analysis from Stanford, where he emphasized organizational theory and economics, and a J.D. from the University of Utah, where he later served as as the Associate Dean of Law.

ANNA V. SHAW SULLIVAN is a doctoral candidate in the Higher Education Administration Program at Peabody College, Vanderbilt University. Her research interests include the college student experience, faculty issues, and institutional/environmental relationships. Prior to beginning her doctoral studies, Sullivan worked in higher education administration for 10 years. She has co-authored two book chapters and published an article in *The Journal of General Education.*

RICHARD A. VOORHEES is director of research and planning for the Colorado Community College and Occupational Education System. His administrative career spans a variety of institutions including tribally controlled, suburban, and urban community colleges, a research university and a comprehensive four-year institution. He has served as an academic dean, chief student affairs officer, and director of institutional research. His publications concentrate on student outcomes, including student persistence, assessment, financial aid, and marketing research. He is currently a consulting editor for *Research in Higher Education* and associate community college editor for *Higher Education: Handbook of Theory and Research.*

PHILLIP K. WOOD is an Associate Professor of Psychology at the University of Missouri-Columbia. His research and teaching interests include quantitative psychology (particularly structural equation models, statistical models of growth and change, and longitudinal methodology), developmental psychology (particularly adult cognitive development), and the assessment of outcomes of higher education. Prior to coming to Missouri, he was a former visiting research scientist at the Max-Planck-Institute for Human Development in Berlin, Germany, and a National Institute of Aging post-doctoral trainee specializing in longitudinal statistical methods at Pennsylvania State University.

WILLIAM ZUMETA is an associate professor in the Graduate School of Public Affairs and the College of Eduction at the University of Washington. His academic interests center on public budgeting and policy analysis, with a particular focus on education. His recent research and writing have focused on public policy and private higher education and on the policy dilemmas posed by the conflict between higher education access imperatives and the fiscal restrictions confronting states. His research has been supported by numerous federal and state agencies and national foundations and organizations, including the National Science Foundation, the U.S. Department of Education, the Lilly Endowment, and the Pew Charitable Trusts. Professor Zumeta's articles have appeared in *The Journal of Higher Education* and other journals in the field, as well as journals in the policy and social sciences and various other outlets. He is the author or co-author of two books and is now at work on a book on public policy and private higher education.

# Technology Transfer from Universities

## Irwin Feller
### *The Pennsylvania State University*

## I. INTRODUCTION

Technology transfer has moved from a contested and peripheral activity among America's research universities to an accepted, indeed valued, part of core missions in the span of about 15 years. The change has been accompanied by pronouncements by university presidents and boards of trustees, revisions in institutional policies, establishment of new offices, expenditures of institutional funds, and alterations in faculty norms and attitudes. The change has produced traceable impacts on selected indicators of technology transfer, and discernible if incompletely traceable impacts on processes of technological innovation and national or regional competitiveness in economic growth.

This review is organized as follows. Section II presents the essay's analytical framework and develops the themes that permeate the selection and distillation of the works reviewed. Section III offers a summary overview of the policy history that placed the topic of academic technology transfer high on the agendas of government, industry, and university officials, and provides a brief exegesis into the definition of technology transfer.

Sections IV and V present what might variously be termed a reversed ordering of intervention and baseline outcomes, or point and counterpoint: the intent of these two sections is to (1) present the workings of both newer and earlier modes of transferring the findings from academic research to commercial uses, and (2) examine the extent to which they complement or compete with one another. Section IV presents recent findings on three of the most visible manifestations of the new order in university technology transfer: (a) patents, licensing activities, and start-ups; (b) university-industry and university-industry-government cooperative R&D programs; and (c) faculty attitudes toward increased involvement in technology transfer. Section V offers a reconsideration of two themes that permeate the problem-setting statements of the 1980s: (a) how the university's mix of applied and basic research activities affects its collaborative relationships with industry, and (b) the efficacy of traditional modes of technology transfer. In this section we also examine (c) industry assessments of the optimal role of universities as contributors to commercially oriented technological innovations. Section VI concludes with an interim assessment of accomplishments to date.

The essay concentrates on the post-1980 literature, referring to other summary works to cover the copious literature of the 1980s. It casts a wide net, thereby concentrating on identifying salient lines of analysis, findings, and policy implications without attempting full or encyclopedic treatment of the issues it notes. Finally, as with the recent literature reviewed here, the essay runs the twofold, if opposite, risks of being outdated by rapidly changing events and of being premature in its conclusions by not allowing for long gestating processes to mature.

## II. ANALYTICAL FRAMEWORK

Three themes—analytical, historical, and evaluative—shape this review. First, it emphasizes processes of technological innovation. Changes in institutional policies and organizational structures to foster the commercial use of academic research, and the effects of the commercialization of academic science on the selection of research projects, the research-graduate education nexus, and the spawning of conflict-of-interest and conflict-of-commitment situations—staples of the literature of the 1980s—are noted, but treated only in passing. Rather, attention is focused on the ways in which the several forms of knowledge emanating from academic research are transferred from the campus to the firm, the value(s) placed by (different) firms on (different) forms of knowledge, and the economic impact of university initiatives.

The rationale for this approach is that issues of university missions and organizational arrangements have already received extensive treatment, while critical examination of what these efforts have amounted to has received less attention. As Fairweather (1988) has written: "Little evidence exists to support or contradict claims about the effectiveness or impact of the newer industry-university relationships" (Fairweather, 1988, p. 13).

Second, the review places the events and commensurate changes of the 1980s into a more historical perspective on the influences shaping relationships between academic researchers and industrial firms. Reflecting recent studies that emphasize helix-like patterns in the waxing and waning of industrial and academic research collaborations, the review seeks to isolate what is new in the form, magnitude, and impact of technology transfer (and thus presumably caused by the policy and program innovations of the 1980s) from the preexisting and continuing means by which knowledge generated by academic research is transmitted to and found of value by firms. In this respect, it treats recent legislative, programmatic, and institutional initiatives as interventions into a continuously evolving set of relationships between industry and universities.

Third, it is evaluative. This tone reflects, in part, the perspective just noted—

the need for assessment and, in part, the programmatic form of support for many recent university initiatives in technology transfer. Federal and state governments financed a substantial portion of the increase in university-industry-government cooperation in research and development; this is especially true of hallmark programs such as the National Science Foundation's Engineering Research Centers or state technology development programs, such as Ohio's Edison Program or New York's Centers for Advanced Technology. The passage of time has increased the demands on the sponsors of these programs for documented accomplishments. The result has been a recent body of formal or semiformal program evaluations.[1]

These evaluations, methodological caveats aside, offer more systematic and larger-scale empirical inquiries than were offered in earlier studies. These studies, represented by Peters and Fusfeld (1983), Johnson (1984), Haller (1984), SRI (1986), Etzkowitz (1989), and Matkin (1990), and summarized effectively by Fairweather (1988), examined the birth processes of the expanded roles for university technology transfer. Accordingly, they focused on and developed typologies of technology transfer roles, modes of delivery, changes in federal legislation and court decisions associated with intellectual property rights, the establishment and restructuring of university patent and technology licensing offices, and the normative issues associated with university and faculty involvement in newer, expanded, and more institutionally aggressive forms of technology transfer. They examined the mutual direct benefits to universities and firms and the larger societal benefits that would flow from improved cooperation (Praeger and Omenn, 1980; Baldwin and Green, 1984). They also catalogued the cultural, organizational, and economic barriers held to be keeping universities and firms from entering into what were otherwise seemingly beneficial collaborations (Geisler and Rubenstein, 1989). Written as events were unfolding, they were often limited to reporting self-congratulatory announcements by the universities or governmental agencies promoting expanded university roles in technology transfer and expanded university-industry cooperation.

The essay's working premise is that with the exception of some continuing critics (e.g., Slaughter, 1990), an expanded form of technology transfer is institutionalized within most research universities. However, use of this premise is not meant to suggest that the current equilibrium is either socially desirable or economically efficient. Indeed, the equibalance of internal and external influences on

---

[1]Relying on program evaluations to determine the magnitude and form of university contributions to technology transfer is not an unmixed blessing. Programs embody theories of technological change. If the underlying theory is inaccurate and incomplete, inaccurate or incomplete measures may be used. The result can be (and has been) concurrent applause for specific outcomes that may have limited economic impact (e.g., number of patents) or disappointment in the nonoccurrence of specific outcomes (e.g., job creation in manufacturing), and handsitting in the face of less visible positive impacts on other aspects of processes of technological innovation/economic growth (e.g., more efficient allocation of industrial R&D funds).

the university's newly assumed responsibilities for technology transfer is fragile. Within the American research university, as the legal and institutional changes initiated in the past decade begin to take hold, as new offices and people charged with responsibility for technology transfer become familiar parts of the campus setting within which faculty operate, and (following the theorem that new ideas triumph not by intellectual power but by the demise of adherents of earlier theories), as faculty socialized in earlier Veblenian norms to eschew commercial incentives in their selection of research agendas (Veblen, 1917) and Mertonian norms to openly communicate their findings in open literatures, retire, technology transfer becomes a routinized part of the internal workings of the research university. This new consensus is supported by episodic institutional successes in securing or licensing patents, increasing license and royalty revenues, launching new start-up firms based on faculty research, or breaking ground/acquiring new tenants for university-sponsored research parks.

This consensus appears strong enough to withstand contrary shocks such as accounts of faculty obfuscation of research findings that conflict with the launching of new firms based on their research, economically problematic investments by universities in start-up firms based on their faculty's research or research parks, and emerging legal battles between universities and their former technology licensing arms (Matkin, 1994; Finn, 1995). For the present at least, with some exception (such as that by the University of Arizona, which, following its payment of $4 million to settle a patent suit, has decided not to allow professors to create companies based on their research [Blumenstyk, 1995a]), universities show little inclination to reduce their commitments to expanded technology transfer missions and activities. Indeed, momentum still seems to be building as ever more universities don the mantle of responsibility for regional economic growth and assume new roles for technology transfer (Southern Technology Council, 1995).

At the same time, the external influences that induced universities to make these expanded commitments to technology transfer have abated. Draconian corporate downsizing and restructuring, improved U.S. export performance, strong U.S. economic performance in comparison with several major international competitors, and reassertion of U.S. technological leadership in selected high-technology industries, such as computer chips, have made international economic competitiveness a simmering but no longer boiling policy imperative. At both federal and state levels, activist government support of university-industry-government collaboration in civilian-oriented research and development has been called into question by ascendant Republican governors and congressional majorities. At both levels of government, the anticipation of launching new university-industry-government R&D partnerships has given way to increased demands for demonstrated economic returns. Program directors and universities have struggled to provide satisfactory quantitative responses to these demands, with only a few programs (for example, New York's Centers for Advanced Technology) offering systematic evidence of program benefits (Feller and Anderson, 1994). The result is that many such programs have experienced budgetary cutbacks, significant redirections, and threats of program termination (Eisinger, 1995). At the same time, industrial funding of academic R&D has stabilized in real dollars; current trends in industrial R&D, which rose from 3 to 7 percent of total academic R&D expenditures between 1971 and 1991 (which themselves increased by 74 percent in real dollars over this period), including the dismantling of central R&D laboratories, the shift to divisionally based research, and a shortening of time horizons, offer ambiguous portents regarding future funding. Although industry may speak of its increasing need for the research capabilities of universities, it shows little indication of underwriting significant increases in support in the near future (Larson, 1994).

This austere funding environment is now compounded by current projections of the dismantling or truncation of civilian-sector, mission-oriented federal R&D and stagnant or declining (in real dollars) federal government support for academic R&D, and contentions that the academic research system is overextended (U.S. Congress, Office of Technology Assessment, 1991; Government-University-Industry Research Roundtable, 1992). Subtly but steadily beneath an unchanging rhetoric, university technology transfer has become less a matter of responsiveness to national or state imperatives, and more one of institutionally initiated and maintained entrepreneurship.

## III. TECHNOLOGY TRANSFER FROM UNIVERSITIES: THE 1980S AND 1990S

### Policy History

As described in an extensive literature, the precipitating events in the early 1980s leading to the crystallization of university technology transfer were increased concern for America's international economic competitiveness, the systematic searching by industry for collaborative R&D partners, the reformulation of state economic development programs to focus on demand creation through technological innovation rather than cost-reducing subsidies (smokestack chasing), and court decisions establishing patent rights in genetic materials (*Diamond v. Chakrabarty*). Permeating these events and leading to heightened attention to universities' role in economic growth was the tighter intertwining of science and technology in the industries—computers, telecommunications, biotechnology—seen as growth sectors. As Richard Nelson has observed:

> ...with the rise of modern science-based technologies, much of science and much of technology have become intertwined....This intertwining, rather than serendipity, is the principal reason why, in many fields, university research is an important contributor to

technical advance, and universities as well as corporate labs are essential parts of the innovation system (Nelson, 1993, p. 7).

A consensus formed about the following propositions: America's basic industries were experiencing structural, not cyclical, contractions; its long-term competitive advantage lay in exploiting the "national" resource of research and development; and its "technological leadership" was slipping because its investment in basic research was not leading to a commensurate introduction and commercialization of new products and processes. In short, America's national system of technological innovation that had evolved since World War II and produced approximately 25 years of economic, scientific, and technological hegemony had hit a choke point. Research findings were bottled up, so to speak, within federal laboratories and university campuses. In terms of Ergas's framework, the United States was following a mission-oriented strategy in which basic research was valued for its contribution to agency missions, as in space or defense, whereas its major international competitors were following a diffusion strategy that emphasized the transformation of basic and applied research, often based on U.S. academic or industrial research, into economic ends (Ergas, 1987). More effective linkage between the institutions that generated new knowledge with those that could convert this knowledge into commercializable products and processes was a universally prescribed solution.

Given this diagnosis, attention quickly became focused on universities, which were the nation's major performers of basic research. In 1980, for example (to select a year that reflects the then current situation), universities were responsible for $5.9 billion of the nation's $8.4 billion in expenditures for basic research, while approximately two-thirds of the $6 billion (current dollars) in research performed by universities was for basic research.

(Repeated citation of these data produced a stylized dichotomy between basic and applied research and between the types of research performed by universities and firms. The statement that universities were the major performers of basic research came to imply that they had little interest in the applications of findings from this research or that they did little applied research. Relatedly, the dichotomy implied that firms did little basic research, or that they were uninterested in the first, most basic pressings of the academic research tree. Neither of these propositions is accurate [Brooks, 1993].)[2]

---

[2]Private firms invest in basic research with full recognition that leakages will occur to the potential (but not necessarily actual) benefit of rival firms (Rosenberg, 1990). They make this investment because basic research both generates new information that can be used in product or process innovation and enhances "the firm's ability to assimilate and exploit existing information" (Cohen and Levinthal, 1989, p. 569. Moreover, firms "...may conduct basic research less for particular results than to be able to identify and exploit potentially useful scientific and technological knowledge generated by universities or government laboratories, and thereby gain a first-mover advantage in exploiting new technologies. Likewise, basic research may permit firms to act as a rapid second mover in the face of spillovers from a competitor's innovation" (ibid., p. 593).

State governments likewise sought to develop new bridges between universities and industry within their borders (Babbitt, 1984) with a goal of creating, retaining, or recruiting (high-tech) "sunrise" industries to compensate for the decline in traditional industries (Lambright and Teich, 1989). Reflecting a general shift towards an entrepreneurial stance that emphasized "demand-creation" as well as traditional smokestack chasing (Fosler, 1988; Eisinger, 1988), states embarked on a number of initiatives to stimulate technology-based economic growth.[3] In almost all cases, this strategy involved universities in central roles, typically in required conjunction with industrial partners.

Adding to, and in many ways complicating, the drive for expanded university attention to the transfer of research findings and technical knowledge was increased attention to the competitiveness of small- and medium-sized manufacturing firms (National Research Council, 1990; U.S. Congress, Office of Technology Assessment, 1990; Shapira, 1990). These firms, which typically either were suppliers to original equipment manufacturing firms or had niche final product markets, were seen to lag behind foreign counterparts in the adoption of recently developed technologies, such as computer-assisted design; also, they were seen as being too small and diverse to provide adequate incentives for private consulting or engineering firms to supply them with technical assistance. The seeming similarities between this atomistic, fragmented market structure and that, historically, of American agriculture were offered as compelling reasons for the need for a national system of manufacturing extension centers. Universities (especially land-grant institutions), because of their experiences with agricultural experiment stations and cooperative extension personnel in integrating research and technology transfer, were seen as uniquely qualified to administer these centers (Cf. Feller, 1993).

The overall effect of these separate but convergent influences was to induce increased university interaction in transferring technologically related knowledge with a broad set of industrial partners: multinational, high-tech firms; embryonic or newly established spin-offs; and manufacturing firms lagging in technological innovativeness.

Universities had long made recognized contributions to specific technological innovations, such as Forrester's invention of magnetic core memories, and to systemic improvements in productivity in selected economic sectors, most notably agriculture (Huffman and Evenson, 1993). What was new about this period, according to Dickson, writing in 1984, was the "depth and intensity that corporate interest in university research has recently acquired, in particular the new stress being placed on the potential value to industry of *basic*, rather than *applied* research" (Dickson, 1984, p. 60). Because of this new emphasis, traditional modes of transferring academic research—publications, consulting arrangements, and project-specific industry-funded research grants—were, in the view of

---

[3]Coburn (1995) provides a compendium of state programs.

many, not adequate to the needs of the times or to latent opportunities.

The inadequacies of the existing system included a "loose" intellectual property rights system for establishing title to findings originating in federally funded academic research, and attitudinal, cultural, or value differences between universities and firms, each of which marched to different drummers, neither convinced that the other understood its rhythms or values. In part, too, the limited ties were held to reflect the power of the federal government-university connection that had developed since the end of World War II: the seemingly abundant flows of federal support, often on a grant basis with few deliverables, were held to be a more attractive lure for faculty than was industry funding. In Derek Bok's words, the worlds of academic and industrial scientists, "drifted apart": "Universities began to look down on the forms of applied research often practiced in corporations, while industrial scientists were persuaded that their university colleagues were too impractical or abstract to be genuinely useful" (Bok, 1982, p. 13).

The actions of the 1980s, spilling over into this decade, may be seen as specific remedies to these ills. These remedies include changes in patent laws to establish an enforceable intellectual property rights regime; organizational structures (and personnel) within the universities to administer new technology transfer responsibilities and to initiate actions in response to new missions; and attitudes conducive to technology transfer on the part of academic faculty and administrators to breath life into new legal and organizational forms.

The legislative history is marked by the following acts: the Stevenson-Wyler Technology Innovation Act (P.L. 96-480) and the Patent and Trademark Amendments of 1980 (P.L. 96-517) (Bayh-Dole Act) and subsequent amendments (P.L. 98-620), and the Federal Technology Transfer Act of 1986 (P.L. 99-502) (Eisenberg, 1995). The Stevenson-Wyler Act provided a new legislative mandate for federal laboratories to pursue technology transfer. The Bayh-Dole Act gave universities and other not-for-profit organizations the right to retain property rights for inventions deriving from federally funded research and eased limitations on the permissible duration of licenses from nonprofit organizations to large businesses. The Federal Technology Transfer Act authorized federal laboratories to enter into cooperative research and development agreements (CRADAs) with public and private sector organizations, and to preassign intellectual property rights.

### Technology Transfer

Technology transfer covers many functions and activities that relate in different ways to the basic and applied research and technical assistance activities of faculty and universities. Matkin (1990) has defined technology transfer as applied to universities as "the transfer of the results of basic and applied research to the design, development, production, and commercialization of new or improved products, services, or processes. That which is transferred often is not really technology but rather a particular kind of knowledge that is a precursor of technology" (Matkin, 1990, p. 5). Similarly, Larsen and Wigand (1987) define technology transfer as "the process through which the results from basic and applied research are communicated to potential users" (Larsen and Wigand, 1987, p. 587).[4]

Each of the above definitions emphasizes processes and results but leaves the concepts behind these results undefined. Moreover, each definition is university-centered; neither offers a concordance to the related issue of defining how university technology transfer activities contribute to the "enhanced technical capabilities of firms."[5]

Technology transfer, according to Matkin, includes "patent and technology licensing offices, investment in start-up companies, research partnerships with industry, liaison programs, business incubators, technical assistance programs, and research parks" (ibid., p. 7). The broader concept of "a particular kind of knowledge" is employed throughout this essay, although the range of activities covered in this review concentrates on patents and licensing, start-ups, and research partnerships, with brief note taken of technical assistance programs and research parks.[6]

## IV. PATENTS, LICENSES, ROYALTIES, AND START-UPS

Patents, licenses, royalties, and start-ups are the most visible manifestations of the university's newly aggressive efforts to foster the commercialization of academic research. The Bayh-Dole Act and related legislation, the lure of industry-establishing patents originating in academic research findings, and the diffusion of new missions, strategies, and best-practices led to the flurry of revisions of institutional policies and establishment of conflict of interest and conflict of commitment policies (American Association of Universities, 1986; Matkin, 1990, 1994). These changes included clarification of ownership policies within the uni-

---

[4]Strikingly absent from either of these definitions is education. A major theme in technology transfer literature, however, is that it is a "contact sport," involving interactions among individuals. An equivalent for universities would be the "moving van" effect: technology is transferred when newly minted Ph.D.s pack belongings and move to their first jobs.

[5]Rahm (1994) expresses the missing elements from these definitions in the following way: "Technology transfer is a nebulous process. The desired end result is apparent but specific implementation activities are hazy," and "Transfer of a technology or a process innovation to firms is usually thought of in a positive sense, but the transfer of negative information may also be beneficial to the firm" (Rahm, 1994, pp. 72-73).

[6]Parsing technology transfer activities from the larger set of research and education activities within which they are nested also leaves untreated the many other ways (e.g., regional impact multipliers from conducting externally funded research; cultural and recreational magnet to attract "footloose," high-tech entrepreneurs) a university's research activities contribute to national and regional economic development activity (see Steinnes, 1987; Malecki, 1991; Goldstein, Maier, and Luger, 1994).

versity, revised formulas for apportioning revenues among faculty inventors, departments and colleges, and central administration with the view toward increasing monetary incentives, movement of patent licensing activities from third-party, external organizations (such as the Research Corporation, the long-standing patent arm of many universities) to in-house staffs, the establishment and expansion of university patent and technology offices, the recruitment of specialized personnel to staff these offices, and the active role played by these offices in informing faculty about the potential and processes for securing patents.

Recent studies provide data on the quantitative impacts of these changes, plus insights into their economic importance. The major trends are an increase in the total number of academic patents, an increase in the number of institutions engaged in patenting, an accentuated concentration of patenting in a small number of patent fields, and a continuing concentration of patents in a small number of universities.

The number of patents awarded to American universities has increased steadily in both absolute and relative terms since the late 1960s. From an average of between 200-300 annually in the late 1960s, the number of patents awarded to universities increased to 350-400 per year in the early 1980s and has risen steadily since then, increasing from 434 patents in 1983 to 1,602 patents in 1993. In percentage terms, universities received 3 percent of total U.S. patents in 1993, up from 1 percent in 1980. University patenting has increased more rapidly than university research spending, leading to a threefold increase in the ratio of university patents to R&D spending. Almost the opposite pattern occurred for U.S. industry: domestic patenting remained relatively constant in the period from the mid-1970s to the mid-1980s, while research spending increased, so that the ratio of patents to spending almost halved. In all, "universities' 'propensity to patent' given their research effort, has been rising significantly at the same time that the overall propensity to patent has been falling" (Henderson, Jaffe, and Trajtenberg, 1995, p. 4).

The number of universities receiving patents increased slowly during the 1970s, and more rapidly and sharply during the 1980s. The total number of institutions receiving patents increased from about 30 in 1965 to 80 in 1980 to 165 in 1993. Two separate patterns are contained within this overall change: first, the percentage of academic patents received by the 100 largest research universities (measured by total research funds) has increased from 80 to 90 percent of total patents. This suggests that a sizable number of institutions receive one or a few patents. Second, within the top 100 institutions, the share of the largest 20 universities has contracted, while those below rank 50 have slowly increased their share. This points both to the development of institutional infrastructures to pursue patent filings among universities formerly passive in their activities and to their increased share of total academic R&D funds (Geiger and Feller, 1995).

Academic patents are heavily concentrated in a small number of patent (utility) classes; the increase in the total number of patents has been strikingly associated with increased concentration of patent activity. In 1969-1973, 80 percent of academic patents were issued in more than 80 different utility classes; by the early 1990s, the 80 percent share was located in 50 utility classes. Three patent classes—435 (Chemistry: molecular biology and microbiology) and 424 and 514 (Drug: bioaffecting and body treating compositions)—represented approximately 25 percent of total academic patents in 1993. Together, these series point to the select number of scientific fields in which academic research is seen to have foreseeable economic impact, and to the concentration of patents in those institutions with strong research programs in the related academic research fields, particularly the life sciences.

Patents, as frequently described, are imperfect measures of technological innovation (Griliches, 1990). Not all forms of new commercially useful knowledge can be patented; moreover, patents are only one of several means (e.g., trade secrets) by which firms establish intellectual property rights. The commercial value of patents is uncertain and dependent on decisions regarding the profitability of further investments in the development of products and markets and the competitive character of the innovation relative to existing products and/or new products, which may or may not be patented. Thus, patents are a limited measure of the extent to which technology, much less scientific and technological knowledge, is being transferred from universities to industry.

Different means exist to assess the commercial importance of academic patents. One is to examine the number of academic patents that are commercialized; another is to compute the total licensing revenues or market values of academic patents; yet another is to test for the importance and generality of patents by examining the extent to which they are cited by other patents. Studies of the pre-1980s period indicated low rates of commercialization of academic patents arising from NSF grants in chemistry and engineering (Marcy and Kosloski, 1982; SRI, 1986). The principal reasons cited were no apparent market for the technology, prohibitive development costs, and supersession by other markets or innovations.

Recent data, although fragmentary and not always comparable, point to higher rates of licensing. A 1994 survey by the Association of University Technology Managers (AUTM), based on responses from 45 of 130 member institutions, reported a total of 440 active licenses for 177 products (Association of University Technology Managers, 1994a,b). This upward trend in part reflects the emerging strategy of university technology licensing officials to identify a licensee before filing a patent application, and to have the licensee pay expenses and fees for patenting the invention (U.S. General Accounting Office, 1992). Thus, that which can be licensed is that which is patented. The trend, as suggested above, likely derives from the strong dependence of the biotechnology industry on academic research in its formative years, and the infusion of funding from both established pharmaceutical and venture capital firms into commercializing academic research (Kenney, 1986). Important, too, was the shift in emphasis from "viewing patents as a necessary means of establishing intellectual property rights, to an aggressive 'marketing' model popularized in the late 1980s and continuing to this day" (Neuer, 1995, p. 8).

A related measure of the economic value of academic patents is license and royalty revenues. As stated by the Southern Technology Council: "The Rubicon of university technology transfer is crossed when faculty inventions are licensed to companies and become expressed in marketable products and services. The invention has moved from protection and hopeful speculation to *commercialization*" (Southern Technology Council, 1995, p. 11).

Technology licensing involves putting together "deals" that exchange the university's newly established intellectual property right for some combination of immediate and future revenues. Various exchanges are possible: some emphasize licensing or royalty payments; others, equity holdings; and still others, industrial support for continued faculty research (Feller, 1990). In each of these exchanges, both the university and the firm take economic risks that the payments may not accurately reflect the market value of the patent. For example, license revenues may overstate the economic value of the knowledge if the firm finds it cannot successfully bring the technology to market; for a patent that leads to a commercially successful innovation, trading greater lump sum payments for running royalties may understate that patent's economic value.

Data on the number and dollar value of licenses are available in scattered form from a set of studies. A GAO report based on a survey of 35 universities for fiscal years 1989 and 1990 reported that these universities received $82 million in income from licenses based on NSF and NIH research (U.S. General Accounting Office, 1992).

Annual surveys conducted by AUTM indicate a steadily increasing level of activity in all aspects of licensing activities. This includes licenses executed, licenses with university equity holdings, licenses/options generating gross royalty receipts, gross royalties received, and license office expenditures (Association of University Technology Managers, 1994a, p. 7). Survey responses from 117 universities, including 85 of the top 100 universities measured in terms of R&D expenditures, indicated gross royalties in FY1993 of $242 million, representing revenues from 3,413 active licenses. Additional revenues were received by U.S. hospitals and research institutes ($74 million) and patent management firms ($59 million) (ibid., p. 15).[7]

Another supporting account of the increased role of licensing is provided by Mitchell's account of the commercialization of academic medical imaging diagnos-

---

[7]The background of rising trends in all aspects of university patenting and licensing may mask a troublesome outlook, according to Jon Sandelin, Office of Technology Licensing, Stanford University. Among the threats cited is proposed congressional legislation that licenses for federally funded pharmaceutical inventions include a provision for the reasonable pricing of any resulting drug products, that all federally funded inventions be put out for competitive bidding, and that a portion of royalties be returned to the federal government (Sandelin, 1994).

tic equipment between 1954 and 1988. Technology transfer is defined as occurring in one of three ways: hands-off, individual contact (e.g., hiring of the researcher or establishment of a start-up firm), and organization contact (e.g., licenses, sponsored projects). Over time, Mitchell finds that the hands-off and individual contact methods of transfer have declined and organizational contact methods have increased in relative incidence, while no significant changes have occurred in the relative incidence of researcher start-ups. As the study covers the time span for the occurrence of changes in federal patent legislation and subsequent modifications in university licensing organizations and policies, it, in a sense, describes transitional events. For example, for the entire sample, licenses were involved in 64 of 183 technologies, yet the underlying behaviors—for corporations to undertake transfer via sponsored research projects and for universities to establish formal patent and license offices—reflect increased reliance on licensing as a transfer method.

Whether licensing leads to an increase in technology transfer, however, is another question, according to Mitchell.[8]

The answer to this question is "fuzzy—probably, but not very much yet, and it needs more study" (Mitchell, 1991, p. 212). Most transfers were to established firms and would have occurred anyway. Only in the few cases of "start-up firms receiving significant organizational assistance from licensing offices" is it likely that manufacture of the technologies would not have occurred in the absence of university initiatives.

Considering only royalties received directly by universities, income is highly concentrated in a small number of institutions. The top 10 recipients received $171 million, or 71 percent of the total. Table 1 lists these institutions.[9]

Not only is the distribution of revenues from patents highly skewed among institutions, but it is also highly skewed among patents: a small percentage of patents generate the largest share of revenues for any university with any appreciable number of patents. Data from the Wisconsin Alumni Research Foundation (WARF) offer one much studied case (Blumenthal, Epstein, and Maxwell, 1986; Wisconsin Alumni Research Foundation, 1986; Feller, 1990). Between 1929 and 1985, WARF received 448 patents from 2,424 invention disclosures. Licenses were issued for 203 patents, but of this total only 100 licenses produced income greater than expenses. Overall, in this period, 10 patents produced approximately 90 percent of the $30 million in royalty income received by WARF. More recent

---

[8]"If technology transfer offices simply capture part of the rent stream of products that would have been commercialized anyway, diverting it into the pockets of the institutions and the researchers, they are doing part of their job. But it may be the smallest part" (Mitchell, 1991, p. 211).

[9]A regionally disaggregated study of university patent experience, an important perspective in the subsequent examination of the regional implications of university technology transfer activities, is presented by the Southern Technology Council's (STC) survey of 41 institutions (including virtually all major research universities and medical centers, plus one state-level organization) in a 14-state region in the southeast. Responding institutions reported a range of active licenses from zero to 304, with a median of 21. For the STC sample of 41, royalty revenues ranged from zero to $6.8 million, with a median of $304,901. The median value increased by 25 percent between 1992-1994.

reviews of patent revenue at MIT, the University of California, and Stanford repeat this pattern. For example, at the University of California, in the 1986-1987 period, 12 of the 161 income-generating patents (of the total 612 patents held by the university) produced 66 percent of the university's income. At Stanford, in the same year, 7 of the 116 income-generating patents produced 75 percent of the income (Matkin, 1990, pp. 120-129; Reimer, 1989).[10]

**TABLE 1. Distribution of License Income—10 Top Universities, FY1993**

| | |
|---|---|
| University of California System | $ 45.4 |
| Stanford University | 31.2 |
| Columbia University | 21.1 |
| WARF/University of Wisconsin-Madison | 15.8 |
| University of Washington/Washington Research Foundation | 14.8 |
| Michigan State University | 14.2 |
| Iowa State University | 11.6 |
| Massachusetts Institute of Technology | 5.8 |
| University of Florida | 5.7 |
| Harvard University | 5.4 |
| Total: Top 10 Recipients | $171.0 |

(Association of University Technology Managers, AUTM Licensing Survey, FY1993, p. 8)

The small number of patents received by many universities and the skewed distribution of revenues from patents raise questions about universities' objectives in pursuing more aggressive patent policies and the strategies they use to transfer patented technology. Even allowing for the economic effectiveness of having prospective licensees reimburse the university for its legal fees in filing and securing patents, the net legal expenses plus administrative costs of technology licensing offices raise questions about their revenue-generating functions. It is questionable whether many offices break even, much less return net revenue. Confirming this assessment are recent statements by several university technology licensing officials: According to Niels Reimers of Stanford University, "With

---

[10]The dependence of patent revenues on single licenses is also shown in the STC data. The percentage of gross revenue obtained from the single most remunerative license ranged from zero to 100 percent, with a median of 52.2 percent.

few exceptions, a ULO (University Licensing Office) is economically viable only if one or more 'big hit' inventions has come along" (quoted in Matkin, 1990, p. 129). Similarly, the president of the Cornell Research Foundation, Cornell University's unit for marketing its technologies, is quoted as follows: "Most patents never make a nickel....Universities aren't in this to make money....Only a few make big money" (Benowitz, 1995, p. 1).

Whether or how bottom-line calculations should or do affect institutional policies is less evident. Patent and technology licensing offices are established to achieve a bundle of objectives—revenue (defined broadly now to include both license income and additional industrial research support), service to faculty, and regional economic development. Patents are seen as means to establishing property rights, which, in turn, may be prerequisites in securing industry support to conduct follow-up research. The costs of patents are thus a cost of doing research.

Moreover, officials from the leading university technology licensing offices have noted frequently that they are not intended primarily as profit centers but rather to serve academic ends. As expressed by Lita Nelson, director of MIT's Technology Licensing Office, "We will not change the academic function for commercialization. We are very careful to convey to potential corporate partners that our primary mission is academic. If we start becoming short-term servants of industry, the country is in trouble" (quoted in Neuer, 1995, p. 8).

The lags between the date of patent issuance and income streams from patents also make any judgments about economic returns premature. Recent increases in patents may be the precursors to outyear booms in revenues for many if not all institutions, with survey data essentially reflecting a bunching of upfront costs that will be amortized over time. Rules of thumb suggest a seven-year lag between patent issuance and sizable revenues; thus, with some legitimacy, university patent offices can contend that any stock-taking on their performance as profit centers is premature, with the best yet to come. Moreover, as noted, royalty income is only one part of the income stream received by universities from their combined research and technology transfer activities. Revenues also may accrue in the form of research grants and contracts to support the work of the faculty member; over time, they may lead to alumni contributions and endowments as successful entrepreneurs capitalize on the benefits they receive from the university's know-how and return it in the form of gifts and bequests. Listing these offsetting factors, however, may simply be goal displacement, whereby the inability of offices to generate sizable net revenues induces a seguing to other, nonincome-generating objectives.

These data on the skewed distribution of revenues and limited net revenues also offer an explanation for emerging university strategies to accept equity holdings in lieu of licenses or royalties. Equity holdings may be less an activist approach to launching new firms than the only recourse to commercial benefits.

Few takers may exist for an institution's patent, either because its technical properties still have to be demonstrated or because of the uncertain economic profitability of producing the product. Equity holdings are one way to increase the utilization of patents, especially in enticing start-up or small firms that would otherwise be unable or unwilling to pay a licensee fee or high running royalties. The strategy also increases the odds of a big hit if and when the firm has a public stock offering.

Henderson, Jaffe, and Trajtenberg's (1995) study of academic patents for the period 1965-1992 offers a third method for assessing the technological importance of academic patents: the frequency with which they are cited in other patents. Their findings indicate that university patents were both more important and more general than the average patent over the whole time period, but that this difference has declined over time over a broad spectrum of technological areas. Accounting for the decline over time was the increase in the percentage of patents receiving no citations in other patents. According to the authors, "This raises the concern that the observed increase in university patenting may reflect an increase in their 'propensity to patent' rather than an increase in the output of 'important' inventions" (Henderson, Jaffe, and Trajtenberg, 1995, pp. 2-3). Put in economic terms, aggressive university technology policies, as least as they relate to patents, may be entering a region of diminishing returns.

## Start-ups

Start-ups represent another form of technology transfer, with the findings of academic research being used to launch new firms. Five separate aspects of this development warrant attention: first, start-ups may be necessary for technology transfer because the new knowledge is not patentable; therefore, the only way the (faculty) inventor can obtain economic rents is through direct commercialization. Second, start-up may be necessary because no existing firm is willing to license the technology and/or there may be significant differences between the view of the university and prospective licensees as to the patent's value. Third, start-ups are a means of regionally appropriating economic benefits within the environs of the university or the state; thus, the approach has singular appeal as a regional economic development outcome relative, say, to licensing.[11]

Fourth, start-ups may be a more effective way of commercializing academic research than licensing (Gregory and Sheahen, 1991). As noted by Gregory and Sheahen:

The statistics for non-university supported spin-off companies seem to be better than

---

[11]Data from the STC survey highlight the possible disconnection between university licensing activities and connections to in-state firms. For 33 institutions in the survey, total license income for the three-year period was $33.7 million. Of this, slightly more than $1 million came from in-state licenses, and $5.1 million came from royalty revenues from licensees located in STC states. Sixteen of the 33 reporting institutions noted zero percent of royalties from companies within their states.

those for licensing. In particular, the spin-off does not require the large income potential that is necessary in licensing operations to make the overall scheme pay. As a result, the spin-off can produce income from more modest inventions. The problem with spin-offs are often related to the usual problems of running a business, and not to the inherent value of the technology—which is similar to the licensing experience (Gregory and Sheahen, 1991, p. 151).

Fifth, start-ups are often seen as tenants for university research parks, and the two developments are sometimes paired. However, again as compared with other methods of transferring technology, start-ups bring with them increased risks associated with conflicts of interest and "allegations of lack of thorough adherence to clinical and scientific investigative standards…," as has occurred with researchers affiliated with Harvard and Johns Hopkins (Samson and Gurdon, 1993).

The emphasis on start-ups in many university technology transfer strategies draws nurturance from the recurrent hope of emulating the Route 128 and Silicon Valley successes, and a research literature that emphasizes the importance of homegrown, indigenous technology-based companies in a region's economic growth and the importance of universities to such firms. Thus, according to Gibson and Smilor (1991), the research university played key roles in the development of the "technopolises" that undergirded the economic growth of Silicon Valley, Austin, Texas, and Phoenix, Arizona. For example, writing about economic development in Austin, Texas, they observe that "of 103 small and medium-sized technology based companies in existence in Austin in 1986, 53— or 52 percent—indicated a direct tie originally to the University of Texas at Austin" (ibid., p. 55). Moreover, "technopolis" is a relative term that need not be restricted to densely populated regions. Montana State University is now performing a similar catalytic role in attracting high-technology economic development to Bozeman, Montana (Blumenstyk, 1995b). The number of high-technology firms in the area has reportedly increased from about 12 to 45 over the last decade. These new firms represent a mix of those started to commercialize ideas developed by the university and those attracted to the region because of access to the university's faculty, students, and specialized equipment.

Data on start-ups are spread across reports issued by universities and reports of federal- and state-sponsored university-industry-government collaborative R&D centers. No single estimate exists for the number, economic characteristics, or viability of university start-up companies. One national estimate is offered in the 1993 AUTM survey, which reports 916 start-up companies formed since 1980 based on licenses from universities and related organizations. This estimate clearly understates the number of start-ups, both because of incomplete coverage and because of the restrictive definition for inclusion.

Complicating any effort to relate the fate of start-up firms to the contribution made by academic research is that the profitability and growth of the firm and the economic value of the initial technology are not inexorably linked. A start-up firm may find little market for its initial technology but manage to redeploy its activities; thus, rather than manufacturing new diagnostic equipment, it may provide clinical testing for other firms or, rather than produce hardware (which itself is not a commercial success), it may find markets for the specialized software developed to operate it. The firm's subsequent growth thus may owe little to the initial set of university initiatives to transfer technology. Conversely, the failure of a university-based firm may not be indicative of the economic value of a technology. Firms fail for many reasons—inadequate capitalization; inability to correctly identify or enter markets; managerial upheavals—not directly connected to the technical and economic superiority of its core technology. Successor or other firms may make better use of it. Lacking at present are business and technological histories that examine these possibilities. Further confounding these relationships among university technology transfer programs, start-up firms, and regional economic growth is the fact that when success does come to the firm it may occur in a different, out-of-state location (Weinberg and Mazey, 1988).

Finally, the connection between university research and the high-technology regional development stories of Silicon Valley and Route 128 is complex, and not necessarily a guide to further university technology transfer strategies. Accounts by Dorfman (1983), Luger and Goldstein (1991), Roberts (1991), and Saxenian (1994) highlight the importance of Stanford University and MIT to their respective regions, but are less about the discrete transfer of specific technologies than about the research infrastructure and attractive power of universities. Dorfman's account of the rise of Route 128 and Silicon Valley where "academic centers" were "at the heart of both local economics" (Dorfman, 1983, p. 312) illustrates the prototypical association between strong university research programs and the spawning of new firms; however, her account also points to the virtually spontaneous character of these developments unaided by efforts on the part of local interest groups or government, or of the direct involvement of either Harvard or MIT. Roberts' (1991) account of the same developments likewise emphasizes the role of MIT (but not Harvard) in the emergence of the Massachusetts computer industry. Strong as the association between MIT and the immediate regional economy was for the computer industry, it did not hold for other groupings of academic research. In a related study of faculty in four MIT departments, Roberts and Peters (1981) concluded that "most mechanical universities have little effect, even few instances of commercially-oriented information transfer, upon neighboring industrial firms" (Roberts and Peters, 1981, p. 109). More recently, Roberts (1991) has suggested that few regions other than Route 128 have experienced any substantial linkages between the start-up of new firms and the area's major universities: "Thus, the MIT-Route 128 model still today remains unusual in its degree of regional entrepreneurial dependence upon one major academic institution. Perhaps other regions need other models if they are to achieve technology-based economic growth" (Roberts, 1991, p. 35).

(Although education is not included in definitions of technology transfer, it should be noted that these studies conclude that the more central role of universities to local economic development is as suppliers of trained personnel to staff the new firms in their environs than as sources of foundation technologies. According to Dorfman, "The most critical manpower need in high technology industries is for scientists, engineers and other technical personnel" (Dorfman, 1983, p. 304). Similar conclusions are reached by Malecki (1991): "The skilled technical and professional workers needed in the non-routine activities are the greatest single location factor for new products and high technology" (Malecki, 1991, p. 264).

## Research Parks

Research (or science/technology) parks are another recent initiative by universities to foster technology transfer and high-tech economic development. Many of these functions extend beyond the immediate scope of this review, and so only a brief outline of the subject is offered. As detailed by Luger and Goldstein (1991), research parks have several objectives, including attracting R&D-intensive firms to increase the density of interaction between tenant firms and faculty and students, and serving as the incubation site of start-up companies (Luger and Goldstein, 1991, pp. 24-25). University involvement in research parks may stem from either development of land already owned or through purchase of land for development as a research park. Several motives may underlie university actions: "Universities do this to earn a positive rate of return, to ensure a supply of space for current and future university expansion, or to have a nearby site for the location of technology-oriented private businesses that can help faculty develop and commercialize technologies" (Luger and Goldstein, 1991, p. 39). However, few "pure" research parks exist; most include tenants engaged in service or production activities. Thus, disaggregated data or careful examination of the experiences of single parks is required to make connections between the commercial success of the park and patterns of university-research park technology transfer.

Luger and Goldstein's work, *Technology in the Garden* (1991), is the major study of the organization and impact of research parks. The authors identified 116 research parks in existence in 1989. The formal and spatial connection between these parks and universities is quite evident. For 72 of these parks for which data were collected, 25 percent were units of public or private universities and 60 percent had a formal or informal affiliation with nearby research or doctoral-granting institutions; and 15 percent had some degree of interaction with faculty members in nearby universities.

Universities participating in research parks enthusiastically endorse such an arrangement's benefits. Faculty at the five universities affiliated with the Research Triangle, University of Utah, and Stanford Research Parks provided an 86 percent approval rating (Luger and Goldstein, 1991, p. 165). Among the benefits received were increased recruiting of research faculty and top graduate students, and "helping to increase the interaction between scientists and researchers in the university and industry" (ibid., p. 165). Almost 25 percent of the 600 survey respondents reported some involvement with firms in the park, "either in joint research or consulting or through the use of specialized facilities and equipment" (ibid.).

However, the "success" of these parks as regional economic development tools is highly variable. Using differences between total employment growth rates both before and after a park had been established between counties with a research park and a control group of counties within a park, Luger and Goldstein judged 16 parks to have been successful under the most stringent criterion, 10 parks to have been successful under a more lenient criterion, and 19 parks to have been unsuccessful. Their case studies of the Research Triangle, Stanford, and Utah University Research Parks suggest that the payoff from new investments in research parks "is slow to be realized" at best, and at worst may be nonexistent as "the park fails to achieve its promise and objective" (ibid., p. 179). Finally, along the lines in the above accounts of the Route 128 and Silicon Valley complexes and in other studies of the regional impacts of academic research (e.g., Glasmeier, 1988; Jaffe, 1989; Markusen, Hall, and Glasmeier, 1986), they call attention to the complex set of interactions between academic research and industrial activities that determine whether a park achieves its intended objectives. Luger and Goldstein write that: "While the synergies between universities and research parks play an important role in the growth-inducement effects that operate through research parks from the economic stimulus from more general university activities….In short, universities, not research parks, may be the 'growth pole'" (ibid., p. 160).

### University-Industry R&D

The growth of university-industry and university-industry-government collaborative R&D programs is the single most important development in the character of university technology transfer endeavors since the early 1980s. University-industry research centers (UIRCs) are the primary vehicle through which industry supports academic R&D: its contribution of $779 million represented 69 percent of industrial support for academic R&D in 1990. UIRCs enlarge and formalize single research awards from firms to universities into consortia-type arrangements or long-term contracts between individual firms and collectivities of faculty. Collaborative R&D programs are also the preferred means for federal and state governments to financially support increased university technology transfer. Finally, these cooperative R&D programs provide for a broad set of interactions between firms and industries, and consequently require attention to be paid to the multiple forms and uses of academic knowledge rather than to patents and start-ups as described above.

Cohen, Florida, and Goe's recent report, *University-Industry Research Centers in the United States* (1992), provides the major examination of the number and magnitude of university-industry research centers. Based on a survey conducted in 1991, the authors report on an estimated 1,056 university-industry R&D centers located at 200 universities in 1990. More than one-half of these centers had been established since 1980 and had spent an estimated $4.12 billion on research and related activities, with approximately $2.53 billion devoted to R&D (or approximately 15.2 percent of total academic R&D expenditures in 1990). Approximately equal shares of this R&D activity were devoted to basic and applied research. Reflecting the federal and state government policy initiatives described above, government support pervades the establishment and operation of these centers. Eighty-six percent received government funding, while more than 70 percent of UIRCs were established either wholly or partly based upon funding from federal or state governments. Reflecting the partnership ethos that surrounds the establishment of these centers, they draw their funding from several sources: federal government—34 percent; state governments—12 percent; industry—31 percent; and universities—18 percent. However, the study clearly points to the entrepreneurial role of universities as the primary, direct impetus in promoting the establishment of such centers.

These funding patterns suggest the mixing and matching of several combinations of partners. Cooperative arrangements may be between universities and firms/industries, or among universities, industry, and government. Given the number of possible combinations and allowing for variations in the interests of specific industrial members of these centers, among state governments and federal agencies, and of the academic participants, differences in expectations held by partners concerning the technology or knowledge transfer outcomes are to be expected. As noted by Cohen, Florida, and Goe (1992), "USRCs also differ importantly in terms of their goals. For example, about one-quarter of UIRCs view improving industry's products and processes as very important, while others pursue more traditional academic objectives removed from commercial objectives" (Cohen, Florida, and Goe, 1992, p. 1).

Almost two-thirds of UIRCs viewed transferring technology to industry as "important." Outputs related to technology transfer are indeed clearly observed in the activities of these centers. In total, responding centers (n=511) reported 679 inventions, 459 patent applications, 211 patents grants, 160 licenses, 464 copyrights, 44 trade secrets, 426 prototypes, 293 new products, and 390 new processes. However, only 6.3 percent of UIRC effort is allocated to technology transfer; centers see their primary goal as advancing scientific and technical knowledge, and their secondary goal as education and training.

The study also bears upon issues raised in a series of empirical and analytical studies of the role of university-industry R&D arrangements on faculty research agendas. Blumenthal et al. (1986) reported a redirection of research priorities among faculty who received research support from industry. Dasgupta and David (1994) and Feller (1990) also have contended that the pursuit of commercialization leads to a redirection of research agendas that essentially blurs the functional specialization of industry and universities. Cohen et al. (1992) report an evident influence on research agenda; UIRC agendas are reported by nearly two-thirds of respondents, with 28 percent reporting a "strong influence."

Federal and state governments have actively sought to promote closer industry-university-government relationships, and have provided funds to catalyze university R&D programs intended to generate findings that would be commercializable, as well as the political prod for universities to expand technology transfer missions.[12] Federal and state strategies have had somewhat different emphases, although each has evolved over time. Federal programs have typically emphasized "pre-competitive" or "generic" research. This newly minted category was close to basic research in being characterized by high degrees of technical and economic uncertainty but was more targeted than basic research by being directed toward product or process development applicable to an entire industry or industries. Pre-competitive research also had dimensions of both private and public goods: it was valuable to many firms within an industry, either competitors or upstream suppliers or downstream customers, but still required investments too large for single firms to underwrite. Recent reviews of these programs offer additional information on the forms and magnitudes of university technology transfer. The earliest of these programs was NSF's Industry-University Cooperative Research Centers, begun in 1972 as part of the Experimental R&D Incentives Program to increase nonfederal investment in R&D and the rate of adoption of R&D findings by both the public and private sectors (Gray et al., 1986). Of three general models of university-industry R&D cooperation tested in the program's early period (1972-1977), consortia arrangements modeled on the Polymer Processing Center at MIT became the template for subsequent university-industry cooperative R&D centers.

The centers are reported to have stimulated technology transfer between university and industry. Again, the type of transfer is important. In most cases, it involved knowledge that could be used directly in its R&D and product development activities rather than in specific products. Evaluations in the mid-1980s noted that companies involved with centers reported investment of additional funds "in their own labs on new projects stimulated by center research. These investments are a clear indication that knowledge transfer is occurring between these two sectors" (Gray et al., 1986, p. 188).

The richness and diversity of the benefits received by firms from participating in these cooperative R&D centers, as well as the different perspectives about the characteristics of technology transfer, are contained in interviews with a cross-sec-

---

[12]State government initiation of technology development programs also "made it imperative," according to Fairweather, "politically and financially for public universities (and for private institutions receiving substantial state subsidies) to seek liaisons with industry" (Fairweather, 1988, p. 44; also see Feller [1992]).

tion of university and industry participants in nine Industry/University Cooperative Research Centers (Scott and Schaad, 1994). Technology transfer is defined to include technology, information, or "know-how." For each center, the larger percentage, ranging from 66 percent to 100 percent of industrial respondents, agreed that the center had helped promote the technical capabilities of their company. For many of the industrial representatives to the centers, successful technology transfer has a literal meaning: successful technology transfer occurs when people use the technology, or when the product is in the commercial marketplace. Other industrial respondents define success differently: successful technology transfer is the generation of independent thoughts regarding different avenues to investigate. "This is valuable as much as a product" (Gray et al., 1986, p. 66).

NSF's Engineering Research Centers represented one of the major federal initiatives of the 1980s to foster the more rapid transfer of academically performed research into the marketplace. Significant here is that ERCs were to accomplish this end by conducting cross-cutting interdisciplinary research and instruction related to complex engineering problems, by conducting research related to "fundamental knowledge," the results of which were to be "useful to industry without being too near-term in focus," and by inculcating students with a broad understanding of what was needed to bring sophisticated products from the laboratory to the market. The striking feature of this agenda is its implicit depictions of the university's distinctive contributions to technological innovations as resting in research on fundamental knowledge and education; and the changes needed within universities to perform this role better. Making the university a more fecund source of commercially useable technology requires increased emphasis on cross-disciplinary studies, greater familiarity with and awareness and attention to R&D management and processes of technological innovation, and closer cooperation with industry. Not included are specific, discrete technological innovations. Initial expectations were that ERCs would not become heavily involved in short-term applied projects, nor would universities become actively involved in commercializing faculty-generated research (Schmitt, 1986).

Reviews of the ERCs have consistently reported that firms belong to them mainly for access to state-of-the-art knowledge, continuing associations with faculty whose work they had previously supported, and graduate students. A GAO study of NSF's ERCs, based on surveys of participating industrial sponsors, indicated that the opportunity to develop patented inventions was the least important of 15 possible reasons for membership. Most important was the match between the firm's interests and the state-of-the art research being done by the ERC (U.S. General Accounting Office, 1988).[13]

---

[13]Bohlander's study of benefits received by firms belonging to the Georgia Institute of Technology's Manufacturing Research Center, a center established to foster the development and transfer of dual use technology, reports similar results. The primary benefit received by firms was "the stimulation provided by the university" (Bohlander, 1994, p. 11).

Feller and Roessner (1995) have recently described the benefits received by firms from participating in ERCs as follows:

...ERCs are of value to firms not because they provide a fixed set of quantifiable bene-fits but because they permit firms to contract for a core set of services and to periodi-cally recontract for specific deliverables simultaneously....Put differently, firm membership in an ERC may be seen less as an investment in one or more separable outcomes, such as a specific research finding or a solution to a problem whose expected value could be compared with the membership fee, and more an investment in a portfolio of outcomes. This 'portfolio' characteristic is all the more attractive as firms perceive that their R&D objectives are variable and changing (Feller and Roessner, 1995, pp. 83-84).

Underlying these assessments of federally supported university-industry coop-erative R&D programs is the proposition advanced by Larsen and Wigand (1987) that "Cooperative research, by its very nature, leads to technology transfer" (Larsen and Wigand, 1987, p. 592).

State programs have been cast as more applied in nature, with the goal of cap-turing "regionally" appropriable benefits, but this is not a full description. State programs in New York, Ohio, and Texas have adopted a portfolio approach that includes support for "cutting edge" research within academic centers, while rely-ing on joint funding by firms or industrial review of projects as forms of insur-ance to the projects' commercial relevance. Others, like Pennsylvania, have emphasized discrete product development.

Each of these state strategies has received legitimization by external review groups, providing de facto endorsement, so to speak, for the type of research knowledge generated by the program and the mode used by the university to transfer technology (National Research Council, 1990; Ben Franklin Partnership Program, 1991; Ebert, Fields, and Syngaarden, 1991; Mount Auburn Associates, 1992).

The evaluations of federal and state programs have given scant treatment to the frictions that have arisen in these programs, particularly those related to the difficulties of simultaneously matching the interests of the firms with the capabil-ities of universities and the administrative strictures of federal or state programs. For example, the evidence cited above suggests that most industrial participants in ERCs view them as sources of broadly usable knowledge. This pattern is not universal. Some firms do expect specific solutions to specific problems delivered within specific time periods. This pattern may be observed for both Fortune 500 companies that participate in ERCs and small firms. The desirability or effective-ness of faculty involvement in such R&D arrangements, however, has repeatedly been questioned.[14]

---

[14]"Except under special circumstances, we think it ill-advised to try to get university researchers to work on specific practical problems of industry, or on particular product or process development efforts" (Rosenberg and Nelson, 1994, p. 346).

In particular, problems have arisen frequently over the effort to involve universities with small firms in technology development programs. Gray et al. (1986) have noted this issue for NSF's UICR programs. Consistent with earlier noted observations about the need for firms to have internal R&D capabilities to effectively utilize externally generated findings, these firms at times require additional detailed assistance to transform research findings into specific R&D lines. Petrick (1995) has described related difficulties for Pennsylvania's Ben Franklin program. Involvement of faculty from Pennsylvania State University's College of Engineering in Ben Franklin Partnership program grants has declined steadily in recent years from a high of over 90 applications in 1989-1990 to between 10 and 20 in recent years. According to Petrick, in the early years, the faculty viewed the program as a viable and desirable source of funds for their research activities. Their experience with projects, however, led them to become so disenchanted that many preferred to seek funding elsewhere. Surveys of faculty and firms also indicated that the participants had different expectations and goals for their joint projects, with mutual disappointment being reported in several cases.

## Technical Assistance

Technical assistance programs are quite a different class of technology transfer activities. These programs typically are directed at small- and medium-sized firms. For the most part, these firms require "off-the-shelf" technology to improve their practices (National Research Council, 1990; Shapira, 1990), augmented to a degree by research directed at solving firm-specific production problems. In practice, university-based manufacturing extension programs ARE operated by specialized staffs: faculty involvement in these centers is limited, often involving the direction of graduate student work on a firm's technical problems as course projects.

As state interest in manufacturing modernization programs quickened in the 1980s, a few existing models were built on first, most notably Georgia Institute of Technology's Industrial Extension Service and Pennsylvania State University's Pennsylvania Technical Assistance Program (PENNTAP). Establishment of Manufacturing Technology Centers (MTCs) as a NIST program under the Omnibus Trade and Competitiveness Act of 1988, followed by the Clinton administration's endorsement of a national system of manufacturing technology centers and manufacturing outreach centers, gave a boost to the establishment of these programs.

There was an initial appeal to locating these new centers with universities. Two of the three original MTCs—the Northeast Manufacturing Technology Center at Rensselaer Polytechnic Institute and the Southeast Manufacturing Technology Center—were initially placed within a university system. This placement reflected a belief as well as statutory language that MTCs would serve as transfer arms for NIST's Advanced Manufacturing Program. Experience with the matching of their intended audience's needs with the activities of MTCs indicated that research universities were not necessarily the best organizational base. There was a limited match between the technical and training needs of small- and medium-sized firms and the capabilities and interests of research universities. Moreover, activities related to "manufacturing modernization" have come to extend well beyond the ambit of traditional technical assistance services—for example, marketing and workforce training. These components are either directly commercial or require a multifunctional span of services; in neither case are universities a superior home base.

The expansion in the number of MTCs and smaller, substate Manufacturing Outreach Centers under the Manufacturing Extension Partnership Program in the Technology Reinvestment Project led these sites to be increasingly placed in state departments of commerce or not-for-profit organizations. Specific data on the organizational forms of the 80 manufacturing modernization centers in place in late 1995 are not available. In general, some form of affiliation exists between approximately 70-80 percent of these centers and colleges and universities, but few universities serve as primary sponsoring organizations. Existing university-based centers have expanded their scale of operations but more as subcontractors to new entities than as lead organizations.

## Faculty Attitudes

Few issues have received as much attention and concern as the impacts of expanded technology transfer initiatives on the values and behaviors of faculty. Critics of these initiatives saw them leading to fundamental changes in the openness of science and as a blurring of the distinctive aspects of academic research (Gibbons and Wittrock, 1987). In contrast, it should be noted that the programs were specifically designed to change the cultures of universities, to make faculty more receptive to the needs of industry, and to have universities change their reward systems for promotion and tenure to reflect the institution's new missions.

How, in fact, have faculty responded to these new initiatives? Specification of a baseline is necessary. Faculty participation in industrially funded research projects is longstanding; consulting activities have always been attractive features of academic life; several major engineering universities (e.g., MIT) were established with ties to industry as a primary objective. Moreover, Etzkowitz (1983) has characterized the emergence of the quasi-firm, the large-scale research group dependent on external funding and directed by entrepreneurial faculty, as only a small step away from overt involvement in technology transfer.

The shift in faculty attitudes towards acceptance of the university's expanded mission in technology transfer and economic development is documented in several studies. Earlier studies (Blumenthal et al., 1986; 3Peters and Etzkowitz, 1990; Matkin, 1990) indicated a general receptivity to new initiatives. As stated by Peters and Etzkowitz in 1990: "Over the last eight years we have seen an increasing legitimizing of university-industry research interactions" (Peters and Etzkowitz, 1990, p. 428).[15]

More recent studies have further documented widespread acceptance by faculty of general emphases on technology transfer as well as continuing concerns that boundary markers, however much they have shifted, nevertheless not be removed. Based on survey responses of approximately 1,000 faculty at 115 randomly selected research-intensive universities, Lee (1995) finds that "...U.S. academics in the 1990s believe that they are more favorably disposed than in the 1980s towards closer university-industry collaboration" (Lee, 1995, p. iii). Lee also reports that "A majority of the respondents supports the idea that their universities participate actively in local and regional economic development, facilitate commercialization of academic research, and encourage faculty consulting for private firms" (ibid.). The apparent line to increased involvement in commercial activities was university involvement in start-up assistance or equity investment in business firms: a majority of respondents were opposed to proposals of this form.

Several variables affect faculty attitudes. Those who fear that university-industry collaboration may adversely affect academic freedom, long-term research, and academic integrity are unlikely to support university transfer; those without such fears are much more likely to support university transfer. Faculties in applied disciplines (e.g., chemical engineering and electrical engineering) are more supportive of transfer alternatives than those in the basic or social sciences. The latter finding is not surprising, and is reminiscent of Matkin's earlier accounts of the opposition by Liberal Arts faculty at Pennsylvania State University to the university's expanded mandate for economic development, and of Nora and Oliva's (1988) findings for research universities in Texas.

The hesitation reported by Lee from faculty in the basic sciences, who by extension of the above discussion on patent data are major contributors to institutional patent counts, is more complex and subject to multiple interpretations. One is that faculty can maintain discordant perspectives, holding different standards for their institutions than for themselves. Another is that faculty in the basic sciences may be accorded greater latitude by industrial sponsors in the setting of research agendas and the conduct of research than in applied fields. Firms that sponsor basic academic research may be self-selecting: their willingness to fund such research is indicative of an understanding of the uncertainties of such work, including the necessity for shifting directions and for openness in specifying project or time deliverables. In turn, this may lead to contractual and collaborative university-industry understandings that remain compatible with paradigmatic notions of unfettered academic research.

---

[15]"Professors with industry connections may conduct more extensive experiments in a particular area if it is of interest to industry, but rarely is there a complete or radical change in research direction. The effect is to enhance or stimulate research, leading at times to new interests" (Peters and Etzkowitz, 1990, p. 430).

There is a bread-and-butter aspect to this change in attitudes that owes less to new conceptualizations than to resource dependence. Faculty who feel pressured to obtain external grants display relatively more favorable attitudes toward transfer alternatives than those who do not.

Lee also reports an inverse relationship between faculty transfer attitudes and measures of institutional prestige. Although a majority of respondents in all prestige groupings support transfer activities, support "is stronger among the faculty in institutions ranked in the lower quartile than those in the top quartile" (Lee, 1995, p. 5). These findings are consistent with Garvin's (1980) view of "prestige-maximizing" and "utility-maximizing" institutions, the closer ties of the latter to local economic constituencies, and Mansfield's (1995) finding that industry representatives frequently view faculty from modestly ranked departments as playing as vital a role in industrial innovation as those from top-ranked departments.

Rahm's (1995) study of faculty behavior includes approximately 2,000 researchers, center directors, and administrative officials from the top 100 universities, ranked by annual R&D expenditures, in science and engineering departments. The study identified differences between those faculty with no technology transfer experiences (university-bound researchers) and those who have interacted with industry in efforts to transfer technology knowledge or know-how (boundary-spanning researchers).

Faculty engaged in technology transfer activities were found far more than university-bound researchers to personally initiate communications with firms, to have informal links with firms, to engage in paid industrial consulting, and to report that "former university students now working in industry sometimes or often contact them regarding firm needs" (Rahm, 1995, p. 271). Rahm observes that "it is clear that many researchers participate willingly in technology transfer activities with firms," and that these researchers "differ from the non-participating, university-bound colleagues in several important ways" (Rahm, 1995, p. 277). Among the differences are that participants "tend to come from departments and universities that provide firm-friendly curricular offerings, organizations and programs"; and are more likely to be crossdisciplinary, to affiliate with research centers, to be less likely to work as independent investigators, and to have personally initiated contacts with a firm regarding their research expertise than university-bound researchers.

A majority of boundary-spanning researchers (59 percent) do not think that an applied research focus hurts basic research. Despite this considerable interaction with industry, a substantial percentage (41 percent) of the boundary-spanning researchers and a majority of the university-bound researchers (54 percent) reported thinking that the emphasis on industrial research was having a negative effect on the basic research mission of the university (ibid., p. 275). The tenor of the findings from these surveys is also found in observations by directors of university technology licensing offices. The director of MIT's Technology Licensing

Office has observed that fewer faculty now believe that involvement in patent and licensing activities contaminates their standing with their academic colleagues or sponsors: "I saw that attitude commonly ten years ago, but not as much any more" (Nelson, as quoted in Katterman, 1995).

Both Lee's and Rahm's studies inquire about the weight accorded to patents in promotion and tenure decisions. In Rahm's study, 44 percent of boundary-spanning researchers and 33 percent of university-bound researchers report that efforts to get patents are rewarded by the university, while the balance of faculty in each class report that these efforts receive no recognition in personnel reviews.

The changes in faculty attitudes reported in these studies are seen by other authors as less wholesome. Brooks (1993), noting that the Cohen et al. study of UIRCs indicates that participating firms have the right to delete information in 35 percent of the centers to delay publication in 53 percent, and the right to do both in 31 percent, terms the trend disturbing; it suggests to him "...an erosion of the academic culture within them" (Brooks, 1993, p. 219). From the different vantage point of land-grant universities performing publicly supported agricultural research, Kleinman and Kloppenburg (1988) contend that the increase in university-industry cooperative R&D and changes in faculty attitudes towards greater acceptance of technology transfer amount to a privatization of publicly funded knowledge. The change in faculty attitudes towards greater acceptance of the commercialization of academic research is a development to be deplored, not applauded, for it sets the private gains of the researcher (and university) ahead of the public sector/social benefits that historically have characterized the mainstream public university.

## V. THE HISTORY OF UNIVERSITY TECHNOLOGY TRANSFER RECONSIDERED

Written as an historical chronology, this section would precede the one above; written as an examination of the evolving terms of a policy debate, it follows. Attention to the university's expanded and more aggressive role in technology transfer, with its attendant markers of patents, licensing, and start-ups, has been balanced by other recent treatments that see expanded university-industry collaboration more as a return to earlier patterns than as a break in university behavior. As noted by Mowery and Rosenberg (1989), "To a great extent, the recent development of closer research ties between universities and industry represents the restoration of a linkage that has been weakened in recent years, rather than a fundamental departure" (Mowery and Rosenberg, 1989, p. 259). This perspective draws from early and continuing engagement of American public universities in problem-driven research, often in response to the needs of local constituents and the historic contribution of universities to technological innovation.

## Applied and Basic Research Reconsidered

In response to the view described above—that new modes of technology transfer are needed to mitigate the research universities' predilection for basic research—Rosenberg and Nelson (1994) have recently provided details on the continuing involvement of American universities in applied, problem-solving, "hands-on" research. Applied research was the dominant form of academic research until about 1920, with basic research appearing only on American campuses in the late nineteenth century, and then only at select institutions (Veysey, 1965; Geiger, 1986; Rosenberg and Nelson, 1994). Throughout the nineteenth century, university research was directed towards agriculture, minerals, and engineering—the mainstays of knowledge-based economic activity of the period. As the new science-based, electrical, and chemical industries emerged towards the end of the nineteenth century, universities quickly responded by establishing new courses and degrees in these fields, providing the skilled personnel necessary to meet growing manpower requirements as well as helping establish the discipline and professions of electrical and chemical engineering. Universities also quickly became engaged in problem-focused research for these industries through grants, consulting, and even "occasionally through the establishment of firms that were headed by academics" (Rosenberg and Nelson, 1994, p. 328). Etzkowitz (1993) describes yet another contribution of universities to technological innovation—the development of core, common research facilities. Early development of commercial aviation depended heavily on the acquisition of experimental data to test the separate and interactive properties of the many component elements in the design of aircraft. Among aeronautics firms in the 1920s, mutual cooperative interests in a neutral ground for cooperative ventures, such as wind tunnels, gave rise to the support of the school of aeronautics at the California Institute of Technology.

The balancing of the university's major historic commitment to problem-focused research with its evolution as an institution predominantly engaged in basic research is not a single story, however. Several competing themes co-exist. One major theme, described in standard histories of the American university and most recently in Geiger's major studies (1986, 1993) is that the emergence of basic research as a major, much less dominant characteristic of the American university involved considerable struggle, especially for public universities. In each of the applied research areas noted above, conflicts existed between faculty interests in developing the underlying knowledge base of their research fields as well as in establishing professional autonomy in setting their own research agendas, and pressures from sponsors for immediate, economically implementable answers to pending technical problems. Scientists in state agricultural experiment stations, established under the Hatch Act of 1888, for example, had to challenge requirements to concentrate on fertilizer tests in order to reallocate resources, including their own time, to conduct more fundamental studies (Marcus, 1985).

The struggle to establish the legitimacy of basic research on their campuses colored faculty responses to subsequent overtures to engage in company-funded research (with perhaps lingering hues to the present). According to Swann (1988) in his account of relationships between academic scientists and the pharmaceutical industry in the early twentieth century: "The high value placed on fundamental research in American universities...helped impede any movement for collaboration with pharmaceutical firms on strictly applied work" (Swann, 1988, p. 30). Cooperative ventures between faculty and firms required adjustments by each. Industry, for its part, began to emphasize the value of research, including support of fundamental research, and began to establish special research laboratories and research institutes, to hire major scientists to head their research departments, and to fund fellowships. Changes by faculty and universities involved acceptance of the legitimacy of industry-sponsored work, and the beginnings of the technology patent and licensing policies that came to characterize the 1980s.[16]

Events of the 1980s may be viewed as a repeat of this earlier pattern, with notable differences. Again, industry's increased investment in basic research, fueled by expectations of profit from breakthrough scientific advances in selected fields in which universities were lead players, appears as a precipitating factor; in this latter period, however, three new sources of fuel were added— national and state government preoccupation with economic competitiveness, venture capital (which could quickly convert latent economic value in new knowledge into capitalized values; Kenney, 1986), and faculty and institutional pursuit of funds to maintain an existing research enterprise in the face of stagnant federal funds.

## Technology Transfer Reconsidered

The earlier statement that universities have long contributed to technological innovation did not address the means by which this contribution occurred. The agenda-building process leading to increased university commitments to technology transfer contained several assumptions that have more recently been challenged. These assumptions were that (1) existing levels of transfer were low; (2) transfer occurred largely through publication of research papers—essentially, an over-the-transom arrangement; and (3) industry sought the new modes of university technology transfer described in section IV.

**Levels of technology transfer.** A 1991 study by Edwin Mansfield, although

---

[16]"As the period between the wars drew to a close, university workers were more receptive to collaborative research with industry and less censorious in their view of industrial works and were themselves pursuing certain commercial practices with respect to medical discoveries formerly decried in academe..." (Swann, 1988, p. 54). In addition, "A rising number of universities, too, were using the patent system by the early 1920s," in part, ostensibly, to prevent pharmaceutical companies from establishing monopolies, but also, according to the President of Columbia University, "to enable the University itself to share in the benefits of the patents, to the end that the funds at its disposal for the promotion of research may be increased" (ibid., p. 55).

not unchallenged, has become the most widely cited confirmation of the "self-evident propositions of economic returns to academic research." The study involved estimates from a sample of 76 major firms in seven industries—information processing, electrical equipment, chemicals, instruments, drugs, metals, and oil. The focus was "academic research occurring within fifteen years of the commercialization of whatever innovation is being considered" (Mansfield, 1991, p. 1). R&D executives were asked to estimate the percentage of new products and processes introduced by these firms between 1975 and 1985 that could not have been developed without substantial delays in the absence of academic research conducted in the previous five years. For the entire sample, 11 percent of the new products and 9 percent of the new processes could not have been developed without such delays. The study's most salient and widely cited finding, albeit studded with caveats, was that the average annual rate of social return to academic research for the entire sample was 28 percent (Mansfield, 1991).[17]

The striking aspect of the Mansfield study is that it offers an independent measure of the economic value of the technology being transferred from universities to firms. The study also suggests that for all the flaws cited of pre-1980 initiatives to strengthen academic technology transfer, knowledge generated by universities was reaching firms and generating economic value to them.

**Technology transfer channels**. Means other than publications or consulting also existed for this transfer; one example was a byproduct of academic research. Eric von Hippel has documented the several ways in which users are frequently the sources of innovation (von Hippel, 1988). In the prototypical user-based sequence of innovation and diffusion, a user perceives that an advance in instrumentation is required, invents the instrument, builds a prototype, proves the prototype's value by applying it, and provides diffused detailed information on both the value of the intention and how the prototype devices can be replicated. Manufacturers then perform product engineering work on the device to improve its reliability and convenience of operation, and manufacture and market the product. Academic researchers are one class of users. Von Hippel's case studies as well as work by Rosenberg (1992) provide several examples of university researchers initiating this user-driven model of technological innovation, especially in scientific instrumentation and medical devices.

The dynamics of this process, enriched by nuanced interactions between faculty and firms, is highlighted in Gelijns and Rosenberg's (1995) account of endoscopic innovations. The invention of flexible endoscopy is credited to Basil Hirschowitz, a gastroenterologist, working in collaboration with C. Wilbur

---

[17]Mansfield's study also points to a mean time lag of seven years between academic research and industrial innovation. This finding is consistent with Ditzel's (1989) estimate, based on experiences at the University of California, that about seven years is required between the invention of a patentable invention by a university and the commencement of a significant royalty income stream. These estimates also underpin earlier statements about the difficulty of assessing the value of patent and technology licensing as profit centers in a period of rapid increases in the number of university patents.

Peters, an optical physicist, and Larry Curtiss, an undergraduate, at the University of Michigan. Their approach involved use of fiber-optic materials; the commercial fiberglass available to them was not adequate, and it was only through connections with the Corning Corporation that they were able to gain access to a supply of optical glass rods, an important step toward the subsequent invention. Their invention at first generated little interest among other researchers or firms in the U.S. or England. Eventually, a commercial firm that had unsuccessfully tried to make fiber-optic bundles undertook the product's manufacture, under license, but only if the three inventors would serve as consultants. As described by Gelijns and Rosenberg:

> It should be particularly noted, then, that the academic/medical trio at the University of Michigan not only solved a critical technological problem with respect to the new device—the cladding of the glass fiber—but they were also instrumental in teaching the industrial firm how to solve some complicated manufacturing problems....This is a drastic departure from what might be regarded as the "normal" division of labor between academics and instrument manufacturers (Gelijns and Rosenberg, 1995, p. 74).

**Modes of university technology transfer sought by industry**. Much of national and state policy promoting increased university technology transfer activities has been based on assumptions about what industry wants and needs from universities to bring new products and processes to the market. But what does the near doubling of industrial support that occurred during the 1980s in fact indicate about industrial firms' desires in the way of knowledge or technology transfer? No single answer is possible given that industries (and firms within industries) differ in their R&D-intensity and in the extent to which they are the sources of process and product innovation (as distinct from having new processes incorporated in the capital goods they purchase from other industries).

Still, a considerable body of research on industrial R&D and business strategy offers a base for some generalizations about the relationship between academic R&D and technological innovation. Industries report their perception that technical advances most often occur through "small incremental improvements to existing products and processes rather than as large technical breakthrough" (Government-University-Industry Research Roundtable, 1991, p. 1). These incremental advances occur most often in industry. Universities, according to the officials, "sometimes" play "a major role following a major breakthrough when it is necessary to establish a base of understanding on which the breakthrough can be bolstered and continue to grow" (ibid.). These views are repeated in the evaluations of major university-industry-government collaborative R&D programs reported above.

Research by economists on processes of technological innovation provides supporting views. The tenor of findings from this work is that academic research may provide new theoretical and empirical findings and new types of instruments essential for the development of a new product, but "Industrial R&D must be carried out to extend, supplement, and focus the findings of the Academic R&D" (Mansfield, 1991, p. 3). Mansfield's studies also reveal that universities are not likely to:

> play a central role or direct role in the development of new products and processes. Most of the new products and processes that could not have been developed (without substantial delay) in the absence of academic research were not invented at colleges or universities; instead, academic research provided new theoretical and empirical findings and new types of instrumentation that were essential for the development of the new product or process, but not the specific invention itself (Mansfield, 1991, p. 12).

David, Mowery, and Steinmueller (1988) express a similar view: "basic research results rarely lead directly to new processes or products with substantial modification….(It) is very difficult to directly attribute to one specific basic research output the economic applications that are separated from it by a substantial period of time, and the intervention of considerable other R&D expenditures)" (David, Mowery, and Steinmueller, 1988, p. 12). Nelson (1993) also has written that "…university research rarely in itself generates new technology; rather, it enhances technological opportunities and the productivity of private research and development, in a way that induces firms to spend more both in the industry in question and upstream" (Nelson, 1993, p. 188). Finally, according to Fusfeld (1994):

> There is no evidence that industry wants universities to use application as an important criteria for their research….There is an enormous difference between university research *being* of great value to industry compared to university research *planning* to be of great value to industry. There is little to be gained and much to lose by encouraging university researchers to think in terms of markets, manufacturing capabilities, or financial requirements. Consideration of those items is the responsibility of industrial research. Universities can maintain their strength in basic research by building bridges with industrial research, not with the marketplace (Fusfeld, 1994, p. 214).

## VI. CONCLUSION

What does recent experience about increased university involvement in technology transfer sum to? Quantitative indicators certainly show increased activity. Federal patent legislation and changes in university policies and structures have stimulated patenting activity, increased licensing, and increased numbers of start-ups. Total license revenues are increasing, and are likely to increase further in the near term as the cumulative impact of recent patent activities takes hold. A small number of institutions are now generating substantial sums of patent-based income; for the larger number of universities currently engaged in active patent and licensing activities, these activities are best described as loss-leaders, serving to induce additional sums of industrial research support, or as public service undertakings.

By themselves, these indicators have modest value in measuring technology transfer or economic impact. The increase in the number of university patents is offset by indications that the economic and technical value of the average patent is declining. License revenues paid by firms to universities may represent unrecovered costs if the processes or products derived from them prove not to be profitable. Lists of start-up firms are not indicators of sustained economic viability. The mortality rate for new firms is high, and there is little evidence to suggest that firms derived from university research fare any better or worse than comparable firms in the industry. Single success stories aside, the aggregate economic impact of most university initiatives in technology transfer is difficult to assess. In part, of course, this assessment reflects the still early stage, indeed infancy, of most university initiatives. It also reflects the poor state of evaluation.

University-industry cooperative R&D programs have become the dominant form for industry support of academic R&D. Both industrial and university participants report a broad set of benefits for these centers, including patents and licenses, but extending well beyond these markers of technology transfer. Firms report benefits from positive and negative findings from academic research, including improved information on the direction of internally performed research and development. The university-industry cooperative model also accommodates considerable variation in the matching of industry and university interests and capabilities. The future for university-industry R&D centers appears now to depend on the constantly evolving character of industrial R&D strategies, in particular (a) the aggregate level of industrial support of academic R&D and (b) decisions by R&D-intensive firms regarding whether to continue participation in such centers or to channel support to a select number of institutions under blanket agreements—an emerging pattern.

Findings on faculty attitudes suggest that they are increasingly accepting the university's commitment to technology transfer and their own involvement with industrially funded R&D. They still profess allegiance to norms of universal science while accepting publications delayed at times and incorporated into industrial R&D support. Not surprising, universities' acceptance of these new relationships is highest among disciplines that have a long association with industry or whose work has an applied orientation, and is least accepted among faculties in arts and sciences. Acceptance of this expanded mission has set the stage for a new set of intra-institutional issues relating to the weight to be accorded to patents and related measures of technology transfer.

Increased university and faculty involvement in commercial activity has been described both as inevitably challenging some of the traditions by which universities function and as irreversible. Matkin (1994) has written of the never ending balancing act that university leaders will need to perform "between the traditions of their institutions and the new demands placed on it by constituencies both inside and outside the university" (Matkin, 1994, p. 383). Campus debates about many issues—pitfalls of greater university involvement in technology transfer-diversion of faculty research agendas; distortion of graduate student dissertation topics; limits on the flow of findings; conflicts of interest; conflicts of commitment; overly optimistic ("winners curse") commitments of institutional funds to indigenous start-ups; loss of social capital as a disinterested source of expertise; and the privatization of knowledge supported by federal agencies—have largely ended. The issues have not gone away, however. A review of technology transfer outputs and outcomes, other than highlighting continuing and building university engagement, is not itself an examination of these concerns or of whether universities have learned how to correctly balance multiple objectives and commitments.

In relation to technology transfer, however, the review does raise new concerns about the ability of universities to achieve, much less maintain, a balance. Even as measures of technology transfer show increased university activity, a constant reminder of the limits to the university's effective role in technological innovation is necessary. The statements are compelling from both industry representatives and scholars: with rare exception, industry does not turn to universities for new commercial products and processes, nor, more importantly, does it want universities to become engaged in such pursuits. From industry's perspective, for universities to become more deeply involved in attempts to bring the fruits of academic research closer to marketable commodities under the rubric of technology transfer carries the risk of confounding competitive relationships among existing firms and of diverting universities from specializing in basic research and education—the things they are seen as doing best.

Technology transfer, however, has the potential to become a self-propelling force within the university. Newly socialized to move its research to market, facing few internal policy or attitudinal barriers, activated by the interests and undertakings of its own newly created offices, and tempted to pursue new financial opportunities to compensate for stagnant revenues from other sources, universities now operate with few clear dividing lines between technology transfer and the commercialization of academic research. The risk is in exaggerating their own capabilities in technology transfer and technological innovation.

### References

Association of American Universities (1986). *Trends in Technology Transfer at Universities*. Washington, DC: Association of American Universities.

Association of University Technology Managers (1994a). *The AUTM Licensing Survey Executive Summary and Selected Data Fiscal Years 1993, 1992, and 1991*. Association of University Technology Managers, Inc.

Association of University Technology Managers (1994b). *AUTM Public Benefits Survey— Summary of Results*. Association of University Technology Managers, Inc.

Babbitt, B. (1984). Grassroots industrial policy. *Issues in Science and Technology* 1: 84-93.

Bagby, J. (1995). *Applied Research Laboratory Technology Transfer and Intellectual Property Project: A Pilot Benchmarking Report*. Final report. University Park, PA: The Pennsylvania State University.

Baldwin, D., and Green, J. (1984-1985). University-industry relations: a review of the literature. *SRA Journal*: 57-77.

Ben Franklin Partnership Program (1991). An analysis of the research and development component of the Ben Franklin partnership program. Report of the Strategic Investment Decision Committee. Harrisburg, PA: Pennsylvania Department of Commerce.

Benowitz, S. (1995). The road to university technology licensing is littered with patents that languish. *The Scientist*, September 18, pp. 1ff.

Blumenstyk, G. (1995a). Turning off spinoffs. *Chronicle of Higher Education*, July 21, pp. A33ff.

Blumenstyk, G. (1995b). The next silicon valley? *Chronicle of Higher Education*, December 1, pp. A43ff.

Blumenstyk, G. (1992). States re-evaluate industrial collaborations built around research grants to universities. *Chronicle of Higher Education*, February 26, pp. 1ff.

Blumenthal, D., Gluck, M., Louis, K.M., and Wise, D. (1986). University-industry research relationships in biotechnology: implications for the university. *Science* 232: 1361-1366.

Blumenthal, D., Epstein, S., and Maxwell, J. (1986). Commercializing university research—lessons from the experience of the Wisconsin Alumni Research Foundation. *New England Journal of Medicine* 25: 1361-1366.

Bohlander, R. A. (1994). *Analysis of Dual Use Technology Development/Technology Transfer at the Georgia Tech Manufacturing Research Center*. Final Technical Report prepared for U.S. Army Missile Command. Atlanta, GA: Georgia Institute of Technology.

Bok, D. (1982). *Beyond The Ivory Tower*. Cambridge, MA: Harvard University Press.

Brooks, H. (1994). The relationship between science and technology. *Research Policy* 23: 477-487.

Brooks, H. (1993). Research universities and the social contract for science. In L. Branscomb (ed.), *Empowering Technology*. Cambridge, MA: MIT Press, pp. 202-234.

Coburn, C., ed. (1995). *Partnerships*. Columbus, OH: Battelle.

Cohen, W., Florida, R., and Goe, R. (1992). *University-Industry Research Centers in the United States*. Pittsburgh, PA: Carnegie Mellon University.

Cohen, W., and Levinthal, D. (1989). Innovation and earning: the two faces of R&D. *Economic Journal* 99: 569-596.

Dasgupta, P., and David, P.A. (1994). Towards a new economics of science. *Research Policy* 23: 487-522.

David, P.A., Mowery, D., and Steinmueller, E. (1994). University-industry research collaborations: managing missions in conflict. Paper presented at the CEPR/AAAS Conference: University Goals, Institutional Mechanisms, and the Industrial Transferability of Research.

David, P.A., Mowery, D., and Steinmueller, E. (1992). Analyzing the economic payoffs from basic research. *Economics of Innovation and New Technology* 2: 73-90.

David, P.A., Mowery, D., and Steinmueller, E. (1988). *The Economic Analysis of Payoffs from Basic Research: An Examination of the Case of Particle Physics Research*. Palo Alto, CA: Stanford University.

Dertouzos, M., Lester, R., and Solow, R. (1989). *Made in America*. Cambridge, MA: MIT Press.

Dickson, D. (1984). *The New Politics of Science*. New York: Pantheon Books.

Dimancescu, D., and Botkin, J. (1986). *The New Alliance*. Cambridge, MA: Ballinger.

Ditzel, R. (1989). The commercialization of university technology in the 1990s. Unpublished manuscript. University of California.

Dorfman, N. (1983). Route 128: the development of a regional high technology economy. *Research Policy* 12: 299-316.

Ebert, J., Fields, C., and Syngaarden, J. (1991). *Evaluation of the Advanced Research and Advanced Technology Programs*. A Report to the Texas Higher Education Coordinating Board.

Eisenberg, R. (1995). *Public Research and Private Development: Patents and Technology Transfer in the Human Genome Project*. Ann Arbor, MI: University of Michigan Law School.

Eisinger, P. (1995). State economic development in the 1990s. *Economic Development Quarterly* 9: 146-158.

Eisinger, P. (1988). *The Rise of the Entrepreneurial State*. Madison, WI: University of Wisconsin Press.

Ergas, H. (1987). The importance of technology policy. In P. Dagupta and P. Stoneman (eds.), *Economic Policy and Technological Performance*. Cambridge, UK: Cambridge University Press.

Etzkowitz, H. (1993). Enterprises from science: the origins of science-based regional economic development. *Minerva* 31: 326-360.

Etzkowitz, H. (1991). Profiting from knowledge: organizational innovations and the evolution of academic norms. *Minerva* 29: 81-95.

Etzkowitz, H. (1983). Entrepreneurial scientists and entrepreneurial universities in American academic science. *Minerva* 21: 198-233.

Fairweather, J. (1988). *Entrepreneurship and Higher Education: Lessons for Colleges, Universities, and Industry*. ASHE-ERIC Higher Education Report No. 6. Washington, DC: Association for the Study of Higher Education.

Feller, I. (1994). The university as an instrument of state and regional economic development—the rhetoric and reality of the U.S. experience. Paper prepared for the Conference on the Industrial Transferability of Research, Stanford University, March 18-20.

Feller, I. (1993). What agricultural extension has to offer as a model for manufacturing modernization. *Journal of Policy Analysis and Management* 12: 574-581.

Feller, I. (1990). Universities as engines of R&D-based economic growth: they think they can. *Research Policy* 19: 335-348.

Feller, I. (1990). University-industry R&D relationships. In J. Schmandt and R. Wilson (eds.), *Growth Policy in the Age of High Technology*. Boston: Unwin Hyman), pp. 313-343.

Feller, I. (1990). University patent and technology-licensing strategies. *Educational Policy* 4: 327-334.

Feller, I., and Anderson, G. (1994). A benefit-cost approach to the evaluation of state technology development programs. *Economic Development Quarterly* 8: 127-140.

Feller, I., and Roessner, J.D. (1995). What does industry expect from university partnerships? *Issues in Science and Technology* 12: 80-84.

Finn, R. (1995). Michigan State University patent dispute illustrates changes in technology transfer. *The Scientist*. October 30, pp. 1ff.

Fosler, S., ed. (1988). *The New Economic Role of the States*. New York: Oxford University Press.

Fusfeld, H. (1994). *Industry's Future: Changing Patterns of Industrial Research*. Washington, DC: American Chemical Society.

Garvin, D.A. (1980). *The Economics of University Behavior*. New York: Academic Press.

Geiger, R. (1993). *Research and Relevant Knowledge*. New York: Oxford University Press.

Geiger, R. (1986). *To Advance Knowledge*. New York: Oxford University Press.

Geiger, R., and Feller, I. (1995). The dispersion of academic research in the 1980s. *Journal of Higher Education* 66: 336-360.

Geisler, E., and Rubenstein, A. (1989). University-industrial relations: a review of the major issues. In A. Link and G. Tassey (eds.), *Cooperative Research and Development: The University-Industry-Government Relationship*. Boston: Kluwer Academic Publishers, pp. 43-62.

Gelijns, A., and Rosenberg, N. (1995). From the scalpel to the scope: endoscopic innovations in gastroenterology, gynecology, and surgery. In N. Rosenberg, A. Gelijns, and H. Dawkins (eds.), *Sources of Medical Technology: Universities and Industry*. Washington, DC: National Academy Press, pp. 67-96.

Gibbons, M., and Wittrock, B., eds. (1987). *Science as a Commodity*. London: Longman.

Gibson, D., and Smilor, R. (1991). The role of the research university in creating and sustaining the U.S. technopolis. In A. Brett, D. Gibson, and R. Smilor (eds.), *University Spin-off Companies*. Savage, MD: Rowman & Littlefield Publishers, pp. 31-70.

Glasmeier, A. (1988). Factors governing the development of high-tech industry agglomerations: a tale of three cities. *Regional Studies* 22(4): 287-301.

Goldstein, H., Maier, G., and Luger, M. (1994). The university as an instrument for economic and business development: U.S. and European comparisons. Paper prepared for "Universities and Society: International Perspectives on Public Policies and Institutional Reform," an invitational symposium in cooperation with and sponsored by the Wirtschaftsuniversitat Wien and the University of North Carolina, Chapel Hill. Vienna, Austria.

Government-University-Industry Research Roundtable (1992). *Fateful Choices: The Future of the U.S. Academic Research Enterprise*. Washington, DC: National Academy of Sciences.

Government-University-Industry Research Roundtable (1991). *Industrial Perspectives on Innovation and Interactions with Universities*. Washington, DC: National Academy Press.

Government-University-Industry Research Roundtable (1986). *New Alliances and Partnerships in American Science and Engineering*. Washington, DC: National Academy of Sciences.

Gray, D., Hetzner, W., Eveland, J.D., and Gidley, T. (1986). NSF's industry-university cooperative research centers program and the innovation process: evaluation based lessons. In D. Gray, W. Hetzner, J.D. Eveland, and T. Gidley (eds.), *Technological Innovation Strategies for a New Partnership*. Amsterdam: North Holland, pp. 175-193.

Gregory, W., and Sheahen, T. (1991). Technology transfer by spin-off companies versus licensing. In A. Brett, D. Gibson, and R. Smilor (eds.), *University Spin-off Companies*. Savage, MD: Rowman & Littlefield Publishers, pp. 133-151.

Griliches, Z. (1990). Patent statistics as economic indicators: a survey. *Journal of Economic Literature* 28: 1661-1707.

Haller, H. (1984). *Examples of University-Industry (Government) Collaborations*. Ithaca, NY: Cornell University Press.

Henderson, R., Jaffe, A., and Trajtenberg, M. (1995). *Universities as a Source of Commercial Technology: A Detailed Analysis of University Patenting 1965-1988*. National Bureau of Economic Research, Working Paper No. 5068.

Hetzner, W., Gidley, T., and Gray, D. (1989). Cooperative research and rising expectations. *Technology in Society* 11: 335-345.

Huffman, W., and Evenson, R. (1993). *Science for Agriculture*. Ames, IA: Iowa State University Press.

Jaffe, A. (1989). Real effects of academic research. *American Economic Review* 79: 957-970.

Johnson, L. (1984). *The High-Tech Connection: Academic-Industrial Cooperation for Economic Growth*. Washington, DC: ASHE-ERIC.

Jones, B., and Vedlitz, A. (1988). Higher education policies and economic growth in the American states. *Economic Development Quarterly* 2: 78-87.

Katterman, L. (1995). University technology offices focus effort on overcoming academic "cultural" barriers. *The Scientist*, June 12, pp. 1ff.

Kenney, M. (1986). *Biotechnology: The University-Industrial Complex*. New Haven, CT: Yale University Press.

Kleinman, D., and Kloppenburg, J., Jr. (1988). Biotechnology and university-industry relations: policy issues in research and the ownership of intellectual property at a land grant university. *Policy Studies Journal* 17: 83-96.

Lambright, H., and Teich, A. (1989). Science, technology and state economic development. *Policy Studies Journal* 18: 135-147.

Larsen, J., and Wigand, R. (1987). Industry-university technology transfer in microelectronics. *Policy Studies Review* 6: 101-115.

Larson, C. (1994). Trends in U.S. industrial research and development. In A. Teich, S. Nelson, and C. McEnaney (eds.), *Science and Technology Policy Handbook-1994*. Washington, DC: American Association for the Advancement of Science), pp. 247-252.

Lee, Y. (1995). *The Academic Climate and Technological Innovation*. Ames, IA: Iowa State University). Final Report to the National Science Foundation.

Luger, M., and Goldstein, H. (1991). *Technology in the Garden*. Chapel Hill, NC: University of North Carolina Press.

Malecki, E. (1991). *Technology and Economic Development*. New York: John Wiley & Sons.

Mansfield, E. (1995). Academic research underlying industrial innovations: sources, characteristics, and financing. *Review of Economics and Statistics* 77: 55-65.

Mansfield, E. (1994). Links between university research and industrial innovation. Paper presented to the Conference of "University Goals, Institutional Mechanisms, and the 'Industrial Transferability' of Research," Stanford University (March).

Mansfield, E. (1991). Academic research and industrial innovation. *Research Policy* 20: 1-12.

Marcus, A. (1985). *Agricultural Science and the Quest for Legitimacy*. Ames, Iowa: Iowa State University Press.

Marcy, W., and Kosloski, B. (1982). *Summary of Patents Resulting from NSF Chemistry Program*. New York: Research Corporation. Report to the National Science Foundation, Office of Audit and Oversight, Contract No. 1 EVL-810-7272.

Markusen, A., Hall, P., and Glasmeier, A. (1986). *High-Tech America*. New York: Allen and Unwin.

Matkin, G. (1994). Technology and public policy: lessons from a case study. *Policy Studies Journal* 22: 371-383.

Matkin, G. (1990). *Technology Transfer and the University*. New York: American Council on Education.

Mitchell, W. (1991). Using academic technology: transfer methods and licensing incidence in the commercialization of american diagnostic imaging equipment research, 1975-1988. *Research Policy* 20: 203-216.

Mount Auburn Associates (1992). *An Evaluation of Ohio's Thomas Edison Technology Centers*. Final Report to the Ohio Department of Development. Somerville, MA.

Mowery, D., and Rosenberg, N. (1989). *Technology and the Pursuit of Economic Growth*. Cambridge: Cambridge University Press.

National Academy of Engineering (1989). *Assessment of the National Science Foundation's Engineering Research Centers Programs*. A report for the National Science Foundation. Washington, DC: National Academy of Engineering.

National Research Council, Commission to Review the Ohio Thomas Edison Technology Centers (1990). *Ohio's Thomas Edison Centers: A 1990 Review*. Washington, DC: National Academy Press.

National Research Council (1993). *Learning to Change*. Washington, DC.

National Science Foundation (1993). *Science and Engineering Indicators—1993*. Washington, DC: National Science Board.

Nelson, R., ed. (1993). *National Innovation Systems: A Comparative Analysis*. New York: Oxford University Press.

Neuer, A. (1995). Academic technology transfer offices evolve into marketing units. *The Scientist*, April 17, pp. 1ff.

*New York Times* (1988). Harvard to seek research profits. September 15, p. A21.

Nora, A., and Olivas, M. (1988). Faculty attitudes toward industrial research on campus. *Research in Higher Education* 29: 125-147.

Peters, L., and Etzkowitz, H. (1990). University-industry connections and academic values. *Technology in Society* 12: 427-440.

Peters, L., and Fusfeld, H. (1983). Current U.S. university/industry research connections. In National Science Foundation, *University-Industry Research Relationships: Selected Studies*. Washington, DC: National Science Board.

Petrick, I. (1995). Empirical evidence on divergent goals and perceptions of success in university-industry research networks. Paper presented to the Technology Transfer Society Annual Meeting. Washington, DC.

Praeger, D., and Omenn, G. (1980). Research, innovation and university-industry linkages. *Science* 207(2980): 379-384.

Rahm, D. (1995). *University-Firm Linkages for Industrial Innovation*. Report to the National Science Foundation, Grant No. SBR-9305591.

Rahm, D. (1994). Academic perceptions of university-firm technology transfer. *Policy Studies Journal* 22: 267-278.

Rahm, D. (1994). U.S. universities and technology transfer. *Industry and Higher Education* (June): 72-78.

Reich, L. (1985). *The Making of American Industrial Research*. Cambridge: Cambridge University Press.

Reimers, N. (1989). Commercialization of ideas in a research environment. Paper presented to the Workshop on Patent Development, University of Missouri-Columbia.

Roberts, E. (1991). *Entrepreneurs in High Technology*. New York: Oxford University Press.

Roberts, E., and Peters, D. (1981). Commercial innovation from university faculty. *Research Policy* 10: 108-126.

Roessner, J. D., and Wise, A. (1994). Industry perspectives on external sources of technology and technical information. *Policy Studies Journal* 22: 349-358.

Rosenberg, N. (1992). Scientific instrumentation and university research. *Research Policy* 21: 381-390.

Rosenberg, N. (1990). Why do firms do basic research with their own money? *Research Policy* 19: 165-174.

Rosenberg, N., and Nelson, R.R. (1994). American universities and technical advance in industry. *Research Policy* 23: 325-348.

Rubenstein, A. (1995). Final report on a study of relations between university-industry interaction and industrial innovation. Center for Information and Telecommunications Technology, Northwestern University. Evanston, IL.

Samson, K., and Gurdon, M. (1993). University scientists as entrepreneurs: a special case of technology transfer and high-tech venturing. *Technovation* 13: 63-71.

Sandelin, J. (1994). University patenting and technology licensing as a mechanism for knowledge transfers. Paper presented at the conference, "University Goals, Institutional Mechanisms, and the 'Industrial Transferability' of Research," Stanford University, March 18-20.

Saxenian, A. (1994). *Regional Advantage*. Boston, MA: Harvard University Press.

Schmitt, R. (1986). Engineering research and international competitiveness. In National Research Council, *The New Engineering Research Centers*. Washington, DC: National Academy Press, pp. 100-106.

Scott, C., and Schaad, D. (1994). *Understanding Technology Transfer in NSF Industry/University Cooperative Research Centers*. Seattle, WA: University of Washington.

Shapira, P. (1990). *Modernizing Manufacturing*. Washington, DC: Economic Policy Institute.

Slaughter, S. (1990). *The Higher Learning & High Technology*. Albany, NY: State University of New York Press.

Southern Technology Council (1995). *Benchmarking University-Industry Technology Transfer in the South: 1993-1994 Data*.

SRI (1986). *The Higher Education-Economic Development Connection*. Washington, DC: American Association of State Colleges and Universities.

SRI (1985). *NSF Engineering Program Patent Study*. Report prepared for the National Science Foundation, Final Report, NSF Contract No. EVL-8319583.

Steinnes, D.N.C. (1987). On understanding and evaluating the university's evolving economic development policy. *Economic Development Quarterly* 1(3): 214-225.

Swann, J. (1988). *Academic Scientists and the Pharmaceutical Industry*. Baltimore, MD: The Johns Hopkins Press.

U.S. Congress, Office of Technology Assessment (1991). *Federally Funded Research: Decisions for a Decade*. Washington, DC: U.S. Government Printing Service.

U.S. Congress, Office of Technology Assessment (1990). *Making Things Better*. OTA-ITE- 443. Washington, DC: U.S. Government Printing Office.

U.S. General Accounting Office (1992). *University Research, Controlling Inappropriate Access to Federally Funded Research Results*. Report to the Chairman, Human Resources and Intergovernmental Relations Subcommittee, Committee on Government Operations, House of Representatives. Washington, DC: U.S. Government Printing Office.

U.S. General Accounting Office (1988). *Engineering Research Centers, NSF Program Management and Industrial Sponsorship*. GAO/RCED-88-177. Washington, DC.

Veblen, T. (1917). *The Higher Learning in America*. New York: Viking Press edition, 1935.

von Hippel, E. (1988). *The Sources of Innovation*. New York: Oxford University Press.

Veysey, L. (1965). *The Emergence of the American University*. Chicago: University of Chicago Press.

Weinberg, M., and Mazey, M.E. (1988). Government-university-industry partnerships in technology development: a case study. *Technovation* 7: 131-142.

Williams, B. (1986). The direct and indirect role of higher education in industrial innovation: what should we expect. *Minerva*: 145-171.

Wisconsin Alumni Research Foundation (1986). Summary Report, Madison, WI.

# State Policy And Private Higher Education:
# Past, Present and Future

## William Zumeta
*University of Washington*

## INTRODUCTION

The title of this chapter implies that there are state policies which affect the private (independent, nonprofit) sector of higher education[1] and that these are worthy of attention. This may not be obvious to the casual observer who might well think that state higher education policies are concerned almost exclusively with public colleges and universities. Recent survey evidence indicates that a surprising number of state policymakers share such a public-only (or at least public-mostly) perspective (Zumeta, 1989; 1992; 1994; Education Commission of the States, 1990).

Nonetheless, as will be explained, many state policies do affect private higher education in important ways and this sector in turn can help to achieve public purposes. To the extent the independent sector is significant in American higher education, or in particular states, it is well that these policies and their impacts be examined. Also, many observers have been concerned for a number of years that the valuable resource represented by the private sector of American higher education has been imperiled by the combined forces of the long decline in the number of high-school graduates, rapid growth in the price of private higher education (especially relative to public alternatives), and the sluggish and erratic growth in federal student aid funding since the early 1980s.[2]

Further, the argument will be made in this chapter that the private sector's role in meeting emerging future demands on higher education—demands that will be increasingly difficult to meet in the accustomed ways—could be quite important,

---

[1]The focus of this chapter is on private, *nonprofit*, or independent, colleges and universities, not (except peripherally) on private, for-profit and vocational postsecondary institutions. Hence, the terms *private* and *independent* higher education will be used interchangeably.

[2] See Carnegie Council (1977), Education Commission of the States (1977; 1990), Breneman and Finn (1978), McPherson and Schapiro (1991), and Breneman (1994).

but only if state policies consciously facilitate this. It will also be argued, however, from both theoretical and empirical perspectives, that in many states there are powerful forces at play that tend to work against such explicit state recognition of the role and potential of private higher education.

## Purposes and Approach of the Chapter

The purposes of this chapter are several. First, I will expand upon the above themes in order to explain why the topic of state policies affecting private higher education is important in an emerging era of increasing demands on higher education but also extreme pressures on its traditional sources of support. Then, I shall trace the development of public policies affecting private higher education historically and comparatively, emphasizing especially the period since about 1970. This review will cover the highlights of the pertinent literature and will attempt to assess in broad terms the consequences of policies, as well as of larger contextual conditions, on private higher education. The coverage includes federal as well as state policies, for in most periods in U.S. history, what the federal government was doing or not doing is critical to understanding the context for state higher education policy.

Next, I will offer a theoretical perspective seeking to comprehend and explain the variability in states' attention to the private higher education sector and, in particular, why many states tend to pay it little heed. I will argue that such a posture has had real consequences in the recent past and will, in general, not serve states well in the years to come, while other feasible postures should work better for many states. Finally, I will suggest key issues for further work in both theory development and empirical research and analysis in this field.

## Why Private Higher Education and State Policies Affecting It Are Important

The private higher education sector in the United States is of historic and, it will be argued here, high current importance. The contributions of the private sector to broad public purposes date back to the colonial period (Rudolph, 1962; Veysey, 1965; Trow, 1993), and are well-known and widely envied around the world, where substantial private sectors are relatively rare (Clark, 1983; Geiger, 1986; Levy, 1986; Kerr, 1991). This admiration is in part due to the high quality of many of America's private institutions, which serves as a benchmark for their public counterparts. Ashby (1971), Clark (1983), and Kerr (1991), among others, have suggested that American private higher education has also provided important models of autonomous but socially responsible governance and behavior to public higher education both here and abroad. These are valuable public purposes served uniquely by independent higher education.

American private colleges and universities are a highly variegated lot, representing a wide variety of cultural, philosophical, and religious, as well as experimental academic, perspectives, and diverse and unusual combinations of subject area specialties. This provides a rich range of choices for students and potential sponsors and supporters that the public sector, with its church-state and other political and bureaucratic limitations, could never match. This is a real virtue in a country as diverse as the contemporary United States. Also, as nongovernmental, largely market-driven entities, private institutions can often respond more quickly— and with more variety, thus serving as a hedge against uncertainty— to new societal needs than can more cumbersome, layered public systems. If some responses prove inappropriate, these can also be more easily allowed to die out or pressured by the environment to adapt than is usually the case in public systems (Thompson and Zumeta, 1981; Birnbaum, 1983).

Moreover, private colleges and universities also do more to serve the equity goals of public policy than is widely appreciated. Nationally, these schools enroll nearly as high a proportion of minority students as do public four-year institutions (National Institute of Independent Colleges and Universities, 1992; Breneman 1994), and graduate a substantially higher percentage of those they enroll (Porter, 1989). Also, according to studies in several states, the family income profile of private college students in the aggregate is very similar to that of students in the four-year public sector and is substantially lower than that of the leading public research universities.[3]

Private higher education institutions are also broadly, if somewhat unevenly, distributed across the country. There are private, nonprofit colleges in the District of Columbia and in 49 of the 50 states. In the fall of 1992, a total of more than 1,800 such institutions enrolled some 2.95 million undergraduate and graduate students (Zumeta, 1994). Even limiting attention to four-year, Carnegie-classified, general-purpose colleges and universities (thereby excluding hundreds of two-year, unclassified and specialized institutions[4]), the aggregate headcount enrollment in this narrowly defined private higher education sector is more than 2.4 million. Although their market share has declined sharply since World War II, private colleges and universities still grant some 28 percent of all baccalaureate degrees, 36 percent of all Ph.D.s, and 60 percent of all first-professional degrees, including a high percentage of teacher education degrees (ECS, 1990).   Thus, the private sector is of real importance to national goals in regard to skilled labor force development.

The proportion of statewide headcount enrollments (including two-year enrollments) in independent colleges and universities is small in some states but ranges to above 50 percent in Massachusetts and to more than 80 percent in the District of Columbia. In the fall of 1992, private sector enrollments were more than a third of

---

[3]In 1993, the estimated median family income of dependent students enrolled at independent colleges and universities was about $46,000. Studies conducted in California, Florida, Minnesota, and Oregon generally show that, contrary to popular belief, the median family income of private-college students tends to be similar to that of students enrolled in four-year public institutions, and below the median income of students attending "flagship" public research universities (National Institute of Independent Colleges and Universities, 1995).

[4]The "specialized" designation includes seminaries, free-standing law and medical schools, and the like.

the statewide total in seven states (plus D.C.) and were 20 percent or more in 17 states plus D.C.[5] The overall "market share" figure for the private higher education sector in the nation was just over 20 percent in 1992, down from around 50 percent just after World War II (McPherson and Schapiro, 1991, p. 22). If two-year institution enrollments are excluded, the nationwide private-sector share in 1992 jumps to 29 percent. It has been estimated that it would cost taxpayers an additional $12 billion annually (1990 dollars) to educate in the public sector all the students now attending private colleges and universities (ECS, 1990, p. 11). Most of this sum, of course, would be paid by state taxpayers.

Thus, there is ample reason for public policy to be concerned with the capacity and vitality of private higher education, given the key societal functions it performs uniquely (or particularly well) and the extent to which it eases burdens on the public fisc in many states. If the private sector continued to perform these functions in the absence of policy intervention or change, there would be no cause for concern. But, as will be argued below, there are reasons to think that important parts of the private sector will be unable to do so, indeed are already visibly slipping in their ability to serve key public purposes.

In light of the limited resources pragmatically available to governments today, the point about reducing burdens on the public fisc takes on added importance. Most importantly, although many state policymakers are not yet fully aware of it, a majority of states will soon face increases—some very substantial increases—in the demand for places in higher education simply by virtue of known demographic trends. In particular, the maturation to college age of the large "baby boom echo" cohort of children born in the 1970s and early 1980s and the effects of recent population growth patterns will be felt very strongly in many states by 2000 and in the years beyond. According to the latest state-by-state projections by the Western Interstate Commission on Higher Education (1993), the number of high-school graduates is projected to increase between 1994-95 and 2004-05 *by thirty percent or more* in ten states (including populous California and Florida), by 15 to 29 percent in 13 more, and by ten percent or more in yet another half-dozen states (Figure 1). These figures are a good rough, though probably conservative, indicator of pressures on enrollment capacity in higher education (hereafter termed simply "demand").[6]

---

[5]The state-level private market share figures reported here were developed by the author with the aid of Dr. Penelope Karovsky, University of Washington, and the National Institute of Independent Colleges and Universities, from the federal Integrated Postsecondary Education Data System (IPEDS) survey data. We have been careful to exclude the private proprietary and vocational schools included by the federal government in its reports from this data base.

[6]The figures are projected from trends in actual data on public and private high-school graduates through 1991-92 (WICHE, 1993). They are probably conservative as indicators of trends in higher education demand because they take no account of recent patterns of increased demand for higher education from older adults and employers seeking worker training, and of the effects of improvements in instructional technology and delivery systems on demand.

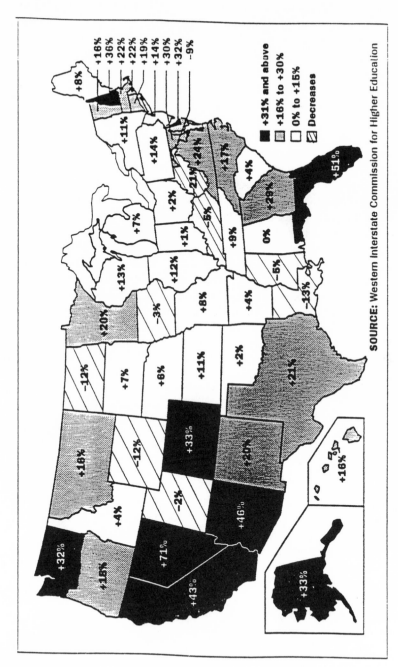

FIGURE 1. Projected Change in the Number of High-school Graduates, 1994–95 to 2004–05

Source: *The Chronicle of Higher Education* Almanac Issue. Sept. 1, 1994

Additional increases in demand for higher education may well be spurred by clear recent signs of strong labor market rewards for college graduates relative to their less-educated peers (Murphy and Welch, 1989), and by the growing interest of employers and employees in higher education as a means of increasing workers' human capital.[7] In many cases high-cost professional school enrollment slots (e.g., in engineering and some health professions) will be in particular demand. Yet, in the face of this growing demand, many public higher education systems are at or near capacity to enroll students and would have to build additional buildings or whole campuses and hire additional faculty to expand enrollments significantly.[8] This is likely to be a very expensive proposition on a per-student basis at a time when public support for taxes and public spending is at a low ebb.

While some public sector expansion will no doubt be necessary in states with growing enrollment demand, many of these same states have private colleges and universities with apparent slack capacity after years of relatively stable or even declining enrollments. Six states[9] showed a decline over the 1980-92 period in undergraduate enrollments in private, four-year colleges and universities, and another seven experienced only modest aggregate increases (less than ten percent) over these twelve years, suggesting that some private institutions in these states may well have additional capacity.[10] Indeed if full-time-equivalent (FTE) enrollment counts are used instead of headcounts, the number of states showing declines in enrollment or only modest increases (<10%) over the 1980-92 period increases to 16.[11] Among these 16 states with sluggish recent enrollments in the

---

[7]There is evidence that the weak job market created by the recession reduced returns on investment for college graduates (Mishel and Bernstein, 1992), though economic returns remain high by historical standards. There is good reason to believe this is a short-term blip in a long-term upward trend in returns to investment in higher education (Marshall and Tucker, 1992).

[8]For example, California, Florida, Virginia, and Washington all face strong pressures to expand their already-full public higher education systems to accommodate large increases in the college-age population (Zumeta and Looney, 1994). Washington also seeks to increase its below average participation rate in upper-division and graduate education (Washington Higher Education Coordinating Board, 1992). Another large state, Pennsylvania, anticipates only modest increases in high-school graduates (14 percent between 1994-95 and 2004-05) but has made increasing participation in higher education a major priority and so is greatly concerned about capacity constraints in its public sector. These cases are only illustrative but they show that capacity constraints in the public sector are not a problem limited to small states or the "Sunbelt."

[9]For these purposes, the District of Columbia is considered a state.

[10]A recent survey by the author of state independent sector association executive officers provides further evidence of underutilized capacity in private higher education (Zumeta, 1994). Of 33 respondents (states) to a question about numbers of additional students that independent colleges and universities in the respondent's state could accept without a major additional investment in facilities and faculty, the median response represented a 10 percent increase over the sector's Fall 1990 enrollment (mean = +13%). When asked how many additional students private institutions *would be willing to accept assuming adequate quality students and government-funded student aid*, the median percentage increase relative to 1990 enrollment jumped to +14% and the mean to +21% (n=31).

[11]This difference, of course, reflects the trend toward greater proportions of part-time enrollments in private institutions (Zumeta, 1994). Significantly, in more than half the states (27), private-sector enrollments of *full-time* students either declined or grew by less than ten percent over the 1980-92 period.

private sector, four anticipate growth in high-school graduates over the next decade (1994-95 through 2004-05) in the twenty percent range or more, and four more expect growth in the 9-14 percent range.

Incremental costs to add students at private institutions with slack capacity should be relatively low, certainly lower than the per-student cost of building additional capacity in the public higher education sector.[12] Moreover, some private institutions wish to grow regardless of slack capacity considerations and it may well be in the taxpayer's interest for them to do so where demand for higher education is strong, even if such growth requires some financial inducement from the state.[13] For present purposes, the primary point is that private higher education's capacity and vitality (that is, quality and capacity to grow) is, if anything, more squarely than ever a legitimate concern of policymakers.

Yet, even as its potential capacity is increasingly needed, private higher education faces threats to its ability to continue to serve public purposes well. These threats trace back, in their most serious form, to around 1980 when the number of high-school graduates began a decline that is just now coming to an end nationally (U.S. Department of Education, 1995); when there began a rapid increase in the private/public "tuition gap" (Clotfelter, 1991); and when the growth in federal student aid funds (particularly grants) slowed dramatically (College Board, 1994). These developments are in all likelihood a factor in the declines in private sector enrollments during the 1980-92 period in several states mentioned above, in the exodus of middle-income students from private institutions identified by Zumeta (1990) and McPherson and Schapiro (1991), and in the sharply increasing trend in private institutions' spending on student aid to attract students (National Institute of Independent Colleges and Universities, 1990; College Board, 1994; Breneman, 1994). These latter trends do suggest potential problems in the ability of the private higher education sector, or at least parts of it, to serve public purposes, problems which are sometimes exacerbated by public policy.[14]

It must be noted, however, that it is not at all clear that private higher education has fared terribly badly with the limited attention it has received from public policy during the recent period of very difficult contextual conditions. Nationwide, full-time-equivalent enrollments in private higher education grew by about eleven percent between 1980 and 1992, not far behind the growth rate over this period in public sector enrollments (Zumeta, 1994). As indicated earlier, there was some enrollment

[12]The comparative cost advantage of the private sector may disappear where public institutions also have slack capacity. Even so, funding arrangements for public institutions may not fully reflect this as they are often tied more closely to average than to marginal costs.

[13]This analysis assumes that the state does not have to pay as much per student-place for private sector capacity as it would pay for new public sector capacity. (It also assumes adequate quality in the private sector.) When the state payments approach a level equal to per-student subsidies (including capital costs) in the public sector, this would be a signal to cap these inducements.

[14]For example, state policies in the area of expansion and pricing of public higher education and in design and funding of student aid programs can have substantial impacts on private institutions. These and other specific policy issue areas are discussed in the analysis which follows.

growth in the private sector in nearly nine-tenths of the states during this period and the coming years promise substantially more favorable underlying demographic trends in most states. In short, the evidence on private higher education's health and prospects is decidedly mixed.[15] The argument for enhanced public policy attention to the private sector thus hinges at least as much on the notion of states seizing an opportunity to meet their emerging needs cost-effectively as on any urgent need to rescue a valued sector of higher education that is in serious trouble.

It will be argued here that state policies toward private higher education have been, for most of U.S. history and with few exceptions, of a generally limited, largely "hands off" character. There are important variations—the major outlines of which will be sketched later—and there has been a clear tendency toward more state involvement in recent years. Still, by and large, most states until quite recently have left private higher education largely alone to both enjoy the benefits of limited state regulation and to weather the storms created by economic recessions and demographic changes. Part of the reason is that independent higher education is a form of private enterprise, which American political and economic philosophy favors leaving alone absent strong reasons to the contrary. And, of course, many in this sector have generally preferred a minimal relationship to government, at least as long as environmental conditions were mostly favorable.[16]

Thus, relatively few states have taken extensive advantage of the opportunities provided by these independent institutions to serve public purposes, beyond simply allowing them to educate as many students as they chose to in the competitive environment created by their coexistence next to heavily subsidized public institutions. The associated norms and habits are rather powerfully embedded in many states still. Hence, it will not be easy for states to behave differently even in circumstances which suggest that more active state partnerships with private institutions might well be cost-effective for higher education in the era now dawning of renewed demand growth but sharp constriction in traditional sources of financial support for the entire postsecondary enterprise. A key purpose of this chapter is to provide both comparative and historical background and a conceptual framework for understanding the state policies that affect private higher education, so as to make possible a broader view of both the possibilities and limitations for use of this sector as an instrument of public policy in this new era.

## State Policies That Affect Private Higher Education

Before proceeding further, it seems appropriate to first describe the major types of state policies that touch private higher education to give the reader some

---

[15]See also Breneman (1994) for a similar conclusion, following exhaustive analysis of financial trends for private liberal arts colleges.

[16]Private higher education's arms-length relationship to government in this country stems in part from the historical sensitivity of church-state relationships, which are often much closer in other countries. Everywhere that private higher education exists, religious motivations have played a part in the establishment of many of the private institutions (Geiger, 1986; Levy, 1986).

concrete referents. This discussion will also seek to provide some practical insights into the varied arrangements by which states currently employ private colleges and universities to serve public purposes by bringing to bear some relevant, fairly recent survey data. Later in this chapter we will consider whether these policies can reasonably be thought of as part of a coherent *state policy posture* vis-a-vis private higher education and will consider some basic empirical evidence indicating that it makes sense to look for patterns of related policies in this field. Then, we will describe and seek to make sense of these state policy postures and their implications, both for policy science and for policy analysis.

A host of state policies affect private colleges and universities in some way. I will provide here a brief overview of these using some of the language of policy instruments familiar to students of public policy (see, for example, Dahl and Lindblom, 1953; Bardach, 1980; Hood, 1983; Elmore, 1987; Linder and Peters, 1989; Howlett, 1991). This language is useful for thinking about whether and how policies in this area intentionally affect their targets or unintentionally impact private colleges and universities when these institutions are not their primary targets.

The empirical data referred to in this section come from three sources.[17] The major source is a pair of national surveys on state policies affecting private colleges and universities. These surveys of state higher education agency directors and statewide private college association heads were conducted by the author for the Education Commission of the States' Task Force on State Policy and Independent Higher Education in 1988.[18] The surveys covered all the major state policies affecting private colleges and universities except student aid funding levels and state policies influencing public institution tuition. These latter topics were well covered by the other two data sources referred to in this section—surveys by the National Association of State Scholarship and Grant Programs[19] and the State Higher Education Executive Officers (1988), respectively, to which I had access for the analyses summarized here.

The discussion below is organized by policy area.

*Student Aid:* According to those who represent them in state capitals (i.e., the state private sector association heads surveyed), the state policies most important to private colleges and universities as a group are, by a wide margin, those in the area of state student aid program design and funding. In response to federal funding incentives, virtually all states now have state student aid programs (i.e., state scholarships and the like) for which needy private college and university students are eligible (National Association of State Scholarship and Grant Programs,

---

[17]Note that these data are used illustratively here. The point of this section is to describe the nature of state policies that touch upon the private higher education sector.

[18]For a complete report on the data from these surveys, see Zumeta (1989).

[19]This survey of state student aid policy and funding by "NASSGP" is conducted annually, most recently for the 1993-94 academic year (NASSGP, 1994).

annual publication).[20] Many of these aid programs function as partial higher education vouchers from the state in that eligible students can carry them to either public or private institutions (including in some cases proprietary schools), and use them to offset tuition charges. But the level of state funding for the awards varies widely across the states, as do such key design features from the standpoint of the private sector as the extent of tuition sensitivity, the maximum award allowed, and the maximum family income level permitted for eligibility.

In addition, states may provide other student aid funds earmarked only for private or only for public college students. Six states provide "tuition equalization" aid grants to private college students regardless of their need status (NASSGP, 1994) on the theory that these students would receive non-need-based state subsidies in the form of below-cost tuition rates if they attended a public college or university. This approach clearly expands the pool of students for whom private institutions can compete and serves to target these state aid funds directly on them, but at the expense of the typical policy goal of targeting aid funds to the needy. With this last consideration in mind, another twelve states make "tuition equalization" grants to private college students contingent on the student's need status.[21] In some states, student aid programs are large enough to, it would seem,[22] make a big difference in terms of the public/private competition for students. But Table 1, which summarizes state student aid funding per-student for the year 1993-94, shows that there is a great range in state funding levels for student aid.

*Direct State Payments to Independent Institutions:* Nearly all the state student aid programs aid private colleges and universities *indirectly* by providing aid to their students or potential students, rather than providing funds directly to the private school. Such funding might logically be regarded as the purchase by the state of student enrollment slots at nonpublic institutions according to eligible students' choices of where to attend rather than as aid to these institutions, although it clearly has both effects and probably in most cases both purposes.

States can also contract *directly* with private colleges and universities to enroll students in particular fields, usually in practice high-cost graduate or professional fields, where the alternative is building additional public sector capacity. In addition, states may contract with private institutions for other services, such as research or technology development in particular fields, for enhancement of academic support programs for disadvantaged students, or for sharing the cost of building a capital facility. A small number of states provide fully discretionary and unabashedly direct aid without any contract involved to private institutions or a subset of them (such as medical or engineering schools which are part of pri-

---

[20]In most cases these aid programs are restricted to undergraduates and about three-fourths of the award dollars are distributed on the basis of the recipient's financial need (NASSGP, 1994, p. 1).

[21]This figure comes from an analysis developed by the author, with the assistance of John Fawcett-Long, from raw data in NASSGP (1994).

[22]This is a judgment, rather than an analytically based conclusion, for a recent survey by the author (Zumeta, 1995a) showed that few states have seriously studied such impacts of their student aid programs.

vate universities) explicitly in the name of preserving their educational capacity and other services to the state.

**TABLE 1. Estimated Grant Dollars to Undergraduates in 1993-94 per Full-Time Undergraduate Enrollment, by State**

| State | Undergraduate Grant Aid | State | Undergraduate Grant Aid |
|---|---|---|---|
| 1. New York | $1,157 | 26. Oregon | $ 158 |
| 2. New Jersey | 996 | 27. Missouri | 153 |
| 3. Minnesota | 783 | 28. Virginia | 151 |
| 4. Illinois | 727 | 29. Rhode Island | 150 |
| 5. Pennsylvania | 543 | 30. Arkansas | 138 |
| 6. Vermont | 504 | 31. Tennessee | 129 |
| 7. Georgia | 375 | 32. West Virginia | 113 |
| 8. Ohio | 356 | 33. Kansas | 109 |
| NATION | 350 | 34. Louisiana | 100 |
| 9. Iowa | 340 | 35. North Dakota | 82 |
| 10. Indiana | *338 | 36. Texas | 66 |
| 11. Florida | 332 | 37. Delaware | 65 |
| 12. Washington | 330 | 38. Alabama | 63 |
| 13. Michigan | 316 | 39. Nebraska | 48 |
| 14. Connecticut | 310 | 40. Alaska | 46 |
| 15. Wisconsin | 297 | 41. Dist. of Columbia | 36 |
| 16. Maryland | 286 | 42. Arizona | 32 |
| 17. Colorado | 269 | 43. South Dakota | 29 |
| 18. California | 268 | 44. Idaho | 28 |
| 19. New Mexico | 222 | 45. Hawaii | 27 |
| 20. Massachusetts | 215 | 46. New Hampshire | 25 |
| 21. Kentucky | 197 | 47. Nevada | 18 |
| 22. North Carolina | 190 | 48. Montana | 16 |
| 23. Oklahoma | 177 | 49. Wyoming | 16 |
| 24. Maine | 175 | 50. Mississippi | 15 |
| 25. South Carolina | 170 | 51. Utah | 14 |

*Grant amounts for 1993-94 were not available. Calculation based on 1992-93 Grant Aid Dollars.

Sources of Data: Grant Aid dollars are from Column 1 and Column 3 in Table 1 of this report. Enrollment data are calculated from the U.S. Department of Education, National Center for Education Statistics, *Digest of Education Statistics, 1993,* Tables 188 and 192, pages 192 and 196. Enrollments for Fall 1992 were not available as this report went to press.

Source: National Association of State Scholarships and Grant Programs, 1994, p. 110

**TABLE 2. Types of Programs of Direct State Payments to Independent Institutions and Their Frequency**

| Type of Program | # of Such Programs | # of States w/Such Programs |
|---|---|---|
| General Institutional Support | 6 | 6:  IL, MD, MI, NJ, NY, PA |
| Support for Health Sciences & Health Professional Programs (Most common fields are medicine, dentistry and nursing) | 22[a] | 14:  AL, FL, IL, MA, MI, NC, NH, NJ, NY, OH, PA, TN, TX, WI |
| Support for EducationalPrograms in Other Specific Fields (Most common fields are education and engineering) | 12[b] | 12:  AL, FL, IL, MD, MO, NC, OH, PA, RI, SC, TN, VA[c] |
| Research/Technology Support | 10 | 7:  FL, GA, LA[d], NJ, NY, OH, TX |
| Program Support for Programs Serving Disadvantaged Students | 6 | 6:  AL, FL, MA, MI, NJ, NY |
| Support for Cooperative Ventures (Excludes technology ventures included above) | 4 | 4:  AL, IL, MA[e], RI[e] |
| Broad-purpose Capital Assistance | 3 | 3:  IL, MD, PA[d] |
| Support for Endowed Chairs Only | 2 | 2:  NJ, NY |
| Support for Instructional Quality Improvement Only | 2 | 2:  LA[c], SC[d] |
| Unclassifiable (Has supported very diverse activities) | 1 | 1:  NJ, (Dept. of Higher Education special-purpose grants) |

Source: Zumeta, 1989.

[a]Includes cases where support for health fields is part of a larger program also supporting other fields.

[b]Includes cases of state appropriations to specialized institutions.

[c]First funding in 1988-89.

[d]Not funded in 1987-88.

[e]Higher education/K-12 cooperation.

In total, according to the survey data, in 1988, 21 of the 50 states provided funds directly to private colleges and universities, whether by contract or other means.[23] Table 2 provides the results on the nature and distribution of these types of programs providing direct state support to private institutions, from the author's 1988 survey of state higher education agency heads. Note that only six

---

[23]Excluded here are direct appropriations or contracts for student aid (to avoid double-counting of state student aid efforts affecting the private sector) and the occasional ad hoc project research grant, though substantial and ongoing research *programs* are included.

states provided general institutional support to a broad range of private institutions. (A few others provided such support to a few schools.)

These data suggest both diversity in states' priorities and needs as these intersect with the capabilities of private colleges and universities, and also considerable variety in legal and fiscal arrangements for providing state support. Before this survey (since no similar survey had been done for many years[24]), it was widely thought that most state programs providing funds to private colleges and universities were contract-based with funding linked to numbers of students enrolled. Also, it was thought that most of these programs were specifically targeted at private colleges.

The survey revealed a considerably more complex picture. Only about half (27) of the 53 programs identified by the survey and with adequate data on funding arrangements for a judgment to be made were found to be *capitation-based* (i.e., funding linked to enrollments or degrees), and only eleven of these involved formal contracts. Another 16 instances of contract arrangements were identified, but in these cases the contracts were for something other than students or degrees, such as for a specific capital project or start-up support for a new program. Finally, ten programs provided support for a wide range of purposes without benefit of either a contract or any capitation formula. Many of these operated on something resembling a grant basis: the state agency solicited proposals and funded the ones it found to best suit state needs, often with quite broad guidelines as to what types of projects might be eligible. A number of states had more than one program encompassing two or more of the above types of arrangements, suggesting again that states have a variety of instruments at their disposal in this policy arena to meet various objectives and state policymaker preferences as to approach.

Significantly and somewhat surprisingly, the survey also revealed that a substantial share of the state programs which provide funds directly to private colleges and universities were *not* limited to funding these institutions. In 29 of the 55 programs (53%) for which the relevant data were available from the survey, only private institutions were eligible for program funds. But in 21 cases (38%), covering 13 different states, the private schools shared eligibility for program funds with public institutions, and in five more cases (9%), covering three different states, for-profit institutions were eligible for state funding as well. The programs for which for-profit schools were eligible were all instances where the state essentially purchased enrollment slots in particular fields, but the programs including both private nonprofits and public institutions encompassed a number with other purposes. Even in the programs involving *only* private nonprofit institutions—most of which were programs in which the state purchased or subsidized enrollment slots, often in high-cost professional fields—the private schools are implicitly competing with public sector alternatives for use of these funds in

---

[24]The previous source was a series of annual surveys conducted by the Education Commission of the States (1971-1982).

that the state university system could be funded to open or expand a program in the field instead.

These data are at variance with the widely assumed view that programs providing state funds to private colleges are essentially "institutional aid." Rather, in many cases the private institutions appear to function more as alternative suppliers of services in a competitive marketplace, with decisions about whom to fund presumably made in substantial measure on the basis of judgments about comparative cost-effectiveness. The distinction is an important one for beginning to understand these state policies.

*Other State Policies:* States typically exempt colleges and universities, both private and public, from property taxes, though such exemptions are increasingly under attack from financially hard-pressed local governments.[25] According to the survey data, they also occasionally provide exemptions from other taxes such as sales taxes, and they typically provide individuals and firms with deductions, or occasionally credits, against state tax liabilities for donations to higher education. Other policies are specifically designed to impact private higher education via creative use of policy instruments available to the state, such as making these institutions eligible for participation in state purchasing pools or eligible to take advantage of state tax-exempt bonding authority.

Also, states may provide by law or practice for private sector representation on the state higher education board itself, for participation in its formal planning activities for higher education, or for private sector participation in state review/approval of new academic programs or locations proposed by public institutions (and occasionally vice versa). There are often high stakes in these state planning and "program review" decisions for the long-term competitive position of private institutions. Yet, the survey evidence showed that many states do not include them very extensively or regularly in their planning and program review policy deliberations. Finally, states may include private colleges and universities more or less in their mandates and regulations governing higher education and in their data collection and analysis efforts. The survey evidence showed that, with the prominent exception of mandates in the area of teacher education, most states did not extensively regulate private higher education nor did they collect or distribute much information about it.[26]

*State Policies Affecting Public Higher Education Tuition:* Another area of state, or at least heavily state-influenced, policy decisions that is of great importance to private colleges and universities is decisions about tuition levels in public higher education.[27] Yet, a separate survey of state higher education agency heads

---

[25] See the discussion and sources cited in Zumeta (1995b, p. 83).

[26] A few states with substantial direct aid to private higher education did more regulation and monitoring of this sector. Also, most states subjected private colleges and universities to state regulation in nonacademic areas, such as labor relations, health and safety, environmental matters, and the like.

[27] Private sector representatives responding to the survey ranked this area second in importance to them behind only state student aid policies (Zumeta, 1989).

showed that impacts on private institutions received little or no consideration in these decisions in all but a very few states (State Higher Education Executive Officers, 1988). So, states seem to use the potent policy instrument of pricing of public higher education services in a way that virtually guarantees unintended consequences for the independent sector.

Thus, in sum, state higher education policymakers can be more or less conscious or strategic in their use of the various types of policy instruments at their disposal—some of which have much broader reach than the private higher education sector alone—heeding or not their impacts on private colleges and universities, as well as on the state's full range of needs and objectives in higher education. In general, policies whose primary targets are within higher education (e.g., student aid programs, tuition policies) can be more easily fine-tuned to take account of impacts on private higher education than can policies (e.g., many general tax and regulatory policies) made by noneducation agencies with multiple targets.

To come at this from another angle, in general, indirect instruments such as portable student aid grants, tax incentives, and information-based instruments[28] have important advantages, where they can get the primary job done, over mandates, regulations and even direct grants because they are less centrally directive and, critically in educational matters, less intrusive on institutional autonomy. They may also be expensive, so there will at times be hard tradeoffs to weigh among effectiveness, cost, and intrusiveness. The argument here is simply that the impacts on private institutions, which affect the ultimate achievement of reasonable state goals in higher education, seem often to get short shrift in the weighing of these tradeoffs. Policies affecting public institution tuition, student aid, program expansion, new initiatives (e.g., in economic development or new instructional technologies), information about higher education, and, sometimes, mandates and regulations tend to be made with the public higher education sector primarily in mind, with little regard to differential effects that may apply to the private sector. This is important background to keep in mind for the remainder of this chapter.

## Structure of Remainder of the Chapter

The remainder of the chapter will proceed as follows. First, I will seek to place private higher education in the U.S. and its relations with government in some comparative perspective by taking a global, though not very fine-grained, view and looking a bit more closely at Japan—a nation of broad interest to the United States and one with an even larger private higher education sector. Next, I will review briefly the highlights of the early history of state-private-higher-education relations in the United States, beginning with the colonial period and continuing

---

[28]Included here, for example, would be information provided to student "consumers" so that they can better choose wisely among postsecondary education options.

up to World War II. This discussion will illustrate the point that, after the *Dartmouth College* case in 1819 established strict limits on state claims on independent institutions, states generally paid little official attention to this sector of higher education, though it represented nearly 50 percent of all enrollments as late as 1950.

Then, the next section will review the postwar period, which saw drastic changes in the scope of higher education in this country (Trow, 1974), with particular attention to the major role of government and public policy in these changes and to their impact on the relative place of the private sector. Because of its significance as the immediate backdrop for current dilemmas, the period since 1980 will receive most emphasis. In particular, in what shape do we now find independent higher education to face an increasingly demanding future, after a decade and a half of competing on uneven terms[29] for a shrinking pool of traditional college-age students? What role have state policies played during this recent period? We will see that it has generally been a limited one, though there is considerable variation from state to state.

The ensuing section will lay out the key dimensions of the future facing higher education in this country. In brief, federal resources will be sorely constrained and almost certainly largely limited to student aid and support for research and some research training. What student aid funding there is may well move even further in the direction of loans and away from grants. At the state level, on the basis of recent experience, governments seem likely to face both uneven potential revenue growth and, in many cases, inability to fully tap potential revenue due to legal or political limitations on taxing and spending (McIntire, 1995). Yet, states face continued powerful demands for spending on such items as replacement of aging physical infrastructure (e.g., roads and bridges), building and operating large amounts of new prison space, meeting the rapidly growing costs of health care for state employees and needy populations (especially through the Medicaid program), and meeting state commitments to fund much of the cost of elementary and secondary education, where demand is again growing rapidly (Zumeta and Fawcett-Long, 1996).

Thus, higher education's competition for state dollars is likely to be much keener than it has been in the past. Yet, as already indicated, in many states the demand for enrollment places in higher education is growing or soon will be (see Figure 1, page 47). And, it can be cogently argued on grounds of both economic efficiency in the knowledge-based economy and equity for newly emerging groups in the population, that participation rates in higher education should be, if anything, targeted to increase. Certainly participation rates should not be allowed to fall, as the set of forces just described that are impinging on states' financial resources would seem to threaten. This section will conclude by observing that,

---

[29]That is, as is documented more fully later, the gap between private and public tuition rates grew sharply and government-provided student aid funds did not keep up with tuition and demand growth.

where they are substantial, independent higher education sectors could have an important role to play here in expanding state capacity to meet demand for higher education, but only if state policies are conducive.

The last major section of the chapter will advance a conceptual framework for thinking about how in the contemporary context state policies interact with (i.e., affect and are affected by) the private higher education sector, and will reflect upon the possible determinants of the different *state policy postures* that are advanced within this framework. The purpose is to provide at least an initial basis for understanding states' policy configurations efficiently and also to provide a tool for assessing the prospects and possible means for changes to make fuller use of this sector. If the above scenario is at all accurate, states will need all the higher education capacity they can muster to respond to the emerging forces at work. This section will also reference empirical evidence supporting the conceptual framework outlined and will suggest a program of research to more fully validate and refine it.

## PRIVATE HIGHER EDUCATION IN THE UNITED STATES IN COMPARATIVE PERSPECTIVE

Research during the 1980s on higher education systems around much of the world found relatively few nations with substantial private collegiate sectors (Clark, 1983; Levy, 1985; 1986; Geiger, 1986). The significant cases are, in addition to the United States, Japan, the Philippines, and several countries in Latin America, notably Brazil (Geiger, 1986; Levy, 1986). The large Western European democracies and Canada sport a few of what Geiger (1986) calls "peripheral" private higher education sectors,[30] although several, including Great Britain and Canada, had more substantial private sectors in the past.

In the developed world outside the U.S. and Japan, most of twentieth century political history has reinforced historic state-centered tendencies in the development of major social institutions, and higher education has been no exception. Most nations have thought quite naturally in terms of national government action to expand educational opportunities and other social goods as their wealth has grown.[31] This fits with traditions emphasizing consistency with national goals and priorities, accountability of major social institutions, and equity across regions. In recent years, equity across other dimensions, in particular the socio-economic class dimension, has become a more prominent concern in many

---

[30]Geiger (1986) classifies the private sectors in Belgium and the Netherlands, with their historical roots in the Roman Catholic Church, as cases of "parallel" public and private sectors (chapter 3). The United States and Japan he terms cases of "mass" private sectors (chapter 2).

[31]Postwar West Germany (now Germany) is a partial exception in that higher education is primarily a responsibility of the *lander* (states) rather than the federal government. Most significantly for purposes of this chapter, the institutions are all public.

nations and, in the main, equity goals are seen as more effectively pursued via national than via subnational (e.g., state) planning and policymaking. Also in recent years, many developing countries have tended to follow a similar path, seeing higher education as an engine of national development and a key part of national policies which at least claim to promote equity across regions, ethnic groups, and socioeconomic classes (Levy, 1986; Geiger, 1986).

Clark's (1983) sweeping analysis of higher education systems and their evolution suggests that such a pattern of development carries significant disadvantages, however. He points out that the presence of a substantial private higher education sector, which he defines as one enrolling at least 15 percent of the nation's college and university students, not only provides more diversity of choice for students and other clients of higher education, but also makes the national system more robust in several important ways. For one, it allows an alternate avenue for expansion of access in periods where this is too costly or politically complex for the public authorities to tackle. Such diversion of rapid growth to a private sector may even enhance public higher education's autonomy by reducing the intense scrutiny it would face under conditions of rapid growth and escalation of spending (Clark, 1983, pp. 161-171).[32]

In other cases, e.g., Japan, the Philippines, Brazil, the private sector has filled in gaps at particular quality tiers where public institutions were wanting (Clark, 1983; Geiger, 1986; Levy, 1986). More generally, the presence of a private sector adds to a system's capacity to innovate and otherwise respond to changing needs in society or the world of knowledge itself.[33] Finally, Clark notes that the presence of a substantial private sector tends to add to the competitive character of higher education systems in terms of the pursuit of academic prestige, which he notes, for all its faults, does serve to reward such values as scientific productivity[34] and high scholarly attainment by students (Clark, 1983, pp. 161-171).

The studies by Geiger (1986), of Japan and the Philippines, and Levy (1985; 1986) of Latin America, provide illustrations of the above point about the private sector's role in filling gaps, particularly gaps in enrollment capacity, left more or less deliberately by public authorities in the face of burgeoning social demand for

---

[32]Elsewhere, Clark has argued that private higher education in the United States has enhanced public sector autonomy in a very fundamental way by providing the initial models for autonomous but public-spirited governance of institutions via independent boards of trustees composed of citizens of stature and influence (1987, pp. 5-6). Kerr (1991) makes a similar point. This governance model has had considerable influence beyond the United States.

[33]This is part of Clark's broader argument that systems with *decentralized authority*, e.g., in public-only systems where states or provinces rather than the national government make the critical decisions in higher education policy, are likely to be more innovative and flexible than systems with a central locus of decisionmaking (Clark, 1983, chapters four, five and six; see also Thompson and Zumeta, 1981).

[34]See also Ben-David and Zloczower (1962) on the point that decentralized and competitive national systems of higher education are likely to be more prone to scientific progress than highly centralized systems.

access to higher education. Japan provides perhaps the readiest comparisons with the United States. According to Geiger's well-documented historical account,[35] the national government in Japan—particularly in response to the surge in demand for higher education after World War II—simply allowed the growing demand to be met by private institutions because of both lack of resources for massive public sector expansion and a concern for the maintenance of academic standards in the state institutions. Thus, by the 1970s, 78 percent of the nation's higher education enrollment was in the private sector.

Not surprisingly, by the late 1960s the trend in this direction had produced strong pressures to both improve standards in the private institutions and to bail them out of serious financial straits, which were leading to rapid escalation in tuition. The government addressed both these concerns simultaneously beginning in the early 1970s[36] with a program of formula-based grants to private colleges and universities designed to help and encourage them (via incentives built into the quite-detailed funding formulas) to spend more on the education of each student and on research and facilities, and to limit enrollments to target ranges established by the national Ministry of Education (Geiger, 1986, pp. 46-47). According to Geiger, the law permitted the government to pay up to 50 percent of the operating expenses of private colleges and universities and in 1980 it actually provided enough to cover about 30 percent of these expenses (p. 47). Thus, the impact of the incentives built into the government's funding formulas could be expected to be quite substantial.

Indeed, Geiger believes that these incentives have had a profound effect on private higher education in Japan. They probably played a role in stabilizing enrollments after years of rapid, rather uncontrolled increases.[37] They also seem to have had the desired effect of improving academic quality—at least to the extent this can be equated with spending on faculty salaries and facilities per student.[38] But, Geiger argues, the incentives built into the funding formulas for private institutions rewarded them for increasing tuition revenue and thus led to sharp growth in tuition rates, not the slackening that government subsidies were expected to produce (p. 49).[39]

---

[35]See Geiger (1986, pp. 17-51).

[36]Prior to this, private institutions were subject to chartering and some other regulation by the national Ministry of Education but were eligible only for limited loans for capital purposes from public funds (Geiger, 1986, pp. 25-26). Few of these institutions had substantial sources of income other than student tuition and fees (which include substantial application and entrance testing fees).

[37]Geiger notes, however, that the period of stability in private sector enrollments coincided with stability in the number of high-school graduates seeking admission (p. 48). Thus, the Ministry's efforts to cap enrollments may have had little independent effect.

[38]But, as Geiger notes, in Japan true changes in the quality of instruction in higher education are particularly hard to effect and to measure. This is so because the academic culture of classroom lecture with little student interaction or out-of-class contact is powerfully entrenched and because perceptions of quality (even by employers) are so closely equated with the test scores of students at entry (pp. 49-50).

Predictably, the private institutions have become increasingly clients of the state and seek aggressively to make their influence felt in the deliberations of both the Ministry of Education and the Ministry of Finance. Finally, Geiger holds that, in spite of explicit efforts to the contrary and some minor successes, the net effect of the government's efforts to bring the private sector into the purview of its planning for higher education "...have powerfully induced greater institutional uniformity" (p. 49) in terms of the nature and aspirations of the institutions. Thus, in Japan public policy toward private higher education has been highly successful in terms of some of its immediate goals, but very likely at the expense of the dynamism and innovativeness of the sector, and certainly in terms of its "private-ness." Geiger sees it as no longer a "mass" private sector in its historic free-form sense, but rather likely to grow only in a limited, controlled way as permitted by national policy (pp. 50-51). Thus, private higher education in Japan has become, in a real sense, an adjunct of the public sector and an important instrument of a carefully planned, if not foolproof, public policy regime in higher education. There may be lessons here for some states in the U.S.

## GOVERNMENT RELATIONS WITH PRIVATE HIGHER EDUCATION IN THE UNITED STATES: EARLY HISTORY

The history of private higher education in the U.S. is quite different from that of most other nations which have sustained nonpublic colleges and universities in the past, or do so in the present. Rather than emerging to fill in gaps left by a dominant public university sector, in America private higher education in a very basic sense came first. This is true in that many of the early colonial colleges— Harvard, Yale, Princeton, Pennsylvania, Dartmouth—are now clearly private institutions, yet, in their early years were at least as much public as private. The early colleges were chartered by colonial, later state, legislatures, from which they received financial subsidies, and for a time had legislatively appointed members on their boards (Rudolph, 1962; Trow, 1993).

But, the early American colleges also possessed important elements of pri-vateness. They were established by the initiative of private, often sectarian, groups separate from the state. As state-chartered corporate entities they had boards made up largely of private citizens which were granted considerable autonomous powers. And, they were not wholly financed by the state but drew their fiscal support from a variety of sources, including both private donations and student fees. These characteristics made them quite different from most European, and in particular English, colleges of the 17th, 18th, and early 19th

---

[39]Geiger observes that this sharp growth in prices may well also have played a role in keeping enrollments from rising in the period after the government subsidies for private colleges and universi-ties were introduced (p. 49).

centuries (Rothblatt and Trow, 1992). Also, the fact that the colonies and states which chartered the early colleges were different from one another led to the establishment of a pattern of differences in many aspects which seemed natural from the beginning in the American context, but which simply did not emerge in smaller countries with much longer common histories and the habit of thinking of higher education in national terms.

Trow (1993) and other authorities (e.g., Herbst, 1982) argue that the central ideas of the American Revolution and the westward expansion of a diverse population into remote areas together made for an environment most conducive to the emergence of a diverse range of higher educational institutions subject to little direction by the state, or by government in any form. Crucially, says Trow, "...the Revolution weakened all agencies of government by stressing the roots of the new nation in popular sovereignty, the subordination of the government to 'the people,' and the primacy of individual and group freedom and initiative" (1993, p. 51). Hence, neither the federal government nor even the states were much disposed to try to create key societal institutions "from the top down."[40] The diversity of the population (in terms of religion, national origin, geographic imperatives, and the like) and the relative sparseness of settlement combined with these ideas to make it inevitable that colleges would be created from the "bottom up" in this society and thus by diverse groups for a wide range of purposes and in diverse ways with limited governmental control. This is thus a rather unique historical backdrop for the emergence of forms of higher education in comparison to other, now-developed nations of the world. And its effects are still strongly felt in attitudes toward private higher education today in many states.

A watershed event in understanding the development of private higher education in the United States and its relationship to state government was the case between Dartmouth College and the New Hampshire legislature (*Dartmouth vs. Woodward*) which came before the U.S. Supreme Court in 1819. The state had chartered the college for the benefit of the public, it argued, and now sought to alter the charter "...to improve the college as a place of learning by modernizing its administration, creating the framework for a university, and encouraging a freer, nonsectarian atmosphere...," while the college resisted this state intervention (Trow, 1993, pp. 55-56). In short, the legislature sought to make its creation more like what we would now call a public institution. Chief Justice John Marshall held for the Court, however, that the legislature must respect the sanctity of its original contract with the college (the charter) and could not change it unilaterally. In an important sense then the American *private* college was born here.

---

[40]An important illustration of this point is the failure of George Washington and his immediate successors in the presidency to generate much interest in chartering a national "University of the United States" (Trow, 1993, pp. 53-55). Such an institution would surely have exerted a powerful standardizing influence on models for higher education in the provinces as have institutions which play a similar role in other countries, such as Tokyo University, the University of the Philippines, or Oxford and Cambridge in England.

Benefactors and trustees could now be sure that the fruits of their toil and treasure would not be taken over by the state, which surely did much to stimulate the subsequent proliferation of private colleges (Trow, 1993, p. 56), and sharp limits were placed on state control over this unique part of higher education.[41]

And great proliferation there was in the ranks of private colleges. In the colonial period, just nine colleges were created. Thirty-six more were added between 1789 and 1830, followed by another 136 before 1865 (Metzger, 1987, cited in Clark, 1987, p. 6), with most of these being what we would now call private institutions. Though many of these mostly small, struggling schools did not survive long, the urge to create institutions of higher education was very strong in America. By 1900 there were nearly 900 private colleges and universities spread out across the country (Clark, 1987, p. 7). At that point, relatively early in the development of the modern university, private higher education *was* much of American higher education, and it developed and thrived through the critical 19th century period with only a little help from government.

The next landmark in the history of American higher education was the Morrill Act of 1862. This Act provided for large-scale land grants to states for the purpose of establishing institutions of higher education.[42] The grants provided remarkable discretion to the states as to how they were to be used, specifying only that, in addition to the traditional, still largely classical, college curriculum of the time, the institutions provide instruction in "agriculture, mechanic arts, and military tactics" (Ross, 1942, cited in Trow, 1993, p. 57). This practical orientation was one of the innovations of American higher education.

Remarkably, the states were also left free to decide to whom the grant would be turned over for use. Thus, in some states private institutions were direct beneficiaries, e.g., Cornell in New York, M.I.T. in Massachusetts, Yale's Sheffield Scientific School in Connecticut. In Kentucky and Oregon private denominational colleges received the money from sale of much of the land grant. In California, an existing private liberal arts college was "merged" with the land-grant endowment to create the University of California (Trow, 1993, p. 57). In many states a new institution was founded, complete with not only a site but an endowment, and so also a new institutional form—the public state university—was solidified.[43] As suggested above, the creation of some form of public institution of higher education was probably made inevitable by the Supreme Court's ruling against the state

---

[41]By so limiting state control over its creations, this decision probably also made the development of the different form we now call "public" colleges and universities inevitable (see Rudolph, 1962, chapter nine).

[42]It is worth noting that these were not the first federal land grants to the states for higher education. The Northwest Ordinance enacted under the Articles of Confederation provided for such land grants, but the Morrill Act grants were far more massive and broadly distributed (Trow, 1993, p. 57).

[43]State institutions of a continuing public character did not begin with the Morrill Act. A few trace their origins to the 18th century (Clark, 1987, p. 8), but it was the federal land-grants of the 19th century which led to the proliferation of this form across the country.

legislature in the Dartmouth College case. A major part of the significance of the Morrill Act—and of particular importance for our purposes in this chapter—was that it once again confirmed that these institutions would be state- rather than federally owned and thus assured that the states would play a key role in higher education policy in this country. As Trow puts it, the federal government simply left the money "...on the stump and walked away..." (1993, pp. 57-58).[44]

In the interest of sticking to the highlights of most pertinence to a survey of public policy and private higher education in the United States, I will now pass over nearly a century of history and turn the reader's attention to the post-World War II period.

## THE POSTWAR PERIOD
### (1945 through the early 1970s)

### The GI Bill and Growth of Public Higher Education

Although it gradually lost "market share" to public institutions as public universities grew, and especially as community colleges began to emerge and the old normal schools became teachers' colleges, private higher education thrived overall under the generally *laissez-faire* state regimes under which it lived during the years of the nation's rapid growth and development. It was not until the middle of the twentieth century that another major turning point was reached in public policy toward higher education that affected the private sector. This was the federal GI Bill[45] and the associated push by the states to greatly expand higher education opportunities for the legions of former soldiers who returned home needing something constructive to do in a peacetime economy.

The GI Bill itself was important not only in providing large scale federal support for higher education, but also for setting a key precedent by directing that support through students—in contrast to the approach taken by the national government in Japan somewhat later when that country faced a surge in demand for higher education—who carried the money to institutions of their choice, rather than supporting institutions directly. Trow points out that in 1944, as in 1862, the federal government opted to forego an opportunity to manage and influence higher education more directly (1993, p. 59). Indeed, it once again exercised only the most limited oversight of the funds as one provision of the law stipulated, "no department, agency, or officer of the United States, in carrying out the provisions [of this Act] shall exercise any supervision or control, whatsoever, over any State,

---

[44]By way of explanation, Trow (1993) points out that there was no federal education bureaucracy to oversee the use of the land grants and, at least as important, there was little agreement in Congress about what the new institutions should look like (p. 58). Thus, as with much else in American history, the key decisions simply were left to the states by a kind of institutionalized default.

[45]The "GI Bill" was known officially as the Servicemen's Readjustment Act of 1944.

educational agency...or any educational or training institution" (Olson, 1974, 17-18, quoted in Trow, 1993, p. 59). Thus, students were allowed to take their GI Bill stipends to a wide range of institutions, including strictly vocational training schools and nonaccredited institutions, and there was some corruption and abuse of the funds (Trow, 1993, p. 59). But, Trow suggests, this tradeoff was a deliberate choice by the federal government to stay out of the details of the operations of higher education. The states did little more in the way of regulation.

The choice to provide GI Bill aid through students rather than institutions can also be seen as a boon to private higher education. It allowed the soldier-students to choose private institutions if they wished and provided many more of them than had ever had it in the past with the wherewithal to afford such a choice.[46] And it provided for this growth in demand without any significant strings attached, thus safeguarding the private sector's privateness. Yet, by initiating the first big surge in demand for higher education and helping to insure that the enterprise became too big and important for government to ignore for long, this first federal student aid program also marked the beginning of the end of the era of true independence from government for much of the private sector.[47]

State governments also reacted to the GI Bill-stimulated surge in demand for higher education with important steps of their own that were to have large, if mostly indirect, impacts on the private sector. After World War II, the pace at which states opened new community colleges, expanded the mission of public four-year institutions (largely the former teachers' colleges), opened new campuses, and expanded enrollments, including graduate enrollments, at their research universities leaped tremendously.[48] Thus, although private higher education enrollments grew at a healthy pace in numbers during the postwar period

---

[46] Of course, since the stipend was not pegged to tuition levels, public institutions with their state-subsidized tuition rates had a price advantage in competing for students funded under the GI Bill. It is not surprising that public institutions increased their share of the higher education market during this period.

[47] Some credit for this should also be assigned to a parallel federal postwar initiative — the development of the federally funded academic research complex. Here too the federal government chose to offer large-scale financing to private and public universities alike on a competitive basis. Given the relative stature of the country's great private universities at the time, this posture assured that they would continue to be key players in the growing research and graduate education enterprise. But it also eventually (one might say inevitably) led to much-increased governmental oversight of the institutions spending the taxpayers' money, private and public alike. (See Wolfle, 1972; Smith, 1990)

[48] Again, the contrast with other developed countries is notable. In Britain and Japan during this period, pressures for growth in the public higher education sector were held firmly in check by the national government for reasons of resource limitations and an effort to maintain high academic standards (Trow, 1993, pp. 58-59; Geiger, 1986, pp. 22-30). In the United States, while federal support was much more generous it was not continuous after the GI Bill expired. Here, competition among states to provide educational opportunities for citizens and for economic development played a key role. Growth in private colleges and universities in the United States was thus overshadowed by the dramatic burgeoning of the public sector, while in Japan the private sector was allowed to grow to alleviate pressure to expand the public segment. In Britain there was no private sector to turn to and participation in higher education remained very low relative to other advanced countries (Trow, 1993, pp. 58-59).

(1945-1970), the era witnessed a precipitous decline in this sector's "market share" of all higher education enrollments. This share fell from 49 percent in 1949 to 26 percent just twenty years later (U.S. Department of Education, 1989, shown in McPherson & Schapiro, 1991, p. 22).[49] These were momentous changes for they meant that higher education now involved far too many citizens and state dollars to escape government's notice any longer and that the responses of governments would, with the exception of a relatively small number of states with still-large private sector shares of the market, largely be shaped by the perceived needs, problems and demands of the public institutions.[50]

Significantly, by and large private higher education, decentralized as it was, passively accepted this development. Most colleges did not want to grow so dramatically as to maintain their market share—small size is part of the "charm" of many of these schools (Breneman, 1994). In any case, even though many new private colleges were founded during this period, it would have been almost impossible for the sector to maintain its overall share through it. The states were adding greatly to the size of the higher education market by opening hundreds of low-priced two-year institutions and building colleges in locations convenient to population centers, as well as by continuing the historic policy of subsidizing the prices of the four-year public schools. Thus, most private institutions were content for their own reasons to grow at a relatively modest pace and, inevitably, the private sector's overall share of the total fell steadily.

The expansion of both public and private higher education during this period was facilitated by reasonably prosperous economic growth with low inflation, and the fact that tuition rates grew only modestly in real terms. The fact that real incomes were rising steadily made it possible for a wider group in the population to consider higher education and to be willing to pay for it. Still, private-sector prices grew substantially faster than public during this period (Clotfelter, 1991, p. 70), and this probably contributed to the private sector's loss of market share.

### The Beginnings of State Aid to Private Institutions and Their Students

This era, in particular the late 1950s and the 1960s, saw the beginnings of significant state student aid programs (Fenske and Boyd, 1981), which have since become a key part of state policy for the private higher education sector (Zumeta 1989; 1992). A few states, such as New York and Illinois, also initiated programs

---

[49]As mentioned earlier, the private nonprofit sector's share of all enrollments in the Fall of 1992 was down to 20 percent. The government figures cited by McPherson and Schapiro include some private, for-profit institutions.

[50]It should be noted that this public sector dominance had always been the case in many of the Western states where private higher education had had little or no time to take root before the *Dartmouth College* decision and the Morrill Act land grants began to shift states' thinking in the direction of public sector provision.

of direct support to private colleges and universities during this period.[51] Both these types of programs reflected a recognition by states—prodded to be sure by private higher education interests—that private higher education served a public purpose in educating students and that both the state and the students were well-served by having access to alternatives to the public system. The issue was, of course, sharpened by the competitive effects of proliferation of low-priced public alternatives to the private schools.

A notable example of recognition of the private higher education sector by a major state is to be found in the famed California Master Plan For Higher Education (Master Plan Survey Team, 1960). This landmark document is best known for its codification of the tripartite "division of labor" in the state's higher education system among the University of California, responsible for doctoral education and research, education in the "major" professions (law, medicine, etc.), and for educating at the undergraduate level the most academically qualified one-eighth of the state's high-school graduates; the California State Colleges (now Universities), responsible for undergraduates down to the top third of the high-school graduates, for education of teachers and for other "lesser" professions, and for some Master's-level programs; and the California Community Colleges, designed to be open-door institutions available to all adults in the state and providing a range of adult and vocational education programs, as well as an accessible route into baccalaureate-level academic education by means of articulated transfer programs (Smelser, 1993). Significantly, the Master Plan also embodied a commitment to very broad access (i.e., no tuition, many campuses spread across the state) and to world-class standards of quality (Pickens, 1995a).

Less widely heralded is that the Master Plan also established a prominent role for the independent sector in California's higher education system and made good on this commitment by establishing a state scholarship program (now called "Cal Grants") under which students could take their state grants to either public or private accredited institutions (Pickens, 1995a). In the early years these grants were clearly designed to facilitate attendance at private institutions. More than 90 percent of the awards in 1961 went to students selecting these schools. Also, the size of maximum grant awards was nearly equal to average tuition at independent colleges and universities as late as 1970 (Pickens, 1995a).[52] Thus, at the time of the Master Plan, the private sector in California was considered a significant

---

[51]However, in some cases (e.g., Alabama, Maryland), such direct state aid to private colleges actually goes back many years (Rudolph, 1962; Zumeta, 1989). Rudolph documents extensive state aid to private colleges in many states in the 19th century, and notes that in at least a few this continued into the early twentieth century (1962, pp. 177-200).

[52]The proportion of Cal Grant awards received by students attending private colleges and universities has fallen steadily over the years, to just over 30 percent in 1994-95. Similarly, the size of the largest grants available has fallen far behind tuition levels in the independent sector (Pickens, 1995a, pp. 10-11; 1995b, unpaginated).

piece of the state's capacity to meet the commitments embodied in the plan in the already-foreseeable impending period of rapid enrollment growth.

California was not alone in taking this view. As indicated above, during the 1950s, and especially in the latter years of the1960s, several other large states initiated substantial programs of aid to private colleges and/or their students. The major examples were states in the eastern half of the country (including the South and Midwest) who faced not only surging demand for higher education but also perceived threats to the viability or financial health of a venerable and well-connected part of the higher education enterprise in the private sector. Their responses included both state aid to students that could be used at private institutions and, in a small number of cases, new or expanded programs of direct state appropriations to private colleges and universities.[53]

### The Higher Education Act of 1965 and Its 1972 Amendments

In 1965 the federal Higher Education Act was enacted. This was historically significant in that it represented, for the first time, a recognition by the federal government of a *permanent* national interest in higher education. The HEA provided for federal support of facilities construction, library development and personnel training, the strengthening of "developing institutions" (primarily, at least originally, the historically black institutions), teacher training, community service and continuing education programs, and financial assistance to students (Keppel, 1987).

Most significant of these provisions for our purposes here were the ones creating broadly based federal student aid programs (grants, loans and work-study under Title IV of the Higher Education Act) and funding them at a substantial level.[54] These were not the first federal student aid programs after the GI Bill, but they were the first to go beyond support of students in fairly narrow fields of specifically identified national need (as in the case of the National Defense Education Act of the 1950s), and were funded at a considerably higher level than the earlier, narrower programs which were limited to loans (Hearn, 1993, pp. 102-103). Reflecting its origins in the Johnson Administration Great Society period, the Act also set an important precedent in targeting federal aid on "needy" students who were thought to be not able to attend college without such aid (Keppel, 1987, pp. 56-57). Still, as is noted by Hearn (1993, p. 102), institutions decided which of their students were eligible and how much they received. Although the 1965 Act actually emphasized institutional aid more than student aid, this marked the high water mark for federal aid to higher education institutions in the United States. The broadly based student aid programs the Higher Education Act created

---

[53]See Fenske and Boyd (1981), NASSGP (1994 and earlier annual survey reports), and Zumeta (1989) on the origins of state programs aiding private institutions of higher education.

[54]Still, the largest authorized spending for FY 1966 under the original Higher Education Act was for the construction of academic facilities for undergraduates. About 32 percent of the original $1.1 billion annual authorization under the Act was for student aid (Keppel, 1987, p. 58).

paved the way for a sharp turn a few years later down the road which had been paved by the GI Bill's student-based approach.

The question of aid to students or aid to institutions was revisited with great intensity during the 1972 debate on major amendments to the Act.[55] There was broad support at this time for a sharp expansion of the federal commitment to higher education in response to then-strong societal commitments to expanding educational opportunities. One source of this support came from advocates of a big expansion of aid to needy students while another key group advocated direct federal aid to colleges and universities. In the latter camp were the national organizations representing the institutions and sectors of higher education as well as some influential members of Congress. But prominent on the side of those arguing for aid through students was the influential Carnegie Commission on Higher Education, led by former University of California President Clark Kerr (Trow, 1993, p. 60).

The Carnegie Commission and others made several telling arguments in favor of the aid-through-students approach. One was that aid to needy students—which was held to be an economic necessity as well as an equal opportunity policy—could be better and more efficiently targeted by federal control of the terms of the aid than if the money went through thousands of different institutions. Indeed, the original idea of the developers of the largest program created by the 1972 amendments, the Basic Educational Opportunity Grants (now Pell Grants) program, was to create a federal entitlement to aid for college for all financially needy students, with need to be established uniformly by a federal formula (Gladieux and Wolanin, 1976; Mumper, 1991, pp. 316-317; Hearn, 1993, pp. 109-110). In addition, less needy students were to have access to federally subsidized and guaranteed loans. Much of this program—with the important exception of the fully funded entitlement—was enacted.

Kerr, economist that he is, and others argued that aid to students rather than to institutions had the advantage of reinforcing market-like incentives for the colleges to respond to student preferences about courses of study and other matters, which they thought would better serve society in the long run than a system where institutional preferences, and inevitably inertia, were more influential. Of course, the GI Bill was cited as a precedent. Perhaps even more important, many on this side of the argument felt that federal aid directly to institutions was not in their own best interest (although the institutions wanted it) in the long run for it would inevitably lead to federal leverage over and interference in educational policymaking.[56] Finally, Trow points out that it was not lost on the advocates of aid-through-students that millions of aided students and their families would

---

[55]For an account of this debate, see Gladieux and Wolanin (1976). See also Hansen (1977); Mumper (1991); Hearn (1993); Trow (1993, pp. 59-60).

[56]For example, there would have been more reason for the government to intervene to press institutions to reallocate resources among areas of study (i.e., manpower planning) were student choices less dominant in this process. Certainly, the national government would have been in a stronger position than it is now to try to influence substantive academic matters for political or bureaucratic reasons.

make a much broader and more effective constituency for continued federal support than would the higher education establishment alone (1993, p. 60).

In addition to whatever force these arguments may have had, chroniclers of the period observe that the institutional interests handled their legislative strategy and tactics quite poorly (Gladieux and Wolanin, 1976; Hansen, 1977; Finn, 1978; Mumper, 1991). The results then seem from this vantage point (with the benefit of hindsight) quite understandable—the major expansion in federal aid to higher education established in the 1972 Higher Education Act amendments routed the support overwhelmingly through students not institutions. Clearly, in the longer historical perspective traced here this seems quite understandable, even predictable, as well. In the United States the national government has paid relatively limited attention to higher education in comparison to the pattern in other countries. What it has paid is money for specific purposes—land grants to start institutions, support for research, aid to students to allow them to pursue higher education, and, more recently, substantial efforts to insure equity in employment practices. But, so far, all this has come with very little direction about what colleges and universities teach, how many of them there are, how much they charge, and so on. And, critically for our purposes, the federal government has welcomed private institutions into its programs[57] and has generally left oversight functions to the states.

One important elaboration on this last point is necessary in the context of the 1972 Higher Education Act amendments (Gladieux and Wolanin, 1976; McGuinness, 1975). This legislation influenced in two significant ways how states dealt with private institutions. First, it required that states strengthen and broaden their planning capacity for higher education as a condition for receipt of federal funds under the Act. In many cases states broadened the membership of their existing state higher education board or commission to qualify, but in some cases a separate planning body (or "1202 Commission" after the section number in the Act) was established with the requisite membership. These bodies were required to produce certain planning documents to satisfy Congress that new federal funds would be well-used.

The main significance for the present purpose is that the membership on the planning body now had to include representatives from both the private, nonprofit collegiate sector and the private postsecondary vocational training sector (often including for-profit institutions). These were new departures in many states—indeed, some had done little or no statewide planning for higher education before—and at least gave the private sector a place at this particular table. As we shall see, this did not necessarily insure that private institutions played a very

---

[57]Notably, from the beginning of the BEOG program (now Pell Grants), the allocation formulas have been designed to insure that the aid funds could cover no more than a fixed percentage (first 50 percent, now 60 percent) of a student's cost of attendance (Mumper, 1993, p. 164). This restricts the amount of funds that might otherwise go to students choosing low-priced public institutions and insures that no student can get all costs covered by the grant.

meaningful role in all subsequent state higher education planning, but it did provide an officially sanctioned starting point.

Second, the 1972 HEA amendments provided modest federal funding for a new program of incentive grants to states, called the State Student Incentive Grant program or SSIG, to establish their own student aid programs (Gladieux and Wolanin, 1976; Hansen, 1979; Fenske and Boyd, 1981). Participating states were required to include students at private institutions in the program. This was a breakthrough for private higher education which had sought to get more states to establish student aid programs for which their students would be eligible. The federal incentive funding has led over the years to virtually all the states establishing such programs (Fenske and Boyd, 1981; Mumper, 1993), with many states providing much more than the required one-for-one match (NASSGP, 1994).[58]

Recent federal efforts to eliminate the SSIG program in the name of budget-cutting and the streamlining of federal student aid programs have cited the program's success in stimulating state student aid efforts as evidence that it is no longer needed.[59] Private higher education interests generally oppose such a step, fearing not only the loss of federal funds but also that some states will drop their need-based aid programs completely, or perhaps no longer assure the eligibility of students attending private colleges. It is widely agreed that the SSIG program has played a significant role in stimulating increased state support for student aid available to both private and public sector students (Hansen, 1979; Fenske and Boyd, 1981; Breneman, 1994). Together with the mandate to include the private sector in state higher education planning and the broader decision represented by the 1965 and 1972 actions on the Higher Education Act to minimize the federal government's direct involvement in higher education policymaking, we can look upon this period of federal action as important in shaping key dimensions of the states' role vis-a-vis private higher education in the succeeding years.

## THE EARLY 1970S TO THE PRESENT

The 1960s, as well as the earlier postwar years to a lesser extent, were years of prosperity in American higher education. Enrollments grew dramatically, supported by expansive state appropriations to the public higher education sector. Strong federal support for research spilled over into support for facilities and graduate education (Smith, 1990). Private higher education was aided at the mar-

---

[58]According to the most recent NASSGP publication (1994), the range across the states in terms of the share of their need-based grants that are provided by federal SSIG funds is from 50 percent (a one-to-one match) in two states, down to just one percent in New York. In addition, one state, Rhode Island, did not participate in the federal program. The figures are estimates for the 1993-94 academic year. States have not, however, always provided the matching funds themselves, but have at times required institutions to put up these funds, a particular problem for private schools.

[59]At this writing, it appears likely that the State Student Incentive Grant (SSIG) program will be eliminated when a budget for fiscal year 1996 is finally agreed upon by Congress and the President.

gins by the beginnings of federal and state student aid programs—and in the case
of the private research universities very much by federal research support—but
prospered primarily because there were plenty of students in the market in a
period when the economy was providing enough for many of them to pay for a
private education. Though, as in earlier periods, a number of private colleges
failed during this period, many more were formed and thrived (Birnbaum, 1983;
Zammuto, 1984).

## The Seventies

But during a period of a few years on either side of 1970 many things changed.
Enrollment growth rates slowed as the "baby boom" children began to graduate
and as economic returns to college education took a nosedive (Freeman, 1976).
Federal research funding also dropped off after a decade of rapid increases
(Smith, 1990), thus making it harder to support graduate students who had provided a source of low-cost teachers of undergraduates. In addition, some graduate students were dissuaded by the first signs of the "Ph.D. glut" (Zumeta,
1982). The Vietnam War and then the first OPEC oil embargo in 1973 ended a
long period of general economic prosperity with relatively low inflation and
began an era during which real earnings have essentially stopped growing
(Marshall and Tucker, 1992). This income stagnation, of course, makes it
harder for students to pay for and donors to support higher education. Initially,
during the 1970s, inflation and interest rates reached very high levels, leading
to problems and dislocations throughout the economy, not least for higher education (Breneman, 1994).

Private colleges and universities in particular faced worrisome fiscal circumstances as they contemplated huge, inflation-driven jumps in costs at a time when
it was harder to recruit both students and private donations (Cheit, 1971; Carnegie Commission, 1973; Wynn, 1974). After several years of economic instability and after studying the projections of high-school graduates into the eighties
and beyond, several groups of distinguished analysts offered a generally gloomy
perspective on the future prospects for a healthy private sector (see Carnegie
Council on Policy Studies in Higher Education, 1977; Education Commission of
the States, 1977; Breneman and Finn, 1978; Behn, 1979). Basically, they feared a
continuing rapid cost spiral with little prospect of offsetting growth in student
revenues in light of the expected leveling and then decline in college-age students
resulting from the "birth dearth" cohort of the 1960s reaching college-age. The
uncertain economy seemed to offer little hope of a dramatic increase in private
donations or help from the states, who would naturally be most concerned about
taking care of "their own" public institutions in an "era of limits."

These analysts did, however, call for states to be attentive to the health of what
they saw as a valuable resource in private higher education, and to help as much
as they could. "Portable" student aid[60] and, significantly, higher and more pre-

dictable tuition rates in public higher education were generally the preferred routes for such help because of their more limited potential, as compared with direct institutional aid, for restricting the autonomy of *independent* institutions.[61]

In fact, while state student aid programs and expenditures grew substantially during the 1970s (McPherson and Schapiro, 1991, p. 29), they remained a modest part of the total student aid picture. Private institutions survived this decade as well as they did in large part because of the rapid growth in student aid from the federal government (Breneman, 1994, pp. 25-30; McPherson and Schapiro, 1991, pp. 25-43). McPherson and Schapiro, citing several sources, note that total federal student aid nearly doubled, after adjusting for inflation, during the 1970s (p. 26).[62] If only generally available aid is counted (thus excluding Social Security and Veterans' educational benefits), the real increase approached 200 percent over the decade, a rate of increase especially beneficial to private institutions with their unsubsidized (at least by the state) tuition rates.

Also during this period, unlike more recent times, federal grant aid grew about as fast as loan aid. An important factor in the rapid growth in federal student aid during this period was the liberalization of aid eligibility standards that culminated in the Middle Income Student Assistance Act (MISAA), enacted in 1978 (Mumper, 1991, pp. 319-320; McPherson and Schapiro, 1991, pp. 31-33; Hearn, 1993, pp. 111-116). MISAA was the product of an effort to head off a powerful movement toward tax credits for higher education tuition, the cost of which would have necessitated major changes in the federal student aid programs. To accomplish this, MISAA's framers raised the maximum family income permitted to qualify for a Pell Grant and, most importantly, removed the income ceiling entirely for federally guaranteed Stafford student loans, thus greatly expanding the federal aid available to middle-income students and families (Mumper, 1991, p. 320). Thus, the last half of the 1970s was a boon to a wide range of students seeking to attend college, including students interested in private institutions, compliments largely of federal largesse.

Meanwhile, in inflation-adjusted dollars, tuition rates grew modestly in the early 1970s, but then declined during the rapid inflationary period of the later years of the decade (McPherson and Schapiro, 1991, pp. 29-30). McPherson and Schapiro's analysis of the combined impact of the tuition and aid trends shows a decline in real net price (inflation-adjusted and net of aid) of higher education from the mid-1970s through 1979 for public institutions and through 1980 for independent schools (pp. 34-37). Thus, though the times were not without serious

---

[60]"Portable" student aid in this context means that the recipient student may use the aid at either a public or an eligible private institution.

[61]On this point, in addition to the sources cited in the previous paragraph, see also Committee for Economic Development (1973) and National Commission on the Financing of Postsecondary Education (1973).

[62]See also Hearn (1993) for thorough documentation of the growth in federal student aid from 1965 through 1990.

economic insecurities—caused by high interest and inflation rates and fears of energy shortages—conditions for higher education in retrospect look comparatively favorable. Also, private colleges and universities in particular were beginning to tap new student markets in earnest during the 1970s as they looked ahead to the period when demographic trends insured that there would be fewer potential students in the traditional age pool. Overall then, during the 1970s private higher education fared relatively well. According to the National Center for Education Statistics, enrollments in this sector climbed by nearly half a million (23%) between 1970 and 1980 (fall to fall), and its "market share" of enrollments in four-year institutions hardly changed (U.S. Department of Education, 1994, p. 177), after two decades of decline.[63]

## The Eighties and Early Nineties

Through the early 1980s, federal student aid policies were quite generous and, if anything, especially so to students attending private colleges and universities. The half-cost limit provision remained in the Pell Grant program (until 1986 when the limit was increased to 60 percent of the costs of attendance), thus preventing students from attending public colleges at little or no out-of-pocket cost, and even students from affluent circumstances were able to obtain government-subsidized loans to attend high-tuition institutions during the MISAA years. But, the environment for the private institutions deteriorated rapidly with the recession of the early 1980s and the sharp changes in federal student aid policies brought about by the Reagan Administration. In addition, after 1980 the number of high-school graduates nationally began to decline, as had been forecast. Thus, although private higher education had staved off the worst of what analysts had predicted for it just a few years earlier, it looked as though this was merely a temporary postponement of the inevitable.

The Reagan Administration clamped down quickly and hard on what had become runaway growth in the guaranteed (Stafford) loan program (Mumper, 1991, p. 323). The Budget Reconciliation Bill of 1981[64] brought back limits on Stafford Loans related to income and educational costs. Also, the Pell Grant program was funded well below its estimated future costs, necessitating caps on the size of grants in subsequent years (*ibid.*). The other generally available student grant programs (Supplemental Educational Opportunity Grants, College Work-Study, and State Student Incentive Grants) were also cut back at this time and have never recovered the constant-dollar funding levels they enjoyed in the 1980s, much less their purchasing power relative to college costs (College Board,

---

[63]Private higher education lost more than two percentage points in *overall* share of enrollments during this decade because of continued rapid growth in public two-year college enrollments.

[64]It should be noted that, because of "forward funding" of student aid programs, the cuts in support for these programs actually took effect in later academic years. Pell Grants and SSIG support, however, first decreased in current dollars in 1980-81 (College Board, 1994).

1994). These cuts occurred just as funds available for student aid from Social Security and veterans' benefits were also declining sharply in magnitude. After a few years of absolute decline in the early 1980s, Pell Grant funding increased somewhat (even in constant-dollar terms) during the later eighties, but has fallen sharply again since 1992-93.[65] Thus, the nominal value of Pell Grants has increased only slightly over the years since 1980 (from $1,800 in 1979-80 to $2,300 in 1993-94), and the proportion of average college costs that the grant covers has declined steadily. For private universities, this proportion is down to ten percent (College Board, p. 3).

For private higher education in particular, the decline in the importance of federal grant programs has increasingly shifted their attention to the government's loan programs (Mumper, 1991), and with considerable success. Mumper points out that, throughout the 1970s, most federal aid was provided to students as grants (1991, p. 326). However, the loan proportion moved upward through most of the eighties, dropped back a bit for a few years when Pell Grant funding picked up, but has jumped sharply in the last couple of years.[66] Since the 1992 reauthorization of the Higher Education Act made substantially more loan funds available, especially to students with moderate rather than very low incomes, the College Board estimates that the dollar volume of federal direct and guaranteed loans has grown by a staggering 50 percent *after adjusting for inflation* between 1992-93 and 1994-95. This is in spite of the fact that a growing proportion of the loans (about one-third in 1994-95) are "unsubsidized" in that the federal government no longer absorbs interest costs for the years the borrower is enrolled (College Board, 1995, p. 3). Thus, although private higher education has aggressively sought access to federal loan funds for its students, student debt levels are now becoming a matter of increasing concern. (College Board, 1995, pp. 3-4; Education Resources Institute and Institute of Higher Education Policy, 1995, cited in Schoenberg, 1995).

A further problem facing the private colleges and universities in regard to federal student aid in the 1980s was the large increase in the proportion of these federal funds going to students attending for-profit postsecondary schools, mostly vocational training schools. At a time when the total available student aid was lagging behind enrollment growth and college costs, the proportion of Pell Grants going to students attending proprietary schools jumped from about 10 percent in

---

[65]According the College Board's latest figures, preliminary current-dollar figures for Pell aid awarded in 1994-95 are $5.65 billion, compared with $6.177 billion in 1992-93 (College Board, 1995). In constant-dollar terms, this is a two-year decline of 13 percent, and even this adjustment understates the true decrease in purchasing power relative to college costs. At this writing (late 1995), it seems all but certain in the current fiscal and political climate that the funding trend for this cornerstone program in the federal government's student aid effort will continue to be flat at best.

[66]The proportion of all student aid in 1994-95, including federal, state, and institutional sources, represented by loans is estimated at 56 percent with grants at 43 percent, compared with 49 percent for loans and 48 percent for grants ten years earlier (College Board, 1995).

1979-80 (up only slightly from 7 percent in 1973-74) to more than 26 percent in 1987-88.[67] The proportion of federal loans awarded to proprietary school students similarly skyrocketed (peaking at 35 percent of Stafford loans in fiscal 1987). These proportions have come down substantially in more recent years, largely as a result of the federal crackdown on schools with high numbers of loan-defaulting students. Nonetheless, proprietary-school students still receive a substantial share of the aid available (College Board, 1995), a development not foreseen by the framers of the federal student aid programs (Keppel, 1987; Mumper, 1991).

Many states made some effort to respond to the slowdown in federal student aid spending in the 1980s, but their efforts were largely cut short early in the decade by the national recession and consequent fiscal squeeze that beset most states. By and large, during the first half of the 1980s states imposed fiscal stringencies on all of higher education, including student aid programs. In many states, this worked a particular hardship on private colleges and universities, whose main (or only) source of state sustenance is these programs. Indeed, overall, student aid programs tended to be cut back more sharply than state appropriations to public colleges and universities, but this was followed by a stronger recovery in state support for them than of state support for public institutions during the generally prosperous years of the later eighties (Zumeta, 1993). Interestingly, during the state fiscal stringencies of the 1990s, states have generally increased the support of their student aid programs quite strongly (Mortenson, 1994a), though much of the increased support has gone to public higher education students to help offset the sharp tuition increases they have faced as state appropriations to their institutions have been cut (NAASGP, 1994; Hines and Pruyne, 1995).

Overall, the state share of all student aid has changed little over the years (6 percent of the total in 1993-94), although the states' share of grant aid has increased somewhat. In total, the states now provide more than $3 billion annually in grants to college students (NASSGP, 1994).[68] Given the likely prospect that the federal government, in its drive to balance its budget, will deemphasize student grants even more in the future, the role of the states in higher education affordability seems destined to become more crucial than ever. For private higher education then, the states' student aid programs are of particular importance in this environment in helping a wide range of students to seriously consider alternatives to low-priced public colleges and universities, should they so choose.

Student aid has taken on great importance in recent years, in large part because of the sharp run-up in tuition prices in both public and private higher

---

[67]Gillespie and Carlson (1983) and College Board (1989), cited in McPherson and Schapiro (1991), p. 28.

[68]More than 98 percent of this state aid goes to undergraduate students (NASSGP, 1994).

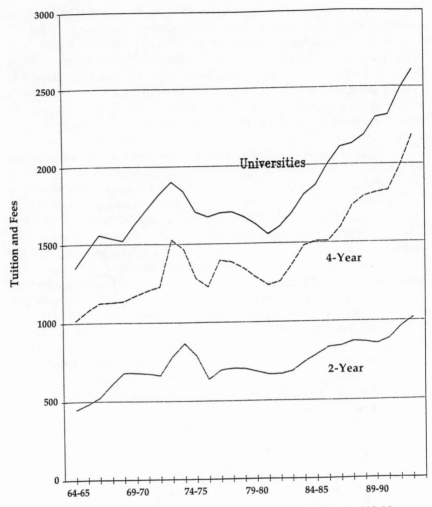

**FIGURE 2. Tuition and Fees at Public Institutions, 1964-65 to 1993-93**

Source: Mortenson, 1994b, p. 6.

education that began around 1980 (See Figures 2 and 3.) These graphs show tuition growth in each sector after adjustment for general price inflation, thus the consistency and overall magnitude of the increases are notable. The increases in the private sector are of particular interest here. Clotfelter (1991) compared tuition and other charges at private and public institutions over nearly three decades and found a long-term growth trend in the ratio of private-to-public tuition and fee levels. This ratio was 4.0 in 1959-60, 4.9 in 1974-75, and 5.9 in 1987-88 (p. 70). In relation to median family income, however, private tuition,

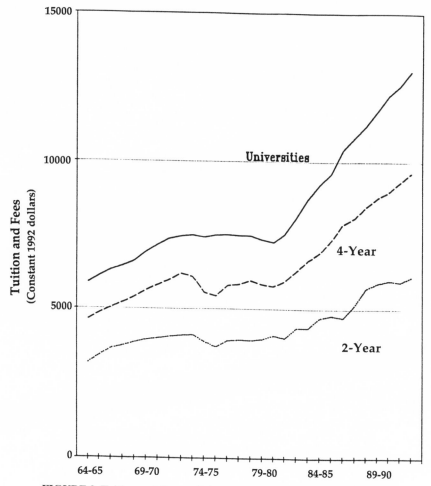

**FIGURE 3. Tuition and Fees at Private Institutions, 1964-65 to 1992-93**

Source: Mortenson, 1994b, p. 7.

room and board charges actually fell from 26.9 percent of income in 1959-60 to 23.4 percent in 1979-80, but then jumped dramatically during the 1980s to 32.3 percent in 1987-88. Average public institution charges as a percentage of family income also increased in the eighties, from 10.3 percent in 1979-80 to 12.3 percent in 1987-88, but remained well below the 14.6 percent level of 1959-60 (Clotfelter, 1991, p. 70).

In the private higher education sector, the rapid price increases of the early eighties were explained as being necessary to permit faculty and institutional maintenance expenditures to "catch up" after the period of dramatic inflation in the late 1970s (Breneman, 1994; St. John, 1994). Public higher education officials attributed large increases in these years to the need to generate revenue to offset recession-induced slowdowns in their state appropriations (St. John, 1994, p. 2).

Nonetheless, year after year of relentless increases, well above the general rate of inflation and extending well beyond the end of the recession period, produced an unprecedented reaction from the federal government. Ronald Reagan's Secretary of Education, William Bennett, a former college professor, and his aides began to aggressively make the argument that colleges and universities were raising tuition and fees so regularly and sharply because they were full of waste and inefficiency and because this allowed them to take advantage of the government student aid available, since up to a point the formulas for distributing aid take tuition and fee levels into account in assessing a student's "need" (McPherson and Schapiro, 1991; Breneman, 1994; St. John, 1994).[69] These arguments certainly struck a populist nerve in some listeners and the point about institutions increasing prices to absorb increased government aid dollars has a superficial plausibility in microeconomic terms. However, the effective limits on income eligibility and grant (and loan) size built into the aid-dispensing formulas raise immediate doubts about the incentive effects on institutional pricing, since in many cases students and their families not aid pools would end up, at the margin, paying for the tuition increases.[70]

Private college interests in particular argued that the recent reductions in government aid simply meant that institutions would have to make up the difference for students, or reduce the number of needy students they enrolled.[71] They pointed to the sharp increases in aid from their own funds that they were providing.[72] They further noted that their main source of revenue for such increases in institutionally funded aid spending had to be tuition increases since this is their main source of flexible revenue. Thus, from the institutions' perspective, their large price increases were mainly attributable to reduced federal aid and their

---

[69]For Secretary Bennett's sentiments unalloyed, see Bennett, 1986; 1987.

[70]For a careful analysis of the likely incentive effects built into the design of the aid programs, see McPherson and Schapiro (1991), pp. 67-69.

[71]With respect to moderate-income students, federally guaranteed loans were available during the 1980s, but the Reagan Administration imposed fairly stringent limits on who could get subsidized loans and how much they could borrow (Mumper, 1991). Thus, private institutions often had to supplement government aid funds heavily or "discount" their tuition prices selectively (whether or not these discounts were labelled officially as scholarships) to remain competitive for many moderate and middle-income students (Breneman, 1994, chapter three). For a helpful analysis of the debate between the Bennett position and that of private and other higher education interests, see St. John (1994, pp. 1-12).

[72]See in particular National Institute of Independent Colleges and Universities (1990); Breneman (1994, chapter three). Breneman, however, is critical of the standard way in which private institutions view and explain the issues at stake here.

desire to continue to enroll diverse student bodies. They further argued that these steady price increases would indeed eventually affect their enrollments (or the income and ethnic composition of their student bodies), especially in an era when the size of the traditional age pool of college students was decreasing each year. One obvious problem is that, if institutions' aid budgets are mainly financed by tuition payments from relatively affluent students, at some point sharp price increases used mainly for redistribution among the student body seem sure to produce growing resistance from those paying the bills (Bowen and Breneman, 1993).

Recent empirical research has made a contribution to sorting out the competing claims here. In order to increase understanding of the relationships between various forms of governmental support, including student aid, and key institutional behavior variables such as tuition pricing and discretionary spending on student aid, McPherson and Schapiro (1991) developed an econometric model incorporating the major financial variables for the fiscal years 1978-79 and 1985-86 to explore relationships among them for various types of colleges and universities (pp. 57-74). Contrary to suggestions by Secretary Bennett, these analysts find no empirical evidence for private four-year institutions of any relationship between federal student aid income and movements in tuition (pp. 70, 72).[73] They find a significant positive relationship between the rate of growth of federal student aid (as well as other income from government both state and federal)[74] and the growth rate of institutional spending on student aid, suggesting that "increased federal aid lowers the cost of admitting needy students sufficiently to allow private institutions to increase their own spending on aid in response…" (p. 72). This implies that the federal aid leverages an increased effect in the desired direction by motivating institutions to take advantage of it by doing more to attract more needy students. Plainly, there is no support here for the Bennett conjectures, though there is also no clear empirical evidence that reduced growth in federal financial support leads institutions to substitute their own funds for aid either.

On the other hand, the (mainly theoretical and conceptual) work of Massy (1990), Zemsky (1990), and Massy and Wilger (1992) also rings true to a considerable extent. These analysts, having observed academe's internal incentive structure and behavioral patterns over a long time and in many settings, point to

---

[73]They do find a positive relationship between federal student aid received and *public* institution tuition pricing, however, probably because these institutions have prices low enough to be able to gain financially from increases in tuition-based aid eligibility of their students (pp. 70-73).

[74]These other relationships are significant because they suggest that private institutions use revenue from such sources as research grants and state appropriations and grants in part to replace some of their own funds spent on the supported activities, and that they move some of the freed-up discretionary funds into student aid (p. 73). According to the McPherson and Schapiro results, they also tend to raise tuition less than they would otherwise. Among public institutions, only the relationship between federal grant and contract funding and institutional student aid spending is statistically significant.

several factors working to drive up costs over time.[75] To summarize briefly, these factors include the labor-intensive character of academic work given traditional definitions of quality based on close faculty-student contact and thus low student-faculty ratios;[76] lack of incentives for cost-saving innovations, in particular in faculty-reducing instructional technology;[77] professorial incentives toward research effort and output at the expense of teaching and advising responsibilities that have spread throughout most of academe and tend to increase costs per student; and incentives for bureaucratic entrepreneurs in academic administration to "build empires" that are costly as a route to advancement.[78] Another factor tending to increase costs on the administrative side is that institutions have had to respond in recent years to more and more mandates, regulation and information demands from federal and state governments.

These "inexorable" cost increases can be passed on to students, as long as they are willing and able to pay. In a macro sense, the availability of some $47 billion in aid annually (College Board, 1995)[79] no doubt does play a role in aggregate willingness to pay, as does the high private returns on investment available in the contemporary economy to those who complete higher education (Murphy and Welch, 1989; Marshall and Tucker, 1992; Breneman, 1994). Thus, there are few strong reasons to attack the powerful forces just described that tend to push costs and prices in higher education up steadily in real terms. (Attacks on these established ways of doing things would, of course, be met with fierce resistance from powerful and eloquent constituencies, so strong reasons are needed to produce impetus to act.)

For public institutions, there are signs that political forces, as well as improvements in the economy, are already bringing a halt to the most recent sharp jumps in tuition levels. (Zumeta and Fawcett-Long, 1996). But for the private sector this simply means that the "tuition gap" (best measured by the private/public price ratio used by Clotfelter, 1991) will likely resume its long-term growth pattern, and thus raises the question, How long will students and families be willing to pay staggering, and seemingly ever-growing, premiums for private higher education? Not surprisingly, the truly elite and most visible private colleges and universities, with plenty of surplus applicants of good quality from high-income families and large endowments, need not worry about this too much, though it does become increasingly expensive for them to maintain diverse student bod-

---

[75]See also Breneman (1994, pp. 32-33).

[76]See Bowen (1980) for a perceptive analysis of how these factors tend to drive up costs in higher education.

[77]Many faculty and institutional leaders are quite interested in investing in the latest educational technologies, but as an addition to the resources used in instruction to enhance quality, not as a way to teach more students per faculty member.

[78]Zemsky's (1990) terms for these last two phenomena are the "academic ratchet" and the "administrative lattice." The other points have been made for a long time by many others.

[79]This figure counts grant and loan aid from all sources, including federal, state, and institutional and private sources.

ies.[80] Less-favored private schools with limited applicant pools and small endowments—the vast, if not very visible, majority of private institutions—have not been able to raise prices nearly as fast as their more-favored counterparts (Clotfelter, 1991), and so have had to be more resourceful in their survival strategies and do live more precariously. In short, many of them have not been averse to pushing aggressively for state assistance and, most importantly, have taken in many cases fairly dramatic steps on their own to revamp their programs and market them effectively to take advantage of whatever student markets they can find (Breneman, 1990; 1994; Zumeta, 1994).

While this resourcefulness in responding to the market is in many ways admirable—and quintessentially American—it is not without its price. With respect to the elite private institutions, there has been a substantial "middle-class melt" as students in this income group have faced steep price increases—even after aid is taken into account—that they have been unable or unwilling to pay (McPherson and Schapiro, 1991, pp. 78-89).[81] Significantly, though, the proportion of low-income students enrolling in these institutions has not decreased much, apparently because these students have continued to be prime targets for what grant aid is available from both governmental and institutional sources. Their proportions continue to be quite modest, however, as are the proportions of minority students in the elite schools (McPherson and Schapiro, 1991; Breneman, 1994). Thus, the place of the middle-income students in the top private schools has evidently been taken by even more students from affluent families who can afford to pay all or nearly all of their high prices (McPherson and Schapiro, 1991, pp. 78-89).[82] And these schools have maintained their liberal arts traditions and, by all accounts, continue to provide an extremely high quality of education to their favored clientele (Breneman, 1994). The elite private universities have also maintained their place in national rankings of quality in graduate education and research. There have been some signs of belt-tightening at some of these institutions (Chira, 1990; "Stanford to Lay Off...," 1990; Manger, 1991; De Palma, 1992; Celis, 1993), but few indications of major changes or that quality has been in any serious way affected.

As suggested above, more problematic (and elusive) are the effects of the difficulties of the recent era (i.e., since 1980) on the nonelite private colleges and

---

[80]McPherson and Schapiro (1994) have documented an apparent decline in proportions of private-college freshmen from high-income families in the last few years (1989-1993), however, suggesting that the point of serious price resistance on the part of such students may have been reached.

[81]McPherson and Schapiro point out (and emphasize further in their 1994 paper) that an important part of the "middle-class melt" phenomenon in private higher education simply results from the decline in the proportion of all students who are from families defined as middle-income (1991, p. 81).

[82]These authors point out that the same type of displacement has occurred in public universities (p. 88). Interestingly, their 1994 paper suggests some recovery in the proportions of private institution freshmen from lower- and middle-income backgrounds at the expense of upper-income students, but this analysis does not distinguish elite from other private institutions, as did the analysis published in 1991. Also, it shows a nearly two-percentage-point decline in the proportion of all freshmen enrolling in private institutions between 1989 and 1993 (1994, Tables 1 and 2).

universities.[83] Surprisingly, there is no evidence that the number of private institutions has declined as many expected it would. On the contrary, a careful comparison of numbers of private, nonprofit, degree-granting colleges and universities reporting enrollments in 1980 and 1992 shows a net increase of more than two hundred.[84] In terms of aggregate enrollments, the private nonprofit sector (including the elite institutions, whose enrollments have grown only a little), gained 13.4 percent in headcount enrollment over these twelve years (Zumeta, 1994).[85] But how have all these institutions survived and even grown in the face of fewer high-school graduates, a growing private/public tuition gap, and a less favorable federal student aid picture?

State student aid has probably helped a bit. After a period of very sluggish growth during the early and mid-1980s, these grant programs have increased quite strongly since the late 1980s (NASSGP, 1994; College Board, 1995). The total of state grant aid in constant dollars is now about twice the 1985-86 level (College Board, 1995).[86] Although public institutions' students have been claiming a gradually growing portion of this aid, especially in the last few years of sharp rises in public sector tuitions, the less-elite private schools, which enroll mainly students from their home state, are prime beneficiaries.[87]

Breneman (1990; 1994) points to the major process at work that accounts for the relative success of the private higher education sector.[88] A great many private institutions once called "liberal arts" colleges or universities have simply moved sharply away from this tradition in their programming in the direction of career-oriented fields. By Breneman's reckoning, by the mid-1980s only about two hundred colleges remained as liberal arts colleges, defined as baccalaureate-granting schools granting at least 40 percent of their degrees in liberal arts as opposed to professional fields. He documents large increases in the proportion of professional degrees awarded by baccalaureate institutions.[89]

---

[83]By this broad term, I mean private institutions lacking substantial endowments and comfortable numbers of "surplus" reasonably qualified applicants for admission.

[84]Calculated by the author with the assistance of Penelope Karovsky from an IPEDS-derived data base maintained at the University of Washington. This data base is the source of the enrollment figures for the private nonprofit sector cited in this section.

[85]These figures exclude Puerto Rico and U.S. territories. Over the same period, public college and university enrollments grew by 20 percent (calculated from NCES, 1994). If only four-year institutions are compared (since the fastest-growing segment in U.S. higher education is the large public community college sector, while private two-year colleges are a small part of the private sector), the two sectors' 1980-1992 growth figures are considerably closer: about 12 percent for the private, four-year institutions and 15 percent for the comparable public institutions.

[86]These are preliminary figures for 1994-95.

[87]Most of the elite private schools have national student bodies, while most state student aid programs restrict eligibility to state-resident students. Thus, it is the locally oriented private schools that depend most on these programs to provide aid to their students.

[88]Breneman (1994) also attributes considerable importance to gains in endowment earnings and fund-raising by private colleges, but these factors are of less import for the nonelite schools than for the best-known schools with large endowments.

Some analysis of recent enrollment trends in the broader private higher education sector is also pertinent. Table 3 (lower panel) shows that, while overall head-count enrollments in U.S. private colleges and universities grew by 13.4 percent over the years 1980-1992, full-time-equivalent (FTE) enrollments gained only 11.1 percent. This is because the strongest growth was in part-time rather than full-time students.[90] Part-time numbers in private colleges and universities grew by a robust 23.1 percent over the twelve years, while full-time students increased by less than half as much (9.6%). Another comparison is equally telling, and related to the first. The number of private-sector undergraduates grew by only 9.0 percent over these twelve years, while graduate and professional enrollments saw much stronger growth, at 28.0 percent. This is, it appears, because a large segment of the private sector has in recent years concentrated on enrolling professionally oriented students in postbaccalaureate programs, often part-time programs targeted at working students.[91]

This conclusion is consistent with Breneman's (1990; 1994) finding that many of the nonelite private colleges have moved away from the liberal arts tradition in terms of their degree offerings. Table 4 provides some additional data that tend to confirm the point. This table shows the trends in private-sector enrollments by (1987) Carnegie classification of private institutions. The fastest-growing category (+30.6%) is the "Liberal Arts II," or less-selective "liberal arts" colleges, which Breneman argues are really small professional institutions (1994, pp. 11-15). Close behind is the "Comprehensive II" institutions category (+25.0%), which are also less-selective institutions dominated by vocationally and professionally oriented programs and students. Specialized private institutions,[92] largely professionally oriented, have also grown rapidly. "Comprehensive I" institutions, which also have substantial professionally oriented programs and students but are more selective than Comprehensive IIs, have also grown significantly (+10.5%). It appears that the strongest group of more traditional private institutions, the "Research I" universities, have also grown at a reasonable rate (+ 10.8%), but the other classifications in the more traditional mold have had sluggish enrollment growth or worse.[93]

---

[89]See Breneman (1994), pp. 138-142 for these trend analyses covering the Carnegie Foundation's Liberal Arts I and II categories of institutions.

[90]For purposes of computing full-time-equivalent enrollments, the National Center For Education Statistics (the source of the data used here) counts three part-time students as equal to one full-time student.

[91]Consistent with this is the finding from the author's (as yet unpublished) analyses of degree award data by field for various Carnegie classes of private institutions, that the fastest-growing fields in the fast-growing classes of institutions during the 1980s and early 1990s have been, by far, business and (since 1985 at least) education, with other professionally oriented fields (e.g., computer science, psychology) also among the leaders in growth rate, though of far less importance in quantitative terms.

[92]This is a composite category composed of a variety of Carnegie categories encompassing seminaries, schools of the arts, free-standing law schools, and various other types of specialized, largely professionally oriented institutions.

[93]Note that the least-demanding classification of doctorate-granting institutions, "Doctorate II" institutions, actually lost six percent of their 1980 enrollments by 1992, and the elite Liberal Arts I institutions gained only 0.5 percent. In the latter case, this enrollment stability appears to be largely by design (Breneman, 1994).

## TABLE 3. Independent College and University Enrollments, 1980, 1985, 1990, & 1992

| | 1980 | 1985 | 1990 | 1992 | 80-85 | 85-90 | 90-92 | 80-92 | % 80-85 | % 85-90 | % 90-92 | %80-92 |
|---|---|---|---|---|---|---|---|---|---|---|---|---|
| Headcount | 2,593,130 | 2,669,553 | 2,852,194 | 2,953,558 | 76,423 | 182,641 | 101,364 | 360,428 | 2.9% | 6.8% | 3.6% | 13.9% |
| Full-Time | 1,867,646 | 1,882,889 | 1,990,062 | 2,060,400 | 15,243 | 107,173 | 70,338 | 192,754 | 0.8% | 5.7% | 3.5% | 10.3% |
| Part-Time | 725,484 | 786,664 | 862,132 | 893,158 | 61,180 | 75,468 | 31,026 | 167,674 | 8.4% | 9.6% | 3.6% | 23.1% |
| FTE | 2,109,474 | 2,145,110 | 2,277,439 | 2,358,119 | 35,636 | 132,329 | 80,680 | 248,645 | 1.7% | 6.2% | 3.5% | 11.8% |
| Undergraduate | 1,983,693 | 2,015,084 | 2,130,764 | 2,174,438 | 31,391 | 115,680 | 43,674 | 190,745 | 1.6% | 5.7% | 2.0% | 9.6% |
| Graduate+First Professional | 605,235 | 648,883 | 721,430 | 779,120 | 43,648 | 72,547 | 57,690 | 173,885 | 7.2% | 11.2% | 8.0% | 28.7% |
| Unclassified | 4,202 | 5,586 | 0 | 0 | | | | | | | | |

### Independent College and University Enrollments, 1980, 1985, 1990, & 1992 (excluding Puerto Rico and territories)

| | 1980 | 1985 | 1990 | 1992 | 80-85 | 85-90 | 90-92 | 80-92 | % 80-85 | % 85-90 | % 90-92 | % 80-92 |
|---|---|---|---|---|---|---|---|---|---|---|---|---|
| Headcount | 2,522,428 | 2,576,223 | 2,763,747 | 2,859,498 | 53,795 | 187,524 | 95,751 | 337,070 | 2.1% | 7.3% | 3.5% | 13.4% |
| Full-Time | 1,813,656 | 1,808,355 | 1,922,393 | 1,987,220 | -5,301 | 114,038 | 64,827 | 173,564 | -0.3% | 6.3% | 3.4% | 9.6% |
| Part-Time | 708,772 | 767,868 | 841,354 | 872,278 | 59,096 | 73,486 | 30,924 | 163,506 | 8.3% | 9.6% | 3.7% | 23.1% |
| FTE | 2,049,913 | 2,064,311 | 2,202,844 | 2,277,979 | 14,398 | 138,533 | 75,135 | 228,066 | 0.7% | 6.7% | 3.4% | 11.1% |
| Undergraduate | 1,915,959 | 1,927,595 | 2,049,104 | 2,088,126 | 11,636 | 121,509 | 39,022 | 172,167 | 0.6% | 6.3% | 1.9% | 9.0% |
| Graduate+First Professional | 602,485 | 643,206 | 714,643 | 771,372 | 40,721 | 71,437 | 56,729 | 168,887 | 6.8% | 11.1% | 7.9% | 28.0% |
| Unclassified | 3,984 | 5,422 | 0 | 0 | | | | | | | | |

Source: Zumeta, 1994.

**TABLE 4. Independent College and University Enrollments**
**Selected Years, 1980 through 1992,**
**by 1987 Carnegie Classification of Institutions**

| HEADCOUNT | 1980 | 1985 | 1990 | 1992 | % 80-85 | % 85-90 | % 90-92 | % 80-92 |
|---|---|---|---|---|---|---|---|---|
| C1 | 608,360 | 634,765 | 665,950 | 672,388 | 4.3% | 4.9% | 1.0% | 10.5% |
| C2 | 222,326 | 230,064 | 261,081 | 277,987 | 3.5% | 13.5% | 6.5% | 25.0% |
| D1 | 188,343 | 184,104 | 196,742 | 200,216 | -2.3% | 6.9% | 1.8% | 6.3% |
| D2 | 183,385 | 178,927 | 172,326 | 172,266 | -2.4% | -3.7% | 0.0% | -6.1% |
| LA1 | 217,263 | 208,557 | 217,585 | 218,242 | -4.0% | 4.3% | 0.3% | 0.5% |
| LA2 | 330,088 | 332,622 | 402,831 | 430,961 | 0.8% | 21.1% | 7.0% | 30.6% |
| R1 | 319,567 | 330,302 | 343,972 | 354,178 | 3.4% | 4.1% | 3.0% | 10.8% |
| R2 | 88,524 | 87,945 | 90,756 | 90,427 | -0.7% | 3.2% | -0.4% | 2.1% |
| **Subtotal** | **2,157,856** | **2,187,286** | **2,351,243** | **2,416,665** | **1.4%** | **7.5%** | **2.8%** | **12.0%** |
| 2yr/Spec/Unc | 364,572 | 388,937 | 412,504 | 442,833 | 6.7% | 6.1% | 7.4% | 21.5% |
| Total | 2,522,428 | 2,576,223 | 2,763,747 | 2,859,498 | 2.1% | 7.3% | 3.5% | 13.4% |

Source: Zumeta, 1994

These patterns suggest that, for institutions not at the top of the traditional quality hierarchy, the successful strategy in the eighties and early nineties has been to emphasize professionally oriented programs accessible to part-time students. The fastest growth has been in such enrollments at the graduate level, but the underlying data (not shown here), as well as the import of Breneman's analysis, indicate that there have been substantial markets at the undergraduate level as well in many fields. It is also important to note, however, that the more traditional classes of private colleges and universities, with the exception of the small Doctorate II group of institutions, have at least held their own in enrollments during a very difficult era. This in itself is a significant accomplishment.

From a public policy perspective, the surprising resourcefulness and vitality of private higher education should be seen, in general, as a positive development. Stronger private-sector enrollments tend to be associated with higher overall participation in higher education and lower costs to state taxpayers (Zumeta, 1996). As suggested earlier, these relationships could be especially significant in the coming era of growing demands for higher education but limited tax revenues. On the other hand, Breneman rightly raises the question as to how small and inaccessible to broad groups of the population we wish to allow the "liberal arts core" of institutions in the country to become (1994, chapter one).[94] Perhaps policymakers should consider taking stronger steps to insure the survival and broader accessibility of more of the distinctively liberal arts institutions.

---

[94] As Breneman and others have pointed out, virtually all liberal arts *colleges* (as distinct from universities with substantial liberal arts programs) are in the private sector. Thus, they are the only apparent source of their particular brand of undergraduate education available to students. These schools have long produced a disproportionate share of the nation's leaders and scholars (Breneman, 1994, ch.1).

Secondly, the vigorous response to the demands of the student market by private institutions that live or die according to their attractiveness to students has potential for abuse, even when the institutions are not-for-profit. Governments, both state and federal, may need to consider creative ways to discharge their duty to the citizenry to insure reasonable quality and truth-in-advertising by these institutions without unduly circumscribing their freedoms as independent organizations and as institutions of higher learning. Certainly this is a difficult balance to strike, but additional places in higher education are of little value if the programs are not sound and the students are not capable of profiting from them. The state role (or potential role) in this area is likely to grow in the foreseeable future as the federal government moves to devolve regulatory responsibilities to the states. States would do well to seek guidance from non-U.S., as well as home-grown, approaches in this delicate area (Geiger, 1986; Dill, 1995; van Vught, 1995).

## WHAT THE FUTURE HOLDS FOR PRIVATE HIGHER EDUCATION

As we look ahead, it is important to think about the future of private higher education broadly, in the context of the challenges facing all of higher education. Indeed, as was suggested earlier, for more than a century it has made little sense in the United States to consider independent higher education separately from the public sector enterprise in this field. Now, as was argued in the early part of this chapter, the demand for higher education is growing for both economic (i.e., the needs of the modern economy) and social (i.e., demographic factors such as the "baby boom echo" and equity concerns) reasons. At the same time, the resources that have traditionally provided the bulk of support for higher education, state tax funds, are increasingly constrained by taxpayer resistance and pressures from other state functions with rapidly growing caseloads and a near-mandatory funding requirement: Medicaid, criminal justice and prisons, and elementary and secondary education. Impending devolution of responsibility for other human services from the federal government to the states adds to the competition for scarce state support.[95] In light of these trends, the prospects for higher education access and adequate funding per-student at the time the next recession hits the states may be grim indeed.

In many states private higher education can provide an important part of the answer to the dilemmas posed by this combination of forces and trends, but only if state policies are conducive. As I shall argue below, however, in a number of states the extant policy framework is not conducive to taking the independent sector seriously as a significant potential contributor to the achievement of state higher education policy goals. In the next section, I will present a conceptual framework for analyzing state policies that affect private higher education and the factors that influence them in an effort to begin to understand and account for the variation in how these institutions are treated in the policymaking process. I will

---

[95]For a more complete analysis of these developments, see Zumeta and Fawcett-Long (1996).

also explain how this framework is helpful in thinking about policy outcomes, such as provision of cost-effective access to higher education in an era of growing demand, and will lay out a theory-building and research agenda related to it, as well as suggest its implications for policy analysis.

## STATE POLICY POSTURES VIS-A-VIS PRIVATE HIGHER EDUCATION

Although state policies that affect private higher education are disparate, there are reasons to believe that within individual states such policies might be related to each other in a more or less coherent fashion. Rational policymakers seeking maximum impact and minimum unintended consequences from the set of policies in place at any given time would be expected to try to select policies that meshed well with policies already in place or simultaneously enacted. Also, although the policies in place at any time have typically emerged during different periods, they arise from policymaking systems and cultures that are likely to be fairly stable over time in important respects (Gardner, Atwell, and Berdahl, 1985). Yet for all its apparent logic, policy coherence is hardly inevitable. Public policymaking processes do not always produce evidently rational results,[96] especially when a set of policies enacted over many years is viewed at a single point in time and in light of contemporary conditions.  Moreover, since many state policies affect private higher education only secondarily in the course of pursuing other, more primary goals, the cumulative array of policies touching this sector could be virtually random.

Howlett (1991) describes a school of thought on the study of policy instruments (the "continuum" school), with its roots in such classics as Dahl and Lindblom (1953) and Kirschen et al (1964), which argues that conceptions of types of policy tools, and thus by extension policy regimes, such as those described in the next section are most useful in understanding instrument choice. The argument is that for most tasks a number of policy tools (e.g., instruments such as grants, mandates, or provision of information) are available, but that policymaker choices among them are driven more by the political, social, economic, and ideological variables at work than by rational assessment of which tool is right for which job. Such analysts as Linder and Peters (1989) in the contemporary "policy design" school, seek to blend the earlier ideas of scholars who emphasized a resource-based notion of policy instruments (i.e., distinguishing direct from indirect grants, information-based strategies from coercive regulations and the like) with those of the continuum school. Howlett concludes a discussion of these efforts by noting: "The basic assumption made by design theorists is that policy instruments are technically substitutable but context-ridden...For the design theo-

---

[96]See in particular Lindblom (1980) for a classic statement of the reasons behind this hoary truth.

rists, then, instrument choice is ultimately a political decision heavily influenced by the nature of beliefs, attitudes and perceptions held by political and bureaucratic decisionmakers" (1991, p. 8).

This line of argument suggests there is indeed some logic in searching for regularities among a state's policies in a particular field, such as those affecting private higher education. Surely, students of higher education are aware that some states pay more attention to their private higher education sector than do others. Elsewhere, I have provided empirical evidence that states' policies in such areas as the presence or absence of state programs providing direct funding to private colleges and universities (whether by contract or direct appropriation); the size of state student aid programs (per-enrolled-student); the level of public institution tuition (a key competitive parameter for private higher education subject to strong state influence); the extent of private-sector involvement in state higher education planning; consideration of impacts on private institutions (often covered under the heading of "program duplication") in state reviews of public sector programs and proposals; and the extent of state mandates, regulation, and data collection affecting private higher education are intercorrelated in predictable ways (Zumeta, 1992).[97] If they were not, there would be little point in searching for comprehensible state "policy postures."

Since there is reason to believe that state policies toward (or affecting) private higher education are not random, the next step is to theorize about how they might be linked and about what factors might determine particular patterns of policies. Conceptually, it seems convenient to begin this process by considering three distinct types of possible state policy orientations or *postures* toward private higher education, which I shall call the *laissez-faire*, *central-planning*, and *market-competitive* state policy postures.[98] Without some such framework concepts it is difficult to think systematically about the wide range of state policies that affect private higher education. Moreover, from a policy analytic standpoint, they facilitate thinking about options for intervening in a state's policy "system" in order to affect policy outcomes and about how to assess the feasibility of possible interventions. Thus, if it could be empirically validated, such a framework would have potentially valuable uses of both the positive and normative variety—i.e., it could help illuminate both policy science in this field and policy analysis.

### The *Laissez-faire* Posture

A state taking the *laissez-faire* posture toward the private higher education sector is essentially choosing to leave this sector to its own devices, while the state pursues its policy ends in higher education strictly through public institutions. At the

---

[97]For example, states with relatively high student aid spending levels are more likely to have programs providing direct state funding to private colleges and universities and to have relatively high tuition levels in public higher education. Each of these variables is also positively correlated with the extent of private-sector participation in state planning for higher education (Zumeta, 1992).

extreme, this would mean little or no state funds for student aid would be available to private college students; no tax incentives aiding private institutions would exist beyond those available to all nonprofits; little or no consideration would be given to independent campuses' concerns in establishing public college tuition and fee structures or their mission and program configurations; the state would provide no funds, either by direct appropriation or by contract, to private institutions for any purpose beyond perhaps the occasional ad hoc research contract for a specific, limited purpose; the private sector would be excluded from a meaningful role in statewide higher education planning; the state would collect minimal information about independent institutions beyond that collected by the federal government; and the state's regulation of private higher education would be of the most limited conceivable scope, i.e., limited to licensing institutions to operate in the state and enforcing on them general state laws not specifically targeted at higher education.

In general, it seems likely that a state policy posture along these *laissez-faire* lines would be most plausible in states with a relatively small (in terms of enrollment share) and politically weak private higher education sector. Regional patterns should be prominent here because of historical factors (some suggested in the earlier discussion) leading to later and more limited development of private higher education west of the Mississippi (Trow, 1993). Other variables at work might include the wealth and general spending propensities of the state, since any proposed aid to private colleges or their students might look to a skeptical legislature much like any other new area of proposed state spending.[99] Also, a state's governance structure for higher education might play a role in that states where the state policy agency is also the governing board for the public institutions—an arrangement that obtains more or

---

[98]For the roots of the latter two constructs, see Breneman (1981) and Spence and Weathersby (1981). In commenting upon a draft of this chapter, James Hearn points out that, if we conceptualize state policy frameworks in terms of a two-by-two matrix (as shown below), a fourth cell is manifest: *bureaucratic/regulatory planning,* which would fit a state that used direct state control mechanisms extensively, but did little in the way of providing incentives or seeking to integrate student aid, tuition, and other policies. I am indebted to Professor Hearn for this interesting suggestion, but will not try to pursue it in this chapter.

USE OF DIRECT
STATE CONTROL

|  |  | Low | High |
|---|---|---|---|
| USE OF DIRECT INCENTIVES | Low | Laissez-Faire | Bureaucratic/Regulatory Planning |
|  | High | Market-Competitive | Comprehensive (Pro-Active) Central Planning |

[99]In fact though, such spending might well offset state spending on public higher education and even lead to a net reduction in state spending on higher education (Zumeta, 1996).

less in a number of states—might be expected to be little concerned with the private sector (i.e., behave as a *laissez-faire* state). On the other hand, other state governance arrangements, such as one of the coordinating board forms where the state agency has a meaningful policy and planning role for both sectors but no line management authority over the public institutions, should be more sensitive to the private sector's role and to potential impacts of policies on it.

What are the likely consequences of a state's pursuing laissez-faire policies vis-a-vis its private higher education sector? As suggested earlier, current competitive conditions facing private institutions, particularly those lacking large pools of surplus applicants and substantial endowments (i.e., the vast majority of private colleges), may imply some untoward consequences from the standpoint of the public interest, such as erosion of quality as funds are increasingly shifted from instruction and plant and equipment to student aid to compete for students; further increases in student debt burdens which may affect their career choices; likely further moves toward more narrow, vocationally oriented curricula; and, perhaps eventually, loss of capacity to enroll students (i.e., to provide access) and provide diversity to a state's institutional mix. If a particular state's private higher education sector is small and weak both academically and politically, the consequences may not be serious, practically speaking. In these circumstances, tragic though it may be for a few institutions and students, little quality enrollment capacity or meaningful diversity may be lost if some private institutions fail to survive the current competitive era without state help.

If, however, a state's independent sector does represent a substantial resource in terms of such publicly useful values as enrollment and research capacity, program quality, meaningful diversity and choice for students and other clients, and successful service to underserved areas and populations, then there is reason for public policy to be concerned about the implications of the laissez-faire posture. These implications should be of concern to policymakers, particularly in states that will soon need all the higher education capacity they can find (see Figure 1, page 47).

### The State *Central-Planning* Posture

At the opposite end of the conceptual continuum from the laissez-faire posture stands state *central-planning*. In this policy posture, instead of ignoring the private sector as in the laissez-faire regime, the state embraces this sector as an integral part of its higher education capacity. This model can only be fully developed in a state that practices strong central planning for its public higher education sector, which typically entails a well-developed "master plan" delineating institutional roles as well as extensive mandates, planning mechanisms, data collection, and use of funding leverage to enforce the grand scheme. In such a regime the private institutions are incorporated integrally in the extensive state planning and management of higher education that exists, get their share of attention when new state initiatives affecting higher education are planned, and receive a substantial share of the state's higher education dollars. Indeed the state's money presumably helps entice them into and cements them within this policy system. To better ensure adherence to its plans and designs, we would expect the central-planning-oriented state to channel some of its dollars directly to independent institutions, indeed perhaps to prefer direct funding of them at the margin to student aid and tax incentives as more effective levers to simultaneously aid and direct the private higher education sector to serve state purposes.

Central-planning also implies as a basic tenet efforts by the planners to limit apparent duplication in institutional missions and programs since this seems unnecessarily expensive.[100] Such efforts can be very significant to the private sector if taken seriously because they mean that duplication of private institution missions, programs, or geographic "turf" become legitimate considerations in state decisions about expansion in public higher education. This addresses one of the private sector's chief state policy concerns in the current competitive era, so this sector can be expected to actively support such vigilance by state authorities. Similarly, in the area of state policies affecting (or determining) public higher education tuition levels, the central-planning-oriented state would be expected to give attention to impacts on private institutions because it is dependent on them to play specific roles in the state's higher education "system." Thus, public tuition levels will tend to be biased upward, though this effect may be moderated by other factors, such as the relative political influence of the public and private sectors.

The price of solicitude from the state in program review matters, and of participation in its planning councils and funding largesse, seems likely to be increased state concern over time with private institutions' missions, program configurations, and performance with state funds.[101] Thus, the state practicing extensive central planning would be expected to collect increasing amounts of data from and about private institutions (as it would about its public institutions), and to oversee their financial operations and their efforts at new program initiatives more closely over time. It would also be likely to come to see these institutions as legitimately subject to more and more state regulation (e.g., with regard to student and institutional assessment, program review, perhaps tuition pricing), as well as to its fiscal largesse.

In short, "independent" institutions which choose to play in the state's game under a central-planning regime run the risk of becoming quasi-public. The negative side of this is that such quasi-public institutions, substantially dependent upon state dollars and subject to various formal and informal state controls, are likely to become less capable of sustaining the diversity of mission and approach, the flexibility and rapid market responsiveness, and the autonomy from a single

---

[100]Whether or not this is always true is another question (Thompson and Zumeta, 1981).

[101]Geiger's (1986) accounts of the evolution of state-private-higher-education relations in Japan, Belgium, the Netherlands, and the Philippines over recent decades are instructive here.

central vision that is an important part of the reason public policy might seek to preserve an independent higher education sector.[102] Also, a centrally focused policy regime will tend to attract some of institutions' creative energies toward influencing the state authorities who control the resources and protections they seek, perhaps at the expense of direct attention to state service needs as reflected in student and market demands.

The state central-planning posture has some advantages as well. It permits the state considerable latitude to aid the independent higher education sector in a time when some (even many) private institutions may need help to continue serving public purposes well. Such aid need not be direct financial assistance from the state to private colleges and universities, though in some cases state help might take this form. Such direct state "institutional aid," more easily than student aid carried indirectly to institutions when students choose them, can be used to target state resources efficiently to particular purposes. Second, such a regime legitimizes use of private institutions to serve public purposes in situations where they may be more cost-effective tools for the particular task than public institutions (e.g., programs serving particular regions or high-cost specialty fields where the private sector already has capacity), or where the two sectors can work cooperatively. This could be increasingly important in an era of limited resources for higher education.

Third, the central-planning approach legitimizes extensive data-gathering on private institutions and their capabilities that should have many uses in managing an integrated state higher education system for optimal results. Fourth, it permits the state authorities to shield private institutions in various ways from subsidized public sector competition, if it is deemed to be in the public interest to do so. Finally, extending the state's regulatory net to include the private sector may have benefits to the extent these efforts succeed in enhancing educational quality, teacher preparedness, and the like, as they seek to do.

States tending in the direction of the central-planning model encompassing the private higher education sector are likely to have historical, cultural, and legal traditions that permit and encourage both strong central-planning and close state-private-sector relations.

Also, the private sector has to be both willing to participate[103] and large enough to be worth taking into account. Empirically, one would tend to look for central-planning-oriented regimes with heavy independent sector involvement in policymaking among states with traditions of active state government and large, politically influential private higher education sectors. These considerations point toward the Northeast and upper Midwest states with large, long-established private sectors and traditions of governmental activism strongly influenced by

---

[102]On these and related points, see Thompson and Zumeta (1981); Birnbaum (1983); Clark (1983); Ware (1989).

[103]For example, nonsectarian and Roman Catholic institutions tend to be less standoffish with respect to state governments than are many Protestant institutions, especially conservative ones.

affected interests. Other likely supportive factors are a coordinating board type of state governance structure, which tends to facilitate private sector involvement more than a statewide "board of regents" arrangement (Zumeta, 1992), and sufficient state wealth to make substantial student aid and programs channeling state funds directly to private colleges and universities seem affordable.

### The *Market-Competitive* State Policy Posture

A third, distinctly different type of state policy posture is possible.[104] In the *market-competitive* regime, rather than letting the chips fall where they may as in the *laissez-faire* model, the state takes a more active posture toward private higher education and private/public relations. Although they avoid the detailed state direction characteristic of the *central-planning* approach just described, state authorities under the *market-competitive* regime nonetheless take a comprehensive view of the state's higher education resources, including its private institutions, but seek primarily to facilitate the workings of the marketplace and to promote evenhanded competition across sectors.

Under the pure market-competitive approach, state intervention would be limited to addressing the various market imperfections which characterize the higher education marketplace.[105] Thus state mandates and regulation would be quite limited. State interventions in this model would likely include tuition and student aid policies designed to more nearly equalize net prices (i.e., after student aid) between private and public institutions;[106] encouragement, or at least no discouragement, of public/private competition not judged to denigrate quality or involve fraudulent claims; and efforts to disseminate widely and facilitate the use by students and their parents of comparative information about institutions' characteristics and performance.[107] This last point is in notable contrast to the central-planning regime where information policy focuses on collecting data for managing the system from the center.

Where the state authorities saw a particular need not being adequately addressed by the public and private institutions (e.g., inadequate production of certain types of trained specialists, a need for new economic development initiatives), the true competitive regime would describe the type of program sought and offer it up for "bids" in a competition open to competent institutions from

---

[104]Of course, so are many others. Empirical research and analysis should be helpful here (see Zumeta, 1996).

[105]These would include widely varying tuition subsidies not systematically related to policy objectives, the existence of near-monopolies in some markets, inadequate or no response to particular state needs by the higher education system, inadequate consumer information, and perhaps some quality control measures beyond information provision, if deemed necessary.

[106]We would expect the competitively oriented state to favor generous, but competitive or "portable" student aid grants tenable at both private and public institutions to *tuition equalization* grants available only to students attending private institutions. The latter, however, do serve to move state subsidies to private and public institution students in the direction of equality.

[107]See also Breneman (1981).

both sectors. Short of this, private institutions would at least routinely be offered the opportunity to compete to fill gaps not of interest to public colleges. Winning bidders would be granted time-limited, performance-based contracts, at least in theory subject to nonrenewal and rebidding, rather than essentially permanent institutional grant programs.[108] This would be the extent of direct state aid to private institutions in the true market-competitive regime, as the state would prefer aid mechanisms where the market selects who gets how much aid, such as tax incentives for donations to institutions of either sector and aid routed through students who can choose which college to attend.

Beyond the specific and carefully targeted interventions to "perfect" the market described above, the pure market-competitive state would, in sharp contrast to the central-planning regime, allow both public and private institutions (a) to plan and modify their own offerings within existing resources without close state regulatory oversight, and (b) to compete directly for students and the resources tied to them. An empirically plausible version of this model would almost certainly, however, entail some restrictions on the program configurations of public institutions (i.e., mission limitations and some state review of new program proposals), and some basic funding guarantees to public institutions independent of enrollments.[109]

One might summarize the differences between the state central-planning model and the market-competitive posture by observing that in the former the private institutions are treated by the state much like the public ones, while in the latter the public institutions face an environment deliberately designed to be somewhat like that now faced by the private schools. The basic point of the latter type of state policy regime is to focus institutions more on reacting to (or even anticipating) societal needs and demands by encouraging them to respond to market or quasi-market signals (i.e., enrollment-driven funding and performance contracting arrangements), and less on working state officials for favored treatment in centrally controlled decisions on missions, programs, and resource allocations.

This model has theoretical appeal but the full-blown market-competitive approach has a number of theoretical and practical difficulties. Two problems are paramount. First, the large costs involved in substantially reducing the effective price gap (tuition gap net of financial aid) between private and public institutions necessary to reduce the privates' sensitivity to direct public sector competition might well be seen as prohibitive in many states, though such expenditures could actually serve to offset in some measure public institutions' need for funds to

---

[108]For a fuller description, see Spence and Weathersby (1981). Several states have recently initiated on a limited basis performance contracting or incentive arrangements with their public institutions that resemble these ideas (Paulson, 1990; Jones and Ewell, 1993; Massy, 1994).

[109]Thus, this model falls short of complete privatization of the public higher education sector, a direction which has been talked about recently in a few states but seems unlikely to come about any time soon.

serve more students (Zumeta, 1996). Public higher education interests will surely argue that they have better uses for the state's limited funds than providing subsidies to more students to attend high-priced private schools. Second, the logic of encouraging in certain ways, rather than uniformly seeking to limit and constrain, intersector competition for students is difficult for many to understand, even in states with relatively strong pro-market attitudes in general. Competition can be noisy and unsettling and the other side of the competition coin is duplication of similar programs, which to many simply looks like waste.[110]

The market-competitive model's approach to information policy—emphasizing the dissemination of information in usable form to consumers to guide their choices rather than amassing it at the state level to inform centrally made decisions—is also unfamiliar to many and relatively untested, though there are recent signs of increased interest in it.[111] There are also legitimate doubts about the sustainability over the long run of a truly open and competitive bidding and rebidding process for performance-based contracts (Spence and Weathersby, 1981; Van Horn, 1991). Finally, one might well wonder what would happen under a market-competitive regime when competition threatened the demise of a public campus, or, for that matter, a politically well-connected private one. In short, the most important open questions about the viability of a market-competitively-oriented policy regime in higher education are likely to be ones of political economy rather than pure economics. Still, the nonintrusive nature of this approach makes it intriguing to those attracted to the market responsiveness, flexibility, and autonomy that characterize many institutions in the private higher education sector.

As with the other state policy posture models discussed here, one would expect historical and cultural factors to play an important role in determining which states might lean in the market-competitive direction with respect to policies toward private higher education. To the extent these factors are captured by regional differences, we might expect to see this posture come closest to fruition in the southern and western states where pro-market values are strong, especially in states where the private sector is large enough to attract policymaker attention but not so large as to successfully take a place in a cartel-like central-planning regime. The connection of the market-competitive orientation to state wealth is not entirely clear *a priori*, but one might expect it to be less attractive to the poorest states, where there will be resistance to large student aid programs benefiting the private sector, and to the wealthiest where concerns with cost-effectiveness in higher education may not be prominent, than to states in the middle-range on

---

[110]On the theory of desirable redundancy in public policy, however, see Landau (1969) and Bendor (1985). In higher education, moreover, programs with similar names may have different foci and serve different types of students, in part because providers seek to differentiate their products.

[111]Recent federal legislation, including the 1992 reauthorization of the Higher Education Act, has emphasized increased quantity and quality of consumer information to include data on student and institutional performance. States are likely to have a key role in enforcing this new policy thrust ("Focus on Accountability," 1994).

wealth measures. Finally, one would expect states with coordinating board governance arrangements to be more attracted to this rather hands-off, level-playing-field approach than would states with a board holding line authority over the public institutions.

## Utility of This Conceptual Framework

As was suggested at the beginning of this section, the type of conceptual framework advanced here seems to provide some useful leverage on the problem of understanding the disparate range of state policies (and nonpolicies) that significantly affect private higher education, while also providing a clear connection to state policies for all of higher education. Each of the ideal-type policy posture constructs proposed is designed to have internal consistency and overall coherence while also not being so far from reality as to seem hopelessly impractical. Therefore, they should be relatively understandable to policymakers. In each case, advantages and disadvantages seem fairly clear, as described above.

Normatively, if a state's policymakers prefer one or another of these ideal types (together with its likely consequences), the framework offered should give them a clearer idea of how to move in that direction, and how to think about modifications to the construct that may be pragmatically necessary. No doubt, the empirical reality of actual state policy configurations will prove considerably more complicated than the simple three-postures framework suggests. Many in-between configurations of policies are obviously plausible and even wholly different conceptualizations of policy coherence are possible, not to mention ad hoc, largely incoherent combinations of policies. The conceptualization sketched here simply represents one possible way of beginning the task of developing understanding of this policy landscape and of laying the groundwork for empirical analysis and testing.[112]

Once state policy postures have been successfully described and classified empirically, the next step would be to learn more about their origins, determinants, and dynamics over time, as well as their implications for policy outcomes of interest. Can *laissez-faire* regimes survive a long period of difficult environmental conditions for private higher education? If so, under what circumstances (e.g., given a small, weak private sector)? What are the consequences for system diversity (nationally as well as at the state level), participation rates in higher education, and costs to the taxpayer? Are *market-competitive* regimes cost-effective, as their proponents would claim? Do such policies undermine public support for public higher education or curtail participation in higher education overall? Is such a regime stable over time, or is it inevitably undermined by the efforts of the players to gain self-serving control over the rules of the game? Can the weaknesses of *market-competitive* and *central-planning* regimes be conquered by a

---

[112]For a preliminary empirical analysis based upon this conceptual framework, see Zumeta (1996).

hybrid approach? Is this what tends to occur to the purer models over time? What are the possible hybrid forms and under what circumstances does each tend to evolve? How will the emerging era of substantially increased demand affect the evolution of policy regimes? This is an agenda for a *policy science* of state higher education policy.

Additionally, this type of analysis, proceeding at once both conceptually and empirically, should help policymakers to think broadly but practically about how to achieve their long-range goals in higher education. In some states, deep-seated attitudes and realities related to historic market shares, constitutional provisions, and entrenched ways of doing things may limit the range of possibilities to those in the neighborhood of one of the above types of policy regimes. Together with precise analysis of the circumstances and needs of a particular state, the framework (especially after it has been validated or modified by empirical studies) should help to illuminate possibilities for modifications of the archetypical approaches that seem to make sense for a particular case. In general, the research program suggested here should eventually make the consequences of possible interventions more susceptible to broad-gauged but empirically grounded analysis, including consequences linked to longer-run political dynamics, as suggested in some of the questions raised in the previous paragraph. Thus, these models and the associated research agenda[113] can also make a contribution to policy *analysis* in higher education.

## CONCLUSION

In this chapter, I have sought to survey the field of state policy and private (nonprofit) higher education. The chapter has provided both a fairly extensive historical and comparative perspective on the role of private higher education, and has indicated the reasons why public policy—in this country, state policy in particular—ought to pay some attention to this intriguing and socially valuable enterprise. I have also sought to make clear that, in current circumstances characterized by a growing private/public price gap not primarily of the private sector's making, by sluggish growth at best in the value of federal student aid, and, until very recently, by a steadily declining pool of traditional students, private higher education, though remarkably resourceful in its responses, has been considerably affected in its capacity to serve public purposes for higher education. In particular, the sector's capacity to serve students between the lowest- and highest-income groups has decreased, its focus on core liberal arts programming has declined dramatically, and, as many institutions have competed desperately for

---

[113]Or, perhaps, an alternative conceptualization that analysts find more compelling. The main point here is to argue for an effort to build and test broad conceptions of states' *approaches* to higher education policy.

students via student aid offers (or tuition discounts) and vocationally oriented programs, it is at least arguable that quality has suffered.[114]

I have further asserted here that, as the demand for higher education rather suddenly turns sharply upward (at least in much of the country) while funds available to states for supporting the enterprise become ever more constricted, we will need all the quality higher education capacity we can get. Thus, more than ever, states need to pay attention to the health of their private colleges and universities, if for no other reason (though several others are offered) than simply to help them meet the coming surge in demand.

Finally, I have offered a preliminary conceptual framework to begin a research-based dialogue about how state policies affecting private higher education are and could be configured. I first suggest that *laissez-faire* state policies vis-a-vis private higher education are likely to have largely undesirable consequences.[115] I suggest that both the *market-competitive-* and *central-planning*-oriented state policy postures have attractions (as well as drawbacks of course), and may be rooted strongly enough in state political traditions and basic attitudes that new interventions may need to be conceived within these broad rubrics in many cases, at least in the near term.[116] I further suggest a research program, following at the same time and in a closely linked fashion both empirical and conceptual lines of development, designed to refine the ideal-type conceptions offered here of how states can approach policymaking affecting private higher education so that such constructs reflect empirical reality more closely and their dynamics over time can be studied and understood.

Such an effort should have payoff for both policy scientists and policymakers and analysts. If the future demands and pressures on higher education are anything like what appears at this juncture to be shaping up,[117] we shall need every bit of understanding we can muster to help make scarce dollars for higher education go as far as they can.

---

[114]This is not to say that all private higher education should be focused on the liberal arts and that professionally oriented programs are necessarily of lower quality. Rather, I mean that the liberal arts core may be shrinking too fast and too much (Breneman, 1990; 1994), and that issues around the quality of the offerings of some of the rapidly growing institutions and programs merit more attention than they are receiving.

[115]For empirical support, see Zumeta (1996).

[116]See Zumeta (1996) for empirical evidence about the relationships between these state postures —and of individual policies within them and of hybrid postures—and such variables of policy interest as state taxpayer spending per capita on higher education, overall adult participation rates, and spending per student in public institutions.

[117]For a fuller discussion of these pressures than could be presented here, see Zumeta and Fawcett-Long (1996).

*The author gratefully acknowledges support from the Lilly Endowment, Pew Charitable Trusts, Education Commission of the States, and National Institute of Independent Colleges and Universities for research relevant to this chapter. He also thanks John Fawcett-Long for research assistance and* Handbook *associate editor James Hearn for encouragement and helpful comments. The author bears sole responsibility for errors of fact or judgment.*

## References

Ashby, E. (1971). *Any Person, Any Study: An Essay on Higher Education in the United States*. First in a Series of Essays Sponsored by the Carnegie Commission on Higher Education. New York: McGraw-Hill.

Bardach, E. (1980). Implementation studies and the study of implements. Paper presented at the Annual Meeting of the American Political Science Association.

Behn, R. D. (1979). *The End of the Growth Era in Higher Education*. Statement presented to the Committee on Labor and Human Resources. United States Senate. Duke University, Institute of Policy Sciences and Public Affairs.

Ben-David, J., and Zloczower, A. (1962). Universities and academic systems in modern societies. *European Journal of Sociology* 3: 45-84.

Bendor, J. B. (1985). *Parallel Systems: Redundancy in Government*. Berkeley: University of California Press.

Bennett, W. J. (1986, November 26). Text of Secretary Bennett's speech on college costs and U.S. student aid. *The Chronicle of Higher Education*: 20.

Bennett, W. J. (1987, February 18). Our greedy colleges. *New York Times*: A31.

Birnbaum, R. (1983). *Maintaining Diversity in Higher Education*. San Francisco: Jossey-Bass.

Bowen, H. R. (1980). *The Costs of Higher Education*. San Francisco: Jossey-Bass.

Bowen, W., and Breneman, D. (1993, Winter). Student aid: price discount or educational investment? *Brookings Review*: 95-97.

Breneman, D. W. (1990, Summer). Are we losing our liberal arts colleges? *The College Board Review*, 156: 16-21, 29.

Breneman, D. W. (1994). *Liberal Arts Colleges: Thriving, Surviving, or Endangered?* Washington, DC: The Brookings Institution.

Breneman, D. W. (1981). Strategies for the 1980s. In J.R. Mingle and Associates (eds.), *Challenges of Retrenchment: Strategies for Consolidating Programs, Cutting Costs, and Reallocating Resources*. San Francisco: Jossey-Bass.

Breneman, D. W., and Finn, C. E., Jr., (eds.), (1978). *Public Policy and Private Higher Education*. Washington, DC: The Brookings Institution.

Carnegie Commission on Higher Education. (1973). *Higher Education: Who Pays? Who Benefits? Who Should Pay?* New York: McGraw-Hill Book Company.

Carnegie Council on Policy Studies in Higher Education. (1977). *The States and Private Higher Education: Problems and Policies in a New Era*. San Francisco: Jossey-Bass.

Celis, W. (1993, October 14). Penn's fiscal plan would cut 3 departments. *New York Times*: A19.

Cheit, E. F. (1971). *The New Depression in Higher Education: A Study of Financial Conditions at 41 Colleges and Universities*. New York: McGraw-Hill Book Company.

Chira, S. (1990, July 9). Stanford takes plunge into budget smashing. *Seattle Post-Intelligencer*: A9.

Clark, B. R. (1983). *The Higher Education System: Academic Organization in Cross-National Perspective.* Berkeley: University of California Press.

Clark, B. R. (1987). *The Academic Life: Small Worlds, Different Worlds.* Princeton: The Carnegie Foundation for the Advancement of Teaching.

Clotfelter, C. T. (1991). Demand for undergraduate education. In Clotfelter, C. T., Ehrenberg, R., Getz, M., and Siegfried, J. (eds.), *Economic Challenges in Higher Education.* Chicago: The University of Chicago Press.

College Board, The. (1989). *Trends in Student Aid, 1980 to 1989.* New York: The College Board.

College Board, The. (1994). *Trends in Student Aid: 1984-1994.* New York: The College Board.

College Board, The. (1995, September 29). *1995-96 Increase in College Costs Averages Six Percent, Upward Trend in Student Borrowing Continues.* News from The College Board, New York, news release.

Committee for Economic Development. (1973). *The Management and Financing of Colleges.* New York: CED.

Dahl, R. A., and Lindblom, C. E. (1953). *Politics, Economics and Welfare: Planning and Politico-Economic Systems Resolved into Basic Social Processes.* New York: Harper.

De Palma, A. (1992, February 3). Hard times force many universities to rethink roles. *New York Times.*

Dill, D. D. (1995). Managerialism versus social capital: the regulation of academic quality in the United Kingdom. Paper presented at the American Association for Policy Analysis and Management, Annual Research Conference, Washington, DC, November 1995.

Education Commission of the States. *Higher Education in the States* series, annual surveys of state support of private higher education. Denver, CO: 1971 to 1982.

Education Commission of the States. (1977). *Final Report and Recommendations: Task Force on State Policy and Independent Higher Education.* Report No. 100. Denver, CO: The Commission.

Education Commission of the States. (1990). *The Preservation of Excellence in American Higher Education: The Essential Role of Private Colleges and Universities.* Report of the ECS Task Force on State Policy and Independent Higher Education. Denver, CO: The Commission.

Education Resources Institute, and Institute of Higher Education Policy. (1995). *College Debt and the American Family.* Boston: Author.

Elmore, R. (1987, Autumn). Instruments and Strategy in Public Policy. *Policy Studies Review* 7: 174-186.

Fenske, R. H., and Boyd, J. D. (1981). *State Need-Based College Scholarship and Grant Programs: A Study of Their Development, 1969-1980.* College Board Report No. 81-7. New York: College Entrance Examination Board.

Finn, C. E., Jr. (1978). *Scholars, Dollars and Bureaucrats.* Washington, DC: The Brookings Institution.

Focus on Accountability: State Accountability Efforts: The Emergence of Report Cards. (1994, March). *SHEEO/NCES Communication Network News* 13.

Freeman, R. B. (1976). *The Over-Educated American.* New York: Academic Press.

Gardner, J. W., Atwell, R. H., and Berdahl, R. O. (1985). *Cooperation and Conflict: The Public and Private Sectors in Higher Education.* AGB Special Report. Washington, DC: Association of Governing Boards of Colleges and Universities.

Geiger, R. L. (1986). *Private Sectors in Higher Education: Structure, Function, and Change in Eight Countries.* Ann Arbor: University of Michigan Press.

Gillespie, D. A., and Carlson, N. (1983). *Trends in Student Aid, 1963 to 1983.* New York: The College Board.

Gladieux, L. E., and Wolanin, T. R. (1976). *Congress and the Colleges: The National Politics of Higher Education.* Lexington, MA: Lexington Books.

Hansen, J. S. (1977). The politics of federal scholarships: A case study of the development of general grant assistance for undergraduates. Unpublished doctoral dissertation, The Woodrow Wilson School, Princeton University.

Hansen, J. S. (1979). *The State Student Incentive Grant Program: An Assessment of the Record and Options for the Future.* New York: College Entrance Examination Board.

Hearn, J. C. (1993). The paradox of growth in federal aid for college students, 1965-1990. In J. C. Smart (ed.), *Higher Education: Handbook of Theory and Research, Volume IX,* Bronx, NY: Agathon Press.

Herbst, J. (1982). *From Crisis to Crisis: American College Government, 1636-1819.* Cambridge, MA, and London, England: Harvard University Press.

Hines, E., and Pruyne, G., (1995). *State Higher Education Appropriations, 1994-95.* Denver: State Higher Education Executive Officers.

Hood, C. C. (1983). *The Tools of Government.* London: Macmillan.

Howlett, M. (1991, Spring). Policy instruments, policy styles and policy implementation: national approaches to theories of instrument choice. *Policy Studies Journal* 19: 1-21.

Jones, D., and Ewell, P. (1993) *The Effect of State Policy on Undergraduate Education.* Denver: Education Commission of the States, March 1993.

Keppel, F. (1987, February). The Higher Education Acts contrasted, 1965-1986: Has federal policy come of age? *Harvard Educational Review* 57: 49-67.

Kerr, C. (1991). *The Great Transformation in American Higher Education, 1960-1980.* Albany, NY: State University of New York Press.

Kirschen, E. S., et al. (1964). *Economic Policy In Our Time.* Amsterdam: North Holland.

Landau, M. (1969, July/August). Redundancy, rationality and the problem of duplication and overlap. *Public Administration Review* 29: 346-358.

Levy, D. C. (ed.), (1985). *Private Education: Studies in Choice and Public Policy.* New York: Oxford University Press.

Levy, D. C. (1986). *Higher Education and the State in Latin America: Private Challenges to Public Dominance.* Chicago: University of Chicago Press.

Lindblom, C. E. (1980). *The Policy-Making Process* (2nd ed.). Englewood Cliffs, NJ: Prentice-Hall.

Linder, S. H., and Peters, B. G. (1989, January-March). Instruments of government: perceptions and contexts. *Journal of Public Policy* 9: 35-38.

Manger, D. (1991, May 15). Smith College plans to cut 85 full-time positions. *The Chronicle of Higher Education*: A2.

Marshall, R., and Tucker, M. (1992). *Thinking For a Living: Education and the Wealth of Nations.* New York: Basic Books.

Massy, W. F. (1990, June). A New Look at the Academic Department. *Pew Policy Perspectives* 2.

Massy, W. F. (1994). Balancing values and market forces: perspectives on resource allocation. Paper presented at the Asia-Pacific Economic Community (APEC) Educational Forum, Chinese Taipei.

Massy, W. F., and Wilger, A. (1992, Winter). Productivity in postsecondary education: a new approach. *Educational Evaluation and Policy Analysis* 14: 361-376.

Master Plan Survey Team (1960). *Master Plan for Higher Education in California, 1960 to 1975.* Sacramento: California State Department of Education.

McGuinness, A. C., Jr. (1975). *The Changing Map of Postsecondary Education, State Postsecondary Education Commission (1202): Their Origin.* Report No. 66. Denver, CO: Education Commission of the States.

McIntire, J. L. (1995). *The Fiscal Policy Environment in Washington State: Trends, Restric-*

*tions, and Implications for Low-Income and Vulnerable Populations.* Seattle, WA: Fiscal Policy Center, Institute for Public Policy and Management, University of Washington.

McPherson, M. S., and Shapiro, M. O. (1991). *Keeping College Affordable: Government and Educational Opportunity.* Washington, DC: The Brookings Institution.

McPherson, M. S., and Schapiro, M. O. (1994). *College Choice and Family Income: Changes Over Time in the Higher Education Destinations of Students From Different Income Backgrounds.* Discussion Paper No. 29. Williams Project on the Economics of Higher Education. Williamstown, MA: Williams College.

Metzger, W. P. (1987). The academic profession in the United States. In Clark, B. R. (ed.), *The Academic Profession: National, Disciplinary, and Institutional Settings* (Berkeley, Los Angeles, London: University of California Press.

Mishel, L., and Bernstein, J. (1992). *Declining Wages for High School and College Graduates.* Economic Policy Institute Briefing Paper. Washington, DC: Economic Policy Institute.

Mortenson, T. (1994a, September). FY1995 state appropriations for higher education: looking better, but that isn't saying much. *Postsecondary Education OPPORTUNITY* 27: 6-11.

Mortenson, T. (1994b, February). Institutional charges. Postsecondary education OPPORTUNITY 20: 10-14.

Mumper, M. (1991, Winter). The transformation of federal aid to college students: dynamics of growth and retrenchment. *Journal of Education Finance* 16: 315-331.

Mumper, M. (1993). The affordability of public higher education: 1970-1990. *The Review of Higher Education* 16: 157-180.

Murphy, K., and Welch, F. (1989, May). Wage premiums for college graduates. *Educational Researcher* 18: 17-26.

The Nation. (1994, September 1). *The Chronicle of Higher Education* XLI(1): 6.

National Association of State Scholarship and Grant Programs. *Annual Survey Report.* Harrisburg, PA: Pennsylvania Higher Education Assistance Agency for NASSGP, annual publication.

National Association of State Scholarship and Grant Programs. (1994). *NASSGP 25th Annual Survey Report, 1993-94 Academic Year.* Harrisburg: Pennsylvania Higher Education Assistance Agency for NAASGP.

National Commission on the Financing of Postsecondary Education. (1973). *Financing Postsecondary Education in the United States.* Washington, DC: National Commission on the Financing of Postsecondary Education.

National Institute of Independent Colleges and Universities. (1990). *A Commitment to Access.* Washington, DC: National Institute of Independent Colleges and Universities.

National Institute of Independent Colleges and Universities. (1992). *Independent Colleges and Universities: A National Profile.* Washington, DC: NIICU.

National Institute of Independent Colleges and Universities. (1995). *Independent Colleges and Universities: A National Profile.* Washington, DC: NIICU.

Olson, K. W. (1974). *The G.I. Bill, the Veterans, and the Colleges.* Lexington: University Press of Kentucky.

Paulson, C. (1990). *State Initiatives in Assessment and Outcome Measurement: Tools for Teaching and Learning.* ECS Working Paper. Denver, CO: Education Commission of the States.

Pickens, W. H. (1995a). Financing the plan: California's master plan for higher education, 1960 to 1994. Report prepared for the California Higher Education Policy Center, San Jose.

Pickens, W. H. (1995b). *Up-Date of Statistics for the Fiscal Data Base Maintained by the California Higher Education Policy Center: Following Adoption of the 1995/96 State Budget Act.* San Jose, CA: California Higher Education Policy Center.

Porter, O. F. (1989). *Undergraduate Completion and Persistence at Four-Year Colleges and Universities.* Washington, DC: National Institute of Independent Colleges and Universities.

Ross, E. D. (1942). *Democracy's College: The Land-Grant Movement in the Formative Stage.* Ames: Iowa State College Press.

Rothblatt, S., and Trow, M. (1992). Government policies and higher education: A comparison of Britain and the United States, 1630-1860. In C. Crouch and A. Heath (eds.), *Social Research and Social Reform: Essays in Honour of A. H. Halsey.* Oxford: Clarendon Press.

Rudolph, F. (1962). *The American College and University.* New York: Vintage Books.

St. John, E. P. (1994). *Prices, Productivity, and Investment: Assessing Financial Strategies in Higher Education.* ASHE-ERIC Higher Education Report No. 3. Washington, DC: The George Washington University, School of Education and Human Development.

Schoenberg, T. (1995, September 29). Student borrowing increases, following changes in federal policy. *The Chronicle of Higher Education* XLII(5): A56.

Smelser, N. J. (1993). California: a multisegment system. In A. Levine (ed.), *Higher Learning in America, 1980-2000.* Baltimore: Johns Hopkins University Press.

Smith, B. L. R. (1990). *American Science Policy Since World War II.* Washington, DC: The Brookings Institution.

Spence, D. S., and Weathersby. G. B. (1981). Changing patterns of state funding. In J. R. Mingle and Associates (eds.), *Challenges of Retrenchment: Strategies for Consolidating Programs, Cutting Costs, and Reallocating Resources.* San Francisco: Jossey-Bass.

Stanford to lay off 150 to 200 employees. (1990, April 25). *The Chronicle of Higher Education*: A2.

State Higher Education Executive Officers. (1988). Survey on Tuition Policy, Costs and Student Aid. Unpublished report. Denver, CO: SHEEO.

Thompson, F., and Zumeta, W. M. (1981, Winter). A regulatory model of governmental coordinating activities in the higher education sector. *Economics of Education Review* 1: 27-52.

Trow, M. (1974). Problems in the transition from elite to mass higher education. In *Policies for Higher Education.* General Report of the Conference on Future Structure of Post-Secondary Education. Paris: Organization for Economic Cooperation and Development.

Trow, M. (1993). Federalism in American higher education. In A. Levine (ed.), *Higher Learning in America, 1980-2000.* Baltimore: Johns Hopkins University Press.

U.S. Department of Education. (1989). *Digest of Education Statistics.* Washington, DC: U.S. Department of Education.

U.S. Department of Education. (1994). *Digest of Education Statistics.* Washington, DC: U.S. Department of Education.

U.S. Department of Education. (1995). *Projections of Education Statistics to 2005.* NCES 95-169. Washington, DC: National Center for Education Statistics.

Van Horn, C. E. (1991). The myths and realities of privatization. In W. T. Gormley, Jr. (ed.), *Privatization and Its Alternatives.* Madison, WI: University of Wisconsin Press.

van Vught, F. A. (1995). The Humboldtian university under pressure: New forms of quality review in Western European higher education. Paper presented at the American Association for Public Policy Analysis and Management, Annual Research Conference, Washington, DC, November 1995.

Veysey, L. R. (1965). *The Emergence of the American University.* Chicago: University of Chicago Press.

Ware, A. (1989). *Between Profit and State: Intermediate Organizations in Britain and the*

*United States.* Princeton: Princeton University Press.

Washington Higher Education Coordinating Board. (1992). *A Commitment to Opportunity: 1992 Update of the Master Plan for Higher Education.* Olympia, WA: Author.

Western Interstate Commission for Higher Education, Teachers Insurance and Annuity Association, and The College Board. (1993). *High School Graduates: Projections by State, 1992-2009.* Boulder, CO: The Commission.

Wolfle, D. L. (1972). *The Home of Science: The Role of the University.* New York: McGraw-Hill.

Wynn, R. G. (1974). *At the Crossroads: A Report on the Financial Condition of the Forty-Eight Liberal Arts Colleges Previously Studied in the Golden Years, The Turning Point.* University of Michigan, Center for the Study of Higher Education.

Zammuto, R. F. (1984, March-April). Are the liberal arts an endangered species? *Journal of Higher Education* 55: 184-211.

Zemsky, R. (1990, July 13). The lattice and the ratchet: toward more efficient higher education systems. Presentation at the Annual Conference of the Education Commission of the States, Seattle, WA.

Zumeta, W. M. (1982). Doctoral programs and the labor market, or how should we respond to the "Ph.D. glut?" *Higher Education* 11: 321-343.

Zumeta, W. M. (1989). *State Policies and Independent Higher Education: A Technical Report.* Report to the Education Commission of the States, Task Force on State Policy and Independent Higher Education. Denver, CO: The Commission.

Zumeta, W. M. (1990, October 19). States and private colleges: new evidence and analysis from the policy arena. Paper presented at the annual Research Conference of the Association for Public Policy Analysis and Management, San Francisco.

Zumeta, W. M. (1992, July/August). State policies and private higher education: policies, correlates and linkages. *Journal of Higher Education* 63: 363-417.

Zumeta, W. M. (1993). Independent higher education and public policy: looking toward 2000. Final report to the Lilly Endowment. Seattle, WA: University of Washington, Institute For Public Policy and Management.

Zumeta, W. M. (1994). *Crisis Or Opportunity? Private Higher Education and Public Policy Looking Toward 2000 and Beyond.* Final Report to the Pew Charitable Trusts. Seattle, WA: University of Washington, Institute For Public Policy and Management.

Zumeta, W. M. (1995a, August 22). Review of Other States' Higher Education Structures and Public Funding for Private Higher Education. Report prepared for JBL Associates, Inc., for the Joint Legislative Budget Committee, State of Arizona.

Zumeta, W. M. (1995b). State policy and budget developments. In H. Wechsler (ed.), *The NEA 1995 Almanac of Higher Education.* Washington, DC: National Education Association.

Zumeta, W. M. (1996). Meeting the demand for higher education without breaking the bank: a framework for the design of state higher education policies for an era of increasing demand. *Journal of Higher Education,* forthcoming.

Zumeta, W. M., and Fawcett-Long, J. A. (in press). State policy and budget developments. In H. Wechsler (ed.), *The NEA 1996 Almanac of Higher Education.* Washington, DC: National Education Association.

Zumeta, W. M., and Looney, J. A. (1994). State policy and budget developments. In H. Wechsler (ed.), *The NEA 1994 Almanac of Higher Education.* Washington, DC: National Education Association.

# Appraising Tinto's Theory of College Student Departure

**John M. Braxton and Anna V. Shaw Sullivan**

*Peabody College, Vanderbilt University*

and

**Robert M. Johnson, Jr.**

*Belmont University*

College student departure generates interest among college and university practitioners as well as scholars. Practitioners' interest grows out of the need to manage individual college and university enrollments. Scholars' interest in college student departure stems from two primary reasons. First, institutional rates of student departure constitute a puzzle, one which might be labeled the departure puzzle. Given the availability of numerous guides on the selection of colleges and universities and the enormous amount of attention that parents, students, and college officials focus upon the college selection process, it is puzzling that almost one-half of students entering two-year colleges and more than one fourth (28.5%) of students entering four-year collegiate institutions depart these institutions at the end of their first year (Tinto, 1993). Even more perplexing, highly selective colleges and universities experience an average first-year departure rate of 8.0% (Tinto, 1993). This rate is surprising given the emergence of what McDonough (1994) terms "admissions management," including private counselors, tutors, and SAT enhancement services, by parents and students who seek admission to highly selective colleges and universities. Underlying such rates of departure are telling facets of human behavior within a social context.

The phenomena of college student departure also provides a window on the academic and social communities within colleges and universities that students experience (Tinto, 1993). Through such a window, our understanding of such topics as college choice (Stage and Rushin, 1993) and the effects of college attendance on student growth and development is enhanced (Terenzini and Wright, 1987). Such is the second reason for scholarly interest in college student departure.

Various theoretical perspectives have been advanced to account for the departure puzzle. These perspectives spring from psychological, societal, economic, organizational, and interactionalist assumptions and formulations about college student departure (Tinto, 1986; 1993). The psychological perspective focuses on the role of such psychological characteristics as maturity to differentiate persisters from departers. An important underlying assumption of this approach is that personality characteristics determine an individual's response to comparable experiences of other students with a college or university. In contrast, the societal approach to understanding student departure focuses not on the individual, but rather on social forces that affect student withdrawal behavior. The weighing of the costs (e.g. tuition, forgone earnings) and benefits (future earnings, status attainment) of college attendance is the crux of the economic theoretical perspective on the college student departure puzzle. The influence of various organizational attributes on student withdrawal decisions is the thrust of the organizational approach to understanding student departure. Organization structure, size, faculty-student ratios and institutional resources, and institutional goals are organizational factors which have been hypothesized to affect student persistence. Characteristic of the interactionalist perspective is the view student departure is a consequence of the interaction between the individual student and the college or university as an organization. Important to such interactions is the meaning the individual student ascribes to their relationship with the formal and informal dimensions of the collegiate organization.

Although role socialization and "person-role fit" can be classified as being interactionalist in their formulations (Pervin and Rubin, 1967; Rootman, 1972), Tinto's (1975;1987;1993) interactionalist model has attracted much greater attention. More than 400 citations to the model by late 1994 as well as the approximately 170 dissertations addressing it by early 1995 indexes such attention.

While assessing the maturity of higher education research, Peterson (1985, p. 8) singled out research on the Tinto model as the most mature. Given its near-paradigmatic status in research on college student departure, several issues spring forth about Tinto's theory.[1] First, 15 testable proposition can be derived from Tinto's theoretical schema. However, little or no attention has focused on the extent to which these propositions are supported by empirical research. An assessment of the magnitude of empirical confirmation of each proposition permits the appraisal of the empirical internal consistency of Tinto's theoretical model. Empirical, internal consistency is particularly important given that 13 of these propositions are logically interconnected and together seek to explain the phenomenon of student persistence.

A second issue pertains to the magnitude of empirical support for each of the 15 propositions across different types of colleges and universities and across dif-

---

[1]Thomas Kuhn (1972) uses the term paradigm to describe consensus in a scholarly field on such matters as theory, methods and problems to be studies. Because Tinto's theory has been extensively tested and cited, one might assume that consensus exists among scholars that this theory is most appropriate for studying the phenomena of college student departure.

ferent groups of students. Because rigorous appraisal of a theory requires that it be tested across different social settings and different social groups (Zetterberg, 1965), this particular issue looms important. Its pursuit also helps us to assess the empirical internal consistency of Tinto's theory across different types of institutions and groups of students. Little or no scholarship has focused on this issue.

Tinto (1986) has discussed the failure of his theoretical schema to take into account other theoretical perspectives. In particular, he points to the need to account for economic and organizational forces within the framework of the interactionalist perspective on student departure decision. Tinto's concern has been addressed by such scholars as Stage (1989), Braxton and Brier (1989), Brower (1992), Cabrera, Nora, and Castaneda, and Hengstler (1992), Cabrera, Nora and Castaneda (1992). How successful have these and other efforts to integrate theory been? This question represents a third issue, and one that has been the focus of little or no scholarship.

Critiques of Tinto's theory by such scholars as Attinasi (1989, 1994) and Tierney (1992), as well Tinto himself (1986), represent the fourth issue. These critiques, however, have not been reviewed and assessed.

Because little or no scholarship has attended to these four issues, this chapter addresses them. Moreover, there has been no assessment of empirical support for Tinto's theory since Terenzini and Pascarella (1980) summarized research testing the construct validity of Tinto's schema. Their appraisal was based on six studies published between 1977 and 1979. Since their summary, researchers have conducted many studies using Tinto's model. Consequently, a thorough assessment of the empirical support for the Tinto model is needed at this juncture. This chapter offers such an assessment, guided by the following four questions:

*1. What is the magnitude of empirical support, in the aggregate, for each of the 15 testable propositions derived from Tinto's Theory?*

*2. Does the magnitude of empirical support for each of the 15 propositions vary across different types of colleges and universities and across different groups of students?*

*3. What attempts have been made to integrate other theoretical perspectives with the Tinto model and how successful have these attempts been?*

*4. What have been the conceptual critiques of Tinto Theory advanced by scholars?*

In pursuit of our four questions, we confined our review to studies that have been subject to peer review. Because peer review is predicated on the assumption that the quality of the research and the contribution made by it are assessed by scholars knowledgeable about the topic of the research (Anderson and Louis, 1991), some confidence in the scholarly quality of the studies reviewed is assured by limiting the review to peer reviewed studies. Thus, this chapter attends to papers presented at annual meetings of scholarly and professional associations and to articles published in refereed academic and professional journals.

Since the initial formulation of the Tinto model in 1975, Tinto has revised it twice (1987, 1993). Ten studies (Allen and Nelson, 1989; Brower, 1992; Cabrera, Stampen, and Hansen, 1990; Cabrera, Nora, and Castaneda, 1992; Cabrera, Castaneda, Nora, and Hengstler, 1992; Cabrera and Nora, 1994; Grossett, 1991; Stage, 1989; Stage and Rushin, 1993; and Pavel, 1991) available to us cited Tinto's 1987 version of the model. Only two of these studies (Allen and Nelson, 1989; Pavel, 1991), however, test a facet of the 1987 model that stands as a revision to the 1975 formulation. Because only two studies tested a construct unique to 1987 schema, we used the 1975 model to address questions 1 through 3 of this chapter. However, the fourth question will encompass a critique of both the 1987 and 1993 revisions of the 1975 seminal model.

Moreover, we used the "box score" approach to determine the magnitude of empirical support for each of the 15 propositions. Empirical support was judged to be "strong" (robust, vigorous) if 66 percent or more of the three or more tests of a given proposition proved to be statistically significant. "Moderate" (modest, middling) support was ascribed if between 34 percent and 65 percent of three or more tests of a given proposition were statistically significant. If 33 percent or less of three or more tests of a given proposition obtained statistical significance, then empirical support was assessed as being "weak" (frail, slight). No support, moderate support, or strong support are the possible categories of affirmation for two tests of a given expected relationship. In addition to these three categories of magnitude of support, two other categories were used. These two additional categories are indeterminate and no support. "Indeterminate (undetermined, uncertain) support" refers to those situations where only one test is made and the results are either statistically significant or nonsignificant. This category is termed indeterminate because subsequent tests may be either affirming or disconfirming. "No support" pertains to two or more tests made that obtained statistically nonsignificant backing for a given proposition.

The measures of the Tinto constructs used by the various studies included in this chapter were also evaluated for their validity by the authors. Thus, only measures of Tinto constructs judged to have face validity are included in our appraisal. Before addressing the questions which guide our assessment of Tinto's interactionalist perspective, we present the formulations of his 1975 model.

## TINTO'S INTERACTIONALIST THEORY

Tinto (1975) postulates that students enter college with various individual characteristics, including those related to family background, individual attributes, and pre-college schooling experiences. Family background characteristics delineated by Tinto are family socioeconomic status, parental educational level, and parental expectations. Examples of individual attributes described by Tinto include academic ability, race, and gender. Pre-college schooling experiences include the characteristics of the student's secondary school, high school academic achievement, and social attainments. These individual entry characteristics are hypothesized to directly influence student departure decisions, as well as students' initial commitments to the institution and to the goal of college graduation. Initial commitment to the institution and commitment to the goal of graduation affect both the level of a student's integration into the academic and social systems of the college or university.

Academic integration is composed of both structural and normative dimensions. Structural integration involves the meeting of explicit standards of the college or university, whereas normative integration pertains more to an individual's identification with the normative structure of the academic system (Tinto, 1975, p.104). Academic performance reflects a student's degree of structural integration into the academic system of a college or university, since grades reflect assessments of a student's ability to meet an institution's values and objectives for student academic achievement. Tinto views intellectual development as an aspect of normative integration because it reflects the student's appraisal of the institution's academic system (1975, p. 104). Tinto also asserts that normative integration takes the form of congruency between the individual's intellectual development and the intellectual environment of the college or university (1975, p. 106).

Social integration refers to the extent of congruency between the individual student and the social system of a college or university. Tinto posits that informal peer group associations, extracurricular activities and interactions with faculty and administrators are mechanisms of social integration (1975, p. 107). Through these mechanisms, individuals receive such important social rewards as social communication, support from peers and faculty, and collective affiliation. Moreover, Tinto points out that social integration does not have to occur at the level of the college or university, but that it can take place within a subculture of the institution (1975, p. 107).

Subsequent commitments—to the institution and to the goal of college graduation—are differentially affected by academic and social integration. The greater the student's level of academic integration, the greater the level of subsequent commitment to the goal of college graduation. Moreover, the greater the student's level of social integration, the greater the level of subsequent commitment to the focal college or university (Tinto, 1975, p. 110). Both subsequent commitments are also shaped by the student's initial level of commitments. In turn, the greater the levels of both subsequent institutional commitment and commitment to the goal of college graduation the greater the likelihood the individual will persist in college. Tinto advances two additional propositions. These propositions are not integral to the longitudinal sequence of the other 13 propositions in accounting for student departure decisions. Moreover, both of these propositions pertain to interactions between constructs of Tinto's theory.

These two additional propositions are as follows: First, Tinto adduces that low levels of institutional commitment can be compensated for by high levels of commitment to the goal of graduation from college and vice versa. He also posits that low levels of academic integration are compensated for by high levels of social integration.

From these formulations, 15 testable propositions are derived—13 primary and two additional propositions. Of the 13 primary hypotheses, we designated five (3, 8, 9, 12, and 13) as fundamental to Tinto's theory because they postulate a direct influence on student departure decisions (3, 12, 13), or because interactions between the individual and the formal and informal academic and social systems of a college or university are of pivotal importance (8, 9). Tinto specifies the direction of the hypothesized influence for propositions 8 through 15, but not for propositions 1 through 7. These propositions are as follows:

1. Student entry characteristics affect the level of initial commitment to the institution.
2. Student entry characteristics affect the level of initial commitment to the goal of graduation from college.
3. Student entry characteristics directly affect the student's likelihood of persistence in college.
4. Initial commitment to the goal of graduation from college affects the level of academic integration.
5. Initial commitment to the goal of graduation from college affects the level of social integration.
6. Initial commitment to the institution affects the level of social integration.
7. Initial commitment to the institution affects the level of academic integration.
8. The greater the level of academic integration, the greater the level of subsequent commitment to the goal of graduation from college.
9. The greater the level of social integration, the greater the level of subsequent commitment to the institution.
10. The initial level of institutional commitment affects the subsequent level of institutional commitment.
11. The initial level of commitment to the goal of graduation from college affects the subsequent level of commitment to the goal of college graduation.
12. The greater the level of subsequent commitment to the goal of college graduation, the greater the likelihood of student persistence in college.
13. The greater the level of subsequent commitment to the institution, the greater the likelihood of student persistence in college.
14. A high level of commitment to the goal of graduation from college compensates for a low level of commitment to the institution, and vice versa, in influencing student persistence in college.
15. A high level of academic integration compensates for a low level of social integration, and vice versa, in influencing student persistence in college.

Figure 1 portrays the interrelationship among the 13 primary propositions of Tinto's theory in longitudinal sequence.

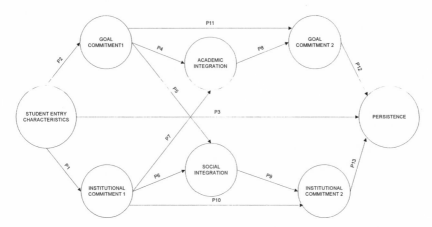

**FIGURE 1. Tinto's 1975 Theoretical Schema: the 13 Primary Propositions**

## Tests of the 15 Propositions

This section addresses the first two guiding questions of this chapter: Given that 15 testable proposition can be derived from Tinto's theoretical schema, what is the aggregated magnitude of empirical support for each of these propositions? Does the magnitude of empirical support for each of the 15 propositions vary across different types of colleges and universities and across different groups of students? We reviewed those studies that have directly tested one or more of the 15 propositions. These studies generally used such structural equation methods as path analysis using multiple linear regression, LISREL, logistic regression. However, multiple regression or discriminant analyses are included in tests of those propositions positing a direct effect on student persistence. All of these statistical methods provide us with an estimate of the independent or net effects of each proposition above and beyond the effects of other constructs.

These studies are multi-institutional or single-institutional in the scope of their samples. Studies focusing on gender and racial/ethnic groups (e.g. African-Americans, Native-Americans) employing structural equations have also been conducted using both multi-institutional and single-institutional settings. Single-institutional studies, however, are most congruent with Tinto's undergirding assumptions. Tinto states that the longitudinal process of student departure within a particular college or university is what his model seeks to explain (Tinto, 1993, p. 112). He further asserts that "it is not a systems model of departure" (1993, p. 112). Because Tinto's interactionalist perspective is a social theory that accounts for student departure from college, empirical tests that maximize variability in the measurement of the theory's constructs are needed. Restricted variance can lead to the failure of some tests of Tinto's propositions to be statistically reliable. Multi-institutional studies are more likely than single-institutional studies to achieve such greater variability (Anderson, 1987). To be consistent with Tinto's assertions, but at the same time recognizing the need for maximum variability in the settings for theory testing, our assessment of empirical support for each of the 15 hypothesized relationships employs both single- and multi-institutional propositional tests. We do, however, make careful distinctions between them.

The magnitude of empirical support for each of the 15 propositions is presented according to support in the aggregate,[2] by institutional type[3], and by student group[4].

**Proposition One: Student entry characteristics affect the level of initial commitment to the institution.[5]**

*Aggregated Support.* A total of six multi-institutional and eight single-institutional tests of this proposition were made. Multi-institutional assessments provide moderate backing, as three of the six tests uphold this proposition (Cash and Bissel, 1985; Pascarella, Smart, and Ethington, 1986(2 tests). Single-institutional appraisals afford strong support given that five of eight tests affirm the hypothesized relationship between student entry characteristics and initial institutional commitment (Pascarella and Terenzini, 1983; Terenzini, Pascarella, Theophilides and Lorang, 1985; Allen, 1986; Braxton, Duster and Pascarella, 1988; and Pascarella, Duby and Iverson, 1983).

*Support by Institutional Type.* Six multi-institutional tests of the effect of student entry characteristics on the level of initial commitment to the institution were made. This relationship was upheld by Cash and Bissel's (1985) study of four-year colleges affiliated with the Seventh Day Adventists. Thus, support for this proposition is indeterminate in liberal arts college. However, assessments conduct using unspecified types of colleges and universities provide strong endorsement, as two of three tests made in this institutional setting found statistically reliable verification for the focal expected relationship (Donovan, 1984; Pavel, 1991). Affirmation is also vigorous in two-year colleges since both tests

---

[2]Aggregate assessments of magnitude of support for a given proposition include all tests of it. Thus, tests carried out in different types of colleges and universities and different groups of students are included.

[3]Support by institutional type includes tests of a given proposition made in a particular type of college and university. Tests for different student groups nested within a particular type of college and university are also included. Thus, the particular type of college or university is the unit of analysis.

[4]Support by student groups includes only those tests conducted focusing on different student groups. The student group is the unit of analysis for support by student group.

[5]Tinto treats student entry characteristics as a general category of variables. Thus, assessments of support for this proposition, as well as for propositions two and three, were conducted with Tinto's categories of family background, individual attributes, and pre-college schooling aggregated with other entry characteristics used by scholars in their tests of propositions one, two and three.

confirm that student entry characteristics affect initial commitment to the institution (Pascarella, Smart, and Ethington, 1986 (2 tests).

Single-institutional tests of this proposition have been carried out with mixed results. The anticipated relationship between entry student characteristics and initial institutional commitment receives moderate affirmation in residential universities, since two of four tests are sustaining (Pascarella and Terenzini, 1983; Terenzini, Pascarella, Theophilides, and Lorang, 1985). However, this relationship is strongly upheld in commuter universities given that three of the four commuter university tests confirm it (Allen, 1986; Braxton, Duster, and Pascarella, 1988; Pascarella, Duby, and Iverson, 1983).

*Support by Student Group.* For both male and female students this particular proposition is modestly upheld. Two assessments were made for both male and female students. Although Pascarella, Smart, and Ethington (1986) found this proposition tenable for both male and female students in their multi-institutional study of two-year colleges, Stage (1988) found it not to be applicable to either male or female students enrolled in a public university.

Moreover, affirmation for this proposition is indeterminate for different racial/ethnic groups. Tests made of the influence of student entry characteristics on initial institutional commitment using both low-income, African Americans (Donovan, 1984) and Native Americans/Alaskan Natives failed to indicate statistical significance. (Pavel, 1991). Both were multi-institutional studies of unspecified types of four-year colleges and universities.

**Proposition Two: Student entry characteristics affect the level of initial commitment to the goal of graduation from college.**

*Aggregated Support.* This proposition was assessed by six multi-institutional and seven single-institutional tests. Multi-institutional assessments strongly uphold the influence of student entry characteristics on initial commitments to the goal of graduation from college, as all six of them sustain this influence (Braxton, Vesper, and Hossler, 1995; Munro, 1981; Cash and Bissel, 1985; Pavel, 1991; Donovan, 1984; and Pascarella, Smart, and Ethington, 1986). However, single-institutional tests afford middling support given that four of seven tests of this proposition empirically sustain it (Allen, 1986; Pascarella, Duby, and Iverson, 1983; Pascarella and Terenzini, 1983; Terenzini, Pascarella, Theophilides, and Lorang, 1985).

*Support by Institutional Type.* Seven multi-institutional assessments of this particular proposition were made. Estimations conducted using unspecified types of colleges and universities furnish strong backing given that all four tests carried out in this setting provide statistically significant support (Donovan, 1984; Braxton, Vesper, and Hossler, 1995; Munro, 1981; Pavel, 1991). Tinto's expectation that student entry characteristics influence initial commitments to the goal of graduation from college garners vigorous confirmation in two-year colleges, as both assessments of this expectation carried out in this type of collegiate institution sustain it (Pascarella, Smart, and Ethington, 1986). Indeterminate affirmation also tends to exist in liberal arts colleges, as the sole test of this proposition in such institutions yielded verifying results (Cash and Bissel, 1985).

Six single-institutional appraisals of the focal proposition were also conducted. This proposition is modestly sustained in residential universities as two out of four tests conducted in this setting uphold it in a statistically significant way (Pascarella and Terenzini, 1983; Terenzini, Pascarella, Theophilides, and Lorang, 1985). In addition, moderate support is rendered by commuter universities because two of the four assessments verified the effect of student entry characteristics on initial goal commitments (Allen, 1986; Pascarella, Duby, and Iverson, 1983).

*Support by Student Group.* Support for the second proposition is undetermined for two different racial/ethnic groups. Pavel's (1991) study done with Native Americans and Alaskan natives, and Donovan's (1984) study made with low-income African Americans both observed statistically significant effects of student entry characteristics on initial goal commitment. Both tests were multi-institutional samples of unspecified types of four-year colleges and universities.

Backing for this proposition is middling, however, for both male and female students. Pascarella, Smart, and Ethington's (1986) study of male and female two-year college students registers support for the focal proposition for both men and women. Yet, Stage's (1988) inquiry conducted in a public university found this proposition untenable for both male and female students.

**Proposition Three: Student entry characteristics directly affect student likelihood of persistence in college.**

*Aggregated Support.* Multi-institutional tests furnish modest support for this expected relationship as 18 of 32 assessments back it (Anderson, 1987 (2 tests); Pascarella and Chapman, 1983a (2 tests); Pascarella and Chapman, 1983b; Cabrera, Stampen, and Hansen, 1990; Williamson and Creamer, 1988; Pascarella, Smart, and Ethington, 1986 (2 tests); Cash and Bissel, 1985; Pascarella, 1985(2 tests); Stoecker, Pascarella, and Wolfle, 1988(3 tests); Donovan, 1984; Pavel, 1991; Stage and Rushin, 1993)). In contrast, single institutional appraisals provide weak affirmation given that the expected direct influence of student entry characteristics on student persistence is upheld by 9 of 27 tests of this proposed influence (Brower, 1992; Getzlaf, Sedlacek, Kearney, and Blackwell, 1984; Halpin, 1987; Voorhees, 1987; Nora, Attinasi, and Matonak, 1990; Pascarella, Duby, and Iverson, 1983; Allen, 1986; and Grossett, 1991(2 tests).

*Support by Institutional Type.* Among multi-institutional tests of Tinto's hypothesis that student entry characteristics directly influence student persistence, those assessments done in commuter universities, two-year colleges, and unspecified types of four-year colleges and universities offer robust confirmation. More specifically, two of three assessments made in commuter universities sustain this proposition (Anderson, 1987; Pascarella and Chapman, 1983a). Of six appraisals carried out in two-year colleges, five uphold this proposition (Pascarella, Smart, and Ethington, 1986 (2 tests), Anderson, 1987, Pascarella and Chapman, 1983a, 1983b). In unspecified types of four-year institutions, twelve tests were performed, and nine of them verify the focal proposition (Cabrera, Stampen, and Hansen, 1990; Williamson and Creamer, 1988; Donovan, 1984; Pavel, 1991; Pascarella, 1985 (2 tests); Stoecker, Pascarella, and Wolfle, 1988 (3 tests). In contrast to these three types of collegiate institutions, residential universities and liberal arts colleges furnish no backing for Tinto's postulation that student entry characteristics exert a direct influence on student departure decisions. Of the three assessments made of this anticipated relationship in residential universities, none of them affirms it (Anderson, 1987; Pascarella and Chapman, 1983a, 1983b). Likewise, none of the three appraisals carried out in liberal arts colleges sustain this proposition (Anderson, 1987; Cash and Bissel, 1985; Pascarella and Chapman, 1983a).

Like multi-institutional assessments, single-institutional appraisals of this proposition made in two-year colleges afford vigorous support. All five of the tests made in this setting confirm the expected relationship between student entry characteristics and student departure (Halpin, 1987; Voorhees, 1987; Nora, Attinasi, and Matonak, 1990; Grossett, 1991 (2 tests)). However, commuter universities accord weak affirmation since two of the six, single-institutional estimations of this proposition performed in this institutional setting uphold it (Allen, 1986; Pascarella, Duby, and Iverson, 1983). Moreover, residential universities offer slight confirmation of the focal hypothesis given that two of ten tests done in this type of university empirically sustain this anticipated influence (Brower, 1991; Getzlaf, Sedlacek, Kearney, and Blackwell, 1984).

*Support by Student Group.* Tests of the focal proposition using female college students weakly affirm it. Of the five tests made employing female students, one of them upholds this proposition (Pascarella, Smart, and Ethington, 1986). However, appraisals of Tinto's hypothesis that student entry characteristics directly influence the likelihood of student persistence in college using male college students offer moderate support given that two of five assessments made bolster this proposition (Pascarella, Smart, and Ethington, 1986; Cash and Bissel, 1985).

Students' race/ethnicity when combined with gender also constitute groups of students. Assessments of the focal proposition using both white male and white females give strong confirmation. The two assessments conducted using these two groups of students verify that student entry characteristics directly affect student departure (Pascarella, 1985; Stoecker, Pascarella, and Wolfle, 1988). Appraisals of this proposition conducted using male African American college students furnish modest support since one of two appraisals carried out sustain it (Stoecker, Pascarella, and Wolfle, 1988). However, tests utilizing female African American college students offer no empirical backing because neither of the two tests conducted confirmed this particular hypothesized relationship (Pascarella, 1985; Stoecker, Pascarella, and Wolfle, 1988).

Appraisals of Tinto's proposed relationship between student entry characteristics and student departure conducted using other student groups—Native American/Alaskan Natives, low-income African Americans, minority and nonminority, younger and older students—provide indeterminate backing for this relationship. More specifically, Pavel's (1991) sole assessment of this proposition using Native Americans/Alaskan natives found support, as did Donovan's (1984) single test of it for low-income African American college students. Likewise, Grossett's (1991) estimation of this proposition carried out utilizing younger and older college students also sustain it. However, Cabrera and Nora's (1994) singular appraisal of this proposition done with minority and non-minority students produced nonaffirming results.

### Proposition Four: Initial commitment to the goal of graduation from college affects the level of academic integration.

*Aggregated Support.* Six multi-institutional and seven single-institutional appraisals of this proposition were conducted. Multi-institutional assessments weakly uphold this proposition since none of the six made affirm it (Cash and Bissel, 1985; Braxton, Vesper, and Hossler, 1995; Pascarella, Smart, and Ethington, 1986 (2 tests); Donovan, 1984; and Pavel, 1991). However, single-institutional tests furnish modest backing as three of the eight tests made verify a relationship between initial commitment to the goal of graduation from college and academic integration (Allen, 1986; Braxton, Duster, and Pascarella, 1988; Pascarella and Terenzini, 1983).

*Support by Institutional Type.* Multi-institutional assessments of this proposition carried out using unspecified types of four-year colleges and universities produce no support for relationship predicted. Three appraisals were made in this setting, and none of them offer statistically significant support (Braxton, Vesper, and Hossler, 1995; Donovan, 1984; Pavel, 1991). Two tests conducted in two-year colleges also fail to uphold this proposition (Pascarella, Smart, and Ethington, 1986). However, Cash and Bissel (1985) made the sole test of Tinto's hypothesis that initial commitment to the goal of graduation from college affects the level of academic integration in liberal arts colleges and obtained nonconfirming results. Thus, liberal arts colleges offer indeterminate backing to this anticipated association.

When considering single-institutional appraisals of this proposition, those tests made in commuter universities render moderate affirmation. To elaborate, two of the four tests conducted in a commuter university render statistically reliable support for the focal proposition (Allen, 1986; Braxton, Duster, and Pascarella, 1988). Although Tinto does not postulate whether the effect of initial goal commitment on academic integration is positive or negative, these two appraisals provide opposite findings on the directional nature of this proposition. Allen

(1986) found this relationship to be positive, whereas Braxton, Duster, and Pascarella (1988) found it to be negative.

In addition, three tests of this proposition were carried out in a residential university (Pascarella and Terenzini, 1983; Terenzini, Pascarella, Theophilides, and Lorang, 1985; Stage, 1988). However, one of these tests produced sustaining results (Pascarella and Terenzini, 1983). Thus, residential universities supply frail support for this particular hypothesized relationship.

*Support by Student Group.* Tests of the influence of initial commitment to the goal of graduation from colleges on academic integration made using various student groups offer no empirically backing for such an influence. More specifically, neither gender differences (Pascarella, Smart, and Ethington, 1986; Stage, 1988) nor racial/ethnic group differences—African American (Donovan, 1984) and Native American/Alaskan native (Pavel, 1991)—were found.

### Proposition Five: Initial commitment to the goal of graduation from college affects the level of social integration.

*Aggregated Support.* Tests of this proposition using multi-institutional samples offer no support for it. Six assessments were conducted, and none of them sustain the focal anticipated relationship (Cash and Bissel, 1985; Munro, 1981; Braxton, Vesper, and Hossler, 1995; Pavel, 1991; Pascarella, Smart, and Ethington, 1986(2 tests). Single-institutional assessments of this posited influence of initial goal commitment on social integration, however, provide moderate confirmation. Of the nine tests made, five of them uphold the focal proposition (Pascarella and Terenzini, 1983 (2 tests); Terenzini, Pascarella, Theophilides, and Lorang, 1985; Pascarella, Terenzini, and Wolfle, 1986; Allen, 1986).

*Support by Institutional Type.* Multi-institutional assessments of Tinto's expectation that initial goal commitments influence social integration done in unspecified types of four-year colleges and universities accord no support for this posited relationship, as three estimations made in this type of institution produced non-affirming results (Munro, 1981; Pavel, 1991; Braxton, Vesper, and Hossler, 1995). Moreover, multi-institutional appraisals of this proposition conducted in two-year colleges also provide no support since both tests made in this setting do not sustain the predicted relationship (Pascarella, Smart, and Ethington, 1986). However, a multi-institutional test of the hypothesized relationship carried out in liberal arts colleges provides indeterminate affirmation as this single test did not uphold this relationship (Cash and Bissel, 1985).

Single-institutional assessments of the predicted influence of initial commitment to the goal of graduation from college on social integration offer a different pattern of empirical support. Residential universities accord robust affirmation given that all three estimations of this proposition carried out in this institutional setting were affirming (Pascarella and Terenzini, 1983; Terenzini, Pascarella, Theophilides, and Lorang, 1985; Pascarella, Terenzini, and Wolfle, 1986). In contrast, single-institutional appraisals done in commuter universities furnish slight support, as one of four such appraisals backs this hypothesized relationship in a statistically significant way (Allen, 1986).

*Support by Student Group.* Assessments of this proposition done with female college students accord modest affirmation, as one of two such appraisals confirmed that initial commitment to the goal of graduation from college affects social integration (Pascarella and Terenzini, 1983). However, tests of this predicted influence made using male college students furnish no support. Neither of the two assessments made sustain this focal proposition (Pascarella, Smart, and Ethington, 1986; Pascarella and Terenzini, 1983).

Tests of the anticipated influence of initial goal commitments on social integration done with Native Americans/Alaskan Native college students afford indeterminate backing. Pavel's (1991) sole test conducted using this group was nonaffirming.

## Proposition Six: Initial commitment to the institution affects the level of social integration.

*Aggregated Support.* Both single- and multi-institutional tests of the focal proposition provide weak empirical backing. Of six multi-institutional assessments conducted, two of these estimations affirm the predicted influence of initial commitment to the institution on social integration (Cash and Bissel, 1985; Donovan, 1984). Eight single-institutional tests were made and two uphold this hypothesized relationship (Stage, 1988 (2 tests).

*Support by Institutional Type.* Single-institutional assessments carried out in residential universities modestly endorse this proposition. More specifically, two of the four tests made in this type of institution statistically verify that initial commitment to the institution affects social integration (Stage, 1988(2 tests). However, estimations done using commuter universities grant no support for this posited influence, as none of the four commuter university tests supply statistically reliable backing (Allen, 1986; Braxton and Brier, 1989; Braxton, Duster, and Pascarella, 1988; Pascarella, Duby, and Iverson, 1983).

Multi-institutional assessments of this proposition were also carried out in liberal arts colleges, two-year colleges and unspecified types of four year colleges and universities. Appraisals made in liberal arts colleges furnish indeterminate affirmation, as the solitary test carried out in this setting detected statistically significant support for the focal proposition (Cash and Bissel, 1985). Moreover, tests of Tinto's hypothesized relationship between initial commitment to the institution and social integration made in both two-year colleges and unspecified types of four-year colleges and universities provide no support for this relationship since both assessments carried out in two-year colleges failed to affirm it (Pascarella, Smart, and Ethington, 1986), as did the three tests made in unspecified types of four-year colleges and universities (Braxton, Vesper, and Hossler, 1995; Donovan, 1984; Pavel, 1991).

*Support by Student Group.* Assessments of the focal proposition conducted using both male and female students offer middling affirmation given that the two tests made using both male and female students yield equivocal results. Pascarella, Smart, and Ethington's (1986) tests of this proposition used a multiple-institutional sample of two-year colleges, and backing was not obtained from their appraisals made with either men or women students. However, Stage (1988) identified statistically reliable support for this proposition utilizing both male and female students in a residential university.

Estimations of the anticipated influence of initial institutional commitment on social integration done using both low-income African American students and Native American/Alaskan native students furnish indeterminate backing for such an influence. The sole test of this proposition using African American students was affirming (Donovan, 1984). Whereas, the single assessment of this proposition made employing Native American/Alaskan native college students was unconfirming (Pavel, 1991).

## Proposition Seven: Initial commitment to the institution affects the level of academic integration.

*Aggregated Support.* Both multi-institutional and single-institutional tests render slight affirmation for this proposition. Of the five multi-institutional appraisals made, one confirms the posited relationship (Cash and Bissel, 1985). Nine single-institutional assessments were carried out and, one of them affords backing for the anticipated influence of initial commitment to the institution on academic integration (Pascarella, Duby and Iverson, 1983).

*Support by Institutional Type.* Multiple appraisals of this proposition in liberal arts colleges, two year colleges and unspecified types of four-year colleges and universities were conducted. Assessments made in both two-year colleges and unspecified types of four-year institutions offer no support to Tinto's proposition that initial commitment to the institutions affects the level of academic integration. Both tests made in two-year colleges were nonsustaining (Pascarella, Smart, and Ethington, 1986), as were the two estimations carried out using unspecified types of four-year colleges and universities (Pavel, 1991; Braxton, Vesper, and Hossler,1995). This proposition is also accorded uncertain affirmation in liberal arts colleges, as Cash and Bissel's (1985) single test in this setting was upholding.

Single institutional appraisals of this proposition were also carried out in two types of collegiate institutions: residential and commuter universities. Tests conducted in residential universities offer no empirical backing given that none of the five estimations made affirmed the expected influence of initial institutional commitment on academic integration (Pascarella and Terenzini, 1983(3 tests); Terenzini, Pascarella, Theophilides, and Lorang, 1985; Pascarella, Terenzini, and Wolfle, 1986). However, this proposition is weakly upheld in commuter universities. Of the four tests made in this setting, one of them confirms the hypothesized relationship (Pascarella, Duby, and Iverson, 1983).

*Support by Student Group.* The focal proposition is not affirmed for either male or female college students. Both tests of the anticipated relationship between initial institutional commitment and academic integration made using males and females fail to uphold it (Pascarella, Smart, and Ethington, 1986; Pascarella and Terenzini, 1983). In addition, tests of this postulated relationship carried out using Native American/Alaskan Native college students render indeterminate support. Pavel's (1991) singular test of this proposition was nonaffirming.

**Proposition Eight: The greater the level of academic integration, the greater the level of subsequent commitment to the goal of graduation from college.**

*Aggregated Support.* Multi-institutional tests of this hypothesis modestly affirmed it. Of the eight tests made, four of them empirically uphold this expected relationship between academic integration and subsequent goal commitment (Braxton, Vesper, and Hossler, 1995; Munro, 1981; Cash and Bissel, 1985; Williamson and Creamer, 1988). Single-institutional assessments also supply moderate support since five of the twelve tests made verify this proposition (Pascarella and Terenzini, 1983; Terenzini, Pascarella, Theophilides, and Lorang, 1985; Allen, 1986; Cabrera, Castaneda, Nora, and Hengstler, 1992; Cabrera, Nora, and Castaneda, 1992).

*Institutional Type.* Among multi-institutional assessments of the posited influence of academic integration on subsequent commitment to the goal of college graduation, the magnitude of support varies across different types of institutions. Four-year colleges and universities as a general category furnish strong backing as two of the three tests conducted in this setting sustain this proposition (Munro, 1981; Braxton, Vesper, and Hossler, in press). However, appraisals made using two-year colleges afford moderate affirmation. Of the two tests made, the one conducted by Williamson and Creamer (1988) supports the focal hypothesized relationship; whereas, Pascarella and Chapman's (1983b) assessment failed to back it.

Single-institutional tests also furnish varying degrees of affirmation for the focal proposition across different types of colleges and universities. Estimations executed using residential universities render middling affirmation as two of the four tests carried out found a statistical significant effect (Pascarella and Terenzini, 1983; Terenzini, Pascarella, Theophilides, and Lorang, 1985). Tests of the expected relationship between academic integration and subsequent goal commitment made in commuter universities also offer moderate backing given that three of the seven assessments carried out affirm this anticipated association (Allen, 1986; Cabrera, Castaneda, Nora, and Hengstler, 1992; Cabrera, Nora, and Castaneda, 1992). However, this proposition receives indeterminate backing in two-year colleges since a single test in a two-year private college failed to affirm it (Allen and Nelson, 1989).

*Student Groups.* Uncertain support for the focal proposition is evidenced when different student groups are considered. In her study of gender differences in student persistence in a residential university, Stage (1988) did not find statistically reliable support for the postulated influence of academic integration on subsequent goal commitment for either male or female students. In addition, Pavel

(1991) reports no support for such an influence for Native-American/Alaskan-native students.

## Proposition Nine: The greater the level of social integration, the greater the level of subsequent commitment to the institution.

*Aggregated Support.* Single- and multi-institutional tests provide different magnitudes of support for this anticipated relationship. Single-institutional assessments offer strong confirmation, as eight of twelve of these estimations empirically uphold Tinto's hypothesis that social integration positively affects subsequent commitment to the institution (Allen and Nelson, 1989 (2 tests)); Allen, 1986; Cabrera, Castaneda, Nora and Hengstler, 1992; Cabrera, Nora, and Castaneda, 1992; Pascarella and Terenzini, 1983; Stage, 1988(2 tests). Multi-institutional tests, however, provide moderate backing since six of the ten appraisals conducted confirm this anticipated influence (Pascarella and Chapman, 1983b (2 tests); Munro, 1981; Braxton, Vesper, and Hossler, 1995; Pascarella, Smart, and Ethington, 1986(2 tests).

*Institutional Type.* Multi-institutional tests of this proposition tend to yield varying degrees of support. Unspecified types of four-year colleges render robust backing for the hypothesized positive relationship between social integration and subsequent institutional commitment since two of three tests conducted in this setting empirically verify this proposition (Munro, 1981; Braxton, Vesper and Hossler, 1995). However, multi-institutional assessments made in two-year colleges render modest confirmation. Of the four estimations conducted, two of them provide statistically reliable verification for the expected influence of social integration on subsequent institutional commitment (Pascarella, Smart, and Ethington, 1986).

Multi-institutional appraisals made in three other types of colleges and universities furnish indeterminate support for the focal proposition. For residential universities, the sole test performed by Pascarella and Chapman (1983b) upheld the hypothesized positive influence of social integration on subsequent institutional commitment. In addition, a solitary assessment conducted in commuter universities also accords indeterminate backing for this posited influence (Pascarella and Chapman, 1983b). An assessment of this proposition in liberal arts colleges also gives indeterminate affirmation, as Cash and Bissel's appraisal of it is unconfirming.

Like multi-institutional appraisals of this proposition, single-institutional tests also give differing degrees of support across different types of colleges and universities. Tests carried out in residential universities render robust affirmation, as three of four estimations executed affirmed the anticipated positive effect of social integration on subsequent institutional commitment (Pascarella and Terenzini, 1983; Stage, 1988 (2 tests). However, commuter universities offer moderate endorsement for this postulated effect given that four of seven assessments made in this type of university sustain it (Allen, 1986; Allen and Nelson, 1989; Cabrera, Castaneda, Nora, and Hengstler, 1992; Cabrera, Nora, and Castaneda,

1992). The magnitude of support for this proposition is uncertain for two-year colleges, as the sole assessment of it was affirming (Allen and Nelson, 1989).

*Student Groups.* When groups of students are considered, the magnitude of support for the hypothesized positive influence of social integration on subsequent commitment to the institution differs for racial/ethnic groups and for males and females. Given that the sole test of this hypothesis using Native Americans/Alaskan natives failed to verify it (Pavel, 1991), the magnitude of backing for this proposition is undetermined. However, appraisals of this predicted positive influence carried-out using male college students offer strong affirmations, as both tests found a statistically reliable effect of social integration on subsequent institutional commitment (Pascarella, Smart, and Ethington, 1986; Stage, 1988). In contrast, tests of this anticipated effect done with female college students furnish moderate confirmation given that one of the two assessments made sustain this effect (Stage, 1988).

## Proposition Ten: The initial level of institutional commitment affects the subsequent level of institutional commitment.

*Aggregated Support.* Both multi-institutional and single-institutional tests of this proposition provide strong backing. More specifically, both multi-institutional tests confirm that initial institutional commitment influences subsequent institutional commitment (Braxton, Vesper, and Hossler, 1995; Cash and Bissel, 1985). All six of the single-institutional appraisals of this proposed relationship also support it (Allen, 1986; Braxton and Brier, 1989; Braxton, Duster, and Pascarella, 1988; Pascarella, Duby, and Iverson, 1983; Pascarella and Terenzini, 1983; Terenzini, Pascarella, Theophilides, and Lorang, 1985).

*Institutional Type.* Multi-institutional tests of this predicted relationship afford contrasting degrees of affirmation across different types of colleges and universities. Assessments done in unspecified types of four-year colleges accord middling support, as one of two estimations of the hypothesized relationship between initial and subsequent institutional commitment sustain this hypothesis (Braxton, Vesper, and Hossler, 1995. However, appraisals executed in two-year colleges furnish no affirmation, as both assessments made failed to statistically verify the focal proposition (Pascarella, Smart, and Ethington, 1986). Moreover, tests carried out using liberal arts colleges afford undetermined confirmation given that the single test of the posited influence of initial institutional commitment on subsequent institutional commitment made in this setting sustained it in a statistically reliable way (Cash and Bissel, 1985).

In addition, eight single-institutional propositional tests were also made. Tests conducted in commuter universities yield strong affirmation. All four assessments of the posited influence of initial institutional commitment on subsequent institutional commitment carried out in this institutional setting provide statistically reliable verification for it (Allen, 1986; Braxton and Brier, 1989; Braxton, Duster, and Pascarella, 1988; Pascarella, Duby, and Iverson, 1983). Estimations of the made in residential universities also provide robust confirmation, as three out of the four checks of this posited influence carried out yield affirming results (Pascarella and Terenzini, 1983; Terenzini, Pascarella, Theophilides, and Lorang, 1985; Stage, 1988).

*Student Groups.* Because Pavel's (1991) singular test of this proposition using Native Americans/Alaskan natives failed to sustain it, indeterminate support is indicated. However, endorsement of the expected influence of initial institutional commitment on subsequent institutional commitment differs between male and female college students. Appraisals done using male college students accord no support, as both tests made are nonaffirming (Pascarella, Smart, and Ethington, 1986; Stage, 1988). In contrast, tests executed using female college students offer middling confirmation since one of the two assessments was affirming (Stage, 1988).

**Proposition Eleven: The initial level of commitment to the goal of graduation from college affects the subsequent level of commitment to the goal of college graduation.**

*Aggregated Support.* Both single- and multiple-institutional appraisals of this proposition provide robust affirmation of it. Of the four multi-institutional tests made, three of them sustain this expected association between initial and subsequent goal commitments (Cash and Bissel, 1985; Munro, 1981; Pavel, 1991). Moreover, six of the eight single-institutional tests made of this hypothesized relationship confirm it (Allen, 1986; Pascarella, Duby, and Iverson, 1983; Pascarella and Terenzini, 1983; Terenzini, Pascarella, Theophilides, and Lorang, 1985; Stage, 1988 (2 tests)).

*Institutional Type.* Multi-institutional estimations of the hypothesized effect of initial goal commitment on subsequent goal commitment offer dissimilar degrees of confirmation. Tests done using unspecified types of four-year colleges and universities accord strong support since two of the three tests conducted using this setting affirm the focal proposition (Munro, 1981; Pavel, 1991). In comparison, assessments of this anticipated effect carried out in liberal arts colleges offer indeterminate affirmation, as Cash and Bissel's (1985) singular multi-institutional test attest to an association between initial goal commitment and subsequent goal commitment.

Single-institutional assessments of this proposition were also carried out. Tests executed in commuter universities provide modest endorsement given that two of the four appraisals carried out using this type of institution offer empirical backing (Allen, 1986; Pascarella, Duby, and Iverson, 1983). However, assessments of the anticipated influence of initial goal commitment on subsequent goal commitment made using residential universities afford strong endorsement since all four tests of this proposition made in this type of institution sustain it (Pascarella and Terenzini, 1983; Terenzini, Pascarella, Theophilides, and Lorang, 1985; Stage, 1988 (2 tests)).

*Student Groups.* Assessments done using Native American/Alaskan-native college students furnish indeterminate backing for the focal postulated relationship. Pavel's (1991) sole test of this proposition for Native American/Alaskan native students upheld it in a statistically reliable way. Likewise, appraisals carried out using male and female college students offer undetermined affirmation for the influence of initial commitment to the goal of graduation from college on subsequent commitment to this goal, as Stage's (1988) tests of this posited influence provides verification for such an influence for both groups.

**Proposition Twelve: The greater the level of subsequent commitment to the goal of college graduation, the greater the likelihood of student persistence in college.**

*Aggregated Support.* Striking differences in the magnitude of support for this proposition are evident. Multi-institutional tests furnish strong affirmation, as 13 of the 18 tests made uphold the anticipated positive influence of subsequent commitment to the goal of graduation from college on college student persistence (Anderson, 1987 (4 tests); Pascarella and Chapman, 1983a (2 tests), 1983b (2 tests); Williamson and Creamer, 1988; Cash and Bissel, 1985; Braxton, Vesper, and Hossler, 1995; Munro, 1981; Pavel, 1991). In contrast, single-institutional tests provide frail confirmation for this hypothesized effect. Of the 19 single-institutional assessments made, four of them sustain the focal proposition in a statistically significant way (Pascarella and Terenzini, 1980; Pascarella and Terenzini, 1983; Terenzini, Lorang, and Pascarella, 1981; Terenzini, Pascarella, Theophilides, and Lorang, 1985).

*Institutional Type.* Multi-institutional assessments of this proposition employing two-year colleges, liberal arts colleges, residential universities, and unspecified types of four-year colleges and universities afford strong affirmation. More specifically, four of five tests made using two-year colleges affirm the anticipated positive influence of subsequent goal commitment on student persistence (Anderson, 1987; Pascarella and Chapman, 1983a, 1983b; Williamson and Creamer, 1988), as do both of the tests made in liberal arts colleges (Anderson, 1987; Cash and Bissel, 1985). All three of the tests made in residential universities also uphold this hypothesis (Anderson, 1987; Pascarella and Chapman, 1983a, 1983b), as do all three of the assessments executed in unspecified types of colleges and universities (Braxton, Vesper, and Hossler, 1995; Munro, 1981; Pavel, 1991).

In comparison, single-institutional appraisals yield differing degrees of affirmation of the hypothesized positive influence of subsequent goal commitment on student persistence. More specifically, tests conducted using commuter universities furnish no support, as none of the nine studies executed in this institutional setting sustains the hypothesized relationship (Allen, 1986; Allen and Nelson, 1989; Braxton and Brier, 1989; Braxton, Brier, and Hossler, 1988; Braxton, Duster, and Pascarella, 1988; Cabrera, Castaneda, Nora, and Hengstler, 1992; Cabrera, Nora, and Castaneda, 1992; Fox, 1986; Pascarella, Duby, and Iverson, 1983). Nevertheless, single-institutional appraisals carried out in residential universities produce modest support since four of the nine tests made using this type of institution support this proposition (Pascarella and Terenzini, 1980; Pascarella and Terenzini, 1983; Terenzini, Lorang, and Pascarella, 1981; Terenzini, Pascarella, Theophilides, and Lorang, 1985). However, estimations of the hypothesized influence done in two-year colleges provide indeterminate backing given that the sole test made in this setting failed to uphold the expected association between subsequent goal commitment and student persistence (Allen and Nelson,1989).

*Student Groups.* Tests of this proposition using Native American/Alaskan natives provide indeterminate confirmation, as the single test using this group of students affords statistically significant backing for the anticipated effect of subsequent goal commitment on college student withdrawal decisions (Pavel, 1991). In addition, assessments of this anticipated influence done employing male and female college students offer no support, as both tests made for each gender do not provide statistically significant affirmation of this particular proposition (Pascarella, Smart, and Ethington, 1986; Stage, 1988).

**Proposition Thirteen: The greater the level of subsequent commitment to the institution, the greater the likelihood of student persistence in college.**

*Aggregated Support.* Single-institutional assessments of this proposed relationship between subsequent institutional commitment and student departure provide robust backing since 13 of the 19 tests made verify this expectation (Allen and Nelson, 1989; Brower, 1991; Mallette and Cabrera, 1991; Pascarella and Terenzini, 1980; Pascarella and Terenzini, 1983; Terenzini, Lorang, and Pascarella, 1981; Terenzini, Pascarella, Theophilides, and Lorang, 1985;Allen and Nelson, 1989; Braxton and Brier, 1989; Braxton, Brier, and Hossler, 1988; Braxton, Duster, and Pascarella, 1988; Stage, 1988 (2 tests)). Multi-institutional appraisals, however, provide moderate support for this proposition, as seven of 13 tests made sustain it (Pascarella and Chapman, 1983a (2 tests); 1983b (3 tests); Cash and Bissel, 1985; Pascarella, Smart, and Ethington, 1986).

*Institutional Type.* Multi-institutional appraisals of this hypothesized relationship between subsequent institutional commitment and student retention made in liberal arts colleges, commuter universities, and residential universities furnish strong affirmation for this hypothesis. To be more specific, both multi-institutional tests made using liberal arts colleges are affirming (Pascarella and Chapman, 1983b; Cash and Bissel, 1985), as are both of the assessments carried out employing commuter universities (Pascarella and Chapman, 1983a, 1983b). The two estimations conducted by Pascarella and Chapman (1983a,1983b) in residential universities also confirm this proposition. However, appraisals of Tinto's postulation of a positive association between subsequent institutional commitment remaining in college done using two-year colleges produced weak support for this postulation, as one of the three tests made sustains it (Pascarella and Chapman, 1983b).

Single-institutional tests of this proposition made utilizing different types of colleges and universities yield a variable pattern of affirmation ranging from indeterminate to strong support for the focal expectation. Tests made using two-year colleges offer indeterminate support as a sole affirming test was conducted (Allen and Nelson, 1989). However, appraisals done with commuter universities furnish moderate backing given that four of nine estimations of the proposed influence of subsequent institutional commitment on student departure decisions affirm such an influence (Allen and Nelson, 1989; Braxton and Brier, 1989; Braxton, Brier and Hossler, 1988; Braxton, Duster, and Pascarella, 1988). Assessments executed using residential universities, however, provide strong confirmation of this postulated influence since six of the seven tests carried-out sustain Proposition 13 (Brower, 1991; Mallette and Cabrera, 1991; Pascarella and Terenzini, 1980; Pascarella and Terenzini, 1983; Terenzini, Lorang, and Pascarella, 1981; Terenzini, Pascarella, Theophilides, and Lorang, 1985).

*Student Groups.* Tests conducted using male and female college students yield modest support for the hypothesized positive influence of subsequent institutional commitment on student persistence in college. Of the two assessments made with female students, one of them upholds this hypothesis (Stage, 1988). Likewise, appraisals executed using male college students also afford moderate confirmation of this particular proposition given that one of the two estimations made verifies the expected influence of subsequent institutional commitment on student departure decisions (Pascarella, Smart, and Ethington, 1986). Tests made using Native American/Alaskan native college students yield indeterminate support for the focal proposition since Pavel's (1991) sole assessment using this group of students found no support for the posited positive relationship between subsequent institutional commitment and the decision to remain in college.

**Proposition Fourteen: A high level of commitment to the goal of graduation from college compensates for a low level of commitment to the institution, and vice versa, in influencing student persistence in college.**

*Aggregated Support.* Two single-institutional tests afford robust support for a compensatory relationship between goal and institutional commitment in influencing student persistence. Both single-institutional assessments of this proposition obtained statistically reliable support for it (Pascarella and Terenzini, 1983; Terenzini, Pascarella, Theophilides, and Lorang (1985). In contrast, four multi-institutional tests provide moderate backing. Two of the four multi-institutional appraisals of this expected compensatory relationship between institutional and goal commitment proposition affirm this expectation (Pascarella and Chapman, 1983a (2 tests).

*Support by Institutional Type.* Single-institutional assessments made in residential universities vigorously uphold Proposition 14, as both tests in this institutional setting afford statistically significant backing (Pascarella and Terenzini, 1983; Terenzini, Pascarella, Theophilides, and Lorang, 1985).

However, multi-institutional appraisals of the proposed compensatory relationship between goal and institutional commitment in affecting student departure made in residential universities, commuter universities, liberal arts colleges, and two-year colleges accord indeterminate support for this postulation. Solitary tests of this proposition were made in each of these four types of colleges and universities. To be specific, the single tests of this proposition conducted in residential universities (Pascarella and Chapman, 1983a) and in liberal arts colleges (Pascarella and Chapman, 1983a) affirmed the expected compensatory relationship. However, the sole assessment made in commuter universities (Pascarella and Chapman, 1983a) and in two-year colleges (Pascarella and Chapman, 1983a) failed to support this proposition.

*Support by Student Group.* Single tests of the hypothesized compensatory association between commitment to the goal of graduation from college and institutional commitment in affecting student persistence made with male and female students yield indeterminate support for this association. Assessments of this proposition made by Pascarella and Terenzini (1983) found it applicable to male student, but not to female students.

**Proposition Fifteen: Academic integration and social integration are mutually interdependent and reciprocal in their influence on student persistence in college.**

Two ways have been used to test this proposition. One method tests whether high levels of academic integration compensate for low levels of social integration in affecting student persistence. The other approach seeks to determine if academic integration directly affects social integration or vice versa.

*Aggregated Support.* The compensatory hypothesis has been the focus of four single-institutional tests. These assessments furnish robust backing for a compensatory interaction between academic and social integration given that three of the four estimations made confirm this facet of Proposition 15 (Pascarella and Terenzini, 1979b; Pascarella and Terenzini, 1983 (2 tests).

Stage (1989a) and Cabrera, Nora, and Castaneda (1992) tested whether academic integration has a direct influence on social integration or vice versa. Stage tested this relationship separately for male and females, whereas Cabreara, Nora, and Castaneda did not make such distinctions. Cabrera, Nora, and Castaneda found that the academic and social integration are related to one another in a statistically reliable way. Stage observed that for males, academic integration positively affects social integration, but not vice versa. In contrast, social integration positively influences academic integration for females. For female students, academic integration does not affect social integration. Although differences between male and female students are observed, vigorous affirmation for this approach to testing the focal proposition is provided.

*Support by Institution.* The compensatory hypothesis variation on Proposition Fifteen is vigorously sustained in the residential university setting, as three of the four tests made empirically uphold it (Pascarella and Terenzini, 1979b; Pascarella and Terenzini, 1983 (2 tests)).

Stage's (1989a) and Cabrera, Nora, and Castaneda's approach to testing this proposition were executed in different types of institutions. Cabrera, Nora, and Castaneda's test was carried out in a commuter university, whereas Stage's test was accomplished in a residential university. Thus, this approach to testing the focal proposition receives indeterminate support in both commuter and residential universities.

*Support by Student Group.* Appraisals of the compensatory hypothesis using female college students render vigorous backing for it since both tests made sustain it (Pascarella and Terenzini, 1979b; Pascarella and Terenzini, 1983). However, an assessment of this variation on Proposition 15 using male college students accords modest support, as one of two tests carried out empirically verifies a compensatory interaction between academic and social integration (Pascarella and Terenzini, 1983).

The hypothesis that academic integration directly affects social integration or vice versa is furnished indeterminate support. Although Stage's assessments of this variation on the focal proposition for men and women is confirming, these tests are the sole ones made. Thus, indeterminate affirmation is indicated.

### Summary: Propositional Tests

The magnitude of support for each of the 15 propositions is summarized in Tables 1, 2-A, 2-B and 3. Table 1 summarizes the aggregated magnitude of empirical backing for each proposition, whereas Tables 2A (multi-institutional tests) and 2B (single-institutional tests) summarize the magnitude of affirmation for each proposition by institutional type. The magnitude of support for each proposition by student group is summarized in Table 3.

*Aggregate Support.* Table 1 shows that two primary propositions are vigorously upheld by both multi-institutional and single-institutional tests. These two propositions are:"(10) the initial level of institutional commitment affects the subsequent level of institutional commitment," and "(11) the initial level of commitment to the goal of graduation from college affects the subsequent level of commitment to the goal of college graduation."

In addition to these two propositions, multi-institutional assessments afford robust backing for two other propositions, whereas single-institutional tests provide strong endorsement for five other propositions are strongly endorsed by single-institutional appraisals. The two additional propositions vigorously sustained by multi-institutional tests are: "(2) student entry characteristics affect the level of initial commitment to the goal of graduation from college", and "(12) the greater the level of subsequent commitment to the goal of college graduation, the greater the likelihood of student persistence in college." Proposition 12 is one of the five core propositions of Tinto's theory.

**TABLE 1. Aggregated Magnitude of Support for Each Proposition by Multiple and Single Institutional Tests**

| Proposition | Multiple | Single |
|---|---|---|
| 1. Student entry characteristics affect the level of initial commitment to the institution. | M | S |
| 2. Student entry characteristics affect the level of initial commitment to the goal of graduation from college. | S | M |
| 3. Student entry characteristics directly affect the student's likelihood of persistence in college. | M | W |
| 4. Initial commitment to the goal of graduation from college affects the level of academic integration. | W | M |
| 5. Initial commitment to the goal of graduation from college affects the level of social integration. | N | M |
| 6. Initial commitment to the institution affects the level of social integration. | W | W |
| 7. Initial commitment to the institution affects the level of academic integration. | W | W |
| 8. The greater the level of academic integration, the greater the level of subsequent commitment to the goal of graduation from college. | M | M |
| 9. The greater the level of social integration, the greater the level of subsequent commitment to the institution. | M | S |
| 10. The initial level of institutional commitment affects the subsequent level of institutional commitment. | S | S |
| 11. The initial level of commitment to the goal of graduation from college affects the subsequent level of commitment to the goal of college graduation. | S | S |
| 12. The greater the level of subsequent commitment to the goal of college graduation, the greater the likelihood of student persistence in college. | S | W |
| 13. The greater the level of subsequent commitment to the institution, the greater the likelihood of student persistence in college. | M | S |
| 14. A high level of commitment to the goal of graduation from college compensates for a low level of commitment to the institution, and vice versa, in influencing student persis- | M | S |
| 15. Academic integration and societal integration are mutually interdependent and reciprocal in their influence on student persistence in college. | NA | S/S* |

*Compensatory test/Stage's and Cabrera et al.'s test
NOTE:S=Strong support
       M=Moderate support
       W=Weak support
       N=No support
       NA=no test made.

**TABLE 2A. Magnitude of Support for Each Proposition by Institutional Type: Multiple Institutional Tests**

| Proposition | Institutional Types | | | | |
|---|---|---|---|---|---|
| | RU | CU | LA | CC | US |
| 1. Student entry characteristics affect the level of initial commitment to the institution. | NA | NA | I | S | S |
| 2. Student entry characteristics affect the level of initial commitment to the goal of graduation from college. | NA | NA | I | S | S |
| 3. Student entry characteristics directly affect the student's likelihood of persistence in college. | N | S | N | S | S |
| 4. Initial commitment to the goal of graduation from college affects the level of academic integration. | NA | NA | I | N | N |
| 5. Initial commitment to the goal of graduation from college affects the level of social integration. | NA | NA | I | N | N |
| 6. Initial commitment to the institution affects the level of social integration. | NA | NA | I | N | N |
| 7. Initial commitment to the institution affects the level of academic integration. | NA | NA | I | N | N |
| 8. The greater the level of academic integration, the greater the level of subsequent commitment to tshe subsequent goal of graduation from college. | NA | NA | NA | M | S |
| 9. The greater the level of social integration, the greater the level of subsequent commitment to the institution. | I | I | I | M | S |
| 10. The initial level of institutional commitment affects the subsequent level of institutional commitment. | NA | NA | I | N | M |
| 11. The initial level of commitment to the goal of ofgraduation from college affects the subsequent level of commitment to the goal of college graduation. | NA | NA | I | NA | S |
| 12. The greater the level of subsequent commitment to the goal of college graduation, the greater the likelihood of student persistence in college. | WS | NA | S | S | S |
| 13. The greater the level of subsequent commitment to the institution, the greater the likelihood of student persistence in college. | S | S | S | W | NA |
| 14. A high level of commitment to the goal of graduation from college compensates for a low level of commitment to the institution, and vice versa, in influencing student persistence in college. | I | I | I | I | NA |
| 15. Academic integration and social integration are mutually interdependent and reciprocal in their influence on student persistence in college. | NA | NA | NA | NA | NA |

RU=Residential university
CU=Commuter University
LA=Liberal Arts College
CC=Two-year college

S=strong support
M=moderate support
W=weak support

N=no support
I=indeterminate support
NA=no test made

# TABLE 2B. Magnitude of Support for Each Proposition by Institutional Type: Single Institutional Tests

| Proposition | Institutional Types | | | | |
| --- | --- | --- | --- | --- | --- |
| | RU | CU | LA | CC | US |
| 1. Student entry characteristics affect the level of initial commitment to the institution. | M | S | NA | NA | NA |
| 2. Student entry characteristics affect the level of initial commitment to the goal of graduation from college. | M | M | NA | NA | NA |
| 3. Student entry characteristics directly affect the student's likelihood of persistence in college. | W | W | NA | S | NA |
| 4. Initial commitment to the goal of graduation from college affects the level of academic integration. | W | M | NA | NA | NA |
| 5. Initial commitment to the goal of graduation from college affects the level of social integration. | S | W | NA | NA | NA |
| 6. Initial commitment to the institution affects the level of social integration. | M | N | NA | NA | NA |
| 7. Initial commitment to the institution affects the level of academic integration. | N | W | NA | NA | NA |
| 8. The greater the level of academic integration, the greater the level of subsequent commitment to tshe subsequent goal of graduation from college. | M | M | NA | I | NA |
| 9. The greater the level of social integration, the greater the level of subsequent commitment to the institution. | S | M | NA | I | NA |
| 10. The initial level of institutional commitment affects the subsequent level of institutional commitment. | S | S | NA | NA | NA |
| 11. The initial level of commitment to the goal of graduation from college affects the subsequent level of commitment to the goal of college graduation. | S | M | NA | I | NA |
| 12. The greater the level of subsequent commitment to the goal of college graduation, the greater the likelihood of student persistence in college. | M | N | NA | I | NA |
| 13. The greater the level of subsequent commitment to the institution, the greater the likelihood of student persistence in college. | S | M | NA | I | NA |
| 14. A high level of commitment to the goal of graduation from college compensates for a low level of commitment to the institution, and vice versa, in influencing student persistence in college. | S | NA | NA | NA | NA |
| 15. Academic integration and social integration are mutually interdependent and reciprocal in their influence on student persistence in college. | S/I* | NA/I** | NA | NA | NA |

RU=Residential university
CU=Commuter University
LA=Liberal Arts College
CC=Two-year college

S=strong support
M=moderate support
W=weak support

N=no support
I=indeterminate support
NA=no test made

*Compensatory test/Stage's test
**Cabrera et al.'s test

## TABLE 3. Magnitude of Support for Each Proposition by Institutional Type: Single Institutional Tests

Student Groups

| Proposition | Male | Female | AAW | AAM | WM | WW | AA | NA/AN | Younger | Older |
|---|---|---|---|---|---|---|---|---|---|---|
| 1. Student entry characteristics affect the level of initial commitment to the institution. | M | M | NA | NA | NA | NA | I | I | NA | NA |
| 2. Student entry characteristics affect the level of initial commitment to the goal of graduation from college. | M | M | NA | NA | NA | NA | I | I | NA | NA |
| 3. Student entry characteristics directly affect the student's likelihood of persistence in college. | M | W | N | M | S | S | I | I | I | I |
| 4. Initial commitment to the goal of graduation from college affects the level of academic integration. | N | N | NA | NA | NA | NA | NA | I | NA | NA |
| 5. Initial commitment to the goal of graduation from college affects the level of social integration. | N | M | NA | NA | NA | NA | NA | I | NA | NA |
| 6. Initial commitment to the institution affects the level of social integration. | M | M | NA | NA | NA | NA | I | I | NA | NA |
| 7. Initial commitment to the institution affects the level of academic integration. | N | N | NA | NA | NA | NA | NA | I | NA | NA |
| 8. The greater the level of academic integration, the greater the level of subsequent commitment to she subsequent goal of graduation from college. | S | M | NA | NA | NA | NA | NA | I | NA | NA |
| 9. The greater the level of social integration, the greater the level of subsequent commitment to the institution. | N | M | NA | NA | NA | NA | NA | I | NA | NA |
| 10. The initial level of institutional commitment affects the subsequent level of institutional commitment. | I | I | NA | NA | NA | NA | NA | I | NA | NA |
| 11. The initial level of commitment to the goal of graduation from college affects the subsequent level of commitment to the goal of college graduation. | I | I | NA | NA | NA | NA | NA | I | NA | NA |
| 12. The greater the level of subsequent commitment to the goal of college graduation, the greater the likelihood of student persistence in college. | N | N | NA | NA | NA | NA | NA | I | NA | NA |
| 13. The greater the level of subsequent commitment to the institution, the greater the likelihood of student persistence in college. | M | M | NA | NA | NA | NA | NA | I | NA | NA |
| 14. A high level of commitment to the goal of graduation from college compensates for a low level of commitment to the institution, and vice versa, in influencing student persistence in college. | I | I | NA | NA | NA | NA | NA | NA | NA | NA |
| 15. Academic integration and social integration are mutually interdependent and reciprocal in their influence on student persistence in college. | M/I* | S/I* | NA | NA | NA | NA | NA | NA | NA | NA. |

M=Male, F=Female
AAW=African American Women, AAM= African American Men
WM=White Males, WW=White Women
AA=African Americans:General
NA/NA=Native American/Alaskan Native
Younger=younger college students
Older=older college Students

*Compensatory test/Stage's test

S=Strong
M=Moderate
W=Weak
N=No support
I=Indeterminate Support
NA=No Test

The five propositions strongly supported by single-institutional tests are as follows: "(1) student entry characteristics affect the level of initial commitment to the institution," "(9) the greater the level of social integration, the greater the level of subsequent commitment to the institution, "(13) the greater the level of subsequent commitment to the institution, the greater the likelihood of student persistence in college," "(14) a high level of commitment to the goal of graduation from college compensates for a low level of commitment to the institution, and vice versa, in influencing student persistence in college, and "(15) academic integration and social integration are mutually interdependent and reciprocal in their influence on student persistence in college.

Of the five hypothesized relationships robustly backed by single-institutional assessments, two of them—9 and 13—are primary propositions. Whereas, two of these five propositions—14 and 15—are adjunctive to Tinto's formulations.

*Support by Institutional Type.* Table 2A demonstrates that multi-institutional tests were not carried out for all of the 13 primary propositions. Consequently, multi-institutional tests conducted for different types of institutions can not be taken into account in assessments of the empirical internal consistency of Tinto's theory across different types of colleges and universities. Moreover, Table 2A also shows that none of the 13 primary propositions are afforded robust support across all of the types of colleges and universities represented in multi-institutional appraisals.

In contrast, single-institutional tests were conducted for each of the 13 primary propositions in two types of college and universities: residential and commuter universities. This observation is evident from Table 2B. Also apparent from Table 2B is the strong support given by both residential and commuter universities to the proposition that "the initial level of institutional commitment affects the subsequent level of institutional commitment (proposition 10)."

In addition, commuter universities furnish vigorous backing to one other hypothesis: "student entry characteristics affect the level of initial commitment to the institution (proposition 1)." Besides proposition 10, residential universities give robust endorsement to the following six expected relationships: "(5) initial commitment to the institution affects   the level of social integration," "(9) the greater the level of social integration, the greater the level of subsequent commitment to the institution," "(11) the initial commitment to the goal of graduation from college affects the subsequent level of commitment to the goal of college graduation," "(13) the greater the level of subsequent commitment to the institution, the greater the likelihood of student persistence in college," (14) a high level of commitment to the goal of   graduation from college compensates for a low level of   commitment to the institution, and vice versa, in   influencing student persistence in college," and "(15)academic integration and social integration are mutually interdependent and reciprocal in their influence on student persistence in college".

Propositions 9 and 13 are core propositions, whereas proposition 14 and 15 are adjunctive propositions.

*Support by Student Group.* Because all 13 primary propositions were assessed using only males and females and not the other student groups exhibited in Table 3, only tests carried out for male and female college students will be considered in our appraisal of the empirical internal consistency of Tinto's formulations across different student groups.

From Table 3, it can be observed that studies involving male college students afford strong support for the proposition that "the greater the level of social integration, the greater the level of subsequent commitment to the institution. This ninth proposition is a core hypothesis of Tinto's theory. In contrast, tests made using female students afford none of the 13 primary propositions robust empirical endorsement. However, one adjunctive proposition is given vigorous backing by them: proposition 15. This proposition reads: academic integration and social integration are mutually interdependent and reciprocal in their influence on student persistence in college.

These possible shortcomings in Tinto's theory do not provide adequate grounds for dismissing it; instead, these gaps point to opportunities for creating stronger theory. In his own acknowledgments of the model's limitations, Tinto warns, "Recognizing theoretical limits should not...constrain us from seeking to improve our existing models or replace them with better ones" (689). Combining theoretical perspectives offers one method for accomplishing this. By drawing upon the works of the French sociologist Durkheim (1951) and the Dutch anthropologist Van Gennep (1960), Tinto provides one example of how works in diverse fields may be combined. In fact, the theories and study of student development reflect an often eclectic, multi-disciplinary nature, utilizing perspectives in sociology, anthropology, psychology, and economics, among others. Kuhn (1970) suggests that such differing perspectives pushes theory development in new directions and offers opportunities for advancing knowledge.

Since the Tinto model has been widely used for two decades, it seems appropriate to ask whether researchers have used additional theoretical perspectives to extend the model. If so, how have those perspectives added to the body of knowledge in the area of student departure? The following section seeks to answer these questions through an analysis of studies that exemplify combined multiple perspectives. It first offers perspectives on theory integration in general as a context for analysis. Second, it reviews integrative studies and seeks to establish whether these studies represent integrative or elaborative works.

## THEORY INTEGRATION AND THE TINTO MODEL

Kerlinger (1973) defines theory as logically interrelated constructs that "present a systematic view of phenomena by specifying relationships among variables, with the purpose of explaining and predicting the phenomena" (p. 9). This definition implies order in the progression of ideas as well as unification of a body of knowledge, with each development building upon and extending the preceding concepts and frameworks. Theoretical *models* move one step beyond the abstract parameters of theory, expanding these to more concrete explications of constructs.

Theories and theoretical models provide scientific tools for researchers and practitioners to gain greater understanding of complex phenomena. Yet, what of such tools when we discover shortcomings in their applicability, utility, or explanatory power? Then, we must either alter the existing tools through integration or elaboration, or develop new ones to fill the gaps in inquiry and unify fragmented areas (Liska, Krohn, and Messner, 1989). When we draw upon existing theory, we build upon a foundation that sometimes has been tested. Adding new concepts then allows us to extend the field in a logical, orderly fashion and to develop theory with stronger explanatory capability. Although no criteria for the successful attainment of such work exists in the higher education literature, researchers in the sociological study of deviance have developed criteria for combining theory via integration and elaboration. Adapting these criteria to our own work enables us to assess this work and its contribution to the field. Our analysis thus requires an additional definition of theory integration, distinguishing it from theory elaboration.

Thornberry (1989) defines integration as "the act of combining two or more sets of logically interrelated propositions into one larger set of interrelated propositions, in order to provide a more comprehensive explanation of a particular phenomenon" (p. 52). This new, logically justified theory must also preserve the beginning causal arguments of the integrated theories (Elliott, 1985). A potential reduction in the clarity and strength of the integrated theory counts among the possible costs inherent in this process by compromising both views.

Elaboration differs from integration since the theorist is not required to reconcile the differences of the perspectives. Instead, the theorist accepts the premises of a single theoretical model and then attempts to build a more comprehensive model through the logical extension of the basic propositions. Thus, clarity and strength remain intact while the inclusion of perspectives taken from other disciplines enhances the explanatory power of the original model.

Based upon these definitions, we apply a total of six criteria for evaluating the levels of integration and elaboration based on the formulations of Farnworth (1989) and Thornberry (1989) to studies using the Tinto model. The *integrated* theory must meet four criteria. It must: first, describe the original theories in terms of their assumptions, level of explanation (macro, micro, individual), propositions, and structure; second, identify the conflicts or competing claims of the theories to be integrated; third, resolve the conflicts in a manner internally consistent with the framework of the integrated model; and, fourth, following modification of the pure forms, combine truncated versions of each theory in a single theoretical model (Farnworth, 1989; Thornberry, 1989). The fifth and sixth criteria relate to *elaborated* theory. This must first begin with a single model, accepting its premises; and, second, extend the model based via inclusion of perspectives taken from other disciplines.

**TABLE 4. Attempts at Theory and Elaboration**

| *Study/Year* | *Classification Criteria* | | | | | |
|---|---|---|---|---|---|---|
| **Category** | **Integration** | | | | **Elaboration** | |
| | *Describes original theories* | *Identifies conflicts/ competing claims* | *Resolves conflicts* | *Modifies for new model* | *Accepts premise of model* | *Extends propositions from perspectives* |
| **Psychological:** Stage, 1989 | N | N | N | N | Y | Y |
| Brower, 1992 | N | N | N | N | Y | Y |
| Peterson, 1993 | N | N | N | N | Y | Y |
| **Environmental:** *Societal* Anderson, 1988 | Y | Y | P | N | N | N |
| *Economic* Braxton, Brier, & Hossler, 1988 | N | N | N | N | Y | Y |
| Cabrera, Stampen & Hansen, 1990 | Y | N | N | N | Y | Y |
| Cabrera, Nora, & Castaneda, 1992 | Y | Y | P | Y | N | N |
| *Organizational* Braxton & Brier, 1989 | Y | N | N | N | Y | Y |
| Cabrera, Castaneda, Nora, & Hengstler, 1992 | Y | Y | P | Y | N | N |
| Cabrera, Nora, & Castaneda, 1993 | Y | Y | Y | Y | N | N |

For the analysis, we group the studies according to the outline established by Tinto (1987, 1993) referenced earlier in the chapter. He labels theories as psychological (1993, p. 84), environmental (1993, p. 86), and interactional (1993, p. 90). He breaks down the environmental category to include societal, economic, and organizational perspectives. In calling for revisions to his theory, Tinto (1986) suggests that alternative or multiple perspectives can strengthen this work. Since Tinto's model is explicitly interactional, we focus upon psychological and environmental perspectives as offering the greatest potential for theory integration. After defining these groups, we categorize the studies according to the criteria for integration and elaboration (see Table 4). The results of the analysis follow.

## Psychological Perspectives

Tinto notes that the psychological category emphasizes the individual's intellectual, personality, motivation, and disposition development. Three studies examine various psychological aspects of student development in conjunction with the Tinto model. The psychological perspectives include motivation (Stage, 1989), life task predominance (Brower, 1992), and self-efficacy (Peterson, 1993).

In the first study, Stage (1989) employed motivational orientations of students in a "Tinto-based study "(p. 385). She examined associations among variables within three distinct typologies to determine the motivational orientations for freshmen, the differing patterns of experiences that might lead to attrition, and the specific patterns of social and academic integration for students within set motivational categories. Using factor analysis to determine the classifications of motivational orientations and LISREL to analyze the relationships among the six constructs of the Tinto model, she found that students' persistence may be impacted by psychosocial differences that affect the influences of environmental factors. Within three subgroups, background characteristics had a direct influence on persistence. She concluded that the "unidimensional" measures (i.e. measures that focus upon demographic while excluding psychosocial factors) used in previous persistence studies limit the applicability of the Tinto model, and called for researchers to use both psychosocial and demographic characterizations of students in future .

In the second study, Brower (1992) meshed concepts of cognitive social psychology with Tinto constructs to explore how students' life-task orientations affect perceptions of their environments and, ultimately, their persistence. This author argued that students commit to seven life task domains, including academic achievement, social interaction, future goal development, autonomy, identity formation, time management, and physical maintenance/well-being (Brower, 1992, p. 446). The pursuit of these domains facilitates or hinders their integration into the life of the institution. Brower hypothesized that the addition of life-task performance to the Tinto model would improve persistence predictions and enable institutional administrators to tailor persistence efforts toward specific types of student profiles (Brower, 1992, p. 449). The researcher used linear regressions to compare the Tinto model constructs of background characteristics, initial commitments, academic integration, social integration, later commitments, and persistence to a life task persistence model. Brower asserted that, while the results support the Tinto theory that student persistence is positively impacted by social and academic integration, students' life-task orientations at specific points provide stronger predictions of persistence. He added, however, that much of the variance in persistence remains unexplained and suggested that researchers should pursue additional studies that will allow them to discover possible indirect effects of the variables selected.

Peterson (1993) utilized psychological factors to explore the relationship between students' perceptions of ability to achieve vocational aspirations within the framework of the Tinto model. She sought to determine whether perceived career decision-making self-efficacy proved significant as a mediating background characteristic in the integration of underprepared students. Using correlation, ANOVA, and multiple regression, Peterson found that variance in the overall, social, and academic integration of her respondents could be explained primarily by the combination of perceived career decision-making self-efficacy and initial goals and commitments. She concluded that career decision-making self-efficacy provides an important variable for use in future research.

Stage (1989), Brower (1992), and Peterson (1993) drew upon the psychological development of students literature in reformulating the Tinto model. Each identified important components that build upon and extend the model, while also identifying shortcomings that can be remedied with the addition of a set of variables rather than with a complete redefinition of the model. Given that theory integration utilizes complete theories with the explicit goal of reconciling differences within competing perspectives, these studies do not appear to meet this definition. They do meet criteria for elaborative works since each accepts the basic premises of the Tinto model and seeks to extend it. Taken together, they provide persuasive evidence of the psycho-social role within Tinto's model. They also increase the applicability of the model when psycho-social profiles are considered along with other variables in the model. As elaborative efforts, they provide strong evidence of the need for future research that adds psychological perspectives to the Tinto model.

## Environmental Perspectives

Tinto includes societal, economic, and organizational perspectives within the broader category of environmental theories (1993, p. 84). Societal perspectives focus upon the process of social attainment, including social status and opportunity structure within the broader society (Tinto, 1993, p. 86). One study (Anderson, 1987) fits into this category. Three studies (Braxton, Brier, and Hossler, 1988; Cabrera, Nora, and Castaneda, 1992; Cabrera, Stampen, and Hansen, 1990) examine the Tinto model using economic theory perspectives; three other studies (Braxton and Brier, 1989; Cabrera, Castaneda, Nora, and Hengstler, 1992; and Cabrera, Nora, and Castaneda, 1993) link organizational perspectives to the Tinto model. The former three studies highlight the "costs and benefits of alternative ways of investing one's scarce economic resources" (Tinto, 1993, p. 87). The latter category of perspectives views student departure "as reflecting the impact that the organization has on the socialization and satisfaction of students" (Tinto, 1993, p. 89).

*Societal Theory.* Anderson (1988) "synthesized the basic ideas from the Tinto (1975) and status-attainment models" (p. 160) to link college persistence to issues of social reproduction and social attainment. She also examined the structural features of the college environment to determine the context in which student involvement and, hence, educational attainment occurs. Her findings indicated that students' background characteristics (and specifically SES) carry direct, continuous effects upon their college choice, extent of involvement, and achievement. Socioeconomic background, rather than prior achievements, predicts students' entry into socially elite institutions. She suggested that SES therefore served to "reemphasize the importance of students' ascribed status background" (p. 174). Further, students' goal commitments and levels of involvement directly influenced their persistence. In addition, institutional commitment contributed to individual involvement. Higher SES students entered institutions characterized by higher SES composition, greater academic orientation, and more cohesive environments. These factors increased students' attainment levels by encouraging involvement and goal commitment. Based on her analyses, Anderson warned that federal policies aimed at diminishing financial opportunities for students may exacerbate socioeconomic imbalances. By examining persistence in combination with status attainment theory, Anderson thus provides perspectives on the role that educational opportunities play in students' ability to attain higher social status or achievement.

Within the societal perspectives, Anderson (1988) combined the Tinto model with the literature on status attainment models. Her schema outlined the differences between the student persistence models and status attainment models and identifies opposing views in both perspectives generally. For example, she noted that status-attainment models focus upon the relationship between colleges and students' experiences and the extent that these mediate effects of ascribed social status. The Tinto model described student social and academic integration as mediating the effects of previous goals and commitments. Anderson did not offer resolution of potential conflicts between these views, nor did she present a proposal for altering the Tinto model. Instead, her results supported the Tinto model notions of integration, commitment, and institutional context while providing new contextual interpretation of these notions as seen through the status attainment lens. Thus, her use of status attainment models serves to elaborate upon and extend the importance of background characteristics without suggesting a need for creating new theory.

*Economic Theory.* The framework of economic perspectives includes financial as well as other types of costs associated with attending college. Within this frame, Braxton, Brier, and Hossler's (1988) work conceptualized "student problems" (p. 242) as costs associated with persistence. They used four variable sets derived from the Tinto model including background characteristics, initial commitment, academic and social integration, and subsequent commitments. Using multiple linear regression, the effects of these were held constant while the additional variable set comprised of student problems was examined for its influence on student withdrawal. The problems included not being able to take desired courses, not being able to enroll in courses at convenient times, difficulty balancing academic workload with home/work demands, being troubled by personal problems, difficulty financing college expenses, and difficulty taking desired courses. They hypothesized that students view these problems much as they might fiscal costs, and opt to drop out if such costs outweigh perceived benefits. The researchers' findings demonstrated indirect support for claims that institutional commitments carry greater weight than personal, psychological, or financial costs in student persistence decisions. Students apparently placed greater weight on the benefits rather than the costs of persistence, since none of the student problems exerted a statistically significant effect on persistence beyond the effects of student background characteristics, initial commitments, academic and social integration, and subsequent commitments.

The second and third studies define costs more directly as immediate fiscal impacts within the Tinto model. Cabrera, Stampen, and Hansen (1990) incorporated ability to pay in the variables of the Tinto model to determine whether it impacted student decisions about college. They hypothesized that ability to pay would moderate the effects of academic and social integration. Variables used in the study included institutional persistence, goal commitment, academic integration, social integration, ability to pay, institutional prestige, significant others' influence, and skills and abilities. Using logistic regression analysis, the three researchers found that students in the uppermost SES quartiles were less likely to withdraw than those in the lower quartiles. In addition, those students aspiring to bachelor's degrees who were satisfied with cost of attendance were slightly more likely to persist than those who were dissatisfied with costs. They found no evidence, however, that ability to pay had an effect on social and academic integration.

The economic analysis completed by Cabrera, Nora, and Castaneda (1992) used all variables of Tinto's (1975, 1987) student integration model but also included those from studies on attrition, significant others, financial aid, and urban commuter settings. The three researchers formulated a structural model with the variables institutional persistence, intent to persist, institutional commitment, goal commitment, academic integration, social integration, precollege academic performance, significant others' influence, and finances. The researchers used LISREL to estimate the parameters of the hypothesized relationships among the constructs and found that financial aid has a significant effect on persistence, impacting students' academic integration, social integration, and goal commitment.

Within the economic perspectives, Braxton, Brier, and Hossler (1988), Cabrera, Stampen, and Hansen (1990), and Cabrera, Nora, and Castaneda (1992) grounded their studies of student persistence in cost-benefit analysis. Results from the two former studies provided new information about the relationship between persistence and costs of acquiring an education. In this respect, they elaborate upon the existing model without creating a new theory of persistence.

The Cabrera, Nora, and Castaneda (1992) analysis, however, suggested a non-causal relationship between financial aid and precollege academic ability (p. 578). The Tinto model does not address such financial concerns specifically. While closer to combining multiple perspectives into an integrated theory, this analysis included constructs of the model without resolving potential differences in competing perspectives. The study did offer a modified version of the Tinto model, despite these drawbacks, suggesting that even though it does not meet the standard for a fully integrative work, additional research in this area may prove fruitful.

*Organizational Theory.* The organization's influence on students' socialization and satisfaction provides the basis for the third environmental grouping (Tinto, 1993, p. 89). Within this category, three articles combine organizational theory with the interactional model outlined by Tinto. All explore possible relationships between these perspectives within four-year institutions.

Braxton and Brier (1989) used five constructs from the Tinto model (1975) and a sixth construct drawn from the work of Price and Mueller (1981) and Bean (1980; 1983). The two researchers hypothesize that students' levels of institutional and goal commitment lead to varying degrees of interaction with three organizational attributes, resulting in academic and social integration. Using path analysis, the Braxton and Brier (1989) causal model predicted paths between the initial institutional and goal commitment and each of the organizational attributes of fairness in enforcing policies and rules, participation in decision-making, and communication. Results showed mixed support for melding the two perspectives: although organizational attributes carried one or more direct effects on social and academic integration, they did not show indirect effects on persistence. The authors speculated that organizational attributes may influence persistence in delayed sequence and suggested the need for further research.

In a similar effort, Cabrera, Castaneda, Nora, and Hengstler (1992) examined the convergent validity between Bean's Student Attrition Model (1982) and Tinto's model (1975, 1987). These researchers indicated that the roles of organizational commitment and students' commitments to the institution in the two models provide complementary functions. They also noted "significant overlap" (p. 159) in Tinto's concept of institutional commitment and Bean's concept of institutional fit and quality. Like Braxton and Brier (1989), noted in the previous study, Cabrera et al. emphasized that combining these two perspectives results in a more comprehensive understanding of the persistence process.

In the third study within this group, Cabrera, Nora, and Castaneda (1993) follow up the 1992 Cabrera, Castaneda, Nora, and Hengstler work. The researchers accomplish this by simultaneously testing Tinto's (1975, 1982) and Bean's (1982) models. They suggest a new baseline model that incorporates both theories. The models were tested via a two-step structural equation modeling strategy using LISREL VII. The final model indicates that the largest total effects on persistence were accounted for by intent to persist (0.485) and GPA (0.463). Institutional commitment (0.562) and encouragement (0.447) exert the larfgest effect on intent to persist. The researchers conclude that the combined theories offer a better understanding of the interplay among institutional, individual, and environmental factors in the persistence process.

Within the organizational studies, Braxton and Brier (1989), Cabrera, Castaneda, Nora, and Hengstler (1992), and Cabrera, Nora, and Castaneda (1993), and Cabrera, Castaneda, Nora, and Hengstler (1992) all specifically sought to mesh organizational and interactional theory. The Braxton and Brier work combined Bean's (1980, 1983) application of Price and Mueller's (1981) work into a single construct to underlie the Tinto model. Bean (1980, 1983) suggested that organizational attributes indirectly affect students' persistence. Braxton and Brier (1989) briefly described the original theories and modified both to develop a model of the student attrition process. They did not identify or resolve conflicts between the two views. Rather than true integration, then, this study appears to consider the Tinto model as the primary focus with Bean's (1980, 1983) constructs of organizational communication, fairness in policy and rule enforcement, and participation in decision-making elaborating these basic constructs. The results do not present a new theory but do indicate the need for additional research to account for potential weaknesses in the study.

Cabrera, Castaneda, Nora, and Hengstler (1992) explored the convergence of Bean's and Tinto's work. They outlined the similarities between the two models, pointing out that both regard persistence as a complex process over time, both regard student entry characteristics as integral to persistence, and both regard persistence as a product of student-institution fit (p. 145). The researchers also noted that the primary differences between the two perspectives regard which variables exert the greatest effect on persistence. Their analysis partially resolved conflicts between the perspectives and proceeded to modify both for inclusion in a new model.

Cabrera, Nora, and Castaneda (1993) followed the former study. They outline similarities and differences in Bean's and Tinto's theories in order to develop a more comprehensive theoretical model. They note the areas of overlap and identify those areas that appear to conflict, then suggest how those conflicts may be resolved. In this way these researchers appear to meet the integrative criteria.

## Summary

As we have seen, these theoretical perspectives result in varying degrees of inclusion and connection with the Tinto model. To some extent, all combine other theoretical views with the foundational theory in attempts to achieve a higher explanatory ability. Three studies examined components of students' psychosocial development within the Tinto theory, while six explored the broad category of environmental perspectives as defined by Tinto (1993). The six studies included a single study which related persistence to social status attainment. Also within the broad category of environmental perspectives, economic theory links to the Tinto model via cost-benefit analysis related to student problems and ability to pay. Organizational perspectives, defined as the impact the organization has on student socialization and satisfaction, comprised the third perspective in the environmental category. This grouping included two studies.

Based upon the criteria established for analyzing theory integration and elaboration, nearly 60 percent (6 of 10) of the reviewed studies match the criteria for elaboration by adding variables and altering constructs in the foundational theory to achieve a stronger explanatory and predictive ability. All three of the psychological category, Stage (1989), Brower (1992), and Peterson (1993) met these criteria. In the environmental category, three met the criteria for elaborative studies. Braxton, Brier, and Hossler (1988) and Cabrera, Stampen, and Hansen (1990) utilized economic theory perspectives to extend the model, while Braxton and Brier (1989) focused upon organizational constructs to elaborate the model. In meeting the criteria for elaborative work, these studies serve an important and significant function in our development of knowledge about the processes of student development, retention, and attrition by extending an existing theory.

Of the remaining studies, three met three or more of the four criteria for integration (see Table 4, page 138). The fourth study answered only two of the four criteria. Cabrera, Nora, and Castaneda's (1992) examination of the role of finances and Cabrera, Castaneda, Nora, and Hengstler's (1992) effort to converge Bean's model and Tinto's model rank close to theory integration. In both studies, the researchers described the original theories, identified the conflicts, and modified the theories to create a new model. They only partially resolved the conflicts and thus fail to meet the integrative criteria fully on this point. Cabrera, Nora, and Castaneda (1993), however, move an additional step forward by not only acknowledging but also consciously resolving conflicts between the two theories. Like the works that meet elaborative criteria, the works that meet integrative criteria build upon a single foundational model. In combining two or more theoretical views, however, these researchers move toward a more robust explanatory model by acknowledging and attempting to resolve potential conflicts between these views.

The fourth study, Anderson's (1988) consideration of status attainment models, met two of the four criteria. She described the original theories and identified the conflicts but neither resolved the conflicts nor modified the theory for a new model. This work also did not meet the criteria for elaboration, however, since it does not accept the premise of the Tinto model. While appearing to criticize Tinto's model as flawed, this work falls short of breaking new ground by integrating opposing views yet also fails to extend the theory. Thus, the researcher misses an important opportunity to add to our body of knowledge about the student departure process.

This analysis offers an alternative method for directing and viewing theoretical work and research. By establishing and applying criteria for assessing efforts to integrate or elaborate theory in the area of student departure, we have attempted to determine how we can make such efforts most useful from a practical as well as a theoretical stance. Individually, each of the reviewed works establishes additional information about persistence. Categorically, they also provide new perspectives and future directions for research. We believe this leads to developing stronger and better theory in future efforts.

## CONCEPTUAL CRITICISMS OF TINTO'S THEORY

In the previous two sections of this chapter we have addressed empirical issues pertaining to Tinto's theory: its internal consistency and efforts to integrate it with other theoretical perspectives. In this section, we turn our attention to conceptual criticisms of the model.

By far, most examinations of Tinto's theory of student departure have been empirical in nature; however, three scholars have focused primarily on conceptual critiques. We discuss and each critique according to its main characteristics and underlying assumptions, appraising the main arguments of the critic. The order of the three critiques reflects both a chronological order and a logical order in that each evaluation of the theory builds upon the previous critique and moves farther from Tinto's original (1975) formulation of the conceptual model.

### Vincent Tinto

The first critic of Tinto's model is Tinto himself; as Tierney (1992, p. 607) notes, "Tinto is the first to acknowledge that his model is not perfect." Tinto (1982, 1986, 1987, 1988, 1993) points out the scope and limitations of the theory. Each critique leads to clarifications and refinements of the previous iterations of the model.

In his first refinement (1982), Tinto notes that the (1975) model explains only certain modes or facets of attrition behaviors and addresses characteristic behaviors of individuals only as they interact with institutions (p. 688). Furthermore, he notes the shortcomings of the theory, stating that it underestimates the role of finances in student departure. He notes also that it fails to distinguish between student behaviors leading to transfer and those leading to dropout (p. 689). He argues as well that the model "fails to highlight important differences in the educational career that mark the experiences of students of different gender, race, and [socioeconomic status]" (p. 689), a point confirmed in our review of research on this model for gender, but unresolved for race/ethnicity. Finally, he notes that the theory is also insensitive to disengagement in the two-year sector (p. 689), a point given indeterminate confirmation in our summary of the empirical evidence. In fact, he states that "from the point of theory and method, differences between groups are sufficient to require separate analyses of group-specific behaviors and therefore separate models of student behavior" (p. 691). Nevertheless, at each point, Tinto refines his theory to take into account these limitations on the earliest statement of the model.

In 1986, Tinto notes that the 1982 improvement of the 1975 model "is also subject to some important limitations" (p. 367). He addresses particularly the failure of the theory in its second iteration to "take explicit account of either the formal organizational or external forces (e.g., external communities) which impact upon student participation in college" (p. 367). Consequently, he argues, the earlier version of the theory is not well suited to the study of non-residential institutions, nor to the study of departure among commuters (p. 367). Moreover, he asserts that the model is not pragmatic enough for strategic planners or policy makers. Third, in 1986, he points to the failure of the 1982 statement of the theory to account for the longitudinal nature of departure behaviors (p. 368). Although departure is longitudinal in nature, Tinto recognizes that his 1982 model does not account for distinctions in that process. In making this critique, he again prefaces an important reformulation of his theory to compensate for such limitations. While he notes that his 1982 model fails to account for the longitudinal nature of departure, he then advances Van Gennep's anthropological notion of tribal rites of passage to reformulate and refine the model. The purpose of each critique, therefore, is to extend the theory to meet the limitations he identifies.

In his 1986 statement, Tinto identifies shortcomings in his 1975 theory based upon research which is indirectly related to his model, drawing on other research as it relates to students' persistence patterns. In 1982, the extent of research based on Tinto's model was not of a volume sufficient to draw inferences for improving the theory. By 1986, however, Tinto did have access to tests of his model in research, although the theory extension and refinement which he performs in 1986 is not based upon empirical evidence derived from tests of his model. As a conceptual theorist, he could have made a stronger case, and perhaps should have made a stronger case for refining and extending his theory by referring to available research based on his theory as it already stood.

In 1987, and later in the second edition of his book, Tinto (1993) further elaborates upon the theoretical foundations set in the 1986 iteration of his model. In 1988, however, Tinto clarifies the nature of the stages of passage, arguing that they are not actual, observable periods, but merely "abstractions that necessarily simplify for purposes of analysis the more complex phenomena we understand as student departure" (p. 448). Tinto argues that his discussion of student problems is "intentionally categorical so as to emphasize the fact that most students are eventually faced with very much the same sorts of problems and experience similar types of difficulties, [which]...are as much a reflection of the process of persistence in college as they are of either the attributes of the persons experiencing them or the institution in which they occur" (p. 449). Tinto does, however, draw a distinction with respect to timing, claiming that the temporal quality of departure can vary for different types of students and institutions (p. 450). In so saying, he rightly acknowledges the simplifications he makes for the sake of the economy of theory and generalization. Whether or not the simplifications and generalizations he makes are justifiable is another matter, and one which is not at all clear from research on his theory. Notably, as in 1986, Tinto does not cite research based on his own model.

In each successive iteration and at each point of his critique, Tinto pursues one of two goals. He identifies weaknesses in the theory with the object of refining and improving various points, or he points them out in order to clarify the limitations for applying the theory. As he states, "Current theory cannot do or explain everything" (1982, p. 688). The limitations he identifies frequently reflect not the conceptual components of the theory but the imperfect or uninformed application of the theory to special situations or populations, such as the persistence of minority students, students at two-year colleges, and students at various points in their college career (1982, p. 689; 1986, p. 378; 1988, p. 450).

To summarize, Tinto fails at each stage in developing his model to use existing research based on an earlier statement of his theory to refine or extend that statement. Consequently, at each stage of refinement and extension, Tinto extends theory that has been empirically tested without using that research and assumes the validity of the theory as it stands. For recommendations on the refinement and extension of Tinto's theory based on empirical evidence of the model, see the recommendations for further scholarship at the end of the chapter.

### Louis C. Attinasi, Jr.

Attinasi offers a second non-empirical or conceptual critique of Tinto's model (1989, 1994) based in the methodological framework of grounded theory (Glaser and Strauss, 1967; Stern, 1980). From this perspective, according to Attinasi (1989, 1992), theories of psychosocial and cultural phenomena, such as departure, in higher education should originate from examination of those constituent populations and not from other cultural groups, such as tribal groups.

Attinasi (1989) states that his motivation for examining Tinto's theory is largely pragmatic. Attinasi cites Pascarella and Chapman's (1983) multi-institutional, path analytic study of Tinto's model to argue that the theory has brought only limited, modest success (pp. 249-50). He attributes the limited success of the model not to the limitations and scope considerations that Tinto enumerates but to the poor fit between the sociological and psychological concepts that Tinto borrows into his theory and the situations to which they are applied. In place of these "alien," tribal concepts borrowed from Van Gennep, Attinasi advocates building theory from "native" concepts drawn from what he terms "sociologies of everyday life" (1989, p. 251). By "native" concepts and "sociologies of everyday life," Attinasi is arguing that one should derive sociological concepts and explanations pertaining to student departure directly from the analysis of college students and not by analogy to concepts and explanations derived from other populations (1989, p. 250). He claims that Tinto's theory, by contrast, relies on rather tenuous analogies between student departure and other social or socio-psychological phenomena, namely, suicide (Durkheim) and tribal dynamics (Van Gennep). However, Attinasi fails to define criteria for drawing legitimate analogies, a key process of traditional theory building.

Attinasi's (1989) critique of Tinto's (1975) model focuses primarily on the manner in which Tinto constructs theory. Like Attinasi, Tinto (1987, 1988, 1993) recognizes the need for qualitative research into the issue of student departure and its connection with culture; however, where Tinto regards qualitative research as a useful tool for complementing and extending theory, Attinasi considers it to be the fundamental mode of theory-building and theory-testing (1989, 1992). Consequently, Attinasi criticizes Tinto's theory as having been "developed on the basis of, and tested with, data collected from institutional records and/or by means of fixed-choice questionnaires...methods of data collection that effectively strip away the context surrounding the student's decision to persist or not to persist in college and exclude from consideration the student's own perceptions of the process" (1989, p. 250). He considers the context of the student's decision and the student's perspective on that context to be the precisely the necessary focus of departure research.

Attinasi's critique of Tinto's theory is not mere nitpicking. He correctly understands Tinto as constructing a theory of student departure as an aspect of college culture and cultural dynamics. He disagrees not with the cultural focus, but on Tinto's means of examining culture, which Attinasi considers overly constrictive. The role of research methodology in Attinasi's argument, therefore, reflects his emphasis on the role of an individual's culture in the process of making meaning. As he states:

> Two assumptions, following from the research perspective, underlay the [more relevant mode of] study: (1) Persistence behavior is the consequence of a process in which the student is an active participant: He or she takes account of various things in his or her everyday world and acts on the basis of how he or she interprets them. (2) Persistence behavior is related to the manner in which the university becomes and remains, through everyday social interaction, a reality for the student. (1989, p. 251).

Consequently, Attinasi shifts the attention away from individuals in a uniform institutional culture to distinct cultures within a single institution.

The effect of Attinasi's perspective on culture and one's mode of research is nowhere more evident than in his discussion of social integration. Whereas Tinto asserts that social integration provides a framework for acquiring norms, morals, and values, Attinasi claims that "students become integrated for distinctly more cognitive, and less moral [i.e. values-oriented] reasons," namely for the formation of "cognitive maps" (1989, p. 268). Cognitive maps, broadly understood, are culturally imprinted means for making sense of one's external environment, personal interactions, and individual expectations and ideologies (Stea, 1969; Herman, Kail, and Siegel, 1979). Because of the nature and significance of one's distinctive culture in the process of cognitive mapping, Attinasi claims that only context-sensitive, grounded analyses are effective in adducing the subtle processes involved in persistence. Attinasi's support for this *a priori* claim is no stronger than Tinto's *a priori* claim that integration serves a normative function for students; each reflects a different perspective on culture and the mode of research. Currently, one cannot make a decisive argument based on the empirical evidence derived from tests of Tinto's theory to reject Tinto's claim or support Attinasi's.

Attinasi's 1994 evaluation of Tinto's theory, specifically, the use of Van Gennep's notion of "rites of passage," demonstrates Attinasi's openness to borrowing conceptual frameworks in order to apply them to his grounded analyses or "sociologies of everyday life." This examination of Tinto's model seems more inclusive of theoretical concepts derived from populations outside of higher education than Attinasi's earlier two articles. Nevertheless, Attinasi consistently maintains his earlier stance on the need for the "development of additional conceptual tools, particularly ones that are grounded in the experiences of students themselves" (p. 11). Tinto, on the other hand, builds his 1975 model on his synthesis of a substantial body of existing research on student departure. Attinasi's rejection of Tinto's model is a rejection both of the methodological means by which Tinto constructs theory as well as a rejection of the particular theoretical lenses through which Tinto analyzes existing student research, namely Durkheim's theory of suicide and Van Gennep's theory of rites of passage.

Although Attinasi's methodological concerns overlap in places with Tinto's own concerns, the conclusions he draws are understandably more radical. Where Tinto refines and clarifies his theory, Attinasi prefers to rebuild it. For Attinasi, Tinto's theory is inherently flawed, performing well only when the institutional culture is relatively homogeneous, a claim supported by Pascarella and Chapman (1983) and to some extent by our review as well. Attinasi's preference for a native or naturalistic mode of inquiry, derived from what he terms "sociologies of life," also reveals a concern for the constrictive effects of those cases in which "fixed data sources" fail to describe adequately the depth of the context (1989, p. 250). Tinto argues that exceptions are inevitable, and that no theory can be extended to cover all cases. Attinasi argues, however, that the exceptions are the most promising grounds for discovery; to ignore or underestimate these exceptions is to ensure only modest success in understanding student departure. Attinasi's verdict, then, is to start over and rebuild the theory conceptually from the ground up.

Attinasi's critique of Tinto's theory changes subtly from 1989 to 1994. The motivations that he claims for the critique are the difference. In 1989, he cites the "modest successes" of Tinto's theory as the evidence for the need to build new theory through different means. As noted earlier, Attinasi supports his claim that Tinto's theory is only modestly successful by citing Pascarella and Chapman's (1983) multi-institutional, path analytic study of Tinto's model, a study whose findings are corroborated by our own review of an even longer history of research; however, Attinasi's critique is much less thorough than the alternative methodology that he designs in response to the study. In 1994, however, Attinasi's conceptual argument follows not from an empirical base of evidence as in 1989, but actually appears to assume some usefulness of Tinto's theory. In this case, Attinasi argues that Tinto's theory is faulty in its details, such as the actual manner in which the integration of students into college society is similar to Van Gennep's tribal group initiations. Attinasi's perspectives on interdisciplinary borrowing and comparative study, therefore, remain implicit in his discussion of grounded theory as a result.

To summarize, Attinasi finds fault with the theoretical foundations of Tinto's model to explain its modest successes. He varies somewhat in the particular aspects of his critique over the course of his commentary. The most significant and consistent element of Attinasi's perspective on student departure, however, is his insistence on adopting a qualitative, grounded analysis in building a new theory. Until Attinasi develops and demonstrates the successes of this theory further, one has little ground outside of *a priori* theoretical or methodological commitments to judge the validity of his critique. In the meantime, quantitative researchers are unlikely to be convinced by Attinasi's distrust of "fixed data sources" or his demands for grounded, naturalistic analysis in spite of the partial success of Tinto's model documented in this chapter.

## William G. Tierney

In his critique of Tinto's model of student departure, Tierney, a critical theorist, offers a radically different conceptual perspective from Tinto and Attinasi. Tierney focuses on the political and ideological implications of the constructs and epistemology undergirding Tinto's theory. As Tierney and Rhoads state: "Fundamental to critical theory is the notion of freedom and justice. The goal of theory is not just to enlighten, but also to enable people to seek justice, freedom, and equality" (Tierney and Rhoads, 1993). This perspective on the role of theory itself is altogether different from that of either Tinto or Attinasi, both of which subscribe to more traditional, mainstream notions of the role of theory (Kerlinger, 1986). Whereas Tinto and Attinasi approach theory with the goals of describing culture and explaining social behavior, the critical theorist also asserts that theory has a prescriptive function to identify marginalizing discourses, which by their nature systematically frame populations as "outsiders," and consequently liberate those populations oppressed by those discourses. Therefore, a fundamental tenet of critical theory is the contention that no theory is exclusively or purely descriptive; rather, one's perceptions of reality both shape and are shaped by one's discourse (Silberstein, 1988; Barrett, 1980; McConnell-Ginet, 1989). Furthermore, the critical theorist argues that to use a theory is to subscribe implicitly to the terms or epistemological foundations of that theory (Tierney 1992, 607). Thus, although Tierney's (1992) and Attinasi's (1989, 1994) critiques overlap a good deal, Tierney's perspective is distinct largely because of its theoretical orientation and consequently its explicitly political character. Tierney's critique is, therefore, a radical challenge of the very rationale undergirding Tinto's theory, attacking the very anthropological constructs which provide simplicity, conceptual elegance, and explanatory power in the sociological model. Tierney argues that these constructs are both prejudicial and invalid.

Tierney's political critique begins with an examination of Tinto's notion of ritual (1992, p. 603, pp. 607-609). He argues that Tinto incorrectly reinterprets this notion in the context of student departure with harmful implications, especially for understanding the persistence and departure of minority students. As Tierney states: "Social integrationists [such as Tinto] assert that all individuals—regardless of race, class, or gender—must undergo a 'rite of passage' in order to achieve full development in society" (1992, p. 607). Tierney (1992, p. 607) claims that this approach places responsibility on the individual to integrate into that set of values and attitudes as a matter of "individual fit" (Tinto, 1987, 1993). Attinasi argues that students who fail to integrate into the dominant culture tend to integrate, nevertheless, into cultural "enclaves" (1994, 11); that is, the nature of integration in an institution is perhaps more complex than either Tinto or Tierney acknowledges.

Tierney also criticizes Tinto's use of the notion of ritual on conceptual grounds. His critique is fourfold. First, Tierney argues that the basis for Tinto's notion of ritual, Van Gennep's "rite of passage," was never intended to refer to the passage of an individual from one culture to another (pp. 608-09). Consequently, he claims that Tinto's use of the notion is not valid in light of the implications for minority students in predominantly white institutions. Framing the college experience as a rite of passage, he argues, theoretically privileges one culture over all others because ritual is culturally specific. Therefore, if going to college is a rite of passage, then it is such only for members of that dominant or mainstream culture. If the college experience is not a rite of passage for the minority student, Tierney insists, then to assume it to be so is to assume that the member of one culture is immature or incomplete without ritual passage into another more valued culture. The difference between Tierney's and Tinto's understandings of the goals and functions of social theory is evident in this case. Attinasi, once again, cuts a useful path through the middle of the theoretical territory by arguing that students who are not members of the dominant society might "also experience college as a rite of passage but in the sense of a territorial movement from stranger to full membership in the college community and, perhaps, to full membership in the larger society" (1994, p. 10). By framing college as a common rite of passage, however, one might underestimate the cultural cost of integration to marginalized students. Both Tierney (1992, p. 616) and Attinasi (1994, p. 10) argue, therefore, for a truly multicultural college community, obviating the need for such a cultural integration in order to persist.

Second, Tierney criticizes the notion that one may "depart" from a ritual (pp. 609-10). As he points out, "Tinto assumes that for one reason or another some students will choose not to participate in a rite of passage and other students will not complete the ritual. Yet when one considers rituals in traditional cultures we find that an initiate neither chooses to participate nor to leave the ritual" (1992, p. 609). Attinasi (1994, pp. 9-10), however, argues that in many cultures, initiation into restricted groups or into foreign territories is often a voluntary rite of passage, and therefore analogous to college attendance. The problem, however, is that voluntary withdrawal from college attendance in Tinto's theory is also analogous to suicide, which is not the case in withdrawal from a rite of passage.

Third, Tierney criticizes Tinto's theory for its focus on college attendance as an individual matter rather than examining the role of groups, which he argues would be more consistent with a cultural theory of student departure (1992, p. 610). Tierney argues that "Tinto has conceptualized college-going at the individualist level rather than the collective one," resulting in the view that conformity is not only the norm, but also the responsibility of the individual (Tierney, 1992, p. 610). Although Tinto recognizes an individual's group membership, the cultural formations of the groups are notably absent from his discussion, although institutional culture plays a vital role in his model. The emphasis is clearly on the "individual" (Tinto 1986, p. 357), "the roots of individual departure," and a "theory of individual departure" (1987) (Tierney, 1992, p. 610). Tinto himself observes the failure of the theory to "highlight important differences in the education career that mark the experiences of students of different gender, race, and socioeconomic status" (1982, p. 689), an observation that our review confirms, but he fails to connect this shortcoming to the emphasis on the individual over the group. As long as Tinto's theory is framed as a cultural theory, Tierney's critique is a valid one; but, how one would rebuild the theory to form a different, more group-oriented analysis is not altogether clear from Tierney's critique.

Fourth, Tierney criticizes Tinto's failure to acknowledge that he brings a nativist or insider's perspective to "native rituals" (1992, p. 610). Tinto analyzes a cultural aspect of higher education as a member of that culture without acknowledging or accounting for how this might affect his analysis. The point that Tierney is making is not that a nativist perspective is invalid, but that Tinto combines that stance with the analytical tools of an non-nativist framework. As Tierney states: "one may reject a cultural model that assumes that reality is socially constructed, but that cannot be done while at the same time one employs analytical tools that derive from those same cultural models" (1992, p. 611). This point again raises the need for considering a grounded theory approach to cultural aspects of student departure, a point made in Attinasi's (1989, 1992, 1994) critiques and mentioned here in Tierney's argument (1992, p. 611).

In his rejection of Tinto's use of the anthropological notion of ritual, Tierney appears to assume certain rules or principles of interdisciplinary borrowing which he neglects to enumerate or elaborate. Although he outlines the invalid use of the anthropological construct of ritual, he fails to demonstrate how one might legitimately use a construct from a related discipline. Additionally, because Tierney's conceptual critique proceeds from different epistemological foundations from those undergirding Tinto's model, his use of theory is unrelated in many instances to Tinto's. Tierney's anthropological critique of Tinto's socio-psychological theory raises questions for evaluating the conceptual underpinnings of that theory within the goals and assumptions Tinto himself appears to adopt. Because of the vast differences in their epistemological foundations, at various points, Tinto and Tierney "talk past each other" (Attinasi,1994, p. 4). Furthermore, Tierney's perspective is so radically different from Tinto's, how Tierney's critique might impact extensions or reformulations of Tinto's theory is not at all clear. Whereas Attinasi provides a middle ground for exploring different conceptualizations of Van Gennep's notion of rites of passage in rebuilding Tinto's model (1994), Tierney offers very little common ground with any earlier statement of the theory.

**Summary**

All three critics agree that more qualitative research should be performed on the phenomenon of student departure. However, the expected effect of this research differs across the three positions. For Tinto (1986, p. 378), the importance of performing qualitative research is to refine the existing theory, just as Tinto's own (1982, 1986, 1987, 1988, 1993) critiques refine and clarify the theory in successive iterations. For Attinasi (1989, 1992), qualitative research is the analytical tool for building a more relevant, more powerful descriptive version of the theory capable of performing better than the "modest successes" of Tinto's theory. This perspective is consistent with Attinasi's (1989, 1992, 1994) critiques, which rebuild and extend the theory from its conceptual underpinnings to the analytical tools to employ. For Tierney (1994, p. 611), qualitative research is necessary to make the cultural observations and analysis prompted by Tinto's important insights into the significance of culture in the phenomenon of student departure. Tierney's goal, however, is not to refine, clarify, or extend Tinto's theory, but to replace it with a cultural, anthropological model which also meets his goals as a critical theorist. Tierney's (1992) critique radically challenges the validity of Tinto's model on the basis of its rationale and internal coherence. A comparable, fully developed model based on a critical theory perspective, however, does not yet exist for scholars to weigh further the potential contributions of critical theory to understanding retention; and, such a theory is needed before scholars can fully determine the value of a student departure model derived from a critical theory perspective.

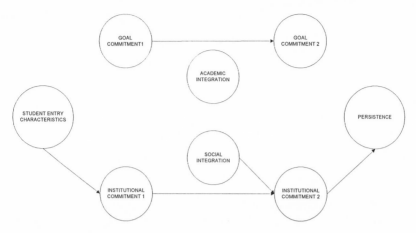

**FIGURE 2. Strongly Supported Propositions: Aggregated Single Institutional Tests**

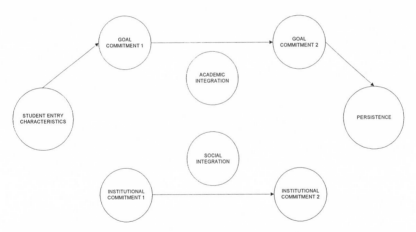

**FIGURE 3. Strongly Supported Propositions: Aggregated Multiple Institutional Tests**

## CONCLUSIONS

We offer the following eight conclusions from our assessment of Tinto's theory of college student departure:

1. In the aggregate, our assessment of empirical evidence regarding the 13 primary propositions indicates partial support for Tinto's theory. Moreover, the five relationships vigorously affirmed by single institutional assessments—including two of Tinto's core hypotheses (9 and 13)—also are logically interconnected with one another, as are three of the four propositions strongly backed by multi-insti-

tutional appraisals. Figures 2 and 3 illustrate this assertion.From the partial support rendered Tinto's theoretical schema, we also gain reliable knowledge about the phenomena of college student departure. Those propositions which are vigorously backed by either single- or multi-institutional appraisals provide such reliable knowledge.

2. Our appraisal also demonstrates partial support for Tinto's theory in residential, but not in commuter universities. Moreover, four of the five primary hypothesized relationships vigorously sustained in residential universities are logically interconnected with one another (5, 9, 10, 13). Two of these four relationships also are core propositions to Tinto's schema (9, 13). Reliable knowledge about the process of college student departure in residential universities also obtains.

3. Tests carried out using male and female college students offer frail support for Tinto's theory. Only one proposition is robustly backed by assessments made with male students, whereas no proposition is vigorously upheld by tests done with female college students.

4. Although Tinto's theoretical perspective possesses logical internal consistency, it lacks, in the aggregate, empirical internal consistency. This conclusion is tenable regardless of whether we consider multi-institutional or single-institutional assessments of the 13 primary propositions, as four of these primary propositions were strongly upheld by multi-institutional tests, and five of these primary propositions were robustly backed by single-institutional appraisals. Figures 2 and 3 graphically demonstrate this conclusion. Thus, revision of Tinto's theoretical formulations is indicated. Suggestions for revision are subsequently made in a later section of this chapter.

5. Given that residential universities afford strong empirical support to five of the 13 primary propositions, and commuter universities furnish robust backing to two of the 13 primary propositions, we conclude that Tinto's theory also lacks empirical internal consistency in both residential and commuter universities.

6. Tinto's theory also lacks empirical internal consistency across two groups of college students: females and males. Tests done with male college students afford strong support for only one of the 13 primary propositions, and assessments conducted using female college students failed to give robust affirmation to any of the 13 primary propositions.

7. From our assessment of the levels of integration and elaboration in studies seeking to extend Tinto's theory, we conclude that only one of these efforts s meet criteria for theory integration, yet others also demonstrate some success in elaborative efforts. They also point toward a need for continued efforts to integrate other perspectives with the Tinto theory in order to resolve some of the problems revealed in the chapter's earlier analysis. The environmental perspective, and specifically the economic and organizational constructs, appears to offer the greatest potential for future integrative efforts. Coupled with the strongly supported prop-

ositions, these perspectives may offer methods for either seriously revising Tinto's theory or for creating new theory with greater internal validity and consistency.

8. The lack of empirical support for many of the propositions in Tinto's theory brings one back to the conceptual critiques for further direction in analyzing the cultural aspects of student departure. Most of the empirical research on Tinto's model actually reflects upon only the earlier (1975, 1982) iterations of the theory. Tinto's later (1986, 1987, 1988, 1993) revisions, however, do not differ from these earlier versions with respect to the weaknesses uncovered empirically. Consequently, one should hesitate before applying Tinto's later refinements and clarifications in order to address these problems in the model.

Although the research fails to empirically support the internal consistency of Tinto's (1975) theory, does the evidence then support Attinasi's (1989, 1992, 1994) critiques? Although Attinasi rebuffs the radical rejection found in Tierney's (1994) critique, he advocates a middle ground between Tinto and Tierney. Without totally rejecting the theory, as Tierney does, Attinasi (1994) finds fault with Tinto's understanding of integration and ritual and appears to reconstruct these notions differently. However, current research does not indicate whether Attinasi's constructs would be any more useful than Tinto's for understanding the cultural aspects of student departure.

In spite of the lack of evidence to support adopting Tinto's later revisions, should one, then, accept Tierney's (1992) critique and directions for further research? Recall that Tierney does not advocate another theory like Tinto's model, but a radically different theory with a completely different set of assumptions. In part, Tierney's critique fits very well with the failure of many of Tinto's propositions as well as with the success of evidence supporting social integration when referring only to members of the dominant culture. What a critical theory perspective on cultural aspects of student departure would entail still remains to be formulated.

## RECOMMENDATIONS FOR FURTHER SCHOLARSHIP

We offer the following six recommendations for further scholarship:

1. Although the empirical internal consistency of Tinto's set of formulations is tenuous, we do not recommend their total abandonment. We do, however, recommend revision. Those logically interrelated propositions which are furnished robust empirical backing provide a starting point for such revision. Figures 2 and 3 could be used as a foundation for such revision.

Such revision might also entail attempts to integrate these strongly backed propositions with the tenets of other theoretical perspectives on student departure. Continued theory elaboration and integration offer opportunities to enhance the theory's explanatory power by continually combining new disciplinary perspectives. The organizational, economic and psychological perspectives on the phenomena of student departure are such possibilities. Such efforts should use the criteria for theory integration and elaboration employed herein.

Psychological, social and organizational forces not directly derived from other theories of student departure might also be used in revision of Tinto's theory. Such forces which directly affect either social integration or subsequent commitments— institutional and goal—are of particular importance.

2. Because academic and social integration are the crux of the interactionalist perspective, scholars should also conduct a review of studies to determine the extent of empirical support for a direct influence of academic and social integration on student persistence. If such backing is substantial, then such a review might also focus on the delineation of those factors which foster or impede academic or social integration. The findings of such an assessment might also assist scholars in their efforts to revise Tinto's theory.

3. Although Tinto's theory lacks empirical internal consistency in residential and commuter universities, such consistency remains an open question for liberal arts colleges and two-year colleges. Tables 2A and 2B (pp. 134-135) attest to indeterminate support for the various propositions, and therefore bolster this contention. Some scholars may want to conduct tests of the 13 primary propositions using liberal arts colleges and two-year colleges to more fully assess the empirical internal consistency of Tinto's theoretical schema in these institutional settings. However, other scholars may decide that the better course of action is to seriously revise Tinto's theoretical schema without making additional propositional appraisals in these two types of colleges and universities.

4. Some scholars may also want to carry out assessments of the 13 primary propositions using different student ethnic/racial groups. As indicated by Table 3, the empirical internal consistency of Tinto's theory is indeterminate for both African Americans and Native Americans/Alaskan natives. Once again, scholars may elect to engage in theory revision rather than further tests of the 13 propositions of Tinto's model. Alternately, some scholars may which to develop and test a theory of minority group student college departure using other theoretical perspectives.

5. Individual researchers should develop ongoing research within defined perspectives, focusing efforts within organizational or economic perspectives, for example. This would allow multiple refinements that continuously build upon previous work, rather than piecemeal efforts that may build toward a stronger theory. Such definition offers the advantages of increasing validity and reliability in designing integrative studies in a variety of settings. It also builds a body of knowledge around specific theoretical perspectives that may ultimately enable us to redefine what we know.

6. As we pursue efforts toward theory integration and elaboration, we must be more explicit in how we address the differences as well as the similarities between disciplines. Identifying and reconciling the differences may lead us in

additional directions for developing student departure theory.

## CLOSING THOUGHTS

Although we recommend revision of Tinto's perspective as a social science theory, we do not suggest that it be abandoned as an organizing framework for institutional research at individual colleges and universities. The 13 primary formulations of Tinto's theory may still be useful to understanding the college student departure process at a given college or university.

Regardless of the future of Tinto's theory, college student departure still remains an important phenomena to be understood.

Through a greater understanding of the departure puzzle, individual colleges and universities can better manage their enrollments. Moreover, scholars will come to better understand not only this phenomena, but also will come to have a window on other facets of the college student experience.

### References

Allen, D.F. (1986). Attrition at a commuter institution: A path analytic validation of Tinto's Theoretical Model of College Withdrawal. Paper presented at the Meeting of the American College Personnel Association, Los Angeles, CA.

Allen, D.F., and Nelson, J.M. (1989). Tinto's model of college withdrawal applied to women in two institutions. *Journal of Research and Development in Education* 22(3): 1-11.

Anderson, K.L. (1987). Persistence, student background and integration/commitment: Variation by definition of persistence and institutional type. Paper presented at the Annual Meeting of the Association for the Study of Higher Education, Baltimore, MD.

Anderson, K.L. (1988). The impact of colleges and the involvement of male and female students. *Sociology of Education* 61: 160-177.

Anderson, M.S., and Louis, K.S. (1991). The changing locus of    control over faculty research: From self-regulation to    dispersed influence. In *Higher Education: Handbook of    Theory and Research*, Vol. 7, edited by J.C. Smart, 57-101. New York: Agathon Press.

Attinasi, L.C., Jr. (1989). Getting in: Mexican Americans' perceptions of university attendance and the implications for freshman year persistence. *Journal of Higher Education* 60: 247- 77.

Attinasi, L.C., Jr. (1992). Rethinking the study of the outcomes of college attendance. *Journal of College Student Development* 33: 61-70.

Attinasi, L.C., Jr. (1994). Is going to college a rite of passage? Paper presented at the Annual Meeting of the American Educational Research Association, New Orleans, LA.

Barrett, M. (1980). *Women's Oppression Today: Problems in Marxist Feminist Analysis.* London: Verso.

Bean, J.P. (1980). Dropouts and turnover: The synthesis and test of a causal model of student attrition. *Research in Higher Education* 12: 155-187.

Bean, J.P. (1982). Conceptual models of student attrition: How theory can help the institutional researcher. In E. T. Pascarella (ed.), *Studying student attrition* (pp. 17-33). San Francisco: Jossey-Bass.

Bean, J.P. (1983). The application of a model of turnover in work organizations to the student attrition process. *Review of Higher Education* 6: 129-148.

Braxton, J.M., and Brier, E.M. (1989). Melding organizational and interactional theories of student attrition: A path analytic study. *Review of Higher Education* 13(1): 47-61.

Braxton, J.M., Brier, E.M., and Hossler, D. (1988). The influence of student problems on student withdrawal decisions: An autopsy on "autopsy studies." *Research in Higher Education* 28(3): 241- 253.

Braxton, J.M., Duster, M., and Pascarella, E.T. (1988). Causal modeling and path analysis: An introduction and an illustration in student attrition research. *Journal of College Student Development, 29*, 263-272

Braxton, J.M., Vesper, N., and Hossler, D. (1995). Expectations for college and student persistence. *Research in Higher Education*36: 595-612.

Brower, A. (1992). The "second half" of student integration. *Journal of Higher Education* 63(4): 441-462.

Cabrera, A.F., Castaneda, M.B., Nora, A., and Hengstler, D. (1992). The convergence between two theories of college persistence. *Journal of Higher Education* 63(2): 143-164.

Cabrera, A., and Nora, A. (1994, November). The role of perceptions of prejudice and discrimination on the adjustment of minority students to college. Paper presented at the Annual Meeting of the Association for the Study of Higher Education, Tucson, AZ.

Cabrera, A.F., Nora, A., and Castaneda, M.B. (1992). The role of finances in the persistence process: A structural model. *Research in Higher Education* 33(5): 571-593.

Cabrera, A.F., Nora, A., and Castaneda, M.B. (1993). College persistence: structural equations modeling test of an integrated model of student integration. *Journal of Higher Education* 64(2): 123-139.

Cabrera, A.F., Stampen, J.O., and Hansen, W.L. (1990). Exploring the effects of ability to pay on persistence in college. *Review of Higher Education* 13(3): 303-336.

Cash, R.W., and Bissel, H.L. (1985). *Testing Tinto's model of attrition on the church-related campus*. Paper presented at the Annual Forum of the Association for Institutional Research, Portland, OR.

Donovan, R. (1984). Path analysis of a theoretical model of persistence in higher education among low-income black youth. *Research in Higher Education* 21(3): 243-259.

Durkheim, E. (1951). *Suicide*. Translated by J. A. Spaulding and G. Simpson. Glencoe: The Free Press.

Elliott, D. (1985). The assumption that theories can be combined with increased explanatory power: Theoretical integrations. In R. F. Meier (ed.), *Theoretical Methods in Criminology* (pp. 123- 150). Beverly Hills, CA: Sage.

Farnworth, M. (1989). Theory integration versus model building. In S. F. Messner, M. D. Krohn, and A.E. Liska (eds.), *Theoretical Integration in the Study of Deviance and Crime* (pp. 93-100). Albany, NY: State University of New York Press.

Fox, R.N. (1986). Application of a conceptual model of college withdrawal to disadvantaged students. *American Educational Research Journal* 23(3): 414-424.

Getzlaf, S.B., Sedlacek, G.M., Kearney, K.A., and Blackwell, J.M. (1984). Two types of voluntary undergraduate attrition: Application of Tinto's model. *Research in Higher Education* 20(3): 257-268.

Glaser, B.G., and Strauss, A.L. (1967). *The Discovery of Grounded Theory: Strategies for Qualitative Research*. New York: Aldine.

Grossett, J.M. (1991). Patterns of integration, commitment, and student characteristics and retention among younger and older students. *Research in Higher Education* 32(2): 159-178.

Halpin, R.L. (1990). An application of the Tinto model to the analysis of freshman persistence in a community college. *Community College Review* 17(4): 22-32.

Hearn, J.C. (1990). Pathways to attendance at the elite colleges. In P.W. Kingston and L.S. Lewis (eds.), *The high-status track: Studies of elite schools and stratification* (pp. 121-146). Albany, NY: State University of New York Press.

Herman, J.F., Kail, R.V., and Siegel, A.W. (1979). Cognitive maps of a college campus: A new look at freshman orientation. *Bulletin of the Psychonomic Society* 13: 183-86.

Kerlinger, F.L. (1986). *Foundations of Behavioral Research* (3rd ed.). New York: Holt, Rinehart, and Winston.

Kuhn, T. (1970). *The Structure of Scientific Revolutions*. Chicago: University of Chicago Press.

Liska, A.E., Krohn, M.D., and Messner, S.F. (1989). Strategies and requisites for theoretical integration in the study of crime and deviance (pp. 1-19). In S.F. Messner, M.D. Krohn, and A.E. Liska (eds.), *Theoretical Integration in the Study of Deviance and Crime: Problems and Prospects*. Albany, NY: State University of New York Press.

Mallette, B.I., and Cabrera, A.F. (1991). Determinants of withdrawal behavior: An Exploratory Study. *Research in Higher Education* 32(2): 179-194.

McConnell-Ginet, S. (1989). The sexual (re)production of meaning: A discourse-based theory. In F. Fank and P. Treichler (eds.), *Language, Gender, and Professional Writing: Theoretical Approaches and Guidelines* (pp. 35-50). New York: Modern Language Association.

McDonough, P.M. (1994). Buying and selling higher education: The social construction of the college applicant. *The Journal of Higher Education* 65(4): 427-446.

Munro, B.H. (1981). Dropouts from higher education: Path analysis of a national sample. *American Educational Research Journal*18(2): 133-141.

Nora, A., Attinasi, L.C., and Matonak, A. (1990). Testing qualitative indicators of precollege factors in Tinto's attrition model: A community college student population. *Review of Higher Education*13(3): 337-355.

Pascarella, E.T. (1985). Racial differences in factors associated with bachelor's degree completion: A nine-year follow- up. *Research in Higher Education* 23(4): 351-373.

Pascarella, E.T., and Chapman, D.W. (1983a). Validation of a theoretical model of college withdrawal: Interaction effects in a multi-institutional sample. *Research in Higher Education* 19(1): 25-48.

Pascarella, E.T., and Chapman, D.W. (1983b). A multi-institutional, path analytic validation of Tinto's model of college withdrawal. *American Educational Research Journal* 20: (1), 87-102.

Pascarella, E. T., Duby, P. B., and Iverson, B. K. (1983). A test and reconceptualization of a theoretical model of college withdrawal in a commuter institution setting. *Sociology of Education* 56: 88-100.

Pascarella, E.T., Smart, J.C., and Ethington, C.A. (1986). Long-term persistence of two-year college students. *Research in Higher Education* 24(1): 47-71.

Pascarella, E.T., and Terenzini, P.T. (1977). Patterns of student-faculty informal interaction beyond the classroom and voluntary freshman attrition. *Journal of Higher Education* 48(5): 540-552.

Pascarella, E.T., and Terenzini, P.T. (1979a). Student-faculty informal contact and college persistence: A further investigation. *Journal of Educational Research* 72(4): 214-218.

Pascarella, E.T., and Terenzini, P.T. (1979b). Interaction effects in Spady's and Tinto's conceptual models of college dropout. *Sociology of Education* 52(4): 197-210.

Pascarella, E.T., and Terenzini, P.T. (1980). Predicting freshmen persistence and voluntary dropout decisions from a theoretical model. *The Journal of Higher Education* 51(1): 60-75.

Pascarella, E.T., and Terenzini, P.T. (1983). Predicting voluntary freshman year persistence/withdrawal behavior in a residential university: A path analytic validation of Tinto's model. *Journal of Educational Psychology* 75(2): 215-226.

Pascarella, E.T., and Terenzini, P.T. (1991). *How College Affects Students*. San Francisco: Jossey Bass.

Pascarella, E.T., Terenzini, P.T., and Wolfle, L.M. (1986). Orientations to college and freshman year persistence/withdrawal decisions. *Journal of Higher Education* 57(2): 156-175.

Pavel, M. (1991). *Assessing Tinto's model of institutional departure using American Indian and Alaskan Native longitudinal data.* Paper presented at the Annual Meeting of the Association for the Study of Higher Education, Boston, MA.

Pervin, L. and Rubin, D. (1967). Student dissatisfaction with college and college dropout: a transactional approach. *The Journal of Social Psychology* 72: 285-295.

Peterson, M.W. (1985). Emerging developments in postsecondary    organization theory and research: fragmentation or    integration. *Educational Researcher* 14: 5-12.

Peterson, S.L. (1993). Career decision-making self-efficacy and institutional integration of underprepared college students. *Research in Higher Education* 34(6): 659-675.

Price, J.L, and Mueller, C.W. (1981). A causal model of turnover for nurses. *Academy of Management Journal* 24: 543-565.

Rootman, I. (1972). Voluntary withdrawal from a total adult socialization organization: a model. *Sociology of Education* 45: 258-270.

Silberstein, S. (1988). Ideology as process: Gender ideology in courtship narratives. In A. Todd and S. Fisher (eds.), *Gender and Discourse: The Power of Talk* (pp. 125-149). Norwood, NJ: Ablex.

Spady, W. (1971). Dropouts from higher education: toward an empirical model. *Interchange* 2: 38-62.

Stage, F.K. (1988). University attrition: LISREL with logistic regression for the persistence criterion. *Research in Higher Education* 29(4): 343-357.

Stage, F.K. (1989a). Reciprocal effects between the academic and social integration of college students. *Research in Higher Education* 30(5): 517-530.

Stage, F.K. (1989b). Motivation, academic and social integration, and the early dropout. *American Educational Research Journal* 26(3): 385-402.

Stage, F.K. (1990). Research on college students: Commonality, difference, and direction. *Review of Higher Education* 13(3): 249- 258.

Stage, F.K., and Rushin, P.W. (1993). A combined model of student predisposition to college and persistence in college. *Journal of College Student Development* 34: 276-281.

Stea, D. (1969). The measurement of mental maps: An experimental model for studying conceptual spaces. In K. R. Cox and R. G. Golledge, *Behavioral Problems in Geography: A Symposium* (Northwestern University Studies in Geography, No. 17), (pp. 228- 53). Evanston, Illinois: Department of Geography, Northwestern University.

Stern, P.N. (1980). Grounded theory methodology: Its uses and processes. *Image* 12: 20-23.

Stoecker, J., Pascarella, E.T., and Wolfle, L.M. (1988). Persistence in higher education: A nine-year test of a theoretical model. *Journal of College Student Development* 29: 196-209.

Sweet, R. (1986). Student dropout in distance education: An application of Tinto's model. *Distance Education* 7(2): 201-213.

Terenzini, P.T. (1994). The good news and bad news: Implications of Strange's propositions for research. *Journal of College Student Development* 35: 422-427.

Terenzini, P.T., Lorang, W.G., and Pascarella, E.T. (1981). Predicting freshman persistence and voluntary dropout decisions: A replication. *Research in Higher Education* 15(2): 109-127.

Terenzini, P.T., and Pascarella, E.T. (1977). Voluntary freshman attrition and patterns of social and academic integration in a university: A test of a conceptual model. *Research in Higher Education* 6: 25-43.

Terenzini, P.T., and Pascarella, E.T. (1978). The relation of students' precollege characteristics and freshman year experience to voluntary attrition. *Research in Higher Education* 9: 347-366.

Terenzini, P.T., and Pascarella, E.T. (1980). Toward a validation of Tinto's model of college attrition: a review of recent    studies. *Research in Higher Education* 12: 271-282.

Terenzini, P.T., Pascarella, E.T., Theophilides, C., and Lorang, W. G. (1985). A replication of a path analytic validation of Tinto's theory of college student attrition. *Review of Higher Education* 8(4): 319-340.

Terenzini, P.T., and Wright, T.M. (1987). Influences on students' academic growth during four years of college. *Research in Higher Education* 26: 161-179.

Thornberry, T.P. (1989). Reflections on the advantages and disadvantages of theoretical integration. In S. F. Messner, M. D. Krohn, and A. E. Liska (eds.), *Theoretical Integration in the Study of Deviance and Crime* (pp. 51-60). Albany, NY: State University of New York Press.

Tierney, W.G. (1989). *Curricular Landscapes, Democratic Vistas: Transformative Leadership in Higher Education*. New York: Praeger.

Tierney, W.G. (1991). *Culture and ideology in higher education: Advancing a critical agenda*. New York: Praeger.

Tierney, W.G. (1992). *OfFicial Encouragement, Institutional Discouragement: Minorities in Academe—the Native American Experience*. Norwood, NJ: Ablex.

Tierney, W.G. (1993). The college experience of Native Americans: A critical analysis. In L. Weis and M. Fine (eds.), *Beyond Silenced Voices: Class, Race, and Gender in United States Schools*. Ithaca, NY: State University of New York Press.

Tierney, W. G., and Rhoads, R. A. (1993). Postmodernism and critical theory in higher education: Implications for research and practice. In J. C. Smart (ed.), *Higher Education: Handbook of Theory and Research,* Vol. 9. New York: Agathon.

Tinto, V. (1975). Dropout from higher education: A theoretical synthesis of recent research. *Review of Educational Research* 45: 89-125.

Tinto, V. (1982). Limits of theory and practice in student attrition. *Journal of Higher Education* 53(6): 687-700.

Tinto, V. (1986). Theories of student departure revisited. In John C. Smart (ed.), *Higher education: Handbook of Theory and Research,* Vol. 2. New York: Agathon Press.

Tinto, V. (1987). *Leaving College: Rethinking the Causes and Cures of Student Attrition*. Chicago: University of Chicago Press.

Tinto, V. (1988). Stages of student departure: Reflections on the longitudinal character of student leaving. *Journal of Higher Education* 59: 438-455.

Tinto, V. (1993). *Leaving College: Rethinking the Causes and Cures of Student Attrition* (2nd ed.). Chicago: University of Chicago Press.

Turner, V. (1977). *The ritual process: Structure and anti- structure*. Ithaca, N. Y.: Cornell University Press.

Van Gennep, A. (1960). *The Rites of Passage*. Translated by M. Vizedon and G. Caffee.

Chicago: University of Chicago Press.

Voorhees, R.A. (1987). Toward building models of community college persistence: A logit analysis. *Research in Higher Education* 26(2): 115-129.

Weidman, J.C., and White, R.N. (1985). Postsecondary "high-tech" training for women on welfare. *The Journal of Higher Education* 56(5): 555-568.

Weis, L. (1985). *Between two worlds*. Boston: Routledge and Kegan Paul.

Williamson, D.R., and Creamer, D.G. (1988). Student attrition in 2- and 4-year colleges: Application of a theoretical model. *Journal of College Student Development* 29: 210-217.

Zetterberg, H.L. (1965). *On Theory and Verification in Sociology*. Totowa, NJ: Bedminster Press.

# A Hierarchical Linear Modeling Approach to Studying College Effects

Corinna A. Ethington[*]

*University of Memphis*

A major flaw in the body of educational research attempting to study school and institutional effects has been the methodological dilemmas due to the hierarchical multilevel character of the majority of data used in such studies. The most comprehensive and possibly influential critique of this research was Leigh Burstein's 1980 article in the *Review of Research in Education* in which he argued that existing statistical models were simply inadequate for estimating the effects of schooling on students. He noted that the models used in school effects research had been single-level and based on the traditional linear model Ordinary Least Squares (OLS) approach which did not adequately match the realities under investigation. That is, the researchers had acknowledged the hierarchical nature of the organization of schooling by gathering data on students, classes, and schools and yet the statistical model reflected only a single level. However, this neglect of the hierarchical or nested nature of the data gathered reflected the limitations of the existing statistical techniques for the estimation of linear models with nested structures rather than a conviction on the part of the researchers that the single-level statistical model was appropriate. There simply were no viable alternatives.

While Burstein's (1980a) discussion focused on the research on school effects at the elementary and secondary level, the methodological concerns are also applicable to research focusing on the influence of college on students. This is perhaps most clearly manifested in the theories and models of student change in college that have been the basis for much of the college effects research. While the earliest research in this area was dominated by psychological developmental models focusing on intra-individual development (e.g., Chickering, 1969; Perry, 1970), the 1980s saw the emergence of college impact models that focus not only

---

[*]The author wishes to acknowledge the helpful comments of James Hearn, Ernest Rakow, and Patrick Terenzini.

on factors associated with individual students but consider the structural and organizational aspects of institutions as well as the climate or environment created by individuals within the institution. For example,

Pascarella's General Model for Assessing Change (1985) is a causal model that considers student learning and cognitive development as a function of student background and precollege characteristics, structural, organizational, and environmental characteristics of the institution, and aspects of student involvement. Similarly, Weidman's (1989) Model of Undergraduate Socialization includes the normative contexts of the academic and social environments of the institution, the major department, and peer groups as influences on student socialization outcomes.

Thus, the models themselves acknowledge the hierarchical character of the influences on college students' growth and development and research based on these models has necessarily involved data with nested structures. This is particularly true for studies utilizing multi-institutional samples of students where both student and institutional measures are considered as influential factors impacting student outcomes. But even single-institution studies could have a hierarchical nature given the organization of postsecondary institutions. Students are nested in classes, in majors, and in departments, schools or colleges within the institution. In *How College Affects Students*, Pascarella and Terenzini (1991) discuss the unit of analysis problem associated with the hierarchical nature of such data in their appendix on methodological and analytical issues, and suggest that differences in the units of analysis used in studies examining similar phenomena may have contributed to the lack of consistency in findings in some areas of research.

Pascarella and Terenzini (1991) go beyond just the unit of analysis issue, however, and even note the disparity in the organizational levels of post-secondary institutions and the type of measures generally used in college effects research. For example, summarizing the research on the influence of institutional characteristics on student learning, Pascarella and Terenzini (1991) review studies that vary in the unit of analysis used. They conclude that for four-year institutions the effects of attending different types of institutions are both small and inconsistent after one statistically controls for the characteristics of students. However, rather than summarily concluding that different types of four-year institutions have essentially the same impact on student learning, they offer alternative explanations for the absence of institutional effects. They point out that student precollege characteristics are not independent of the institution attended, and that the level of measurement of the institutional variables may be inappropriate. That is, the global college environment measure may have little impact on students given the subenvironments existing within institutions such as different majors and different living arrangements. They essentially are acknowledging the multilevel nature of the organization of schooling in postsecondary institutions and its impact on research on college effects.

As noted, higher education researchers have recognized the multilevel character of their data and have often grappled with the unit of analysis problem in studying the effects of institutional characteristics on student level outcomes. Some have chosen to use the student as the unit of analysis (the most common approach), assigning common institutional measures to each student within an institution. Others have aggregated student level data within institutions and estimated models based on the aggregate or institutional level data. But each of these approaches is unsatisfactory. Disaggregating higher order variables to the individual level violates the assumption of independence of observations that is a basic assumption for the classical OLS approach. The analyses fail to capture the positive intraclass correlations that result from the interdependencies among students within the same institutions, classes, majors, etc. These interdependencies are brought about by the common experiences of students within the same institutions and result in misestimated standard errors. Using institutional level variables to predict individual level outcomes also forces researchers to assume that all individuals within an institution are identically affected by the institutional level characteristics. This is an obvious error because even financial resources are differentially allocated to departments and colleges within institutions.

Aggregating the individual-level variables to a higher level and using that level as the unit of analysis introduces the aggregation bias problem where aggregate relationships generally are much stronger and can be quite different than those at the individual level. This is because the within-group variability that is often as much as 80 to 90 percent of the total variation is lost (for a more detailed discussion of the statistical limitations of using aggregate data see Hannan and Burstein, 1974, and Burstein, 1980a). The aggregation of variables is also problematic conceptually since disaggregated measures change their meaning when aggregated. Take for example the relationship between socioeconomic background and educational attainment. The student's socioeconomic background is a standard measure used in school effects research. It is considered to be a measure of the student's social class and a proxy for the educational and financial resources and experiences provided by the student's family. However, the average socioeconomic status of a student body represents a normative environment of the *institution* and this aggregate measure can have an impact on student attainment over and beyond that of the individual's background.

An early proposed solution to the analytical problems associated with multilevel data was what has become known as the "slopes as outcomes" approach to regression (Burstein, 1980a, 1980b; Burstein, Linn, and Capell, 1978; Burstein and Miller, 1980). Burstein and his colleagues recommended estimating a separate Ordinary Least Squares (OLS) regression equation for each school using only student-level predictors for a student-level outcome, and then using the regression coefficients from these equations as outcomes to be explained by school-level characteristics. This approach was very appealing in that it allowed the relationships among the student-level measures to be uniquely determined for each group utilizing only within-group variability, and the variability predicted by the school-level measures represented between-school variability without the noise from the within-school variance affecting the between-school equations. Burstein's approach also allowed the modeling of the interaction between the two levels; that is, how school-level characteristics affected the relationships among student-level characteristics.

However, this approach utilizing OLS regression was also incomplete. Because OLS regression coefficients are usually estimated with considerable error, one is limited in detecting effects of between-group characteristics. The variance of the coefficients consists of both true parameter variance and error. This coefficient variance needs to be separated into its components in order to accurately test the group-level effects, and the statistical model needs to be able to analyze this complex variance-covariance structure which OLS regression is unable to do. Thus, Burstein's proposal was not without its own difficulties and was abandoned in favor of more sophisticated estimation procedures that could more accurately model the structure of the data. A more complete discussion of the problems associated with Burstein's OLS "slopes as outcomes" approach can be found in Raudenbush and Bryk (1986).

The 1980s saw considerable advances in statistical theory and estimation procedures that led to a new class of statistical methods based on what has become known as multilevel or hierarchical linear models (see ]Bock, 1989 for an introduction to the alternative statistical methods). These statistical models more accurately represent the hierarchical organization of educational systems, and Dempster, Laird, and Rubin's (1977) EM algorithm provided the approach for the estimation of the covariance components. Today there are a number of statistical computing programs available for estimating multilevel models including BMDP-5V (Schluchter, 1988), GENMOD (Mason, Anderson, and Hayat, 1988), HLM (Bryk, Raudenbush, Seltzer, and Congdon, 1988; Bryk, Raudenbush, and Congdon, 1994), ML2 (Rabash, Prosser, and Goldstein, 1989), and VARCL (Longford, 1986). Kreft, de Leeuw, and van der Leeden (1994) compare and contrast these five programs and note that HLM is by far the most popular program used in the United States. It is the HLM approach to multilevel modeling that will be illustrated in the following sections. Statistical estimation and inference within this approach are based on the Bayesian estimation of linear models that was developed by Lindley and Smith (1972) and Smith (1973), and the variance component estimation procedure utilizes the Dempster et al. EM algorithm.

The approach utilized in Bryk et al.'s HLM (Hierarchical Linear Modeling) program is fully detailed in Raudenbush and Bryk (1986) and Bryk and Raudenbush (1992) and overcomes the most commonly encountered difficulties faced with multilevel data. Perhaps most importantly, the *unit of analysis* issue is not a problem. It is not necessary to worry about whether to use the student as the unit of analysis spreading institutional characteristics across students or to aggregate data to the institutional level. Multilevel modeling resolves the aggregation bias problem by decomposing any observed relationships between variables into separate student-level and institutional-level components. The *dependence among individuals* within groups which results in misestimated standard errors is not a problem because multilevel modeling estimates a separate equation within each group incorporating into the statistical model a unique random effect for each organizational unit and the variability in these random effects is taken into account when estimating standard errors; that is, parameter and error variances are estimated separately. *Heterogeneity of regression* (i.e., the magnitude of the effect being different for different groups) is specifically tested by examining the variation of the coefficients across groups and modeling any variation in coefficients as a function of group or institutional characteristics. Finally, the *different meanings and effects* of a variable resulting from using different levels of aggregation can be included in one model by using both the individual and aggregate measures.

## CONCEPTUAL UNDERPINNING OF HIERARCHICAL LINEAR MODELS

Since multilevel modeling is an extension of OLS regression, it is helpful to build an understanding of the HLM approach by first considering a simplistic bivariate OLS example, the classic example of the relationship between socioeconomic status and educational attainment. *Do students from higher socioeconomic backgrounds tend to reach higher levels of educational attainment than their lower-status peers, and is this tendency more likely in some types of institutions?* To answer the first part of our question we could estimate the bivariate regression equation,

$$EDATT = b_0 + b_1 (SES),$$

where the slope, $b_1$, indicates the amount of change in educational attainment for a unit change in socioeconomic status and the intercept, $b_0$, is the educational attainment for an individual whose socioeconomic status has a value of 0. This intercept is usually ignored in standard regression studies for it is usually meaningless. For example, suppose the SAT verbal score were used to predict educational attainment. The intercept would be the predicted attainment for a student who had an SAT of 0, but is meaningless since the minimum score on the verbal SAT is 200. A technique that allows the intercept to have substantive meaning is to rescale the independent variable so that a value of 0 represents its average value. This is often accomplished by standardizing the variable (converting all measures to z-scores), but one loses the metric in which the variable is measured. Another approach is to center the independent variable by subtracting the mean from each subjects' measure. With this scaling a value of 0 on SES represents average socioeconomic status and the intercept can then be interpreted as the predicted attainment for a student with average socioeconomic status. This interpretation is an important one in the HLM approach to multilevel modeling since it allows the intercept to be interpreted as the predicted outcome for the "average" student. For this reason all independent variables have been centered in the examples to follow.

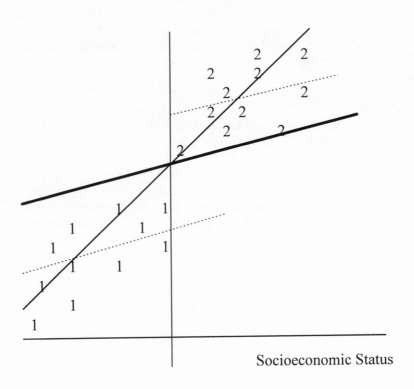

Attainment

Socioeconomic Status

——— Regression ignoring institutions
········ Separate within-institution regressions
▬▬▬ Average within-institution regression

**FIGURE 1. Within- and Between-Institution Socioeconomic Status-Attainment Relationship**

Attainment

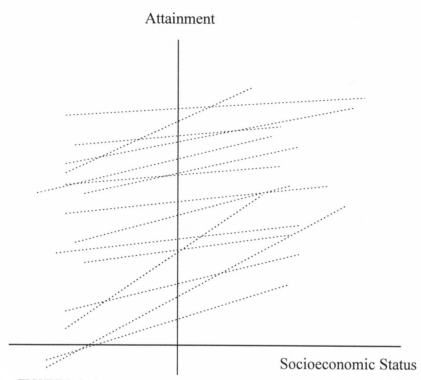

Socioeconomic Status

**FIGURE 2. Socioeconomic Status-Attainment Relationship for Students in Fifteen Institutions**

Suppose we have a sample of students from two institutions with measures on both their socioeconomic background and educational attainment and estimate the above equation, ignoring the fact that the sample represented two different groups of students, resulting in

$$EDATT = 2.09 + .45 (SES),$$

which indicates that there is a positive relationship between SES and EDATT with each unit increase in SES associated with a .45 increase in EDATT, and that a student of average SES has a predicted EDATT value of 2.09. This equation represents the relationship for the entire sample of students and does not recognize that the students come from different schools. The question then arises as to whether this is an accurate summary of the data for the sample of students. Examining a scatterplot of the data (Figure 1) we see that the two institutions are serving different student populations, one with lower socioeconomic status than the other. We also note that the relationship between the two variables is the same for each of these two schools (the slope of the dotted lines within each group is the same and the lines are parallel). The relationship is not as strong **within** each institution (the within school slopes are flatter than the slope of the composite sample, which ignores institutional membership), and it is evident that the composite relationship is inflated (the slope is steeper) when we ignore institutional make-up. The average within-institution regression more accurately reflects the relationship between socioeconomic status and educational attainment.

Even the pooled within-institution regression may be misleading because the relationship between the variables may differ across institutions (i.e., the slopes of the within-institution regressions could be different.) If we extend this example to the multi-institutional situation that is more usual in college effects research and estimate a separate equation for each institution, the plot of those equations might appear as in Figure 2. The institution whose regression is depicted at the top of the figure could be said to be a more egalitarian institution. Students within that institution reach comparable levels of attainment, regardless of their socioeconomic status, indicating an absence of a relationship between the two variables. The equations for several other institutions have relatively steep slopes, suggesting a stronger relationship between socioeconomic status and attainment. Thus, to answer our original question we must respond that whether or not socioeconomic status is related to educational attainment depends on the institution that students attend. We see some institutions with strong relationships, some with moderate, and some with almost none.

Examining the points at which the lines intersect the vertical axis (the intercepts), we also note that there are considerable differences in the attainment levels of students with average socioeconomic status across the various institutions (remembering that our data are centered and the intercept represents the predicted attainment of a student with average SES.) It can also be seen that differences between attainment levels of high and low SES students within a single institution (evidenced by the steepness of some slopes) are almost as great as that between institutions (comparing intercepts between institutions.) Thus, we see that the attainment levels differ across institutions as well as the relationships between socioeconomic status and attainment. The natural question then is what is it about the institutions that causes these differences. There is obvious variability in the slopes and intercepts of these equations, and it is this variability that is modeled in HLM using institutional level measures. Modeling the intercepts examines the question of how institutional practices or characteristics affect the average attainment levels of students, and modeling the slopes identifies those practices or characteristics that contribute to a more or less egalitarian institution.

## OVERVIEW OF THE HIERARCHICAL LINEAR MODEL

Multilevel modeling using the HLM approach for this example would first estimate the following regression equation for each institution:

$$\text{EDATT}_{ij} = \beta_{0j} + \beta_{1j}(\text{SES}_{ij}) + r_{ij}$$

where $i = 1,..., n_j$ students in institution j, and $j = 1,..., J$ schools. $EDATT_{ij}$ is the educational attainment for student i in institution j, $SES_{ij}$ is the socioeconomic status of student i in institution j, $r_{ij}$ is random error, and $\beta_{1j}$ is the relationship between SES and EDATT in institution j. This is a within-institution or Level-1 model and appears to be a standard OLS regression equation except that the within-institution regression coefficients are allowed to vary across institutions. The "average" coefficient is then tested to determine whether it is significantly different from 0. In the instances where an institution has too few students represented in the sample, the HLM approach improves the estimation of effects for small sample sizes by adjusting the estimates to be more similar to the estimation of effects for the total sample. That is, each coefficient is weighted proportional to its precision and for institutions with few students, the coefficient for that institution is estimated by "borrowing" information from the other data since similar estimates exist for other, larger groups (see Bryk and Raudenbush, 1992 or Raudenbush and Bryk, 1986 for a detailed explication of these estimation procedures.)

After the parameters of the equation have been estimated for each institution, the variance of the parameters across institutions is calculated and tested with a chi-square statistic to determine if the estimates are really different across institutions or if the variability is only due to chance. If there is non-random variability in estimates, a between-institution or Level-2 model is estimated. This model uses institutional measures to predict the coefficients of the Level-1 model. Given the apparent variability in both the intercept and the slopes across the institutions in our example, we could examine the possibility that the selectivity of the institution (or any other characteristics of the institution for which we have data) might impact the average attainment levels (the intercept) and the socioeconomic-attainment relationship (the slope) by estimating the following two equations:

$$\beta_{0j} = \gamma_{00} + g_{01} (SELECT_j) + u_{0j},$$

where

$\gamma_{00}$ is the overall intercept;

$\gamma_{01}$ is the relationship between selectivity of an institution and the average attainment of its students;

$u_{0j}$ is the unique effect of school j on average attainment holding selectivity constant;

and

$$\beta_{1j} = \gamma_{10} + \gamma_{11} (SELECT_j) + u_{1j},$$

where

$\gamma_{10}$ is the main effect of student socioeconomic status;

$\gamma_{11}$ is the effect of selectivity on the within-institution relationship between socioeconomic status and attainment;

$u_{1j}$ is the unique effect of school j on the socioeconomic-attainment slope holding selectivity constant.

As can be seen, this approach expands on the work of Burstein (1980a) and his "slopes as outcomes" conceptualization and goes beyond the OLS regression methods. The general HLM model is represented by a Level-1 model in which the student outcome is considered a function of student measures:

$$Y_{ij} = \beta_{0j} + \beta_{1j} X_{1ij} + \beta_{2j} X_{2ij} + \ldots + \beta_{Qj} X_{Qij} + r_{ij}$$

where

$Y_{ij}$ is the outcome for student i in institution j;

$X_{qij}$ are the values on the student-level independent variables measured for student i in institution j;

$\beta_{qj}$ are the intercept and regression coefficients representing the effects of the student-level independent variables on the outcome in institution j;

$r_{ij}$ represents random error,

and the Level-2 model where each Level-1 coefficient is considered a function of group characteristics:

$$\beta_{qj} = \gamma_{q0} + \gamma_{q1} W_{1j} + \gamma_{q2} W_{2j} + \ldots + \gamma_{qS} W_{Sj} + u_{qj}$$

where

$\beta_{qj}$ is the regression coefficient in school j;

$W_{sj}$ are the values on the institution level variables measured for institution j;

$\gamma_{qs}$ are the regression coefficients representing the effects of the institution-level variables on the within-institution relationships, $\beta_{qj}$;

$u_{qj}$ represents random error.

By centering the independent variables measured at the student-level (the $X_{qij}$) about their respective group means, the intercepts, $\beta_{0j}$, represent the mean outcome in respective institutions. Thus, modeling the intercepts in the between-institution Level-2 model examines the effects of institutional variables on average student outcomes. Modeling the remaining coefficients examines the extent to which the within-institution relationships are influenced by institutional characteristics. While the latest version of HLM can estimate models containing three levels (e.g., departments within schools/colleges within institutions), that representation is not illustrated in this chapter due to lack of access to data containing three organizational levels. The modeling of the third level is a straight-forward extension of the previous conceptualization in which the parameters of the Level-2 model are estimated by Level-3 measures and their variability examined across the Level-3 units.

In addition to the parameter estimation and significance tests, the reliability of the Level-1 coefficients, analogous to that of classical measurement theory, can be calculated by

$$\text{reliability of } (\beta_q) = (1/J) \ \Sigma \tau_{qq} / (\tau_{qq} + v_{qqj})$$

where $\tau_{qq}$ is the parameter variance and $v_{qqj}$ is error variance. These reliabilities will be close to 1 when the parameters vary substantially across Level-2 units or when the Level-2 sample sizes ($n_j$) are large.

# COLLEGE EFFECTS ON EDUCATIONAL ATTAINMENT: AN HLM EXAMPLE

To illustrate the process of multilevel modeling with the HLM framework, let's extend the original example of the relationship between student socioeconomic status and educational attainment. This example uses data from the 1971-1980 Cooperative Institutional Research Program surveys (Astin, 1982). Since the HLM program requires two raw data files as input and does not have the capability for general exploration and manipulation of data, all preliminary analyses checking, cleaning, and exploring the data and recoding and transforming variables were conducted using SPSS. Two raw data files were then created. The first dataset contained information on individual college students (the Level-1 file) while the second contained information on the characteristics of the institutions that those students attended (the Level-2 file). Each student's record must contain a common Level-2 ID that links the student to a particular Level-2 institution. While HLM contains two options for handling missing data in the Level-1 file, all Level-2 data must be complete. For ease of operation, the data sets created for this example contained only those subjects and institutions having complete data on the variables selected. The Level-1 sample consists of 3109 students attending four-year institutions, and the Level-2 sample consists of the 173 institutions attended by the above students.

The dependent variable used in the analyses is student educational attainment nine years after college matriculation and is measured on a scale ranging from 1 = high school graduate to 5 = Ph.D. or advanced professional degree. The Level-1 predictors of educational attainment represent both pre-college characteristics and measures of the college experience: socioeconomic status (SES), high school academic performance (HSACAD), college grade point average (COLGPA), college social involvement (SOCIAL), and a measure of general satisfaction with college (SATIS). The Level-2 variables included selectivity (SELECT), size (SIZE), percent graduate enrollment (PERGRAD), per pupil expenditure (EXPEND), student/faculty ratio (RATIO), and control (CONTROL, with 1 = public, 2 = private.) The analyses were conducted using HLM/2L (Bryk, Raudenbush, and Congdon, 1994).

## The Oneway Random-effects ANOVA Base Model

Three stages of modeling were incorporated in these analyses. The analyses began by first estimating a base model that is equivalent to a oneway random-effects ANOVA. This model has no Level-1 or Level-2 predictors, and the purpose is to model student-level variance in educational attainment as a function of variability within institutions or among students (pooling variances calculated within each institution) and variability due to between-institution differences. This decomposition of the total variance in attainment allows the determination of what proportion of that total variance is due to individual differences and what proportion is due to institutional differences. The within-institution variance component is then the basis for the calculation of the proportion of variance explained by student characteristics. This Level-1 equation is

$$EDATT_{ij} = \beta_{0j} + r_{ij},$$

where each student's attainment is characterized as a function of his or her institutional average attainment, $\beta_{0j}$, and a random effect, $r_{ij}$, that is unique to each individual. The variance of the random effects is denoted $\sigma^2$ and represents the pooled within-institution variance (or variance among students.)

At Level-2, the model is

$$\beta_{0j} = \gamma_{00} + u_{0j},$$

where each institution's average attainment, $\beta_{0j}$, is considered to be a function of the grand mean, $\gamma_{00}$, and a random error associated with each institution, $u_{0j}$. The variance of the institutional random effects is denoted $\tau_{00}$ and represents the between-institution variance, or variance of institutional means. This model is often referred to as a fully unconditional model since there are no student characteristics used as predictors at Level-1 nor any institutional characteristics used as predictors at Level-2. Table 1 presents the results of the estimation of this initial base model.

**Table 1: Estimation of Oneway Random-effects ANOVA Base Model of Educational Attainment**

| Fixed Effect | Coefficient | S.E. | t-ratio | Reliability |
|---|---|---|---|---|
| Institutional mean attainment ($\gamma_{00}$) | 3.095 | .032 | 97.71*** | .688 |
| Random Effects | Variance | DF | Chi-square | |
| Between institution ($\tau_{00}$) (variance of intercepts) | .119 | 172 | 655.80*** | |
| Within institution ($\sigma^2$) | .781 | | | |

*** p < .001

The estimate of the grand mean of educational attainment across all institutions (the fixed effect) is 3.095 representing an average of approximately a bachelor's degree, and the overall reliability with which the institutional means are measured is .688. The estimates for the between- and within-institution variances (the random effects) are .119 and .781, respectively. This between-institution variance represents the variance of the intercepts, $\beta_{0j}$, or the variability of the mean educational attainment levels across institutions. Using these parameter estimates the intraclass correlation can be calculated, which in this instance represents the proportion of variance in educational attainment that is due to between-institution differences:

$$\rho = \tau_{00}/(\tau_{00} + \sigma^2) = .119/(.119 + .781) = .132.$$

Thus, we see that 13 percent of the variance in attainment is a function of between institution differences ($\tau_{00}$ represents the variance of the intercepts and $\sigma^2$ is the pooled within-institution variance). The large-sample chi-square test on the between-institution variance component is significantly different from 0 at p < .001 indicating that the average educational attainment of students within institutions varies significantly across institutions. This variability of institutional means will subsequently be modeled by using institutional measures to predict the $\beta_{0j}$.

## A Random-Coefficients Model

The second model estimated is a full Level-1 model using the students' characteristics to predict the students' educational attainment. Considering students' educational attainment to be a function of socioeconomic background, high school academic performance, college academic performance, college social involvement, and general satisfaction with experiences at the institution, the following equation is estimated for each institution:

$$EDATT_{ij} = \beta_{0j} + \beta_{1j}(SES_{ij}) + \beta_{2j}(HSACAD_{ij}) + \beta_{3j}(COLGPA_{ij}) + \beta_{4j}(SOCIAL_{ij}) + \beta_{5j}(SATIS_{ij}) + r_{ij}.$$

Since each of the student-level predictors is centered about the institutional mean, the intercepts still represent the institution mean attainment levels. This model is referred to as a random coefficients model since each of the $\beta_{qj}$ are allowed to vary across the institutions and are considered to be a function of only a grand mean and a random error:

$$\beta_{qj} = \gamma_{q0} + u_{qj}.$$

The parameters of the Level-1 equations are averaged across schools and the average within-institution regression equation is presented in Table 2 as the *fixed effects*. Since we do not assume that the student-level effects are constant across institutions (there is an option within HLM to specify that they **not** be allowed to vary), the variance of the coefficients is calculated, separating parameter variance from error variance, and is tested to determine whether the effects of the student measures vary across institutions. These variances and the chi-square tests are also presented in Table 2 as the *random effects*.

**Table 2: Estimation of Random-coefficients Model of Educational Attainment**

| Fixed Effects | Coefficient | S.E. | t-ratio | Reliability |
|---|---|---|---|---|
| Institutional mean attainment ($\gamma_{00}$) (intercept) | 3.093 | .032 | 97.75*** | .767 |
| Effects of student-level variables | | | | |
| SES ($\gamma_{10}$) | .056 | .022 | 2.53* | .097 |
| HSACAD ($\gamma_{20}$) | .016 | .024 | .67 | .087 |
| COLGPA ($\gamma_{30}$) | .296 | .019 | 15.37*** | .106 |
| SOCIAL ($\gamma_{40}$) | .124 | .016 | 7.64*** | .079 |
| SATIS ($\gamma_{50}$) | .061 | .045 | 1.33 | .160 |
| Random Effects | Variance | DF | Chi-square | |
| Between institution ($\tau_{00}$) (variance of intercepts) | .129 | 160 | 786.24*** | |
| SES slope | .010 | 160 | 174.09 | |
| HSACAD slope | .010 | 160 | 140.12 | |
| COLGPA slope | .008 | 160 | 170.25 | |
| SOCIAL slope | .004 | 160 | 152.41 | |
| SATIS slope | .069 | 160 | 164.70 | |
| Within institution ($\sigma^2$) | .628 | | | |

\* p < .05; \*\*\* p < .001

Examining the fixed effects, we see again that the average attainment level is approximately a bachelor's degree (3.093) and that one's socioeconomic background, college grade point average, and social involvement all have positive significant effects on educational attainment. The within-institution or student-level variance is now .628. Remembering that in the base Oneway ANOVA model where we decomposed the total variance in educational attainment into a component due to within-institution or individual differences and a component due to between-institution differences, the within-institution variance estimate was .781 (see Table 1, p. 176). The reduction in this within-institution variance represents the student-level variance that is explained by the student-level measures. Thus, the proportion of variance explained is

Proportion explained = (.781 - .628)/.781 = .195

Thus, the five student measures have explained approximately 19.5 percent of the pooled within-institution variability in educational attainment. The between-institution variance is .129 (the difference between this value and the previous estimate of .119 is due the fact that the random effects model has more equations defining the model and more parameters to estimate and is within normal random error variability) and is significant, again indicating that there are still true differences in the mean educational attainment levels across institutions. However, the variances of the slopes of the five student measures are all non-significant, indicating that their variability across institutions is noise and not true parameter variance. Substantively, this indicates that the importance of any of these student characteristics to educational attainment is not a function of the type of institution attended, but is consistent regardless of the institution. The reliability indices indicate that the mean attainment levels are highly reliable, .767. Since there is no variability of the remaining coefficients across institutions, as expected, the coefficients are less reliable indicating that the variance in the parameters is due to sampling variance.

## The Random-intercept Model

The third and final analysis contains both student-level and institutional level variables. The student-level model (Level-1) remains the same as before. However, since none of the coefficients for the student measures varied across institutions, the variances of those coefficients are now specified to be 0 and there are no Level-2 predictors for these parameters. That is, after first allowing the coefficients to vary across institutions in the previous analysis and seeing by the chi-square test that there is no parameter variance, the option to specify no variability in the coefficients across institutions is invoked in this analysis. Only the intercept or mean institutional attainment is modeled by the six institutional characteristics since the chi-square test indicated that the value of the intercept did vary across institutions. This is a random-intercept model since only the intercept is allowed to vary across institutions, and both the student and institutional variables are centered allowing the intercept to be interpreted as the average attainment across institutions. The following equations describe the model estimated in this final stage of the analyses:

Level-1 Model

$$EDATT_{ij} = \beta_{0j} + \beta_{1j}(SES_{ij}) + \beta_{2j}(HSACAD_{ij}) + \beta_{3j}(COLGPA_{ij}) + \beta_{4j}(SOCIAL_{ij})$$
$$+ \beta_{5j}(SATIS_{ij}) + r_{ij}.$$

Level-2 Model

$$\beta_{0j} = \gamma_{00} + \gamma_{01} SELECT_j + \gamma_{02} SIZE_j + \gamma_{03} PERGRAD_j + \gamma_{04} EXPEND_j$$
$$+ \gamma_{05} RATIO_j + \gamma_{06} CONTROL_j + u_{0j}$$
$$\beta_{1j} = \gamma_{10}$$
$$\beta_{2j} = \gamma_{20}$$
$$\beta_{3j} = \gamma_{30}$$
$$\beta_{4j} = \gamma_{40}$$
$$\beta_{5j} = \gamma_{50}$$

The results of this final analysis are given in Table 3. The between institution variance is now .035. This represents the residual variance in the mean educational attainment after including the six institutional measures in the equation for the intercept. To determine the proportion of variance explained in mean institutional attainment levels as a function of the six institutional measures, the between-institution variance estimate from the random-coefficient model (Table 2), .129, is the basis for the calculation.

$$\text{Proportion explained} = (.129 - .035)/.129 = .729$$

Thus, the six institutional measures explain approximately 72.9 percent of the variance in attainment levels across institutions.[*] This is a substantially larger proportion of variance explained than is usually seen in college effects studies and is possibly because of the separation of the within-student and between-institution variability. However, the remaining unexplained variability (.035, which represents 29.1 percent of the original between-institution variability) is still significant ($X^2 = 320.13$, $p < .001$) indicating that there are still significant differences among the mean attainment levels of institutions not explained by the six variables. Of these variables, selectivity, percent graduate enrollment, per student expenditure, and control each have positive significant effects on the average educational attainment of institutions. The effect of control indicates that students attending private institutions have higher average attainment levels than their peers in public institutions, controlling for the other five institutional measures. The parameter estimates from the Level-1 model are essentially the same as from the previous analysis with the slight differences in the numerical values again a function of randomness and the more complicated structure of the final model. No reliabilities are reported for these parameters since their variances were fixed to be 0.

The HLM approach utilized in the above example has three distinct advantages over the methodologies previously applied in examining institutional effects on students. First, by acknowledging the multilevel nature of the data, selecting a unit of analysis and dependency among responses is not problematic. Second, the structural relationships both within and between institutions can be modeled by student and institutional variables used separately in the Level-1 and Level-2 models. Finally, through the decomposition of variance components (both within and between institutions and separating sampling variability from parameter variability) there is a greater ability to explain or describe relationships. In essence, this approach more accurately reflects the type and structure of data commonly used in such studies.

From the decomposition of the variability in educational attainment we see

---

[*]It is important to remember that since the independent variables have been centered, the intercept represents the average educational attainment level for an institution and the coefficient presented is the average of the intercepts across institutions. In this Level-2 model, we are trying to determine what institutional characteristics affect institutional mean attainment levels or why they vary across institutions. Student-level measures do not affect institutional-level outcomes and, as such, it is not appropriate to talk of "controlling for student characteristics." Control for student characteristics is done at Level-1. Control for **student body characteristics** (e.g., selectivity) is done at Level-2.

that by far the more important sources of variability are those associated with characteristics of individual students (see Table 1, p. 176.) That is, differences in the educational attainment levels of students is to a far greater extent the result of individual differences than it is differences in the types of institutions they attend. Only 13 percent of the variance (.119) is explained by institutional differences whereas 87 percent is explained by differences among students (.781.) After including student characteristics in the Level-1 model, we see that we explain 19.5 percent of the differences among students within institutions using the five student measures. However, almost three-quarters of the between-institution variability is accounted for by the six institutional measures considered in this example.

**Table 3: Estimation of Random-intercept Model of Educational Attainment**

| Fixed Effects | Coefficient | S.E. | t-ratio | Reliability |
|---|---|---|---|---|
| Model for institutional mean attainment | | | | |
| Institutional mean attainment ($\gamma_{00}$) | 3.086 | .021 | 145.62*** | .455 |
| Effects of institution-level variables | | | | |
| SELECT ($\gamma_{01}$) | .008 | .002 | 3.85*** | |
| SIZE ($\gamma_{02}$) | −.005 | .021 | −.25 | |
| PERGRAD ($\gamma_{03}$) | .048 | .013 | 3.82*** | |
| EXPEND ($\gamma_{04}$) | .047 | .016 | 3.05** | |
| RATIO ($\gamma_{05}$) | −.018 | .017 | −1.07 | |
| CONTROL ($\gamma_{06}$) | .243 | .063 | 3.88*** | |
| Effects of student-level variables | | | | |
| SES ($\gamma_{10}$) | .045 | .020 | 2.31* | |
| HSACAD ($\gamma_{20}$) | .027 | .022 | 1.22 | |
| COLGPA ($\gamma_{30}$) | .303 | .018 | 17.24*** | |
| SOCIAL ($\gamma_{40}$) | .123 | .015 | 8.02*** | |
| SATIS ($\gamma_{50}$) | .068 | .040 | 1.68 | |
| Random Effects | Variance | DF | Chi-square | |
| Between institution($\tau_{00}$) | .035 | 166 | 320.13*** | |
| (variance of intercepts) | | | | |
| Within institution ($\sigma^2$) | .653 | | | |

* p < .05; ** p < .01; *** p < .001

There were no interactive effects found in this example. There was no variability in the effects of the five student measures on individual attainment levels across the institutions which indicated that while socioeconomic background, college academic performance, and social experiences within an institution enhance attainment, and high school academic performance and general satisfaction with an institution have no direct influences on attainment, these influences are consistent regardless of the characteristics of the institution attended. Thus, the possibility that the importance of grades and background would be more pronounced for some types of institutions is not substantiated. For this sample of student, it appears that it does make a difference where one attends college. In particular, after controlling for the other institutional characteristics we see that students attending selective or private institutions are advantaged in terms of likelihood of higher educational attainments since the average attainment levels of students attending these institutions is higher, but the importance of their own attributes in reaching higher levels of attainment is not different from that of students attending less selective or public institutions.

But is there a net advantage of attending a private school over and beyond the entering characteristics of students attending such institutions? The measure of selectivity used in this analysis is the average SAT or ACT equivalent of students within an institution. As such, it represents not only an indicator of the selectivity of the institution in its admissions standards but also a measure of the academic aptitude of the student body. The effect of institutional control indicates that there are differences in the average attainment levels of students attending public and private institutions after controlling for their academic abilities. Thus, differences in the academic abilities of students attending public and private institutions do not explain the differences in attainment levels. However, it could well be that other student precollege characteristics (e.g., socioeconomic status, degree aspirations) might explain the public/private differential. To test this supposition, one would aggregate those student characteristics at the institutional level and include them in the Level-2 model. If the significant effect of control disappeared after including these aggregate measures one would conclude that the public/private differential in attainment levels was dominantly a result of the differences in the characteristics of the student bodies.

## EFFECTS OF COLLEGE MAJOR, QUALITY, AND PERFORMANCE ON EARNINGS: AN HLM EXAMPLE

The second example illustrating how hierarchical linear modeling is used to study college effects comes from Rumberger and Thomas (1991). Their study was focused on the economic returns of college and examined the impact of college academic performance, gender, and institutional characteristics on the earnings of recent college graduates for selected majors. Their student-level data were drawn from the 1987 Survey of Recent College Graduates administered by the U. S. Department of Education and the institutional-level data were drawn from the Annual Survey of Colleges 1985-1986 supplemented by Astin's institutional selectivity ratings (Astin and Henson, 1977) updated in 1983. Only portions of their results for business majors are presented in this example due to space limitations.

Based on the results of running a series of OLS analyses, they specified a random-coefficients model with Level-1 defined by

$$EARNINGS_{ij} = \beta_{0j} + \beta_{1j} (FEMALE) + \beta_{2j} (GPA) + r_{ij}$$

and Level-2

$$\beta_{qj} = \gamma_{q0} + u_{qj}.$$

Thus, individual earnings were specified to be a function of the individual's gender and college grade point average. The variable FEMALE was an indicator dummy variable with 1 representing females and 0 representing males. GPA was the student's self-reported college grade point average measured on a scale from 0 (low) to 4 (high). Both student-level variables were centered allowing the intercept to be interpreted as the average earnings per institution. The coefficient for FEMALE represents the differential in earnings received by females relative to males. The results of the estimation of this model are shown in Table 4.

**Table 4: Random-coefficients Model of Recent Business Graduates' Earnings[a]**

| Fixed Effects | Coefficient | S.E. | Reliability |
|---|---|---|---|
| Institutional mean earnings($\gamma_{00}$) | 20,754.34*** | 288.25 | .532 |
| Effects of student-level variables | | | |
| FEMALE ($\gamma_{10}$) | –3,201.71*** | 499.58 | .147 |
| GPA ($\gamma_{20}$) | 2,732.85*** | 585.51 | .178 |
| Random Effects | Variance | DF | Chi-square |
| Institutional means | 94304.71 | 175 | 458.18*** |
| FEMALE slope | 105739.54 | 175 | 201.78 (p=.081) |
| GPA slope | 201459.36 | 175 | 236.26** |

[a] Adapted from Rumberger and Thomas (1991)
** p < .01; *** p < .001

The average of the mean institutional earnings of this sample of business graduates is $20,754.34, but the chi-square test indicates that this salary is not representative of all institutions since there is significant variability across institutions. The regression coefficients indicate that female business majors earn approximately $3,200 less than their male peers, and that there is a positive, significant relationship between college grade point average and earnings. Each one point increase in grade point average is associated with an increment of approximately $2,700 in salary. Using a .05 criteria, the female differential in salary does not vary across institutions ($X^2 = 201.78$, p = .081) indicating that regardless of the type of post-secondary institution attended, female business majors on average earn \$3,200 less than male business majors. However, the effect of academic performance *is* conditional on type of institution given the significant chi-square for the coefficient of grade point average ($X^2 = 236.26$, $p < .01$). Rumberger and Thomas considered the .081 level seen for the chi-square testing the variability of the coefficients for FEMALE to be significant and subsequently modeled each of the three parameters in the Level-1 equation with two institution-level measures that had been used in previous studies and were found significant in their OLS analyses. Thus, their next model was an intercept- and slopes-as-outcomes model in which both the intercept and the two Level-1 regression coefficients were allowed to vary across institutions and that variability modeled by two Level-2 predictors. The Level-1 equation is the same as before

$$\text{EARNINGS}_{ij} = \beta_{0j} + \beta_{1j} (\text{FEMALE}) + \beta_{2j} (\text{GPA}) + r_{ij},$$

but the Level-2 equations now contain the two institutional measures:

$$\beta_{0j} = \gamma_{00} + \gamma_{01} \text{SELECT}_j + \gamma_{02} \text{PRIVATE} + u_{oj}$$

$$\beta_{1j} = \gamma_{10} + \gamma_{11} \text{SELECT}_j + \gamma_{12} \text{PRIVATE} + u_{1j}$$

$$\beta_{2j} = \gamma_{20} + \gamma_{21} \text{SELECT}_j + \gamma_{22} \text{PRIVATE} + u_{2j}$$

where SELECT represents the average SAT scores of incoming freshmen and PRIVATE was a dummy variable with a value of 1 indicating private schools. They did not center the Level-2 variables. Results of this model for the business majors is given in Table 5.

Examining the estimates of the equations for each of the three parameters in the Level-1 equation ($\beta_{0j}$, $\beta_{1j}$, $\beta_{2j}$), we see that the selectivity of the institution has a significant coefficient in the equations for the intercept ($\beta_0$) and the GPA slope ($\beta_2$). This indicates that the selectivity of the institution explains some of the between-institution differences in mean earnings and the effect of GPA on earnings. Specifically, the effect of selectivity on mean earnings (8.23) indicates that a one hundred point increase in selectivity is associated with a \$823 increase in average salary. However, the effect of selectivity on the GPA-earnings relationship is negative (-16.30) indicating that the GPA slope is smaller for more selective institutions. This means that for comparable increases in grade point averages, students attending more selective institutions receive lower average increases in salary than their peers in less selective institutions. Rumberger and Thomas (1991) interpret this selectivity-grade point average relationship with respect to earnings as suggesting that "employers may be more sensitive to GPA differences for students from less selective institutions as a way of distinguishing between them, but are less concerned with such differences for students attending more selective institutions" (p. 15). The control of the institution was non-significant in all three equations indicating that after controlling for the selectivity of an institution, there were no differences in mean earnings, the female differential, or the GPA differential between students attending public and private institutions.

**Table 5: Intercept- and Slopes-as-outcomes Model of Recent Business Graduates' Earnings[a]**

| Fixed Effects | Coefficient | Reliability |
|---|---|---|
| Model for institutional mean earnings ($\beta_0$) | | |
| Intercept ($\gamma_{00}$) | 12,580.39*** | .495 |
| SELECT ($\gamma_{01}$) | 8.23* | |
| PRIVATE ($\gamma_{02}$) | 1,064.96 | |
| Model for FEMALE slope ($\beta_1$) | | |
| Intercept ($\gamma_{10}$) | –3,110.54 | .185 |
| SELECT ($\gamma_{11}$) | –0.07 | |
| PRIVATE ($\gamma_{12}$) | –303.97 | |
| Model for GPA slope ($\beta_2$) | | |
| Intercept ($\gamma_{20}$) | 17,329.05* | .119 |
| SELECT ($\gamma_{21}$) | –16.30* | |
| PRIVATE ($\gamma_{22}$) | 2,229.34 | |

| Random Effects | Variance | DF | Chi-Square |
|---|---|---|---|
| Institutional means | 81821.84 | 173 | 405.78 |
| FEMALE slope | 140605.49 | 173 | 200.49 (p=.075) |
| GPA slope | 125897.05 | 173 | 229.86** |

[a] Adapted from Rumberger and Thomas (1991)
* $p < .05$; ** $p < .01$; *** $p < .001$

The chi-square tests indicate that there are still significant differences in the parameters across institutions (again, they considered the test for the variability of the coefficient for FEMALE to be significant.) They subsequently estimated a second Level-2 model that included twelve institutional measures as predictors of the three Level-1 coefficients. In addition to selectivity and control, they included the percentage of minority undergraduates (%MINORITY), mean educational level of students' fathers (MEAN FAED), number of applications divided by the number of students (ATTRACT), percent of applications accepted (ACCEPT), student-faculty ratio (RATIO), percent of faculty with Ph.D.s (%PHD), percent of faculty who are full-time (%FACFT), percent of undergraduates attending full-time (%UFT), percent of students who are undergraduates (%UG), and the total number of students (SIZE).

Given the number of Level-2 predictors, initially the equation for each Level-1 coefficient was estimated separately to avoid non-convergence problems given the large number of random effects to be estimated. For their final model, they included all Level-2 variables in the equation for mean earnings, but limited the variables in the equations for the FEMALE and GPA parameters to include only those proving to be significant in the intermediate stages of modeling the Level-1 coefficients separately (although they left PRIVATE in the equation for the coefficient for GPA even though it was non-significant.) Results of their final model estimation are shown in Table 6.

**Table 6: Full Intercept- and Slopes-as-outcomes Model of Recent Business Graduates' Earnings[a]**

| *Fixed Effects* | *Coefficient* | *Reliability* | |
|---|---|---|---|
| Model for institutional mean earnings ($\beta_0$) | | | |
| Intercept ($\gamma_{00}$) | 32,656.69*** | .409 | |
| SELECT ($\gamma_{01}$) | 11.23* | | |
| PRIVATE ($\gamma_{02}$) | 612.67 | | |
| %MINORITY | 68.44* | | |
| MEAN FAED | −979.69* | | |
| ATTRACT | 352.92 | | |
| ACCEPT | −49.81* | | |
| RATIO | −48.93 | | |
| %PHD | 3.50 | | |
| %FACFT | −23.69 | | |
| %UFT | −6.05 | | |
| %UG | −4,204.86 | | |
| SIZE | 2.62 | | |
| Model for FEMALE slope ($\beta_1$) | | | |
| Intercept ($\gamma_{10}$) | −1,308.71 | .172 | |
| %PHD | −43.10* | | |
| Model for GPA slope ($\beta_2$) | | | |
| Intercept ($\gamma_{20}$) | 17,329.05* | .116 | |
| SELECT | −15.97* | | |
| PRIVATE | 2,239.88 | | |
| *Random Effects* | *Variance* | *DF* | *Chi-Square* |
| Institutional means | 57990.54 | 163 | 324.87*** |
| FEMALE slope | 128914.16 | 174 | 192.66 (p=.158) |
| GPA slope | 122806.64 | 173 | 229.95** |

[a]Adapted from Rumberger and Thomas (1991)
*p <.05; **P <.01; ***p <.001

Their results show that four variables are significant in explaining the variability in mean earnings across institutions: three variables representing the social composition of the student body (selectivity, percent minority undergraduates, and average father's education) and the percent of applications accepted. The additional ten institutional characteristics were not as effective in explaining the variability in the female differential or the effect of GPA on earnings. The percent of faculty with Ph.D.'s has a significant negative effect on the female differential indicating that the higher the proportion of faculty with Ph.D.'s, the smaller the gap between male and female business graduates average earnings. The selectivity of the institution continued to have a negative effect on the GPA coefficient.

The variability of the three coefficients (intercept, FEMALE slope, and GPA slope) across institutions was reduced but remained significant for mean earnings and for the GPA coefficient indicating that while the institutional measures do contribute to the explanation of variance in the parameters, there is still significant variability across institutions. To calculate the proportion of variance in the parameters that is explained by the institutional measures, the variance estimates from the random-coefficients model are used (Table 4, p. 183). The reduction in the variance of mean earnings is

Proportion explained in mean earnings = (94304.71 - 57990.54)/94304.71 = .385

and that for the variance of the GPA coefficient is

Proportion explained in GPA slope = (201459.36 - 122806.64)/201459.36 = .390

Thus, approximately 39 percent of the variance in both mean earnings and the GPA-earnings relationship is explained by the institutional characteristics. However, after introducing the Level-2 variables into the equation for the coefficient for FEMALE there is an *increase* in variability of that parameter across institutions (change from 105739.54 in random-coefficients model to 140605.49 in slopes-as-outcome model). Since the chi-square test initially indicated that there was no true parameter variance across institutions, that parameter would normally have been specified to be 0 in subsequent analyses since attempts to model that variability would be attempting to model randomness. This, combined with the increased complexity of the model and the low reliability of that parameter lends to instability in the estimates of that random effect.

## COMPARING MULTI-LEVEL AND TRADITIONAL RESULTS

This chapter began with a brief discussion of the methodological problems that have plagued school effects research at both the pre- and post-secondary level. Most simply it is the multilevel, hierarchical character of much of the data used in such studies that lead to the shortcomings associated with the conventional OLS analytical procedures that are dominantly used. What was subsequently presented was an introduction to the HLM conceptualization described by Raudenbush and Bryk (1986) that utilizes a maximum-likelihood empirical Bayes approach for the estimation of multilevel models. This approach overcomes some of the most commonly encountered difficulties faced with multilevel data such as the unit of analysis question, dependency among individuals within units, heterogeneity of regression, and the different meanings and effects of variables at different levels of aggregation.

Given the advantages of hierarchical modeling, the question arises as to how the results of such modeling differs from OLS approaches. In Chapter 5 of their book, Bryk and Raudenbush (1992) illustrate the advantages to HLM modeling by comparing the results of three analyses of the same data: one taking the hierarchical approach, one utilizing the individual as the unit of analysis, and one aggregating the individual data to the group level. They examined the relationship between school characteristics and teachers' sense of efficacy in their work. The comparison of the three analyses showed that the estimates of the regression coefficients were somewhat similar in each of the three methods, but the hierarchical estimates were closer to those produced at the individual-level. Variations is the size of the coefficients across the three methods will depend on the degree to which the sample sizes within each group are different. If the sample sizes are the same in each group, the coefficients will be identical regardless of which method is used. Because the hierarchical and individual level analyses both weight as a function of group sample size (although the weightings used are different), the estimates from these procedures will generally be close. On the other hand, using aggregate data, the analysis is unweighted and a group with very small sample size could become a very influential data point. Given the limited information about the group, the aggregate measure is not stable, but the weighting used in HLM and individual-level analyses avoids this instability.

The standard errors for the coefficients were approximately the same for the hierarchical analysis and the group-level analysis, but were generally one-third smaller in the individual-level analysis. It is usually the case that the individual-level standard errors will be underestimated because of the dependence among individuals within groups, and, thus, one would be more likely to conclude that an effect was statistically significant in an individual-level analysis. The analysis using aggregate data avoids the dependency problem and only considers between-group variability. The within variability is lost along with the dependencies among individuals. However, HLM retains both sources of variability, decomposing the total to within- and between-variability. When group sample sizes are the same, the HLM and aggregate analyses will produce identical standard errors.

Substantively, these comparisons of methods indicate that if the individual is used as the unit of analysis, the magnitude of the coefficients is robust and generally similar to what would be obtained through an HLM analysis. Thus, the assessment of the magnitude of the effect of a variable on some outcome is generally accurate. However, that effect is more likely to be statistically significant in the individual-level analysis and incorrect conclusions would be drawn relative to the importance of a variable in predicting the outcome. Using aggregate data, the coefficients are not robust (except in the presence of balanced data which is rarely the case in college effects research), so the fact that the standard errors are more accurate is immaterial given that one cannot trust the parameter estimate. Bryk and Raudenbush (1992) note that the hierarchical approach captures the best features of each of the other two approaches by providing the most unbiased and efficient estimates of the coefficients and the proper standard errors regardless of the degree of dependency within groups.

However, it was in the proportions of variance explained that the most dramatic differences among the analyses were seen. In their analysis using individual-level data only 5.4 percent of the variance in the dependent variable was explained by the school characteristics because at that level the total variability was used as the denominator for the calculation. That is, the reduction in the *combined* between- and within-group variability was considered the proportion explained. Using aggregate data, the proportion explained was 42.6 percent because the variability among individuals was lost and only between group variability was used. Thus a more appropriate variance estimate is used as the basis for the calculation, but this is still not the best estimate because of the unreliability of the parameters; the between-group variance estimate also carries error associated with unreliability. In the hierarchical analysis the proportion explained was 63.1 percent. This latter variance-explained statistic provides the best estimate because it is unaffected by the dependencies among individuals within units and by the unreliability of the parameters using aggregate data.

## CONCLUSION

Given the arguments made about the inadequacies of traditional approaches to studying college effects and the advantages gained by utilizing the methodological advances made in this area over the past two decades, it may appear that multilevel modeling is the be-all and end-all in school and college effects research, but this is not the case. As with any new development, questions arise as to the adequacy of multilevel modeling in different research scenarios and what the approach can and cannot do for researchers. Because of the enthusiastic adoption of multilevel modeling, Ita Kreft and Hilary Saner felt that the time was ripe for a full discussion of the merits of the method. Calling together some of the most well-known researchers in the field and the producers of software utilized in estimating multilevel models, they organized a conference held at the RAND Corporation in Santa Monica in October of 1993 on "Hierarchical Linear Models:

Problems and Prospects." Papers presented at that conference along with discussions of those papers appeared as a special issue of the *Journal of Educational and Behavioral Statistics (JEBS)* appearing Summer, 1995. In his paper, Draper (1995) notes that multilevel modeling in the social sciences has unquestionable usefulness but that it is associated with (1) an increase in the complexity of analysis and (2) the possibility of confusion and overstatement of evidence. He strongly questions the uncritical use of such modeling, raising issues related to the validity of inferences made from data that may be questionable. de Leeuw and Kreft (1995) caution that in many instances multilevel modeling of random coefficients is not really necessary, even given the multilevel character of a data set. With very large groups and small intraclass correlations nothing is gained from the more complicated modeling since more traditional approaches perform equally well and are less sensitive to model assumptions. They point out also that if researchers are interested only in the regression coefficients, they can be reliably estimated with any weighted or unweighted least squares method (Busing, 1993; van der Leeden and Busing, 1994; Kim, 1990.) Morris (1995) points out that when the number of Level-2 units is small, the maximum likelihood methods do *not* provide better variance estimates or measures of uncertainty, and Raudenbush (1995) notes that even the Level-2 coefficients can be misleading when the number of subjects varies substantially between units.

Burstein, Kim, and Delandshere (1989) suggest that more studies need to be conducted comparing analytical procedures using common sets of simulated data in order to examine the robustness of these procedures because the gains made in the analytical power and precision could possibly be associated with potentially incorrect results should the data only partially satisfy assumptions. They further suggest that the data used in substantive research be examined from multiple perspectives in order to have more confidence in results. Researchers interested in utilizing these multilevel modeling approaches in their research would be well-advised to read the series of papers in this special issue of *JEBS* as well as the Kreft, de Leeuw, and van der Leeden (1994) review of computer programs. While these papers tend to be of a more statistical nature, the discussions are easily read.

But beyond the statistical issues are conceptual and data issues. The availability of appropriate statistical models and analytical techniques for use in studying college effects does not relieve one from appropriately conceptualizing the research. Murchan and Sloane (1994) argue that research models consist of two overlapping submodels: a conceptual or theoretical model and a statistical model. The theoretical model describes the researcher's view of the world and the statistical model describes that view mathematically and is used to test the theoretical model. In order to most appropriately utilize the multilevel statistical models, it is imperative that the conceptual or theoretical model accurately reflects the organization of the phenomena studied. Many of the college effects models currently used acknowledge the multiple levels of influence on students. Weidman's (1989) model clearly differentiates these multiple sources. There are influences at the student-level from individual characteristics and parental socialization measures; at the institutional-level from global measures such as institutional mission, size, and quality; and also at subenvironment levels such as major, department, peer groups, and organizations. Thus, college effects research *does* involve propositions about relationships among constructs at different organizational levels, but those relationships have not been adequately modeled by the methodologies employed.

But we have had problems with our data as well. Returning to Pascarella and Terenzini's (1991) concern about the subenvironments within institutions and the possibility that the more global measures of institutional characteristics currently used in college effects research may not adequately reflect the more immediate influences on students, we need to be more concerned about what we are trying to measure. For example, the selectivity of an institution certainly is an indication of the normative academic environment of the entire institution. But even within an institution, different departments and majors have more or less stringent requirements for entry. The environment *within* the department or major should have more immediate influence on students than that of the institution as a whole. In fact, it may be that *both* influence students in either complementary or competing manners.

We often try to control for the influence of major by including dichotomous variables in OLS regression, but this is by far an imperfect measure of the *influence* of major since the coefficient only represents differences between majors on the outcome. It is also difficult to consider multiple majors with the use of dichotomous variables. One approach is to collapse majors into groups based on some degree of similarity (e.g., quantitative versus non-quantitative), losing variability among majors. Another approach is to use a dummy variable for each major, in which case the $R^2$ is artificially increased and degrees of freedom are squandered. Still another way to capture the influence of major would be to use compositional variables in which a measure of the environment of a major is simply the average of characteristics of students within the major. This is consistent with Holland's (1966, 1985) perspective in which individuals create their common environment as a function of their similar characteristics. These compositional variables which measure the proximal environment of students capture the more immediate influences on students and can have an effect over and beyond the characteristics of an individual.

In essence, in conceptualizing and planning the research, the multiple levels acknowledged in the theoretical models should be adequately reflected in the data gathered. We have the theoretical models and we have the appropriate statistical methods to test the propositions implied by the theory, but the models and statistical results are only as good as our data. With the multilevel modeling techniques the problems of unit of analysis, dependencies among groups of individuals, misestimated standard errors, and non-robust parameter estimates that plague OLS approaches are generally resolved if appropriate data are used. We can more adequately address the structure of the data and determine whether relationships between the student characteristics and the student outcomes differ as a function of different types of institutions. We now must concentrate on the adequacy of our data.

However, a final caution is necessary and cannot be expressed better than the words of Goldstein (1995):

> There is a danger, and this paper reminds us of it, that multilevel modeling will become so fashionable that its use will be a requirement of journal editors, or even worse, that the mere fact of having fitted a multilevel model will become a certificate of statistical probity. That would be a great pity. These models are as good as the data they fit; they are powerful tools, not universal panaceas (p. 202).

## REFERENCES

Astin, A. (1982). *Minorities in American Higher Education*. San Francisco: Jossey-Bass.

Astin, A., and Henson, J.W. (1977). New measures of college selectivity. *Research in Higher Education* 6: 1-9.

Bock, R.D. (1989). *Multilevel Analysis of Educational Data*. San Diego: Academic Press.

Bryk, A.S., and Raudenbush, S.W. (1992). *Hierarchical Linear Models: Applications and Data Analysis Methods*. Newbury Park, CA: SAGE Publications.

Bryk, A.S., Raudenbush, S.W., and Congdon, R.T. (1994). *Hierarchical Linear Modeling with the HLM/2L and HLM/3L Programs*. Chicago: Scientific Software International.

Bryk, A.S., Raudenbush, S.W., Seltzer, M. and Congdon, R.T. (1988). *An Introduction to HLM: Computer Program and User's Guide* (2nd edition). Chicago: University of Chicago Department of Education.

Burstein, L. (1980a). The analysis of multilevel data in educational research and evaluation. In D. C. Berliner (ed.), *Review of Research in Education* (Vol. 8). Washington, DC: American Educational Research Association.

Burstein, L. (1980b). The role of levels of analysis in the specification of educational effects. In R. Dreeben and J. A. Thomas (eds.), *The Analysis of Educational Productivity, Vol. I: Issues in Microanalysis*. Cambridge, MA: Balinger.

Burstein, L., Kim, K.-S., and Delandshere, G. (1989). Multilevel investigations of systematically varying slopes: Issues, alternatives, and consequences. In D. Bock (ed.), *Multilevel Analysis of Educational Data*. San Diego: Academic Press.

Burstein, L., Linn, R.L., and Capell, F.J. (1978). Analyzing multi-level data in the presence of heterogeneous within-class regressions. *Journal of Educational Statistics* 3: 347-389.

Burstein, L., and Miller, M.D. (1980). Regression-based analysis of multi-level educational data. *New Directions for Methodology of Social and Behavioral Sciences* 6: 194-211.

Busing, F.M.T.A. (1993). *Distribution Characteristics of Variance Estimates in Two-level Models* (Technical Report No. PRM 93-04). Leiden, The Netherlands: University of Leiden, Department of Psychometrics.

Chickering, A. (1969). *Education and Identity*. San Francisco: Jossey Bass.

de Leeuw, J., and Kreft, I.G.G. (1995). Questioning multilevel models. *Journal of Educa-*

*tional and Behavioral Statistics* 20: 171-189.

Dempster, A.P., Laird, N.M., and Rubin, D.B. (1977). Maximum likelihood from incomplete data via the EM algorithm. *Journal of the Royal Statistical Society, Series B* 38: 1-38.

Draper, D. (1995). Inference and hierarchical modeling in the social sciences. *Journal of Educational and Behavioral Statistics* 20: 115-147.

Goldstein, H. (1995). Hierarchical data modeling in the social sciences. *Journal of Educational and Behavioral Statistics* 20: 201-204.

Hannan, M., and Burstein, L. (1974). Estimation from grouped observations. *American Sociological Review* 39: 374-392.

Holland, J. (1966). *The Psychology of Vocational Choice: A Theory of Personality Types and Model Environments*. Waltham, MA: Blaisdell.

Holland, J. (1985). *Making Vocational Choices: A Theory of Vocational Personalities and Work Environments*. Englewood Cliffs, NJ: Prentice-Hall.

Kim, K.-S. (1990). Multilevel data analysis: A comparison of analytical alternatives. Unpublished doctoral dissertation, University of California, Los Angeles.

Kreft, I.G.G., de Leeuw, J., and van der Leeden, R. (1994). Review of five multilevel analysis programs: BMDP-5V, GENMOD, HLM, ML3, and VARCL. *The American Statistician* 48: 324-335.

Lindley, D.V., and Smith, A.F.M. (1972). Bayes estimates for the linear model. *Journal of the Royal Statistical Society, Series B* 34: 1-41.

Longford, N.T. (1986). VARCL - Interactive software for variance component analysis. *The Professional Statistician* 5: 28-32.

Mason, W.M., Anderson, A.F., and Hayat, N. (1988). *Manual for GENMOD*. Ann Arbor: University of Michigan, Population Studies Center.

Morris, C.N. (1995). Hierarchical models for educational data: An overview. *Journal of Educational and Behavioral Statistics* 20: 190-200.

Murchan, D.P., and Sloane, F.C. (1994). Conceptual and statistical problems in the study of school and classroom effects: An introduction to multilevel modeling techniques. In I. Westbury, C. A. Ethington, L. A. Sosniak, and D. P. Baker (eds.), *In Search of More Effective Mathematics Education*. Norwood, NJ: Ablex Publishing Corp.

Pascarella, E.T. (1985). College environmental influences on learning and cognitive development: A critical review and synthesis. In J. Smart (ed.), *Higher Education: Handbook of Theory and Research* (Vol. 1). New York: Agathon Press.

Pascarella, E.T., and Terenzini, P.T. (1991). *How College Affects Students*. San Francisco: Jossey-Bass Publishers.

Perry, W. (1970). *Forms of Intellectual and Ethical Development in the College Years: A Scheme*. New York: Holt, Rinehart & Winston.

Rabash, J., Prosser, R., and Goldstein, H. (1989*). ML2: Software for Two-level Analysis. Users' guide*. London: University of London, Institute of Education.

Raudenbush, S.W. (1995). Reexamining, reaffirming, and improving application of hierarchical models. *Journal of Educational and Behavioral Statistics* 20: 210-220.

Raudenbush, S., and Bryk, A.S. (1986). A hierarchical model for studying school effects. *Sociology of Education* 59: 1-17.

Rumberger, R.W., and Thomas, S.L. (1991). The economic returns to college major, quality, and performance: A multilevel analysis of recent graduates. Paper presented at the Annual Meeting of the American Educational Research Association, Chicago, April 1991.

Schluchter, M. (1988). *Technical Report 86: BMDP-5V - Unbalanced Repeated Measures Models with Structured Covariance Matrices*. Los Angeles: BMDP Statistical Software, Inc.

Smith, A.F.M. (1973). A general Bayesian linear model. *Journal of the Royal Statistical Society, Series B* 35: 61-75.

van der Leeden, R., and Busing, F.M.T.A. (1994). *First Iteration Versus IGLS/RIGLS Estimates in Two-level Models: A Monte Carlo Study with ML3*. (Technical Report No. PRM 94-02). Leiden, The Netherlands: University of Leiden, Department of Psychometrics.

Weidman, J. (1989). Undergraduate socialization: A conceptual approach. In J. Smart (ed.), *Higher Education: Handbook of Theory and Research* (Vol. 5). New York:

# The Cost-Effectiveness of American Higher Education:
# The United States Can Afford Its Colleges and Universities

### Jeffery E. Olson
*St. John's University*

The organizational environment of higher education is becoming increasingly hostile. Government regulation is increasing. Government support is being withdrawn. Many people are scrutinizing internal operations more intensely. Cost increases are widely believed to reflect organizational pathologies. People suspect higher education boards and administrators of being weak and institutions of being ineffective. These conditions raise the question of whether higher education merits the level of public financial support that it presently enjoys. The discussion of this question is organized around six sub-questions. Two relate to higher education's economic effectiveness, two relate to its costs, and two relate to cost and effectiveness:

## Effectiveness

Has education in general, higher education in particular, been economically effective?

Is faculty scholarship worth society's continuing support?

## Costs

Do higher education cost increases result primarily from internal organizational pathologies or external environmental changes?

Should government continue to subsidize higher education at present levels?

## Cost-Effectiveness

Does higher education produce enough economic growth to justify funding increases that exceed inflation?

Do present funding mechanisms match the economic benefits and burdens of higher education?

Economic considerations are emphasized because funding questions are primarily economic and the discussion would quickly become unwieldy if non- economic benefits and costs were considered too specifically; nevertheless, the non-economic considerations are also important.

An organizational cost-effectiveness framework provides a basis for the analysis. It borrows somewhat loosely from economics and organizational theory. The looseness results from the gaps and inconsistencies in the studies and data. The pieces used to respond to the questions do not all come from an internally coherent set of studies and concepts.

## ORGANIZATIONAL COST-EFFECTIVENESS FRAMEWORK

Organizational costs can be related to organizational effectiveness by combining cost theory from economics with an effectiveness framework from organizational theory. Scott (1992, Chapter 13) provides a useful basis for the effectiveness piece of the framework. It can be applied to any level of organizational activity. He identifies three types of effectiveness indicators that correspond to the organizational elements of effectiveness: structurE, process, and outcome. Outcomes include goods and services produced as well as personal and social changes resulting from the goods and services. The outcomes flow from the processes, which are based on the structure. You cannot have the outcomes if you do not have the processes that lead to them, and you cannot have the processes if you do not have the structure that leads to them. The distribution of outcomes among individuals and groups is the distribution of organizational benefits.

Through cost theory, costs and their burdens can be related to the effectiveness piece of the framework. The costs are a function of the ingredients of the structure and their prices. The ingredients are the participants, raw materials, goods, and services that together comprise the structure. The distribution of costs among individuals and groups is the distribution of organizational burdens.

The organization's technical and institutional environments affect both cost and effectiveness in important ways (Scott, 1992; Meyer and Scott, 1983). The technical environment is the environment of an organization that produces a product that competes in a market. The market imposes some level of rationality, of technical efficiency. Applied to higher education economics it consists of natural limitations or constraints on organization. By natural I mean the kinds of phenomena that natural scientists study (Olson, 1994). This includes the limitations that neo-classical economists would consider, particularly the scarcity of resources.

The institutional environment is the environment of organizations that must conform to some level of social norms to maintain their legitimacy (Scott, 1992). It consists of social limitations or constraints on organizations (Olson, 1994). These include shared beliefs, norms, laws, agreements, and customs. Organizations need to conform more or less to these social limitations to maintain their legitimacy and continue functioning with a minimum of external interference.

Usually the technical and institutional environments interact to constrain organizations. For example, custom and law define currency and financing mechanisms as well as the conditions under which a particular market, say the market for undergraduate students, operates. These constrain a college's behavior and students' behavior. Once the market is defined, then the technical constraint of the scarcity of students of various kinds and of financing further limits the college's behavior. These organizational environments constrain the revenues, costs (including expenditures), prices, ingredients, structure, processes, and outcomes of organizations.

The outcomes or products can be either technical or institutional (Olson, 1994). Technical outcomes have a natural or physical basis. They include changes in mental abilities or physical characteristics, transportation of an object from one place to another, and reorganization of parts into a new whole. The actual socialization of a student, the enhancing of a student's cognitive ability, and custodial care of a student are educational examples of technical outcomes or products.

On the other hand, institutional outcomes involve social relabeling, which might or might not accompany a technical change. For example, when a person receives a college degree, society treats the graduate differently, whether or not the person has changed in any way. This is an institutional outcome. If the person does in fact know more or have different habits resulting from the education, these would be technical outcomes. Certification for a particular form of employment is an institutional outcome that might or might not accompany technical outcomes.

This framework provides a basis for analyzing an organization's cost-effectiveness. Institutional outcomes depend only on conformity of the organization's structures and processes to the expectations of the institutional environment. For example, if a college is organized and operated according to social expectations of a college and a student successfully participates in the necessary courses for receipt of a degree, people in society treat the person as a graduate whether the person learned anything or not. The status of a graduate is not a technical outcome. This means that resources can be increased or decreased, structures changed, or processes changed and the people completing a course of study will still be treated the same as graduates as long as the structures and processes continue to conform to social expectations of how to structure and operate a legitimate degree program of that particular level of quality.

On the other hand, technical outcomes actually result from technical processes, technical processes actually depend on technical structural requirements, and technical structural requirements actually require the necessary resources. But, the converse is not the case. The presence of the resources does not guarantee the presence of the structure, the structure does not guarantee the necessary processes, and the processes do not guarantee the technical outcomes. If the organization does not use the resources, the structure, or the processes properly, organizational effectiveness will not result.

Obviously costs can increase or decrease without affecting technical or institutional effectiveness. If costs increase through increased prices, they do not necessarily affect the ingredients, the structure, the processes, the outcomes or the technical effectiveness at all, but they might affect the institutional outcomes, for example, through causing people to believe that the college is not well run and to question the quality of its graduates. Costs could also increase through adding ingredients to the organization without effectively incorporating the ingredients in the structure, increasing organizational slack. Again, technical effectiveness would not be enhanced. Costs could decrease through reducing slack without reducing technical effectiveness.

Economists focus attention on three levels of analysis: the social level, the level of the entire society; the private level, the level of individuals and households; and the firm level, the level of a higher education enterprise. Different levels of analysis provide answers to different questions. Answers to questions about the overall effectiveness and affordability of higher education enterprises lie primarily at the social and private levels. Answers to the questions about the nature of cost increases lie primarily at the enterprise level.

Productivity is discussed throughout this analysis. It is itself a measurement of cost-effectiveness. Productivity is a ratio of value produced to value used in production (Wallhaus, 1975, p.1). Value need not be monetary. It can be measured in many ways (Debreu, 1959; Olson, 1994). Three common ways in cost-effectiveness are monetary value, counts, and subjective judgments of utility (Levin, 1983). The term gross productivity refers to productivity ratios in which the products are measured by counts. Labor productivity refers to productivity ratios in which the labor used is measured by counts. Faculty productivity is an example of a labor productivity measure.

There are many types of productivity ratios (Olson, 1994). They differ in three ways: Does a single product or multiple products appear in the ratio? does a single input or multiple inputs appear in the ratio? is the ratio average or marginal? Productivity ratios and cost ratios are equivalent. They are the inverse of each other. If product is the numerator and resource the denominator, then it is a productivity ratio. If the resource is the numerator and the product the denominator, then it is a cost ratio. The most important ratios used here are gross productivity or cost, labor productivity or cost, capital productivity, and multi-factor productivity.

In higher education there are two dimensions to production (Hopkins and Massy, 1981) or productivity: quantity and quality. Quantity is measured by counts, for example, student-teacher ratios, and quality is usually measured by monetary value or subjective utility. Price is sometimes used as an indicator of quality: a more expensive item implies a higher social value. An example of a subjective utility indicator of quality would be a reputational ranking. Gross productivity or cost is a quantity ratio. It is particularly valuable in analyzing budgets or structural requirements where quality constraints do not apply or have already been applied. For example, a student-teacher ratio is a gross productivity measure where quality might have constrained the selection of students and faculty.

For convenience, in this study higher education assumes three primary functions or sets of processes: instruction, scholarship, and service. Instruction has four main elements: cognitive development, socialization, credentialing, and custody. Cognitive development includes the outcomes of knowledge transfer and enhancement of cognitive functions. Socialization is the process by which students become members of society in general and members of academic disciplines or professions in particular by internalizing beliefs, norms, and values and learning roles. Educational institutions have the responsibility of socializing students into personal and professional values appropriate for citizens and workers. Credentialing provides the institutional outcome of labeling students as having successfully participated in particular cognitive development and socialization processes; enabling employers, prospective spouses, and others to screen them for social roles. Credentialing has been an important function from higher education's earliest years. For example, in Ferruolo's (1985) history of the formation of the University of Paris, one of the inducements to student enrollment was the preference that the kings of France and England gave to graduates. Custody involves the physical maintenance of students. Traditionally, a reason that parents sent their children to college was for their care and maintenance away from home.

Scholarship includes the development, integration, and refinement of knowledge bases. Scholarship includes research, which focuses on development of new knowledge. Of the many important functions, scholarship may be higher education's most important one. Individual and organizational rational processes and instruction depend on knowledge bases for their effectiveness. They can be no more effective than the knowledge underlying them. All of education–elementary, secondary, higher, extension, individual study–is no better than the scholarship at its base. All rational processes–manufacturing, agriculture, information and other services, management, politics–depend on the knowledge at their base.

As information technologies facilitate access to knowledge bases, scholarship will become increasingly important. The many gaps and inconsistencies in society's knowledge will become increasingly visible and unacceptable. Other enterprises will more readily compete in knowledge transmission, but they lack the concentration of knowledge expertise to compete effectively in scholarship. Also, the public nature of knowledge interferes with its commercialization, except for limited areas protected by intellectual property. This makes broad-based scholarship commercially unattractive despite its social and private importance. Within the instructional function, socialization and credentialing also give higher education competitive advantages

The final primary mission of higher education is service. It encompasses organizational service such as cooperative and extension services, and individual service such as faculty consulting. Individual service sometimes includes service to the higher education enterprise as well as to external enterprises. Economists have noted particularly that higher education service often involves knowledge transmission and transfer.

## EFFECTIVENESS—IS FACULTY SCHOLARSHIP WORTH SOCIETY'S CONTINUING SUPPORT?

As previously discussed, scholarship includes the development, integration, and refinement of knowledge bases. Scholarship includes research, which focuses on development of new knowledge. While there is evidence that scholarship is increasingly important in all types of higher education enterprises, doctoral–particularly research–universities have the primary responsibility for developing, integrating, refining, and testing the knowledge bases. In particular, they have the primary responsibility for basic research. Corporations are not likely to undertake this responsibility without government support even though the economic benefits of basic research exceed those of applied research (Balderstone, 1990). The economic obstacles to making basic research attractive to industry are that the research is very expensive, the results are uncertain, and the exclusionary principle can be applied only for a few types of developmental research. Corporations cannot readily justify the expense and the risk if they cannot retain the economic benefit from the outcomes. Only where the results are applied enough in nature to be patentable, can the expenditures be justified.

University-based research has enhanced the American economy. Part of the genius of American universities is that their primary mission is not instruction but the integration of scholarship, instruction, and service (Balderstone, 1990). University faculty members develop, transmit, and transfer knowledge simultaneously. The magic of the productivity is in the mix.

University-based multi-output production permits the educational needs of the students to influence scholarship, and the research findings to be transmitted throughout the educational system and transferred to industrial and other organizations more readily. Faculty members take the knowledge to other organizations through their consulting and collaborative research. They also share it at professional meetings and through scholarly journals with similarly educated corporate employees. Their graduating students take it to their employers. Most faculty members of every type of college come from doctoral universities and transmit their knowledge to their students. In turn it can pass to school teachers and through them to their students.

Economists focus more attention on the economic benefits of research and development in the natural sciences and related professions than in the social sciences and humanities and their related professions. Some commentators are even threatened by scholarship in the social sciences and humanities. Their concerns actually underscore the importance of social science and humanities scholarship. If it had little potential impact, it would likely raise less concern. External research is much more limited in these fields than in the natural sciences, despite the importance of these knowledge bases to education and rational processes. Much more research is needed on the uses in society of scholarship from the humanities, social sciences, and related professions.

I have not found many explanations of the relationship between scholarship and knowledge base development. A deep understanding of this process is important to the economics of higher education. Many authors and even some faculty suggest that the structure is overdeveloped, that too many or too many inadequately competent participants are involved (Massy and Wilger, 1995, p. 16). This process may be explained in several conflicting ways with different implications for the cost- effectiveness of higher education. They are the genius theory, the public meeting theory, the construction theory, and the mining theory.

## Possible Explanations

### The Genius Theory

First, there are a few geniuses who publish articles and books that are worthwhile. No one's work is really needed. If we could just identify these few and support them, we would not need to waste resources supporting any of the others.

### The Public Meeting Theory

Second, knowledge development is a conversation, a public meeting, some contributions are more valuable than others, but the benefit comes from the on-going dialogue, with as many participating as possible. The contributions are of many types. Questions are valuable, not just answers. Requests for clarification are valuable too. Valuable points come from unlikely sources. Some participants are effective at summarizing and others at integrating other people's ideas into creative new ones. A synergy operates. The whole builds together.

### The Construction Theory

Third, it is like constructing a building. Some people produce more visible and more challenging pieces, but everyone who pounds a nail or saws a board contributes to the whole. Not all the contributions can or need be made by geniuses.

### The Mining Theory

Fourth, it is like mining. To obtain the gold from the ore you must mine much ore, with only a small percentage of the valuable mineral resulting. The effectiveness of the enterprise is evaluated by the amount of earth moved and refined mineral produced, not by the overburden.

If knowledge depends only on the work of geniuses, then society can find them, support them and let all other scholars go. They just get in the way. On the other hand, if scholarship is a town meeting, a community-based process, then society should engage as many people as it can afford and be grateful for their willingness to participate. If it is a construction project, with different people performing different but related functions, many of which do not require genius, then society hires as many of each type as it needs and can afford. If it is like mining, with much overburden, then society needs to be careful and not evaluate its effectiveness based on individual articles or books, but on the overall productivity of the enterprise. We need more research to determine the nature of the process.

## University-Industry Relationships

While the relationship between scholarship and society generally has received little attention, the relationship between university research and industry has received a good deal of attention. Geiger (1992) provides a history and overview of these relationships. He reviews the three primary approaches to university-industry research and development relationships. First, there are consultants. Second, there are separate industrial research laboratories in universities that receive contracts. These decreased in importance as industry expanded their own laboratories, then increased again during the eighties and are decreasing again. Third, federal and state governments fund university-industry partnerships with the hope that they will continue with funding from the partners, which has not often happened. Sometimes the state government has stepped in to take the federal government's place. All three approaches depend on corporations having their own research and development component to be able to take advantage of the academic research, to make the technology transfer. These corporate researchers received the same training, read the same journals and participated in the same meetings. This is the essential linkage of technology transfer. He says that there undoubtedly are high social rates of return; however, the evidence comes primarily from high prestige institutions, such as MIT, the University of North Carolina at Chapel Hill, and Stanford.

Geiger cites Nelson (1989) as offering some "plausible and helpful distinctions on [technological change]." Nelson divides technology into generic knowledge, which is relatively public, and practiced techniques, which are acquired through investment and experience and are more private. The most advantageous circumstance for corporations is a head-start in developing practiced techniques from the generic knowledge. Close relationships with university scholars enables this head-start.

Geiger concludes that industry will never be able to invest much in basic research and that there is limited value to industrial research based in universities. Industry-supported research has gone up and down from an average of about 30 percent of GNP since 1960.  Less than 5 percent of this is university-based. The percentage of university-based research supported by industry reached a high of 8.0 percent in 1955. In 1989 it was 6.6 percent. The roles of universities and industry in research and development are well demarcated for good economic reasons.

## Separately Budgeted Research and Development and Economic Growth

Studies of separately budgeted research and development reveal that economic growth results more from basic than applied research (Bureau of Labor Statistics, 1989) and that most basic research is done in universities (Geiger, 1992). Researchers have quite consistently found that research and development is successful in stimulating economic growth (Bureau of Labor Statistics, 1989; Geiger, 1992; Gordon, 1985; Griliches, 1985; Brooks, 1985; Clark and Griliches, 1984). The Bureau of Labor Statistics (1989) found that research and development is the strongest and most consistent influence observed on multi-factor productivity growth. It contributes .2 or .3 percent annually to productivity growth directly and even more when indirect effects are considered.  Gordon (1985) also found very high returns to research and development investment. Griliches (1985) found that the federal contribution has had a less obvious effect than privately financed research and development. Brooks (1985) showed that even when government research and development was undertaken for non-market reasons, the results were commercially successful. In addition to basic research being primarily university based, Becker and Lewis (1992) say that most high-tech research and development is associated with higher education in one way or another.

These results appear to hold despite the methodological problems inherent in the studies. Jaffe (1985) outlined the difficulties of measuring research and development contributions, but the difficulties biased the results against the importance of the contributions. The methods actually underestimate the importance of research and development.

McMahon (1992) concluded from a study of 11 OECD nations that higher education and university-based research and development together contributed about 13 percent of economic growth. He notes that this means that the real rate of return to higher education must be augmented for research and development substantially beyond the instruction rate of between 7 percent and 9.7 percent. He also found evidence of complementarity in the inputs into national economic growth so that some investment in every form of input is needed.

These studies are limited to separately budgeted research. Much of higher education's scholarship is not separately budgeted, but departmental, particularly in the humanities, social sciences and related professions. The benefits of departmental research are not directly included in the estimated benefits presented above.

In addition to its transmission through instruction and transfer through collaborative research, the knowledge developed through scholarship is transferred through service, particularly consulting. Even fewer studies have focused on the economics of these activities.

## Conclusions

Of the many important functions of higher education, scholarship may be the most important one. Instruction depends on scholarship: cognitive development is no better than its knowledge base. Individual and organizational rational processes also depend on the knowledge base for their effectiveness. They can be no more effective than the knowledge underlying them. All of education–elementary, secondary, higher, extension, individual study–is no better than the scholarship at its base. All rational processes in the society–manufacturing, agriculture, law, information, other services, management–depend on their respective knowledge bases. This is one reason that scholarship leads to prestige in higher education

The indirect nature of scholarship's benefits makes them harder to recognize. CEO's do not necessarily recognize the benefit of the research even if they recognize the benefit of the instruction, because they do not usually use the research directly. They receive the benefit of the research primarily through the education of their employees and the advice of their consultants.

The research affects all Americans through the instruction they receive. While not all are educated in doctoral universities, most faculty in higher education institutions received their terminal degrees from doctoral universities. Through them the results of university-based research flow throughout the higher education community. In turn, almost all school teachers are educated by them, and they in turn educate all children in our society. This is a relatively short-linked network that connects all Americans to the research and scholarly activities of doctoral universities. Even if they were the only schools to subscribe to scholarly journals, the journals would potentially affect the entire society. Additionally, essential knowledge transfer connections between higher education and other public and private enterprises are between higher education faculty members and their research-credentialed counterparts in other enterprises.

We should not precipitously act to weaken the research enterprise. Knowledge bases are increasingly important and scholarship is primarily responsible for them.

## HAS EDUCATION IN GENERAL, HIGHER EDUCATION IN PARTICULAR, BEEN ECONOMICALLY EFFECTIVE?

### Beliefs

Explanations and studies of higher education's social and private effectiveness are more readily understood through grouping them according to the social functions that they emphasize: general (or multi-function), instruction, scholarship, and service. Scholarship has been discussed and the economics of service have received attention. This section will focus on effectiveness in general and then on instruction. Then they will be considered together with scholarship to answer the question.

## General (Multi-Function)

### Explanations

Becker and Lewis (1992) provide an excellent review of the literature on the contributions of higher education to economic growth. It is quite consistent with the framework already presented. First, higher education is the primary producer of the knowledge base on which technological change depends. Second, higher education faculty members and other professionals participate in consulting, publishing, conferences and other activities that disseminate the knowledge. Third, higher education transmits the knowledge to students through various teaching activities. It also screens students for prospective employers. These activities lead to the enhancement of people's abilities to be productive and to the improvement of the capital, machines and equipment with whom people interact in production, and to the ability of prospective employers to select the most appropriate employees. They also note that higher education contributes to the national economy through consumption as well as investment by providing learning, entertainment, culture, and group activities benefiting their communities.

Knowledge development, transfer, and transmission change society's normative structures, making possible other changes in structures, processes, and outcomes. Economists and other social scientists have various theories about precisely how they affect society, but additional scholarship is needed to confirm and refine them. Nevertheless, the evidence of their overall effectiveness is strong.

### Evidence of Overall Effectiveness

According to Becker and Lewis, Pencavel (1992) provides "a selective, non-technical, review of research on the contribution of education, and especially higher education, to economic growth and efficient resource allocation." He poses and answers three major questions. "First, what is known about the role of education in economic growth?" Second, what is the effect of college education on individual earnings? Third, "...to what extent is the supply of well-educated labor responsive to earnings." In response to the first question he concludes that two types of evidence support the proposition that increases in rates of school completion and improvements in education quality have contributed to the growth in U.S. labor productivity. He has found that school enrollment rates (including those of higher education) and economic growth rates are correlated across countries, and that industries in the United States with the most rapid technical progress make the most use of highly educated labor. In response to the second question he concludes that earnings of college educated labor rose much more quickly than non-college educated labor during the 1980s. These suggest that higher education does enhance earnings although the mechanisms are not well understood. As to the third question, he finds evidence to support the proposition that the supply of new graduates, the rate of attrition to a profession, and the rate of reentry to a profession all respond to earnings differentials and other monetary incentives.

Baumol, Blackman, and Wolff (1989) review studies of American economic growth and conclude that technological development and a highly educated labor force separate the world's leading economic nations from the others. The United States is the world's economic leader. The only nations that remain competitive are ones that are also highly developed technologically and have the educated labor force to be so.

Economists conduct four basic types of studies relating education to social and private economic benefits: Growth accounting studies, economic impact studies, rate of return studies, and wage studies. The first two relate primarily to general effects of education. Results from education studies and higher education studies are presented because the separate effects are not easy to disentangle.

Growth accounting studies relate the factors believed to underlie overall economic growth to changes in Gross Domestic Product, a measurement of the dollar value of all final goods and services, including education, produced in the U.S. economy in a given period. Labor and capital are the two most important factors considered. Labor composition (a measurement of education) and research and development (a narrow measurement of scholarship) are often included as well. They provide estimates of education's contributions to economic growth.

Economic impact studies trace the benefit that an institution adds to a particular community or region by tracing the flow of additional revenues resulting from the institution's presence in the community. The focus is on additional revenues because the other revenues would already be in the community. These studies have focused on regional economics because students came primarily from within the United States, so they added nothing to the national economy. They would have spent their money somewhere within the nation anyhow. The influx of foreign students to American colleges and universities is making a national economic impact study more meaningful.

Rate of return studies relate the economic return of investment in education to the economic cost of the investment. They have been used primarily to study returns to instruction and so will be discussed under that heading.

### Growth Accounting

Becker and Lewis (1992) note that early growth accounting studies included only the relationships between the quantities of labor and capital and assumed that the residual was due to education. More recent models include specific variables for education and research and development. Becker and Lewis conclude that the returns to education and research are very positive, in the range of 15 to 21 percent and growing.

The Bureau of Labor Statistics (1993) has concluded that labor composition and research and development, the two factors related most directly to higher education, have been important since at least 1948 and increasingly important since at least 1979 in enhancing productivity (p.11). Productivity per hour of all persons in the business sector grew at a rate of 2 percent between 1950 and 1992 in the non-farm business sector and of 1.6 percent in the business sector (p. 4). Multi-factor productivity grew at an average rate of 1.3 percent between 1950 and 1990. Output per unit of capital declined at a rate of 0.5 percent during that same time period (p. 8) Average annual contributions of factor inputs to aggregate input show that labor composition is becoming more important, and that research and development is higher during higher productivity periods (p. 55). Productivity growth slowed during 1973-1979. Various factors are suspected of causing the slowdown including a leveling off in research and development expenditures (p. 6).

Education generally and higher education specifically have produced far more increase in gross domestic product than the increases in their expenditures. Not only does higher education affect national economic growth, it also affects regional economic growth. These effects have been studied primarily through economic impact studies, focusing on public colleges and universities.

## Economic Impact Studies

Smith and Drabenstott (1992) provided a valuable review of these studies and concluded that "Publicly supported colleges and universities play a critical role in economic development, but that role is neither well defined nor easily understood." They note that the key linkages are complex, hard to quantify, and subject to change over time. The studies they cited concluded that higher education contributes strongly to local economies. For example, Plaut and Pluta (1983) found a positive relationship between state industrial growth and total education expenditures after controlling for the effects of other relevant market, labor, land, tax, and expenditure variables. Wasylenko and McGuire (1985) found a statistically significant, positive relationship between total employment growth and state spending on education. Jones and Vedlitz (1988) concluded that the levels of state spending for higher education and the level of educational quality are positively related to state economic growth.

Jones and Vedlitz also found "solid support for the idea that business creation is a critical component of the economic growth process, in that it is causally prior to employment growth." Second, they "...found that spending for higher education in the states affects business creation but not job growth." Job growth occurs indirectly as the created businesses grow. They caution that migration of educated individuals from the state will attenuate the effects. "States that focus resources on their flagship research universities seem to fare better than those employing more of a scattersite approach."

Much of higher education's community support arises from beliefs about the regional economic impact of each institution. Leslie and Slaughter (1992) evaluate studies of higher education's regional economic impact. They note that jobs and wealth are the two major direct economic contributions of higher education to communities, and the major indirect economic impact is in the earnings and spending of all college graduates.

Not only do higher education expenditures benefit the local economy, but there is evidence that the benefits offset the increased tax burden. Helms (1985) presented evidence that the disincentive effects of state and local taxes on business location may be overcome when tax revenue is used to finance improved public services such as education, highways, and public health and safety. In particular, the author showed that state spending on higher education has a positive and statistically significant relationship to a state's personal income, a relationship large enough to outweigh the negative effect on growth of the taxes used to finance the expenditures.

## Quality Productivity

Economic growth studies have a qualitative component to them because they measure growth in monetary terms. Spending decisions also have a qualitative component to them, but the quality dimension of economic growth is not fully reflected in expenditures. Baumol, Blackman and Wolff (1989) compare life in the 19th century with contemporary life. The comparison illustrates concretely how knowledge-based technological development has changed life quality for most people. Fewer children die. People eat better. They work fewer hours for life's necessities. They have more discretionary time. They can more readily move to follow opportunities. They can communicate with and visit friends and family more frequently at much lower cost. Designer dress styles are quickly available to most consumers. Of course, economic freedom brings responsibility for choices that make life worse as well as better.

Economic factors enable and constrain us but there are many other factors that influence the quality of our lives, particularly social and spiritual factors. The increased potential for meaningful lives also increases the potential for less meaningful lives depending on the choices we make as individuals and groups. Education can be an important tool in making wiser choices, further underscoring its importance.

## Instruction

There are many theories about the relationship between instruction and economic outcomes. They were developed for education generally, but relate to higher education as well.

The studies of the relationship between the structures and processes of formal instruction and social-level and private-level economic outcomes support the importance of education to outcomes at both levels. Productivity is enhanced at the social level and job opportunities and income are enhanced at the private level. While economists continue to disagree about the mechanisms, the evidence provides a meaningful pattern. Education is associated with productivity and compensation growth, but the relationship is not perfect.

## Explanations

Economists have provided various explanations for the relationship between instruction and social and private economic outcomes. These theories differ in several ways. They differ about whether job structures adapt to differences in individual potential, whether education causes economic outcomes or is merely statistically associated with them, in other words, whether educational outcomes are technical or just institutional. They differ in assumptions about the adaptability of job structures; in other words, do job structures adjust to enable people to use their increased capacities or not? They differ as to whether private economic returns follow personal productivity; in other words, do markets ultimately require owners and managers to reward employees for their productivity?

### Human capital theories

The most important theory about the economic relationship between education and society is human-capital theory. It has a long history in economic thought. Adam Smith (1776/1976) referred to the basic concept in *On the Wealth of Nations,* but 20th century economists really developed it (for example, Becker 1964/1993; Denison, 1962; Schultz, 1963). At the social level, the theory is that education endows individuals with habits, knowledge, attitudes, and other capacities that enable them to be more productive. At the social level, firms take advantage of the increased capacity to produce more and better goods and services, increasing the total wealth of society. At the private level, individuals' increased productivity leads to their increased compensation.

Human capital theory has been a primary basis for governmental policy. For example, it was one of the justifications for the investment in education in Lyndon Johnson's War on Poverty. It has also been a basis for World Bank decisions about where to invest. Most other theories about the economic relationship between education and society respond to human capital theory. Human capital theories led economists to conduct rate of return studies that provide strong evidence of economic returns to education. Although, the exact nature of education's contributions remains controversial.

### Screening

Many economists and sociologists have questioned human capital theory. The major alternative among economists is screening theory (for example, Arrow, 1973; Spence, 1973). It is that education does not endow individuals with enhanced habits, knowledge, capacities, and attitudes but merely screens individuals to determine how productive they will be, enabling firms to identify them more readily and put them to work, increasing the quantity and quality of goods and services in society. Both of these are examples of technical as well as institutional production because they involve a social recognition of an actual difference in the physical basis of the people. Screening theory is often confused with credentialing theory, which does not assume a technical difference in people's capabilities.

## Credentialing

A related theory involving only institutional production is that education does not necessarily identify the most able, it merely credentials people (Berg, 1971). Society believes in the credentials and gives credentialed people better opportunities. This results not in increased quantity and quality of goods and services, but in private returns to the credentialed individuals.

## Chartering

A variant of credentialing theory is chartering. Chartering adds an additional element to credentialing that can enhance social outcomes. In its simplest form, Meyer (1970) says, because people believe in educational credentials they expect credentialed individuals to be different or to perform better, and credentialed individuals expect themselves to perform better. They are more likely to accept socialization and to make special efforts to satisfy others' expectations. For example, people might expect a Harvard graduate to "do better than that," which might lead the graduate to do so.

## Job-queuing theory

Lester Thurow (1972) has argued that human capital theory does not adequately capture the effect of education. He notes that people's increased capacities do not lead to increased productivity unless the structure of jobs in the economy permits use of the increased capacities. When the job structure is sticky–does not smoothly adjust–there is no increased productivity in society. The credentials merely alter people's positions in the queue for jobs, redistributing the private returns but not enhancing the economy.

## Overeducation or underemployment

Thurow's recognition that the job structure needs to adjust to take advantage of employees' increased capacity raises an important issue involving education and society, the issue of overeducation. The basic idea is that individuals with more education than a job requires might be less productive than those meeting the minimum requirements (Tsang and Levin, 1985). They are not as challenged or do not take the job as seriously, perhaps because they feel the job is beneath them.

Tsang (1987) found that employees that exceeded the minimum educational requirements for jobs had lower levels of productivity than those who barely met the educational requirements. They appeared to be overeducated for the jobs and the overeducation led to reduced productivity. The prospect of reduced productivity due to overeducation is a concern in a society that is seeing people with college degrees taking jobs formerly occupied by people with high school degrees.

The corollary theory is underemployment. The idea is that employees do not need to be less productive because they are overeducated. The employer could make them more productive by modifying the job structure to permit them to take advantage of their additional capacity to be productive. This requires a flexibility often associated with participatory management strategies.

### Radical economic theory

Bowles and Gintis (1975, 1976) imply that education leads to increased productivity in society but at a social cost. Formal education socializes people into acceptance of economic roles in society. For most people, the roles require them to learn to submit to authority, perform personally meaningless tasks for extrinsic rewards, and accept social inequalities as fair returns to merit even when they are not. These economists imply that the changes in personal characteristics do lead to increased productivity within a capitalist structure, but the returns to the productivity go primarily to the managers and owners not the employees, and the job structure alienates employees from the intrinsic value of their work.

### Importance of Education to Productivity

Human capital, job-queuing, chartering, and radical economic theory all support a technical relationship between education and productivity, but the relationships differ. Human capital, job queuing, and radical economic theories assume that education produces technical outcomes, making the person different in capacities, beliefs, role understanding, or in other ways that enhance the person's potential for productive labor. These theories differ in terms of consequences. Human capital theory implicitly assumes that the job structure will adjust to take advantage of participants' increased capacities. Radical economic theory assumes that education socializes participants into being willing to submit to the job structure. Job queuing theory does not assume that the structure will adjust. If it does not, then education becomes merely a credential that alters people's positions in the queue for jobs, leaving people underemployed and their productive potential undeveloped, an ineffective outcome. Human capital theory and radical economic theory differ in their assumptions about who receives the benefits from the increased productivity. Human capital theory assumes that in the long run markets will adjust to equalize productivity and compensation. Radical economic theory assumes that owners and managers will capture more than their share of the economic outcomes.

Chartering theory does not make the assumption that education enhances individuals' productive capacity. Instead, it assumes an institutional outcome to education, that increased productivity might result from conforming to the label that society has attached of being a graduate of a particular kind.

These theories are not all mutually exclusive. Each provides potential insights into the economic relationships between education and society. Underlying almost all of the theories is an assumption that education is associated with higher levels of productivity either because it increases people's productive capacity directly or because it causes them to raise their levels of productivity to conform to others' expectations. Whatever the reason, most economists agree that education is one of the primary factors that determines the quality and quantity of goods and services in society.

Whether instruction provides additional capacities or not remains a question, but some evidence does support the human capital assumption. Psacharopolous (1984) supports the view that better educated people are more productive and rejects attacks on the schooling link to productivity, and Kiker and Roberts (1984) find that human capital depreciates without continued investment. The longer people have been away from formal schooling the lower the returns. Depreciation makes little sense for a screening effect. Credentialing could have a depreciation effect if credentials lose their meaning over time, but that would be a very subtle use of credentials.

Mitch (1990) suggests that formal education is not as indispensable to economic growth as theorists assume, just as the railroad was not as indispensable as earlier economists had assumed. He suggests that experience and informal capacity development are substitutes. At present this is not the case. The socialization, screening, and credentialing roles of formal education cannot be accomplished through informal capacity development, and experience is difficult to obtain without credentials. Anyone seeking substitutes for formal education will need to address the socialization, screening, and credentialing requirements of prospective employers or alter the institutional environment that supports credentialing.

See Becker and Lewis (1993), Cohn and Geske (1990), Leslie and Brinkman (1988) for general discussions of the various theories and empirical studies about the economic benefits of education. See also Dean (1984) for a focus on the relation of education to productivity growth.

## Importance of Education to Employment and Wages

The evidence relating education to economic outcomes is circumstantial, but the statistical associations are strong and varied. Higher education is statistically associated with increased compensation, systematic differences in compensation by college major, increased opportunities for job training, reduced probability of unemployment, and differences in relationships to technology, including whether capital generally replaces labor. It is also associated with substantial non-market and non-economic benefits.

### Internal rates of return

In internal rate of return studies, a person's lifetime stream of income is related to the cost of college including forgone employment, both discounted to present value, to compute the rate of return that would equate the present value of income and costs. Critics have viewed the results of these studies with skepticism, primarily because they have many weaknesses, but most of the weaknesses lead them to understate the returns. They do not capture the indirect economic benefits. They also do not capture the non-economic benefits. Estimates can be overstated as well. Hoenack (1990) has warned that much of the work on internal rates of return is subject to selectivity bias because most of the people who go to college would have earned more anyhow.

In a meta-analysis of rate-of-return studies, Leslie and Brinkman (1988) concluded that the internal rate of return to a four-year degree was in the range of 11.8 to 13.4 percent. The rates differed depending upon the assumptions of the method. They concluded that the rates of return decreased with educational level, the return to a master's degree being about 7.2 percent and to a Ph.D. about 6.6 percent. A primary reason for the decline in returns to more advanced degrees is that the opportunity cost of obtaining further education increases dramatically with the increases in income potential resulting from the prior education.

Rate-of-return studies were conducted primarily before the demand for college educated labor increased dramatically in the late 1980s and 1990s. Wage studies corroborate the high private rates of return and provide evidence of the dramatically increased demand for college labor in the 1980s and 1990s.

## Wage and compensation studies

Becker (1992) found solid evidence for a dramatic difference in compensation between college educated and non-college educated labor. After reviewing the literature and presenting proposed explanations for the differences, he concludes that higher education is an investment that yields a respectable financial return to both society and the individual.

Murphy and Welch (1989) reviewed 25 years of data on wages to college graduates. They found that the returns increased between 1963 and 1971, declined between 1971 and 1979, and increased since then. They suggest that the decline during the 1970s resulted from an oversupply of college-educated labor. They believe that the subsequent increases appear to be due to an increasing demand for college educated labor and a reduced supply. They speculate that the increased demand might result from changing patterns of international and national trade, structural changes in the domestic economy (shifts to service sector jobs), and changes in production technologies within industries (shifts to flexible production and increased use of computer aided technologies).

Traditionally, real compensation has increased with productivity, but that connection has weakened in recent years. Real compensation per hour and output per hour rose at about the same rate between 1950 and 1988 (3.0 and 2.8 percent) (Bureau of Labor Statistics, 1993, p. 39). Between 1974 and 1979 they grew at exactly the same rate (0.7 percent). Since then labor productivity has increased much faster than real compensation (1.0 percent versus 0.2 percent) (p. 38). The weakened relationship between productivity and compensation has become an important concern.

## Education and technology

Mincer (1989) reviewed the relationship between education and adaptation to technology. He reports that Bartel and Lichtenberg (1987) found that more educated workers were used in industries using more recently developed equipment. This effect was magnified in research and development intensive industries. The effects held for workers with relatively recent vintages of education. They were not significant for workers above 45. He also reported that Gill (1988) related proportions of full-time workers with specified education levels to Jorgenson's measures of multi-factor productivity growth in 28 industries covering the whole economy over the periods 1960-1979 and 1970-1979. "Correlations were positive for workers with more than high school, negative for high school dropouts, and zero for high school graduates. Gill also found that the proportion of more educated workers was greater in technologically progressive industries within each of eight broad occupation groups.

Mincer (1989) also found, "Proportions of workers whose education exceeded high school were larger in industries in which productivity growth was more rapid." "As productivity growth stops and so, presumably, technology ages, fewer educated workers are needed to handle it. Evidently, worker training substitutes for the use of more educated workers…" This conclusion is more consistent with human capital theory than screening or credentialing theories.

## Unemployment rates

Howe (1992) reviewed the literature and did an empirical analysis of higher education's effect on unemployment rates. He concluded: "More education has always reduced the probability of being unemployed. And, it has become an increasingly important criterion of job market access over time." The demand for college graduates has increased over time largely at the expense of the demand for high school graduates. "In addition, skills possessed by high-school graduates often have not matched the skills required for available jobs in a growing economy. This is particularly a problem for many older workers displaced from dying or stagnant industries." High school graduates accounted for over 66 percent of the rise in unemployment between 1968 and 1988 while college graduates accounted for only 15 percent. "It is likely that the competitive advantage held by college graduates will continue into the future," particularly during downturns in the business cycle.

## Job training

Levels of formal instruction also affect job training opportunities. Mincer (1989) summarized a number of studies of job training. The studies found quite consistently that the likelihood of respondents' receiving job training increased with education, declined with age and length of seniority, was greater for married men and smaller for married women, and is greater in large firms and where the machinery is more costly. The studies also found that job training increases employee's wage growth. The rates of growth were higher for more recently graduated workers.

## Technological development and labor

Becker and Lewis (1992) note that there is a disagreement about whether capital development complements or substitutes for labor. They say that capital-skill complementarity is well known in the economics literature, and that several authors have shown that more educated individuals are better able to absorb new information, take initiative, and adopt new technologies (Bartel and Lichtenberg, 1987; Jamison and Lau, 1982). Becker (1992) discusses briefly the relationship between educated labor and capital. He cites Hamermesh (1986) as claiming solid support for the idea that unskilled labor is primarily a substitute for physical capital while skilled labor is primarily a complement, but Pencavel (1992) points to the work of Weiss (1977) and Denny and Fuss (1983) to conclude that the evidence is mixed.

## Non-market and non-economic impacts

Cohn and Geske (1992) surveyed research on the non-market effects of education. They found that despite fluctuations over time, the internal rates of return to education have remained remarkably stable, especially over the long run. The private rates of return for a four-year degree ranged from 10 to 21 percent. The internal rates of return for graduate education are typically much smaller. Estimates in the United States run from negative to 23.6 percent, with the bulk of estimates under 10 percent.

Cohn and Geske speculate that societies invest in higher education primarily for the non-market and non-monetary returns, which they conclude are considerable. They examined economic studies of some of these outcomes and found returns to family life, health, consumption behavior, asset management, and culture and values, among other things.

Anderson and Hearn (1992) reviewed studies of equity outcomes in higher education and concluded that inequities remain but progress has been made for women and ethnic minorities. The problems remain most severe for those from low socioeconomic backgrounds: "Repeatedly, the research literature suggests that coming from a socio-economically disadvantaged background limits educational attainments and limits the positive effects of college attendance on occupational and income attainments." (p. 327)

In a footnote Cohn and Geske (1992) acknowledge the existence of substantial external benefits. They cite Ehrlich (1975) and Webb (1977) on reduced crime participation, and Taylor and Wolfe (1971) and Stapleton (1976) on political participation. Substantial impacts of many types have also been found in non- economic studies of higher education. See for example, Feldman and Newcomb (1973) and Pascarella and Terenzini (1991).

## Conclusions

While the evidence is ex post facto and the causal relations are still debated, the strong association between education in general, higher education in particular, and positive economic outcomes is overwhelming. Higher education instruction has become increasingly important. Demand has increased for educated labor, and higher productivity and increased earnings and opportunities are all associated with college education.

Additionally, higher education contributes scholarship to the instruction. It primarily provides the knowledge bases for all formal and informal instruction and all social rational processes, political and cultural as well as economic. Almost all technological progress, increased social awareness, and economic productivity have higher education scholarship at their base.

The combination of instruction and scholarship, not to mention service, makes education, particularly higher education, one of society's most economically effective set of enterprises. Despite extensive anecdotes of organizational inefficiencies, widespread public criticism, and increasingly detailed proposals for reform, formal education provides a combination of cognitive development, socialization, screening, credentialing, and chartering associated with important and consistently positive private and social outcomes. Possible explanations for causality are strong. In fact, most explanations, even critical ones, assume some form of causality.

## COSTS—DO HIGHER EDUCATION COST INCREASES RESULT PRIMARILY FROM INTERNAL ORGANIZATIONAL PATHOLOGIES OR EXTERNAL ENVIRONMENTAL CHANGES?

Concerns about the increasing costs of higher education have been widely expressed in the media. In particular they assume that institutions of higher education are inefficient because they do not keep their cost increases from exceeding inflation. The inefficiencies are assumed to reflect organizational pathologies even by many scholars and higher education participants (Getz and Siegfried, 1991; Gumport and Pusser, 1995; Leslie and Rhoades, 1995; Massy, 1991a and 1991b; Massy and Wilger, 1995). Americans are reluctant to support enterprises that they believe do not work.

Scott (1992, Chapter 12) defines organizational pathologies through providing examples. They are grouped according to the people they most affect. One set affects organizational participants and the other, organizational publics. The pathologies for participants are alienation, inequity, and over-conformity or ritualism. For publics, they are unresponsiveness, inefficiency, and relentlessness.

Massy (1991a, pp. 4-5) provides three possible explanations of cost increases in administration and student services and five of academic costs. For administration and student services, the explanations are build-up of organizational slack, accretion of unnecessary tasks, and function lust. The latter two he groups with other explanations under the heading of the administrative lattice. For academic costs, they are the cost disease, the growth force, organizational slack, output creep, and situation-specific factors, such as government regulation or the cost of energy during the oil crisis (Massy, 1991b, pp. 1-5). He describes all of these as pathological except the cost disease, the growth force, and situation-specific factors. These three result from changes in the environment.

Getz and Siegfried (1991, pp. 262-268) provide six possible explanations of cost increases in higher education: increased student demand for services, increased institutional competition for inputs, the cost disease, status-seeking, weak management, and increased governmental regulation. Status-seeking and weak management are pathological. The others reflect changes in the environment.

Leslie and Rhoades (1995) provide 11 propositions about administrative cost increases in higher education for empirical testing. They are increased support for alternative revenue generation, increased governmental regulation, increased organizational complexity, shifts of responsibilities from faculty, increases in participatory management, self-perpetuation, imitation of other institution's successes, imitation of state-of-the-art structures, proximity to budget decision-makers, proximity to high status external organizations, and personal characteristics of administrators. All are described as basically internally pathological except increased governmental regulation.

Gumport and Pusser (1995, pp. 501-505) note the increases in administrative expenditures and in counts of administrators in the University of California between 1966-1967 and 1991-1992. They call these increases bureaucratic accretion. They suggest six explanations and empirically test some of them. The explanations are the additive explanation, adaptation to complexity, adaptation to institutional forces for legitimacy, tactical administrative growth, mission as policy, and administrative maximizers. All are described in pathological terms, except perhaps adaptation to complexity and adaptation to institutional forces for legitimacy.

These explanations and others are described next, as much as possible in the words of their authors. The pathologies are presented first, then the responses to environmental changes. Then the explanations are compared with empirical evidence to determine how well they fit the data.

## Organizational Pathologies

Most explanations of cost increases fit clearly into one of Scott's (1992) classifications. A few could fit into more than one. The administrative lattice has complexities that fit unresponsiveness as well as relentlessness. Massy (1991a) notes that the administrators themselves think they are fulfilling their responsibilities, a kind of relentlessness.

### Unresponsiveness

Scott (1992) notes that Max Weber and other past and present political analysts have expressed concern about how societies could maintain control over expanding public bureaucracies. "'More and more the specialized knowledge of the expert became the foundation for the power position of the officeholder '(1946 trans., p. 235)."

### Status-seeking

Getz and Siegfried (1991, p. 265) write, "Under the constraints of not-for- profit organization, it seems plausible to assume that the compensation of those in control, as well as the prestige of being associated with the institution may play a prominent role among the institution's objectives....Under such circumstances, and with limitations on free entry into the market, institutions are likely to provide greater quality (smaller classes, higher admission standards, greater emphasis on research) than would accommodate consumer tastes in a competitive for-profit market (Newhouse, 1970)."

### Output creep (Massy, 1991b, p. 2)

Massy defines output creep as, "...the creep of higher education's output mix toward more of what faculty want to produce as opposed to what payers want to buy." It is most likely to manifest itself in lower student-faculty ratios, lower student- teaching assistant ratios, lower course-loads, and larger class sizes.

### Inefficiency

Scott's discussion focuses on inefficiencies in organizations not facing market discipline and incentives.   In particular, he discusses  Olson's (1965 and 1982) arguments about self-interest interfering with organizational efficiency. They do not relate specifically to higher education, but the concern about organizational efficiency is shared by higher education's critics.

### Weak management (Getz and Siegfried, 1991, p. 266)

"If institutions do not carefully assess costs and benefits when making decisions, if purchase decisions are not made in a way that induces vendors to give attractive prices, and if rewards are little associated with performance, then indeed costs will be higher without the college's services being more attractive to students or improving faculty welfare....To account for rising college and university costs in the 1980's, however, the quality of management must have deteriorated vis-â-vis earlier periods." Weak management would result in higher prices for the same ingredients, among other things.

### Mission as policy (Gumport and Pusser, 1995, pp. 504-505)

"...under certain circumstances, the university mission may stand in for explicit university policy. The university mission provides few clear institutional mechanisms for selecting among priorities or making resource allocation decisions in accord with those priorities....Mission as policy in a time of abundant resources may lead to unanticipated, capital-intensive consequences."

### Increased organizational slack (Massy, 1991a and 1991b)

Organizational slack is excess organizational capacity. Some slack is necessary to enable an organization to accommodate disturbances in its environment but too much slack is inefficient (Scott, 1992, p. 235). If increases in organizational slack are a source of the problem, then resources per student will be increasing.

### The additive explanation (Gumport and Pusser, 1995, pp. 501-502)

Blau (1973) and Gumport and Pusser (1995) found that the economies of scale enjoyed in higher education administration decreased over time. Gumport and Pusser speculate that this results from the Durkheimian tendency "...in times of rising revenue intraorganization conflicts may be mediated by adding positions and resources rather than making exclusive choices."

### Relentlessness

Scott regards relentlessness as the most important pathology facing contemporary organizations. He quotes Coleman (1974, p. 49), "Decisions about the employment of resources are more and more removed from the multiplicity of dampening and modifying interests of which a real person is composed–more and more the resultant of a balance of narrow interests of which corporate actors are composed."

### Administrative maximizers (Gumport and Pusser, 1995)

"...budget maximization is an essential pursuit and...those who do not maximize will not persist." Quoting from Meyer et al., "Concepts of rational administration themselves generate complexity beyond that imposed by task demands." "In a time of increasing resources, growth becomes less a possibility than an inevitability of inertia."

### Tactical administrative growth (Gumport and Pusser, 1995)

"...refers to administrative responses to perceived political economic pressures for short-run excellence....In the case of UC, one perspective suggests that the University may have increasingly directed resources to managing perceptions of quality and utility at some cost to core quality processes....In this scenario, reputation and resource acquisition respond more to administrative interventions than to instructional interventions."

### The administrative lattice (Massy, 1991c, pp. 7-8)

"'The administrative lattice' is the process by which administrative staff proliferates and gets entrenched...the phenomenon is systemic rather than being the result of any particular policy or intent." Among other things it includes the following three elements:

*Accretion of unnecessary tasks* (Massy, 1991a, pp. 5-6). "'The supply of administrators creates its own demand.'" "A good person is hired to perform a task. This task results in the discovery of new problems, creating the need to perform additional tasks. Others in the organization are drawn in, since they must respond to or defend against the new initiatives. Problems of coordination increase and more time is spent in meetings. Soon additional people must be hired to keep up with the increased workload."

*Function lust* (Massy, 1991a, p. 5). Professionals think their roles are important and see a need for more of it. Their motives are pure, but the result is an expansion of their functions, a self-perpetuating growth is the label of Leslie and Rhoades (1995). "Increases in administrative costs are a function of the self-perpetuating growth of administration."

*Responsibility shifts from faculty to administration* (Massy, 1991b; Leslie and Rhoades, 1995). Leslie and Rhoades propose, "Increases in administrative costs are a function of administrators taking on functions formerly performed by faculty." This enables faculty members to concentrate on their preferred activities. It could enable enterprise costs to rise without student-faculty ratios rising. Student-administrator costs would rise instead.

### Increased costs from participatory management (Massy and Wilger, 1991, p. 7; Leslie and Rhoades, 1995, p. 197)

"...increases in administrative costs are a function of the growth of consensus management in administration." (Leslie and Rhoades, 1995).

### Diversifying revenue sources (Leslie and Rhoades, 1995)

"The more an institution emphasizes the generation of alternative revenues, the greater the proportion of resources that are directed to administrative units perceived as (potentially) generating such revenues." (p. 193) This explanation is included as pathological because of the emphasis on perception and potential. All levels of government have reduced their higher education support creating a need for additional revenues. If the search is sensible, then it is a response to environmental changes. If it is relentless, then it is pathological. Leslie and Rhoades describe it as too extreme, based on perceptions and potentiality, rather than reality.

### Academic ratchet (Massy, 1991a)

Massy says that faculty members increase the costs of instruction by arguing for more discretionary time for research and consulting. They seek smaller classes and lighter teaching loads. The effect of these requests is to ratchet up the cost of higher education. If the academic ratchet is working, student-teacher ratios, student- teaching assistant ratios or class sizes would continually increase.

### Inequity

Scott (1992) notes, "Formal organizations are expected to be fair in their treatment of personnel...achievement is supposed to replace ascription as the basis for distributing rewards." (p. 323) The focus of Scott's concern is inequities from ascription to organizational participants, but he is also concerned with structural inequities (pp. 324-325). These might well encompass inequities from differences in structural position.

## *Budget proximity* (Leslie and Rhoades, 1995)

"The greater the organizational distance between the unit and the budgetary decision maker, the smaller will be the proportional increase in the resource allocation to that unit."

## *Administrative connection to external power and privilege* (Leslie and Rhoades, 1995)

"Increases in administrative costs will be proportionate to the unit's perceived closeness to the high technology and corporate marketplaces." "The ascribed characteristics of administrators and their clients (ethnicity, gender, and social-class background) will have an effect on increases in administrative costs among central administrative units and among academic units."

### External Demands

Costs do not necessarily increase because of organizational pathologies. They also increase because of external demands. The technical or institutional environment changes and the organization needs to adapt to the changes.

### The Technical Environment

The technical environment includes market forces of supply and demand. As demand or supply for resources or products changes, organizations need to adapt to survive. Sometimes this means raising costs. For example, increased competition for resources usually increases the resources' prices. In turn organizational costs increase unless the organization can substitute lower priced resources, because higher education enterprises operate in competitive markets for students and other essential resources (Rothschild and White, 1993).

## *Increased demand for inputs* (Getz and Siegfried, 1991, pp. 264-265)

Higher education has experienced a variety of changes in demand for resources and services that have affected costs. The most important of these has the unfortunate rubric of the cost disease, which makes it sound pathological when it is not. It is really just the increased demand for organizational resources resulting from their increased productivity elsewhere in society.

*Increased demand because of an increasingly productive economy–the cost disease.* Baumol and Blackman (1983) have shown that the per unit cost of an activity that has a relatively fixed ratio of inputs to outputs will increase if the larger economy becomes more productive because relatively less output is being produced by the inputs. The increasing productivity of the economy increases demand for the resources so their prices rise. The fixed ratio of inputs means that the price increases in the inputs become cost increases in the product. Our society has defined education so that it has a fixed ratio of inputs to outputs. In fact, society probably requires universities to increase the ratio of all resources to students, further increasing the cost. This means that the economic growth that higher education causes increases higher education costs faster than inflation. The more effectively universities contribute to economic growth, the more their cost problems increase.

Saying that our society requires universities to maintain a fixed ratio of inputs to outputs means that as a society we evaluate the quality of higher education enterprises at least partially on the basis of ratios of resources to students, such as faculty-student ratios and study carrel-student ratios. Such ratios are also used by accrediting agencies in their determinations. University employees play important roles in these processes, and they are not completely disinterested.

The cost disease would predict that expenditures per student would rise at a rate roughly equaling inflation plus the rate of economic growth. This would mean that higher education instructional expenditures would increase on average about 3 percent per year from 1960 to 1993. They actually increased at a rate of only 1.6 percent.   The cost disease alone would more than explain this increase.

Faculty salaries would also increase faster than inflation for comparably situated faculty members, but this is not the case. Faculty salaries have barely held their own in real terms (Getz and Siegfried, 1991), despite salary increases from increasing average faculty age.

Costs can be measured in terms other than dollars. When measured in terms of faculty the cost of higher education has not changed dramatically over time. From the fall of 1976 until the fall of 1991, the last year for which statistics are readily available, the ratio of students to faculty (including research faculty) decreased from 16.6 to 16.4 (National Center for Education Statistics, Table 214, p. 227). This is not a dramatic increase. The ratio of students to all staff decreased more substantially from 5.4 to 4.9, but this could be very misleading. The variety of services that higher education enterprises provide has expanded greatly during this time period. These additional staff members are not necessarily supporting instruction.

*Increased demand for students.* Undergraduate enrollment is the most important single source of revenues for higher education and is central to the academic mission. Enrollment declines were widely predicted because of the reduction in number and quality of high school graduates. Higher education enterprises have needed to compete for the available students in ways that might well have increased costs. More underprepared students might have been admitted. More student services have been needed to assist the underprepared students and to compete for all students. Enrollments have also shifted toward graduate programs to compensate for decreased undergraduate enrollment and to meet increasing graduate student demand.

*Student demand for services* (Getz and Siegfried, 1991, pp. 262-264). "One explanation holds that the market is competitive and that institutions must therefore meet market tests to survive and prosper. Prospective students may be attracted by faculties with stronger reputations, better facilities, a stronger marketing program, and services that improve students' chances of success or that enhance their experience." On the other hand, competition for students may require institutions to keep costs down.

### Enrollment shifts to graduate programs

Universities have been criticized for shifting their attention to graduate education (for example, Massy, 1991b, p. 3), but that is where the enrollment is shifting. They are also criticized for layering program on program but that is also where enrollment is shifting. The contemporary knowledge base is becoming more complex. It is not surprising that academic programs mirror that complexity. They help create it and help disseminate it. Students are not required to major in these new programs. The programs are market based and students shift to respond to market opportunities.

Student-teacher ratios are smaller on average for graduate students, and faculty teaching loads for graduate courses are often lighter with the rationale that graduate faculty members need to spend more time keeping current in their fields. This means that graduate education is more expensive. As higher education enrollments shift more from undergraduate to graduate education, student-teacher ratios decrease and higher education costs increase. Also, graduate programs typically require more library, laboratory, computer, and other instructional resources for students and faculty, further increasing the cost of higher education as enrollments shift toward graduate education. Increased graduate enrollment can also increase costs because undergraduate instruction and graduate instruction are substitutes, at least within particular service mixes (Cohn, Rhine, and Santos, 1989; Nerlove, 1972; Olson, 1994).

### Efficiency of resource mix

Nerlove (1972) theorizes about the complementarity and substitutability of undergraduate education and research and graduate education. He assumes that they complement each other where one of the activities clearly dominates the other, but in the range of more equal production of both they are substitutes. This means that if higher education institutions are shifting from undergraduate education dominating graduate education to more of a balance, the costs of higher education will increase. If this is a source of cost increases, student-teacher ratios should be decreasing. He treats graduate education and research as one integral activity.

In a study of faculty gross productivity, Olson (1994) found economies of scale and scope for undergraduate instruction and research, and for undergraduate and graduate instruction. Brinkman (1990) found economies of scale and scope in universities. He theorized that norms for faculty create a fixed-cost situation. As enrollments increase, marginal costs decrease. But Getz and Siegfried (1991) warn that economies of scale might be an artifact of the transitional nature of the resulting resource-student ratios. It takes longer to increase faculty appointments and other enterprise resources than student enrollments. In the interim there appear to be economies of scale.

Cohn, Rhine, and Santos (1989) studied 1,887 institutions of higher education for the academic year 1981-1982. Their results differed from Nerlove's hypothesis but were largely consistent with Olson's findings about faculty. They found economies of scope for teaching and research, suggesting that they are complementary at those customary levels. They suggest that growth appears efficient only when it involves multiple outputs.

### Increased demand for expanded organizational activities

Many estimates of university expenditures per student are very misleading because they implicitly assume that all educational and general expenditures are for instruction. When doctoral university expenditures are allocated to their final cost objectives the instructional expenditures per student are dramatically lower. These adjustments are particularly important for research universities, some of which receive more revenue from research grants and contracts than from tuition (Olson, 1996).

Doctoral university faculty members spend more time engaged in university activities than faculty members at any other level. Their workloads appear to be lighter because teaching is only one of their responsibilities and it takes much more time to remain competent to teach at an advanced level.   They also have responsibility to develop and test the knowledge bases for their disciplines.

### The growth force (Massy, 1991b)

Knowledge and information technology are continually expanding. New knowledge and new technology do not necessarily replace the old, but often augment it. Colleges and universities need to support new programs as well as old ones. Libraries expand, course offerings expand, departments divide, faculty develop new specialties, new departments are created, new equipment is needed. The growth force manifests itself in additional courses, programs, disciplines, faculty, library materials, and specialized facilities and equipment. The growth force would result in increased costs because of an increase in resources per student, if not at the level of academic programs, then perhaps at the levels that administer and support the more complex array of programs. In instruction, higher education might have more faculty per student, more staff per student, more teaching assistants per student, more space per student, more equipment per student, and so forth. Brinkman (1990) found that the expansion of number of departments led to increased marginal costs, perhaps in evidence of the growth force.

### Resource uncertainties and cost

Costs increase as institutions manage their environments, institutionally and technically. Proactive administrations require resources to conduct their activities. The enterprise may act more effectively, develop its opportunities more completely, but the per student costs will increase.

*Diversifying revenue sources* (Leslie and Rhoades, 1995). "The more an institution emphasizes the generation of alternative revenues, the greater the proportion of resources that are directed to administrative units perceived as (potentially) generating such revenues."

*Adaptation to complexity* (Gumport and Pusser, 1995). This adaptation to complexity can be both technical and institutional in nature. The technical adaptation is the growth necessitated by the need to coordinate the complexity, to make it work. The institutional adaptation is the need to add units that are needed to maintain the legitimacy of the university, the appropriate vice presidential offices, the appropriate student service offices, the ones that society expects a legitimate university to have. The institutional ones are inefficient from a narrow technical perspective, because they are not necessarily needed to do the work, but they are efficient from an institutional perspective because the university will have greater difficulty attracting students, faculty, staff, and donor support if its legitimacy as a university is called into question.

Gumport and Pusser (1995) propose that the administrative component of higher education institutions might grow merely as a response to the complexity of the external environment, responding to external demands to perform more and more tasks. This explanation might also apply to the instruction, research, service, and auxiliary components as well. They say that little empirical work has been done in this area, but cite Brinkman and Leslie (1986) as finding that greater complexity is associated with higher administrative cost. They also provide some evidence from their study of University of California expenditures. Gumport and Pusser also propose that administrative structures grow to adapt to institutional forces for legitimacy.

This is related to Leslie and Rhoades proposals about mimetic addition to administrative structure: "Faced with increased environmental uncertainty and with unclear technologies for achieving organizational ends, managers will increasingly adopt the administrative structures developed by successful organizations," and "The more that administrators become involved in professional associations, the more they and their institutions will tend to adopt normative administrative structures and practices."

*Organizational complexity and administrative cost* (Leslie and Rhoades, 1995). The more complex an institution becomes, the greater the share of its expenditures that will be devoted to administration."

*Reduced supply of government funding.* Ironically, the continually decreasing supply of government funding reduces the certainty of resources in the environment creating a need to develop alternative sources, which increases costs. New units need establishment and coordination. Not all of them will succeed. Other institutions compete for the resources, increasing the need for sophistication to succeed.

Yet this circumstance is expected to continue. Robert Atwell, President of the American Council on Education (1992) says that

...higher education should not expect to increase its share of GDP or state or federal funding because of competition from Medicaid, welfare, prisons, highways, and K-12 education. The claims of many of these other claimants are supported by government mandates or court orders. My point is not that higher education does not face this obstacle, but that it faces this obstacle with a misperception by most of the community including many of its spokespeople that it cannot justify its support. It is functioning very well, being very productive internally and externally, for its graduates and American society. There are problems as with any enterprise and they should be addressed. There are opportunities for improvement and they should be explored and developed as appropriate. But, the enterprise is sound. Its demands are sensible. It justifies its funding. Its research is as central to its effectiveness as its instruction. It is the combination of the two that is important. Mission creep is not necessarily a problem. It is the development of an opportunity in the face of a need for increased interaction between knowledge and instruction.

Atwell (1992, p. 7B) adds

Best of all, our prospects could improve if we could convince the citizenry and its elected representatives that investment in education yields both economic and social returns that exceed virtually any of the alternatives. The reality is that society needs us and is turning to us for help more than it ever has, yet our resources are inadequate to fulfill the expectations.

Government subsidies have declined consistently at all levels in recent years. This has shifted the cost burden of instruction increasingly to the institution and the student. It has also shifted the indirect cost burden of research increasingly to the institution. Schneider (1985) studied trends in indirect cost policy and concluded that the universities were underrecovering indirect costs. This means that the other activities in the university are subsidizing current sponsored research.

**The Institutional Environment**

The institutional environment changes with changes in legal requirements, including governmental regulations, or social expectations.

*Aging faculty*

A major factor in the price of faculty is that they are older. The institutional environment of our society includes a strong expectation that people receive rewards for their seniority independently of their productivity.

*More mandates and expectations*

Society's expectations of colleges and universities have increased. These enterprises are expected to instruct students in all of the same basics as before in addition to contemporary knowledge and skill and do it all in the same amount of time. They also need to interact with regulatory agencies and conform to their demands.

### Government regulation and cost increases (Getz and Siegfried, 1991; Leslie and Rhoades, 1995)

Getz and Siegfried note, "Occupational Safety and Health Administration regulations, Affirmative Action programs, requirement for access and services for the handicapped, requirements for coequal facilities for intercollegiate athletics for females, and increased requirements for cost sharing in many research, training, and other program grants might be cited as examples of regulations that impose cost burdens on institutions, usually without commensurate revenue offsets." Leslie and Rhoades (1995, p. 194) propose: "Increased state and federal regulatory pressure on higher education is associated with the growth of administrative staff and expenditure."

A recent indirect cost controversy led to a bureaucratic response requiring increased accounting by both the government and colleges for instruction and research This resulted in an increased demand for university accountants even though few institutions were accused of misconduct and accusations were limited to research programs. Ironically, concerns about indirect costs resulted primarily in increasing indirect costs.

### Imitation of state of the art structures (Leslie and Rhoades, 1995, p. 199)

"Faced with increased environmental uncertainty and with unclear technologies for achieving organizational ends, managers will increasingly adopt the administrative structures developed by successful organizations."

"The more that administrators become involved in professional associations, the more they and their institutions will tend to adopt normative administrative structures and practices."

### Adaptation to institutional forces for legitimacy (Gumport and Pusser, 1995)

"...in the pursuit of legitimacy a university will emulate structural forms of successful organizations in its organizational field, leading to similar structures across universities..." This explanation is pathological if the effort is overdone, but this behavior is not necessarily pathological. An organization must conform to the normative demands of its institutional environment to remain legitimate, and it must remain legitimate to continue to receive resources. Legitimacy maintenance is as important as satisfying market constraints. Failure to operate within either set of constraints leads to organizational failure. Institutional demands vary in their importance and flexibility, but failure for an organization to conform to social expectations can bring severe consequences rapidly.

*Resistance to faculty substitutes and other changes in institutionalized indicators of quality*

This is from the external environment as well as from the faculty members themselves. Instruction by full-time faculty costs more than instruction by doctoral students or part-time faculty, but the institutional environment of higher education responds negatively to substitutes for full-time faculty particularly in prestigious colleges and universities. In fact, the proportion of courses taught by full-time faculty is an institutionalized indicator of quality. Nevertheless, the proportion of part-time faculty has increased to reduce costs (National Science Foundation, 1994).

## Evidence and Conclusions

While there are many possible explanations of cost increases, the evidence to discriminate between them remains inadequate. However, some conclusions can be reached. First, the nonpathological explanations adequately explain the overall increases. Second, the explanations that assume increases resulting from deteriorating student-faculty ratios or real increases in faculty salaries, or instruction costs do not find support in the available evidence, at least not for higher education as a whole. Evidence might exist for particular institutions or types of institutions. Third, increases are primarily in administration and student services. Fourth, the hardest cost increases to explain except through pathologies are in the dramatic increase in the number of administrators. Fifth, there is some explanation for the effect of uncertain resources on higher education costs.

### Overall Cost Increases

Instructional expenditures have not increased at unreasonable rates even when we include indirect costs, such as administration, maintenance and student services. Getz and Siegfried (1991) analyzed HEGIS/IPEDS data for the period from 1978-79 to 1985-86 to identify the magnitude of the increases during the period. They used an estimate of university expenditures that they labeled adjusted education and general expenditures (AE&G). It included separately accounted for expenditures for instruction, public service, academic support, student services, institutional support, operation and maintenance of plant, unrestricted scholarships, and mandatory transfers. It excluded sponsored research and restricted scholarships. They found that costs per student increased 2.7 percent faster than the general price level for all of higher education. They found that market forces bear heavily on institutions of higher education. The other elements of AE&G grew faster than instruction.

Getz and Siegfried state that cost increases due to the cost disease will approximate the cost of living plus the growth in productivity. If we use the GDP price deflator as the measurement of inflation and GDP growth as the measurement of productivity growth, we find that higher education expenditures should have increased approximately 3 percent per student per year since about 1960, the real rate of GDP increase (National Center for Education Statistics, 1995, Table 30). In fact, expenditures increased only about 1.3 percent per student per year (Olson, 1996), dramatically less than one would expect from the cost disease. The best explanation for the smaller increase is the likelihood that the cost increases in higher education were artificially deflated by the social unacceptability of higher increases. This relaxed briefly during the mid-1980s as a result of widespread changes in beliefs about the need to increase funding for education to enable the nation to compete economically. These changes led to federal and state legislative actions to restore cuts in real funding.

### Faculty-Based Explanations

Many critics of higher education speak as if costs have increased because of faculty, but higher education cost increases do not appear to be faculty-related, at least for higher education as a whole. Getz and Siegfried found that faculty salaries increased by 1.6 percent per year above the rate of increase in the general price level. This is below the level of economic growth and so is less than would be expected from the cost disease. They found that the proportion of the instructional budget devoted to full-time faculty declined by 1.1 percent per year. Faculty salaries have probably declined after controlling for the aging of faculty because salaries are age dependent. Increasing salaries at the rate of inflation merely enables faculty members to purchase the same goods and services as before. They do not participate in the economic growth associated with higher education. Student-faculty ratios (National Center for Education Statistics, 1995) and student-teaching assistant ratios (National Science Foundation, 1994) have not deteriorated either.

Increases in costs generally have been surprisingly low, given changes in the external environment, particularly the cost disease and the growth force. Costs have increased at a reasonable rate for a fixed resource technology; in fact, faculty salaries have probably been artificially depressed. Higher education markets are heavily influenced by public perceptions. If society feels that faculty compensation is increasing too fast or that increases cannot be afforded, then it is more difficult for legislatures and boards of trustees to increase faculty salaries even if appropriate. Faculty members are then required to choose between their scholarly activities at a stagnant income or other activities. Many choose the stagnant incomes to retain the scholarly life.

### Administration and Student Services

There has been an increase in the number of administrative personnel and staff in colleges and universities (Getz and Siegfried, 1991; Massy, 1991a; Gumport and Pusser, 1995). With higher education costs remaining so far below what one would expect from all of the possible explanations, it is premature to assume that the growth in administration and student services is pathological. Higher education markets enjoy competitive discipline. Salaries do not increase at the rate that the cost disease would predict. They do not increase at the rate that the growth force would predict. It is hard to understand how costs can be controlled in other respects but not for administrators. Additional study is needed.

In the meantime higher education institutions should explore opportunities to use new technologies to make the same productivity gains, but the increases do not necessarily reflect inefficiency or mean that colleges and universities were in some sense broken.

### Less Certain Resources

Brinkman (1990) discusses revenues, prices, technological change, and social change as environmental factors affecting the stability of institutions of higher education (IHEs). He also discusses evidence of financial adjustments, providing tables of estimates of the proportion of four-year colleges that reduced instructional and education and general expenditures per FTE student between 1975 and 1984. Of course 1984 was near the bottom of the financial low afflicting higher education before *A Nation at Risk* and other national reports restored public acceptance of revenue increases for education. He also discusses the mechanisms that IHEs use to respond to revenue reductions. He classifies them as either resistance or adaptation strategies (Mingle and Norris, 1981). Resistance strategies include increasing student recruitment, improving student retention, increasing tuition, and diversifying revenue sources (ACE estimated that two-thirds of all IHEs experiencing revenue shortfalls during the last few years, particularly  public IHEs, reacted in all these ways except increasing tuition). Mixed strategies include one-time cost cutting. This one is almost universally adopted initially. Adaptation strategies include reducing the rate of growth of some budget categories, across-the-board cuts, selective cuts, reallocation of resources, and enhancing management and planning capabilities (Smith, 1980) such as program review, formal planning structures, cash-management techniques, and contingency funds (the first three of these can now be found in three-fourths of the nation's campuses while contingency funds are used at half (Andersen, 1985)). Instructional budgets are often protected during the first round of cost-cutting. Hyatt, Shulman, and Santiago (1984) found that the duration of the fiscal crisis, the degree of management flexibility available to the institution, the diversification of institutional revenue sources, the historical level of recurring program support, and the ability of administration to communicate with all of the institution's constituent groups influence how an IHE will respond.

### SHOULD GOVERNMENT CONTINUE TO SUBSIDIZE HIGHER EDUCATION AT PRESENT LEVELS?

Among the most important issues about higher education costs are subsidy issues: Who should subsidize whom and how should they do it? Federal, state, and local levels of government subsidize higher education instruction through establishment and support of public institutions of higher education and through scholarships, grants, and loans to students. The government and other sponsoring agencies that provide indirect cost revenues for sponsored research and other programs that exceed actual costs subsidize other activities of the institutions, perhaps instruction. Where indirect cost revenues do not cover indirect costs, other activities of the institution subsidize the research. All institutional donors subsidize various institutional activities. Undergraduate students subsidize other university activities, perhaps graduate and professional instruction or faculty research, if their tuition exceeds their instructional costs. Some support of research is an appropriate sharing of the cost of developing the knowledge bases of the instruction. Student tuition subsidizes auxiliaries if auxiliaries do not recover their full (direct and indirect) costs. Students in lower-cost majors subsidize students in higher-cost majors unless the institution has adopted discriminatory pricing. Students needing fewer services subsidize students needing more services. Institutions whose faculty enhance the knowledge bases of their disciplines through research and publishing subsidize institutions whose faculties do not. Institutions that subsidize the costs of educating students probably subsidize the institutions that hire them and the students themselves. Students who only pay the full instructional costs of their education have received subsidies from the developers of the knowledge bases of their instruction. Deferred maintenance results in the future subsidizing the past.

American higher education enjoys government subsidies. These shift some of the cost burden to taxpayers. They are sensible if they represent corrections needed for imperfect markets. Markets may need correction for imperfect information, spillovers, or inability to apply the exclusion principle. Information is imperfect if people would choose differently if they had a perfect understanding of all of the alternatives and their choices. A review of the popular literature, even the business literature, demonstrates the imperfect information about higher education. Spillovers are consequences of production or exchange that are not born by the decision-makers themselves. They can be positive or negative. Higher education theorists often argue for government subsidies because of the positive spillovers. Pollution is an example of a negative spillover. Application of the exclusion principle means that someone can exclude the benefits of an action from others. For example, a radio broadcast using conventional technology cannot be excluded from anyone within range who has a radio receiver. An important example in education is general knowledge. Its application cannot readily be excluded from use by anyone aware of it. All three of these market imperfections exist in higher education.

Freeman (1976, 1980) argued against expanding higher education during a period that productivity growth in the United States was relatively stagnant. He believed that government had oversubsidized higher education causing it to expand beyond the socially desirable point, so that higher education might actually be drawing away resources from other more productive activities and hindering America's economic growth.

Becker and Lewis (1992) presented five "countervailing arguments" against Freeman's contention of overinvestment. First, recent estimates of current and projected returns to higher education are not low (Berger, 1992; Murphy and Welch, 1989; and Becker, 1992). Second, Cohn and Geske (1990), Denison (1962), and Miller (1967) have argued effectively that expenditures on education compete primarily with consumption expenditures rather than with savings and so do not detract from physical capital investment. Therefore, they "can make a net contribution to growth even if the social rate of return might be lower for education than for physical capital." Third, the efficient system for college loans in the United States has facilitated market efficiencies that narrow the differences between alternative rates of return. These estimates of return are more meaningful than the aggregate rates on which Freeman based his contention. Fourth, the apparent social rate of return is misleading because the costs of education rise faster than other costs for purely structural reasons (the cost disease). In fact, higher education contributes to increasing productivity which in turn increases the relative cost of higher education. Fifth, rate-of-return studies ignore the productivity that results from higher education's interaction with other forms of investment. Higher education contributes in many ways to the increased productivity of capital and these complementary effects are overlooked in computing rates of return. For example, Griliches (1969), Fallon and Layard (1975), and Baumol, Blackman, and Wolff (1989) have shown that "primary level education is not enough to foster and maintain economic growth." Becker and Lewis (1992) note that higher education contributes to allocation efficiency. More educated individuals are better able to absorb new information, take initiative, and adopt new technologies (Bartel and Lichtenberg, 1988; and Jamison and Lau, 1982).

Lott (1987) summarizes eight hypotheses for why education is provided publicly, examines their weaknesses, and recommends an alternative to them, namely that public education enables the government to increase its legitimacy in ways that reduce the cost of acting (in terms of resistance from citizens), particularly in transferring wealth.

Important economic, psychological, and social consequences follow the choice of mechanisms for the subsidies, including the likelihood that a subsidy will occur, the voluntary nature of the subsidies, and the repayment burdens, among others. For example, subsidized loans increase the number of students who can be helped adequately while keeping the primary burden on the students. They reflect the investment nature of education. However, they also place a major emotional burden on student households and constrain the career choices that a graduate can make. The graduate needs to obtain enough compensation, combined with that of other household members, to support a household and pay the loans.

Becker (1990) says that a growing number of economists have claimed that low postsecondary tuition as a public policy is both inefficient and inequitable, but Pechman (1970) and a number of other economists disagree. Using a different methodology, they arrive at the opposite result. This controversy remains unresolved.

The decline of government support for education reflects widespread changes in the institutional environment. Education competes with other government programs for increasingly scarce tax dollars, but there is good evidence that education funding is justifiable. Aschauer (1992) used macromodels to determine if public education contributed more to private sector productivity and growth than other public expenditures. His previous research supported the contention that a government investment in a core economic infrastructure contributes to private sector productivity, profitability and investment: "...a rise in public nonmilitary investment raises the rate of return to private capital, thereby boosting productivity, and spurs private investment and economic growth. Public consumption, on the other hand, does seem to be negatively related to productivity growth and private investment." His previous studies of education did not find any relationship between public education and private sector productivity growth. He suspected that the problem was the often indirect nature of the contributions and the difficulty he had determining the appropriate lag. This study found that public education expenditures provide an important contribution to private sector productivity growth. Apparently public sector expenditures for education are part of the core economic infrastructure.

Government subsidies are especially important for scholarship. As previously mentioned, corporations are not likely to undertake this responsibility without government support even though the economic benefits of basic research exceed those of applied research (Balderstone, 1990). The economic obstacles to making basic research attractive to industry are that the research is very expensive, the results are uncertain, and the exclusionary principle can be applied for only a few types of research. Corporations cannot readily justify the expense if they cannot retain the economic benefit from the outcomes. Only where the results are applied enough in nature to be patentable, can the expenditures be justified. Yet, scholarship develops and enhances the knowledge bases on which informal and formal instruction at all levels, and all rational processes depend.

The imperfections of higher education markets for instruction, scholarship, and service support continuing governmental subsidies. Society will underinvest in instruction, scholarship, and service without these subsidies. Support for government subsidies is reinforced by Aschauer's (1992) finding that governmental funding for higher education enhances the social infrastructure for private sector economic growth.

## COST-EFFECTIVENESS—DOES HIGHER EDUCATION PRODUCE ENOUGH ECONOMIC GROWTH TO JUSTIFY FUNDING INCREASES THAT EXCEED INFLATION?

Growth accounting studies conclude consistently that American education, including higher education, contributes importantly to the nation's economic growth. Although educational expenditures comprise only 7.5 percent of Gross Domestic Product (National Center for Education Statistics, 1995), education is credited with between 15 and 21 percent of total economic growth (Becker and Lewis, 1992). Higher education expenditures comprise 3.0 percent of GDP, but higher education is credited with much of the return to research, which the Bureau of Labor statistics found directly accounted for 10 to 15% of economic growth. Higher education also shares in the returns to instruction. Clearly, higher education generates enough economic growth to justify continuing expenditures in excess of inflation.

In fact, until someone develops technologies for higher education that move it beyond fixed or even increasing ratios of resources to students, higher education needs to receive expenditures in excess of inflation to enable participants and providers of resources to share in the economic growth that higher education generates. If expenditures do not exceed inflation, they will at most be able to purchase the same bundle of goods and services as before even though they participated in an enterprise that directly provided 15 to 21 percent of economic growth.

No sector of the economy competes with education and education-based research in direct and indirect contributions to economic growth because economic development relies on rational processes, and knowledge development, transmission, and transfer are essential to rational processes. For example, growth in electronics depends on knowledge development, transmission, and transfer in electronics. Growth in pharmaceuticals and other health care industries also depends on knowledge development, transmission, and transfer. Corporate finance, corporate structuring, mining, environmental conservation and regulation, entertainment, and communications all depend on the development, integration, testing, and refinement of relevant knowledge bases.

The nature of university activity makes universities appear to be more inefficient than they are. People also assume that all human activities ought to be more efficient than they can be. They too easily ignore the inefficiencies in their own organizations and too easily ignore the value of apparently inefficient activities that actually are efficient, such as slack and renewal activities. They do not understand the nature of academic work. They see too little of what faculty members do. They assume that faculty members are not working unless they are in class teaching. They have trouble believing that they can really be committed enough to work hard when they are not more closely supervised. They feel threatened by the controversial things that faculty members are reported to have produced. The exception dictates the public impression, as is so often true in the present media environment, where controversy sells news.

When higher education cost increases result from productivity increases in society produced by higher education, the increased productivity more than covers the increased costs. It is more efficient to fund the productivity enhancing activities than not to do so, despite their increasing costs. Up to a point, the value that the increasingly costly activities add more than justifies the increasing costs.

At the social level the increased costs of higher education are clearly feasible, despite common beliefs to the contrary. The increase in higher education expenditures from one year to the next has averaged less than 4 percent of the increase in Gross Domestic Product (National Center for Education Statistics, 1995, Table 30), substantially below all but the most conservative estimates of what it produces. At the private level the situation is more complicated, as explained in the next section.

## DO PRESENT FUNDING MECHANISMS MATCH THE ECONOMIC BENEFITS AND BURDENS OF HIGHER EDUCATION?

One of the major obstacles to persuading people that society can continue to afford the cost increases of universities is that the benefits of the productivity gains do not flow directly to the people who are asked to pay the higher costs. For people to afford the cost increases, the distribution of burdens of sales, income and property taxes, and tuition and fees would need to match the distribution of economic benefits from higher education enterprises. This is difficult to accomplish.

Tuition and fees can at most match the private returns to instruction. Other funding methods are needed to match the private returns to other peoples' instruction and to scholarship. As previously noted, compensation increases no longer follow labor productivity increases. The benefits of productivity gains from education are not necessarily awarded to the employee. Tuition and fees do not follow these benefits. Also, scholarship produces a public good that anyone can tap. The complementarities of higher education make scholarship and instruction more effective to produce together, but the benefits of scholarship extend far beyond higher education, far beyond tuition and fees.

The gains often go to entrepreneurs, or their investors, who recognize how to tap the benefits of the enhanced resources. For example, entrepreneurs have made fortunes from computers and related technologies. Their success is built on university developed knowledge, technology, and human capital. They might donate to higher education, but rarely at a rate equal to the benefit that they have derived. Few people who benefit from higher education attribute the benefit adequately to their or other people's education or to scholarship. These benefits are too indirect.

The burdens and benefits should ideally match temporally as well, an impossibility. Scholarship, instruction, and service precede their economic benefits, usually by many years. Entrepreneurs have difficulty funding research and development and employees' instruction from revenues not yet received. Students and their families have difficulty paying for future benefits from present resources. Even where loans are available, the returns are uncertain. Market imperfections reduce private incentives to invest and public investment faces political obstacles.

Some problems are geographic. Employees educated in Maine are productive in Seattle. When these results are systematic, communities can face a drain on their resources, through the education of people who leave. The communities enjoy indirect benefits, but not equal to the burdens.

The problem is becoming worse because the cost burden of higher education to students and their families is increasing even faster than the costs of education. On average, the direct costs of higher education per student (as measured by expenditures) increased by 1.3 percent per year, but each student's burden increased faster because all levels of government have reduced subsidies to education (National Center for Educational Statistics, 1995, Table 318). The total cost to students is more than inflation and living expenses. It includes the opportunity cost of attending college. These costs have decreased in relative terms because compensation to non- college educated labor has declined.

Few students paid the full instructional cost, but tuition's share is increasing. Between 1981 and 1992, tuition's share of total current fund revenue rose from 21 to 26.5 percent (National Center for Education Statistics, 1995, Table 318) and tuition increased in real dollars at the same time. During that same period higher education revenues from governmental agencies declined as a percentage of total revenues from 48 percent to 40 percent. Federal non-research revenue per student decreased from $950 to $880 between 1981 and 1991 but increased to $980 in 1993.

There is even a question about how completely to match benefits and burdens. The many arguments for using higher education to increase social equity encourage some redistribution.

The obstacles to matching benefits and burdens are enormous, but some principles seem to apply. First, government subsidies are essential. Presently, markets cannot capture the benefits of scholarship that is not embodied in print or applied enough to patent. And markets are too imperfect to capture the social returns to instruction and the private returns to an employee's instruction. Second, higher education benefits are primarily global or at least national, so the federal government should play an important role. Students instructed in one community migrate to other communities. Scholarship has few geographical limits. Nevertheless, states and local governments do benefit from the economic impact of higher education institutions, particularly flagship universities, so some degree of state and local role remains important. Where more students remain within the state or locality, the role becomes more important. Also, state and local funding is more important where states and localities want to retain control. Third, higher education's contributions are capital and human capital contributions. The benefits have largely been identified in terms of economic growth. Some form of taxation related to capital gains might well provide a better match than some present funding mechanisms.

## CONCLUSION

Higher education clearly merits the present level of public support. No set of activities has more importance for a knowledge society than scholarship and instruction. No enterprises enjoy the concentration of expertise and other resources and possess the organizational structures and processes to develop, integrate, refine, test, transfer, and transmit knowledge than does higher education. With all their idiosyncrasies and possible weaknesses, they are among society's most effective institutions. They contribute more to the economic quality and quantity of goods and services in American society than any other type of institution.

Their scholarship provides the primary knowledge bases for the educated labor, technological development, rational processes, and even social conscience of all private and public enterprises. Through some combination of genius, public conversation, and knowledge construction and mining, they develop new concepts for individual and social action. They integrate these with prior knowledge. They refine the knowledge for more effective transfer and transmission. They test it to determine the effectiveness of its interaction with social and physical reality: its dependability for providing meaning and producing desired outcomes.

They also provide the formal advanced instruction associated with the most positive personal and social economic outcomes. Through some combination of cognitive development, citizen and professional socialization, screening, credentialing, and chartering, they enable their graduates to be more likely to obtain a job, to receive better compensation, to receive more training on the job, and to enjoy positive nonmarket and noneconomic outcomes. Their employment is generally associated with their employers' higher productivity and greater productivity growth. This combination of scholarly research and instruction are also associated with private and social opportunities. While debate continues about the causal direction of these relationships between education and outcomes. Their strength and consistency should make Americans very cautious about reducing public support to any degree.

## REFERENCES

Andersen, C.J. (1985). *Conditions Affecting College and University Financial Strength.* Washington, DC: American Council on Education.

Anderson, M.S., and Hearn, J.C. (1992). Equity issues in higher education outcomes. In W. E. Becker and D. R. Lewis (eds.), *The Economics of American Higher Education.* Norwell, MA: Kluwer Academic Publishers.

Arrow, K.J. (1973). Higher education as a filter. *Journal of Public Economics* 2(July), 193-216.

Aschauer, D.A. (1992). Is public education productive? In W. E. Becker and D. R. Lewis (eds.), *Higher Education and Economic Growth.* Norwell, MA: Kluwer Academic Publishers.

Atwell, R.H. (1992). Financial prospects for higher education. *Policy Perspectives* 4(3), 5B-7B.

Balderstone, F.E. (1990). Organization, funding, incentives, and initiatives for university research: A university management perspective. In S. A. Hoenack and E. L. Collins (eds.), *The Economics of American Universities: Management, Operations, and Fiscal Environment.* Albany, NY: State University of New York Press.

Bartel, A.P., and Lichtenberg, F.R. (1988). The comparative advantage of educated workers in implementing new technology. *Review of Economics and Statistics* 69(1): 1-11.

Baumol, W.J., and Blackman, S.A.B. (1983). Electronics, the cost disease, and the operation of libraries. *Journal of the American Society for Information Sciences* 34: 181-191.

Baumol, W.J., Blackman, S.A.B., and Wolff, E.N. (1989). *Productivity and American Leadership: The Long View.* Cambridge: The MIT Press.

Becker, G.S. (1964/1993). *Human Capital: A Theoretical and Empirical Analysis with Special Reference to Education.* Chicago: University of Chicago Press.

Becker, W.E. and Lewis, D.R. (1992). Preview of higher education and economic growth. In W.E. Becker and D.R. Lewis (eds.), *Higher Education and Economic Growth.* Norwell, MA: Kluwer Academic Publishers.

Becker, W.E. (1990). The demand for higher education. In S. A. Hoenack and E. L. Collins (eds.), *The Economics of American Universities: Management, Operations, and Fiscal Environment* (pp. 129-153). Albany, NY: State University of New York Press.

Becker, W.E. (1992). Why go to college? The value of an investment in higher education. In W.E. Becker and D.R. Lewis (eds.), *The Economics of American Higher Education.* Norwell, MA: Kluwer Academic Publishers.

Berg, I. (1971). *Education and Jobs: The Great Training Robbery.* Boston: Beacon Press.

Berger, M.C. (1992). Private returns to specific college majors. In W.E. Becker and D.R. Lewis (eds.), *The Economics of American Higher Education.* Norwell, MA: Kluwer Academic Publishers.

Blau, P.M. (1973). *The Organization of Academic Work.* New York: John Wiley.

Bowles, S., and Gintis, H. (1975). The problem with human capital theory—A Marxian critique. *American Economic Review* 65: 74-82.

Bowles, S., and Gintis, H. (1976). *Schooling in Capitalist America: Educational Reform and the Contradictions of Economic Life.* New York: Basic Books.

Brinkman, P.T. (1990). College and university adjustments to a changing financial environment. In S.A. Hoenack and E.L. Collins (eds.), *The Economics of American Universities: Management, Operations, and Fiscal Environment.* Albany, NY: State University of New York Press.

Brinkman, P.T., and Leslie, L.L. (1986). Economies of scale in higher education: Sixty years of research. *Review of Higher Education* 10(1): 1-28.

Brooks, H. (1985). Science policy and commercial innovation. *The Bridge*, summer, pp. 7-13.

Bureau of Labor Statistics. (September 1989). *The Impact of Research and Development on Productivity Growth.* Bulletin 2331. Washington, DC: U.S. Government Printing Office.

Bureau of Labor Statistics. (September 1993). *Productivity and the Economy: A Chartbook.* Bulletin 2431. Washington, DC: U.S. Government Printing Office.

Clark, K.P., and Griliches, Z. (1984). Productivity growth and R&D at the business level: Results from the PIMS database. In Z. Griliches (ed.), *R&D, Patents, and Productivity.* Chicago: The University of Chicago Press.

Cohn, E., and Geske, T.G. (1992). Private nonmonetary returns to investment in higher education. In W.E. Becker and D.R. Lewis (eds.), *The Economics of American Higher Education.* Norwell, MA: Kluwer Academic Publishers.

Cohn, E., and Geske, T.G. (1990). Education and economic growth. *The Economics of Education*, (3rd ed.), Chapter 6. Pergamon Press: New York.

Cohn, E., Rhine, S.L.W., and Santos, M.C. (1989). Institutions of higher education as multi-product firms: Economies of scale and scope. *Review of Economics and Statistics* (May): 283-290.

Coleman, J.S. (1974). *Power and the Structure of Society.* New York: W. W. Norton and Co., Inc.

Dean, E. (ed.). (1984). *Education and Economic Productivity.* Cambridge, MA: Harper and Row Ballinger.

Debreu, G. (1959). *Theory of Value.* New York: Wiley.

Denison, E.F. (1962). The sources of economic growth in the U.S. and the alternatives before us. Supplementary Paper No. 13. New York: Committee for Economic Development.

Denny, M., and Fuss, M. (1983). The effect of factor prices and technological change on the occupational demand for labor: Evidence from Canadian telecommunications. *Journal of Human Resources* 18(2): 161-176.

Ehrlich, I. (1975). On the relation between education and crime. In F.T. Juster (ed.), *Education, Income and Human Behavior.* New York: McGraw-Hill.

Fallon, R.P., and Layard, R. (1975). Capital-skill complementarity, income distribution and growth accounting. *Journal of Political Economy* 83: 279-301.

Feldman, K.A., and Newcomb, T.M. (1973). *The Impact of College on Students,* Volume I. San Francisco: Jossey-Bass Publishers.

Ferruolo, S.C. (1985). *The Origins of the University of Paris.* Stanford, CA: Stanford University Press.

Freeman, R. (1976). *The Overeducated American.* New York: Academic Press.

Freeman, R. (1980). The facts about the declining value of college. *Journal of Human Resources* 14: 289-318.

Geiger, R.L. (1992). The ambiguous link: Private industry and university research. In W.E. Becker and D.R. Lewis (eds.), *The Economics of American Higher Education.* Norwell, MA: Kluwer Academic Publishers.

Getz, M., and Siegfried, J.J. (1991). Costs and productivity in American colleges and universities. In C.T. Clotfelter, R.G. Ehrenberg, M. Getz, and J.J. Siegfried (eds.), *Economic Challenges in Higher Education* (Part III, pp. 259-392). Chicago: The University of Chicago Press.

Gill, I. (1988). Technological change, education, and obsolescence of human capital. Unpublished manuscript, University of Chicago.

Gordon, R.H. (April 1985). Estimating the effects of R&D on Bell system productivity. Working paper No. 1607. Cambridge, MA: National Bureau of Economic Research.

Griliches, Z. (1969). Capital-skill complementarity. *Review of Economics and Statistics* 51: 465-468.

Griliches, Z. (1985). Productivity, R&D, and basic research at the firm level in the 1970's. Working paper no. 1547. Cambridge, MA: National Bureau of Economic Research.

Gumport, P.J., and Pusser, B. (1995). A case of bureaucratic accretion: Context and consequences. *The Journal of Higher Education* 66(5): 493-520.

H.mermesh, D. S. (1986). The demand for labor in the long run. In O. Aschenfelter and R. Layard (eds.), *Handbook for Labor Economics* (Volume 1). New York: North Holland Press.

Helms, L.J. (1985). The effect of state and local taxes on economic growth: A time series-cross section approach. *The Review of Economics and Statistics* 67, 574-582.

Hoenack, S.A. (1990). Introduction. In S. A. Hoenack and E. L. Collins (eds.), *The Economics of American Universities: Management, Operations, and Fiscal Environment.* Albany, NY: State University of New York Press.

Hopkins, D.S.P. and Massy, W.F. 1981. *Planning Models for Colleges and Universities.* Stanford, CA: Stanford University Press.

Howe, W.J. (1992). The effects of higher education on unemployment rates. In W.E. Becker and D.R. Lewis (eds.), *Higher Education and Economic Growth.* Norwell, MA: Kluwer Academic Publishers.

Hyatt, J.A., Shulman, C.H., and Santiago, A.A. (1984). *Reallocation Strategies for Effective Resource Management.* Washington, DC: National Association of College and University Business Officers.

Jaffe, A.B. (1985). Quantifying the effects of technological opportunity and research spillovers in industrial innovation. Doctoral dissertation presented to Harvard University.

Jamison, D.T., and Lau, L.J. (1982). *Farmer Education and Farm Efficiency.* Washington, DC: World Bank.

Jones, B.D. and Vedlitz, A. (1988). Higher education policies and economic growth in the American states. *Economic Development Quarterly 2,* 78-87.

Kiker, B.F. and Roberts, R.B. (1984). The durability of human capital: Some new evidence. *Economic Inquiry,* April, 269-281.

Leslie, L.L., and S.A. Slaughter. (1992). Higher education and regional development. In W. E. Becker and D. R. Lewis (eds.), *The Economics of American Higher Education.* Norwell, MA: Kluwer Academic Publishers.

Leslie, L.L., and Rhoades, G.(1995). Rising administrative costs: Seeking explanations. *The Journal of Higher Education* 66(2): 187-212.

Leslie, L.L., and Brinkman, P.T. (1988). *The Economic Value of Higher Education.* New York: Macmillan.

Levin, H.M. (1983). *Cost-Effectiveness: A Primer.* Beverly Hills, CA: Sage Publications.

Lott, J.R., Jr. (1987). Why is education publicly provided? A critical survey. *Cato Journal* 7(2): 475-501. (Reprinted in M. Blaug, Mark (ed. ). *The Economic Value of Education.*)

Massy, W.F. (1991a). Improving productivity in higher education: Administration and support costs. *Capital Ideas* 6(1).

Massy, W.F. (1991b). Improving academic productivity: The next frontier. *Capital Ideas* 6(2).

Massy, W.F. (1991c). Rebuilding the fiscal bridges to the twenty-first century. Stanford Institute for Higher Research discussion paper, Stanford University.

Massy, W.F., and Wilger, A.K. (1991). Productivity in postsecondary education: a new approach. Stanford Institute for Higher Research discussion paper, Stanford University.

Massy, W.F., and Wilger, A.K. (1995). Improving productivity: What faculty think about it--And its effect on quality. *Change,* July/August, 10-20.

McMahon, W.W. (1992). The contribution of higher education to R&D and productivity growth. In W.E. Becker, and D.R. Lewis, *Higher Education and Economic Growth.* Norwell, MA: Kluwer Academic Publishers.

Meyer, J.W. (1970). The charter: Conditions of diffuse socialization in schools. In W. R. Scott (ed.), *Social Processes and Social Structures.* New York: Holt, Rinehart and Winston.

Meyer, J.W., and Scott, W.R. (1983). *Organizational Environments: Ritual and Reality.* Beverly Hills, CA: Sage Publications, Inc.

Miller, W.L. (1967). Education as a source of economic growth. *Journal of Economic Issues.* 1 (December): 280-296.

Mincer, J. (1989). Human capital and the labor market: A review of current research. *Educational Researcher*, May, 27-34.

Mingle, J.R., and Norris, D.M. 1981. Institutional strategies for responding to decline. In James Mingle and Associates, *Challenges of Retrenchment.* San Francisco: Jossey-Bass Publishers.

Mitch, D. (1990). Education and economic growth: Another axiom of indispensability? From human capital to human capabilities. In G. Tortella (ed.), *Education and Economic Development Since the Industrial Revolution.* Valencia, Spain: Generalitat Valenciana.

Murphy, K. M., and Welch, F. (1989). Wage premiums for college graduates: Recent growth and possible explanations. *Educational Researcher* 18(4): 17-26; reprinted with modification as: Wages of college graduates. In W.E. Becker and D.L. Lewis (eds.) *The Economics of American Higher Education*, 1992. Norwell: Kluwer Academic Publishing.

National Center for Education Statistics. (1995). *Digest of Education Statistics.* Washington, DC: National Center for Education Statistics.

National Science Foundation. (1994). *Computer Aided Science Policy Analysis and Research Database System.*

Nelson, R.R. (1989). What is private and what is public about technology. *Science, Technology, and Human Values* 14: 229-241.

Nerlove, M. (1972). On tuition and the costs of higher education: Prolegomena to a conceptual framework. *Journal of Political Economy 80*(3) (May-June), S178-S218.

Newhouse, J.F. (1970). Toward a theory of nonprofit institutions: An economic model of a hospital. *American Economic Review*, 60(March), 64-74.

Olson, J. E. (1994). Institutional and technical constraints on faculty gross productivity in American doctoral universities. *Research in Higher Education* 35(5): 549-567.

Olson, J.E. (1996). The subsidization of research and instruction in American universities. Paper for the Annual Meeting of the American Educational Research Association, New York City.

Olson, M., Jr. (1965). *The Logic of Collective Action.* Cambridge, MA: Harvard University Press.

Olson, M. Jr. (1982). *The Rise and Decline of Nations: Economic Growth, Stagflation, and Social Rigidities.* New Haven: Yale University Press.

Pascarella, E.T., and Terenzini, P.T. (1991). *How College Affects Students.* San Francisco: Jossey-Bass Publishers

Pechman, J.A. (1970). The distributional effects of public higher education in California. *Journal of Human Resources* 5: 361-370.

Pencavel, J. (1992). Higher education, economic growth, and earnings. In W. E. Becker and D. R. Lewis (eds.), *Higher Education and Economic Growth.* Norwell, MA: Kluwer Academic Publishers.

Plaut, T.R., and Pluta, J.E. (1983). Business climate, taxes and expenditures, and state industrial growth in the U.S. *Southern Economic Journal* 50: 99-119.

Psacharopolous, G. (1984). The contribution of education to economic growth: International comparisons. In J. W. Kendrick (ed.), *International Comparisons of Productivity and Causes of the Slowdown*. Cambridge, MA: Ballinger.

Rothschild, M., and White, L.J. (1993). The university in the marketplace. In C.T. Clotfelter and M. Rothschild (eds.), *Studies of Supply and Demand in Higher Education*. Chicago: The University of Chicago Press.

Schneider, R.W. (1985). Unraveling the indirect cost tangle--An analysis of indirect cost trends and policy issues, 1972-1984. Unpublished doctoral dissertation, University of Delaware.

Schultz, T. (1963). *The Economic Value of Education*. New York: Columbia University Press.

Scott, W.R. 1992. *Organizations: Rational, Natural, and Open Systems* (3rd ed.). Englewood Cliffs, NJ: Prentice-Hall, Inc.

Smith, A. (1776/1976). *An Inquiry into the Nature and Causes of the Wealth of Nations*. Oxford: Clarendon Press.

Smith, D.K. (1980). *Preparing for a Decade of Enrollment Decline: the Experience of the University of Wisconsin System*. Atlanta, GA: Southern Regional Education Board.

Smith, T.R. and Drabenstott, M. (1992). The role of universities in regional economic development. In William E. Becker and Darrell R. Lewis (eds.), *The Economics of American Higher Education*. Norwell, MA: Kluwer Academic Publishers.

Spence, D. (1973). Job market signaling. *Quarterly Journal of Economics* 87(August): 355-374.

Stapleton, D.C. (1976). Social benefits of education: An assessment of the effect of education on political participation (Workshop Paper 7606). Social Systems Research Institute, University of Wisconsin, Madison.

Taylor, E.K., and Wolfe, A.C. (1971). Political behavior. In S.B. Withey (ed.), *A Degree and What Else? Correlates and Consequences of a College Education*. New York: McGraw-Hill.

Thurow, L. (1972). Education and economic inequality. *The Public Interest* 28(Summer): 66-81.

Tsang, M. C. (1987). The impact of underutilization of education on productivity: A case study of the U.S. Bell Companies. *Economics of Education Review* 6(3): 239-254.

Tsang, M.C., and Levin, H.M. (1985). The economics of overeducation. *Economics of Education Review* 4(2): 93-104.

Wallhaus, R.A. (1975). The many dimensions of productivity. *New Directions for Institutional Research* 8: 1-16.

Wasylenko, M., and McGuire, T. (1985). Jobs and taxes: The effect of business climate on states' employment growth rates. *National Tax Journal* 38: 497-511.

Webb, L.D. 1977. Savings to society by investing in adult education. *In Economic and Social Perspectives on Adult Illiteracy: A Conference Report*. Tallahassee, FL: Florida Dept. of Education.

Weber, M. (1946 trans.). *From Max Weber: Essays in Sociology*, ed. Hans Gerth and C Wright Mills. New York: Oxford University Press.

Weiss, R.D. (1977). Elasticities of substitution among capital and occupations in U.S. manufacturing. *Journal of the American Statistical Association* 72(360): 764-771.

# A Secondary Analysis of Claims Regarding the Reflective Judgment Interview: Internal Consistency, Sequentiality and Intra-Individual Differences in Ill-Structured Problem Solving

**Phillip K. Wood**
*University of Missouri-Columbia*

In recent years, calls for educational reform at the post-secondary level have focused on the need for college students to reason complexly about issues which have no single correct answer. Specifically, such calls have concentrated on cultivating student awareness about difficult real-world problems and justifying these positions in a rational, defensible manner. Specifically, students who solve such real world problems must attend to the reasons for multiple positions with respect to a problem:

> By attending to the knowledge claims of the major over time and by treating increasingly complex matters from multiple points of view, students discover that nothing is self-evident, that nothing is simply "there," that questions and answers are chosen and created - not given - and that they are always are framed by context; for that reason, they always are contingent (Association of American Colleges, 1991, p. 13)

Such awareness of multiple perspectives is not sufficient, however. Colleges claim that students should also be able to produce a defensible position which takes this complexity into account:

> Students need to learn...what the difference is between developing and justifying a position and merely asserting one; and how to develop and provide warrants for their own interpretations and judgments" (Association for American Colleges, 1991, p. 14)

Finally, educated students should be able evaluate their own and other reasoned perspectives on the issue:

> Students cannot be allowed to be content with the notion that issues may be addressed by any number of equally valid formulations among which they cannot choose. They

must learn to discriminate by arguing, and they must realize that arguments exist for the purpose of clarifying and making choices (Association of American Colleges, 1991, p. 14).

### Table 1 . The Reflective Judgment Model: Stage Related Assumptions about Knowing[1]

**Stage 1—A person knows what she or he has observed. Facts and judgments are not differentiated.**

*View of Knowledge:* Knowledge is assumed to exist absolutely and concretely. It can be obtained with absolute certainty by direct observation.

*Concept of Justification:* Beliefs need no justification since there is assumed to be an absolute correspondence between what is believed and what is true. Alternatives to one's view are not perceived.

*Typical Judgment:* "I know what I have seen."

**Stage 2—Authorities and facts are related: authority figures are sources of facts and, therefore, truth.**

*View of Knowledge:* Knowledge is assumed to be absolutely certain, or certain but not immediately available. Knowledge can be obtained directly through the senses (such as direct observation) or via authority figures.

*Concept of Justification:* Beliefs are unexamined and unjustified, or justified by their correspondence with the beliefs of an authority figure (such as a teacher or parent). Most issues are assumed to have a right answer, so there is little or no conflict in making decisions about disputed issues.

*Typical Judgment:* "If it is on the news, it has to be true."

**Stage 3— Absolute answers are assumed to exist, but to be temporarily inaccessible. In the absence of absolute truth, facts, and personal beliefs are seen as equally valid.**

*View of Knowledge:* Knowledge is assumed to be absolutely certain or temporarily uncertain. In area of temporary uncertainty, only personal beliefs can be known until absolute knowledge is obtained. In areas of absolute certainty, knowledge is obtained from authorities.

*Concept of Justification:* In cases in which certain answers exist, beliefs are justified by reference to the authorities views. In areas in which answer do not exist, beliefs are defended as personal opinion since the link between evidence and beliefs is unclear.

*Typical Judgment:* "When there is evidence that people can give to convince everybody one way or another, then it will be knowledge; until then, it's just a guess."

**Stage 4— Evidence is now seen as important to the construction of knowledge claims, along with the acknowledgment that a belief cannot be known with absolute certainty for pragmatic reasons. Thus, knowledge claims are idiosyncratic to the individual.**

*View of Knowledge:* Knowledge is uncertain and knowledge claims are idiosyncratic to the individual since situational variables (e.g., incorrect reporting of data, data lost over time or disparities in access to information) dictate that knowing always involves an element of ambiguity.

*Concept of Justification:* Beliefs are justified by giving reasons and using evidence, but the arguments and choice of evidence are idiosyncratic, for example, choosing evidence that fits an established belief.

*Typical Judgment:* "I'd be more inclined to believe evolution if they had proof. It's just like the pyramids: I don't think we'll ever know. Who are you going to ask? No one was there."

**Table 1 *(continued)*. The Reflective Judgment Model: Stage Related Assumptions about Knowing[1]**

**Stage 5—Types of evidence are differentiated within perspectives (e.g., historical or scientific evidence). Further, different rules of inquiry across perspectives or disciplines are recognized. Quality of evidence is also evaluated as strong/weak, relevant/irrelevant, etc. Evidence is not an end in itself, but is used to construct interpretations.**

*View of Knowledge:* Knowledge is contextual and subjective since it is filtered through a person's perceptions and criteria for judgment. Only interpretations of evidence, events or issues may be known.

*Concept of Justification:* Beliefs are justified within a particular context using the rules of inquiry for that context and by context specific interpretations of evidence. Specific beliefs are assumed to be context-specific or are balanced against other interpretations, which complicates (and sometimes delays) conclusions.

*Typical Judgment:* "People think differently and so they attack the problem differently. Other theories could be as true as my own, but based on different evidence."

**Stage 6—Generalized rules of inquiry may be applied across perspectives (e.g., the weight of the argument, likelihood of the conclusion being correct, acknowledgment that judgments are tentative). Interpretations are subject to critique and judgment for coherency, consistency with the evidence, explanatory power, etc.**

*View of Knowledge:* Knowledge is constructed into individual conclusions about ill-structured problems based on information from a variety of sources. Interpretations that are based on evaluations of evidence across contexts and on the evaluated opinions of reputable others can be known.

*Concept of Justification:* Beliefs are justified by comparing evidence and opinion from different perspectives on an issue or across contexts, and by constructing solutions that are evaluated by criteria, such as the weight of the evidence, the utility of the solution or the pragmatic need for action.

*Typical Judgment:* "It's very difficult in this life to be sure. There are degrees of sureness. You come to a point at which you are sure enough for a personal stance on an issue."

**Stage 7—Judgments are seen as the outcome of a process of rational inquiry; they are based on a variety of interpretive considerations (e.g., the explanatory value of the interpretations, the risks of an erroneous conclusion, consequences of alternative judgments) and the interrelationships of these factors.**

*View of Knowledge:* Knowledge is the outcome of a process of reasoned inquiry in which solutions to ill-structured problems are constructed. The adequacy of those solutions is evaluated in terms of what is most reasonable or probable based on the current evidence, and is reevaluated when relevant new evidence, perspectives, or tools of inquiry become available.

*Concept of Justification:* Beliefs are justified probabilistically based on a variety of interpretive considerations, such as the weight of the evidence, the explanatory value of the interpretations, the risk of erroneous conclusions, consequences of alternative judgments, and the interrelationships of these factors. Conclusions are defended as representing the most complete, plausible, or compelling understanding of an issue, based on the available evidence.

*Typical Judgment:* "One can judge arguments by how well thought out the positions are, what kinds of reasoning and evidence are used to support it, and how consistent the way one argues on this topic is as compared with other topics."

[1]Adapted from King and Kitchener (1994)

## THE REFLECTIVE JUDGMENT MODEL

In recent years, the Reflective Judgment Model (Kitchener and King 1981) has gained increased acceptance as a measure of college students' ability to reason about such problems. Pascarella and Terenzini (1991), in their review of twenty years of educational research describe the Reflective Judgment model as "...the best known and most extensively studied" model of post-formal operations (p. 123).[1] Broadly seen, the model systematically documents the emerging abilities of students to deal with complex problems according to the three themes outlined above. At early levels of Reflective Judgment, subjects fail to appreciate that a given complex problem may allow of more than a single correct answer which is "simply 'there.'" At intermediate levels of Reflective Judgment, subjects are aware that some problems may not have single correct answers, but have substantial difficulty differentiating arbitrary personal preferences from organized and developed interpretations and judgments. At advanced levels of Reflective Judgment, subjects move from the ability to formulate a valid approach to a problem to the ability to evaluate the general adequacy of an approach relative to other logical, internally consistent approaches. The Reflective Judgment model and the assessment instrument based on it, the Reflective Judgment Interview (RJI), describe these differences in terms of seven qualitative levels in students' abilities to understand complex problems and to justify their point of view. Table 1 describes these assumptions in general terms as well as in terms of the view that students have of knowledge and basis for students' justification of their positions.

Generally, the research conducted to date (discussed in more detail below) has helped to establish that the RJI documents a type of reasoning which develops during college. This research, conducted both longitudinally and cross-sectionally, has also demonstrated that these gains do not appear attributable to gains in general verbal ability, pre-existing student differences, or test/retest effects. Given these encouraging aspects to RJI research, it seems reasonable to consider the utility of the RJ model for greater application as a measure of college outcomes. Unfortunately, the extensive resources required to administer and score the RJI have prohibited research which attempts to assess institutional, cohort, and/or classroom differences in Reflective Judgment. Although repeated claims have been made that Reflective Judgment documents an important inter-individual differences in ability, little is known about whether reliable student differences exist within a classroom that may be relatively homogeneous in terms of educational level. Such information would seem critical if the Reflective Judgment model is to be used as the basis for educational interventions within an aptitude-treatment design, for example. Finally, although general summaries of the research using the RJI have been made, little attempt has been made to assess whether the different and sometimes conflict-

---

[1]It should be noted that King and Kitchener (1994) do not describe Reflective Judgment as a measure of post-formal reasoning, since reasoning about the well-structured problems by means of formal operations and epistemic cognitions about ill-structured problems are distinct content areas.

ing claims regarding the RJI represent actual differences as a function of cohort or subpopulation or some failure of RJI administration or scoring to produce comparable data across studies. The data have not been analyzed in a consistent fashion which allows direct comparison of such conclusions. Obviously, the next steps in Reflective Judgment research should involve production of educational interventions designed to promote reflective thinking and development of an assessment measure which more efficiently assesses differences in students' reflective judgment as a function of student characteristics, campus learning environments, and educational institutions. Before these steps are undertaken, however, it is profitable to re-examine the existing research using the RJI to examine whether the construct holds promise for these extensions.

To these ends, this paper will first briefly discuss important aspects of Reflective Judgment research and theory, and how Reflective Judgment differs from other, similarly named or related constructs in educational and psychological research on problem solving. Since the RJI is a rather unique semi-structured interview, its format and scoring will then be described. These points serve as a prologue to the major purpose of the paper: To re-analyze all available data from research using the RJI in order to examine whether the Reflective Judgment is a complex developmental model which holds promise as a type of general outcomes measure of education. Such an examination entails several objectives. Specifically, given the available data: (1) Does the RJI provide psychometrically comparable data across studies?; (2) Can the scoring of the RJI be improved?; (3) Although differences in the RJI as a function of educational level have been replicated several times, is variability in Reflective Judgment roughly the same across individuals at various levels of educational attainment or is performance variation greater for some educational levels than others?; (4) How large are the differences in Reflective Judgment between subpopulations of students and what student or institutional characteristics appear to be associated with these differences?; (5) Do students reason differently across the four content areas of the RJI?; (6) Does the Reflective Judgment model document a progression of sequential changes in reasoning, or is there evidence for skipping levels of the model or regression over time?; and, (7) Is it the case that change in Reflective Judgment occurs slowly, or do some individuals demonstrate patterns of rapid change? Finally, the act of gathering and organizing these data led to two somewhat broader issues of relevance to educational research in general: (8) How accurate are the research data and analyses on which these claims are based?; and (9) How adequately have the data been analyzed? Before addressing these objectives, however, a short summary of past psychometric and research claims for the instrument will be presented to provide a context for the analyses to be reported.

## Reflective Judgment as Reasoning about Ill-Structured Problems

Wood (1983) described ill-structured problems as those for which there does not exist a single correct answer. The Reflective Judgment model does not make a claim to being a comprehensive model for all types of problem solving behaviors which are valuable college outcomes. It is not even a model of all types of ill-structured problems and does not evaluate the factual accuracy of students' evidence or argument. . Rather, the Reflective Judgment model is an evaluation of the epistemic cognitions which subjects make when faced with an "ill-structured problem" for which conflicting sources of information currently exist and about which even qualified experts can be expected to disagree. The Reflective Judgment model has been differentiated from simple declarative cognitions about a problem or even meta-cognitive processes of self-evaluation of performance (Kitchener, 1983). Wood (1983) also conceptually differentiates the ill-structured problems of the Reflective Judgment Model from processes involving statistical inference, utility, and risk. While no study has directly compared statistical reasoning with Reflective Judgment, King et al. (1990) found supporting evidence for this claim in that mathematics and computer science graduate students performed lower on the RJI than graduate students in the social sciences (composed of psychology, sociology, and educational measurement). Finally, ill-structured problems differ from "ill-defined" problem spaces typified by researchers who examine the role of "insight" in real-world problem solving (e.g., Duncker, 1945; Maier, 1933; Hoffman et al., 1963 also discussed in Sternberg, 1982) in that "ill-defined" problems, while not allowing of a clear deductive solution strategy, nevertheless allow of single correct answers about which qualified experts would not disagree.

## Relationships of Reflective Judgment to Other Types of Problem Solving

Many studies and discussions of Reflective Judgment have had as their goal the differentiation of Reflective Judgment from competing or similar intellectual ability constructs which deal with the ability to solve "well-structured" problems (those having a single, correct answer) which are more commonly used in educational assessment. The consensus appears to be that although the RJI is related to traditional problem solving measures, it is conceptually distinct. For example, Brabeck and Wood (1990), Wood (1990) have argued that traditional measures of critical thinking (such as the Watson-Glaser Critical Thinking Appraisal) are a necessary but not sufficient condition for Reflective Judgment. Specifically, Wood (1990) employed a statistical test to determine that low levels of critical thinking were accompanied by low levels of Reflective Judgment, while high levels of critical thinking are accompanied by moderately higher performance in Reflective Judgment as well as by a dramatic increase in variability in performance. Wood and Games (1991) found a similar necessary but not sufficient pattern of increasing heteroscedasticity using Terman's Concept Mastery Test, a general measure of verbal ability. Mines et al. (1990) used discriminant analyses to differentiate particular critical thinking skills related to particular levels of Reflective Judgment.

Table 2. Traditional Reflective Judgment Dilemmas

| Topic | Text |
|-------|------|
| Evolution. | Many religions of the world have creation stories, These stories suggest that a divine being created the earth and its people. Scientists claim, however, that people evolved from lower animals forms (some of which were similar to apes) into the human forms known today. |
| Food Additives. | There have been frequent reports about the relationship between chemicals that are added to foods and the safety of these foods. Some studies indicate that such chemicals can cause cancer, making these foods unsafe to eat. Other studies, however, show that chemical additives are not harmful, and actually make the foods containing them more safe to eat. |
| News. | Some people believe that news stories represent unbiased, objective reporting of news events. Others say that there is no such thing as unbiased, objective reporting and that even in reporting the facts, news reporters project their own interpretations into what they write. |
| Pyramids. | Most historians claim that the pyramids were built as tombs for kinds by the ancient Egyptians, using human labor, and aided by ropes, pulleys and rollers. Others have suggested that the Egyptians could not by themselves have build such huge structures, for they had neither the mathematical knowledge, the necessary tools, nor an adequate source of power. They claim that the Egyptians were aided by visitors from other planets. |

## Relationships to Other Constructs

Additional studies have sought to differentiate the RJI from more developmentally based constructs. For example, Kitchener and Kitchener (1981) argued that, logically, development in Piagetian formal operations was insufficient to account for differences in Reflective Thinking ability. King (1977, also discussed in King, 1986) noted that, 91% subjects in her study scored as formal operational while modal Reflective Judgment scores ranged from Stage 2 through Stage 7. King et al. (1989) also examined the relationship of RJI to constructs such as moral development (as assessed by Rest's (1979) Defining Issues Test), ego development (as measured by Loevinger's Sentence Completion Test (Loevinger et al., 1970), and other measures of psycho-social development. (Glatfelter, 1982; Polkosnik and Winston, 1989). King and Kitchener (1994) summarize the results of these studies by noting that Reflective Judgment appears to develop independently of ego development and is only moderately or unrelated to measures of psycho-social development.

## The Reflective Judgment Interview and Dilemmas

The Reflective Judgment model of justification for beliefs and the RJI assessment procedure are most easily understood by an overview of the interview and

Reflective Judgment Stage descriptions. The RJI consists of the presentation (in random order) of a brief complex issue (hereafter "dilemma"). These dilemmas represent an ill-structured problem dealing with an on-going controversy. Most Reflective Judgment studies have used four traditional dilemmas given in Table 2. The subject is then asked to explain his/her position in response to a series of standardized probe questions given in Table 3. These questions are posed by a trained, certified interviewer who probes subject responses in order to secure an unambiguous summary of the subject's approach to the problem.

### Table 3 . Reflective Judgment Interview—Probe Questions[1]

| Probe Questions | Rationale/Purpose |
| --- | --- |
| **What do you think about these statements?** | How did you come to hold that point of view? |
| **To allow the participant to share an initial reaction to the problem presented. Most respondents state which point of view is closer to their own (e.g., that the Egyptians built the pyramids, that news reported is biased).** | To find out how the interviewee arrived at the point of view, and whether and how it has evolved from other positions on the issue. |
| **On what do you base that point of view?** | To elicit the basis of a participant's point of view, for example, a personal evaluation of the data, consistency with an expert's point of view, a specific experience, etc. |
| **Can you ever know for sure that your position on this is correct? How or why not?** | To better understand the participant's assumptions about whether issues like this can be known absolutely, what s/he would do in order to increase the certainty, or why that wouldn't be possible. |
| **When two people differ about matters such as this, is it the case that one opinion is right and the other one is wrong? If yes, what do you mean by "right"? If no, can you say that one opinion is in some way better than the other? What do you mean by "better"?** | The question is not designed to assess moral rightness, but factual accuracy. The first purpose is to see if the respondent hold a dichotomous, either/or view of the issue (characteristic of the early stages). The second purpose is to allow the participant to give criteria by which s/he evaluates the adequacy of arguments (information that helps differentiate high from middle-level stage responses). |

Table 3 *(continued).* **Reflective Judgment Interview—Probe Questions[1]**

| Probe Questions | Rationale/Purpose |
|---|---|
| **How is it possible that people have such different points of view about this subject?** | This question is designed to elicit comments about the participant's understanding of differences in perspectives and opinions (what they are based on and why there exists such diversity of opinion about the issue). |
| **How is it possible that experts in the field could disagree about this subject?** | This question is not designed to tap their view of experts and authorities in terms of their decision-making about controversial issues, such as what role experts might play (if any), whether their viewpoints are weighted differently, and if so, why this would be done. |

**If the person does not take a stand on the issue (does not endorse a particular point of view) on the first question, the following questions are asked:**

**1. Could you ever say which was the better position? How/Why not?**
**2. How would you go about making a decision about this issue?**
**3. Will we ever know for sure which is the better position? How/Why not?**
**4. When people differ about matters such as this, is it the case that one opinion is right and one is wrong?**
**(If yes) What do you mean by "right"?**
**(If no) Can you say one opinion is in some way better than the other? What do you mean by better?**
**5. How is it possible that people can have such different points of view about this subject?**
**6. What does it mean when experts in the field disagree about this subject?**

[1] Adapted from King and Kitchener (1994).

## Scoring of Reflective Judgment Protocols

Details regarding the scoring of Reflective Judgment protocols are given in more detail elsewhere (Kitchener and King, 1981, 1985; King and Kitchener, 1994), but a brief description of the rating process will be given here. Each dilemma given to a subject is transcribed and all references to the educational level and gender of the subject are removed from the transcript. Transcripts of each dilemma are then given in random order to two trained raters who assign a Reflective Judgment rating by means of a three-digit scoring system. If only one style of reasoning is present in a given transcript, raters assign the same score to all three digits (e.g., if the transcript contained evidence for only Stage 3 reasoning, the rating would be

333). Occasionally, a transcript contains evidence of another level of reasoning in addition to the most predominant style. In these cases, the first digit of this rating represents the predominant style of reasoning in the protocol, with the less-evident stage occupying the second or third digits. The dominant stage is then repeated in the remaining stage. (For example, legitimate multiple stage ratings would be 334 or 343.) To obtain a Reflective Judgment score under this system, the three digits assigned by a rater are averaged. Scores, then follow the measurement scale in thirds (e.g., scores of 3, 3.3, 3.6, and 4 are possible). Transcript ratings are averaged across raters to form a final score for a dilemma. Finally, composite scores for the interview are formed by averaging across all four dilemmas.

Since Reflective Judgment scores are meant to convey evidence for a particular stage of reasoning in a transcript, safeguards have been built into the procedure to assure the final score assigned to a given dilemma actually reflects to a level of reasoning observed by the raters and not an average of ratings from other levels. For example, the rerating system for scoring the RJI ensures that it is not possible for a final rating of rating of 4 to occur for a dilemma by averaging a three-digit rating of 3-3-3 from one rater with a three-digit rating of 5-5-5 from the other. Under the rerating system, raters are asked to re-rate a transcript if the ratings assigned by both raters differ by one full stage or more. These discrepant transcripts are combined with transcripts which were initially in agreement and these transcripts are then rerated. If, on rerating the scores are still discrepant by at least one stage, the raters discuss the transcript in question and assign a final score to the transcript. For each transcript then, three possible scores are possible, Round 1 (or initial) ratings, Round 2 (composed of rerated transcripts and transcripts which were initially in agreement) ratings, and Resolved (composed of Round 2 ratings and final scores as assigned after rater discussion) ratings.

Traditionally, measures of inter-rater agreement (the proportion of times that the two raters assigned scores within a stage of each other) is based on Round 1 and Round 2 scores. Internal consistency estimates based on the four dilemmas (such as coefficient alpha) are based on resolved ratings averaged across both raters, since these are thought to represent the most accurate estimates of a subject's score on the dilemma.[2]

## Psychometric and Conceptual Claims for the Reflective Judgment and the RJI.

As noted below, 30 studies involving longitudinal and cross-sectional designs have been conducted to date which used the RJI. This represents a total of 2033 individuals. Based on these studies several general claims regarding the psychometric properties of the RJI and the general nature of Reflective Judgment ability have been made. A secondary analysis of the available RJI data allows for a

---

[2]It should be noted that some reports of internal consistency for the RJI have been based on Round 1 scores, evidently in the belief that such estimates are a more conservative estimate than use of Round 2 or Resolved scores. As shown below, this is not the case.

closer examination of these claims. These claims concern: 1.) the adequacy of the existing rating rules and certification procedure to produce reliable, accurate data which are comparable across studies; 2.) the sequential nature of the Reflective Judgment model; 3.) claims concerning the gradual nature of change in Reflective Judgment over time; 4.) the view that the RJI dilemmas constitute essentially parallel forms; and 5.) the relationship of educational level to Reflective Judgment. These claims are discussed in turn below. For each of these claims, an effort will be made to note general consensus on some claims, discrepancies and their basis, as well as areas of inquiry which have not yet been addressed.

Before doing so, however, it is worthwhile to note that efforts to evaluate the data across studies to date also allows an investigation of whether the three-digit scoring procedure can be improved. As noted before, RJI scores to date have consisted of a simple average of the three digits of assigned by a rater and many or most ratings contain a mixture of two adjacent stages. In many cases the relative position of the minor stage conveys information about the relative salience of the minor level. For example, a rating of 343 is thought to contain more Stage 4 reasoning than a rating of 334. Below a new and simple scoring scheme is introduced which allows for more fine-grained scaling of Reflective Judgment ability. This improvement results in a slight gain in internal consistency of the instrument as well as permitting the computation of stage utilization scores which can be used to assess the sequentiality of the model.

## The Rating and Certification Procedures for Reflective Judgment Assure That RJI Data Is Comparable Across Studies

This claim is not explicitly addressed in RJI research, but is implicit in attempts to compare and interpret RJI performance across studies. Three ways of addressing the comparability of RJI scores have been attempted to date; comparison of general conclusions from several RJI studies; comparison of reported psychometric characteristics of the RJI across studies; and explorations of possible rater bias. Each of these approaches will be discussed and evaluated in turn.

Several studies have attempted to evaluate the overall performance of the RJI across studies and to summarize salient differences between subjects (such as educational level) (Kitchener, 1986; Kitchener and King, 1990; King and Kitchener, 1994). These studies have accepted the reported data and analyses "as is" without an examination of possible data entry errors or errors of analysis which could have occurred. In cases where scored transcripts or entered data were available, data integrity and the accuracy of reported statistical analyses can be examined. Specifically, in many cases, it is possible to determine whether errors occurred by proofreading coding sheets or scored transcripts. In other cases, errors can only be identified by examining the data for coded values outside the permissible range, and by writing computer programs to check whether discrepant scores of raters were overlooked in the rerating process.

After the data have been checked for accuracy, a closer examination of the psychometric properties of the RJI can be undertaken. Generally, as reported in the literature, the reliability of the for published RJI studies has been very good to exceptional (e.g., King, et al., 1990; King and Kitchener, 1994; Kitchener et al., 1989; Brabeck and Wood, 1990). King and Kitchener (1994), summarized the reported agreement and internal consistency estimates across all known RJI studies. For the thirty studies which reported agreements, the median agreement rates of 77%. Forty percent of the studies reported an agreement level of 87% and one quarter reported agreement levels of at least 90%. Interestingly, of the four studies which reported an agreement levels less than 70%, King and Kitchener note that three were from samples that included adult learners and nonstudent adults. King and Kitchener also report a median coefficient alpha of .85 across studies which report it, with a range across studies from .50 to .96.

The findings regarding reported agreement and internal consistency, while informative, can be profitably supplemented by a reanalysis of the existing data. In examining the reported psychometric properties, four difficulties or ambiguities of interpretation present themselves: 1.) The reported internal consistency and agreement indices across studies are based on data composed of a variety of educational levels in some instances and relatively few in others; 2.) The internal consistency estimates reported in all studies, coefficient alpha or inter-rater correlations, assume that raters constitute a fixed effect, rather than a random effect, meaning that no effort has been made to assess the generalizability of the internal consistency to a larger pool of certified raters. 3.) The definition of inter-rater agreement seems slightly different across studies (discussed in more detail below); and 4.) The possibility of rater bias, agreement, and reliability information has not always been investigated across studies.

**Heterogeneity of RJI Ability across Studies**
It is not, strictly speaking, possible to compare the agreement and internal consistency coefficients across all studies as reported in King et al. (1994) since some studies reported these statistics based on extremely small, homogeneous sample sizes used in a particular study, while other studies reported reliabilities taken across a variety of educational levels. If the RJI is to be used to promote educational interventions in particular educational settings it is necessary to understand how reliably individuals within a given educational level may be discriminated using the RJI. Also, while the reported reliabilities of the RJI in published articles are quite high, it is not known whether comparable psychometric properties are found for RJI studies which did not report them. Some notes from unpublished studies suggest this might be a problem. For example, Van Tine (1990) noted an initial 62% agreement rate for an early subset of her data which necessitated a recalibration of the raters before rating could continue.

Some research has investigated the use of the RJI within a given educational level, or as a result of educational interventions or environmental support (e.g.,

Kitchener et al., 1993; Lynch, 1990; Sakalys, 1984). In addition to investigating the range of observed RJI scores of given educational levels (discussed below) it is also appropriate to investigate the internal consistency of the RJI within educational level, as opposed to internal consistency estimates which are based on a population of widely different levels of educational attainment. While it is expected that such internal consistency estimates would be lower, it is not known whether the decrease in internal consistency prohibits the use of the RJI for groups of students who are all at a given educational level.

### Raters as Random Effects

Conceptually, however, there is also some question as to whether the internal consistency estimate, coefficient alpha, is appropriate for assessing internal consistency across raters. Coefficient alpha assumes a fixed effect model of reliability and the estimates of internal consistency may not be used to generalize to a larger universe of interest (in this case, the larger universe consists of the pool of certified raters). Also, simple comparisons of coefficient alpha estimates across studies do not take into account the issue of sampling variation in the reliability estimate. For example, heterogeneity of reliability estimates studies examining a particular educational level may identify important differences across samples in the internal consistency of the RJI, or may be attributable merely to sampling variation in the reliability estimate. To address these issues, internal consistency estimates using the random effects intraclass correlation coefficient (ICC, Shrout and Fleiss, 1979) will be computed. Random effects ICC's differ from fixed effects ICC's (which include coefficient alpha as a special case) in that they take into account the sampling variation between raters. Finally, it is also possible to calculate approximate confidence intervals in order to assess whether the RJI possesses differential internal consistency across samples.

### Rater Agreement Criterion Differences

There is also some evidence that different criteria for rater agreement have been used across studies. For example, Welfel (1979) describes a three-point difference between raters as being in agreement, while other researchers report a three point difference as being discrepant (e.g., Brabeck, 1983; Glatfelter, 1982; King et al., 1983; King et al., 1990). In addition, some studies appear to assume that the ratings of a given transcript may only consist of at most two stages (such as 4-3-4, 4-4-3, and 3-4-3), while other studies mention that, on rare occasions, three stage ratings have been used (such as 4-5-6).[3]

---

[3]It should be noted that some examples of the scoring of the RJI indicate that three-stage ratings are acceptable, although rare (e.g., Kitchener, 1986). In rater training workshops, however, raters have been instructed not to assign three-stage ratings without additional confirmation. Some raters contacted personally by the author indicated that they didn't believe that three stage ratings were allowed.

## Rater Bias

The issue of possible rater bias has been relatively under-explored in RJI research. Only two studies have investigated this possibility: Brabeck (1980) conducted an extensive comparison of the scores from both raters used in her study in an effort to identify possible rater bias and found a small but statistically significant difference between overall raters (difference=.1, p. 114). This bias appeared to be unrelated to educational level. Dale (1995) found a statistically significant rater by dilemma interaction, but argued that the magnitude of the interaction was of little practical importance. Kelly (1993), using a Rasch measurement model, found no statistically significant differences between raters in King and Kitchener's (1994) 10 year longitudinal data.

## Reflective Judgment Documents a Uniform Series Of Sequential Changes In the Ability to Reason About Ill-structured Problems

The Reflective Judgment model is a complex stage theory, meaning that individuals are assumed to function at a variety of levels in addition to their predominant or preferred level of response (King and Kitchener, 1994; Rest, 1979). The sequential nature of the construct was first investigated based on Kitchener and King's (1981) initial cross-sectional study of advanced doctoral students, college juniors and high school juniors who were matched on verbal ability. Davison (1979) proposed a sequentiality test which revealed that subjects responded at levels adjacent to their predominant level (a property which this sample did not demonstrate for other developmental measures except for Rest's (1979) Defining Issues Test) (Davison et al., 1980). This form of "cross-sectional" sequentiality for the RJI was replicated on other samples of undergraduate and graduate students (Strange and King, 1981; Welfel, 1982). This type of sequentiality has been applied to longitudinal studies as well (Brabeck and Wood, 1990; King et al., 1983). In addition, longitudinal research involving two or three times of testing has reported increases or no change in performance between 84-100% of individuals (Brabeck and Wood, 1990; King et al. 1983; Kitchener et al. 1990; Kitchener et al. 1989; Sakalys, 1984; Schmidt, 1983, 1985; Welfel and Davison, 1986). To date, no evidence of stage skipping has been found. King and Kitchener (1994, Table B6-2) report none of the three educational levels in their longitudinal study increased one and a half stages or more between adjacent testings over the course of their 10 year longitudinal study. A reanalysis of all available longitudinal data described below under the proposed revised scoring scheme generally confirms this observation at the level of individuals, except that testings from three individuals in the Kitchener and King (1981) study and one individual from Kitchener et al. (1993) study showed evidence of stage increases between 2.1 and 2.45 stages.

The reported data on sequentiality is in agreement and appears to hold for cross-sectional as well as longitudinal data. Such analyses have not been conducted in all applications of the model, raising the possibility that some populations might be identified for which the model may not hold. In a related vein, the relatively small sample size employed in most studies of Reflective Judgment (all studies employed samples less than 200 subjects), does not allow a more fine-grained examination of the stage and sequence of Reflective Judgment. It could well be, for example, that certain stages of Reflective Judgment are characterized by single approaches to ill-structured problems, while at other levels of Reflective Judgment, subjects exhibit much more variability in performance in addition to their preferred level of response. Specifically, no examination has been made looking at whether the complex stage model of the RJI represents a single level of response at some levels while showing more variability in response at other levels.

### Growth in Reflective Judgment Ability Is Not Due to a Test/retest Effect and Is Gradual

Five additional studies have investigated whether the obtained upward trend in scores in longitudinal studies could be due to a test-retest effect for the instrument. Kitchener and King (1990) report minimal differences between the traditional Reflective Judgment dilemmas and a new dilemma topic concerning nuclear energy in the 10 year follow-up testing of their subjects. Kitchener et al. (1993) found no differences in a two week follow-up assessment of the RJI, even when subjects received extensive information about the Reflective Judgment construct and studied examples of higher level responses. This pattern has been replicated in studies which employed relatively short assessment intervals. Sakalys (1984) reports small nonsignificant (growth=.1) gains in RJI score over a four month period. Polkosnik and Winston (1989) report a statistically significant change of .19 for a six month longitudinal study.[4] Thompson (1995) found no gains in Reflective Judgment as a result of a longitudinal study designed to assess an educational intervention in biology designed to promote Reflective Judgment. Kronholm (1993) is one exception to this pattern. In an experimental intervention designed to promote Reflective Judgment, she reports significant gains of approximately .3 of a stage while a control group changed negligibly. King and Kitchener (1994) report that all longitudinal studies employing at least a year's duration found statistically significant increases, particularly among those involved in collegiate programs. A reanalysis of some of the longitudinal data with short testing intervals (such as Kitchener et al., 1993 and Brabeck and Wood's (1990) longitudinal data) could inform researchers whether the test/retest reliability is similar across different studies and samples and the degree to which short-term fluctuation can be expected in Reflective Judgment scores.

### Differences in Reflective Judgment as a Function of Educational Level Have Documented a Generally Increasing Pattern of Reflective Judgment

Early undergraduate samples tend to score at about 3.5 on the RJI, indicating that at times subjects believe these issues are a merely a function of opinion and at

---

[4]Which, as shown below, is *not* statistically significant.

other times they believe that opinions must be justified by facts, but are unsure of how to incorporate discrepant information. Undergraduate juniors and seniors, by contrast, score at about level 4, indicating that, on the average, they recognize the importance of facts in supporting an opinion, but do not systematically organize these facts into any logical internally consistent approach relative to a particular discipline or theory. Beginning graduate students generally score at about 4.5, indicating that they at times do not organize their views in terms of any internally consistent fashion, and at other times appear able to organize the information in an area in terms of a particular discipline or theory, but have no criteria for choosing between available alternative explanations/theories. Samples of advanced doctoral students score at about level 5.5, indicating that they at times appreciate that a synthesis across disciplines/theories is possible, but they do not produce these syntheses themselves. At other times, these students appear able to organize the material only in terns of a particular theory or discipline.

King et al. (1994) summarized the reported patterns in all known RJI studies by educational level and found generally common patterns of RJI scores within educational level. A secondary analysis of available data could be used to more accurately assess the performance within and across educational levels. For example, the magnitude of institutional differences in Reflective Judgment ability and/or differences in RJI ability as a function of educational level can reveal important interindividual differences in students which would have direct implications for the structure and approach of teaching for Reflective Judgment. The relationship of educational level to Reflective Judgment could be explored to see whether it shows a necessary but not sufficient pattern, providing preliminary evidence for the presence of differential trajectories of growth in Reflective Judgment over time, the presence of distinct subgroups which have different overall levels of RJI scores, or the presence of some unmeasured variable(s) which interact(s) with educational level to produce a functional model of RJI ability (Wood, 1994).

### Differences in Performance Across RJI Dilemmas Are Either Nonsignificant or Negligible

The overall RJI score for an individual is composed of a simple average across all four dilemmas, implying that RJI scores for each dilemma represent strictly parallel measures composed of equal amounts of error and true score variability. Some studies provide indirect support for this view. For example, Kitchener et al. (1989) report that individual's modal score was consistent across problems 75% of the time. The remainder of the time, the mode was no more than one stage discrepant. Kelly (1993), employing a generalized Rasch model, found no dilemma differences across the four dilemmas for longitudinal data based on Kitchener and King's (1981) study. Other researchers, however, have found differences between dilemmas. Welfel (1979) examined the issue of dilemma differences from an analysis of variance framework and found that statistically significant differences did exist between dilemmas, but that the magnitude of these differences was quite small (.1 of a stage) and found that the creation evolution dilemma was lower than the other three.Brabeck (1980, p. 114) reported that average scores on the chemicals dilemma were .2 higher than on the other three dilemmas (which were identical to one decimal place) but did not test to see whether these differences were statistically significant. Dale (1995) found a difference of almost .4 of a stage between the news reporting and creation/evolution dilemmas in a study of students and faculty at a conservative Christian college.

No study to date has attempted to directly explore the psychometric properties of the RJI from a classical test theory model. King et al. (1994) examined previously published inter-dilemma correlations for RJI studies and concluded that the magnitude of the correlations appeared to be the same for each of the four dilemmas, although no statistical test of this conclusion was made. The process of deriving an overall Reflective Judgment score for an individual, composed of the simple average of scores on all four dilemmas, assumes that each dilemma should have equal weight in computing a composite score. In psychometric terms, all research to date has assumed that the four dilemmas of the RJI are strictly parallel measures, and have not examined whether the dilemmas are parallel forms which are perhaps only tau-equivalent (equivalent in terms of the true-score which is estimated containing different amounts of error variance, Lord and Novick, 1968) or congeneric (i.e., not equivalent in terms of the level of the true score estimated, but still indicators of the same underlying construct). Such explorations into the properties and utility of dilemma scores as parallel measures could result in improved scoring and interpretation of RJI data.

While all research to date converges on the view that overall differences in performance are, if present, quite small, the pattern of dilemma differences differs from study to study. No research to date has investigated whether these observed differences by dilemma could be due to other rater phenomena such as rater bias. An examination of several data sets could be used to decide whether the observed differences between dilemmas are related to issues of rater bias or whether the obtained differences are the product of chance sampling variation in subjects. Further, all studies to date have examined the issue of dilemma differences based only on global samples spanning a wide range of educational levels. It seems reasonable to explore whether a differential pattern of differences across dilemmas may obtain for individuals as a function of educational experience. Finally, all tests of differences across dilemmas to date have sought to uncover systematic differences in performance on the dilemmas which obtain systematically across individuals. Although some studies have sought to explore whether interindividual differences in these dilemmas exist (by analyzing whether differences in level exist across curricular or education groups), no studies have sought to examine whether systematic intra-individual differences in performance exist which are unrelated to intact observable groups. Since it seems reasonable to believe that individuals may differ considerably in their interest and exposure to the dilemma topics, the issue of systematic intra-individual performance patterns across the RJI dilemmas will also be explored using an hierarchical factor model.

## DATA COLLECTION

### Identification of Existing Studies of Reflective Judgment

An initial pool of existing studies employing the RJI was constructed by contacting raters and researchers known to the author and other Reflective Judgment researchers. In addition, computerized literature searches using Dissertation Abstracts International, PsychLit and ERIC were conducted. Twenty-three studies were identified through this process. The general design, sample sizes, and reported results from these studies are reported in King et al. (1994). Seven additional studies were also identified by personal contact subsequent to those outlined in King et al. (1994) through personal contact with the author or other raters. Seven studies were identified in the computerized searches but were not used in the present study because studies did not involve the use of the traditional RJI and did not use trained raters. Of the 30 studies identified which used the RJI, data sets from twenty studies were gathered. Of the seven longitudinal studies identified, six studies were ascertained. Ten of the twenty studies ascertained were unpublished reports or dissertations/theses. Of the studies not available, one was a presented paper, two were published in scholarly journals, and seven were unpublished dissertations/theses. In all, Reflective Judgment data from 1,509 subjects were obtained, representing $11,676^6$ rater judgments of $6,620^5$ dilemmas ratings.

### Identification of Subject Samples and Sample Sizes

The experimental designs of all studies were then examined in an effort to examine the discrete samples which were taken in each study and the number of subjects assessed. For example, the King et al. (1990) study of critical thinking examined the performance of twenty freshmen, and seniors and graduate students taken from either the social sciences or the natural sciences. This study, then, was counted as containing five samples of students. All samples were then totaled across studies to arrive at a number of individuals in the study (100). Studies, samples, and subjects who were ascertained and unavailable were grouped according to general educational level and are presented in Table 4. The ascertainment procedures were most successful for the High School and Graduate populations, where 100% of the available data were included. Sixty-nine percent of the subjects taking the RJI interview were undergraduates. Only two of the six known studies using the RJI on nonstudent populations were available, represent-

---

[5]Number includes longitudinal testings and so is not a multiple of the number of subjects.

ing roughly 33% of the available population. Overall, 74% of the available subject data was collected, an acceptable rate, given the fact that the studies employed were conducted over the past eighteen years. In addition, as will be discussed, average level and range of performance for individual grades are very similar to figures based on a meta-analysis of all reported results in King, et al. (1994). In two cases, separate studies investigated the performance of the same individuals. Dove (1990) administered the remaining two dilemmas to a sample of subjects in the Kitchener et al. (1993) study. Van Tine (1990) involved a retest of selected subjects in McKinney (1985). Data from these studies were merged in order to provide more complete records for each subject and to prevent a given individual from being included twice in the data set.

**Table 4. Study, Sample and Subject Ascertainment Rates by Educational Level**

| Education Level | Number of Studies | Number of Samples | Number of Subjects |
|---|---|---|---|
| *High School*<br>(8th Grade - 12th Grade) | | | |
| Ascertained | 5 | 12 | 175 |
| | (100)[1] | (100) | (100) |
| Not Ascertained | 0 | 0 | 0 |
| *Undergraduate*[2]<br>(Freshman - Senior | | | |
| Ascertained | 21 | 42 | 991 |
| | (75) | (68) | (69) |
| Not Ascertained | 7 | 20 | 428 |
| *Graduate*<br>(Masters and Doctoral | | | |
| Ascertained | 9 | 15 | 263 |
| | (100) | (100) | (100) |
| Not Ascertained | 0 | 0 | 0 |
| *Non-Student Populations* | | | |
| Ascertained | 2 | 3 | 58 |
| | (33) | (38) | (30) |
| Not Ascertained | 4 | 5 | 136 |
| *Total* | | | |
| Ascertained | 20[3] | 82 | 1509 |
| | (66) | (73) | (74) |
| Not Ascertained | 10 | 25 | 524 |

[1]Numbers in parentheses indicate percentages

[2]Includes data from Traditionally and Nontraditionally aged student

[3]Study numbers do not total since many studies investigated students from many education levels. Dove counted as a separate study in Undergraduate, but not recorded in Total, since these subjects were the same as in Kitchener et al.(1993).

Although attempts to secure raw data over such a long time period are infrequently attempted in psychology, it appears that the proportion of data secured from available data is quite good. By comparison, the ascertainment rates of 74% overall and even the 30% of nonstudent populations and 69% of undergraduate samples compare favorably with Wolins (1962), where only 24% of the data sets from a sample of 37 published studies over a three year period were made available for secondary analysis.

## RESULTS

### Accuracy Checks

*Data Verification.* The first step in conducting any secondary analysis is to check the accuracy of the received data sets. For the present study, it was possible to secure original coding sheets and data sets only for eleven studies. Three studies were reentered from coding sheets or tables. For the remaining studies, accuracy checking for these data sets was confined to: Checking to make sure that all RJI ratings were within reasonable bounds, proofreading the input formats for statistical programs which accompanied the data sets, and replicating the major analyses reported for each study. For all studies, it appears that random miskeypunching did not occur, since all ratings for all dilemmas for all individuals fell within the range 1-7. Although no keypunching errors were found, in three instances a subject had ratings for one rater on a dilemma, and the second rater assigned only a single digit. This problem was encountered once each in Kitchener, et al. (1993), Van Tine, (1990) and Strange and King (1981). No corrections for these codings were found in the computer programs, making data from these ratings invalid. In these cases, it seemed most reasonable to code these ratings as three digits corresponding to the single digit rating. Finally, one rating from Kitchener and King (1981) Time 1 data was entered in the wrong column. The correct entry for this resolved score was ascertained by pulling the data from the original transcripts. The raw data sheets from Friedman (1995) were somewhat difficult to check. Raw coding sheets from Round 1 were provided separately by each dilemma. The master data set on which Friedman's analyses were based contained only summary dilemma scores across both raters. When these two data sets scores were reconciled, it seemed that several times dilemma topics were transposed for some subjects. This did not affect overall scores for the subjects, which were based on composites across all dilemmas. In addition, the rater agreement from the coding sheets was somewhat higher than that reported in Friedman (1995), indicating an over 95% agreement rate. For these reasons it was decided to code only the raw data, but not to include these data in round one agreement statistics. Where the Round 1 scores for Friedman's data indicated a discrepancy, resolved ratings were assigned which were consonant with the numerical value in Friedman's final master data set.

*Errors of Analysis in Previous Research.* Proofreading the input formats for the data sets revealed an analysis error for the results reported in Strange and King (1981). For these data, the input format statement for the food additives dilemma, resolved (consensus rating) was off by one column, resulting in an RJI dilemma score which was the sum of two digits divided by three, instead of all three digits. Rerunning the analysis of variance reported in Strange and King (1981) and Strange (1978) based on corrected data revealed the same pattern of statistical significance, however the significance levels of independent variables used to predict the RJI were uniformly higher than that reported. In addition, Polkosnik and Winston (1989) reported statistically significant growth in scores over a three month period for a sample of sixteen college students from the University of Georgia. Although it was possible to reproduce the Time 1 and Time 2 means for these two groups (3.42 and 3.44, respectively), this difference was nowhere near statistical significance using a repeated measures analysis of variance. This error appears to be due to an incorrect calculation of the Mean Square Error for the analysis. Although the descriptive statistics in Friedman's study of undergraduate and graduate students were replicated, several of the analyses of variance F statistics were different. To some extent similar results could be obtained by deliberately miscalculating the experimental design as if it were a balanced one, suggesting that some of the failure to reconcile the two data sets may be due to inaccuracies in statistical software. The pattern of statistical significance remained the same, however. Three minor errors of reportage or analysis in other studies were also found.[6]

Kronholm's longitudinal study evaluated an educational intervention designed to promote Reflective Judgment presented some difficulties. While the statistical analyses were not in error, the claim that the intervention alone is responsible for gains of .3 of a stage in Reflective Judgment seems open to question. Using a 2 (intervention versus control conditions) by 2 (times of measurement) design, Kronholm found a time by condition interaction existed for the data (which was replicated). However, follow-up analyses of this interaction yielded a puzzling pattern of means: The post-test means for both groups were almost identical (3.46 for the control versus 3.53 for the intervention groups, respectively; $t(76)=-1.17$; $p=.25$). The pretest means for these two groups revealed large differences, however (3.58 for the control versus 3.23 for intervention; $t(78)=4.60$; $p<.0001$). Much of the statistical significance for the time by condition interaction in the study appears due to the nonequivalence of these two groups on pretest. Several analyses examining background academic aptitude, achievement,

---

[6] 1.) Davison (1979) incorrectly states that the Reflective Judgment scale has 9 levels but that no individuals were identified at levels 1, 8, and 9. 2.) Welfel (1982, p. 495) incorrectly reports the degrees of freedom for an analysis of covariance as a one way design when it should have been a 2x2 design. The corrected test of the overall model analysis of covariance was $F(3,58)=2.88$, $p<.01$, retaining the significant educational level effect ($F(1,58)=10.75$, $p<.01$) 3.) Wood and Games (1991) incorrectly refer to the overall Concept Mastery Test scores as a vocabulary subtest of the measure.

and background variables failed to identify possible reasons for this large initial difference between groups.

*Rater Discrepancies.* With three exceptions, raters in these studies were trained to a criterion agreement rate of 80% using a two point agreement criterion. Some irregularities occurred across studies as to how discrepant raters could be before this divergence could be counted as a disagreement. Kitchener and King's sample at Time 1 contained seventeen scores which were discrepant by exactly three points. At Time 2 sixteen scores were discrepant by exactly three points. Welfel (1982) Time 1, and Kitchener and Wood (1987) defined disagreement as more than a three point discrepancy between ratings. All remaining available data sets ( to the extent that it was possible to check) appear to have defined discrepancy as a difference of three points or more (including Welfel (1982) time 2, and Kitchener and King Times 3 and 4).[7] One rating from McKinney (1985) was discrepant by three points and was not resolved. Examination of the patterns of rating and rerating revealed that, on other occasions, raters had rerated transcripts discrepant by three points, so this discrepant rating appears to be an oversight.

In summary, the examination of data accuracy and rater discrepancies revealed that data entry, computer programming, or failure to resolve discrepant scores resulted in incorrect data for 18 dilemmas. 17.85 percent of the studies contained some coding error. Expressed as a function of the total number of dilemmas which were rated, the overall error rate for the studies was .33 percent. This also represents a 1.35 percent error rate of the data for any individual associated with a particular measurement occasion. Although the error rates noted for these studies must be interpreted as conservative estimates (since it was not possible to investigate all studies from original data), the error rates compare favorably with those found in previous psychological research. Rosenthal (1978), for example, notes a 1 percent error rate at the data entry level, which is much higher than the .33 percent error rate for individual dilemmas found here and is lower than all studies reviewed except one reviewed by Rosenthal (1978).

## Scoring Issues

*Multi-Stage Ratings.* A second minor source of diversity in the scoring of Reflective Judgment across studies occurs when some raters assigned three separate digits to indicate their rating of a protocol. For example, in these situations, raters assigned the ratings such as 4-5-6 to a protocol, indicating that the predominant reasoning style in the transcript was Stage 4 with evidence of reasoning belonging to Stages 5 and 6. These ratings occurred in the Kitchener and King (1981)

---

[7]It is rather unusual that the Kitchener and King (1981) and Welfel and Davison (1986) studies would change their definitions of rater agreement from one time to another without documenting this fact. This finding appears to point to some early and undocumented variability in the operational definition of rater agreement.

data set, the McKinney (1985), Dale (1993), and Van Tine (1990). Examination of available Round 1 ratings from all studies found that out of a total of 6620 available ratings, 1.45 percent (96) contained ratings from at least one judge which contained three different stages. Although (as discussed below) subjects may frequently show evidence of more than two levels across the four dilemmas of the RJI, an examination of the response patterns across judges reveals that such three-stage ratings are not advisable at the transcript level on two grounds: First, raters do not seem to be able to reliably detect more than two types of reasoning in a given protocol. Based on Round 1 ratings, judges never agreed that all three stages were present. In only one resolved rating session were judges able to agree that three stages were present in the protocol and even in that one, neither judge initially assigned three separate stages in their initial rating. Second, the practice of allowing more than three stages to be present in a protocol poses some difficulties for notions of rater agreement. Since discrepancy is defined as a three or more point difference between ratings, this means that a rating of 4-5-6 is discrepant with a rating of 4-4-4, even though both judges agree on the major level of reasoning in the transcript. Similarly, a 4-5-6 is counted as being in agreement with a rating of 6-6-5 even though the major level of reasoning in the protocol is different by two levels.

*Proposed Overall and Stage Utilization Measures.* As noted before, the score for a given protocol, dilemma, and interview consists of the average of the three-digit codes across raters. As noted above, this scheme, which measures ability in one third of a stage increments, does not take into account the relative position of the second stages assigned to a protocol. For example, the ratings 343 and 334 are possible ratings with the same average score (3.3). The first rating, however, is used by raters to indicate more Stage 4 reasoning in the protocol than the second. In addition, it is at times useful to examine protocol ratings in order to assess the percent of times in an interview that a given level of reasoning is present. Under the current system of averages, it is not possible to do this and a subject who receives an average score of 4.0 on the RJI based on four pure examples of Level 4 reasoning is not distinguished from a subject who reasons at Level 3 on two dilemmas and at Level 5 on the other two.

In order to enable a more fine-grained scale and in order to compute rough measures of subjects' stage utilization measures, compositing weight measures were assigned to each of the three digits of a rating. The first and second digits were assigned a weight of .4 and the third was assigned a weight of .2. These values were multiplied by the stage levels and then summed across the three digits to form a composite score. For example, a rating of 334 would receive a value of $(3 \times .4) + (3 \times .4) + (4 \times .2) = 3.2$. Scale intervals are then measured in even increments of one fifth (Ratings of 333, 334, 343, 434, 443, and 444 would be 3, 3.2, 3.4, 3.6, 3.8, and 4.0, respectively). In addition, for those rare dilemmas which were assigned three different stages by a rater, the end rating reflects the major level assigned to the protocol (e.g., a rating of 456 receives an overall score of 4.8 instead of 5.0). This more fine grained scale provides modest improvements in the internal consistency of the RJI as will be described below.

In addition to providing a finer scale of measurement, it is also possible to calculate approximate stage utilization scores for ratings. A rating of 334 indicates 80 percent Stage 3 utilization and 20 percent Stage 4 utilization. A rating of 343 indicates 60 percent stage 3 utilization, and 40 percent Stage 4 utilization. Such stage utilization scores are similar to the utilization scores developed for Rest's (1979) Defining Issues Test and allow an examination of subject's response repertoire which is not possible given only simple averages.

## Psychometric Properties of the RJI.

Previous reviews of the RJI have emphasized the high reliability and internal consistency of the measure. Unfortunately, it difficult to judge whether the multiple pass rating system employed in the RJI results in improved reliability and internal consistency or to assess the degree to which the RJI possesses the same internal consistency and agreement rates across samples and educational levels; Some studies reported agreement only for Round 1 scores, some calculated these statistics only for the experiment as a whole and not for particular educational levels, and some studies sampled a wide variety of educational levels while others concentrated on students of relatively homogenous educational levels. Additionally, as noted above, some studies employed a two-point agreement criterion in ratings, while others employed a three-point agreement. In order to make a statement of the psychometric properties of the instrument, the available raw data from Round 1, Round 2 and Resolved ratings were re-examined.

Psychometric properties for the RJI may be divided into three general areas: Internal consistency, inter-rater agreement, and intraclass correlations between raters. Internal consistency as measured by coefficient alpha, which indicates the reliability of the RJI treating the four topic of the interview as separate items. Item scores are based on the average across the two raters for each topic. Agreement rates are estimates of the proportion of times that one rater assigns a score within one stage of the other rater. Intraclass correlations represent the proportion of true score variability between two raters. As such, two estimates of intraclass correlations can be considered, the intraclass correlation between raters for the overall score across all four dilemmas, and the intraclass correlation across raters across the individual dilemmas of the RJI.

*Internal Consistency.* The second column of Table 5 shows the internal consistency of the RJI for all available studies. In the top half of the table, alphas for studies using all four topics are presented. The bottom half of the table shows alphas for those studies which used some subset of the standard RJI topics. The internal consistency estimates are presented based on resolved data, since resolved scores represent the raters' best estimate of the score for a particular topic. Numbers in parentheses indicate overall internal consistencies based on Round 1 ratings, where available. As can be seen, many studies show little, if any improvement in internal consistency as a result of the rating process. Three studies (DeBord (1993), McKinney (1985) Time 2, and Thompson (1995) Time 2 Control) showed a decrease in internal consistency as a result of the rating process, while only three studies note an increase in internal consistency (Kitchener and Wood, 1987; Kitchener and King, 1981 Time 4, and Thompson (1995) Time 2 Experimental).[8].

Notably, the internal consistency estimates from two studies appear markedly different from the others, even taking into account the small sample sizes employed. Data from Kronholm's (1993) intervention study and King, Taylor, and Ottinger's (1989) study of black undergraduates revealed much lower internal consistency estimates than the remaining studies. In both cases, the raters involved did not go on to rate additional studies, making it difficult to determine if these patterns point to legitimate concerns regarding the use of the RJI with minority and some types of undergraduate populations, or if these two studies represent a failures of the rater certification process to ensure reliable rating.

The internal consistency estimates in Table 5 are, in most cases, slightly higher than those reported in the original studies, possibly due to the increased precision of measurement afforded by the finer-grained scoring procedure noted above. Van Tine's (1990) reported alpha of .87 is much higher than the .78 found for this study and may constitute a transposition error. Polkosnik and Winston's (1989) reported alpha of .89 is higher than the .80 found for the Time 1 data, but may be due to the internal consistency estimate being based on all times of assessment.

It is not possible to directly compare the internal consistency estimates across all studies directly as a measure of the quality of RJI ratings, since some studies included a wide range of educational levels (e.g., Kitchener and King, 1981), while other studies examined only a narrow range of educational levels (e.g., McKinney's study of high school students). In order to facilitate comparisons across studies, separate internal consistency estimates were computed for each study by educational level and the resulting internal consistency estimates and confidence intervals were examined in an effort to detect possible patterns of differential internal consistency across studies. With one exception (noted below) the studies which employed all four standard dilemmas were roughly equivalent. Data were then grouped according to educational level and the resultant coefficient alpha estimates based on Time 1 data by educational level, accompanied by a 95 percent confidence interval are given in Table 6.

---

[8]The increase in internal consistency for the Kitchener and Wood (1987) study is probably due to the poor agreement rates for these data (discussed below). The relatively slight change in coefficient alpha for the Kitchener and King (1981 Time 4) study may be due to the use of a split rating scheme involving three raters.

## Table 5 . Internal Consistency Estimates Based on Topics of the RJI for All Available Studies[1]

| Study | N | Coefficient Alpha | 95% Confidence Interval | | Raw Agree-ment | Kappa | Bangdi wala |
|---|---|---|---|---|---|---|---|
| | | | Lower | Higher | | | |
| *Studies Using All Four Dilemmas* | | | | | | | |
| Brabeck (1983) | 119 | .76(.75) | .68 | .82 | .79 | .67 | .77 |
| Time 2 | 25 | .77(.76) | .58 | .89 | .82 | .69 | .80 |
| Time 3[2] | 22 | .84(.86) | .70 | .93 | .84 | .72 | .85 |
| Dove (1990) Time 1[3] | 44 | .91(.89) | .86 | .95 | .80 | .70 | .71 |
| Friedman (1995) | 41 | .92 | .87 | .95 | n.a.[4] | | |
| Kelton and Griffith (1986) | 16 | .95 | .89 | .98 | n.a. | | |
| King, Wood and Mines (1990) | 91 | .89(.90) | .84 | .92 | .72 | .62 | .66 |
| Kitchener and King (1981) | 80 | .95(.95) | .93 | .97 | .87 | .84 | .82 |
| Time 2[5] | 58 | .96(.95) | .93 | .97 | .78 | .71 | .75 |
| Time 3[6] | 54 | .92(.92) | .87 | .95 | .75 | .67 | .60 |
| Time 4[7] | 50 | .88(.83) | .81 | .93 | .76 | .69 | .60 |
| Lawson (1980) | 80 | .81 | .73 | .87 | n.a. | | |
| McKinney (1985) | 56 | .54(.55) | .30 | .71 | .98 | .96 | .97 |
| Time 2[8] | 21 | .77(.86) | .55 | .90 | .70 | .42 | .59 |
| Van Tine (1990) | 42 | .79(.82) | .67 | .88 | .90 | .81 | .83 |
| Welfel (1982) | 64 | .63 | .45 | .76 | n.a. | | |
| Time 2[9] | 25 | .76 | .55 | .88 | n.a. | | |
| *Studies Not Using All Four Dilemmas* | | | | | | | |
| Dale (1995)[10] | 52 | .85 | .77 | .91 | .89 | .83 | .94 |
| DeBord (1993)[11] | 42 | .83(.94) | .68 | .91 | .73 | .57 | .66 |
| Glatfelter (1982)[11] | 80 | .87(.85) | .79 | .91 | .97 | .94 | .97 |
| Kelton and Griffith (1986)[12] | 125 | .95 | .94 | .97 | n.a. | | |
| Kitchener et al. (1993)[13] | 112 | .86(.88) | .80 | .90 | .79 | .71 | .75 |
| Time 2 Control | 53 | .90(.91) | .83 | .94 | .85 | .79 | .83 |
| Time 2 Experimental | 104 | .93(.94) | .89 | .95 | .83 | .77 | .74 |
| Kitchener and Wood (1987)[14] | 48 | .88(.79) | .80 | .93 | .61 | .49 | .48 |
| King, Taylor and Ottinger (1989)[15] | 146 | .53(.53) | .38 | .65 | 1.00 | .99 | 1.00 |
| Kronholm (1993) Time 1 Control[16] | 52 | .36 | .00 | .61 | n.a. | | |
| Time 1 Experimental | 28 | .23 | .00 | .62 | n.a. | | |
| Time 2 Control | 50 | .30 | .00 | .58 | n.a. | | |
| Time 2 Experimental | 28 | * | | | n.a. | | |
| Polkosnik and Winston (1989)[15] | 19 | .80 | .58 | .92 | n.a. | | |
| Time 2 | 15 | .89 | .73 | .96 | n.a. | | |
| Time 3 | 15 | .94 | .86 | .98 | n.a. | | |
| Strange and King (1981)[17] | 64 | .72(.73) | .58 | .82 | .75 | .64 | .67 |
| Reed and McGaffic (1994)[18] | 48 | .76 | .58 | .87 | n.a. | | |
| Thompson (1995)[19] | 49 | .91(.91) | .84 | .95 | .87 | .72 | .92 |
| Time 2 Control | 27 | .85(.90) | .68 | .93 | .89 | .78 | .86 |
| Time 2 Experimental | 22 | .83(.67) | .60 | .93 | .80 | .54 | .79 |

[1]Coefficient alpha based on Resolved Scores (numbers in parentheses indicate Round 1 alphas), Agreement measures based on Round 1 data

[2]Published in Brabeck and Wood (1990).

[3]Data from Kitchener et al. (1993) were merged with Dove (1990) to form complete records.

[4]Data were not available because Round 1 ratings were not coded in the data set. For two studies, agreement information is unavailable because only one rater was used (Kelton and Griffith, 1986; Polkosnik and Winston, 1989).

[5]Published in King, Kitchener, Davison, Parker and Wood (1983)

[6]Published in Kitchener, King, Wood and Davison (1989).

[7]Published in Kitchener and King (1990).

[8]Conducted by and reported in Van Tine (1990)

[9]Published in Welfel and Davison (1986)

[10]Based on Pyramids, Evolution and Additives dilemmas

[11]Based on two randomly selected dilemmas

[12]Based on three randomly selected dilemmas individuals with all four dilemmas not included

[13]Based on subjects not included in Dove (1990) having only Additives and Pyramids dilemma. Experimental and control groups combined since Time 1 assessment is a pretest.

[14]Based on Pyramids, News, and Additives Dilemmas

[15]Based on News, Evolution, and Additives dilemmas Time 2 Experimental variance/covariance matrix contained negative values, preventing calculation of coefficient alpha

[16]Based on Pyramids, Evolution and Additives dilemmas

[17]Based on Pyramids, News, and Evolution dilemmas

[18]Based on News and Pyramids dilemmas

[19]Based on Pyramids and Evolutions dilemmas

In order to identify possible differences across studies within educational level, coefficient alpha estimates were generated separately by study within each educational level. In general, samples taken from restricted ranges of high verbal ability (such as the undergraduate and high school samples in Kitchener and King (1977) which were matched on verbal ability to a graduate sample and Kitchener et al. (1993) which were also sampled on the basis of high verbal ability) were not different in terms of internal consistency than samples which were selected for high variability (such as Brabeck's samples of high and low critical thinkers, or McKinny's sample of high and low academic achievement high school students). Internal consistency estimates from one sample were, however, markedly different than remaining samples: The college freshman data from Welfel (1982) were markedly lower than that of other studies (coefficient alpha for these 32 subjects was .13). Accordingly, coefficient alpha was recomputed for the college freshmen excluding this sample.

Overall, the coefficient alpha within educational level ranges from .73 to .85 for undergraduate samples, and about the mid .80s for graduate samples. These internal consistencies are generally representative of the internal consistencies found when coefficient alpha was calculated for each educational level separately for each study. While these internal consistencies are helpful in informing an instructor or educational researcher as to the internal consistency which may be expected when the RJI is administered to individuals within a given educational level (as might happen in research using educational interventions to promote Reflective Judgment), it is also helpful to estimate the internal consistency of the instrument based on selected ranges of educational levels of interest (as might occur in studies which seek to document outcomes of higher education tied to the undergraduate or graduate experience, for example. Coefficient alpha based on resolved ratings across all undergraduate data was .81 (95% Confidence interval .77-.84). Coefficient alpha based on all graduate data was .87 (95% Confidence interval .83-.90). Based on only 8th-12th grade data coefficient alpha was .81 (95% Confidence interval .76-.86). When coefficient alpha is based on all individuals who completed all four dilemmas, coefficient alpha is .94.

**Table 6. Internal Consistency Estimates Based on Topics as Items[1]**

| Education level | N | Coefficient Alpha | 95% Confidence Interval | |
|---|---|---|---|---|
| | | | Lower | Higher |
| High School[2] | | | | |
| 9th grade | 53 | .84 | .76 | .90 |
| 11th Grade | 44 | .90 | .84 | .94 |
| 12th Grade | 62 | .72 | .58 | .82 |
| Undergraduate | | | | |
| Freshman | 64 | .51 | .27 | .68 |
| Freshmen w/o Welfel (1982) | 32 | .79 | .64 | .89 |
| Sophomore | 32 | .73 | .53 | .85 |
| Junior | 77 | .85 | .78 | .90 |
| Senior | 132 | .77 | .70 | .83 |
| Graduate Students | | | | |
| Masters/Beginning Doctorate | 107 | .84 | .79 | .89 |
| Advanced Doctoral | 55 | .86 | .78 | .91 |

[1]Studies not using all four dilemmas not included in Education Level alphas. Based on Resolved scores.

[2]Data from 8th and 10th grades excluded since some dilemma covariances contained negative values, yielding an invalid estimate for coefficient alpha.

Of course, the internal consistency estimates presented here by educational level must be interpreted with some caution. On the one hand, these internal consistency estimates may represent overestimates relative to what a researcher may expect, in that they include institutional level differences and thus may reflect a larger range of variability than that found in any particular sample. On the other hand, these estimates may represent underestimates of the reliability that would be found in any given study, since unequal numbers of individuals were sampled at each educational level. If a researcher were to gather an equal number of data points at each educational level, the observed coefficient alpha would be higher than found in such unbalanced samples. Nevertheless, it seems reasonable to employ these figures as summary estimates of internal consistency since they so closely parallel the estimates arrived at based on individual samples. Additionally, those studies which did sample ranges such as freshman-senior or high school samples appear to have similar overall internal consistency estimates to the estimates based on such ranges of educational level.

*Rater Agreement.* Previously, two raw agreement measures have been calculated for the RJI: Raw agreement, the proportion of times that raters were less than three points discrepant in their ratings and agreement rates corrected for chance using Tinsley and Weiss' (1975) T-coefficient. Since Tinsley and Weiss' T-coefficient is a special case of the more general kappa coefficient, and since kappa does not take into account unequal marginal frequencies in its correction for chance agreement, it was decided to calculate three measures of agreement across studies: Raw agreement (defined as the percent of times that a composite score for a transcript from one rater was one level or more discrepant than the other rater's score), an unweighted kappa statistic, and a weighted kappa statistic which takes into account different marginal frequencies in the data (Bangdiwala, 1985). These agreement coefficients for each study are given in the right hand of Table 5. Overall, raw agreement rates for the individual studies fall between .7 and .8, with half of the studies containing a raw agreement rate 80 percent or higher. Only one study (Kitchener and Wood, 1987) contained an error rate lower than 70 percent. Two reasons exist for this low agreement rate: This study employed a three-point (as opposed to a two-point) agreement criterion between raters. Transcripts from this study were also translated from the original German, introducing a possible source of ambiguity in the transcripts. Kappa coefficients were uniformly lower than raw agreements, since these agreements contain a correction for chance agreement, with 55 percent of the samples demonstrating agreement rates of .70 or higher. Two studies, Kitchener and Wood (1987) and Van Tine's (1990) retest of a sample drawn from McKinney (1985) provided extremely low corrected agreement rates.

When these agreement rates are compared to those reported in the separate studies, the same raw agreement values were found with a few exceptions: King, Wood, and Mines (1990) reported an agreement rate of .90, which was based on the agreement rates of the composites of the two raters, and not on individual dilemma agreement. The agreement rates for Times 1 and 2 of Kitchener and King (1977) (.87 and .78) are higher than the reported .77 and .72, respectively. These differences could be due to a conservative approach to scoring agreement for transcripts which contained three stages of response.

Raw agreement rates were also examined separately for each study within educational level and then examined before being combined. Generally, no substantial differences by study obtained for agreement rates and so agreements calculated separately by each educational level are presented in Table 7. As can be seen, raw agreement rates for each educational level appears to run from 80 percent to 100 percent, with Masters/Beginning doctorate students showing a 82 percent agreement rate, suggesting that these data are slightly more difficult for raters to agree on. Kappa for these data ranged from .75-1.00. In most cases

Bangdiwala's weighted kappa yielded estimates between unweighted kappa and the raw agreement.

**Table 7. Agreement Estimates for Individual Dilemmas by Educational Level[1]**

| Education level | N Dilemmas | Raw Agreement | Kappa | Bangdiwala |
|---|---|---|---|---|
| *High School* | | | | |
| 8th grade | 20 | 1.00 | 1.00 | 1.00 |
| 9th grade | 220 | .95 | .91 | .91 |
| 10th Grade | 40 | 1.00 | 1.00 | 1.00 |
| 11th Grade | 112 | .96 | .93 | .92 |
| 12th Grade | 306 | .91 | .85 | .90 |
| *Undergraduate* | | | | |
| Freshman | 1061 | .97 | .96 | .96 |
| Sophomore | 290 | .93 | .87 | .90 |
| Junior | 484 | .86 | .78 | .84 |
| Senior | 1070 | .93 | .90 | .92 |
| *Graduate Students* | | | | |
| Masters/Beginning Doctorate | 589 | .82 | .75 | .77 |
| Advanced Doctoral | 322 | .88 | .84 | .82 |

[1]Based on all studies with available Round 1 data and calculated on a per dilemma basis. More individuals included in this table than in Table 5 because individuals were included who had one or more missing dilemmas for some items.

*Internal Consistency between Raters.* The internal consistency across raters for RJI, the degree to which the overall RJI score of one rater is consistent with that of another rater, has been traditionally assessed as the correlation between the summary scores of two raters (or, using raters as "items" the square root of this correlation, coefficient alpha, has been reported). This approach results in an overestimate of the degree of internal consistency between raters, because it assumes that raters constitute a "fixed effect" as if the internal consistency of interest was composed of only a single pair of raters. In this study, however, it makes conceptual sense to estimate internal consistency taking into account the fact that raters were drawn from a larger pool of certified raters and it is to this pool that researchers wish to generalize their findings. The intra-class correlation coefficient (ICC, Shrout and Fleiss, 1979), a measure of internal consistency drawn from generalizability theory, is just such an internal consistency measure.[9] Under the assumption that raters are a fixed effect (and not randomly drawn from some larger population) the ICC is equal to coefficient alpha. Two forms of the ICC were calculated based on the present data. The ICC based on the composite rating for one rater with another was calculated. This estimate was also recalcu-

[9]The ICC formula used assumed that the same raters rated all transcripts within a given study. For studies which employed a three rater system, ICC's reported here are based on a rearrangement of the data records to create two ratings for each dilemma. No discrepancies in ICC between combinations of raters within such studies were found.

lated based on the individual dilemmas. Since no significant differences were found at the level of the individual dilemma, these dilemma-based ICC's were calculated across all available dilemmas. Since sample size varied substantially from one sample to the next, a Satterthwaite approximate 95 percent confidence interval was also calculated based on the formulae in Fleiss and Shrout (1978).

Based on the composite, internal consistency between raters appears quite high for studies which employed a wide range of educational levels (ranging from .73 to .97).The exceptions to this pattern were Kitchener and Wood (1987) (a study which employed a range of undergraduate and graduate subjects), with an ICC of .63, King, Taylor and Ottinger (1989) a study of black undergraduate students (ICC=.34), and some of the groups in Kronholm's (1993) and Thompson's (1995) intervention studies. Internal consistency estimates calculated separately by the four undergraduate levels for the King et al. (1989) study were particularly low, ranging from .13 to .64. While the low internal consistency of the Kitchener and Wood (1987) study appears to be due to the difficulties of translation (since one of the raters went on to successfully rate other studies) the ICC values for King et al. (1989), Kronholm (1993), and Thompson (1995) studies are again more difficult to interpret. As mentioned above, the King et al. (1989) study findings could be due to difficulties in rating transcripts from black undergraduates, or could be a failure of the rater certification process. It is interesting to note that both intervention studies which employed a curricular intervention in a college course, the Time 2 experimental conditions had markedly lower internal consistency estimates based on raters. Perhaps this indicates that some subjects are able to mimic some higher stage responses in an interview, making these data more difficult to rate. For the remaining studies, it appears, as expected, that samples with restricted ranges of Reflective Judgment have lower internal consistency (ranging from .12 to .57)

When these values are compared with reported coefficient alphas (or transformed, based on reported correlations), ICC's are generally .1 to .15 lower than their fixed effects counterparts. This discrepancy was less pronounced for studies with wide ranges in educational level.

When ICC's are based on the individual dilemmas of the RJI, these ICC's are much lower, due to the smaller amount of information present for raters to judge.[10] Exceptions to this pattern are Dale (1995), and Kronholm (1993). Interestingly, when one compares the observed ICC based on the composite with a predicted ICC based on a Spearman-Brown estimate drawn from the individual dilemma-level, we find that the observed reliability of the composite is consistently lower by anywhere from .05 to .2 than the observed composite ICC. The exceptions to this pattern are King and Kitchener Time 1 and Glatfelter (1982), which yielded the same ICC and

---

[10]Exceptions to this pattern are Dale (1995), and Kronholm (1993). Recall that these studies only employed two raters for a minority of ratings, making it difficult to compare rater composite and dilemma patterns.

King and Kitchener, Time 4, which yielded a value .18 lower than that found for the composite. This pattern will be interpreted in light of the investigation of the RJI's dilemmas as parallel forms described below..

**Table 8 . Internal Consistency Estimates Based on Raters of the RJI for All Available Studies[1]**

| Study | N | Based on Composite | | | Based on Dilemma | | |
|---|---|---|---|---|---|---|---|
| | | Intra-Class Corre-lation | 95% Conf. Interval | | Intra-Class Corre-lation | 95% Conf. Interval | |
| | | | Lower | Higher | | Lower | Higher |
| *Studies Using All Four Dilemmas* | | | | | | | |
| Brabeck (1983) | 119 | .88 | .81 | .92 | .50 | .43 | .56 |
| Time 2 | 25 | .48 | .19 | .71 | .31 | .14 | .46 |
| Time 3[2] | 22 | .57 | .20 | .80 | .38 | .18 | .54 |
| Dove (1990)[3] | 44 | .81 | .62 | .90 | .60 | .50 | .69 |
| Friedman (1995) | 43 | .97 | .58 | .99 | .93 | .89 | .96 |
| King, Wood and Mines (1990) | 91 | .83 | .75 | .89 | .65 | .58 | .70 |
| Kitchener and King (1981) | 80 | .97 | .81 | .99 | .90 | .87 | .92 |
| Time 2[4] | 58 | .93 | .79 | .97 | .81 | .76 | .85 |
| Time 3[5] | 54 | .80 | .64 | .88 | .62 | .53 | .70 |
| Time 4[6] | 53 | .89 | .71 | .95 | .38 | .18 | .54 |
| McKinney (1985) | 56 | .75 | .60 | .85 | .65 | .57 | .72 |
| Time 2[7] | 21 | .12 | .05 | .38 | .11 | .00 | .24 |
| Van Tine (1990) | 42 | .22 | .04 | .43 | .24 | .13 | .35 |
| Welfel (1982) | 45 | .63 | .41 | .78 | .52 | .41 | .62 |
| *Studies Not Using All Four Dilemmas* | | | | | | | |
| Dale (1995)[8] | 35 | .92 | .64 | .97 | .94 | .76 | .97 |
| DeBord (1993)[8] | 42 | .89 | .70 | .95 | .84 | .74 | .90 |
| Glatfelter (1982)[9] | 80 | .66 | .51 | .77 | .27 | .15 | .39 |
| Kitchener et al. (1993)[10] | 112 | .73 | .62 | .81 | .69 | .71 | .75 |
| Time 2 Control[9] | 53 | .82 | .66 | .90 | .78 | .68 | .85 |
| Time 2 Experimental[9] | 104 | .84 | .76 | .89 | .79 | .73 | .84 |
| Kitchener and Wood (1987)[11] | 47 | .63 | .41 | .78 | .59 | .41 | .73 |
| King, Taylor and Ottinger (1989)[12] | 146 | .34 | .19 | .48 | .31 | .22 | .39 |
| Kronholm (1993) Time 1 Control[13] | 38 | .47 | .19 | .68 | .57 | .43 | .69 |
| Time 1 Experimental | 28 | .68 | .39 | .84 | .64 | .49 | .76 |
| Time 2 Control | 22 | .38 | .00 | .70 | .76 | .60 | .86 |
| Time 2 Experimental | 8 | .12 | .00 | .70 | .70 | .38 | .86 |
| Strange and King (1981)[14] | 21 | .65 | .29 | .84 | .59 | .41 | .73 |
| Thompson (1995)[15] | 49 | .44 | .19 | .64 | .37 | .19 | .52 |
| Time 2 Control | 22 | .63 | .28 | .83 | .54 | .29 | .72 |
| Time 2 Experimental | 27 | .22 | .00 | .54 | .17 | .00 | .41 |

[1]Coefficient alpha based on Resolved Scores Numbers of individuals do not correspond to number in study since only one rater was used for many subjects

[2]Published in Brabeck and Wood (1990).

[3]Data from Kitchener et al. (1993) were merged with Dove (1990) for form complete records. Experimental and Control conditions combined since Time 1 assessment is a pretest.

[4]Published in King, Kitchener, Davison, Parker and Wood (1983).

[5]Published in Kitchener, King, Wood and Davison (1989).

[6]Published in Kitchener and King (1990).

[7]Conducted by and reported in Van Tine (1990)

[8]Based on Pyramids, Evolution and Additives dilemmas

[9]Based on two randomly selected dilemmas

[10]Based on subjects not included in Dove (1990) having only Additives and Pyramids dilemma. Experimental and control groups combined since Time 1 assessment is a pretest.

[11]Based on Pyramids, News, and Additives Dilemmas

[12]Based on News, Evolution, and Additives dilemmas

[13]Based on Pyramids, Evolution and Additives dilemmas

[14]Based on Pyramids, News, and Evolution dilemmas

[15]Based on Pyramids and Evolutions dilemmas

Internal consistency estimates computed separately by educational level ranged from .67-.92, and do not appear to vary systematically as a function of educational level, when the confidence intervals for these ICC's are examined (Table 9). ICC's associated with individual dilemmas appear to generally run from .56 to .87.[11]

Taken together, the agreement rates and internal consistency estimates from these data indicate that, with a few notable exceptions, the Reflective Judgment Interview can be reliably and accurately scored by trained raters. Although the process of blindly rerating transcripts which are initially discrepant improves the agreement levels of the interview, the improvements in internal consistency based on these reratings is slight, suggesting that rater differences on a particular transcript "average out" over the four dilemmas yielding an acceptable indication of an individual's overall ability. In light of these patterns, the finding that some studies employed a three-point criterion for rater agreement versus the two-point criterion is probably not a significant threat to the quality of the data. For example, the lower agreement rate found for Kitchener and Wood (1987) does not appear to result in a dramatically different estimate of internal consistency based on coefficient alpha. Some notable exceptions were found, however. In four studies, internal consistency and agreement rates of the data appear to be quite low compared with other studies. Welfel's (1982) freshman data appear to have a much lower internal consistency than other freshman samples. This could be due to raters scoring these data first, causing some calibration errors or rater bias (discussed below) to

---

[11]Although Welfel's freshman sample demonstrated a significantly lower pattern of internal consistency across dilemmas, this differential pattern was not found for the ICC's. Recalculating the ICC values for freshmen without this sample resulted in no noticeable improvement.

come to light. In addition, King et al. (1989) found exceptionally low internal consistency in a study of undergraduate black students at Bowling Green State University. Both studies which used a curricular intervention in a given class demonstrated some difficulties in internal consistency, although Thompson's (1995) study produced an acceptable internal consistency based on topics as items. These studies could pose a threat to the generalizability of the RJI and its scoring to minority populations or could point out some difficulties in using the RJI for intervention research. Alternatively, given that a single rater was used in the Kronholm (1993) study and the raters of the King et al. (1989) study did not rate other studies, it could mean that the certification process is not stringent enough or that rater "drift" occurs, with raters becoming less reliable after a period of time after certification.

**Table 9. Internal Consistency Estimates Based on Raters of the RJI by Education Level[1]**

| Educational Level | N | Based on Composite | | | Based on Dilemma | | |
|---|---|---|---|---|---|---|---|
| | | Intra-Class Corre-lation | 95% Conf. Interval | | Intra-Class Corre-lation | 95% Conf. Interval | |
| | | | Lower | Higher | | Lower | Higher |
| *High School* | | | | | | | |
| 9th Grade | 57 | .83 | .68 | .90 | .75 | .68 | .80 |
| 10th Grade | 15 | .83 | .29 | .95 | .56 | .31 | .74 |
| 11th Grade | 33 | .88 | .63 | .95 | .78 | .68 | .84 |
| 12th Grade | 83 | .83 | .73 | .90 | .78 | .73 | .82 |
| *Undergraduate* | | | | | | | |
| Freshman | 246 | .74 | .68 | .79 | .65 | .61 | .70 |
| Sophomore | 111 | .67 | .55 | .76 | .68 | .62 | .74 |
| Junior | 154 | .82 | .76 | .87 | .74 | .70 | .78 |
| Senior | 186 | .87 | .82 | .90 | .84 | .81 | .87 |
| *Graduate* | | | | | | | |
| Masters/Early Ph.D. | 159 | .92 | .87 | .95 | .87 | .84 | .89 |
| Advanced Graduate/ Ph.D. | 69 | .88 | .77 | .93 | .82 | .77 | .86 |

[1]Agreement measures based on Round 1 data Sample sizes do not total to all complete studies since McKinney Time 2 data were included as 11th graders, and eight 8th graders are not included in this table.

*Rater Bias.* As noted above, few studies have explored whether some raters assign statistically significantly higher or lower values in their transcript ratings.

Rater bias in this study was operationally defined within an analysis of variance framework as the presence of two effects: An overall main effect for rater (indicating that one rater awarded systematically higher scores than the other) and a Rater by Dilemma interaction (indicating that one rater assigned higher or lower scores than the other for particular dilemmas, but not necessarily over all dilemmas). In order to assess the presence of bias and its possible differential effect across studies and or educational levels a general linear model was specified using the 658 protocols from individuals with two ratings on all four dilemmas across all occasions specifying as a dependent variable the Reflective Judgment score and using as independent variables of Dilemma (4) x Study (12), educational level (11), and Rater (2). (Supplemental analyses based on Roun1 and and Round 2 data not reported here revealed the same pattern of statistical significance.)This analysis revealed a significant rater by dilemma by study interaction (p<.01), and a significant effect for study, but no significant effects for Dilemma, study x dilemma interactions and no interactions involving educational level (all p's>.1).

Although this analysis is based only on protocols for which all four dilemmas are present, they may be taken as evidence that the dilemmas of the RJI do not differ systematically. It also points out a class of alternative explanations to claims that dilemma differences exist for the RJI, namely that they appear to be a function of rater bias in some studies. Examined individually and based on all data for which dilemma scores were available (i.e., not restricting the analysis to only those studies which used all four dilemmas and used two raters), none of the studies found a main effect for Rater. Eight studies contained a statistically significant Dilemma effect. However, as indicated by the interaction of Dilemma with Study, the pattern of dilemma differences was not consistent across studies. Across most studies, regardless of statistical significance, the magnitude of overall dilemma differences never exceeded .15 of a stage, except for Dale's study, discussed below. Four studies, (Kitchener and Wood, 1987 and Welfel, 1982) found a statistically significant interaction between Dilemma and Rater indicating differential rater bias across dilemma. For the Welfel (1982) data, one judge consistently rated the creation/evolution dilemma lower than the remaining three dilemmas (lower by .33 than the average across the remaining three dilemmas) while the other rater's scores were relatively the same.[12] For the Kitchener and Wood (1987) data, one rater awarded scores on the Pyramids dilemma which were on the average .47 higher than the other rater, while dilemma scores were comparable across the remaining dilemmas. In Dale's (1995) study, two raters were used on only a few transcripts. Based on Round 1 data, the second rater,

---

[12]Given the markedly poorer internal consistency of the Welfel (1982) data for the freshman sample, additional follow-up analyses were run including educational level as a separate effect and also investigating whether the bias patterns were different for the freshman and senior samples. These merely confirmed the general pattern of bias in the study as a whole, but did not uncover a significant educational level by rater by dilemma interaction. No rater by dilemma interactions significant for either educational level group, presumably due to the lower statistical power of these analyses.

described as a novice rater, assigned scores on the average .82 higher than the other rater for the News dilemma, and .34 higher on the food additives dilemma. Based on resolved data, these differences were much lower (.2 for the News dilemma and .27 for the Food Additives dilemma). Rater 1's scores, while comparable across all dilemmas on Round 1, increased .23 when based on resolved scores. Since gains of .3 to .4 of a stage represent the average two year gain for some populations (see Table 11, p. 292) the magnitude of the interactions found for these studies is practically significant.

Taken together, these data also suggest that such idiosyncratic rater bias effects may be reduced by the rerating procedure. When separate analyses of variance similar to the ones described above were conducted on Round 1 data, a significant ($p<.05$) Rater effect was found for two studies, Brabeck (1983) and Van Tine (1990). In the Brabeck (1983) data, one rater awarded slightly higher scores than the other (.09). For the Van Tine (1990) data, one rater awarded overall scores .13 higher than the other.

To summarize, little evidence was found for systematic rater bias in these data as a whole. Some evidence exists, however, that some raters assign differentially high or low scores to a given dilemma within the interview, suggesting that the existing certification procedures should be expanded to incorporate more examples of each dilemma at each level of Reflective Judgment. The statistically significant dilemma differences were not consistent across studies, suggesting either that small differences in expertise exist across the populations researched with the RJI, or that rater bias, if it exists, consists of a small and systematic bias at the level of individual dilemmas.

### Level and Variability of RJI Scores as a Function of Educational Level.

In several studies, level of educational attainment has been the strongest correlate of Reflective Judgment. However, this general association does not communicate whether some educational levels are fairly limited in variability in RJI, whether outliers are likely to systematically occur, or where the largest differences between educational levels occur. In order to address these questions, RJI scores were organized as a function of educational level and a box plot of final (resolved) composite RJI scores was formed for each group. For convenience, these distributions of scores are grouped into High School grades 8, 9, and 10, High School grades 11 and 12, four undergraduate levels (Freshmen through Senior), and Beginning and Advanced doctoral students. Figure 1 shows the resulting distributions.

Since box plots are infrequently reported, a word of explanation regarding their design is appropriate. Box plots are designed to summarize the characteristics of level and shape of distributions. They convey five important features of a set of data: typical or central value, variability, shape (symmetry or skewness), outlying data points, and behavior in the tails of the distribution. The central box for each educational level extends from the lower quartile (Q1) to the upper quartile (Q3). Thus, the length of the box is the interquartile range showing the middle 50 percent of the observations. Behavior in the tails of the distribution (often termed "adjacent values") is indicated by the single lines above and below the central box. If the inter-quartile range (Q3-Q1) is denoted by IQR, these adjacent values are computed as: Q3+1.5IQR and Q1-1.5IQR, respectively. If the data are normally distributed, this range corresponds roughly to the 99 percentile range for the data. Median values (Q2) are denoted by a middle line in the box.

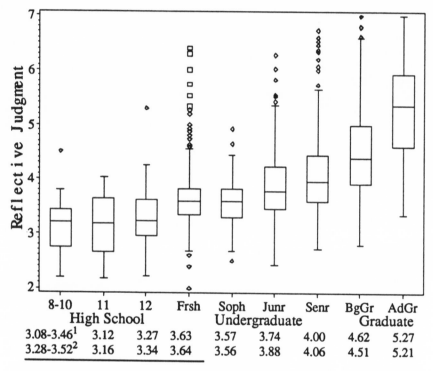

| | | | | | | | | |
|---|---|---|---|---|---|---|---|---|
| 8-10 | 11 | 12 | Frsh | Soph | Junr | Senr | BgGr | AdGr |
| | High School | | | | Undergraduate | | | Graduate |
| 3.08-3.46[1] | 3.12 | 3.27 | 3.63 | 3.57 | 3.74 | 4.00 | 4.62 | 5.27 |
| 3.28-3.52[2] | 3.16 | 3.34 | 3.64 | 3.56 | 3.88 | 4.06 | 4.51 | 5.21 |

1. Weighted means reported in King et al. (1944) from traditionally aged college students. 8th Grade means not reported.
2. Means computed from secondary analysis based on traditionally and nontraditionally aged students. Based on resolved scores using revised scoring scheme.

**FIGURE 1. Box Plots of Overall Reflective Judgment Level as a Function of Educational Level**

These univariate statistics conveyed via the box plots reveal a pattern of systematically increasing trends in RJI score as a function of educational level. The college samples appear higher than the high school samples, but are lower than the graduate samples. The overall performance of Freshmen appears roughly the same as sophomores, while the Junior and Senior groups, with the median senior performance being slightly higher than the 75th percentile of freshman perfor-mance. In addition, as one compares higher educational level students to lower educational level students, it is apparent that the distribution of scores becomes simultaneously more variable. Mean scores by educational level given at the bot-tom of the figure are quite similar to those based on reported means based on a survey of all available studies reported in King et al. (1994, Tables B6-3 through B6-6). It is also interesting to note that the college freshman distribution appears positively skewed, with several individuals scoring as outliers above the norm for the group. Some of this pattern may be due to the fact that many freshman sam-ples in the data set were matched on verbal or critical thinking ability to graduate populations (e.g., Kitchener and King, 1981; Brabeck, 1983). It is interesting to note that, although the Advanced Graduate sample shows a large amount of vari-ability in RJI scores, few differences were found between samples at the Advanced Graduate level (discussed below), suggesting that substantial variabil-ity exists in individual samples of Advanced Graduate students.

Part of the reason that these distributions increase in variability could also be due to the increased variability of samples across the studies examined. In order to examine the relative magnitude of between sample differences, separate analyses of variance were conducted on the data for each educational level, treating each sample of interest as an independent variable (High School samples in the 8th grade and the 10th grade were only examined in one study and were therefore excluded from these analyses). (A single Manova of these data was not possible, given the fact that not all studies explored all educational levels.) Samples within a given study were based on the experimental design used and were defined as fol-lows: First, analyses of variance within educational level were conducted sepa-rately for each study investigating a sample characteristic of interest (e.g., in Brabeck's study of High versus Low Critical thinkers, the objective of the analysis of variance was to determine if the data should be grouped together into one sam-ple, or should be split into two groups). If, the sample sizes were larger than 5, and the differences between samples statistically significant, then data from a study was broken according to that category. In Friedman's study of dispositional cate-gories, it was decided to break the sample according to area of study and not dis-position, since no differences were found as a function of disposition after adjusting for area, and other studies had also investigated the role of area of study to Reflective Judgment. Dale's (1995) study contained the only faculty sample to date and so it was decided to include this sample in the Advanced Graduate group.

Each sample so defined was compared against all other available samples of the same educational level. The results of these analyses must be interpreted with caution, since the design of the analysis is extremely unbalanced with sample sizes as small as eight individuals being included with studies as large as 67. Neverthe-less, some common patterns emerged across these analyses. First, differences across samples within educational levels were statistically significant in all cases (p<.01) except in the high school 8th and 10th grades (where only data from Kitchener et al. (1993) was available for experimental and control conditions[13]).

Within each educational level, statistically significant differences across samples appeared practically significant as well $R^2$ for high school groups appeared to be higher (ranging from .43 to .56) than those from undergraduates (college sophomores and juniors were .31 and .38, respectively, while college freshman and college seniors were .11 and .12, respectively). The $R^2$ for Beginning graduate students was .32 while for advanced graduate groups it was .13. For each of the educational levels average scores for each sample and the standard error of the mean are expressed as a dot plot in Figure 2. For this figure, a dot represents the mean associated with the group, and the horizontal line expresses the standard error associated with the mean. For some samples (e.g., Polkosnik and Winston's (1989) study of University of Georgia students, Kitchener et al.'s (1993) study of Colorado students) the standard errors are quite large, due to the small sample sizes associated with these studies within educational level. Reed and McGaffic's (1994) study of elderly samples was included in Figure 2, but not included in the analyses of variance, mainly to provide a comparison of this group with current students.[14] Vertical or diagonal lines in the figure indicate which samples were not significantly different from each other. If a sample does not share a vertical or diagonal line with another sample within educational level, this means that these two samples are different.

*High School Samples.* For the 9th grade high school samples, data taken from Kitchener et al.'s (1993) study were higher than the McKinney (1985) students who were identified as high academic achievement students. These students were, in turn, higher than those identified as low academic achievement from McKinney's study. This pattern is expected, given that the Kitchener et al. (1993) data were taken from students of high verbal ability. For high school juniors, Kitchener and King's (1981) sample (mean=2.8) were lower than data from Kitchener et al. (1993) (mean=3.7). This is unusual, given the fact that both of these samples were selected for high verbal ability. This pattern may demonstrate either large sample to sample differences in Reflective Judgment for this educational level, or a substantial cohort effect. For the high school senior data, Kitchener et al.'s (1993) seniors were higher than all other samples, McKinney's (1985) low and high achieving seniors were lower than the other samples, and Brabeck's (1983) high critical thinking sample scored higher than her low critical thinking sample, with Glatfelter's (1982) sample falling between these two groups.

---

[13]Preliminary analyses of variance examining only the experimental and control pre-test conditions for the Kitchener et al. (1993) study revealed no Time 1 differences between experimental and control conditions for any educational level.

[14]Educational attainment in this study was scored as years of study, and not degree attainment per se. For that reason, the data from this study were classified as high school if they indicated 12 years of education, college freshman if they indicated 13 years of education, and as college senior if they indicated 16 years or more of college education.

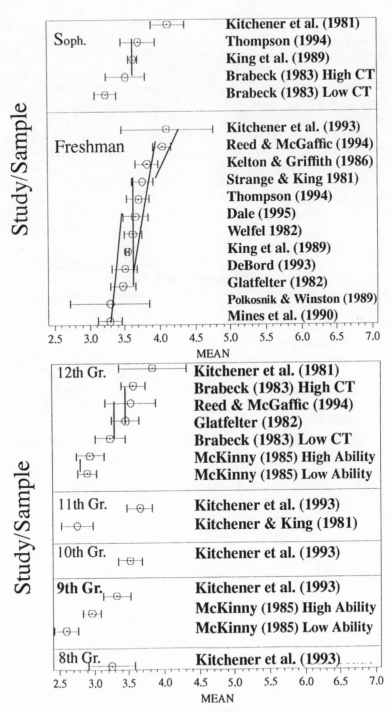

FIGURE 2. Dot Plots of Differences between Sample Groups by Educational Level

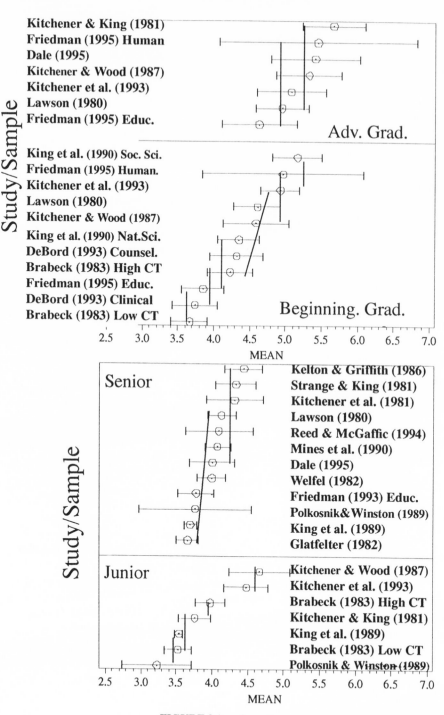

**FIGURE 2 (continued)**

*College Freshmen.* Less clear-cut differences were found between freshmen samples. Kitchener et al.'s (1993) study was higher than eight other samples; Kelton and Griffith's (1986) studies performed higher than Glatfelter's (1982) study of re-entrant college women in Utah; and Polkosnik and Winston's (1989) study of University of Georgia students and Mines et al. (1990) study of University of Iowa freshmen scored lower than four other studies. To the extent that Kitchener et al.'s (1993) and Kelton and Griffith's (1986) study used students from private institutions, this suggests that freshmen from selective private institutions score roughly .4 to .5 of a stage higher on the RJI than their public university counterparts. The finding that two samples taken from the University of Iowa (Strange and King, 1981 and Mines et al. (1990) differ by .4 of a stage may be due to the fact that neither the Mines et al. (1990) study nor the Strange and King (1981) study were random samples from the freshman population. The freshman sample for the Mines et al. (1990) study were drawn from an Introductory Rhetoric class, a course which many college freshmen are able to test out of by demonstrating successful writing skills. Data from the Strange and King (1981) study were closely matched on the basis of ACT composite score to a sample of seniors. To the extent that attrition may be related to academic aptitude as defined by the ACT, Strange and King's (1981) sample of freshmen may be composed of higher academic aptitude students than the freshman sample as a whole.

*College Sophomores.* Three distinct groups emerged for the college sophomore samples: . Brabeck's (1983) sample of low critical thinking students taken from institutions described as small, private Catholic institutions in New England scored lower than the other four samples, while Kitchener et al.'s (1981) study was higher than the other samples. The average scores of Thompson's (1994), Brabeck's (1983) high critical thinking students, and King et al.'s (1989) study of black students from Bowling Green State University were not different from each other.

*College Juniors.* For the college junior data, data from Kitchener and Wood's (1987) study of German university students and Kitchener et al.'s (1993) study of Denver University students were comparable. Data from Brabeck's (1983) high critical thinking sample and Kitchener and King's (1981) study were higher than Polkosnik and Winston's (1989) study of University of Georgia students. Brabeck's (1983) high critical thinking sample was also higher than King et al.'s (1989) study of black students at Bowling Green State University.

*College Seniors.* For the college senior data, samples from Kelton and Griffith (1986), Strange and King (1981), and Kitchener et al. (1993) were higher than five other samples. The pattern of higher performance in RJI by private institution samples was not as pronounced in the senior data, but again this could be somewhat due to the fact that several studies from public institutions selected seniors who were matched to graduate samples on the basis of educational aptitude/verbal ability.

*Beginning Graduate Students.* Beginning graduate students were defined as either entering, master's level, or beginning doctoral level. King et al.'s study of social science doctoral students scored higher than eight other samples. Similarly, Friedman's (1995) study of Humanities students scored higher than six other samples. King et al. (1993), Lawson (1980), and Kitchener and Wood (1987) scored higher than three other samples. To some extent, the King et al. sample although ascertaining beginning graduate students may contain some advanced graduate students, since such students were not explicitly excluded from the sample. Brabeck's (1983) low critical thinking sample, DeBord's (1993) sample of clinical psychology graduate students, and Friedman's (1995) study of education graduate students were low. While the overall pattern of means replicates King et al.'s finding of higher scores for graduate students in the social sciences relative to graduate students in the natural sciences, the finding that DeBord's clinical sample and Friedman's education sample were low indicates that students in the social sciences are not automatically high in Reflective Judgment, as might be the case if reflective students self-selected for the social sciences. DeBord's clinical psychology sample psychology student sample was lower than the natural science sample in King et al. (1990). There is some reason to believe that level of educational attainment within this group is responsible for much of the observed sample differences. DeBord's (1993) clinical sample consisted entirely of first semester doctoral students. His sample of counseling psychology graduate students contained several individuals (10 out of the 15 studied) who had masters degrees, but were enrolled for the first time in the doctoral program in counseling. As such, this pattern of samples (taken together with the longitudinal change patterns discussed below) suggests that early levels of graduate study, particularly in the social sciences, may be accompanied by relatively rapid growth in the ability to reason about ill-structured problems.

*Summary of Educational Level and Sample Differences.* Overall, patterns of differences across the individual samples are striking. Although the general pattern of performance across all samples reveals a distinct upward trend as a function of educational level as shown in Figure 1, the range of samples for many undergraduate levels is large and roughly a stage, ranging from stage 3 to stage 4. The magnitude of differences between these samples is substantial: Recall that differences of .4 of a stage are about the same size as the two year longitudinal effect for the instrument, and differences of a full stage constitute roughly changes associated with six to ten years of longitudinal growth in Reflective Judgment. As such, when applying Reflective Judgment theory to a particular institution or classroom, it would be misleading to classify a particular classroom or sample of students as scoring at a given level in the absence of RJI data. This points to the need for assessment of Reflective Judgment level before proceeding with educational interventions geared to a particular level of Reflective Judgment reasoning. These is also some evidence to suggest that students from selective private institutions score higher than samples taken from public universities. Such a pattern, however, may be due to admissions criteria and not institutional effects per se. The absence of longitudinal data and lack of detailed information on institutional admissions and attrition patterns precludes any clear resolution of the issue. It seems reasonable to conclude, though, that educational institutions who wish to use to RJI as an instrument to document institutional effectiveness must also carefully attend to issues of student characteristics (such as major and critical thinking level), attrition, and institutional admissions criteria before claiming a superior performance of their students as a result of their educational experiences at a particular institution.

## General Sequentiality of the RJI

The next section examines claims regarding the sequentiality of the Reflective Judgment and its status as a complex stage theory model of development. A complex stage theory model assumes that individuals progress according to the ordered stages proposed by the theory, but does not assume that subjects reason at the same stage in all situations due to differential task demands or random subject performance variation. Under a complex stage model, response patterns from developmental data conform to the sequentiality hypothesis if the second most frequently used stage is adjacent to the first, if the third most frequently used stage is adjacent to either the first or the second stage, etc.

Davison (1979) proposed a test of the sequentiality for such complex developmental sequences by means of a probabilistic unfolding model. Davison's test involves the modeling of a contingency table of the major or predominant stage which an individual demonstrates by their minor, or second most frequently used stage. By definition, the contingency table which results has zeros on the diagonal. For this test, the contingency table was calculated based on the percent stage utilization scores described above for a data set composed of all resolved RJI data across all measurement occasions and represents data from 2102 records. This contingency table of major and minor stage is given in Table 10. The data reported in Table 10 contains 2002 records, since 100 records contained evidence for only one stage of Reflective Judgment and were excluded from this analysis. For seven individuals, ties resulted which could be broken in either a favorable or unfavorable manner to the sequentiality hypothesis. Since the analyses presented here found that the Reflective Judgment model was differentially sequential, the results reported here are based on breaking these ties randomly. Results based on breaking the ties favorably or excluding tied data from the analysis were identical.[15] As can be seen from Table 10, the data from 58 individuals not consonant with the sequentiality hypothesis and are located in cells 2/4, 2/5, 3/5, 4/2, 4/6, 4/

---

[15]It should be noted, however, that when the analyses are rerun based on data which break ties unfavorably, that the analyses are the same except that the $\chi^2$ for the modified sequentiality hypothesis remains significant. Analyses which either exclude such ties as ambiguous data or break such ties randomly seem a more appropriate test of sequentiality.

7, 5/3, 5/7, 6/3, 6/4, 7/4 and 7/5. These 46 observations represent only 2.90% of the data on which the sequentiality test was based.

**Table 10. Observed and Expected Response Pattern Frequencies for Combined Reflective Judgment Interview Data**

| Minor Stage | | 2 | 3 | 4 | 5 | 6 | 7 |
|---|---|---|---|---|---|---|---|
| Predominant Stage | 2 | –[1] | 26[2] | 4 | 1 | 0 | 0 |
| | | | 28.62[3] | 1.10 | .35 | .61 | .32 |
| | | | 26[4] | 2.45 | 2.14 | .28 | .13 |
| | | | 9.26[5] | 15.22 | 4.31 | 1.50 | .70 |
| | 3 | 115 | – | 482 | 4 | 1 | 0 |
| | | 112.94 | | 476.10 | 3.52 | 6.16 | 3.28 |
| | | 115 | | 482 | 4.20 | .54 | .26 |
| | | 32.61 | | 398.69 | 112.99 | 39.24 | 18.46 |
| | 4 | 6 | 637 | – | 321 | 16 | 6 |
| | | 5.77 | 632.52 | | 327.11 | 13.44 | 7.16 |
| | | 4.16 | 637 | | 321 | 16.18 | 7.67 |
| | | 72.10 | 536.54 | | 249.78 | 86.75 | 40.82 |
| | 5 | 0 | 3 | 120 | – | 76 | 5 |
| | | .72 | 1.85 | 129.21 | | 71.33 | .89 |
| | | 1.60 | 3.46 | 120 | | 76 | 2.94 |
| | | 9.09 | 67.66 | 111.16 | | 10.94 | 5.15 |
| | 6 | 0 | 1 | 5 | 62 | – | 57 |
| | | 1.07 | 2.74 | 4.49 | 60.36 | | 56.34 |
| | | .16 | .35 | 5.49 | 62 | | 57 |
| | | 5.06 | 37.66 | 61.87 | 17.53 | | 2.86 |
| | 7 | 0 | 0 | 2 | 4 | 48 | – |
| | | .50 | 1.28 | 2.10 | .66 | 49.46 | |
| | | .09 | .19 | 3.05 | 2.66 | 48 | |
| | | 2.13 | 15.86 | 26.06 | 7.38 | 2.56 | |

[1]Dashes indicate response patterns (cells) which cannot occur.
[2]The First number in each cell represents the observed frequency.
[3]Second numbers indicate predicted cell frequencies under Davison's sequentiality model.
[4]Third numbers indicate predicted cell frequencies under differential sequentiality model.
[5]Fourth numbers indicate predicted cell frequencies under quasi-independence model.

Davison (1979) proposed a two-step process for determining whether the response frequencies correspond with those predicted by a given developmental sequence. The first step involves testing whether the data conform to a quasi-independence model, which assumes no sequentiality in the data. The predicted frequencies from this model form the basis of a $\chi^2$ test. If this $\chi^2$ is statistically significant, the data are tested in a second step against a sequential model, which includes a single sequentiality parameter for adjacent stages and indicates an added probability of occurrence predicted by the developmental sequence. If the $\chi^2$ from this model is not statistically significant, this is taken as confirmation of the sequential nature of the data. For these data, the independence $\chi^2$ is highly significant ($\chi_{19}^2=3150.41$; p<.001) but Davison's sequential model was also statistically significant ($\chi_{18}^2=60.94$; p<.01). An examination of the actual and predicted frequencies under the sequential model (shown in the first and second columns of Table 10) revealed that the largest discrepancies from the data occurred in the sequential cells of the table and in situations where Davison's model predicted more nonsequential responses on the basis of chance than in fact occurred. Conceptually, lower Reflective Judgment stages appear more clear-cut than more advanced stages. Individuals with dominant scores of 3 or 4 appear to have fewer upper-stage responses than one would expect under the sequentiaility model, while individuals with dominant stages of 5 and 6 had fewer adjacent stage frequencies than expected under the sequential model. A small modification of Davison's test was made to test this possibility: separate response frequencies for adjacent stages were modeled for each dominant stage. This fit of this model was also statistically significant, indicating the probabilities of dominant and subdominant stages were different, even within major stage ($\chi_{13}^2=32.00$, p<.01). An additional sequential model was also specified which allowed the adjacent stages to be of unequal frequencies for each level. By definition, this model results in a perfect fit of the adjacent stages, while fitting an independence model to the remaining cells. Predicted frequencies for the modified sequentiality model are given as the fourth entry in the table cells of Table 10. The Reflective Judgment data conformed well to this modified sequential model ($\chi_9^2=9.67$; p=.38).

Even though no nonsequential cells of the contingency table differed from rates predicted under chance by more than 3, it is helpful to examine which studies contained stage discrepant ratings in an effort to understand if certain populations or studies contained higher rates of nonsequential ratings. Nonsequential ratings, though rare, seemed to occur most frequently in three studies: testings based on King and Kitchener's (1981) longitudinal study, King, Wood, and Mines' (1990) study of mathematics and social science graduate students, and Kitchener and Wood's (1987) study of German university students.[16].

Taken together, the results of the sequentiality analyses show that the Reflective Judgment interview and scoring system document a complex developmental sequence. Nonsequential responses are quite rare and, given that some of the nonsequential responses occurred predominantly in three of the studies, suggests that these deviations may be the result of minor scoring variability between rat-

---

[16]Five of the 11 4/6 ratings were taken from longitudinal tests from Kitchener and King's (1981) study; Two of the four 7/5 ratings, two of the five 5/7 ratings were taken from King et al. (1990); and the two 7/4 ratings, three of the five 4/7 ratings, and one of the four 6/4 ratings were from Kitchener and Wood (1987)

ers. Given the translation required for Kitchener and Wood's study of German university students, it is also possible that these few deviations represent difficult or ambiguous translations. To date, these results stand in contrast to previous applications of Davison's test to other developmental theories, which have failed to reject the quasi-independence model. The finding differential sequentiality by dominant levels of Reflective Judgment is discussed in the context of spline regressions discussed below.

### Stage Utilization as a Function of Reflective Judgment Level.

One of the reasons for the patterns of increased variability as a function of Reflective Judgment level may be that bjects are more stage-homogeneous in their responses at earlier levels of the model and show a greater variability in performance on the RJI at higher levels. To explore this, a series of spline regressions was conducted on the data predicted stage utilization scores for Levels 2-7 as a function of overall rescaled RJI score. (Since Reflective Judgment Level 1 responses occur only rarely, they were excluded from the present analysis). The results of these regressions are given in Figure 3.

Generally, Figure 3 shows that stage utilization patterns are more diverse for more advanced levels (stages 5 and 6) of Reflective Judgment than for earlier levels. For example, the average percent stage utilization for individuals with an overall score of 5.0 is only 50 percent, with the final score reflecting a composite of Level 4 and Level 6 reasoning. It is worthwhile to note that no individuals evidenced nonadjacent stage utilization patterns (e.g., no protocols contained examples of only Level 4 and Level 6 reasoning), suggesting that it is reasonable to assume that the data for higher levels, while showing a greater variability in performance, can be described as sequential. High percent stage utilization scores for levels 2, 3, 6, and 7 may be due to the fact their location at the ends of the measure and not reflective of the degree of high stage utilization for these levels (e.g., it is mathematically possible to have an overall score of 6.9 on the RJI only if a substantial proportion of the dilemma scores are at level 7).

*Growth and Stability of the RJI over Time.* Is growth in Reflective Judgment uniformly slow for students at all educational levels? Is the test/retest reliability of the instrument the same across educational levels, or is there evidence of retest effects or differential growth, dependent on initial level of educational attainment? In order to address these questions, data from the longitudinal studies were examined. Samples were again calculated on the basis of whether they contained at least five individuals in the group, and whether either a main effect for an independent variable was observed or an interaction over time. Table 11 shows the samples broken out by educational attainment and lists the initial mean score for the sample, the difference between time 2 and time 1 for the sample, the test/retest correlation between occasions, and the time interval associated with the retesting.

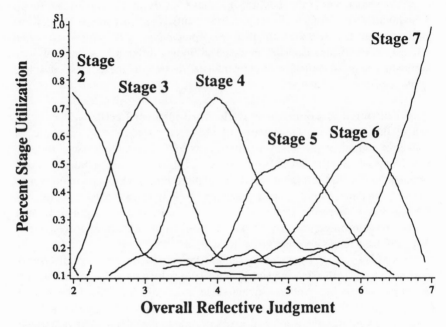

**FIGURE 3. Spline Regressions of Stage Utilizations Scores as a Function of Overall Reflective Judgment Level.**

Three general patterns emerge from an examination of the table: First, as expected, the test/retest correlations go down as a function of the length of time between testings. In order to assess the relative comparability of these correlations, it is possible to generate estimates of the test/retest correlation for a year's duration (Rindskopf, 1984). These estimates appear for all testings of length six months through 10 years in parentheses after the test/retest correlations. When these annualized correlations are examined, it appears that longitudinal data based Kitchener and King's (1981) study show estimated test/retest correlations between .85-.98. Data taken from other studies show a lower pattern of test/retest correlation. Notably, Brabeck's (1983), Polkosnik and Winston (1989), Kitchener et al.'s (1993) control group all demonstrated only moderate test/retest correlation, generally in the .5 to .6 range. Two of the intervention studies, Kronholm (1993) and Thompson (1995) revealed substantially lower test/retest correlations. Particularly, Kronholm's (1993) control groups showed statistically significant *decreases* on retesting. These decreases, coupled with the low internal consistency found for the study, give some additional reason to be cautious about the conclusions of the study. The three intervention studies (except for Kronholm's late undergraduate group) report a consistent pattern in that those samples which report a substantial gain in overall RJI score also have substantially lower test/

retest correlations, suggesting that if change does occur as a result of educational interventions to promote Reflective Judgment, it does not occur uniformly for all individuals in the group.

An examination of patterns of average change between testings also provides some insight as to whether differential trajectories of growth obtained on the RJI as a function of initial educational level. Kitchener and King's (1981) study showed that initial level of educational attainment is inversely related to amount of change over time. High school students generally changed an average of .41 per year over the first two years of the study, compared with .21 for the late undergraduate sample, and .08 for the advanced graduate sample. The magnitude of change from other studies, however, is much less than this: Brabeck's (1983) longitudinal data showed almost no growth. Since Brabeck's study involved samples of high and lower critical thinkers, perhaps this difference in growth rates could be due to a differential growth rate for high ability students, whereby they gain more on Reflective Judgment than their lower verbal ability counterparts.

For the graduate samples, test/retest correlations were much higher. Data from Kitchener et al. (1993) was higher than would be expected based on an examination of change patterns for earlier educational levels from the same study. The 24 early graduate students in the study showed a difference of .59 over the period of two weeks, an indication of a possible test/retest effect of the RJI for this population, or evidence that the educational intervention presented in Kitchener et al. (1993) was particularly effective for this group. Even though the difference score for the 13 control individuals in this group did not show much gain, replication of a test/retest study for these individuals seems warranted. Similarly, for advanced graduate students, the gains in overall RJI score for the Kitchener et al. (1993) data are much higher than would be expected from the Kitchener and King (1981) data. Some of this difference could, however, be also due to the fact that these subjects tested much lower at time 1 than the subjects in Kitchener and King (1981)When separate analyses of variance of the Kitchener et al. (1993) data was conducted separately for the experimental and control groups, the main effect for time for the control group (.013) was not significant, while the main effect for time in the experimental group (.23) was statistically significant. These results must be interpreted with caution, since a general linear model of the combined data failed to find a condition by time interaction. It is interesting to note however that a comparable analysis of variance which employed chronological age as opposed to educational level failed to find these patterns of significance. As such, these analyses may be taken to support the previous general finding in Reflective Judgment research that educational experience, as opposed to chronological age, is a more important determinant of level of Reflective Judgment.

In summary, four aspects of the time-related change in Reflective Judgment are evident from the longitudinal data: (1) The magnitude of gain in Reflective Judgment is inversely related to students' level of educational attainment; (2)

Change in Reflective Judgment (particularly as a result of educational intervention) does not appear to be uniformly efficacious for all students, even within a particular educational level; (3) Initial transitions to a subsequent new educational setting (e.g., from high school to college; from college to graduate study) appear to be associated with larger gains in Reflective Judgment; and (4) retest effects for the instrument, if present, appear to be confined to graduate samples..

**Table 11 . Test/Rest Correlations and Growth in Reflective Judgment[1]**

| Education Level | N | Time Interval | Test/Retest Correlation | Difference | Mean Initial Score |
|---|---|---|---|---|---|
| *Junior High/Early High School (8th-10th Grades)* | | | | | |
| Kitchener et al. (1993) | | | | | |
| Control | 11 | 2 wks. | .59† | –.19* | 3.45 |
| Experimental | 20 | 2 wks. | .63** | .11 | 3.38 |
| McKinney (1985)[2] | 21 | 2 yrs. | .43†(.66)[3] | .50** | 2.76 |
| *Late High School (Grades 11 and 12)* | | | | | |
| Kitchener et al. (1993) | | | | | |
| Control | 7 | 2 wks. | .37 | –.00 | 3.67 |
| Experimental | 15 | 2 wks. | .87** | .09 | 3.77 |
| Brabeck (1983) | | | | | |
| Times 1 and 2 | 25 | 1 yr. | .52** | .15† | 3.40 |
| Times 1 and 3 | 22 | 2 yrs. | .44*(.66) | .02 | 3.44 |
| Kitchener and King (1981) | | | | | |
| Times 1 and 2 | 17 | 2 yrs. | .85**(.92) | .82** | 2.78 |
| Times 1 and 3 | 15 | 6 yrs. | .54*(.90) | 2.09** | 2.84 |
| Times 1 and 4 | 13 | 10 yrs. | .59*(.95) | 2.35** | 2.82 |
| *Early Undergraduate (Freshman and Sophomore)* | | | | | |
| Kitchener et al. (1993) | | | | | |
| Control | 6 | 2 wks. | .61 | .25 | 3.85 |
| Experimental | 14 | 2 wks. | .26 | .06 | 4.23 |
| Kronholm (1993) | | | | | |
| Control | 22 | 3 mo. | .80**(.41) | –.09* | 3.49 |
| Experimental | 18 | 3 mo. | .31(.01) | .30** | 3.19 |
| Polkosnik and Winston (1989) | | | | | |
| Times 1 and 2 | 8 | 3 mo. | .88**(.60) | .08 | 3.29 |
| Times 1 and 3 | 7 | 6 mo. | .46(.21) | .11 | 3.39 |
| Thompson (1995) Freshmen | | | | | |
| Control | 6 | 3 mo. | .67†(.20) | –.03 | 3.61 |
| Experimental | 14 | 3 mo. | .16(.00) | .17 | 3.75 |
| Thompson (1995) Sophomore | | | | | |
| Control | 11 | 3 mo. | .54†(.09) | –.02 | 3.79 |
| Experimental | 8 | 3 mo. | .73*(.28) | –.07 | 3.59 |

**Table 11** *(continued).* **Test/Rest Correlations and Growth in Reflective Judgment**[1]

| Education Level | N | Time Interval | Test/Retest Correlation | Difference | Mean Initial Score |
|---|---|---|---|---|---|
| Welfel and Davison (1986) | | | | | |
| Times 1 and 2 | 25 | 4 yrs. | .20(.67) | .54 | 3.64 |
| Table 11 (cont.) | | | | | |
| *Late Undergraduate (Junior and Senior)* | | | | | |
| Kitchener and King (1981) | | | | | |
| Times 1 and 2 | 27 | 2 yrs. | .77**(.88) | .42** | 3.74 |
| Times 1 and 3 | 27 | 6 yrs. | .51**(.89) | 1.14** | 3.76 |
| Times 1 and 4 | 26 | 10 yrs. | .54**(.94) | 1.03** | 3.87 |
| Kitchener et al. (1993) | | | | | |
| Control | 13 | 2 wks. | .94** | −.06 | 4.45 |
| Experimental | 19 | 2 wks. | .45† | .10 | 4.38 |
| Kronholm (1993) | | | | | |
| Control | 28 | 3 mo. | .42*(.03) | −.17* | 3.66 |
| Experimental | 10 | 3 mo. | .55(.09) | .28** | 3.32 |
| Polkosnik and Winston (1989) | | | | | |
| Times 1 and 2 | 19 | 3 mo. | .86*(.55) | .07 | 3.37 |
| Times 1 and 3 | 8 | 6 mo. | .92**(.85) | .30** | 3.45 |
| *Early Graduate* | | | | | |
| Kitchener et al. (1993) | | | | | |
| Control | 13 | 2 wks. | .68** | −.02 | 4.95 |
| Experimental | 24 | 2 wks. | .65** | .59** | 4.91 |
| *Advanced Graduate* | | | | | |
| Kitchener et al. (1993) | | | | | |
| Control | 3 | 2 wks. | 1.00** | .33* | 4.42 |
| Experimental | 11 | 2 wks. | .69* | .32 | 5.26 |
| Kitchener and King (1981) | | | | | |
| Times 1 and 2 | 15 | 2 yrs. | .81**(.90) | .19† | 6.03 |
| Times 1 and 3 | 13 | 6 yrs. | .87**(.98) | .22† | 6.00 |
| Times 1 and 4 | 14 | 10 yrs. | .83**(.98) | .09 | 5.93 |

[1]Based on Resolved Scores. Time intervals involving other than Time 1 as an initial score not included since many subjects changed educational level from one time to another.

†=p<.1, *=p<.05, **=p<.01

[2]Time 2 Conducted by and reported in Van Tine (1990).

[3]Numbers in parentheses indicate annualized test/retest correlations

## Reflective Judgment: Inter and Intra-Individual Differences by Dilemma.

A structural equations approach was designed to test whether the RJI represents a single psychological construct (as argued from the internal consistency estimates and previous research discussed above). The structural equation approach proposed here also allows an assessment of the relative magnitude of rater bias and systematic differences in Reflective Judgment as a function of dilemma topic. Before discussing a classical test theory approach to Reflective Judgment, it helps to examine some properties of the instrument which have not been examined or explained thus far in the paper. As noted in Table 6 (p. 270), the items of the RJI demonstrate a rough general item equivalence by educational level. If any trend can be extracted from these data, it would appear that the instrument is more internally consistent for advanced undergraduates (college juniors and seniors) and graduate students than for early undergraduates. If the RJI measures a single ability, one would expect to find that dilemma scores for the RJI would be closer to each other for more advanced educational levels than for earlier educational levels. An examination of the patterns of scores assigned to individual dilemmas, however, finds that the opposite is the case. In an examination of the distribution of dilemma scores, it was found that 21.75 percent of individuals demonstrated dilemma scores which were at more than one major level and that multiple stage ratings were more common among advanced educational levels. For the junior, senior, beginning graduate and advanced graduate samples, the percentages of individuals with dilemma scores at more than one level of reasoning were 17%, 20%, 14%, and 16% respectively. Although 14% of the college freshman sample contained more than one stage rating across dilemmas, for no other group did more than 7% of the individuals show evidence of more than one stage. It is paradoxical, then, that groups which appear to show the largest variability in performance across dilemmas (which would normally indicate the presence of increased measurement error) would demonstrate the greatest amount of internal consistency. The structural equation approach outlined below is designed to assess whether the variability in performance in ratings across dilemmas constitutes measurement error, systematic differences in Reflective Judgment ability as a function of dilemma topic, or some pattern of unmeasured systematic bias in the rating of the RJI.

Structural equation modeling has enjoyed increased popularity with psychologists as a way of testing form equivalence (Lord and Novick, 1968; Loehlin, 1992). In parallel forms models, performance on each observed variable (in this case the rater's evaluation of a dilemma transcript) is thought to be a product of an unobservable true score (or scores) and a unique component of the variable due to measurement error. For models in which all variables are measures of the same underlying construct, these relationships may be represented by means of a path diagram such as that found in Figure 4. As can be seen, such models demonstrate the close relationship between classical test theory and confirmatory factor analysis. For the present study, a set of initial models was tested using all available data where all four RJI dilemmas were available from two raters (N=668). Eight observed variables were measured for this model, each rater's scores on each of the four dilemmas. All structural models presented below are maximum likelihood estimates.

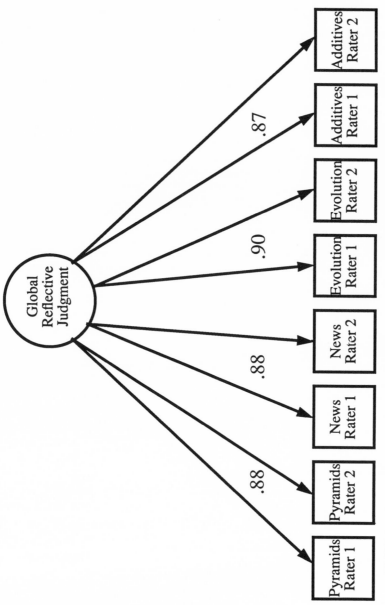

FIGURE 4. Structural Model Representing Reflective Judgment Dilemmas as Congeneric Parallel Forms

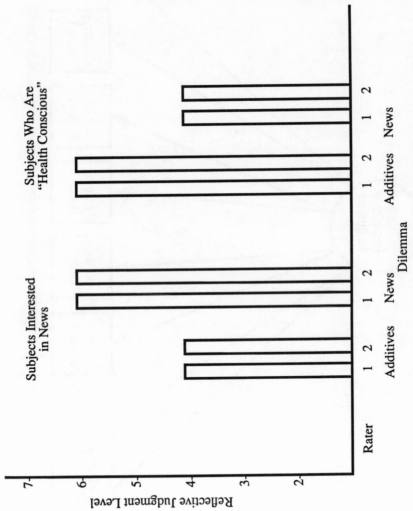

FIGURE 5. Hypothetical Dilemma Differences in Reflective Judgment for Two Groups

*RJI Dilemmas a Tau-Equivalent versus Congeneric Parallel Forms.* As an initial test, two models drawn from classical test theory are compared. In the first model, RJI ratings across dilemmas and raters were through to represent tau-equivalent measures, meaning that each rater's score on each dilemma is roughly the same in terms of its efficacy as a measure of underlying Reflective Judgment ability. Each dilemma rating may, however, contain a different amount of error variance. This model of Reflective Judgment ability may then be compared with a model of congeneric parallel forms, in which each variable is thought to be related to the underlying construct of Reflective Judgment, but variables differ in their relative strength as indicators of Reflective Judgment. If a congeneric model of Reflective Judgment were true, compositing weights for the different dilemmas could then be used so that more reliable Reflective Judgment dilemmas would be more heavily weighted in the estimation of overall Reflective Judgment ability. Congeneric models failed to improve the fit of the model by reference to Type II fit measures (TLI$=-.10$, SBC$_2=-.01$, AIC$_2=.00$[17]). In contrast to the factor loadings shown in Figure 4 which show the congeneric factor model, unstandardized factor loadings for the tau-equivalent model were .85 across all dilemmas.

*Identification of Topic-Specific and Rater-Specific Sources of Covariation.* Given the eight indicator variables of this study, it is also possible to estimate the relative magnitude of rater bias and systematic effects due to dilemma topic by means of a Schmid-Leiman transformation (Schmid and Leiman, 1957). Since the issue of dilemma differences and rater bias has been explored by means of analysis of variance models (e.g., Brabeck 1980; Wood, 1981; Welfel, 1979) some explanation and justification for the present approach is necessary. The means for the four traditional dilemmas for the 668 subject data pool were almost identical (means were 4.06, 4.08, 4.00 and 4.05 for the Pyramids, News, Evolution, and Food Additives dilemmas respectively[18]). This means that, across all individuals, no dilemma appears to be systematically easier or more difficult than any other. Such statistics, though, may mask important sources of interindividual differences across dilemmas. For example, suppose that, unknown to the researcher, exactly half of the individuals in this study were very health conscious and as a result scored quite highly on the Food Additives dilemma. Further suppose that the other half of these subjects were quite interested in news reporting and thought quite a bit about whether it was biased. This state of affairs is shown graphically in Figure 5. The average scores by dilemma across these two groups might appear nearly identical. Clearly, if the researcher did not have access to information about these sources of expertise or interest, she might conclude that, on the average no differences existed between these two dilemmas when, in fact, quite dramatic unmeasured interindividual differences in exper-

---

[17]It should be noted that the fit measures here are Type II fit measures relative to the null model of tau-equivalence and not to the independence model which is the usual basis for fit measures. See Marsh et al. (1988) for a discussion of the superior performance on Type II fit measures and their computational definitions.

[18]These means are based on all available data with four dilemmas and is a larger sample than that discussed in the structural models below. Overall means taken from studies with two raters for all dilemmas yielded identical mean values to two decimal places.

tise were evident. In analogous fashion, it is also possible to identify previously unmeasured effects at the rater level by examining common patterns of high or low assignment across all dilemmas of a particular rater by examining whether any significant covariation between the four dilemmas rated by a particular rater exists above and beyond that explained by reference to the overall Reflective Judgment Level (or dilemma-specific factors) found in the data.

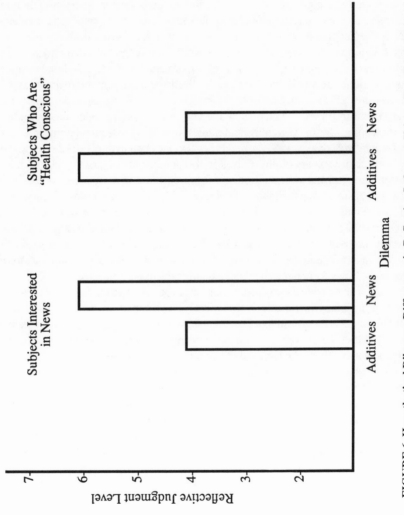

FIGURE 6. Hypothetical Dilemma Differences in Reflective Judgment Using a Two Rater System

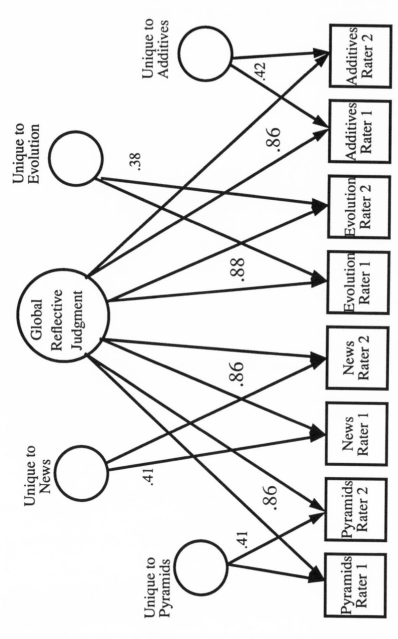

FIGURE 7. Hierarchical Factor Model of Overall Reflective Judgment and Dilemma-Specific Abilities

Although it is not possible in this present study to detect level of interest/involvement or differential expertise across these dilemmas, some estimate of the presence and extent of such context effects can be gleaned from consideration of the data from two raters of these dilemmas. Figure 6, for example, shows the bar chart patterns of the scores of two raters for these unmeasured groups, indicating that, even though the unmeasured variable of subject interest/experience is not included in the study, some evidence for such effects can be gleaned correlationally. Specifically, if context effects exist, we should expect to find that one rater's score for a dilemma transcript should correlate with another rater's score for the same transcript above and beyond the score one could expect based on overall Reflective Judgment ability.

In terms of a structural equation model, then, a Schmid-Leiman (1957) hierarchical factor analysis was used to determine if specific dilemma effects were present in the data in addition to an overall Reflective Judgment ability. Patterns of covariation between rater's scores for a dilemma over and above global Reflective Judgment ability were investigated by testing whether a significant improvement in model fit resulted from the addition of latent variables which had, as their indicators, only a particular dilemma. Two types of dilemma-specific Reflective Judgment models were explored: One which forced dilemma effects to be equal for all dilemmas, and another which allowed such effects to vary from one dilemma to another.[19]

In like fashion, the issue of unmeasured rater bias for certain types of individuals can be explored by testing to see whether a given rater's scores across the four dilemmas share common patterns of covariation beyond that accounted for by overall Reflective Judgment ability. These patterns of bias could, conceivably, be different for the four dilemmas of the RJI.

Since models which include topic specific and rater specific effects above and beyond overall Reflective Judgment ability are nested with the single factor Reflective Judgment model, it is possible to compare the incremental fit for nested model by reference of Type II incremental fits. Using the tau-equivalent model of Reflective Judgment as a null model, and an incremental fit criterion of .9 (Marsh et al., 1988), the structural model indicating that Reflective Judgment is a tau equivalent model with context effects unique to each dilemma (set equal across each dilemma) yielded a superior fit (TLI = .97, $SBC_2$ = .95; $AIC_2$ = .97). The standardized solution for these data are given in Figure 7. As can be seen, overall, each RJI rating is a relatively strong indicator of overall Reflective Judgment ability. (The standardized factor loading for overall Reflective Judgment level may be interpreted as a measure of the internal consistency of a given judge's rating of a particular dilemma. When adjusted for the effects of the length

---

[19]Since each of the context effect factors contained only two indicators, it was necessary to constrain the context effects to be the same for each dilemma and factor variances for these factors were set to 1 in order to obtain mathematically identified solutions.

of the instrument, this value (.95) closely approximates the values of coefficient alpha for the overall group reported above. In addition to this overall ability, however, a substantial context effect also exists for the data (.46) but such context effects are not as reliably indicated as overall Reflective Judgment ability.[20]

Consonant with the overall estimates of rater bias using analysis of variance described above, little evidence was found for rater bias under this intra-individual differences model (defined as two unmeasured variables which had as manifest variables, all of the dilemma ratings associated with a particular rater. TLI increments for the effects of rater bias above the proposed model were all <=.6) The magnitude of these effects when estimated accounted for less that .03 percent of the variability in Reflective Judgment scores, a practically nonsignificant amount.

Of course, given the substantial literature and theory assuming the Reflective Judgment is a single ability, supplementary analyses were conducted to determine if the observed dilemma effects could be due to other characteristics of the data, such as differential gender effects, sampling variation, or differential reliability induced by the inclusion of data with lower internal consistencies.[21] Analyses which excluded suspiciously low reliability or unusually high- and low-scoring samples relative to other studies yielded the same choice of reliability model as the general analysis as well as similar factor loadings. Separate follow-up analyses based on general educational level (collapsed into high school, freshman and sophomore undergraduate, junior and senior undergraduate, and graduate samples to provide a minimally satisfactory sample size), revealed that the RJI is more reliable measure of overall ability for graduate samples (evidenced by a factor loading of .90 as opposed to .82 for the general model) and that dilemma effects were more pronounced for this group as well (.68 as opposed to .46 for the general model). As such, these analyses can be seen as a corresponding to the results from the spline regressions of stage utilization, which suggested that higher stages of Reflective Judgment are accompanied by more variability in response than lower levels of Reflective Judgment. In addition, the Type II fit measures were less clear-cut for the High School and Beginning Undergraduate analyses (TLI=.81, $SBC_2$=.56, $AIC_2$=.81 and TLI=.88, $SBC_2$=.72 and $AIC_2$=.88 for the Beginning Undergraduate and High School samples, respectively). These fit patterns also indicate that, for lower levels of RJI ability, the salience of unique dilemma effects and the assessment of Reflective Judgment as

---

[20]Additional analyses were also conducted which employed the Schmid-Leiman transformation outlined here, except that dilemma effects were allowed to vary as well as factor loadings for the general RJI factor. This analysis generated fit measures similar to the TLI indices for the model described here, and incremental fit measures of this target model using the model adopted here did not reveal any incremental improvement in fit (TLI=−.06, $SBC_2$=−.28, and $AIC_2$=.09).

[21]Specifically, the data were rerun excluding the data of Welfel's (1982) freshman sample, Van Tine's (1990) data and retest of McKinney (1985). Computer runs excluding low- or high-scoring samples excluded Kitchener et al. (1993), Strange and King (1981), DeBord (1993), and Brabeck (1983).

a single ability are less pronounced (loadings associated with overall Reflective Judgment were .67 and dilemma-specific effects were .55). Some caution, however, is appropriate in making this interpretation, since these patterns could also arise due to the smaller range of ability in the high school and beginning undergraduate samples relative to the graduate samples.

## DISCUSSION

Taken as a whole, this study this study has some implications for behavioral research generally, in that it examined a the accuracy of the data and conclusions from a relatively large number of studies. The substantive conclusions from the analyses also have broad implications for the assessment of general cognitive outcomes of higher education, both in terms of the properties of a construct such as Reflective Judgment, and the relative magnitude of sample-to-sample and cohort differences in ability. Finally, this study points the need for future research needed using the Reflective Judgment model.

### How Valid Are Our Data and Conclusions?

In earlier days of behavioral research, analysis consisted of labor intensive and often tedious entry of data which was followed by equally labor intensive statistical calculation. It should be noted that the amount of labor involved often forced, the design and statistical analyses of the time to be rudimentary compared to the complexity of some of the studies reviewed here. Because of the labor intensive nature of research at the time, it was quite appropriate for investigations of data quality (e.g., Rosenthal, 1978; Wolins, 1962) to concentrate on data entry and calculation errors. To the extent that the studies reviewed here are representative of behavioral research in general, it seems that the advent of microcomputers and statistical software packages in educational research is responsible for reducing such clerical errors. The computer programming required to operate statistical software packages and the increased complexity of research designs, however, underscore the need for researchers to attend to other errors which are arguably more serious threats to the quality of research data and conclusions.

*Accuracy of Data and Statistical Analyses.* The advent of both more user-friendly statistical analysis packages and more complex experimental designs means that different opportunities are now present for clerical error to occur (in the input formats for the statistical package, computer programs used to score the data, and in programs written to produce statistical analyses). Obviously, it bears noting that these programs should be proofread as well and that such errors generally worked *against* the hypothesis of interest. Even if proofread, however, the data should be further explored with an eye to accuracy. Researchers should graph their data and produce descriptive statistics with an eye to investigating whether errors in data entry, programming, or analysis have occurred. In statistical consultations I have had with both graduate students and faculty, this step often neglected in the haste to analyze and report the data. If researchers hope to improve their accuracy beyond that found here, however, they must adopt a more skeptical attitude toward their data, especially if they hope to "catch" errors that occur with a low base rate.

*Data Management Issues.* The detail and complexity involved in long-term, multi-wave longitudinal research is much more than that involved in merely conducting three or four separate cross-sectional studies. Much of the unnecessary labor expended in bringing the existing data sets into a common format (not discussed here), was the result of a small set of questionable data management decisions which occurred across multiple studies. Three recommendations seem appropriate: (1) Analyses and data sets should be based on a version of the data as close to the original raw data as possible. The expense of computer storage and scoring are no longer a consideration in data analysis especially for relatively small studies such as those reviewed here. Letting the computer do the scoring minimizes the possibility of human calculation errors, makes it easier to understand and check the scoring of the raw data, and allows the researcher flexibility in developing future alternative scoring strategies. (2) Partial duplicates of study variables should not be made across data sets. Even in some cross-sectional studies, researchers would create different computer files of the same data in order to produce different statistical analyses. Not only does this practice make it difficult for a subsequent follow-up of the study, the possibility is much greater than corrections to the data are not applied thoroughly to all affected data points. A master data set should be made for a study and, if subsequent data becomes available, can be merged with the master data set to produce a new data set. (3) Coding schemes in the data should reflect the design of the study. For example, coding a 2 x 2 experimental design with a single variable numbered from 1 to 4 makes it more difficult to analyze the data using statistical software and increases the possibility that the data will be analyzed incorrectly.

*Methodological Skepticism.* Although many of the conclusions using the RJI were consistent across studies, some of the conflicting patterns of conclusions across studies were due to the fact that the researchers failed to consider plausible alternative explanations that a reasonable skeptic might raise. For example, the finding of mean level differences on the topics of the RJI using a repeated measures anova found in some studies seems largely due to rater bias on the individual topics of the RJI. The dramatic levels of growth found in Kronholm's (1993) could be due to the use of non-equivalent groups, and not to the experimental intervention per se. Researchers (especially those investigating Reflective Judgment!) should investigate the reasonableness of a proposed statistical analysis in terms of what can and cannot be concluded, given the limitations of the data. Researchers should beware of drawing inferences and making conclusions only within the context of only their own, and not competing, research perspectives.

To fail to consider alternatives to a proposed interpretation is to run the risk of "coming not to bury Caesar but the praise him."

## Implications for the General Assessment of Cognitive Outcomes of Higher Education

Taken together, patterns of performance within and across samples by educational level reveal a number of interesting properties in the RJI which may well generalize to other broad measures of cognitive outcomes of higher education.

### Institutional/Sample Differences

Differences between samples in Reflective Judgment appear more pronounced at lower levels of educational attainment than at higher levels. Specifically, samples which were selected for higher academic achievement and/or verbal ability performed much better than samples selected for low academic achievement or critical thinking. This pattern is consistent with the view that traditional measures of verbal ability constitute a necessary but not sufficient condition for advanced levels of Reflective Judgment. The magnitude of these differences, however, may be artifactual, since many of the collegiate samples were to some extent random samples of ability, while the high school samples were selected for high versus low academic ability or critical thinking.

In collegiate samples, it appears that students from smaller, more selective institutions performed higher on Reflective Judgment than students from public universities. It is difficult at this point to attribute these differences to the educational institutions per se, because this pattern could be due to the greater selectivity of admissions in the smaller private institutions. Future research in institutional effects on constructs such as these should control for and incorporate this source of student differences.

### Expertise and Topic Effects

The pattern of RJI scores at higher levels of educational attainment is quite different than that at lower levels. Differences between graduate student samples as a function of area of study are more pronounced than at lower levels. These differences do not appear to be an artifact of general verbal ability differences across disciplines, since some beginning social science samples scored quite low in Reflective Judgment and many of the natural science/mathematics samples scored higher than the social science samples on measures of verbal reasoning and critical thinking. Intra-individual differences (in the form of variability in performance) are more pronounced for beginning and advanced graduate students than for undergraduate samples, meaning that variability in performance as a function of topic is more pronounced for graduate students than undergraduates. The question of whether these intra-individual differences describe a general pattern of expertise relative to the content area or general decalage in performance remains to be seen.

This general pattern of results has several implications for the general assessment of cognitive outcomes of higher education. First, although developmental constructs are often described as "process" of reasoning which are relatively independent of problem content, the general pattern of findings described here reveals that is only partially true: Individuals at lower levels of Reflective Judgment shows a great consistency across the four topics of the RJI, but individuals in advanced undergraduate and graduate samples show a greater variability in performance on the topics. This finding is particularly interesting given DeBord's (1993) finding that graduate students in psychology scored significantly higher on the RJI when the topics dealt with ill-structured psychological dilemmas as opposed to the usual dilemma topics. It remains an open question as to whether the lower scores for natural science/mathematics graduate students would remain if ill-structured topics in mathematics and the sciences were explored.

Given that the content area of the problem is more important in the assessment of more advanced students, it appears essential that sampling of general cognitive outcomes should have a definite content area, in order to control for the discipline and intra-individual differences found here. Specifically, asking students to reason generally "about problems encountered in courses they have had," "problems which are important to them" or asking students to reason about "topics from the course which was the most important to them" as is done in some developmental measures of reasoning unnecessarily confounds students' personal interests, and curricular experiences with discipline differences general patterns of growth and change over time. For assessment instruments which require raters to assign scores, the practice of using two raters to assign scores provides valuable information concerning possible rater bias and drift. Pending the development of more easily scored computer or paper-and-pencil measures, such safeguards appear necessary.

## Implications for Reflective Judgment Research

*Psychometric Properties*

Seen as a developmental construct, it appears that the RJI represents a complex model of how individuals change in their ability to reason about ill-structured problems. Although safeguards exist for assuring the internal consistency of raters and the psychometric properties of the instrument were acceptable for many studies, improvements are clearly needed. In a minority of studies the internal consistency of the RJI was quite low, and this seems to explain the discrepant patterns in educational level differences and/or change found in those studies. Although the RJI usually performs more reliably than similar measures, it seems advisable for researchers to supply initial calibration ratings of interviews prior to rating study data in order to control for possible rater drift. Even if the raters employed provide acceptable ratings, it also appears that early undergraduate samples provide less internally consistent data than advanced undergraduate and graduate populations, suggesting that more extensive assessment of early under-graduates may be necessary, particularly if students are to participate in an intervention designed to promote reflective thinking based on their initial level of reasoning.

### Design of Intervention Studies

Given the variety of studies using the RJI on college samples, this study several additional areas of research are needed: First, researchers wishing to investigate the efficacy of educational interventions to promote reflective thinking should carefully attend to the students' levels of educational attainment and initial level of Reflective Judgment. As such, the value of hierarchical linear models which simultaneously assess group effects across institutions and classrooms while incorporating student differences in verbal ability and educational attainment seem clear. The pattern of longitudinal differences in Reflective Judgment appears directly related to educational attainment. Students at earlier levels of educational attainment show more dramatic growth over time than individuals initially assessed when they are advanced undergraduate and graduate students.

### Under-researched Student Populations

Research in the psychometric properties and growth patterns associated with three populations seems particularly warranted: college freshmen minority students, and faculty. It is rather surprising, given the large number of studies using the RJI and research which describes rather large changes in reasoning during the freshman year (Pascarella and Terenzini, 1991) that more longitudinal research using freshmen has not been conducted. King et al.'s (1989) study of black undergraduate students provided data that were much less internally consistent than other undergraduate studies. It remains to be seen whether this finding is due to the use of relatively inexperienced raters or describes a serious limitation in the reliability of the RJI with minority populations. Lastly, Dale's (1995) study of college faculty (and examination of some of King and Kitchener's (1994) advanced doctoral students who went on to become faculty members not discussed here) revealed that even faculty do not uniformly reason about ill-structured problems in a probabilistic fashion, a finding similar to Basseches (1984) interviews designed to assess dialectical thinking in college faculty. If faculty are unable to model probabilistic reasoning, it seems unsurprising that even graduate students are unable to reason probabilistically.

**Intra-individual and discipline differences.** The finding that significant intra-individual differences exist in the dilemmas of the RJI have important implications for both future research and design of educational interventions to promote reflective thinking. First, as noted above, the discipline difference between social science and mathematics/natural science graduate students could be due to social science graduate students' greater exposure to/expertise with ill-structured problems. Alternatively, these differences could also be an artifact of the fact that the dilemmas of the RJI are more strongly related to social science questions and ill-structured problems taken from mathematics and the natural sciences could produce a very different pattern of discipline differences in reflective thinking.

Alternatively, it may be that significant differences across dilemma topics at the individual level can be used to design more effective educational interventions tailored to promote individual students' reflective thinking. Given that advanced undergraduate and graduate students vary considerably in their ability to reason about ill-structured problems across dilemmas, a teacher who wishes to promote reflective thinking may begin by conducting informal assessments of ill-structured problems from a variety of areas. One set of educational objectives for the student would consist of demonstrating how an ill-structured problem from one area is isomorphic to another type of ill-structured problem. If it is the case that students may be better able to reason about some everyday ill-structured problems than issues those with which they are less familiar, instructors may be better able to bring students to reason within a curricular context.

## SUMMARY

Although the psychometric properties of the RJI appear promising, the labor and expense involved probably prohibit its wider use as a measure of a general cognitive outcome of a college education. However, more care must be taken in the design of college outcomes studies using the instrument. Specifically, student characteristics of general verbal ability, educational attainment, and area of study appear to be related to reflective thinking. The selectivity and size of educational institutions also appear related to reflective thinking, although it is difficult to determine which of these is more closely related to higher levels of reflective thinking. It seems an open question whether even the RJI possesses sufficient internal consistency to be used as grouping variable within an aptitude-treatment study. The sample size necessary to detect such interactions is probably greater than previously thought, given the lower internal consistency of the measure within educational level.

As mentioned in the introduction, the development of a more efficient and easily scored measure to assess Reflective Judgment is a next logical step. Contrary to previous descriptions of the model and instrument, however, such an instrument should not be designed to assess a single construct of Reflective Judgment. Because significant intra-individual differences in reflective thinking exist, the curricular context chosen for the ill-structured problems used to measure Reflective Judgment is probably very important, particularly for graduate students.

Future measures of Reflective Judgment should employ a variety of specific ill-structured problems, some of which are drawn from students' area of study in order to secure a better picture of students' ability to reason about ill-structured problems.

*The author would like to thank Patricia King and Karen Kitchener for their assistance in securing the data. The author would also like to thank P. Paul Heppner, Jeanne Hinkelman, and two reviewers for their constructive comments. Reprint requests should be sent to:*

Phillip K. Wood
210 McAlester Hall
University of Missouri-Columbia
Columbia, MO 65211

## References

Association of American Colleges (1991). *The challenge of connecting learning.* Project on Liberal Learning, Study-in-Depth, and the Arts and sciences Major. Washington, D.C: Association of American Colleges.

Bangdiwala, S.I. (1985). A graphical test for observer agreement. *Proceedings of the 45th Session of the International Statistical Institute,* Amsterdam, Holland, 307-308.

Baltes, P.B., Reese, H.W., and Nesselroade, J.R. (1977). *Life-span Developmental Psychology: Introduction to Research Methods.* Monterey, CA: Brooks/Cole.

Basseches, M. (1984). *Dialectical Thinking and Adult Development.* Norwood, NJ: Ablex.

Brabeck, M.M. (1980). The relationship between critical thinking skills and development of reflective judgment among adolescent and adult women. Doctoral dissertation, University of Minnesota, *Dissertation Abstracts International 41/11A,* p. 4647.

Brabeck, M.M. (1983). Critical thinking skills and reflective judgment development: Redefining the aims of higher education. *Journal of Applied Developmental Psychology* 4: 23-34.

Brabeck, M.M. and Wood, P.K. (1990). Cross-sectional and longitudinal evidence for differences between well-structured and ill-structured problem solving abilities. In M.L. Commons, C. Armon, L. Kohlberg, F.A. Richards, T.A. Grotzer, and J.D. Sinnott (eds.) *Adult Development 2: Models and Methods in the Study of Adolescent and Adult Thought.* (pp. 133-146) New York: Praeger.

Dale, J. L. (1995). Reflective Judgment in a conservative Christian college for clergy education. (Doctoral dissertation, University of Denver)

Darlington, R.B. (1990). *Regression and Linear Models.* New York: McGraw-Hill.

Davison, M.L. (1979). Testing a metric unidimensional qualitative unfolding model for attitudinal or developmental data. *Psychometrika* 44: 179-194.

Davison, M.L., King, P.M., Kitchener, K.S. and Parker, C.A. (1980). The stage sequence concept in cognitive social development. *Developmental Psychology* 16:121-131.

DeBord (1993). Promoting Reflective Judgment in counseling psychology graduate education. Unpublished masters thesis. University of Missouri-Columbia.

Dove, W.R. (1990).The identification of ill-structured problems by young adults. (Doctoral dissertation, University of Denver, 1990). *Dissertation Abstracts International 51-06B,* 3156-3358.

Duncker, K. (1945). On problem-solving. *Psychological Monographs* 58: 5 (Whole No. 270).

Fleiss, J.L., and Shrout, P.E. (1978). Approximate interval estimation for a certain intraclass correlation coefficient. *Psychometrika* 43: 259-262.

Glatfelter, M. (1982). Identity development, intellectual development, and their relationship in reentry women students. Doctoral dissertation, University of Minnesota. *Dissertation Abstracts International* 43, p. 3543A.

Hoffman, L.R., Burke, R.J. and Maier, N.R.F. (1963). Does training with differential reinforcement on similar problems help in solving a new problem? *Psychological Reports* 13: 147-154.

Kelly, C. (1993). The fundamental measurement of Reflective Judgment. Unpublished doctoral dissertation, University of Denver.

Kelton, J., and Griffith, J.V. (1986). The learning context questionnaire for assessing intellectual development. Unpublished manuscript.

Kenny, D.A. and Judd, C.M. (1984). Estimating the nonlinear and interactive effects of latent variables. *Psychological Bulletin* 96: 201-210.

King, P.M. (1977). The development of reflective judgment and formal operational thinking in adolescents and young adults. Doctoral dissertation, University of Minnesota. *Dissertation Abstracts International* 38, p. 7233A.

King, P.M. (1986). Formal reasoning in adults: A review and critique. In R. Mines and K. Kitchener (eds.), *Adult Cognitive Development*. Praeger: New York.

King, P.M. and Kitchener, K.S. (1994). *The Development of Reflective Judgment in Adolescence and Adulthood.* Jossey-Bass: San Francisco.

King, P.M., Kitchener, K.S., Davison, M.L., Parker, C.A., and Wood, P.K. (1983). The justification of beliefs in young adults: A longitudinal study. *Human Development* 26: 106-116.

King, P.M., Kitchener, K.S. and Wood, P.K. (1994). Research on the Reflective Judgment model. In King, P.M. and Kitchener, K.S. *The Development of Reflective Judgment in Adolescence and Adulthood.* Jossey-Bass: San Francisco.

King, P.M., Kitchener, K.S., Wood, P.K., and Davison, M.L. (1989). Relationships across developmental domains: A longitudinal study of intellectual, moral, and ego development. In M.L. Commons, J.D. Sinnott, F.A. Richards and C. Armon (eds.), *Adult Development: Vol. 1. Comparisons and Applications of Developmental Models* (pp. 57-72). New York: Praeger, 1989.

King, P.M., Taylor, J.A. and Ottinger, D.C. (1989, November). Intellectual development of black college students on a predominantly white campus. Paper presented at the meeting of the Association for the Study of Higher Education, Atlanta, Georgia.

King, P.M., Wood, P.K. and Mines, R.A. (1990). Critical thinking among college and graduate students. *The Review of Higher Education* 13(2): 167-186.

Kitchener, K.S. (1983). Cognition, metacognition and epistemic cognition: A three-level model of cognitive processing. *Human Development* 4: 222-232.

Kitchener, K.S. (1986). The reflective judgment model: Characteristics, evidence, and measurement. In R.A. Mines and K.S. Kitchener (eds.), *Adult Cognitive Development: Methods and Models* (pp. 76-91). New York: Praeger, 1986.

Kitchener, K.S., and King, P.M. (1981). Reflective judgment: Concepts of justification and their relationship to age and education. *Journal of Applied Developmental Psychology* 2: 89-116.

Kitchener, K.S., and King, P.M. (1985). Reflective judgment scoring manual. (Available from K.S. Kitchener, School of Education, University of Denver, Denver, CO 80208 or P.M. King, Department of Higher Education and Student Affairs, Bowling Green State University, Bowling Green, OH 43403.)

Kitchener, K.S., and King, P.M. (1990). The reflective judgment model: Ten years of research. In M.L. Commons, C. Armon, L. Kohlberg, F.A. Richards, T.A. Grotzer, and J.D. Sinnott. *Adult Development: Vol. 2. Models and Methods in the Study of adolescent and Adult Thought.* (pp. 63-78) New York: Praeger.

Kitchener, K.S., King, P.M., Wood, P.K., and Davison, M.L. (1989). Consistency and sequentiality in the development of reflective judgment: A six year longitudinal study. *Journal of Applied Developmental Psychology* 10: 73-95.

Kitchener, K.S., and Kitchener, R.F. (1981). The development of natural rationality: Can formal operations account for it? *Contributions to Human Development: Social Development in Youth: Structure and Content,* 5. Karger: Basel, Switzerland.

Kitchener, K.S., Lynch, C.L., Fischer, K.W., and Wood, P.K. (1993). Developmental range of reflective judgment: The effect of contextual support and practice on developmental stage. *Developmental Psychology* 29: 893-906.

Kitchener, K.S. and Wood, P.K. (1987). Development of concepts of justification in German university students. *International Journal of Behavioral Development* 10: 171-185.

Kronholm, M. M. (1993). The impact of a developmental instruction approach to environmental education at the undergraduate level on development of reflective judgment (Doctoral dissertation, Southern Illinois University at Carbondale, 1993). *Dissertation Abstracts International* 54: 4417B.

Lamiell, J.T. (1981). Toward an idiothetic psychology of personality. *American Psychologist* 36: 276-289.

Lawson, J.M. (1980). The relationship between graduate education and the development of Reflective Judgment: A function of Age or Educational Experience. Doctoral dissertation, University of Minnesota. *Dissertation Abstracts International* 47: 402B.

Loehlin, J.C. (1992). *Latent Variables Models (2nd Ed.).* Hillsdale, NJ: Lawrence Erlbaum.

Loevinger, J., Wessler, R,. and Redmore, C. (1970). *Measuring Ego Development.* Jossey-Bass: San Francisco.

Lord, F.M,. and Novick, M.R. (1968). *Statistical Theories of Mental Test Scores.* Reading, MA: Addison-Wesley

Lynch, C.L. (1990). The impact of a high support condition on the exhibition of reflective judgment. (Doctoral dissertation, University of Denver). *Dissertation Abstracts International* 50/09: p. 4246.

McKinney, M. (1985). Reflective judgment: An aspect of adolescent cognitive development (Intelligence, Wechsler, Verbal Achievement, Ability). Intellectual development of younger adolescents. (Doctoral dissertation, University of Denver). *Dissertation Abstracts International* 47: 402B.

Maier, N.R.F. (1933). An aspect of human reasoning. *British Journal of Psychology* 24: 144-155.

Marsh, H.W., Balla, J.R. and McDonald, R.P. (1988). Goodness-of-fit indexes in confirmatory factor analysis: The effect of sample size. *Psychological Bulletin* 103: 391-410.

Mines, R.A., King, P.M., Hood, A.B. and Wood, P.K. (1990) Stages of intellectual development and associated critical thinking skills in college students. *Journal of College Student Development* 31: 537-547.

Pascarella, E. and Terenzini, P. (1991). *How College Affects Students: Findings and insights from Twenty Years of Research.* San Francisco: Jossey-Bass.

Polkosnik, M.C. and Winston, R.B. (1989). Relationships between students' intellectual and psychological development: An exploratory investigation. *Journal of College Student Development* 30: 10-19.

Reed, P.G., and McGaffic, C. (1994, May). Postformal reasoning as a mental health resource in later life. Paper presented at the Western Society for Research in Nursing Conference, Phoenix, AZ.

Rest, J. (1979). *Development in Judging Moral Issues.* University of Minnesota: Minneapolis.

Rindskopf, D. (1984). Using phantom and imaginary latent variables to parameterize constraints in linear structural models. *Pychometrika* 49: 37-47.

Rosenthal, R. (1978). How often are our numbers wrong? *American Psychologist* 33: 1005-1008.

Sakalys, J.A. (1984). Effects of an undergraduate research course on cognitive development. *Nursing Research* 33: 290-295.

Schmid, J. and Leiman, J.M. (1957). The development of hierarchical factor solutions. *Psychometrika* 22: 53-61.

Schmidt, J.A. (1983). The intellectual development of traditionally and nontraditionally aged college students: A cross-sectional study with longitudinal follow-up. (Doctoral dissertation, University of Minnesota). *Dissertation Abstracts International* 44/09, p. 2681.

Schmidt, J.A. (1985). Older and wiser? A longitudinal study of the impact of college on intellectual development. *Journal of College Student Personnel* 26: 388-394.

Shrout, P.E. and Fleiss, J.L. (1979). Intraclass correlations: Uses in assessing rater reliability. *Psychological Bulletin* 86: 420-428.

Sternberg, R.J. (1982). *Handbook of Human Intelligence.* New York: Cambridge University Press.

Strange, C.C. (1978). Intellectual development, motive for education and learning styles during the college years: A comparison of adult and traditional-age college students. (Doctoral dissertation, University of Iowa). *Dissertation Abstracts International,* 39/08A, p. 4768.

Strange, C.C. and King, P.M. (1981). Intellectual development and its relationship to maturation during the college years. *Journal of Applied Developmental Psychology* 2: 281-295.

Tinsley, H.E.A. and Weiss, D.J. (1975). Inter-rater reliability and agreement of subjective judgments. *Journal of Counseling Psychology* 22: 358-376.

Van Tine, N.B. (1990). The development of reflective judgment in adolescents. (Doctoral dissertation, University of Denver), *Dissertation Abstracts International* 51/08A, p. 2659.

Welfel, E.R. (1979). The development of Reflective Judgment: Its relationship to year in college, academic major, and satisfaction with major among college students (Doctoral dissertation, University of Minnesota). *Dissertation Abstracts International* 40/09A, p. 4949.

Welfel, E.R. (1982). How students make judgments: Do educational level and academic major make a difference? *Journal of College Student Personnel* 23: 490-497.

Welfel, E.R. and Davison, M.L. (1986). The development of reflective judgment in the college years: A four year longitudinal study. *Journal of College Student Personnel* 27: 209-216.

Wolins, L. (1962). Responsibility for raw data. *American Psychologist* 22: 657-658.

Wood, P.K. (1983). Inquiring systems and problem structure: Implications for cognitive development. *Human Development* 26: 249-265.

Wood, P.K. (1990). Construct validity and theories of adult development: Testing for necessary but not sufficient relationships. In M.L. Commons, C. Armon, L. Kohlberg, F.A. Richards, T.A. Grotzer, and J.D. Sinnott (eds.), *Adult Development: Vol. 2. Models And Methods in the Study of Adolescent and Adult Thought.* (pp. 113-132). New York: Praeger.

Wood, P. K. (1994). The effect of unmeasured variables and their interactions on structural models. In A. von Eye and C. Clogg (eds.), *Analysis of Latent Variables in Developmental Research.* (pp. 109-130) Beverly Hills, CA: Sage.

Wood, P.K., and Games, P. (1991). Rationale, detection and implications of interactions between independent variables and unmeasured variables in linear models. *Multivariate Behavioral Research* 25: 295-311.

# Student Learning and Cognitive Development in the Community College

### Richard A. Voorhees

*Colorado Community College and Occupational Education System*

Research on student learning and cognitive development has not fully considered the community college. While two lengthy reviews in the past decade (Pascarella, 1985; McMillan, 1987) have served to illuminate the general connections between institutions of higher education and student learning outcomes, neither has isolated the contribution of community colleges. A first aim of the present work, then, is to provide a current review of student learning research as it might pertain to the community college. A second purpose is to examine new literature that may cause a re-evaluation of the community college's role in student learning. In contrast to previous research that has been only associational in nature, new studies represent clear advances in methodology and design. A third purpose is to propose a new model for assessing student learning and cognitive development in the community college. This model includes variables and concepts the literature connects to student learning experiences within the community college and posits relationships among those variables in new ways.

The debate about whether community colleges produce quality learning outcomes is customarily acted out by comparing learning outcomes ascribed to 4-year institutions. Accordingly, this chapter begins by contrasting student and faculty characteristics between the 2-year and 4-year sectors, a useful springboard for analyzing the traditional criticisms of student learning within the community college. Critics root their assumptions in political and social terms that invariably conclude that students attending community colleges achieve inferior learning outcomes. It is argued here that these assertions are often methodologically and conceptually lacking. When coupled with recent findings reviewed in this chapter, these shortcomings call for a longer look at community college learning outcomes. To help define that debate, a brief review of the conceptual literature of student learning and cognitive development is offered. Theories of student learning, of course, do not envision community college students and their learning environments as separate from the mainstream of higher education. However, where practical, connections between developmental theory and community college characteristics are proposed.

A section discussing measurement issues in assessing student learning and cognitive development provides an overview of the statistical and conceptual issues that are encountered in attempts to isolate student learning. Research methodology in this area has improved dramatically over the past several years, a hopeful sign for untangling the complex interplay of factors associated with student learning and cognitive development. In tandem with the contextual review that precedes it, this section provides the framework for the review of studies that follow.

The bulk of this chapter is devoted to contemporary studies that examine student learning and cognitive development within higher education. Although only a handful focus on the community college, an accumulation of recent studies comparing learning outcomes between sectors forms a promising corner in the literature. These studies receive particular scrutiny since their findings lead to new conceptualizations of the community college and its students. A synthesis of this chapter is presented by a general model of student learning and cognitive development in the community college.

Elements of this model are drawn from the literature of community college characteristics and factors which may influence student learning encountered both within and outside the community college. This model combines theoretical underpinnings about how students learn in general with the practical, daily experiences common to most community college students. The press of demands that compete directly with the learning process has not been considered within previous efforts to estimate models of student learning. This chapter concludes in the pursuit of a model that more fully captures the learning experiences of students at the community college.

## Distinctions among Terms

Semantical differences pervade the literature. It is important for the task at hand to strike demarcations among academic achievement, student learning, cognitive development, and critical thinking. As used here, academic achievement refers to quantitative measures of students' cumulative performance in classes, usually represented by grade point average (GPA), or receipt of a postsecondary degree or certificate. Both, for reasons reviewed below, are disputable measures of student achievement but appear frequently in the literature as proxies for student learning. Student learning as used throughout this chapter refers to the acquisition of skills and knowledge independent of either GPA or certification. Cognitive development refers to the process of acquiring those skills thought to be arranged hierarchically according to Bloom's Taxonomy (Bloom, Englehart, Furst, Hill, and Krathwohl, 1956). Cognitive development, then, occurs under the broader category of student learning. Critical thinking refers to a set of cognitive skills and abilities that also is subsumed under the broad umbrella of student learning. Pascarella and Terenzini (1991) define critical thinking as:

...the individual's ability to do some or all of the following: identify central issues and assumptions in an argument, recognize important relationships, make correct inferences from data, deduce conclusions from information or data provided, interpret whether conclusions are warranted on the basis of the data given, and evaluate evidence or authority. (p. 118)

Having established this chapter's connotations for student learning and cognitive development, attention is turned to the context of the community college learning debate. Attacks on the community college have not been based on deepseated understandings of community college characteristics and how they might set the community college apart from other sectors of higher education. Community college critics now have the upper hand in the current debate, although the parameters are changing because of shifts in student demographics and the evolution of sharper methods of inquiry.

## THE CONTEXT OF THE COMMUNITY COLLEGE LEARNING DEBATE

### Community College Characteristics
In the fall of 1991, 1,399 public 2-year colleges enrolled nearly 5.4 million students, representing 48 percent of public enrollments in higher education and 35 percent of total enrollment across public, private, and proprietary postsecondary education (National Center for Education Statistics [NCES], 1994, p. 177). According to NCES the share of public enrollments in community colleges has steadily increased each fall since 1970, when 2.3 million students were enrolled. In contrast, enrollment increases by 1,986 4-year public institutions—4.2 million in the fall of 1970 to 5.9 million in the fall of 1991—have not been commensurate with increases at 2-year public colleges (NCES, 1994, p. 177). This enrollment gap has been fueled by part-time enrollment, chiefly by females. Overall, the part-time proportion of community college enrollments has risen from 48 percent in the fall of 1970 to 65 percent in the fall of 1991. The part-time proportion of public 4-year enrollments has increased only modestly during this time, from 27 percent to 30 percent (NCES, 1994, p. 178).

Community college students are also more diverse. They are older and more likely to be female and minority group members. Nearly 60 percent of total undergraduate public 4-year enrollments were under 24 years old in the fall of 1991 (NCES, 1994, p. 179). The corresponding figure for public 2-year colleges was 42 percent.[1] Community colleges also serve higher proportions of undergraduate females (57.5%) and minority students (23.5%) than public 4-year institutions (52.9% female and 13.7% minorities).

---

[1] This statistic probably is influenced by the higher proportion of unknown student ages (12.3%) reported to NCES by 2-year colleges than by 4-year colleges (3.1%).

Over the past two decades the community college has replaced 4-year colleges as the access point to higher education for first-time students. Slightly over one million students began their college experience at public two-year institutions in the fall of 1991, compared with 718,000 in the public 4-year sector and 393,000 in the private 4-year sector (NCES, 1994, p. 185). There are substantial differences, on average, between the high school preparation of those first-time freshmen choosing the community college and those choosing 4-year institutions. For example, data available from the Higher Education Research Institute at the University of California at Los Angeles drawn from the annual Cooperative Institutional Research Program (CIRP) survey suggests that 24.7 percent of first-time students bring self-reported high school GPAs of C or lower to the community college. The corresponding figure for private and public 4-year colleges is 14.2 percent (Higher Education Research Institute, 1992).[2]

Community colleges also serve the needs of under-prepared learners to an extent greater than 4-year institutions. The National Center for Education Statistics (1991) reports that in 1989 at least one remedial course was offered by 90 percent of two-year colleges, 64 percent of four-year colleges, and 58 percent of private colleges. While NCES reports that 30 percent of all college freshmen took at least one remedial course in the fall of 1989, it appears that remedial coursework is not evenly spread throughout higher education. That is, 55 percent of those freshmen at colleges enrolling predominately minority students took at least one remedial class. Indications are that demand for remedial education is increasing, and may outstrip the community college's ability to keep pace. Accelerated demand, particularly in those community colleges serving higher proportions of minority students has given credence to the assertion that current students represent the first generation to reach the community college less prepared than those that preceded them (Rouche and Rouche, 1993).

There were about 91,000 full-time regular faculty at public community colleges in the fall of 1987 (NCES, 1994). Full-time community college faculty are proportionately older. Over 80 percent of public community college faculty were 40 years or older compared with 74 percent of 4-year sector faculty. About 44 percent of community college faculty are employed part-time and 56 percent full-time (American Association of Community Colleges [AACC], 1995). The mix of part-time to full-time faculty in the community colleges has been linked to issues of quality in learning outcomes. So, too, might the ratio of full-time regular faculty to graduate teaching assistants been of concern in assessing quality of lower-division coursework in the 4-year sector.

National data documenting the number of part-time instructors, chiefly graduate teaching assistants, employed by 4-year institutions are not available. Neither

---

[2] Whether these proportions are representative of first-time students at all community colleges in the United States is doubtful since the CIRP participation rate for 4-year schools dwarfs current participation rates for community colleges.

are national data available which compare average class sizes at 2-year institutions and 4-year institutions. One must turn to institutional or state-wide studies to draw preliminary conclusions about faculty employment status and workload between sectors. A recent statewide study (Chisholm, 1994) of public faculty workload in Colorado documents substantial differences between sectors. Average freshman and sophomore class sizes for lecture classes were highest at research universities (34) and lowest at community colleges (14 in urban community colleges and 11 in rural community colleges). Chisholm also demonstrates substantial differences in equivalent number of 3-credit hour classes taught during an academic year by full-time research university faculty (4.1) versus full-time community college faculty (11.3 in urban community colleges and 14.6 in rural colleges). Teaching assistants culled from the ranks of graduate students accounted for nearly 18 percent of faculty-student contact time in traditional classes at research universities. Community colleges, in contrast, employed no teaching assistants but employed more part-time faculty (59% at urban community colleges and 31% at rural colleges) than research universities (14%).

The level of faculty preparation is usually ignored in explaining student learning. If it can be advanced that part-time faculty employed by community colleges hold, at a minimum, master's degrees while instruction at the lower division at 4-year doctoral-granting institutions is conducted by graduate teaching assistants, a substantial gap in the academic preparation of faculty exists. This gap may influence student learning outcomes. If faculty characteristics reported by Chisholm typify national data, and there is no reason to believe otherwise, they should be considered in efforts to illuminate differences in learning outcomes between sectors.

### Criticism of the Community College's Academic Credibility

Previous reports that seek to ascertain the role of community colleges in producing student learning and cognitive development outcomes have not always overflowed with praise. Yet, the assumptions underlying these critical narratives have not been particularly precise or praiseworthy, especially since student learning outcomes are not assessed directly. Instead, attacks on the community college's academic credibility are marshalled on two wide fronts: baccalaureate completion rates and socioeconomic attainment outcomes. It is generally acknowledged that community college students do not complete baccalaureate degree programs in the same proportion as students who begin their careers at 4-year institutions. For example, recent research (Whitaker and Pascarella, 1994) estimates the effect on total educational attainment attributed to initial attendance at a 2-year college to be 15 percent. Evidence to buttress the second line of attack, socioeconomic attainment outcomes, is less convincing and is contradicted in the literature by studies using superior methodologies. In the past, critics may have been forced to rely on surrogates because these data that estimate student learning have been unavailable. However, as data become available, indirect criticisms should not persist. The connections between indirect measures and student learning in the community college are reviewed below.

## Baccalaureate Completion Rates

Alba and Lavin (1981) underscore the debate about whether community colleges students' low rates of transfer and higher rates of dropout are attributable to negative community college influences or to the students who enter them. They compared the academic careers of students assigned to 4-year schools with those assigned to 2-year schools in the City University of New York (CUNY), a system of commuter institutions. The students in Alba and Lavin's study first applied to CUNY's 4-year colleges; one group was granted admission, the other was assigned to 2-year schools. The authors report that both groups held the same aspirations for the baccalaureate degree as determined by their initial application to a 4-year school and a subsequent survey. Assignment decisions were based primarily on high school grade averages. The sample was limited to those applicants whose high school averages were less than 80 percent as calculated by grades earned in college preparatory classes. This exclusion results in selection of a 4-year sample that is unrepresentative of the 4-year study population with respect to prior academic achievement.

The authors report that while the groups were similar with respect to high school averages, they were unalike in high school rank. Community college assignees were significantly less likely to rank in the upper half of their high school graduating class, to have completed an equivalent number of high school preparatory classes, and to have completed an academic high school program. Socioeconomic status and minority status were not significantly different between groups although Alba and Lavin note that Catholic ethnics were over-represented in the community college group while Jewish students were overrepresented in the 4-year college group. Both groups were characterized as from modest or low income families. Although the community college group came from families with proportionately higher incomes, differences between groups were not significant.

Controlling for high school background, Alba and Lavin report that five years after entry only 40 percent of initial community college entrants had transferred to a senior college and were about 50 percent less likely than the 4-year sample to have earned a baccalaureate degree. There were significant differences across community colleges. Students entering certain community colleges within the CUNY system achieved baccalaureate rates superior to students entering certain 4-year colleges. This suggests that institutions exert effects independent of student prematriculation characteristics although Alba and Lavin were unable to disentangle this effect.

Those students initially placed at a community college earned significantly fewer credits during the first three years and differed significantly from their 4-

year counterparts in academic performance after the first year. By the end of the third year, some of the most academically talented community college students had transferred, suppressing subsequent average academic performance statistics at the community college. Based on the superior grades earned by the community college sample during the first two years, Alba and Lavin speculate that 4-year schools were more rigorous. Differences in grading, coupled with lower rates of baccalaureate attainment, led Alba and Lavin to conclude the community college produces deleterious effects on students. Their findings, however, focus on students who were presumed to have baccalaureate intentions at the time they applied to college. Whether baccalaureate intentions endured beyond matriculation is not known. Students initially assigned to the community college may have redirected their goals during their studies. These findings are also now dated and do not generalize easily to the increasing number of part-time students at the community college.

Grubb (1991) offers a descriptive analysis of transfer rates from the community college to 4-year institutions drawn from the National Longitudinal Study of the Class 1972 (NLS-72, NCES, 1981) and the High School and Beyond Study (HSB, NCES, 1985).[3] Grubb reports that transfer rates are falling for all groups of students entering the community college. The decline is steepest for women, Blacks, Hispanics, and those with low aspirations. Grubb examined upward shifts in the proportion of women, minorities, and students from low and middle socioeconomic classes entering the community college and downward shifts in the proportion of students who had pursued academic tracks in high school and those indicating baccalaureate aspirations. He concludes these shifts account for between one-quarter and one-third of the decline in transfer rates.

Grubb also castigates the community college for lower baccalaureate completion rates by reasoning that academic Associate degree programs have weakened since the 1970s. Because these programs are ineffective, they fail to produce students who might transfer to earn degrees at the 4-year level. Almost paradoxically, Grubb suggests that depressed rates also can be traced, in part, to those who

---

[3] The National Longitudinal Survey of the High School Class of 1972 was conducted under the auspices of the National Center for Educational Statistics, U. S. Department of Education. It was formed by a two-stage sampling process in which schools first were sampled, then individual students within those schools were surveyed during the spring of 1972. Educational Testing Service administered a test battery and base-year questionnaire to 16,683 seniors enrolled in 1,070 public, private, and parochial schools in the fifty states and District of Columbia. The sampling scheme employed ensured that schools in low-income areas and schools serving large proportions of minorities would be sampled at double the normal rate. Four follow-up surveys were conducted. The first follow-up occurred in academic year 1973-74, the second in the fall of 1974, the third in the fall of 1976, and the fourth in the fall of 1979.

The High School and Beyond study was initiated by NCES to compliment the NLS-72 study . HSB studied high school students enrolled in 1980. Like NLS-72, this database studied seniors. Unlike NLS-72 it also included a sophomore cohort. The initial national sample was larger than the NLS-72 and contains initial data on 30,000 seniors and 28,000 sophomores. Follow-ups occurred in 1982, 1984, 1986, and 1992.

transfer without completing an Associate degree, a transfer group which would be less influenced by the ineffectual nature of community college transfer programs. Grubb does not demonstrate that students native to 4-year institutions receive degrees at a higher rate during the identical period of this study. Nor does he offer quantitative or qualitative evidence to support his characterizations of eroding quality in the community college's academic programs. Grubb's data also cannot capture student interactions with faculty, curricula, or external pressures either at the community college or subsequently in 4-year colleges. Finally, no weight is given to the ages or employment status of students. It is almost certain that older adults or those employed during their studies could not pursue the linear, lock-step progression to the baccalaureate that Grubb envisions.

Velez (1985) uses the NLS-72 database to determine the odds that high school seniors will earn a bachelor's degree. Using logit analysis, Velez concludes that students enrolled in academic programs (non-vocational programs) who begin their careers at a 4-year college enjoy a 19 percent higher probability of finishing a baccalaureate than students who started in a 2-year college. This finding may be seen as damning to some community college supporters and mildly indicative of noncomparable learning outcomes between community colleges and 4-year institutions. Yet, several sampling issues may recast these findings.

First, like Alba and Lavin's study, it is not known whether 2-year college students in the sample were pursuing a bachelor's degree after they entered the community college. Degree aspirations were sampled during respondents' senior year of high school and not after that. Also unknown is the number of high school seniors within the sample who intended to begin their career at the community college and later transfer to a 4-year college in pursuit of a bachelor's degree. Student intentions can be expected to change as result of interactions with the collegiate environment and can lead to behavior which is different from that originally predicted. Changing student goals coupled with the heterogeneous range of student intentions found at the community college are factors which can influence outcome studies but are usually overlooked.

Community college students express a wider range of educational goals than their 4-year counterparts. For example, a tally of reasons students choose to enroll at the community college can include: academic degree with no transfer, academic degree with transfer, vocational degree with no transfer, vocational degree with transfer, no degree intentions, classes for personal interest, and classes to upgrade employment skills. The profile of student intentions may vary from community college to community college and may overlap as students pursue multiple goals. In contrast, almost all students entering 4-year institutions are likely to express baccalaureate degree intentions. If one accepts the premise that intentions shape future behavior, the utility of examining the behavior of those students expressing intentions that might forecast goal attainment appears evident. Although research documenting the role of student reported intentions in forecasting community college success is equivocal (see, for example, Bers and Smith, 1991; Voorhees, 1987), disregard of the range of student intentions at the community college in this instance undercuts accurate generalizations.

Velez also included students in his sample who had not graduated from high school during the same year as their college matriculation. The proportion of those students who delayed their college is unreported as is their initial choice of institution. On average, students who delay their entry to higher education for one year after high school graduation do not persist at the same rate as those who enter higher education directly after high school graduation (Pascarella and Terenzini, 1991). Given the community college's traditional open admission status, it is probable that "late" starting students most easily entered the community college, a factor which by itself might suppress baccalaureate attainment rates.

Other factors besides bachelor degree completion distinguished the 2-year college sample from the 4-year college sample in Velez's study. Community college students, on average, measured lower on prematriculation characteristics including socioeconomic status (SES), high school curriculum, math, high school grades, and aptitude. These factors might provide alternate explanations for low baccalaureate degree attainment for initial entrants. Post-matriculation academic performance, as captured by grades, was almost identical for 2-year and 4-year students. Thus, despite lower aptitude, high school grades, and prior engagement in curricula described as less than academic in high school, 2-year college students appeared to reached parity in academic performance. The use of grades as a proxy for measuring learning should be approached with appropriate caution. Even so, the contrast in post-matriculation academic performance between 2-year and 4-year students in Velez's study is striking. If, in fact, students at both levels perform academically at the same level as measured by GPA, there can exist little room to castigate the community college academic environment except, possibly, to assert that grade inflation runs rampant at the community college. Velez is silent on this point.

These criticisms call for a re-examination of Velez's conclusions. However, the post-hoc nature of research using NLS-72 and HSB databases would constrain such efforts. Secondary databases do not permit operationalization of key variables that have been collected for other purposes. Even if all data were available, it is not probable that nuances and meaning can be captured by a simple logit regression. This study does point to a considerable opportunity for those who might use lower baccalaureate degree attainment as a lever to attack its academic credibility of the community college. This challenge might be met in understanding the fuller spectrum of student and institutional characteristics influencing community college student learning and cognitive development.

Dougherty (1994) reviews a range of studies—chiefly efforts to find out why more community college students do not earn baccalaureate degrees—and argues that the community college provides inferior lower division preparation. Dougherty concedes that factors which explain why transfer students do not earn the baccalaureate degrees are complex. These factors include neglect of the academic program at the community college in favor of increased vocationalism, fewer opportunities for social integration, and lower selectivity and academic prestige. Other impediments cited include students' difficulty in moving to strange new colleges, the difficulty in securing acceptance and financial aid, and loss of credits. The most pointed criticism bearing on the present work, however, is the suggestion that the community college offers instruction that is not up to 4-year college standards. Citing work examining the transfer function (Cohen and Brawer, 1987; Richardson and Bender, 1987), Dougherty points to lack of faculty encouragement for students to transfer and faculty failure to express and enforce high academic student expectations. Community college faculty are seen by Dougherty as more likely to assign grades to meet class norms than their university counterparts, to cover less material in class, and less likely to assign difficult readings and essay exams.

Declining rigor, according to Dougherty, is due to the influx of students who are less prepared academically, are not interested in transfer, and yet enroll in transfer programs. Institutional culture degenerates when community college faculty become discouraged with their students. Dougherty presents no hard data to gird his speculations about academic quality at the community college. Whereas Dougherty recognizes most of the difficulties facing community college transfer students in their pursuit of the baccalaureate, he fails to acknowledge that these difficulties cannot be a surrogate measure of the effectiveness of community college instructional outcomes. Two studies reviewed here (Bohr, Pascarella, Nora, Zusman, Jacobs, Desler, and Bulakowski, 1994; Pascarella, Bohr, Nora, and Terenzini, 1995) which focus directly on differences between 2-year institutions and 4-year institutions in student learning and cognitive development provide strong evidence that Dougherty's conclusions are premature.

*Socioeconomic Attainment and Occupational Status Outcomes*
A second surrogate for measuring student learning and cognitive development is measurement of socioeconomic and occupational status outcomes. A comprehensive study executed by Sewell and Hauser (1975) using path analytic techniques serves as a touchstone for gauging the impact of higher education on earnings and occupations. Sewell and Hauser surveyed all Wisconsin high school seniors in 1957 and followed this group up in 1964. The initial survey produced a 95 percent response rate. Since subsequent earning data were available only for males, Sewell and Hauser's 1975 analyses exclude females. Though gender representation could not be accomplished, two findings in this study are particularly notable. First, high school rank was nearly as important as scores on a standardized test of mental ability administered in high school in explaining subsequent occupational status. Second, the sons of parents with only grade school education obtained on average one and one-fourth fewer years of higher education that the

sons of parents who were college graduates even when their fathers had similar jobs and their families had similar incomes. Sewell and Hauser's seemingly disparate findings bear directly on learning research for students served by the community college. It might appear that prior achievement in secondary school can overcome deficits in measured mental ability in future attainment, but the effects of being a first-generation college attendee may be more difficult to surmount. Sewell and Hauser also report future earnings disadvantages linked to initial community college attendance, although their sample was quite small and included not just community colleges, but bible institutes and foreign colleges. Their general conclusion, however, is that the process of socioeconomic attainment appears to work in essentially the same way irrespective of what college students choose.

Despite these findings, the community college continues to be linked to low prestige, less desirable occupations (Breneman and Nelson, 1981; Grubb, 1984). When initial student characteristics and educational attainment are statistically controlled, however, these reports are less than conclusive (see, for example, Smart and Ethington, 1985; Whitaker and Pascarella, 1994). Comparing the effects of 2-year and 4-year college attendance, Whitaker and Pascarella used the 1986 follow-up of the NLS-72 database to focus on gender, race, socioeconomic origins, age, secondary school performance, precollege self-esteem, and precollege educational and occupational aspirations on subsequent socioeconomic attainments. With the exception of educational and occupational aspirations, no conditional effects were uncovered. Their general conclusion is that status attainment disadvantages experienced by 2-year college graduates are attributable largely to the effects of educational attainment, not to 2-year college effects. Further, Whitaker and Pascarella suggest that when educational attainment was controlled, there was general parity in prestige and earnings between those who began their academic careers in 2-year or 4-year colleges. An unknown in the Whitaker and Pascarella investigation is whether students in either the 4-year or 2-year samples completed their educational or vocational programs. Not drawn, also, are the connections between initial attendance decisions and subsequent interaction with those institutional characteristics that influence student career development. Several studies (Smart and Hamm, 1993a; Smart and Hamm, 1993b) examine those institutional effectiveness measures at community colleges that have been linked with superior student career development opportunities.

Whitaker and Pascarella conclude that contrary to earlier research suggesting that 2-year college students are disadvantaged in relation to baccalaureate degree attainment, the effect of students' initial attendance decisions are not irreversible. They report earnings parity between 2-year and 4-year college entrants after 13 years, a considerably longer time span than that used in earlier studies. Of allied significance was the finding that those students who expressed the highest levels of educational and occupational aspirations were more likely to attend a 4-year institution and were more likely to derive greater socioeconomic benefit from attending a 4-year institution. This finding highlights the general impact of self-selection in initial institutional choice and may suggest that community college students arrive with diminished baccalaureate degree expectations. Important, also, are the questions this finding raises about the 2-year college environment. For example, it is not now known whether initial lower levels of educational and occupational aspirations persist throughout 2-year college students' careers or whether parity in aspirations is reached only after transfer to a 4-year institution.

In further analysis of the NLS-72 database, Smart and Ethington (1985) examine the effect of institutional type on early career employment outcomes for subjects who had either begun their academic career at the community college or at a 4-year institution and had completed baccalaureate degrees within four years after high school graduation. Controlling for academic ability, socioeconomic status, intended occupational status, and years employed, the authors found no significant differences for either males or females who began their academic careers at the community college or 4-year institutions in early job status, stability, or satisfaction. There also were no significant differences in the early career outcomes and the number of years spent at the community college. Smart and Ethington speculate that if short-term disadvantage does beset students initially matriculating at the community college as traditionally advanced, such disadvantages do not persist after attainment of the baccalaureate.

Smart and Ethington did not tackle the issue of progression to the baccalaureate as targeted in other reviews (Alba and Lavin, 1981; Dougherty, 1994; Grubb, 1991). Yet, it would appear that those students who made "on-time" progression to the baccalaureate were prepared adequately, if not comparably, at the community college for their subsequent academic pursuits and entry into the labor market. Smart and Ethington conclude that previous efforts which show lower aggregate success rates at community colleges than 4-year institutions may be the result of initial student differences rather than the failure of the community college to provide learning environments that promote student learning.

Minority occupational attainment also has received play in the literature. Pascarella, Smart and Stoecker (1989) use the NLS-72 database to examine the effect of institutional type on early status attainment of Blacks. Controlling for gender interaction with other influences by developing separate structural equation models for Black men and women, they addressed the question whether students were influenced in early educational, occupational, and economic attainments by attending predominantly Black versus a predominantly White institution. The structural model allowed for simultaneous control of all variables on the ultimate dependent variables, permitting focused comparison of the influence of competing factors on early status attainment. For example, net of social origins, secondary school attainments, initial aspirations, institutional quality, and academic and social experiences, the differences in early educational, occupational, and economic attainments between Black men attending predominantly Black institutions versus those attending White institutions were slight. Black women, on the other hand, appeared to derive positive effects on both educational attainment and occupational status from attendance at Black institutions. Remarkably, the influence of attending a Black college on occupational status was reported to be nine times stronger for women than for men.

Beyond the impact of institutional type, the authors observe that the most consistent positive effect on early status attainment was collegiate academic achievement, a two-item scale consisting of self-reported GPA and membership in a scholastic honor society. Net of other causes, academic achievement had no direct effect on occupational status or income; academic achievement did, however, exert significant indirect effects on occupational status for both sexes and on income for women through degree completion. College academic achievement produced the most potent positive effect on bachelor degree attainment for both sexes, underscoring the criticality of performance in the classroom for Black students. Secondary school academic achievement, as measured by high school grades and class rank, exercised the largest zero-order correlation coefficient with collegiate academic performance. The resulting bridge between Pascarella, Smart, and Stoecker's results and the present study may be regional in nature. The greatest access to higher education for Blacks living in the South is through predominantly Black institutions, whereas community colleges provide the greatest access for Blacks outside the South (Mow and Nettles, 1990).

*Summary of Indirect Criticisms*
Reports disparaging the community college's ability to produce quality academic outcomes and a general tendency in the academic community to accept the face validity of such reports overlook several factors. As an access point to higher education, and perhaps despite the obstacles to educational attainment inherent in the characteristics students bring with them, the community college plays an indisputable role as a mechanism for individuals to better themselves. Critics are not able to substantiate with data their claims that the community college cultivates learning environments which are substandard. Instead, reliance on baccalaureate completion rates and socioeconomic outcomes serves as convenient proxies for a true evaluation of the community college learning environment.

**Theoretical Underpinnings of Student Learning and Cognitive Development**
This section deals with the conceptual basis for addressing student learning as informed both by the traditional roots of cognitive science and by recent formulations that seek to examine learning among adults. In the main, cognitive development research traces its beginnings to the pioneering work of Piaget (1950). Piaget studied cognitive development in children and concluded that this development was age-linked, culminating with formal reasoning. Formal reasoning is the basis for scientific reasoning in problem solving. Other researchers have sub-

sequently identified a still later stage occurring in the adult years which draws upon all previous stages and allow for relativistic thinking. This has been labeled as postformal reasoning. Drawing upon a synthesis of research, Pascarella and Terenzini (1991) estimate that only about 55 percent of all college students operate at the formal reasoning level. Further, Pascarella and Terenzini estimate 85 percent of the gain in formal reasoning occurring between the freshman and senior year occurs during the freshman and sophomore year.

Piaget also was the first to speculate that learning occurs as a process in which an individual balances his or her experiences with his or her cognitive structure. This balancing, or seeking equilibrium, coupled with age-linked progression in human development are consistent themes throughout cognitive development literature. Recent literature is useful for purposes of their chapter because it provides the opportunity to match adolescent and adult learning theory with those characteristics of community college students reviewed above. The proportion of older students at the community college, for example, ensures that more variability in age-linked cognitive development will be present in the community college learning environment.

*Developmental Theories of Learning*
Loevinger (1976) offers a scheme in which cognitive development cuts across time and forms a coherent frame of reference or world view for the individual. These stages are uniform and include presocial, symbiotic, impulsive, self-protective, conformist, conscientious, individualistic, autonomous, and integrated. Loevinger describes these stages as multicultural in application. Ego development is considered a master trait, second only to intelligence in determining an individual's response to situations. Loevinger's theory does not, however, stress potential interventions or purposefully constructed situations where ego development can be maximized. As a result, little insight exists in this theoretical orientation about how higher education might influence or accelerate individual ego development.

Kohlberg (1973) advances a cognitive development theory of moral reasoning in which individuals move through stages that serve as frames of reference from which they analyze and judge courses of action in moral situations. Kohlberg groups his developmental schema in three levels: preconventional, conventional, and postconventional. Preconventional reasoning is egocentric in nature and moral principles are largely derived from individual needs. Conventional reasoning is depicted as a stage when the individual possesses shared moral values that underlie society. At the last stage, the postconventional level, individuals construct moral principles that are universal in application. Kohlberg believes that change is caused if environmental challenges are posed at one stage above where an individual is currently functioning. The challenge to institutions of higher education is to design interventions either through the curriculum or extracurriculum to increase levels of moral reasoning.

Kolb (1984) describes learning as the process by which knowledge is created through the transformation of experience. Kolb describes the learning process as consisting of two dimensions: grasping information and transforming information. Grasping information occurs either through concrete experience or through abstract conceptualization. Concrete experience focuses on tangible involvement in immediate experience and often involves feelings. Abstract conceptualization represents a less personal interpretation of experience related more to thinking than to feeling. Transforming information occurs either through reflective judgment or through active experimentation. Reflective observation represents an internal attempt to understand the world, often by watching, whereas active experimentation represents an external attempt to influence the world by active involvement in experience. According to Kolb the combination of possibilities for grasping and transforming information results in a distinct learning style. Kolb also speculates that differing patterns of learning development emerge from female and male socialization.

Piaget's (1950) explanation that cognitive development occurs through a continual balancing of experience and cognitive structures serve as the point of departure for most developmental theories of student learning. Perry's (1970) theory of intellectual development, for example, identifies three general stages of intellectual development that can be used to characterize the moral reasoning of college students: dualism, relativism, and commitment. The first structure is characterized by the belief that all knowledge is known. Uncertainty of knowledge is a temporary phenomenon when authority figures conceal the truth temporarily to promote exercises that are good for students. Progression on Perry's scale leads to discovery that some knowledge is not known now, but is tempered by a belief that it will be known in the future. As students continue to encounter areas of uncertainty, they come to believe that most, if not all, knowledge is uncertain. This perspective leads to a shift from finding the truth to ways of thinking about knowledge. Knowledge eventually becomes contextual and students construct their perspectives and make commitments based on a critical review of the relevant evidence. Subsequent investigations using Perry's scheme suggest that the most potent predictor of placement on Perry's scale is the number of years of exposure to college (Pascarella and Terenzini, 1991). Of the cognitive theorists, Perry's scheme has received the most attention in higher education, particularly to isolate cognitive development in higher education environments (in this review, Baxter Magolda, 1989; Durham, Hays, and Martinez, 1994; Buczynski, 1991).

Modern theories of cognitive development lend a framework from which empirical findings which appear disjointed can be reconciled. Those theories reviewed above are not inclusive of the range of developmental theories of student learning. However, what can be gained for purposes of this chapter from this cursory review is an appreciation that cognitive development, while linked to chronological age, does not occur as a matter of course. Institutions can design strategies to enhance moral, ego, and reasoning development. Simultaneously, the design of such interventions will be complicated at institutions such as community colleges which serve a wider range of student ages and levels of academic preparedness. The literature of student learning and cognitive development has usually ignored the influence of student age and preparedness and links to corresponding cognitive stages. Student learning outcomes can be associated with developmental equilibria that mitigate either for, or against, attainment of knowledge and skills.

## MEASUREMENT ISSUES IN STUDENT LEARNING AND COGNITIVE DEVELOPMENT

Most research in the social and behavioral sciences is correlational and non-experimental. The study of student learning and cognitive development is no exception although recent studies have incorporated at least some statistical techniques that result in extending previous research. The nonexperimental nature of higher education research occurs because of the difficulty, both politically and ethically, of assigning students to control and treatment groups. In combination with imprecise terminology, correlational and nonexperimental techniques have produced a bewildering array of results in the area of student learning and cognitive development.

The route to assessing student learning in any institution is marked with pitfalls and assumptions about the process of learning itself. The central question that should occupy the attention of researchers and policy-makers alike is: what types of students change in which types of ways at which types of institutions? To date, the response from the higher education community to this question at best has been spotty. Previous research suffers from an inability to distinguish between the effects on student learning attributable to student prematriculation characteristics and those attributable to institutions. Reports from the community college sector, in particular, are sketchy and only in recent studies have controls been inserted for those variables that can confound results.

Studies that review the impact of selected variables on student learning and cognitive development but fail to employ the statistical controls necessary to isolate student learning are of little value. A secondary technique involves controlling for the influence of student pretest characteristics by matching subjects. Either choice of technique invites particular concerns at the community college where students may absent themselves from study cohorts as they pursue other opportunities. Matched group designs have not yet illuminated the contribution to student learning and cognitive development attributable to enrolling in a community college versus enrolling in a 4-year institution or not enrolling in higher education. The single study (Pascarella, 1989) in the literature that uses a control group of non-students and a treatment group of students did not incorporate community college students, nor did it present demographic data that might allow extrapolation of its results to the community college.

Illustrative of the difficulties in apprehending research in this area is the review of critical thinking published by McMillan (1987). Drawing chiefly from the published results of correlational studies, McMillan concludes that little evidence exists to support setting up instructional changes to enhance student critical thinking. However, he does not dismiss the potential of specific programs producing critical thinking gains. Instead, his conclusion is based on several shortcomings within the literature. First, the typical one-semester study period common to research in this area may represent insufficient time in which gains in critical thinking can occur. Second, measures of critical thinking probably should be curriculum-specific. That is, broad general assessments of critical thinking measure only small parts of the curriculum, making it difficult to tie gains in critical thinking to a specific course or program. Third, the unit of analysis in studies reviewed by McMillan typically was classes, not students. Comparisons between classes allow only a small unit of analysis for statistical replications, diminishing the opportunities to find significant differences.

## Statistical Issues

Prediction equation studies pose a distinct advantage over single correlational studies since they introduce many variables into a single equation. A major advantage is that they allow a way to "partial out" those associations that can confound statistical analysis so that "true" effects of independent variables can be estimated. Still, single equations are intended only to predict, not to explain. The mindset of single equation is to reduce to a manageable number the variables that might influence a dependent variable. A single equation model posited to predict student learning and cognitive development can easily obscure more complex explanations. Yet, because of its reductionist nature, single equation models also might provide a basis for examining associations among variables influencing student learning in new ways. However, the review of the literature in this study suggests that the process by which students learn is not linear, but instead might best be captured by a system of equations, or models, depicting the influence of multiple factors interacting from multiple perspectives during multiple time frames.

Previous research, particularly when student grade-point average or achievement test scores have been removed from regression equations predicting student learning, generally has produced multiple squared correlations ($R^2$) which are modest at best. These studies have pointed to ideas and factors that bear on student learning and cognitive development that can form a valuable framework for future analysis. However, a total picture quickly eludes a single equation, especially when time-linked causes that predate the measurement of the dependent variable are at play. Such causes, especially when conceived as constituting sets of variables, are best analyzed by a series of equations.

Research using stepwise multiple regression is particularly counterproductive to efforts to understand student learning and cognitive development. Use of stepwise analyses suggest that little is known either conceptually or from previous empirical studies about the effect of various factors on student learning and cognitive development. This orientation holds that it is necessary to rely on computer software for judgment about the strongest associations among predictive variables, rather than the researcher assuming the obligation to pose underlying structural relationships gleaned from the literature. Research in the area of student learning and cognitive development has developed an accumulation of findings over the past several years that negate the heuristic stance one must claim to appropriately use stepwise regression.

Analysis of covariance provides a useful tool within multiple correlational studies to adjust for initial differences in student characteristics. In studies of student learning, covariance techniques are also used to control statistically for the effects of those independent variables thought to interact to produce corresponding changes in R2 values. Covariance techniques help in "leveling the playing field" by allowing an even comparison between groups on student learning dimensions through the control of prematriculation or other characteristics. In instances where a pretest score is the most potent predictor of post-test scores, it becomes necessary to equate both control and treatment groups on pretest scores to isolate on that part of post-test performance that can be attributed to other factors.

Yet another useful technique is the entry of cross-product terms entered as covariates within regression equations to estimate the influence of interactions between independent variables. Cross product terms are optionally entered by the researcher when it is thought that an independent variable or variables exert nonlinear effects on a dependent variable. Nonlinear effects indicate statistical interactions between independent variables. In student learning research cross product terms are most frequently entered for race and gender (see, for example, Pascarella et al., 1995). While use of covariance and cross-product terms entered as covariates extend the usefulness of single equation studies, other techniques, such as structural equation models, appear more capable of explaining the rich processes that underlie student learning.

Path analysis represents a utilitarian approach for estimating the effects of variables posited to influence dependent variables such as student learning and cognitive development. This is accomplished by posing models in which variables thought to affect student learning and cognitive development are depicted as causally antecedent. Depicting time relationships can help to illuminate the complex interplay of factors that ultimately may influence student learning and cognitive development. The use of path analysis also creates the obligation for the researcher to depict *a priori* relationships for variables under study. Ideally, this depiction is based on theoretical considerations and careful evaluation of findings from previous research. Kaufman and Creamer (1991), for example, estimated a model of student learning and development utilizing Ordinary Least Squares (OLS) regression in a path analytic framework. They found statistically significant changes in R2 associated with several antecedent variables within the model. However, their study is conceptually limited because lack of goodness of fit indices negate an understanding of how well their model fits the data. Consequently, it is not known if the model was specified in such a way to capture the underlying relationships for the variables studied, nor how it might have been altered to improve its fit in view of theoretical constructs.

Structural equation modeling techniques such as Linear Structural Relationships (LISREL), (Jöreskog and Sörbom, 1984) offer distinct advantages in disentangling the process of student learning and cognitive development. The largest advantage of structural equation modeling for analyzing relationships that affect student learning is its ability to *simultaneously* solve equations within a posited model. LISREL also provides researchers a way to easily employ multiple measures of latent variables. Latent variables are those measures that are conceptual, such as SES, which are constructed by the variance contributed by other variables, such as family income, fathers' education, occupational status, etc. Additionally, models can be specified in which variables share error variance to capture more fully the relationships of factors occurring outside the model and their potential impact on relationships inside the model. This allows estimation of relationships between variables that are not causally antecedent. If a relationship is not posed as causal in OLS path analysis, it is not estimated, thereby increasing unexplained variance.

Multicolinearity also is a ubiquitous concern in OLS driven path analytic models and can result in deletion of one or more variables whose shared variance is thought to skew levels of the dependent variable. In contrast, structural equation models can correlate residual variance, allowing highly correlated variables to be included within a model and to control for the effect of that relationship on dependent variables (see, for example, Knight, 1993, cited below). LISREL provides methods to handle causal relationships and residual relationships that are unavailable under path analysis utilizing OLS.

## Conceptual Issues

### Sources of Measurement

Almost all research purporting to disentangle student learning and cognitive development outcomes uses test data. Those studies which seek to compare these outcomes across institutions and sectors rely on standardized, commercial examinations that are typically multiple-choice protocols designed for group administrations. These examinations have many advantages, including external validity, quick implementation cycles, and relatively low institutional or faculty effort in their design. Disadvantages include disallowance of specific institutional or program curricular goals, and lack of institutional and student "fit" within the comparison groups which were combined to provide norm-referenced data. Standardized tests also mask learning experiences for individual students. The number, nature, and quality of student experiences within and outside institutions will vary from one student to another. Experiences associated with learning outcomes cannot be the same for all students, nor can group averages reflect individual student experiences.

Reports of research utilizing locally developed examinations, either objective or subjective tests designed chiefly by faculty, to capture student learning and cognitive development are scarce. These examinations can capture student learning within a particular program because they can be geared to specific curricular goals and objectives. Because of design flexibility, locally developed tests can also capture institutional and student influences on learning. The central disadvantage is the perceived lack of objectivity necessary for external review and comparison. As evidenced above, external groups have little trouble in questioning the academic credibility of the community college. Consequently, the liabilities associated with commercial, standardized testing are perhaps not insurmountable if research or policy goals include the need to provide comparable information across sectors.

Besides locally developed examinations, other learning assessment techniques in varying levels of use across higher education include student interviews, student self-reports, demonstrations, simulations, oral examinations, and behavioral observations. Like locally developed examinations, these assessment methods are more closely aligned with curricular content at a given institution, but their results are not reported widely in the literature. The suspicion here is that results from nonstandardized examinations are not widely published because the judgment of journal editors is that they lack generalizability in settings other than those from which they arise and that nonuniform measurement goals—and perhaps the measurement protocols themselves— make replication difficult. Here the downside is that a significant body of knowledge—a collection of results that might supplement what is gleaned from standardized examinations—does not receive the exposure which might inform larger efforts.

*Measurement Strategies*

A major obstacle to understanding group changes in student learning and cognitive development is the misuse of gain scores. Part of any gain on a measure over time is often an artifact of initial pretest scores. Those students scoring initially lower typically exhibit greater gains through regression-to-mean than those with initially high scores. This statistical artifact often provides a misleading picture of community college students who initially may not score as high as their 4-year college counterparts on prematriculation measures of student learning and cognitive development, but who may subsequently make larger, more statistically significant gains.

Pike (1992) provides a wide overview of methodologies most often used to measure change in college students. Those methodologies include gain scores, residual scores, and repeated measures. According to Pike, the largest issue in measuring change arises from qualitative differences in growth for students at different levels of initial ability. Despite shortcomings inherent in each methodology, Pike recommends employment of repeated measures techniques because the greater number of data elements collected provide more opportunities to assess change along a continuum. No studies reviewed for this chapter utilized repeated measures techniques.

Estimates of gains in student learning and cognitive development in institutions of higher education also can obscure the effects of maturation and self-selection. A central challenge to assessing gains accurately is to account for that growth attributable to the maturation process separate from that part attributable to institutional influences. This problem is frequently addressed in nonexperimental research through the statistical controls, including analysis of covariance. Self-selection occurs chiefly in studies where students have enrolled in a particular program or course outside the control of the researcher. In these instances, students bring to the study environment a predisposition to treatment effects. An example occurs when academically able students enroll in challenging courses which produce large critical thinking gains, but for which their predispositions for critical thinking are uncontrolled in subsequent analyses. Undeserved conclusions may result.

Another community college characteristic that serves to limit studies of student learning and cognitive development is the effect of short-term persistence rates and part-time attendance patterns on sample size. It is well known that on average community college students persist at rates less than rates at 4-year institutions. The result can be incomplete group information on post-test assessments for those members of student cohorts who drop out, stop out, or transfer to other institutions before completion of the sampling period. Missing data for voluntary leavers in post-test measures may not skew group averages as much as missing data for those students who were asked to leave for academic reasons. Yet another potential pitfall in studies of student learning and cognitive development is the preponderance of students who attend the community college on a part-time basis. Part-time students usually are not selected to participate in gain studies since it is typically thought that the college and its learning environment would have less of a chance to produce changes in students whose exposure was not maximized in the same way as full-time students. The result is that student learning and cognitive development measures are unavailable for part-time students, a group representing most of the nation's community college students. Additionally, attendance patterns of students who attended full-time during the pretest gathering phase but later attended only part-time has not been entertained in the research literature. Subsequent part-time attendance might provide fewer learning opportunities compared with those students who continued to attend on a full-time basis. Community college attendance patterns also may be sporadic, during which a semester of full-time attendance can be followed one or more by part-time attendance. Because the duration of exposure may be a concern in estimating the true influence of the institution on the extent of student learning and cognitive development, it is somewhat puzzling that no study analyzed in this review controlled for subsequent attendance patterns.

It is not surprising that research that investigates student learning typically focuses on the freshman year, especially since the largest gains in critical thinking during a collegiate career occur between the beginning and end of the freshman year (Pascarella and Terenzini, 1991). What is surprising, however, is that little focus is placed on the impact of student adjustment during this time. While research on student learning has considered the effect of demographic variables, environmental or institutional variables, and indices of student effort, scant attention has been paid to the complexities associated with student transitions to college and the effect such transitions might have on attainment of student learning and cognitive development outcomes. An accounting for the psychosocial press of influences bearing on student learning and cognitive development—including self-concept, motivation, and quality of effort—during the first critical exposure to higher education might inform both practice and theory.

No review of conceptual issues associated with student learning and cognitive development would be complete without mention of student diversity. Diverse persons would include persons of color, differentially abled, and non-U.S. citizens. Since assessment is not a value-free exercise, it would be well to consider the purposes for which assessment is operationalized and whether assessment results represent all students. Issues of cultural fairness in testing, adaptability of testing procedures for differentially abled students, and lack of English language proficiency are potential stumbling blocks. Learning gains reported by ethnicity, for example, can produce useful dialog about improving the teaching and learning environment. However, concerns about the fairness of the assessment selected for use may cloud the practical application of results. Issues of culture and educational attainment are also largely unaddressed in the student learning literature. By way of illustration of issues of cultural diversity, one might ask what does it mean to be a learner? Answers to this question may mean different things for different people. It is important also that assessments provide each student an equal opportunity to show his or her proficiency on the skill being measured rather than skill at negotiating the assessment's language base or the physical capacity necessary to respond to test items. To date, the literature of student learning and cognitive development has not incorporated these issues.

## STUDENT LEARNING AND COGNITIVE DEVELOPMENT

Studies that investigate student learning, unlike those dealing with student persistence, are not numerous in the literature of higher education. There is heightened interest in this area in the decade of the 1990s. The research reviewed here was selected for inclusion based on several criteria. First, those multicorrelational studies drawing from a conceptual base which deal with student learning in the community college were included. This vein includes several studies encouraging to community colleges (Bohr, et al., 1994; Pascarella et al., 1995). Second, studies that appear frequently in other reviews were included if they applied to the community college, either directly or by a process of extrapolation. Several studies cited in this review arise from other higher education settings that tangentially bear on the community college but have potential to inform study in this area. Also, a few persistence studies have been incorporated here since it is difficult to separate the literature of persistence from student cognitive development. Together, these findings have been used to suggest broader associations with student learning in the community college. The organization of this section is categorical, representing the connections between institutional influences, faculty and curricula, and student characteristics on student learning and cognitive development.

### Institutional Influences

Our ability to describe institutional learning environments by referencing key variables may only result in approximations of that environment. Demographic and other information can reveal a great deal about learning environments, but simple descriptions of institutions can be misleading. Baird (1988) points to the folly at hand when one decides institutions of similar size create the same learning environment. Size, student characteristics, expenditures per full-time equivalent student, and library holdings provide valuable information about the institution, but do little to depict the environment in which those factors operate and interact. Such variables operate in institutional environments, but cannot be synonymous, themselves, with that environment. Prior to discussing what types of college environments are conducive to learning outcomes, it is important to review whether it can be shown that college attendance, net of other influences can be associated with learning outcomes.

Pascarella (1989) sought to determine whether the college experience makes a difference in learning outcomes acquired by young adults. Pascarella offers the literature's first, and apparently only, pretest and post-test comparison of differences in critical thinking between academically able young adults who attended college and those that did not. Pascarella used a control group that was unexposed to collegiate influences, a strategy which eliminates threats to internal validity including maturation, testing, instrumentation, and, possibly, regression to the mean. Subjects completed the Watson Glaser Critical Thinking Appraisal (CTA) (Watson and Glaser, 1980) during their senior year of high school. The CTA consists of objective items comprising five subtests: inference, recognition of assumptions, deduction, interpretation, and evaluation of arguments. College participants were matched with non-college participants on ethnicity (White versus non-White), high school senior CTA total score, American College Testing (ACT) composite score, and family socioeconomic status. Both groups were given the CTA approximately one year later. The college group was also given a 10-item questionnaire designed to profile collegiate experiences and involvements.

When high school CTA scores, ACT composite scores, secondary school grades, family SES, and educational aspirations (to control for the interaction between self-selection and maturation) were posed as covariates, Pascarella found significantly higher scores on total CTA score and on the interpretation and evaluation of arguments subscales for the college group. To test for the effects of the college experience on critical thinking, partial correlations were calculated for the ten college experience variables and CTA total and subscale scores. None were significant, suggesting that no single college experience could account for the development of critical thinking gains. However, when seven items representing student involvement were extracted, standardized, and summed to form a composite variable, a different picture emerged.

Pascarella entered this scale, a measure of overall involvement, with the five covariates and a measure of institutional selectivity. This analysis produced a significant partial correlation between total involvement and CTA total scores and subscores for inference, recognition, and interpretation. Because it incorporates a non-college control group matched to a college attending group, Pascarella's (1989) study serves as a touchstone for examining college effects on critical thinking during the first year of college. However, because descriptive data about colleges in the study are lacking, it is not possible to use these results to assess the developmental potential of a particular institutional type.

In an earlier study seeking to trace influences of institutional type, Nichols (1964) compares the effects of precollege characteristics and college type on Graduate Record Examination (GRE) verbal (V) and quantitative (Q) scores. The subjects were National Merit Finalists who graduated from college on-time, four years after high school graduation. Precollege characteristics include gender, Scholastic Aptitude Test (SAT) score, high school rank, high school class size, percent of high school class attending college, student organizational office held in high school, fathers' education, mothers' education, fathers' occupational status, mean scores on GRE subtests and total score for career choice group, career choice, and teacher ratings.[4] College type included northeastern men's colleges, technical institutes, state

---

[4]There were five initial career categories entered into the multiple regression equations. Teaching, scientific research, and engineering also were included as dichotomized variables in the analyses because they were most common major choices for the sample. Professions (medicine, dentistry, law, etc.) and the "all other" category were not dichotomized.

universities, women's colleges, high budget coed liberal arts colleges, low budget coed liberal arts colleges, private universities, and other (Notre Dame, Rice, and Marquette). Community colleges were not included.

By calculating partial correlations among independent variables, Nichols found that GRE score differs significantly with college type. He reports that technical colleges and state universities tended to increase predicted Q scores compared with predicted V scores and that northeastern men's colleges increased predicted V scores compared with the predicted Q score. The two major fields with the most influence on GRE performance were engineering, which increased predicted Q scores and decreased predicted V scores, and English, which produced an opposite effect. Correcting for the influence of major on GRE scores reduced the effect of college type but did not change its statistically significant effect. Faculty-to-student ratio, library books per student, the average ability levels of students, and college affluence were unrelated to GRE scores. Nichols concludes that colleges direct student abilities into verbal or qualitative channels rather than affecting overall levels of ability.

Individual student interactions within institutions may exert more influence on student learning outcomes than any total effect ascribed to a particular institution. Franklin (1995), for example, studied perceptions of learning and cognitive development held by 4-year college alumni. Student precollege traits, quality of student effort, and interactions with faculty and peers were more powerful predictors of perceptions of cognitive development and influences on learning than either institutional characteristics or institutional environment. Drawing data from the Cooperative Institutional Research Program (CIRP) initial and follow-up surveys of 2,165 students at 4-year institutions, Franklin tested Pascarella's (1985) general causal model for assessing the effects of college environments on student learning and cognitive development.

Structural and organizational characteristics were posed as a three-variable set consisting of institutional control, institutional type (4-year college or university), and institutional selectivity (selective or nonselective). This variable set was exogenous, or occurring outside the model, and was not posited to have a direct effect on student perceptions of cognitive development and influences on learning. Institutional environment was operationalized from 20 items in the CIRP that captured student perceptions about the social and academic press of an institution and was posited to exert direct effects on quality of student effort and only indirect effects on perceived academic learning and student perceptions of cognitive development.

Variables exerting the largest total effect on student perceptions of learning in Franklin's study, as measured by self-reported college GPA, were high school GPA, quality of student effort, interactions with faculty, Scholastic Aptitude Test (SAT) score, and predicted success. Variables exerting the largest total effect on perceived cognitive development were interactions with peers, quality of student effort, predicted success, interactions with faculty, and SAT score. Franklin's analyses highlight the shortcomings of using multiple regression-based path analysis to decompose structural models. Lacking are measures of model fit and corresponding efforts to improve the fit of the model to these data.

*Commuter Institutions*

Reports that institutional characteristics and environments have only modest influence on student perceptions of learning and cognitive development in 4-year institutions probably do not bode well for community colleges if one accepts the proposition that residential living environments which are most often found in his sector promote closer ties to the campus and provide multiple opportunities for student learning and cognitive development to occur. The 1986 Postsecondary Student Aid Study found that less than 2 percent of public 2-year college students live in school-owned housing (NCES, 1989). Comparable percentages for public doctoral-granting institutions are 30 percent and nearly 47 percent for private doctoral universities (Choy and Gifford, 1990). It would appear, therefore, that the learning gains that might accrue in residential living environments are not a potent factor at the community college. Nonetheless, at those community college campuses with residential facilities, chiefly rural colleges, this effect should be evident in the same way as at residential 4-year institutions.

One quite recent study deals directly with commuter students and student learning, although not in a community college setting. Terenzini, Springer, Pascarella, and Nora (1995b) analyzed the factors that influence learning, cognitive development, and orientations toward college and their effect on critical thinking skills development for freshmen at an urban, commuter university. It was not surprising that precollege initial critical thinking ability was the most significant predictor of critical thinking ability measured at conclusion the first academic year. Using OLS regression, the authors estimated the effect on critical thinking with precollege critical thinking ability included and excluded in separate equations. Terenzini et al. report college experiences explained between 7 percent (with precollege critical thinking included) and 17 percent (with precollege critical thinking excluded) of the variance. The unique variance attributable to out-of-class experiences was higher than class-related experiences, a suggestion at odds with the conventional wisdom about commuter institutions' ability to exert learning influences beyond the classroom. In a finding which must be disconcerting to those who advance the efficacy of academic and social integration as predictors of student success, the authors state that students who characterized their relationships with peers as "friendly, supportive, (or) a sense of belonging" were less likely to show gains in critical thinking ability than were students who characterized their peer relationships as "competitive, uninvolved...alienated." This study considered the number of undergraduate courses taken as a critical thinking predictor but did not examine course-taking patterns.

*Community Colleges*

The ability of the community college as a unique institution in influencing student learning can be approached from the perspectives of faculty and administrators employed there. Smart and Hamm (1993a) trace four dominant organizational culture types at 2-year colleges and their relationship with nine measures of institutional effectiveness as first proposed by Cameron (1978). Among other effectiveness measures, they report that those colleges with a dominant adhocracy culture have significantly higher adjusted means on administrator and faculty perceptions of student educational satisfaction, student academic development, student career and personal development, professional development and quality of the faculty, system openness and community interaction and the ability to find resources. Adhocracy cultures emphasize entrepreneurship, growth, and adaptability in which leadership is seen as innovative and risk-taking.

The least effective environment in promoting student educational satisfaction and student academic development was the hierarchical culture. Lowest in effectiveness for reported student career development was the clan culture. Hierarchical cultures are marked by norms and values associated with the bureaucracy and are dependent on stated roles and enforced through rules and regulations. A clan structure emphasizes shared goals and values in which internal transactions are guided by tradition, beliefs, and trust. The proportions of adhocracy, hierarchical, and clan cultures are unknown in American community colleges, but these labels can be helpful in describing learning environments.

Smart and Hamm (1993b) also relate the mission orientation of community colleges to Cameron's (1978) measures of institutional effectiveness. They report those community colleges that operate under tripartite missions, that is, transfer and college parallel programs, technical and career programs, and adult and continuing programs were the most effective according to Cameron's scheme. Those colleges that reflect a singular mission, chiefly technical and career programs, were second most effective. Least effective were those colleges with dual missions. Administrators and faculty at tripartite mission institutions rated student academic development and student personal development most effective in their institutions. As might be anticipated, those institutions with single purpose career and technical programs perceived themselves as most effective in student career development.

Smart and Hamm (1993a, 1993b) were only able to estimate the learning environment through surveys of teachers and administrators. A closer look at community college environments and their influence on student learning would include direct measures of student learning and their perceptions of the learning environment. Although this challenge awaits, we might begin to approximate its eventual results by reference to existing research which ties student persistence to academic integration at the community college. Bers and Smith (1991) analyzed a sample of the entire population of a suburban community college to examine academic and social integration effects on student persistence. Using discriminant analysis, a general non-theory based statistical technique, the authors found significant differences between persisters and nonpersisters as measured by academic and social integration. Social integration made a larger contribution to group discrimination than academic integration. For purposes of this review, however, it is significant to note that intent to re-enroll, educational objective at entry, and employment status were more efficient discriminators. This is consistent with previous research on nontraditional students (Bean and Metzner, 1986: Voorhees, 1987) which suggests that prematriculation and student environmental effects exert a direct, or unmediated, effect on student persistence.

Establishing direct effects for prematriculation characteristics, of course, calls into question the general influence that the community college might exert on students and their experiences. Yet, the level of student engagement within an individual community college would seem to produce significant associations with student learning. Bers and Smith report high levels of association between academic and intellectual development and interactions with faculty, suggesting that community college students may rely on faculty to an extent greater than previously thought (see, for example, Voorhees, 1987). Underscoring the difficulty in obtaining self-reported student data at a community college, only 37 percent of the 1,142 students in the initial study group provided social security numbers, thereby excluding a significant portion of the enrolled student population from the study sample.

It appears almost obvious that different levels of student engagement within an institution might produce different levels of student learning. Little is known, however, about student engagement across institutional type. Baird (1990) compares student college activity across five institutional types, doctoral granting universities, comprehensive colleges and universities, selective liberal arts colleges, general liberal arts colleges, and community colleges. Institutions in the sample numbered 42, including 13 community colleges. Using the results from College Student Experiences Questionnaire (CSEQ) (Pace, 1984) follow-up administrations in a national, multi-institutional sample consisting of sophomores, juniors, and seniors, Baird reports that the most frequently occurring activities are course learning, writing, student acquaintances, personal experiences, and student union activities. Least frequent activities were art, music, and theater, library usage, science or technology, clubs and organizations, and athletics and recreation. In comparing institutional type, Baird reports community college students, while generally the least involved in many out-of-class activities, were more likely to be involved than their counterparts at other institutions in library usage and writing. Moreover, community college students were approximately equal to other students in self-reported estimates of learning and interactions with faculty. Baird reports that students reported academic experiences commensurate with other institutions in the study.

*4-year Institutions Versus Community College Learning Outcomes*

Direct institutional comparisons of student learning and cognitive development have only recently surfaced in the literature. These studies contrast outcomes between 4-year institutions and community colleges and promise to be pivotal in the learning debate. Bohr et al. (1994) compare reading comprehension, mathematics, and critical thinking skills of students attending a community college and those attending a 4-year university, both located in metropolitan areas. To control for the effects of place of residence in the freshman year, residential students were excluded from the 4-year sample. The College Assessment of Academic Proficiency (CAAP) developed by ACT was administered during their first semester of attendance to freshmen who were enrolled for six (6) or more credit hours. An alternate form of the CAAP was administered in the spring of the same academic year. To control for those gains that were artifacts of initial ability, Bohr et al. statistically equated all students on initial CAAP scores. Age, total credit hours enrolled in both semesters of the freshman year, and the total number of hours of employment also were entered as covariates. Age was thought to influence the amount of cognitive change that might occur due to maturation. Total credit hours were thought to influence the total exposure to formal academic programs and hours of employment were thought to affect students' level of involvement and commitment to studying and academic tasks. The resulting mean adjusted gain scores for students from both types of institutions showed no significant differences between sectors. Each subject had to volunteer to participate in the study and completed the freshman year, two factors that might contribute to self-selection bias which, in combination with a narrow, two-institution study, limits generalizability.

By widening the number of 4-year and 2-year institutions selected for study, Pascarella et al. (1995) sought to extend the generalizability of the Bohr et al. (1994) findings. Their study included eighteen 4-year and five 2-year colleges from throughout the nation. Institutions were selected to be representative of institutional type and control. The population of students attending the resulting sample of schools approximated the national student population in ethnicity and gender. Because of the diversity of institutions in the study, Pascarella et al. excluded those 4-year institutions whose student precollege academic preparation characteristics were not consonant with the 2-year colleges in the study. The result was that six 4-year institutions were matched with the five 2-year institutions. A more sweeping set of controls was tested than in the Bohr et al. (1994) analyses by adding ethnicity, family social origin, academic motivation, on- or off-campus residence, and level of academic aptitude of the freshman class as measured by the average precollege CAAP scores at each of the eleven institutions to sex, age, and employment status. Cross product terms testing for interactions with institutional type were entered into the main effect regression model to test for conditional effects. This yielded two conditional effects for race and gender. At community college level, non-White students appeared to derive the more cognitive benefit in reading, mathematics, and critical thinking than White students. Pascarella et al. report that females appear to benefit more in reading, critical thinking, and composite achievement from attending a 4-year college.

## Faculty and Curricula

In the community college, the instructor's major role is teaching. In the past, it was not unusual for community college instructors to have had teaching experience at the secondary school level and therefore, at least some exposure to the importance of the study of teaching. Because of the oversupply of Ph.D. graduates in some fields during recent years, more community college instructors have earned doctorates and, like their 4-year college and university colleagues, probably have had little opportunity during their academic training to systematically probe the effects of their behavior on students.

In a study of intellectual functioning in college classrooms, Fisher and Grant (1983) found that class size made a significant difference in the information-processing skills applied by instructors. In larger classes, the lower levels of Bloom's taxonomy, that is, recall skills, are most often applied. In medium-sized classes, those with 16 to 45 students, instructors employ the lower three cognitive levels least often. Fisher and Grant also found that class size was related to students' opportunity to apply a variety of cognitive skills. Students in classes of fifteen or fewer made significantly greater use of higher-order thinking processes— analysis, synthesis, and evaluation—than students in large classes. In Fisher and Grant's study, institutional size was also significantly related to cognitive development. Students attending small institutions made most frequent use of the lowest cognitive levels, while those attending large institutions performed most often at the third level, interpretation. Teaching style also was related to students' cognitive functioning. Under direct teaching, student discourse decreased and students became less likely to use a fuller range of cognitive levels.

Wilson, Gaff, Dienst, Wood, and Bavry (1975) report that while community college faculty undoubtedly share educational goals with their counterparts at universities, it appears that the methods by which they attempt to reach these goals are moderated by the influence of their colleagues. Wilson et al. found that university faculty are likely to adopt lectures and note taking as teaching practices. Community college faculty, on the other hand, are student-centered and more willing to individualize their teaching. Teaching behavior also may be shaped by teacher perception of students taught. Reciprocally, academic motivation of students may be expected to shape the kinds of teaching strategies employed. For example, community college faculty see themselves in a position where they must motivate students to learn (Wilson et al., 1975). In contrast, university faculty view their students as challenged by subject matter. Because community college faculty are more likely to agree that their students need motivation, Wilson et al. speculate they also are more likely to endorse a need for pedagogy and to believe that prospective faculty should receive training in teaching skills. University faculty, on the other hand, show the least interest in pedagogy.

Students also have preferences for faculty teaching styles. Emanuel and Potter (1992) analyzed differences in student preferences in learning styles and faculty communication styles between high school students and upper division college students. Both groups were selected from single institutions and examined for preferences among dependent, collaborative, participative, competitive, and independent styles. Emanuel and Potter report that college students exhibit a wider range of preferences for faculty communication styles than high school students but that preferences for collaborative learning styles diminished among college students. Females, both adolescent and college-aged, displayed preferences for participative learning styles. The authors also examine learning style preferences by student major. They report engineering students favored a dependent learning style while creative arts students rated it lowest. Conversely, engineering students rated participative and competitive styles lowest while creative arts students rated them highest. Faculty communication style preferences also varied by major. Social science majors favored the dramatic style while engineering students rated the precise faculty communication style highest. The role of maturation in these findings is not clear. However, as applied to the community college, with its older students, one might anticipate a still wider range of preferences for faculty communication styles.

General education curricula and course taking patterns have also been the focus of student learning research. Knight (1993) tested a LISREL model to determine freshmen to senior general education gains across 4-year institutions offering different patterns of general education. Based on a nationwide sample, Knight reports that students attending institutions where less than 40 percent of the curriculum consisted of general education and where the general education requirement was unevenly distributed across majors, exhibited significantly greater gains than students attending institutions with other patterns of general education. Controlling for precollege ability, Knight reports that across institutions students with the same precollege ability exhibit different levels of freshmen general education achievement. Knight accounts for this by pointing to self-selection of students into different types of institutions which accent different environments. The model used in this study represents concerted effort to more efficiently capture residual error than previous gain score research.

Adams and Fitch (1983) explore psychosocial effects of academic departments on identity and ego stage development in a sample of 294 students attending a comprehensive state university over two academic years. Student identity status was estimated during interviews using an ego-identity protocol developed by Marcia (1966). The result was categorization of students in one of four categories: (a) diffusion or absence of crisis or commitment, (b) foreclosure or absences of crisis with commitment, (c) moratorium or crisis without commitment and (d) identity achievement or previous crisis with established commitment. Ego development was assessed using a sentence completion test (Loevinger and Wessler, 1970) and resulted in placing students along a continuum comprising, in ascending order, impulsive and self-protective, conformists, conscientious, autonomous, and integrated stages. College environment was assessed from student perceptions of departmental or relational thrusts and from peer assessments of the university environment as captured by the College and University Environmental Scale (Pace, 1969) administered to 20 graduating seniors from each of the eight departments selected for study.

Adams and Fitch used stepwise discriminant analysis to differentiate between identity and ego stage development across academic departments. They found that different departments appear to recruit students with similar personality patterns. Academic-oriented departments draw or attract students whose identities are more developed. Those academic-oriented departments that were less practical or community-oriented attracted males committed to a specific identity (foreclosed and achieved) while academic-oriented departments which de-emphasized practical or social awareness attracted females with more committed identities. Once enrolled in these departments, efforts by faculty and fellow students in promoting societal awareness produced either stability or advancement in identity formation.

Adams and Fitch were unable to demonstrate ego stage growth attributable to departmental press, a finding which these authors suggest may result from a pervasive need among adolescents to consolidate rather than change. General adolescent press may override the influence that departments can exert over ego development. Similarly, physical and emotional separation from parents also may wield more influence than the psychosocial influence of the academic environment. Because of its single institution, single sample design, this study provides only modest evidence that the academic structure of an institution can influence students at different developmental stages in dissimilar ways. Unknown, for purposes of this work, are the impacts of nontraditional age, ethnicity, and academic ability—factors more proportionately operable in the community college—on the culture of academic departments and their ability to impart changes in ego stage and identity status. The connections between student attraction to specific departments and resultant changes in ego stage development may be a ripe field for exploration in the community college.

Kember and Gow (1994) explore teaching orientations and their effect on student approaches to learning among faculty and students at two polytechnic institutions in Hong Kong. Teaching orientations were categorized as learning facilitation and knowledge transmission. Facilitating teachers view themselves as guiding student learning, utilizing interactive classroom techniques, and possessing a caring attitude toward students. Factorially derived subscales for learning facilitation were problem solving, interactive teaching, facilitative teaching, pastoral interest, and motivator of students. Knowledge transmission teachers view knowledge of the discipline or subject as the most important requirement for an academic. In this view, teaching is a matter of presenting knowledge as clearly and accurately as possible. The primary student experience is verbatim copying of teacher-presented material. Subscales for knowledge transmission were training for specific jobs, use of media, imparting information, and subject area knowledge.

Student orientations to learning were operationalized as deep approach, surface approach, and achieving approach. According to Kember and Gow, the deep approach is typical of students who have an intrinsic interest in their subject and search for personal meaning in learning activities. Surface approach students are extrinsically motivated and reduce their work by concentrating on study tasks defined by their teachers. Achieving approach students have a motivational component characterized by organized study skills. Students were surveyed at the beginning of their departmental coursework and near its conclusion to calculate change-in-approach scores. Kember and Gow tested zero-order correlation coefficients and found that in those departments where the predominant orientation is toward knowledge transmission, students' use of deep approach was likely to decline from course beginning through its conclusion. Conversely, departments with a propensity toward learning facilitation discourage the use of surface approaches. In those departments where teachers believe that their role is to impart knowledge a corresponding suppressor effect for both deep and achieving student learning orientations was observed. Due to smaller class sizes, then, community colleges may have greater opportunities to promote deep and achieving approaches to student learning than do 4-year colleges.

*Out-of-Class Learning*

Kuh (1995) examines the connection between out-of-class experiences and student learning and development. Kuh and associates conducted interviews with 149 seniors at 12 institutions with reputations for providing rich learning opportunities beyond the classroom. Students were selected for interviews by institutional personnel who were asked to provide a group of 10 to 12 seniors who reflected a range of involvement in the campus. It was requested that no more than half of these students would be highly visible (involved in student government, newspaper, etc.). The final sample included students from underrepresented racial and ethnic groups. Two 4-year institutions, located in metropolitan areas, were asked to select older, part-time, and commuting students. In the first stage, transcripts of interviews were analyzed and eight categories of out-of-class experiences and fourteen categories of outcomes emerged. In the second stage, the fourteen outcomes were recoded into five outcome domains derived by factor analysis. These were interpersonal competence, practical competence, cognitive complexity, knowledge and academic skills, and humanitarianism. These were compared with student experience dimensions posed as antecedent to learning outcomes including leadership responsibilities, interactions with peers, academics, institutional ethos, work, faculty contacts, travel, and other experiences.

Kuh found that gains in knowledge and academic skills were most influenced by academic out-of-class experiences and faculty contact outside the classroom. Cognitive complexity was influenced by interactions with peers and academic out-of-class experiences. These findings amplify the role of out-of-class academic experiences as reinforcers for in-class learning. Kuh reports there were no differences in sex, race, or institutional type with respect to participating in out-of-class academic activities. More men than women associated their gains in cognitive complexity with faculty contact. Women, in contrast, were more likely to associate gains in cognitive complexity with peers than were men. Minority students were more likely to associate gains in cognitive complexity with faculty contact than non-minority students. Students at independent colleges were more likely to associate gains in cognitive complexity with peer interaction than their counterparts at state institutions.

## Student Characteristics

### Age

It is commonly accepted that the physiological process of aging places no limit on learning until about the age of 75 when the body begins to deteriorate (Kidd, 1973). Physiological factors influence learning before this age, certainly, but can be compensated for by assistive devices including eyeglasses and hearing aids. Speed of response also appears to diminish over the life-span, but this, too, can be overcome by controlling the pace at which information is presented. There also is general agreement that memory deficits accompany aging (Cross, 1981), but that such decrements are minor and appear related to the original purposes for which information was first memorized.

Given that age, by itself and up to at least the eighth decade, appears not to influence student learning in ways that cannot be overcome, it is interesting that few studies have incorporated it as a factor worthy of study. Schmidt (1985) sought to detect whether age or education had the greatest impact on the intellectual development of college students of traditional and nontraditional age at a large Midwestern university. Schmidt assessed reflective judgment, general vocabulary, and verbal reasoning of an academically able sample of traditional (approximately age 18) and nontraditional first year students (approximately age 21), and traditional (approximately age 21) juniors. Utilizing Analysis of Variance (ANOVA), Schmidt reports that juniors scored higher than either group of freshmen and that the nontraditional freshmen scored higher on all dependent variables than traditional freshmen. The magnitude of difference in reflective judgment scores between freshmen and juniors was attributable to higher increases for women. The average reflective judgment score of the nontraditional freshmen was less than that of the traditional freshmen and juniors, suggesting erosion in this element of cognitive development that might be associated with a lack of exposure to formal schooling in intervening years between high school and college. As applied here, Schmidt's findings would suggest that, on average, older students entering higher education for the first time by way of the community college may be at a disadvantage in cognitive skills compared to those students entering directly from secondary schools, a finding consistent with Pascarella's (1989) findings of critical thinking deficits in a non-college control group.

*Gender*

Baxter Magolda (1989) examines gender differences in approaches to learning and perspectives on learning. Academically able, traditional-aged freshmen women and men at a large Midwestern state university were selected for interviews and administered the Learning Style Inventory (LSI) developed by Kolb (1985) and the Measure of Epistemological Reflection (MER) developed by Taylor (1983) to assess intellectual development according to Perry's (1970) scheme.[5] No significant gender differences were found in these quantitative measures. Baxter Magolda reports qualitative differences, however. Women scored lower on authority in Position Three than men, were more prone to collect others' ideas rather than debate opinions, and placed greater emphasis on personal interpretation than did men. There was no support for the conventional proposition that women prefer concrete experiences to abstract conceptualization. Women took less initiative in learning than did men and relied more on authority in Perry's Position Two.

Bar-Haim and Wilkes (1989) examined the sciences and the roles scientists play to study cognitive skills, specifically "differentiation" and "remote association," in females who might be attracted to careers in science. Differentiation is related to the ability to recognize and formulate research problems. Low differentiators are thought to be bound by their preconceptions and view the world homogeneously. It is harder for low differentiators to accept the unanticipated as fact. Remote association is not related to differentiation, but is a measure of problem-solving skills thought to be associated with mental flexibility.

Bar-Haim and Wilkes report that remote associators see connections and devise original integrative solutions. Students low in both domains are more likely to be the "technicians" of science. Those who score high on differentiation and low on remote association are likely to be good "problem finders." Those who score high on remote association and low on differentiation are probably good "problem solvers." Students who score high on both cognitive abilities have the broadest range of abilities and will probably be good "integrators," able to find problems and to solve them. The authors characterize science

[5]See Baxter Magolda and Porterfield (1985) for a full discussion on efforts to validate the MER instrument.

as pervasively populated by low-differentiating, problem-solving men, with whom high-differentiating high remote associating women are likely to first come into conflict. Bar-Haim and Wilkes suggest that the underrepresentation of women in science fields arise from prevailing sex-role definitions that, in turn, discourage the potential women problem solvers from attempting a scientific career. They suggest that although problem-solving women are most likely to thrive on a career committed to research, they are for the same reason mostly traditional and unlikely to aspire to such a career. These findings help to illuminate the interaction between gender and student choice of major, particularly in hard sciences. They also may be used as indications that students functioning at varying cognitive levels may be attracted to certain majors, but for a variety of reasons—some of which might include socialization—may not pursue those choices.

*Minority Status*

The connections between minority status and student learning and cognitive development are not direct. Most of the literature on minority student learning and cognitive outcomes uses indirect measures of learning including persistence and degree attainment. Nora (1993), considering the community college as a focal point, concludes that irrespective of study design or statistical technique, research on minority student success generally reaches the same dismal conclusion. Minority students have not fared well over the years in persistence, degree attainment, and transfer. Nora also concludes that were it not for the community college few minority students would be enrolled in higher education. Nora's review does not particularly inform the present study because it does not examine academic learning or performance. However, his conclusions about future research agendas are of note. He observes that models of educational attainment ought not be developed specifically for minorities, but should be global in the sense they capture those influences common to minority and majority students. Global models could show how institutions influence learning for all students, thereby providing a framework for elevating the total institutional environment, an outcome that would aid minority student attainment.

Mow and Nettles (1990) in an extensive review of the literature of minority students in higher education conclude that non-Asian minority students have lower performance and persistence in college. Blacks were found to have lower retention rates, slower rates of progression, and lower grades than Whites. Hispanics have lower retention rates than Blacks, but their grades may be higher. According to Mow and Nettles, lower academic performance and progression of Black students may be explained by their average lower high school GPAs, lower scores on standardized admission tests, and lower SES. A conclusion emerging from Mow and Nettles' review is that minority status, by itself, does not explain academic performance. Surrogate measures of student learning—degree attainment and retention rates—are also unexplained by minority status. Interaction with institutional structures and peers may be more important in explaining minority student success.

In a direct study of minority student cognitive outcomes, Durham, Hays, and Martinez (1994) examine differences for matched samples of White and first-generation Chicano sophomores and juniors. Responses to essays comprising the Measure of Intellectual Development (MID) designed to locate students' position on Perry's (1970) continuum were available for both groups. For Chicano students, the Learning Environment Preference (LEP) and a questionnaire designed to elicit socioeconomic background data was administered. The MID and LEP are nationally normed instruments designed specifically to assess positions on Perry's scheme. The essays that students wrote for the MID also were used to assess holistic writing skills apart from Perry's scheme.

Chicano students were participants in a program to promote greater minority participation in graduate and professional education. As prerequisites for admission to the program, Chicano students had to possess a cumulative GPA of 2.75 or better, eligibility for financial aid, and sophomore status at a college or university. Chicano students were matched to a sample of White students on age, gender, sophomore or junior status, holistic writing scores, and Perry scheme ratings drawn from a national database. In testing for significance among zero-order correlation coefficients, Durham et al. report a series of complex interactions for Anglo students but merely one significant association for Chicano students between the holistic score on the essay and position on Perry's scale. The authors conclude that Chicano student intellectual performance is independent of their experiences within the college's academic structure. Durham et al. suggest that different sociocultural support networks are at work for Chicano and Anglo students. Chicano students receive parental encouragement to attend college from their families similar to that provided by Anglo parents, but little practical information can be imparted between generations because of lack of Chicano parental experience with college. There were seven significant zero-order correlation coefficients for the White sample, age-gender, age-academic class, age-holistic writing, gender-Perry level, academic class-holistic writing, academic class-Perry level, and Perry level-holistic writing level. These findings are of some consequence given that groups were matched on these variables, suggesting there are significant perceptual differences in how first-generation Chicano students regard their academic experiences. It is not known whether White students also were first-generation college attendees, nor was it possible to detect what other factors associated with SES might influence level of Perry functioning.

Tracey and Sedlacek (1987) in a cross-sectional study suggest that quite different processes and experiential backgrounds determine academic achievement for White and Black students attending a predominantly White, large university campus with liberal admissions policies. Examining the relationship between noncognitive attributes and academic success, they report substantial differences in the experiences of successful Black and White students. Tracey and Sedlacek estimated separate LISREL models for Black and White students in which persistence and first-semester GPA were the ultimate dependent variables. Exogenous variables were support, community service leadership, racism, self-concept, long-range goals, realistic self-appraisal, and academic ability. They found that academic ability, as measured by SAT scores, had a significant direct effect on first semester GPA for both Black and White students. However, for Black students, the only other variable positively associated with first semester GPA was support. For White students, first semester GPA was affected by self-concept. First semester GPA was related to subsequent persistence for the White sample, but unrelated for the Black sample.

The structural model presented in Tracey and Sedlacek's study did not pose institutional experience variables as intervening between the noncognitive predictors and GPA or persistence. Thus, in the jargon of path analysis the model as posited by Tracey and Sedlacek is "just identified," meaning that it will reproduce the correlation matrix exactly. This situation occurs when it is thought no theoretical structure underlies the relationships depicted by the model. Absent trimming the model by constraining parameters, the possibility exists that factors and relationships for factors which might explain minority academic achievement are not fully explored.

In a study of academic dismissal and satisfactory progress with two cohorts of first-time students conducted at a state university, Ott (1988) found a negative relationship between high school GPA and probability of academic dismissal. SAT scores were not a consistent predictor of academic dismissal. After controlling for student ability and precollege achievement, Ott reports that race and undergraduate choice of college within the university structure were statistically significant predictors of academic performance. These results suggest that freshmen with the same high school GPAs and equal SAT scores were more likely to encounter academic failure if they were minority or enrolled in curricula that had more math and science requirements. Ott found no predictive power for sex, on-campus residence, or attendance status. This study used only several variables and presupposed no causal relationships among predictor variables. Although the choice of technique, logistic regression, appears appropriate given the categorical nature of the data, the complex interplay between race and choice of program of study was not captured and is an area ripe for further study.

In a study of the connections between planned transfer behavior and choice of curricula Nora and Rendon (1990) sampled Hispanic and White community college students in class sections thought to enroll students with transfer intentions. Nora and Rendon hoped to detect which student characteristics were associated with predispositions to transfer. Using LISREL, the authors found that academic integration, a multiple indicator variable composed of academic perceptions, transfer perceptions, participation in academic and career counseling, and participation in the institution's academic life, exerted the largest total effect on predispositions to transfer. Level of initial institutional commitment was positively related to levels of academic integration irrespective of ethnicity. Controlling for the influence of all variables in the model, Nora and Rendon report that ethnicity was not statistically related to predisposition to transfer.

Using another structural equation model, Nora and Horvath (1990) reported significant variation in course-taking patterns of White and Hispanic male and females in six 2-year institutions in the Southwest. The model specified by the authors traced high school grades, encouragement by others, parent's education, attitudes toward math and science, and high school preparation on enrollment patterns in community college math and science classes. Whereas Nora and Horvath's model fits the data well for females, it inexplicably failed to capture any variance in course-taking patterns for males. White female students who did well in high school were more likely to enroll in community college math and science classes than were Hispanic females. Mathematics and science courses generate outcomes linked closely with the development of critical thinking skills (Bar-Haim and Wilkes, 1989; Winter and McClelland, 1978). Consequently, Nora and Horvath's findings assume importance for future studies of community college course-taking behavior and gains in critical thinking skills for both minority and non-minority students.

*Student employment*
Pascarella, Bohr, Nora, Desler, and Zusman (1994) examine the effect of on-campus and off-campus work on first-year cognitive outcomes for 210 first-year students enrolled at an urban research university. They report no significant differences between students working either on- or off-campus and those students who did not work in student learning and cognitive development outcomes as measured by the CAAP in mathematics, reading comprehension, and critical thinking. Covariates were initial CAAP scores, initial student motivation, student ages, total credit hours taken during both semesters of enrollment, and on-campus residence. Gender was not posed as a covariate. During a second stage of the analysis, quadratic terms were entered into equations predicting reading comprehension, mathematics, and critical thinking. Hours worked per week on-campus and hours worked per week off-campus were squared and entered within the regression equation to estimate whether the relationship between these variables and cognitive outcomes was curvilinear. Only the quadratic term for hours worked per week on campus was significant in increasing the $R^2$ for reading comprehension. A flat relationship for reading comprehension existed at the 10-hour level for on-campus work, but a negative relationship was detected when employment hours increased beyond 10. To illuminate further the connection between employment and cognitive growth, the authors entered study time in the quadratic and linear equations. Although a significant, negative relationship between hours worked off-campus and time studying was found, they found no corresponding significant changes in cognitive growth.

## Commuting

Pascarella, Bohr, Nora, Zusman, Inman, and Desler (1993) examine gains in reading comprehension, mathematics, and critical thinking skills— as measured by the CAAP—between commuter freshmen and freshmen living on-campus. Controlling for precollege cognitive level, academic motivation, age, work responsibilities, and the number of freshmen-year credit hours took, significant gains in critical thinking during the freshman year were found. Gains in critical thinking between commuter and residential students were in the same positive direction, but between group differences were statistically insignificant. The authors suggest that unlike gains in mathematics and reading comprehension that occur by exposure to specific parts of the college curricula, gains in critical thinking are, perhaps, supplemented by the residential living experience. This study is limited by the single institution sample, but provides support for the effects of residential living on the development of critical thinking skills.

## Identity

Buczynski (1991) examined the connections between student identity and intellectual development with a sample of freshman students enrolled at a midsized comprehensive university. She used two instruments to measure student identity, the Erwin Identity Scale and the Scale of Intellectual Development (SID). The SID is based on Perry's (1970) scheme, Buczynski reports that identity at the beginning of a student's freshman year has a direct influence on intellectual development at the end of the sophomore year. Those students with a less developed sense of identity appear to develop intellectual skills to a lesser extent than those with strong initial identity. Buczynski speculates that those students with a strong identity are less anxious in an academic setting and participate more fully in classroom discussions and are more likely to seek out instructors for assistance outside class.

## Satisfaction

Pike (1991a) tested a model of academic achievement and satisfaction for senior students enrolled in a public research university. Pike reports that academic satisfaction exerts a positive direct effect on academic performance, but that academic performance does not significantly affect academic satisfaction. This finding implying a nonreciprocal relationship between performance and satisfaction may suggest that satisfaction should be a causally antecedent factor used to predict academic performance, at least for the upperclass students enrolled at this setting.

Pike (1991b) examines self reports of learning development by seniors and alumni from a single institution and its relationship to satisfaction. Pike utilized two structural equation models to find out whether perceptions of learning were associated with general institutional satisfaction, that is, the "halo" effect. Pike's results were equivocal indicating that although the halo effect model did not fit the data better than the non-halo model, there was insufficient evidence to dismiss the halo effect. Pike argues that satisfaction with the institution may be inseparable from satisfaction with perceived learning outcomes.

*Cognitive Complexity*

Winter and McClelland (1978) investigated undergraduate ability to form complex concepts that discriminate between abstract data and an ability to express these concepts or put them into clear language. The authors developed the Test of Thematic Analysis (TTA) to gauge the effect of college on the ability to form concepts. This instrument asks subjects to generate and articulate complex concepts in response to several stories that do not involve any specialized knowledge or experience by the subject. The TTA was administered to students at a prestigious liberal arts college, a 4-year state supported institution with a career focus, and a community college. The community college was described as serving students who were similar to the 4-year state institution, but with a more pronounced liberal arts orientation. Winter and McClelland report statistically significant differences in mean scores between freshmen and seniors at the selective liberal arts institution, slight but nonsignificant gains at the 4-year institution, and no differences between freshmen and sophomores at the community college. Sample sizes at the 4-year institution (68) and community college (n=64) were less than one-quarter the selective liberal arts sample (221) and may be a factor in determining differences. No controls were made for student age nor student attrition. Winter and McClelland report that certain majors—mathematics, physics, and engineering—were responsible at the selective liberal arts institution for gains in thematic scores net of maturation or self-selection bias. Winter and McClelland did not use the same subjects in a classic pretest post-test paradigm. Thus, their findings represent only modest estimates on which potentially confounding influences are uncontrolled.

*Self-concept and Adjustment*

Livengood (1992) in a study of traditional-aged freshmen education and human development majors at a selective private university reports that students with low confidence in their abilities are performance-goal oriented. That is, they take on activities that are performance-oriented, rather than learning-oriented, to validate their abilities. Confident students, on the other hand, sought out opportunities to learn and activities in which their competence would be developed, even at risk of earning lower grades. This could suggest that low-confidence students at the community college would benefit from a supportive learning environment that rewarded day-to-day performance while seeking to expand opportunities for students to become learner-directed.

Kanoy, Wester, and Latta (1989) predict female freshman students' second term GPA from traditional predictors, in particular the SAT and high school GPA, and nontraditional predictors including locus of control and self-concept. The sample consisted of 70 volunteer students at a 2-year liberal arts college with an emphasis on transfer to 4-year institutions. Students were segregated in two groups, based on their GPAs as predicted from traditional measures. Students were given an assessment of internal versus external locus of control, based on Perry's (1970) scheme, and a scale to detect their academic self-concepts. Not surprisingly, traditional measures accounted for 50 percent of the variance in second semester GPA for those students predicted to be high achieving. Traditional measures, however, failed to predict GPA for the lower-performing group. Stepwise multiple regression was used to estimate the effect of internality, cognitive complexity, and academic self-concept. These variables were added to the model along with significant variables from the first regressions. Only two predictors were significant for the higher achieving group, high school GPA and academic self-concept. For low-performing students, Kanoy et al. report that self-concept was negatively related to self-reported prospects for achievement but positively related to academic effort. Kanoy et al. suggest that the negative relationship between perceived achievement success and second semester GPA can be accounted for by students' locus of control. The more internal the student, the more likely they are to take more responsibility for their academic experiences and to do better in the classroom.

Brooks and DuBois (1995) use several measures to assess student adjustment to college, including academic, social, personal/emotional, and total adjustment. The sample was traditional-aged, academically able freshmen attending a Midwestern university on a full-time basis. Only two minority students were included in a sample of 56. Questionnaire data were collected during the subjects' second semester of attendance. Older students in the sample reported lower anticipated grades and lower anticipated adjustment. The mean age of the sample (18.7) and a tight standard deviation (.95) suggest that even small differences in age can produce doubts about successful transitions to higher education. ACT score was positively associated with anticipated GPA and a standardized measure of adjustment, but negatively associated with psychological symptoms. A measure of emotional stability was negatively associated with manifestations of psychological symptoms and positively with personal/emotional and total adjustment. Similarly, a factorially derived measure of intellect also was positively associated with total adjustment and negatively associated with psychological symptoms. A low self-rating on problem-solving skills, the only variable having a significant relationship with academic adjustment was negatively correlated with academic adjustment. Hierarchical stepwise regression analyses indicate that while ACT scores account for a .21 increase in R2 predicting anticipated grades, student satisfaction and social support also produced significant positive changes in R2. Given the restricted age ranges and cross-sectional design of this study, Brooks and DuBois' findings provide modest indication that students' anticipated grades and self-reported academic adjustment can be related to age.

## Quality of Effort and Motivation
Terenzini, Springer, Pascarella, and Nora (1995a) analyze two concepts intrinsically related to student learning motivation—interest in academic learning and

intrinsic value of learning—in a single institution longitudinal panel study conducted with new students at a 4-year urban commuter university. Interest in academic learning may be conceived as students' perceptions of the utilitarian benefit of their academic progress. Intrinsic value of learning, in contrast, can be linked to "learning for learning's own sake." Using a path analytic, hierarchical regression approach, Terenzini et al. examined the effect of antecedent variable sets including precollege characteristics, types of courses enrolled (technical and preprofessional or sciences), class-related experiences, and out-of-class experiences on interest in academic learning and intrinsic value of learning. The CAAP was administered at the beginning and conclusion of one academic year to provide estimates of students' gain in reading, mathematics, writing, science reasoning, and critical thinking. A questionnaire designed to capture student perceptions about orientations toward learning was part of both administrations. Terenzini et al. partitioned the variance attributable to the college experience variable set and calculated the influence of each set on interest in academic learning and intrinsic value of learning in two ways.

In the first iteration, student precollege orientation to learning was included in the precollege characteristics variable set. In the second iteration, precollege orientation to learning was excluded. While both the "in" and "out" models explained significant variance in interest in academic learning and intrinsic value of learning, predictably, the "in" model explained more. The precollege characteristics variable set only reached significance in both equations when orientations to learning were included. In estimating statistical significance, course learning experiences and hours spent studying were positively related to interest in academic learning while hours spent socializing with friends was negatively associated. The most potent predictor—by a factor of more than two—was course learning, the extent of involvement in total class activities. None of these variables, on the other hand, were significant predictors of intrinsic value of learning. Within the class related experiences variable set, students' contact with faculty members made the largest positive contribution to both "in" and "out" equations while library usage, inexplicably, made a negative contribution.

As anticipated from the literature of student involvement (Astin, 1984) and quality of effort (Pace, 1984), participation in art, music, and theater and the number of unassigned books read exerted a significantly positive effect on intrinsic value of learning. The item factor loadings for the interest in academic learning and intrinsic value of learning factors are quite modest (±.40 to ±.63) and were concomitant with low reliability statistics (.67 and .56, respectively). There also were no estimates of direct or indirect effects for independent variables on learning outcomes, nor did the path analytic techniques permit an estimate of the fit of the data to the model. Nonetheless, this study does suggest that post-enrollment experiences in an urban 4-year commuter institution have greater effects than precollege personal and academic characteristics when precollege orientation to learning is considered. However, whether the range of precollege personal and academic characteristics was restricted within the sample is unknown. The result is that extrapolation of these findings to the community college where open admissions policies produce a more heterogeneous range of student characteristics— including learning orientations—becomes problematic.

Ames and Ames (1989) underscore the role that learning styles and culture play in student motivation. They hypothesize that student learning styles may be the primary psychological variable through which culture exerts influence on student learning. Since culture and learning styles both may be characterized as ordering and regulating perception, their role cannot be overlooked in explaining student motivation. Potential learning styles cited by Ames and Ames were taken from Entwhistle (1981) and include: meaning-oriented, reproduction-oriented, and achievement-oriented. If motivation and learning styles are interwoven, they can explain, in part, why certain types of students choose, or are motivated, to pursue learning at different rates and with different ends in mind. Similarly, the connections between cognitive structures and motivation pose intriguing questions about the learning process.

Hancock (1994) compares motivation between low conceptual level (LCL) and high conceptual level (HCL) students among 63 academically able students at the United States Military Academy. LCL learners are characterized as having relatively few cognitive structures and avoid or reduce ambiguity. HCL learners, in contrast, are more complex and are more likely to use alternative learning processes. Hancock tested the proposition that LCL learners should be matched with direct-instruction treatment and HCL learners matched with nondirect instruction. Hancock reports no statistical differences between the HCL and LCL groups with respect to motivation to learn course content, perhaps as a result of the homogeneity of the population, including self-selection factors which almost certainly accompany entrance into a military academy. Motivation also might be affected by the socializing effect inherent in military education. No significant differences in motivation to learn course material were reported for students taught using direct instruction methods versus those taught using nondirect methods. He did, however, find a significant interaction between instructional method and conceptual level; the motivation to learn course content was maximized for the LCL students exposed to direct instructional methods. The opposite was true for HCL learners. Although Hancock's findings are limited by its cross-sectional design and homogeneous sample, it does present the basis for examining closely the connections between student motivation and instructional type.

According to Erekson (1992), only the quality of effort exerted by students in faculty interaction produces a significant effect on student achievement. After estimating a model predicting grade-point averages at the end of the first semester of university study by testing effects of student effort, library effort, course learning, and contact with faculty he suggests that only a limited number of factors can be linked to student achievement. The mere presence of quality libraries, faculty, or classroom learning opportunities does not ensure student achievement. He cautions that the quality of student effort in producing significant positive effects on academic achievement by way of faculty interaction should not be license for faculty to expect students to seek them out in a oneway relationship. Rather, faculty interaction may be a proxy for student interest in subject matter, student adjustment to grading practices, or student efforts to curry faculty favor.

From estimates of a path analytic model developed to explore both academic and personal-social gains of freshmen university students, Kaufman and Creamer (1991) report degree aspiration level has a significant but indirect effect on intellectual gains in a sample of university freshmen. Students were administered a locally developed questionnaire that captured their perceptions of important goals in college and the CSEQ (Pace, 1984). The authors report a response rate of 32.5%. Degree aspiration and major certainty were posited in this model as causally antecedent to academic experiences; neither variable was depicted as influencing intellectual gains. Females in the sample were significantly more likely to report higher intellectual gains and personal growth. Although gender yielded significant effects in both variables, its effect was indirect. Because the model was decomposed with OLS, no statistics are available that would indicate whether the model fit the data.

## RECOMMENDATIONS FOR NEEDED RESEARCH

Since community colleges are organizations unlike 4-year institutions, if only because of the wider range of student characteristics one finds, development of a new model of student learning and cognitive development seems propitious. Such a model would capture more fully not just the characteristics students bring with them to the institution, but also their experiences both inside and outside the institution after matriculation. Figure 1 presents a general causal model of the antecedents of student learning and cognitive development that might be worthy of estimating in a community college environment. This model draws upon the work of Pascarella (1985) who suggested structural modeling as a technique for disentangling the complex relationships that influence student learning and cognitive development. Also tapped was Bean and Metzner's (1985) model of student persistence because it suggests that nontraditional student background characteristics exert direct effects on outcomes independent of, or unmediated by, the college environment. Franklin's (1995) findings that structural and organizational characteristics lack influence on learning and cognitive development also informs this model. That is, Franklin suggests that these variables ought to be deleted in pursuit of a more parsimonious model. Given that the present model calls for estimations of student learning and cognitive development by commu-

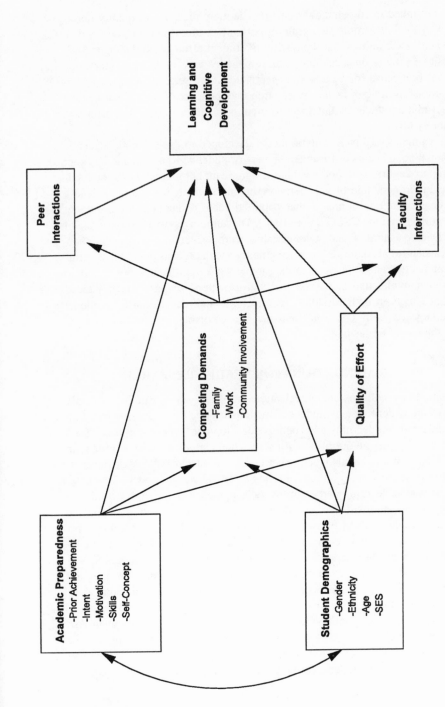

FIGURE 1. A Model for Assessing Community College Student Learning and Cognitive Development

nity college students, omitting institutional characteristics seems appropriate. However, there exists some evidence that community college cultures are divergent with respect to administrator and faculty opinions about effectiveness as operationalized by student learning opportunities (Smart and Hamm, 1993a, 1993b). For this reason, the proposed model is perhaps best estimated for a single institution or a set of institutions similar in learning orientations.

The model presented here also incorporates chief elements from a model of adult participation in education proposed by Cross (1981). The Cross model views opportunities and barriers to participating in education as mediating between an adult's perceptions of goal importance and expectations that participation will satisfy those goals. Cross' model also accentuates the role of age-linked life transitions as exerting direct influence on perceptions of educational value. The key to Cross' model is individual motivation to participate, a concept which is entwined with self-concept and accurate self-evaluation. The chief contribution of Cross' model to the present model is acknowledgment that older students perceive the learning environment as one possibility among competing and perhaps equally compelling opportunities.

This model depicts student learning and cognitive development in the community college as a function of the direct and indirect influences of six major blocks of variables. Student experiences within and outside the community college environment are seen as influenced by academic preparedness (academic skills, intent, motivation, and prior achievement) and student demographics (age, ethnicity, gender, and socioeconomic status). These exogenous variables influence students' competing demands (work, family and community) and quality of student effort. In turn, competing demands and quality of student effort are depicted as influencing peer and faculty interactions. Peer interactions are influenced directly by the press of competing demands and indirectly through competing demands by academic preparedness and student demographics. Faculty interactions are influenced directly by competing demands and quality of student effort and indirectly through competing demands by student demographics and academic preparedness. Ultimately, learning and cognitive development are directly influenced by academic preparedness, student demographics, quality of student effort, competing demands, peer interactions, and faculty interactions.

The use of competing demands as an indicator of the press which community college students encounter sets this model apart from other proposed models of student learning and cognitive development. Competing demands is the conceptual counterweight to the academic and social structures that have received wide currency in the literature as key conceptual components within 4-year institutions to explain student integration. These structures, however, have shown only weak potency in explaining community college student success (Voorhees, 1987). While competing demands is a structure that operates outside the community college environment, it is hypothesized to affect all students through its impact on student behavior within, and attitude toward, the community college environment and subsequent effects on student learning and cognitive development. Within the milieu of the community college competing demands may represent a cultural norm in which beliefs and attitudes about work, community involvement, and family assume an institutional dimension.[6]

**TABLE 1. Direct Effects Predicted Among the Variables Comprising the Model of Community College Student Learning and Cognitive Development**

|  | Quality of Student Effort | Competing Demands | Peer Inter-actions | Faculty Inter-actions | Learning and Cognitive Develop-ment |
|---|---|---|---|---|---|
| **Academic Preparedness** |  |  |  |  |  |
| Academic skills | ? | + | n/a | n/a | + |
| Intent | + | + | n/a | n/a | + |
| Motivation | + | + | n/a | n/a | + |
| Prior achievement | + | + | n/a | n/a | + |
| **Student Demographics** |  |  |  |  |  |
| Age | + | + | n/a | n/a | + |
| Ethnicity | ? | ? | n/a | n/a | ? |
| Gender | ? | ? | n/a | n/a | ? |
| SES | + | ? | n/a | n/a | + |
| **Quality of Student Effort** | n/a | n/a | n/a | + | + |
| **Competing Demands** |  |  |  |  |  |
| Community involvement | n/a | n/a | − | − | ? |
| Family | n/a | n/a | − | − | ? |
| Work | n/a | n/a | − | − | ? |
| **Peer Interactions** | n/a | n/a | n/a | n/a | ? |
| **Faculty Interactions** | n/a | n/a | n/a | n/a | + |

[6]See Baird (1988) for an excellent discussion on the transmission of interpersonal environmental effects by institutional type.

Table 1 displays the predicted relationships for the six variable blocks and their ultimate relationships with student learning and cognitive development. Where possible these predictions have been informed by the literature reviewed in this work. Where the literature is not helpful, question marks appear. Testing of the model with community college students will help in defining its parameters and suggesting where it might be improved.

As Table 1 indicates, the relationships between the individual variables comprising academic preparedness and quality of student effort are mixed. Clearly, intent and motivation should exert a positive effect student learning and cognitive development through a positive effect on quality of student effort (Buczynski, 1991; Kaufman and Creamer, 1991; Knight, 1993; Nora and Rendon, 1990). No irrefutable evidence exists at this juncture to predict either a positive or negative relationship between academic skills and quality of effort. It is reasonable to predict that prior achievement would affect quality of effort in the same positive way in which it should affect student learning and cognitive development (Ott, 1988).

Academic preparedness is also thought to be consonant with a level of cognitive structure that enables students to deal with the press of competing demands. In this regard, academic skills, intent, motivation, and prior achievement are thought to produce effects on competing demands and, in turn, on learning and cognitive development. Those students who are better prepared to handle academic work also should cope more effectively with community, family, and work obligations. The depiction of academic preparedness as having a direct or unmediated effect on student learning and cognitive development suggests that a positive effect for this variable set may exist despite the effect of other internal or external factors.

*Student Demographics*
The relationships for student demographics are more mixed. Although their collective effect on quality of student effort is not clear, the relationship between socioeconomic status and quality of student effort is thought to be positive. Because of advantages that accrue to students from higher SES backgrounds, including a peer culture that uniformly supports success, SES should be positively associated with quality of student effort. This prediction, however, is speculative and will only be known when the model is tested with community college students. Age is considered the only clear positive relationship predicted between student demographics and competing demands. It is thought that age, and attendant maturation, will enable students to balance their academic commitments with other social and familial roles. Similarly, age is predicted to positively influence student learning and cognitive development (Bohr et al., 1994; Brooks and DuBois, 1995; Pascarella et al., 1995). The ambiguous prediction for gender stems from contradictory findings in the literature about its direct effect on student learning and cognitive development. Bar-Haim and Wilkes' (1989) study, for

one such example, would suggest that female status interacts to a significant degree with academic achievement.

### Quality of Student Effort

This set is hypothesized as exerting direct effects on faculty interactions and the ultimate dependent variable, student learning and cognitive development. Franklin (1995), working with a sample of 4-year students, found significantly positive relationships between student learning and cognitive development and faculty interactions and the quality of student effort. Whether such results will hold for the community college environment is not now known. As a mediating variable for the effects of academic preparedness and student demographic characteristics, each of which also influence student learning and cognitive development directly, estimations of quality of student effort in a community college environment might extend the present understanding of community college student involvement (Astin, 1984).

### Competing Demands

Since most students attend the community college on a part-time basis, other agendas and obligations must consume most of their lives. This separates the community college in fundamental ways from the 4-year institution. The press of competing demands in this model is influenced by academic preparedness and student demographic characteristics and serves as a mediated effect for these variables' effect on student learning and cognitive development. Pascarella et al. (1994) found no significant differences in freshman year cognitive outcomes between students working on- and off-campus although the effect on reading comprehension appeared to flatten as hours worked increased. Family obligations within the model might also represent the wider effects of peer and subculture norms on academic behavior thought to be independent of subsequent peer influences that occur in the collegiate environment. There is some evidence to suggest that family culture plays a role in student learning and cognitive development (Durham, Hays, and Martinez, 1994: Nora and Horvath, 1990). Little is known about the press of community involvements, but the civic orientation of those students similarly inclined may also produce significant out-of-class gains in student learning and cognitive development (see, for example, Pascarella, Ethington, and Smart, 1988). Students' perception of locus of control may also influence how competing demands are addressed and their subsequent effects on student learning (Kanoy, Wester, and Latta, 1989). Since minority students are also more likely to attend the community college part-time, live at home, and work while going to college than their White counterparts (Mow and Nettles, 1990), they are more likely to have a wide range of external pressures competing for their time and energies.

Ultimately, the very process of gathering assessment information from students, or otherwise eliciting their participation in an assessment program, can be detrimentally influenced by competing demands. Burdened with jobs, family, and community responsibilities, besides pursuing their educations, community college students might rightfully resent the extra time required to participate in entry assessment. After receiving a degree or certificate, or simply completing a sequence of classes they have identified as meeting their needs, they may be even more reluctant to devote time to further testing or assessment activities.

*Peer Interactions*
This model depicts the effect of peer interactions on student learning and cognitive development ambiguously. Terenzini et al. (1995b) suggest that supportive peer interactions among students at a commuter institution may not be associated with gains in student learning and cognitive as large as those associated with peer interactions characterized as competitive or uninvolved. Franklin (1995), on the other hand, suggests that positive peer interactions are positively associated with gains in student learning. Mow and Nettles (1990) speculate that minority students at the community college would have less time available for interacting with other students, a tentative relationship captured in this model by the indirect relationship depicted between ethnicity and peer interactions as mediated by competing demands. Hanson (1994) reports that positive peer influences can ameliorate the deleterious effect of race, class, and gender on youth's educational attainment. In this model, competing demands would determine the influence of peer influences on student learning and cognitive development.

*Faculty Interactions*
Faculty interactions are thought to positively influence student learning and cognitive development. Evidence exists in the literature (Endo and Harpel, 1982; Erekson, 1992; Franklin, 1995; Hancock, 1994) that faculty interactions produce positive gains in student learning and cognitive development. The relationship depicted by the model is direct and mediates the effect of student quality of effort on the ultimate dependent variable. Minority community college students are thought to be influenced by the press of competing demands (Mow and Nettles, 1990) to the detriment of potential faculty interactions, a relationship represented by indirect effects of minority status on faculty interactions. Quality of effort is an antecedent variable which similarly mediates the influence of academic preparedness and student demographics on faculty interactions.

*Model Summary*
The causal model advanced represents a departure from previous models of student learning and cognitive development. Its differences are intended to be responsive to the community college through postulating that factors external to the institution can be as important in mediating student learning as those factors that occur inside the community college. It also is argued that competing demands influence the normative culture of the community college, creating a structure that can help explain the process of student learning in contextual terms. The proposed model also is unique in that it does not depict direct effects for aca-

demic preparedness or student demographics on either faculty interactions or peer interactions. It is submitted that, together, the influence of these prematriculation characteristics assumes meaning only through the press of competing demands and the quality of student effort. Faculty interactions are influenced by prematriculation characteristics through competing demands and through quality of student effort. The effect of prematriculation characteristics on peer interactions occurs solely through the press of competing demands. Conceptually, then, the key components of the community college's learning structure are posited as peer and faculty interactions. These factors accrue influence over student learning and cognitive development through the press of family, work, and community involvement, and through the quality of student effort.

## FINAL THOUGHTS

Attempts to understand student learning and cognitive development have only scratched the porous surface of possibilities. With several notable exceptions, the bulk of findings reviewed above is only tangentially related to the study of student learning and cognitive development at the community college. While this chapter represents an effort to tie existing research to the community college and to highlight new findings that extend the learning debate, it probably cannot overcome the inconsistencies in the previous research base. Conflicting findings have been a traditional frustration besetting attempts to unify this line of inquiry. With adequate sampling techniques, carefully posed definitions, consideration of the entire spectrum of student characteristics, and use of statistical techniques such as structural modeling, perhaps progress in this area can be ushered forward. Clearly, more careful delineation of student inputs within the learning environment at the community college is needed to advance this agenda.

Research across all sectors is hampered by a dearth of data about student learning outcomes both individually within institutions and collectively throughout higher education. Much of what we now know about student learning and cognitive development comes from studies using samples drawn from one, or perhaps several institutions. One notable exception reviewed in this chapter (Pascarella, et al., 1995) looks at student learning across a multi-institutional sample and represents the genre of research that ought to be encouraged. On a wider scale, the federal government, through the National Center for Education Statistics, has expressed an interest in advancing a national assessment of student learning (NCES, 1993). Such an effort, designed and executed across higher education, would represent a monumental accomplishment. The availability of data from a national study of student learning outcomes would provide sorely needed information that could improve practice and theory. As one might expect, commissioning of such work must await consensus on target skills and abilities to be measured and must consider the heterogeneity of American higher education.

Differences across institutions can include curricula, grading practices, faculty preparation, and types of students served.

Advancing a research agenda in student learning and cognitive development cannot operate outside political realities. Serious questions are posed by state governors and legislatures about the quality of learning. A recent report entitled "Making Quality Count in Undergraduate Education," authored by the Education Commission of the States (ECS, 1995) and representative of the views of state, regional, and national policymakers, presents a series of pointed recommendations to the higher education community. Foremost, among these are that institutions should develop and use better ways to measure and monitor institutional performance. Consensus is found in this report by the statement, "If the [higher] education process often lags behind changing expectations and knowledge, existing measurement and assessment techniques are even further behind" (ECS, 1995, p. 24). Whether this represents general contempt for research methodology or simply frustration at unavailability of information is not known. However, there is little sympathy for judging institutional quality by the number of credit hours or student majors produced, or institutional student-faculty ratios. It is clear instead that those who hold the purse strings now are interested in results from assessments of learning and competencies. While most community college educators, particularly in vocational areas, would be quick to point to the link between their curricula and competencies, few examples appear in the wider literature which might trace this important connection. Dissecting the curriculum in relation to learning outcomes represents a fundamental challenge to those in the research community and to the institutions they serve. While this opportunity is before all of higher education, the suggestions which follow are intended to sharpen the research agenda for student learning and cognitive development at the community college.

There are many unknowns about the community college which should be entertained in future research. The influence of academic departments on undergraduate learning outcomes, for example, may be worth estimating at the community college. The extent to which a departmental structure transmits learning effects at a 4-year institution may be buttressed by the availability of graduate assistants. The applicability of this "within" college effect to the community college where traditional academic departmental structures are not always present might be of interest.

The connections between learning gains in student learning and cognitive development and proportions of professional faculty would also be of considerable benefit to understanding the learning process. Contrasted in particular to research universities, where graduate teaching assistants typically are responsible for delivering instruction in lower division courses, the community college ostensibly has relied in the academic areas on faculty who have completed at least one level of graduate training (AACC, September, 1995). The differences in types of teachers across institutions has not been explored, but might serve to illuminate further research comparing student learning and cognitive outcomes.

As the nation's chief vehicle for the education of minority students the community college must bear responsibility for documentation of learning outcomes for all students. A useful research agenda here could apprehend those instances where student learning interventions might be helpful. Nora's (1993) suggestion is that models of attainment should incorporate all students so that minority student achievement is understood in context. A result would be that interventions designed for students based on general institutional attainment would be beneficial in particular to minority students. Research conducted with all students would use the contribution to learning assessment by minority students in order to ask the fundamental question posed by this chapter: What types of students change in which types of ways at which types of institutions?

Finally, there have been no studies which estimate the contribution of community colleges, by themselves, to student learning and cognitive development versus those who do not attend college. Pascarella (1989) approximates the effects of higher education on critical thinking by comparing a control group of noncollege young adults to a group who entered college. Pascarella was able to show significant gains in critical thinking for the group that attended college. Although matching samples, as was done in Pascarella's study, is probably not superior to statistical control for prematriculation characteristics, such a study awaits completion in the community college sector. Positive findings here, in tandem with recent reports that show no inter-sector differences in student learning outcomes, would help to complete a picture of the contribution of community colleges to student learning and cognitive development.

### References

Adams, G., and Fitch, S. (1983). Psychological environments of university departments: Effects on college students' identity status and ego stage development. *Journal of Personality and Social Psychology* 43: 1266-1275.

Alba, R.D., and Lavin, D.E. (1981). Community colleges and tracking in higher education. *Sociology of Education* 54: 223-237.

American Association of Community Colleges (1995). *AACC Annual: 1995-96 State-by-State Analysis of Community College Trends and Statistics.* Washington, DC: AACC.

American Association of Community Colleges (September, 1995). *AACC Research and Data.* (Research Report). Washington, DC: AACC.

Ames, C, and Ames, R. (1989). *Research on Motivation in Education: Goals and Cognitions. Volume 3.* New York: Academic Press.

Astin, A.W. (1984). Student involvement: A developmental theory for higher education. *Journal of College Student Personnel* 25: 297-308.

Baird, L.L. (1988). The college environment revisited: A review of research and theory. In J. C. Smart (ed.) *Higher Education: Handbook of Theory and Research*, Vol. 4. New York: Agathon.

Baird, L.L. (1990). The undergraduate experience: Commonalities and differences among colleges. *Research in Higher Education* 31: 271-278.

Bar-Haim, G., and Wilkes, J.M. (1989). Cognitive interpretation of the marginality and underrepresentation of women in science. *Journal of Higher Education* 60: 371-387.

Baxter Magolda, M.B. (1989). Gender differences in cognitive development: An analysis of cognitive complexity and learning styles. *Journal of College Student Development* 30: 213-220.

Baxter Magolda, M.B., and Poterfield, W. D. (1985). A new approach to assess intellectual development on the Perry scheme. *Journal of College Student Personnel* 26: 343-351.

Bean, J.P., and Metzner, B.S. (1985). A conceptual model of nontraditional undergraduate student attrition. *Review of Educational Research* 55: 485-540.

Bers, T.H., and Smith, K.E. (1991). Persistence of community college students: The influence of student intent and academic and social integration. *Research in Higher Education* 32: 539-556.

Bloom, B.S., Englehart, M., Furst, E., Hill, W., and Krathwohl, D. (1956). *Taxonomy of Educational Objectives: Handbook I. Cognitive Domain.* New York: David McKay.

Bohr, L., Pascarella, E.T., Nora, A., Zusman, B., Jacobs, M., Desler, M., and Bulakowski, C. (1994). Cognitive effects of two-year and four-year institutions: A preliminary study. *Community College Review* 22: 4-11.

Breneman, D., and Nelson, S. (1981). *Financing the Community College: An Economic Perspective.* Washington, DC: Brookings Institution.

Brooks, J.H., and DuBois, D.L. (1995). Individual and environmental predictors of adjustment during the first year of college. *Journal of College Student Development* 36: 347-360.

Buczynski, P.L. (1991). Longitudinal relations among intellectual development and identity during the first two years of college: A structural equation modeling analysis. *Research in Higher Education* 32: 571-583.

Cameron, K.S. (1978). Measuring organizational effectiveness in institutions of higher education. *Administrative Science Quarterly* 23: 604-632.

Chisholm, M.P. (1994). *Faculty Instructional Workload.* (Research Report). Denver, Colo: Colorado Commission on Higher Education.

Choy, S. P., and Gifford A. G. (1990). *Profile of Undergraduates in American Postsecondary Institutions.* (NCES 90-353). Washington, DC: Government Printing Office. (ASI 1990 4846-3.9)

Cohen, A.M., and Brawer, F.B. (1987). *The Collegiate Function of the Community College.* San Francisco: Jossey-Bass.

Cross, K.P. (1981). *Adults as Learners.* San Francisco: Jossey-Bass.

Dougherty, K.J. (1994). *The Contradictory College: The Conflicting Origins, Impacts, and Futures of the Community College.* Albany: State University of New York Press.

Durham, R.L., Hays, J., and Martinez, R. (1994). Socio-cognitive development among Chicano and Anglo American college students. *Journal of College Student Development* 35: 178-182.

Education Commission of the States (1995). *Making Quality Count.* Denver: CO

Emanuel, R.C., and Potter, W.J. (1992). Do students' style preferences differ by grade level, orientation toward college, and academic major? *Research in Higher Education* 33: 395-414.

Endo, J.J., and Harpel, R.L. (1982). The effect of student-faculty interaction on students' educational outcomes. *Research in Higher Education* 16: 115-138.

Entwhistle, N. (1981). *Styles of Learning and Teaching.* New York: Wiley.

Erekson, O.H. (1992). Joint determination of college student achievement and effort: Implications for college teaching. *Research in Higher Education* 33: 433-446.

Fisher, C., and Grant, G. (1983). Intellectual levels in college classrooms. In C. Ellner and C. Barnes (eds.), *Studies of College Teaching: Experimental Results, Theoretical Interpretations, and New Perspectives.* Lexington, MA: D.C. Heath.

Franklin, M. (1995). The effects of differential college environments on academic learning and student perceptions of cognitive development. *Research in Higher Education* 36: 127-153.

Grubb, W.N. (1984). The bandwagon once more: vocational preparation for high-tech occupations. *Harvard Educational Review* 54: 429-451.

Grubb, W.N. (1991). The decline of community college transfer rates: Evidence from national longitudinal surveys. *Journal of Higher Education* 62: 194-217.

Hancock, D.R. (1994). Motivating adults to learn academic course content. *Journal of Educational Research* 88: 102-108.

Hanson, S.L. (1994). Lost talent: Unrealized educational aspirations and expectations among U. S. youths. *Sociology of Education* 67: 159-183.

Higher Education Research Institute (1992). *American Freshman: National Norms for Fall 1992*. Los Angeles: University of California at Los Angeles, Higher Education Research Institute.

Jöreskog, K., and Sörbom, D. (1984). *LISREL V: Analysis of Linear Structural Relationships by Maximum Likelihood and Least Squares Methods*. Mooresville, IN: Scientific Software, Inc.

Kanoy, K.W., Wester, J., and Latta, M. (1989). Predicting college success of freshman using traditional, cognitive and psychological measures. *Journal of Research and Development in Education* 22:3, 65-70.

Kaufman, M.A., and Creamer, D.G. (1991). Influences of student goals for college on freshman-year quality of effort and growth. *Journal of College Student Development* 32: 197-206.

Kember, D., and Gow, L. (1994). Orientations to teaching and their effect on the quality of student learning. *Journal of Higher Education* 65: 58-74.

Kidd, J.R. (1973). *How adults learn*. Chicago: Association Press.

Knight, W.E. (1993). An examination of freshmen to senior general education gains across a national sample of institutions with different general education requirements using a mix-effect structural equation model. *Research in Higher Education* 34: 41-54.

Kohlberg, L. (1973). Continuities in childhood and adult moral development revisited. In D.A. Goslin (ed.), *Life-Span Developmental Psychology: Personality and Socialization*. San Francisco: Jossey-Bass.

Kolb, D.A. (1984). *Learning Style Inventory*. Boston: McBer and Company.

Kolb, D.A. (1985). *Experiential Learning: Experiences as the Source of Learning and Development*. Englewood Cliffs, NJ: Prentice-Hall.

Kuh, G. (1995). The other curriculum: Out-of-class experience associated with student learning and personal development. *Journal of Higher Education* 66: 123-155.

Livengood, J.M. (1992). Students' motivational goals and beliefs about effort and ability as they relate to college academic success. *Research in Higher Education* 33: 247-262.

Loevinger, J. (1976). *Ego Development: Conceptions and Theories*. San Francisco: Jossey-Bass.

Loevinger, J., and Wessler, R. (1970). *Measuring Ego Development I: Construction and Use of a Sentence Completion Test*. San Francisco: Jossey-Bass.

Marcia, J.E. (1966). Development and validation of ego identity status. *Journal of Personality and Social Psychology*. 3: 551-558.

McMillan, J.H. (1987). Enhancing college students' critical thinking: A review of studies. *Research in Higher Education* 26: 3-29.

Mow, S.L., and Nettles, M.T. (1990). Minority student access to, and persistence and performance in, college: A review of the trends and research literature. In J. Smart (ed.), *Higher Education: Handbook of Theory and Research*, Vol. 6. New York: Agathon Press.

National Center for Education Statistics (1981). *National Longitudinal Study: Base Year*

*(1972) Through Fourth Follow-up (1979) Data File Users Manual.* Washington, DC: U. S. Government Printing Office.

National Center for Education Statistics (1985). *High School and Beyond 1980 Senior Cohort Second Follow-up (1984) Data File User's Manual.* Washington, DC: U. S. Government Printing Office.

National Center for Education Statistics (1989). *Digest of Educational Statistics, 1989.* Washington, DC: Government Printing Office.

National Center for Education Statistics (1991). *College-Level Remedial Education in the Fall of 1989.* Washington, DC: Government Printing Office.

National Center for Education Statistics (1993). *National Assessment of College Student Learning: Getting Started.* Washington, DC: Government Printing Office.

National Center for Education Statistics (1994). *Digest of Educational Statistics, 1994.* Washington, DC: Government Printing Office.

Nichols, R. C. (1964). Effects of various college characteristics on student aptitude tests scores. *Journal of Educational Psychology* 55(1): 45-54.

Nora, A. (1993). Two-year colleges and minority students' educational aspirations: Help or Hindrance? In J. Smart (ed.), *Higher Education: Handbook of Theory and Research,* Vol. 9. New York: Agathon Press.

Nora, A., and Horvath, F. (1990). Structural pattern differences in course enrolment rates among community college students. *Research in Higher Education* 31: 539-554.

Nora, A., and Rendon, L.I. (1990). Determinants of predisposition to transfer among community college students: a structural model. *Research in Higher Education* 31: 235-255.

Ott, M.D. (1988). An analysis of predictors of early academic dismissal. *Research in Higher Education* 28: 34-48.

Pace, C.R. (1969). *College and University Environment Scales: Technical Manual (2nd ed.).* Princeton, N. J.: Institutional Research Program for Higher Education.

Pace, C.R. (1984). *Measuring the Quality of College Student Experiences.* Los Angeles: Higher Education Research Institute, UCLA.

Pascarella, E.T. (1985). College environmental influences on learning and cognitive development: A critical review and synthesis. In J. C. Smart (ed.) *Higher Education: Handbook of Theory and Research,* Vol. 1. New York: Agathon.

Pascarella, E.T. (1989). The development of critical thinking: Does college make a difference? *Journal of College Student Development* 30: 19-26.

Pascarella, E.T., Bohr, L., Nora, A., Desler, M,. and Zusman, B. (1994). Impacts of on-campus and off-campus work on first year cognitive outcomes. *Journal of College Student Development* 35: 364-370.

Pascarella, E.T., Bohr, L., Nora, A., and Terenzini, P.T. (1995). Cognitive effects of 2-year and 4-year colleges: new evidence. *Educational Evaluation and Policy Analysis* 17: 83-96.

Pascarella, E.T., Bohr, L., Nora, A., Zusman, B., Inman, P., and Desler, M. (1993). Cognitive impacts of living on campus versus commuting to college. *Journal of College Student Development* 34: 216-220.

Pascarella, E.T., Ethington, C.A., and Smart, J.C. (1988). The influence of college on humanitarian/civic involvement values. *Journal of Higher Education* 59: 412-437.

Pascarella, E.T., Smart, J.C., and Stoecker, J. (1989). College race and the early status attainment of black students. *Journal of Higher Education* 60: 82-107.

Pascarella, E.T., and Terenzini, P.T. (1991). *How college affects students. Findings and insights from twenty years of research.* Jossey-Bass: San Francisco.

Perry, W.G. (1970). *Forms of Intellectual and Ethical Development in the College Years: A Scheme.* New York: Holt, Rinehart, and Winston.

Piaget, J. (1950). *The Psychology of Intelligence*. New York: Harcourt Brace Jovanovich.

Pike, G. R. (1991a). The effects of background, coursework, and involvement on students' grades and satisfaction. *Research in Higher Education* 32: 15-30.

Pike, G.R. (1991b). Using structural equation models with latent variables to study student growth and development. *Research in Higher Education* 32: 499-524

Pike, G.R. (1992). Lies, damn lies, and statistics revisited: A comparison of three methods of representing change. *Research in Higher Education* 33: 71-84.

Richardson, R.C., and Bender, L.W. (1987). *Fostering Minority Access and Achievement in Higher Education: The Role of Urban Community Colleges and Universities*. San Francisco: Jossey-Bass.

Rouche, J.E., and Rouche, S.D. (1993). *Between a Rock and a Hard Place: The At-Risk Student in the Open-Door College*. American Association of Community Colleges: Washington, DC

Schmidt, J.A. (1985). Older and wiser? A longitudinal study of the impact of college on intellectual development. *Journal of College Student Personnel* 26: 388-394.

Sewell, W.H., and Hauser, R.M. (1975). *Education Occupation, and Earnings. Achievement in the Early Career* New York: Academic Press.

Smart, J.C., and Ethington, C.A. (1985). Early career outcomes of baccalaureate recipients: a study of native 4-year and transfer 2-early college students. *Research in Higher Education* 22: 185-193.

Smart J.C., and Hamm, R.E. (1993a). Organizational culture and effectiveness in two-year colleges. *Research in Higher Education* 34: 95-106.

Smart J.C., and Hamm, R.E. (1993b). Organizational effectiveness and mission orientation of two-year colleges. *Research in Higher Education* 34: 489-502.

Taylor, M.B. (1983). The development of the Measure of Epistemological Reflection. *Dissertations Abstracts International* 44: 1065A. (University Microfilms No. Da 83-18, 441)

Terenzini, P.T., Springer, L., Pascarella, E.T., and Nora, A. (1995a). Academic and out-of-class influences on students' intellectual orientations. *Review of Higher Education* 19: 23-44.

Terenzini, P.T., Springer, L., Pascarella, E.T., and Nora, A. (1995b). Influences affecting the development of students' critical thinking skills. *Research in Higher Education* 36: 23-40.

Tracey, R.J., and Sedlacek, W.E. (1987). A comparison of white and black student academic success using noncognitive variables: A LISREL analysis. *Research in Higher Education* 27: 333-348.

Velez, W. (1985). Finishing college: The effects of college type. *Sociology of Education*, 58: 191-200.

Voorhees, R.A. (1987). Toward building models of community college persistence: A logit analysis. *Research in Higher Education* 26: 115-129.

Watson, G., and Glaser, E. (1980). *Watson-Glaser Critical Thinking Appraisal*. San Antonio, TX: The Psychological Corporation.

Whitaker, D.G., and Pascarella, E.T. (1994). Two-year college attendance and socioeconomic attainment: some additional evidence. *Journal of Higher Education* 65: 194-210.

Wilson, R.C., Gaff, J.G., Dienst, E.R., Wood, L., and Bavry, J.L. (1975). *College Professors and Their Impact on Students*. New York: John Wiley and Sons.

Winter, D.G., and McClelland, D.C. (1978). Thematic analysis: An empirically derived measure of the effects of liberal arts education. *Journal of Educational Psychology* 70: 8-16

# What Discourages Research-Practitioners in Faculty Development

**Bob Boice**

*State University of New York at Stony Brook*

Research-practitioners, those individuals whose practice is research-based, are relatively uncommon in any discipline. Even in psychotherapy, where I often work, the enormous numbers of practitioners include only a minority who scientifically test and report what they do:

> Throughout the human service professions, the term *scientist-practitioner* and its variants has been seen as an ideal seldom fulfilled. This idea refers to a clinician who can not only directly assist people with their problems, based on knowledge developed within his or her profession, but also contribute to our collective knowledge, thereby improving our practice (Barlow, Hayes, and Nelson, 1984, p. xi).

Still, fields like psychotherapy and medicine are often led by research-practitioners. Seligman's (1991, 1994) influential notions about depression and pessimistic explanatory styles came, in large part, from his own laboratory research and research-based interventions with real patients. Masters and Johnson's (1970) pioneering information on human sexual responses and dysfunctions came from their own data collected in systematic observations and treatments with patients.

In those arenas, so far as I know, research-practitioners are not discouraged by colleagues whose work is more exclusively pure or applied. Instead, these research-practitioners are encouraged from both directions: By pure researchers (who want practical, meaningful tests of their findings); and by the great bulk of practitioners who do no research (but who want new directions). Practitioners attribute their own relative noninvolvement in data collection to practical limitations, not to disdain for researchers.

Consider the implication for faculty development (commonly known by its narrower labels: teaching improvement; instructional development). Ours is a field some three decades old and still growing; generally it does just as its name suggests—it assists the professoriate and its apprentices in their work (see Menges and Mathis, 1988, for an overview of its definition, evolution, and litera-

*371*

ture). And ours is a field peculiar in its treatment of research-practitioners. We can point to very few of us who conduct assessed interventions, fewer in influential roles. We admit to an unusually large chasm between what our pure researchers report and what our everyday practitioners do. We even, however unintentionally, do things to discourage research-practitioners who conduct *measurably* effective interventions in faculty development. (Unassessed interventions occur routinely—as in consultations with teachers about their student evaluations—and without hindrance from colleagues in faculty development. But because most faculty developers shun measurement, we cannot know how their outcomes compare to assessed interventions.) Not surprisingly, then, our closest and most caring judges conclude that we have made little progress (Weimer and Lenze, 1991).

In this chapter, I aim first to explain the reasons and costs for a tradition that keeps our research and practice so separate. We have yet to face up to this shortcoming. Second, I review literatures from outside the usual purview of higher education to help explain our ambivalence about interventions with measurable changes. Third, I draw out examples of research-based projects with needy faculty members and suggest reasons why these studies mark progress over usual, unevaluated practice. To really help faculty thrive, I conclude, we need to coach them out of their usual procrastinative habits (particularly the inefficiencies that hamper teaching). Fourth, I detail actual instances of resistance to doing and reporting such practical research; the problem is that most such interventions require pointing out and modifying poor work habits of faculty (and, worse yet, recognizing our own). There is, I argue, an unspoken taboo against dealing with procrastination and its opposite, efficiency, in our field (consider how rarely we talk about efficiencies of teaching). Fifth, I suggest ways of helping our young, formative field move past these unhappy, counterproductive attitudes and customs by explaining how usual reluctances to deal with procrastination lie at the heart of our inertia. And sixth, I overview the little-known literature on procrastination in the belief that we need to understand and confront its mechanisms if we are to ever to become accountable, comfortable interventionists. Without measured and meaningful interventions, it seems to me, there can be no real research-practice. I finish all this with a list of what I think are classic myths that keep faculty developers from appreciating the importance of measured interventions—mistaken beliefs that leaders and administrators need to question.

## THE RESEARCH-PRACTICE DIVIDE IN FACULTY DEVELOPMENT

As faculty developers, we already sense some of the things we do that elicit skepticism from critics of our efforts. Our usual applied programs tend to attract the very teachers who least need help; by preaching to the converted, we may convince ourselves that our strategies work when they do not (Eble and McKeachie,

1985). Our leaders often express disdain for research on faculty development with comments like this one: "We don't need researchers to tell us what to do. We know what works" (Garth, 1992). (Members of the Flat Earth Society would applaud that assertion.) We sometimes seem too undisciplined, even too lazy, to measure the effectiveness of what we do. At one major campus I visited a year ago, its faculty developer lamented the administrative and budgetary changes that now necessitated accountability for her programs: "It's a pity. Things were so nice before. Now we have to measure things that can only get in the way of doing things that we did so well before."

To an extent, this pessimism can be realistic. Perry (1991) points out that when some practitioners are forced to incorporate operational definitions of instruction in their projects, what gets measured is so artificial that resulting changes have no bearing on reality. But such missteps are not necessary. The bigger problem, Perry concludes, is that practitioners, when they consult the research literature at all, do so without careful consideration of contextual and other constraints that would help make teaching improvement meaningful and enduring.

What keeps research unread and misused? The problem isn't the lack of publications; there is an enormous literature available on research about teaching, one spanning at least two-thirds of a century (McKeachie, 1990). The divide between research and practice may be mostly a matter of tradition. Perry (1991) draws this modestly pessimistic conclusion about the customary standoff:

> Unfortunately, those who teach are frequently unaware of this literature and do not use it; and those who are responsible for assisting teachers in these matters, instructional developers, largely ignore it....Similarly, college administrators routinely fail to consult the empirical evidence when making instruction or personnel decisions about class size, course assignments, grading distributions, or teacher evaluations....Inattentiveness to this literature is also evident in researchers...no empirical evidence is provided to verify that the manipulation has legitimate educational consequences (p. 15).

Even upon seeing this reminder of the research-practice gulf, we might wonder if it really matters. After all, research on teaching may seem difficult to apply to real-life settings. Practitioners often romanticize teaching as an art, not a science; presumably the mere act of trying to dissect and control teaching may make its essences disappear. And, despite criticisms, faculty development continues to grow and prosper on American campuses. Those of us veteran at observing and assisting college teachers might suppose that outsiders, particularly researchers, have little that is new or useful to tell us.

One place to witness this anti-empirical attitude is in the publications of faculty developers. Scan the pages of any of its central periodicals (e.g., *To Improve the Academy*; *The Journal of Staff, Program and Organizational Development*) and the same pattern emerges:

1. Most articles are reports of informal, short-term teaching improvement projects on a single campus (e.g., "Putting Empowerment in the Classroom"), of

untested ideas of what might help improve teaching (e.g., "Incorporating Values and Beliefs to Construct a Wise University"), or cheerful reminders about why teaching is important (e.g., "Loving Teaching").

2. Almost none of these articles include data or controls or replications. Those few that do measure supposed progress rarely go beyond teacher/participant estimates of satisfaction with the program or of how, say, their newly uncovered learning/teaching styles (or renewed commitments, etc.) *might* eventually augment their teaching.

3. The majority of project descriptions omit mention of most precedent, relevant scholarship; even ongoing programs at other campuses doing similar things are ignored. Apparently, practitioners suppose that programs of teaching improvement should be reinvented each time they are implemented; clearly, they surmise that their interventions need no informing from other programs about what worked and what did not.

4. Without true accountability for instructional development programs, there is no evidence of progress, even of which strategies (e.g., workshops versus faculty grants) might be most effective. And none of us can claim that the presence of faculty development programs, often for several decades, has generally improved teaching on our campuses. We cannot even profess a common direction or goal.   As Menges and Mathis (1988) conclude in their analysis of this literature, there is no central theme or guiding theory in faculty development. What happens seems scattered, unconnected, inconsequential.

How general is this distancing of practitioners from research? It certainly extends to the primary funding agency for teaching improvement, the Fund for the Improvement of Postsecondary Education (FIPSE). I know of instances where investigators, to get a proposal for a project approved by FIPSE, first had to agree to remove almost all measures of ongoing progress (e.g., records of activities to be filled out by mentors and mentees). Agency experts supposed that the measures would get in the way of changes that mattered. Most FIPSE projects go unpublished once completed; few seem to induce widespread change in how faculty developers work. FIPSE is one of several powerful institutions that helps perpetuate the oral, old-girl tradition of communicating what gets done in faculty development. Similar pressures against research/publishing/scholarship extend even more clearly to the national organization for faculty developers, POD (Professional & Organizational Development Network in Higher Education). Presentations at its annual conferences almost completely exclude mention of research or data. Instructions for submitting proposals to a recent conference (1994), for example, took on these emphases:

> The challenge for you will be to design a session that encourages dialogue and collaborative discovery with tangible outcomes....Sessions in this category might inspire a commitment to experimentation/action on the part of participants that could be reported at subsequent POD conferences or through POD publications....These ses-

sions are not intended to be the traditional "show and tell" [i.e., research] program descriptions.

I could sense, from directions like these, that data presentations should be low-keyed but I didn't realize how much so until a graduate student and I successfully navigated the first part of the review process with a proposal. Our conference presentation (on the experiences of new graduate TAs and of interventions to improve their teaching) would have needed complete recasting—into an entirely experiential format, with the audience put in the roles of new GTAs. Such a format left no room to report what we had learned in our own systematic program (the "show and tell" approach disparaged in the instructions for proposals). Instead our role-played interaction was somehow supposed to bring audience members to their own, idiosyncratic conclusions about how to carry out teaching improvement projects on their campuses.

A colleague of mine with research-practitioner inclinations at another campus experienced a similar reaction from POD reviewers (she has given me permission to quote the comments she was mailed):

> According to the description of the presentation methodology, large amounts of time will be spent on listening to audiotape excerpts, reading selected student's feedback and pair discussion. I don't think it a good way to spend participant's time on. Instead, the presenter can summarize these components and briefly share with the audience.

The recipient of this discouraging comment described her reactions to the review in her letter to me:

> My proposal states that I will be sharing the results of a POD funded project. In my attempt to make the session interactive, I thought it would help to share some data with participants—to let them draw some conclusions before I present my own conclusions. The reviewer did not see it this way. [she repeats the comments from the proposal review form, above]....I have several responses to this comment. First, without looking at the data itself, my conclusions lose some of their meaning. The qualitative, grounded theory-type research I did makes much more sense (especially to people to who don't engage in such research) when seeing some of the data. And second, showing PODers what information I gathered just might convince some of them that they already *have* such data at their fingertips, that research is not such a difficult undertaking, and that they only need to set aside time to analyze the data they have already collected for teaching improvement to do some research of their own.

I could go on with other testimonials from research-oriented practitioners whose proposals were slighted or rejected by PODers (I know of several) but the point is, I trust, clear. The leaders of POD, all of them highly influential in the field as a whole, discourage research on faculty development.

Still, the anti-research stance of POD conferences has its seeming merits. Suppose, as PODers sometimes do, that their conferences are justifiably oriented to experiential, confirming, humanistic exchanges and that actual reports of program progress belong in their annual publication, *To Improve the Academy.* Its calls for published papers, though, never mention data, controls, or replications. Instead:

> Typical manuscripts range from descriptions of methods, reflections upon practice, and sample materials or exercises, to theoretical and conceptual discussions and practical applications of research-based studies (Wadsworth, 1994).

Does this journal simply not encourage research or does it actually discourage it? It has published few data-based studies with interventions that helped faculty make documented, enduring changes. And those exceptions were not cheered. In one case I know of, three of five reviewers for *To Improve the Academy* concluded that the report was not about faculty development. During my own stint as associate editor for that journal, no suggestions that authors of manuscripts add scholarly reviews of precedents or informal data about project outcomes were honored. In its e-mail network, its leaders continue to issue "POD-Correct" statements about why topics like helping faculty with their writing are not properly part of "POD Spirit."

So, can we legitimately argue that approaches like POD's advance faculty development? They, at the least, provide social support and stimulating ideas for working professionals in an often underfunded, isolating practice. Perhaps by putting a premium on humanistic development by way of consulting and networking, POD brings subtle progress to teaching improvement that only its most involved practitioners can detect.

### Is There Real Progress in Faculty Development?

Weimer, an experienced practitioner and champion of accountability in higher education, provides a striking answer to the question just posed. Her initial presentations, in a POD invited address (Weimer, 1992) and in a chapter with a colleague (Weimer and Lenze, 1991, 1997) ruffled some feathers. (She dared go to POD and make some surprising comments about the emperor's old clothes). The conclusions she and Lenze drew from their own careful study and from its precedents bear another look here.

The move to open criticism of the area began well before Weimer's public reports, as a part of the analyses of research in higher education conducted by Menges and his colleagues and students. Levinson-Rose and Menges (1981), for instance, scrutinized accounts of interventions that presumably improve college teaching (faculty grants, workshops, feedback from student ratings, and teaching-training protocols). Almost all such studies were clouded by conceptual and methodological problems. Workshops, for instance, were the most commonly employed strategy in teaching improvement but were almost never carefully evaluated. Moreover, workshops rarely included follow-up activities that might have encouraged lasting changes in teachers. Menges was typically gentle in stating his conclusions but the message was clear: There was no substantial evidence that teaching improvement programs make a difference in what faculty do over the long run.

A decade later Weimer and Lenze (1991, 1997) presented their analysis of the same categories from a much larger literature. Accounts of faculty development and instructional improvement programs had grown by leaps and bounds. Had its proof of progress done likewise? Weimer and Lenze's most startling finding was the continuing near absence of research, any kind of research, on instructional improvement:

> In colleges and universities across this country and others, instructional interventions are being used with virtually no empirical justification as to their effectiveness. They have become the "traditional" and "customary" means of intervening to improve instruction. This is not to denigrate unnecessarily the wisdom of practice and the voice of experience present in the literature....The problem is simply that they are not enough (p. 327).

The second finding followed from the first. In a culture where few practitioners feel compelled to prove the effectiveness of their interventions, even the unusual efforts where research is carried out often come up as less than ideal:

> Granted, on some of the interventions reviewed...any evidence would be an improvement, but for most of the interventions, evidence which does more than collect and summarize self- reported attitudes is essential. Favorable attitudes do not guarantee what is in fact needed if instruction is to be improved. Faculty must change what they do in class. Those changes must be obvious to independent observers....In other words, the effects of instructional interventions in these substantive realms must be established before any definitive claim can be made about current efforts to improve instruction (p. 328).

And finally, Weimer and Lenze's call for more rigorous inquiry adds a reminder about how we could in fact learn more from our work—by examining a) the relative effectiveness of individual interventions and b) their comparability across the different kinds of teachers that faculty developers encounter:

> Stronger justification would include evidence that interventions like the ones reviewed in this study are effective in changing the behaviors, student assessments, and learning outcomes in the faculty in these groups. More specific evidence would identify which of the interventions are most successful for each target group [e.g., TAs and new faculty compared with other, less captive samples of teachers] (p. 328).

What effect did Weimer's clarion call to POD have on subsequent practice? Little is yet apparent. In a subsequent lead article in *To Improve the Academy*, Wright and O'Neill (1994) reported results of a survey of POD members asked to rate the potential usefulness of 36 practices for teaching improvement. The limitation involved in relying on mere estimates of confidence in strategies is recognized (perhaps as a concession to pressures from research-practitioners like Weimer):

The results do not, then, actually measure the tangible outcomes of the various elements of an instructional development program, nor do they directly assess the impact of institutional policy and academic enterprise in higher education (p.33).

So their main finding, of a consensus about the use of and confidence in a limited number of interventions, proves nothing about what actually helps improve teaching. What remains a mystery about Wright and O'Neill's study is why they didn't at least ask practitioners if they had actually tested the efficacy of any of these strategies. The topic of research-based interventions continues to be a taboo in faculty development.

## Is the Lack of Progress Due Mostly to Practitioners?

The temptation in overviewing these failings of practitioners is this: We might imagine that the deficit in information about interventions originates almost exclusively in practitioners' conferences and publications. Not so. The great divide between research and practice in faculty development is diligently maintained by both sides.

Consider the journals and organizations in higher education that most openly stand for research. Surely, we might think, they must be more supportive of applied research on topics like teaching improvement. Sometimes they are; more often they are not. Until recently, one leading journal in higher education simply returned manuscripts on applied research about faculty development with the comment, "We do not accept papers about interventions."

At the recent meetings of ASHE (1994), our most stringently research-oriented organization, not one paper on the program included data about interventions where the behaviors of teachers/professors were modified. Instead, the expanding numbers of empirical papers about faculty life (e.g., the kinds of advice, good and otherwise, that new faculty hear from senior colleagues) remain almost purely descriptive. Without application of what we learn about why some colleagues fail as teachers, of what use is this information? (I return to this question anon; for the moment I ask another that helps conclude my initial point about the lack of empirical demonstrations of interventions in journals of higher education.)

How many research articles exist that provide proof of improved teaching? The number is only a handful and the instances are not well-known (e.g., Boice, 1984, 1995a; Carroll, 1977; Erickson and Erickson, 1980; Murray and Lawrence, 1980; Perry and Struthers, 1994). Even the most thoroughgoing reviews of the field (e.g., Menges and Mathis, 1988; Weimer and Lenze, 1991, 1997; and my own on-line examination of the education and psychology literatures) uncover little or no mention of such outcomes  The conspicuous absence of such reports might indicate a powerful prohibition against them.

## COSTS TO FACULTY DEVELOPMENT OF THE
## RESEARCH-PRACTICE DIVIDE

To an extent, we already know the costs. (And none of us probably feels like listening to another lecture about the value of science in terms of improved techniques for preventing and correcting problems such as diabetes.) I'll try to be mercifully brief in sampling some of the sacrifices I have documented first-hand.

### Costs to Faculty Development Practitioners

I have, for over a decade, consulted at several campuses, particularly as an observer, evaluator, and advisor to their faculty developers. These are, in my experience, bright, hard-working, and well-intentioned individuals. And generally, in my view, they operate amidst a painful uncertainty about the future of their positions and their programs/centers. Why? Usual campus politics always enter the picture at some point; faculty developers often do not know if incoming administrators will be supportive. Faculty developers who do little research or publishing in respected journals rarely qualify for tenure. Sometimes other campus agencies or developers compete for recognition and support. But when I interview the faculty on campus committees and the higher administrators to whom faculty developers report, a different factor emerges. Faculty, particularly the considerable numbers who value research and empirical accountability, wonder if their local faculty development centers make a difference that merits the budget they get. Administrators, many with similar leanings, hear the faculty's reservations and worry that developmental funds might better be spent elsewhere, say on encouraging faculty to write more grant proposals to funding agencies (the results of which definitely do get measured). For instance, the chair of a campus advisory committee said this to me: "It's hard to tell what they [the Teaching Center] do or if the director is very efficient. How many people do they actually help each year? How much do they really improve the teaching of their clients? Who knows?" Said the higher administrator listening to that comment: "Well I certainly don't. All I know is that I like [the faculty developer], even if she does seem a bit scattered, and I know how much this thing costs us each year. I don't know if I can continue to justify it."

### Costs to Faculty

Here too the data are few and the topic is one usually avoided in polite conversation. I highlight a case I knew about first-hand, a sudden administrative withdrawal of support for a research-based program that mentored new faculty as teachers. The project at a large comprehensive campus had been a success for three consecutive years; its 25 formal mentoring pairs evidenced clear advantages for new teachers compared to nonparticipants. Among those were improved estimates and counts of involvement in social support networks and reliably higher ratings of classroom teaching (Boice, 1990). In the fourth year, the incoming higher administration on that campus decided the project could be continued without a faculty developer or the funds that had supported research-based structures and accounts of mentor-mentee participation. Said one: "This isn't about research, it's about teaching." The mentoring program quickly became nonfunctional; few new mentoring pairs continued to meet regularly and where they did, benefits were obscure. More important, experienced mentors and mentees agreed in estimating that incoming new faculty without the formal mentoring program were faring less well in dimensions including teaching, scholarship, and collegiality. What had been perceived as a broadly effective climate of acceptance and support for new hires seemed to vanish with surprising quickness. Why? Observers of the change in administrative support agreed on a single factor: Prior, the mentoring pairs had kept meeting (despite initial feelings of busyness and awkwardness) because the project was so highly structured, data-oriented, and effective. Pairs tempted to skip a mentoring meeting met to be able to contribute data, to be able to respond comfortably to weekly calls from experimenters. Pairs in the project felt themselves contributing to an important research study and they constantly saw interim summaries of the data that showed how well the program worked.

I could cite a variety of other demonstrations that research-based programs make a difference but one other stands out for me. On two campuses I have tracked individuals who had been considered for positions as newcomers on the tenure track but did not accept job offers. My emphasis has been on women and minorities and on the difference between campus locations where faculty development for new faculty was carried out as well-publicized research project and where it was not. By my counts, newcomers who would have been in marginal roles (e.g., sole women or minorities in a department) were over twice as likely to decline tenure-track positions when faculty development programs played no demonstrable role in helping newcomers survive and thrive. Typical comments of withdrawers essentially reflected an awareness that success in things that mattered for retention/tenure would be difficult without strong, systematic support from colleagues and campus agencies. They told me that they opted for other academic positions (or even more often for business careers) because they could not see: a) the support networks and mechanisms for new faculty (including mentoring and fast-track programs) in place, and b) the evidence that developmental programs helped marginal newcomers in proactive ways. When women and minorities did opt for membership in departments and on campuses where they were effectively social isolates, their indices of success were clearly lower than for peers who found more early support and success (Boice, 1993a).

# WHAT DISCOURAGES RESEARCH-PRACTITIONERS IN FACULTY DEVELOPMENT?

In their own criticism of research on teaching improvement, Weimer and Lenze make a point we have not yet considered here. There is no gain in merely blaming practitioners (or pure researchers). To move beyond this stubborn tradition of separatism and prejudice, we must do more to understand its underlying mechanisms.

We need, it seems, to uncover things that actually discourage research-practitioners from pursuing the middle-course of trying to reconcile research and practice. Here too we are woefully short of empirical information. We know little about our editorial and other gatekeeping processes—especially about how our leaders act to encourage some kinds of emphases in favor of others. I know of only one effort by a journal in this area to examine its favoritisms towards topics of manuscripts submitted for publication (*Journal of Excellence in College Teaching*). I know of none that examines the fairness or openness of our journal reviewers in faculty development or higher education. In particular we know little about the fate of rejected manuscripts and authors (although a prominent editor, Silverman, 1977, proposed more attention to such matters). So, if gatekeepers do discourage the authors of research-based manuscripts based on assessed interventions with faculty, how would we know it?

Ordinarily we would not. Some rejected, discouraged authors probably leave the field or find more socially acceptable topics to research and report. Others, no doubt, keep quiet about their rejections from conferences, funding agencies, journals, and book publishers. There is no adaptive pride in being found wanting by one's leading colleagues. But an unusually open, tolerant format like this one allows me to make a bold, risky move. Herein I present a sampling of my own rejections (and acceptances) to show how differently reviewers behave towards manuscripts and proposals that emphasize data-based interventions versus those that do not. Why? I hope not only to stimulate a reexamination of how badly we sometimes treat colleagues with nontraditional approaches, but also to encourage more disclosure of discouragements experienced by other research-practitioners. (Other research-practitioners in faculty development have told me of their own similar experiences, privately.) As things stand now, for instance, there are only vague safeguards against reviewers acting capriciously, with political motives dominating matters of substance.

## Journal Submissions

I'll start on a positive note. When my own manuscripts, often based on studies of new faculty, are purely descriptive, they are almost always well-received by reviewers in higher education. Consider the course of a paper dealing strictly with the experiences of new faculty. An early version of a paper that was eventually titled "New Faculty as Teachers" was rejected but, I thought, reasonably. The main criticism was that my sample relied too heavily on observations at a single campus. The revised version, expanded to extensive observations at two campuses (Boice, 1991), was accepted in friendly, supportive fashion. The only real demand for change was a proviso that conditions at my study campuses for new faculty might have been less ideal than at other campuses. (Also a reasonable criticism, I thought, and one I readily complied with.) In another descriptive account of faculty behaviors, this time on factors of writing productivity, my manuscript was accepted with compliments and with no suggestions of change (Boice, 1993c). At times like these I felt highly encouraged to persist in my research in higher education.

Papers that focused on interventions fared differently. One of them, about a programmatic, evaluated way of enhancing both teaching and scholarly writing, is the most obviously experimental test of interventions I submitted. (A tolerant editor decided to publish it despite reviewer complaints—Boice, 1995a). It elicited the most discouraging criticisms I have experienced in 30 years of publishing in scholarly journals. Consider these comments from one reviewer for this leading *research* journal. The first complaint is about the confusing nature of my paper:

> ...the ms. is simply too long and awkward in its structure. For example,....On page 57, the author(s) drops in another study (i.e., non-participants in the study). Why does this manuscript become so tedious?

What this reviewer failed to recognize was that the "other study," with its non-participants was nothing but a control group against whom I compared the progress of my experimental participants. Here was a reviewer who wanted to reject my report of several years' effort because he or she claimed not to understand the function of a control group in an experiment.

The main criticism from this reviewer may have been more telling. She or he simply objected to doing empirical research on teaching and writing:

> Finally, is writing or teaching as scientific as you make it out to be? Is there no room for the art? The heavy emphasis on measurement, and trying to reduce writing, to specific tasks and activities, without recognizing the inexact nature of the process, overlooks an important variable in the equation.

In other words, things like teaching and writing are inexact arts, not amenable to the "trite" manipulations of researchers. How, then, can faculty developers learn what works to help improve teaching without measuring specific tasks and activities? The reviewer did not say.

Now, it isn't that I object to criticism per se (although I prefer praise); most of my publications have been improved by critics' questions and suggestions. But I do object to criticisms that offer no constructive suggestions for change, that seem more political than substantial.

Because reviewer comments about research-based interventions in teaching improvement are so atypically political and impolite, I suspect they reflect reactions to the violation of a great, unspoken taboo. Before I examine that powerful prohibition, I present one more sampling of reviewer comments. It was here that the insight about interventions as taboo became clear to me.

## Proposals for Books

My second book on faculty development, *The New Faculty Member* (1992), is largely descriptive and it received almost uniformly positive, helpful critiques about how to improve its organization and usefulness. Its emphasis on data initially made the editor, a primary gatekeeper of books on faculty development, anxious ("how about putting all that in an appendix?"), but she did publish the book. Only one reviewer, after publication, disliked the book; he, as a pure research psychologist who works only in laboratories, took offense at the qualitative, field-based aspects of my research (Kraus, 1993).

My most recent attempt to publish a book in this area might have been entitled *Advice for New Faculty.* Its long, detailed proposal is heavily oriented to information about usual pitfalls facing new hires and on interventions that have been effective in helping them survive and thrive. In assembling several versions of a prospectus, I anticipated trouble. I would be treading on another old prohibition, the one about giving new faculty specific, empirically based advice. Consider that books of advice for new professors are almost always based on the personal experiences of the writer (who is always the proud possessor of a laudable career in the professoriate, who always presents advice confidently but with no proof of its generality or usefulness—e.g., Gibson, 1992; Rheingold, 1994). Where can newcomers learn about the faculty who failed, about reliable turning points in early careers, about real predictors of success in the retention/tenure process, or about the unique perils facing nontraditional people on the margins? What, specifically, can they do to ensure success and satisfaction? Except for the unreliable medium of gossip, there are no readily available sources that provide this sort of information.

The reviews of my lengthy, detailed proposal for this book surprised even me. Consider this one from a POD leader who used the same comments to prevent acceptance with two different publishing houses:

> Reviewing Bob Boice's new proposal on "rules" for new faculty was harder than I thought....I have tried to categorize the aspects of this proposal that I find problematic [three single-spaced pages of criticisms follow].

One of her objections was that the topic of new faculty has already been completely covered, that nothing more needs saying:

> ...there has been a fairly exhaustive coverage of new faculty concerns and strategies for success. I have to wonder is there is any new thing to say or if old issues will reappear in new attire.

Then she turned to a more heartfelt objection. She disliked the tone of a book that would inform new faculty about the downside of professorial life:

Put simply, it is pessimistic. As a faculty developer who sees faculty finding great satisfaction (and, of course, stress) in their work, the tenor of the proposal was disquieting....[then she quotes my proposal]: "We acknowledge that too many of us spend our careers in a disappointing state of collegial isolation and neglect. This is what I want readers to face up to." He [referring to me] then devotes considerable time and attention to strategies to overcome mental problems evidenced by faculty....I am much more optimistic about faculty life. Further, my and others' many years of practice and research on faculty satisfaction do not support these broad and depressing generalizations about faculty life.

Then she turns to a deeper criticism. She is also sure that my methods will not work and that faculty would not accept them even if they did:

I work directly with faculty on teaching and faculty development issues on a daily basis and am in touch with faculty developers across the country on an almost daily basis (thanks to POD e-mail listserve). Perhaps I have missed something but I don't think the big issues we are grappling with and the strategies we are working on resonate with ASRP [the acronym then used for the proposal]. It just does not strike me a [sic] particularly meaningful tool for faculty or teaching development.

Why? She concludes that the strategies are "unrealistic." She imagines that neither she nor any faculty developer could be expected to help new faculty learn "mental strategies" like relaxation exercises and that faculty would laugh at the suggestion of doing so.

Finally:

And having said all of the above, I honestly don't know how to suggest revision for this proposal....I hope I have not been too harsh.

My immediate temptation, upon rereading these criticisms, is to dispute them. First, there *is* more to be said about new faculty and how they can be helped; the higher education literature on this topic proliferates, usually with worthwhile new findings. She condemns new work by many other researchers in the field before having seen it. Second, there *is* reason to inform new faculty about how many of their counterparts fail and why, particularly for newcomers on the margin. Faculty developers who imagine that most new hires thrive and that most of our colleagues experience fulfilling careers are deluding themselves. And third, the techniques *have* in fact proven widely effective in helping new faculty at several campuses succeed in domains that mattered to them and their committees. Claims by this reviewer that the strategies will not work are unsupported by data. I could go on...

### Getting to the Real Point

I think, once I resume a calm and objective stance, that the content of criticisms like these is not the point. It symptomizes something else, something that has offended reviewers in ways that even they may not fully appreciate. It is, I believe, a problem general to the field, not just idiosyncratic to me.

I came to that realization after first rereading this stinging, hurtful review, when I recalled that the same reviewer had strongly, constructively supported my earlier, descriptive accounts of faculty behavior. Here, evidently, I had stepped out of bounds and the response was overwhelming, perhaps even to her ("I hope I have not been too harsh").

But, eventually, this trauma proved helpful in some ways. It led me to look beyond my seeming mistreatment to the problem of *assessed* interventions themselves and why they are so adamantly opposed in areas like faculty development. Therein—figuring why measured interventions are taboo—may lie some useful insights. Perhaps it will help ease the way to an inevitable acceptance of research-practitioners and even proven interventions in faculty development. Hereafter the tenor turns more to discovery and hope of change; I am sometimes a pessimist and a complainer, but not usually for long. I'd rather get some work done.

## WHY EFFECTIVE INTERVENTIONS ARE TABOO

### The First Clue: Attempts to Change Behavior are Taboo

The realization that criticisms of my interventionism were not necessarily personal to me came in perusing a recent article about why experimentally, academically oriented psychologists (not psychotherapists) resist practicing interventions (Kipnis, 1994). These are psychologists who value themselves above all as pure scientists. In their culture, moving beyond descriptions and explanations to attempts to change behavior is not socially acceptable (or even a matter of polite discussion). Why? Kipnis concludes that scientists in western culture are educated to simply contemplate knowledge, not to use it. To apply scientific knowledge raises questions about what kinds of changes are desirable and about who the controller will be. Particular suspicion and hostility are directed against behavior technologists because their strategies are obviously, powerfully, effective and hard to refuse, once their systems are in place.

No matter, Kipnis notes, that behavior technologists are miscast as coercers of change (instead, behaviorists prefer to reduce constraints against change and to fully inform patients/clients of likely outcomes in advance). The important things about interventions are that they seem to devalue the person who is getting help and that they surely give power to individuals who decide that change is important. A curious fact about objections to interventions is that they are resisted most vehemently and irrationally by leaders when offered to individuals marginal to the traditional system, who would probably fail without them. The real problem with interventions and behavior technology, Kipnis concludes, may be their threat to change the status quo; experimental psychologists (and faculty develop-

ers) may unknowingly act in conservative ways to ensure that tradition is not significantly changed.

In fields like psychology and faculty development, where researchers and
practitioners see themselves as enlightened and progressive liberals, Kipnis'
deductions are discomfiting and seemingly wrong-headed. Could academe be
quietly committed to preserving traditions including the social Darwinism that
selects only those individuals with the right stuff for survival (i.e., who need no
obvious help or interventions)? Expert observers of the professoriate such as
Clark (1987) support such an unpalatable assumption:

> ...faculty choice is naturally much more problematic for the vast majority who labor
> without the benefit of a major research reputation...many are treated badly....Such
> hierarchies are an affront to democratic instincts. They produce large numbers of have-
> nots....The whole wild business of competition in American higher education may
> begin with survival, but above that threshold it is a struggle to first maintain status and
> then to enhance it. With no monetary profit marker by which to judge success, prestige
> is the required coin (pp. 58, 60).

What kinds of unfair patterns exist in this tradition? Among them, Clark notes,
are traditionally downward-tilting disciplines like composition teaching whose
members are relatively more common at lower status, lower paying campuses.
(Downward tilt means a disproportionately higher representation toward the
lower end of the continuum; an example of an upward-tilting discipline is physics.) What, according to Clark's careful studies, helps determine status in the professoriate? One thing is the obvious divide between research and teaching.
Another is the related distinction between pure research and applied work. Like
them or not, these are the entrenched values of academe. The surprise in this is
that faculty developers (ourselves members of a downward-tilting discipline)
may work with especial, if unconscious, vigor to help maintain and enhance the
very traditions that bring us perpetually low status and slow progress.

How could the same people who stand for improving the perceived worth of
teaching vis-a-vis research be guilty of keeping the status of teaching secondary?
How could practitioners who genuinely want faculty (and student) welfare to
improve be accused of impeding its progress? We have seen suggestions.
Because of our prejudice against research (as though it can only be promoted at
the expense of good teaching), we help keep studies of teaching from acquiring a
credibly empirical base. So long as teaching must be treated as an inexact art,
with no specifiable skills, it will remain less legitimate, seemingly less difficult to
do than research. So long as the worth of faculty development interventions has
to be judged politely, by what ingroups of practitioners feel is most effective and
socially acceptable (but not by empirical proof), instructional development will
retain its tentative, apparently superficial appearance in an academe that values
facts and status most. So long as its few research-practitioners who deal empirically with interventions are treated rudely and discouraged from reporting and

publishing, faculty development will continue to make little tangible progress. Faculty developers would fare better in the long run by meeting the chemist or biologist on her/his own grounds—by arguing for the scientific integrity of the data from faculty development, by speaking the language of most of academic culture.

## A Second Clue: The Social Impropriety of Examining Excuses and Failures

In these first attempts to make sense of faculty development's irrational exclusion of proven interventions (and thus, of research-practitioners), we may have gained some notion of why we are stuck. Interventionists, at least those who make their actions public and measurable, elicit a long-standing resistance from others, particularly in arenas where research and practice are usually kept separate. Still, we have not fully answered a more basic question. What *really* makes interventions so objectionable? True, they are often misrepresented by critics. And interventions do place decisions about what changes need making in the hands of supposed experts (a position that anyone who counsels teachers must also assume). If most of us, as teachers and practitioners, already intervene at times, why is what we ordinarily do acceptable? I have hinted at the answer: When we merely intervene informally, without measuring and reporting the changes we induce, we do not seem like evil, manipulative controllers. When we intervene with apparent inefficiency and incompleteness, we leave credit for change (among the few who improve) to the actors or to the changed environment (Skinner, 1971).

But why oppose proven inventions that can help needy, deserving faculty survive when they will otherwise suffer and fail (particularly when many of our new hires would be eager volunteers)? Why, instead, insist on mere descriptions or models of faculty experience (for researchers) or on vague assurances that interventions work (for practitioners)? Clearly something deeper, something we rarely talk about, is going on here. A taboo.

Social psychologists have only recently suggested the answer. To closely examine someone's excuse for not managing to be efficient (e.g., "I'm too busy to work on my teaching") is a social impropriety (Snyder and Higgins, 1988). Similarly, exposing one's own inefficiencies and irrationalities is an impropriety…if doing so puts others in the self-conscious position of recognizing that they too are sometimes guilty of the same embarrassing failing. (Most of us may know an analogue, the feeling of embarrassment for an anxious speaker and the even greater discomfort of someone other than the speaker pointing out the speaker's failing.)   Is there an advantage to this tradition of not examining excuses? Snyder and Higgins confirm it in their research. So long as we and others overlook the wastefulness of our busyness and indecision and dilatoriness, we can perpetuate polite, attractive images of ourselves and others as too lovably disorganized and impressively harried to do important things. Excuses work because they minimize self-focus and embarrassment. Making excuses also confirms the social contract implicit in all this: socially skilled audiences prefer to overlook improprieties. When they acknowledge them at all, they do so politely, indirectly, even humorously. To an extent, maintaining illusions about others' and one's own progress can be adaptive. But excuses (and our usual politeness about them) rarely bring progress.

Consider how the illusion promoted by politeness about excuses can be costly. In academe, and elsewhere, we attribute intelligence and genius to the extent that we cannot see how people get things done (Langer, 1989). As teachers we judge the brilliance of our students to the degree they can succeed without obvious structure or direction (Astin, 1985). So it is, according to the research-practitioner Sternberg (1985), that we let schoolchildren fail because we assume they lack talent (and because we politely accept and foster their excuses). Instead, he and his co-researchers find, failing students lack only the tacit knowledge of how to succeed in school, an entirely teachable and learnable kind of knowledge (Sternberg, Okagaki, and Jackson, 1990). In traditional approaches to teaching, we assume that students with the right stuff somehow acquire this tacit knowledge on their own or with the help of incomplete, vague instruction (Tobias, 1990). Why do we rarely follow Sternberg's example of teaching survival skills to students? Teachers apparently find the prospect of having to coach basics embarrassing, to themselves and, presumably, to students. They (much as did my harshest critic) assume that students will laugh at and rebel against programs designed to change how they think and behave. There is also an elitist prejudice at work here. Teachers traditionally believe that the best students need little help, that teaching time is not well-invested in students who somehow lack the motivation and sophistication to learn. (Faculty developers often brag about working only with teachers who want and readily accept help, with the same group of colleagues who faithfully attend workshops and the like.)

Does the same taboo act for faculty developers as for teachers? Consider why subjecting faculty to simple strategies that would make them more efficient, less procrastinative, in their work might embarrass everyone involved. No group I can think of puts greater value on expertise, on not making mistakes in public than professors. None other matches their valuing of autonomy, freedom, and self-correction. None other is more at peril of procrastinating or of paying a professional price for it.

So, it follows, the professoriate is a place where the tacit skills of efficiency are seldom taught systematically, even discussed. It is a place where common failings of procrastinating the writing, teaching improvement, and collegial networking that ensure success are hardly mentioned, and then only in dark humor. It is a place, where, as a rule, faculty developers are selected and reinforced for skills of cheerfulness, counseling skills, and social leadership, not for prowess at research or success in faculty careers. Why would coaching faculty in the skills of efficient work help? Teachers induce more comfort (in themselves and their students) and learning when they learn to display "prosocial motivators" (e.g., forward leans, smiles, and other signs of approachability). They make points more memorably when they pace themselves, change gait for emphasis, and stop in timely fashion (Boice, 1995b; 1996a). Who would be in the best position to effect this coaching in proven ways? Research-practitioners. Who would be best able to point out the need for learning these usually neglected skills to faculty? Same answer.

And who is more likely than faculty developers, given the scenario just overviewed, to suppose themselves unqualified as interventionists, as disinclined to point out the kinds of failings that faculty typically excuse? Who would be more opposed to inducing faculty to participate in research-based programs that show the simple, correctable nature of usually troublesome faculty problems like procrastination and its inefficiency? No one else, as of yet.

So, it seems to me, the real taboo about interventions (and research-practitioners) in faculty development amounts to this: Society in general discourages close examinations of excuses, notably when they cover our common failings like procrastination/inefficiency that could suggest a weakness of character. Academe is particularly unlikely to scrutinize excuses, specifically procrastination. It is, accordingly, highly likely to suppose that people who fail deserve to fail; presumably, newcomers to the professoriate who need significant, measurable help to survive do not belong. The problem with doing research-based interventions with faculty is that the interventions point out the embarrassing failings of professors, cast doubt on the traditionally polite and inefficient interventions popular with faculty developers, and (closest to home of all) remind faculty developers that their own busy inefficiencies and procrastinations could easily be corrected. Research-practitioners in faculty development, if they are to prosper, need to confront procrastination/inefficiency in order to help their colleagues in demonstrably effective ways. I provide evidence to that effect anon.

How, historically, have societies dealt with violations of taboos? By way of social disapproval, punishment, sometimes with banishment. More tellingly, reactions have maintained the status quo, often against needed progress. One of the colleagues who examined reviewer comments in response to my manuscripts about interventions, herself a black woman, said to me: "You're being treated just like me, and you're a white man. They're finding reasons to exclude you that say more about them than about you." She added another thought: "This is why, you know, they can claim they have programs to help underrepresented people while the affirmative hires, one after another, fail. They really don't let anything important change."

In the next section of this chapter, then, I examine that greatest of taboos, the topic we have yet to consider objectively in higher education: Procrastination and inefficiency. No other major problem in academic performance can claim a smaller literature, or fewer proven interventions. None other is so unnecessarily, counterproductively neglected and discouraged. None other is more centrally related to our reluctance to accept meaningful interventions (because most interventions for faculty are about the potentially embarrassing topic of procrastination and inefficiency). Indeed the topic is so uncommonly connected to what we do that I expect you to react, at least initially, with disbelief, impatience, and annoyance. Not for long, I hope.

## QUESTIONS ABOUT PROCRASTINATION'S RELEVANCE

By procrastination I mean more than putting off important things until they are hurried under deadlines or not done at all. I mean the inefficiencies (even of the unintentional sort) that come in avoiding the discomfort in doing something difficult that can be delayed. I mean the inefficient, tiring busyness that comes with doing other, easier, more immediately rewarding things while never quite catching up with what really needs doing. I mean the narrowness that keeps us from learning to be organized and efficient because we mistakenly suppose we perform better with impulsivity and intuition. I'll explain as we move along.

But first, what does procrastination have to do with traditional failings of faculty development to accept research-practitioners? We procrastinate when we avoid the uncomfortable topic of measuring what we do and of doing something that matters to teachers. We reinforce that procrastination when we excuse our noninterventionism by claiming that teaching is an art and by supposing that faculty could not profit in learning to be efficient. We put off the necessary help for our colleagues, especially those on the margins, by worrying more about what might embarrass them or us in the short run. We shirk our real responsibility when we suppose that assessing the effectiveness or our programs would necessitate coercive, sinister interventions that are qualitatively different from what we already do more subtly. Instead, we opt for the easy and the immediately rewarding. We even procrastinate facing up to the topic of procrastination. (So it is, I think, that some early readers of this manuscript saw what comes next as completely unrelated. It isn't. But it is unfamiliar and discomfiting. Please be patient as I try to describe what I learned as a research-practitioner.)

I begin by responding to common excuse for attending to procrastination: Some people in our field suppose the topic is already covered in sufficient detail.

### First Question: Is Procrastination Really Neglected and Excused?

Several things help confirm the assumption that procrastination is an impolite subject of serious study. In fact, it has mustered only a small, scattered, obscure literature (compared, say, with problems of test anxiety or to ways of teaching critical thinking). It is rarely defined in clear, operational ways. Almost all its accounts are speculative; there are as few research-based demonstrations of enduring interventions for procrastination as for teaching improvement. Most of characterizations of procrastination are amiable and portray it as forgivable. And its most memorable accounts in scholarly sources are humorous. For example: Murray's (1978) Law of Delay ("That which can be delayed, will be"); Upper's (1974) article, "An unsuccessful treatment of a writer's block," which is a title over a blank page.

In the midst of all this amiability and indefiniteness, there is much worth noting if we are to move to more tolerance of research-practitioners and of their inevitable emphasis on interventions. In what follows I try to show why most of what has been written on procrastination is narrowly superficial and easily ignored. I suggest links between procrastination and working in efficacious ways (procrastination is the opposite of efficacy). And I attempt to illumine its true nature by linking it to phenomena like self-defeating behaviors, bingeing, depression, and pessimistic explanatory styles. By the end, I hope to manage two other things: To show how interventions can be made more socially acceptable by modeling them after expert behaviors. And to have lessened some of the unthinking embarrassment associated with interventions, with their usual target of procrastination, and with research-practitioners.

### Second Question: How Do We Underestimate Procrastination (and So, the Need for Interventions)?

Only recently did researchers dare point out the thing we have already seen a hint of: Most explanations of procrastination make it seem socially acceptable. Most rely on the unreflective self-reports of procrastinators for understanding of the problem. So, when students explain why they put off studying for tests, they endorse researchers' categories such as fear of failure, an excuse that carries no social opprobrium (Schouwenberg, 1992). And when professors cannot write, they most often claim busyness, an especially excusable excuse in our profession. How can we tell that these socially acceptable excuses are not the real causes of procrastination? Procrastinators' self-reports of things like fear of failure do not directly predict trait measures of procrastination (Lay, 1992; Milgram, Batori, and Mowrer, 1993; Silverman and Lay, in press). New faculty who claim they are too busy to keep up with their writing have as much accessible time as peers who write more productively (Boice, 1993c). The problem lies elsewhere, beyond the ready appreciation of procrastinators themselves.

Not only have most researchers relied on procrastinators' self-serving explanations of dilatoriness, they have also studied it under conditions that minimize its seriousness. Few reports of procrastination depict the costs of putting off imaging tests for symptoms of cancer or of delaying writing under the demands of retention/tenure systems. Most, instead, test notions of procrastination on introductory students in contrived school settings. These fall short of reality in terms of representing either truly important time pressures or the maladaptive effects of serious procrastination (Dweck, 1986). They say even less about how procrastinators often conspire to discourage research-practitioners from implementing effective interventions to help make them more efficient.

### Third Question: Do We Actually Value Procrastination (quietly, perhaps unintentionally)?

The answer to that question is yes. Procrastination offers short-lived, powerful rewards; most of us know them but we uncommonly discuss their temporary delightfulness. These are some of the most common: autonomy, excitement, retribution, relief, and relieving excuses—in the short run. Writers, for example, who consistently wait and then rush to finish under deadlines report the highest levels of enjoying the excitement and risk of not really knowing if they can make it (Boice, 1994). Teachers, similarly, express the greatest excitement with teaching when they say so much that they rush and run overtime (Boice, 1996b). (Procrastination is as much a problem of not knowing how to stop as of struggling to start.) Procrastinators, studied closely, can be seen to delay and to withhold as a means of controlling other people, even of getting revenge (Nelson, 1988). Procrastination offers well-documented benefits of hiding abilities and avoiding evaluations, all for the sake of presenting a favorable self-image (Ferrari, 1991). Procrastinators are also most likely to complain about others exercising control over them; the benefits they ascribe to avoiding people who advocate efficiency include a seeming sense of freedom. Procrastination even offers special, illusory magic: Procrastinators are more likely to wait for Muses and magic (Boice, 1994), even for effortless solutions and inspirations during sleep (Ross, 1985; Epel, 1993). Finally, procrastinators are commonly depicted as particularly lovable and nonthreatening by writers who are, themselves, admitted procrastinators (e.g., Hamada, 1986). One POD leader with whom I conducted a workshop arrived late and harried and boasted of her busyness. The audience of faculty cheered her.

Some of our traditional fondness for procrastination owes to confusion about when procrastination can be adaptive. There are times (while checking to collect materials, to reset directions) when proactive waiting helps (Mills, 1959; Murray, 1978). And we may block and delay further when we suffer from overexposure and fatigue, at times where we need rest or help (Leader, 1991). But these adaptive delays occur mostly with people who suffer no real problems with the kind of procrastination that brings worrisome, unproductive pauses. One little-known fact about procrastination is that highly successful adults indulge in very little of it (Wagner and Sternberg, 1986). Another is that most patterns of procrastination cause serious damage long afterward (Dweck, 1986). A basic problem of appreciating the potential seriousness of some kinds of procrastination is that many of us seem to succeed, more or less, despite engaging in them. Again, tradition reserves special acclaim for academics who apparently thrive despite a lovable disorderliness and an impressive lack of help (Langer, 1989; Sternberg, 1985). What tradition usually overlooks is the result for faculty, especially those excluded from usual support networks, who procrastinate excessively. They wash-out in the tenure process or they squeak-past in ways that undermine their self-esteem and motivation (Boice, 1993a).

Something else helps keep procrastination overvalued and underestimated. We have already seen the oppressiveness and immorality ascribed to those who would intervene in it. And we know the peculiar prejudice against efficiency in higher education (Solomon and Solomon, 1993). So it is that academics shy away from an image of being well-organized and disciplined. Sometimes we even imagine that orderliness is tantamount to pathological kinds of obsessive-compulsiveness (Bond and Feather, 1988). It can be, but only in excess. The same issues come up when the topic turns to the necessarily intrusive, controlling nature of interventions (Kipnis, 1994). Those who conduct them, as we saw earlier, are assumed to be overly organized, overly efficient, heartless people. Faculty developers have a cherished tradition of supposing, with suspect evidence, that interventions cannot work because they would rob faculty of their autonomy (Menges, 1991):

> By way of example, I suggest one concept that deserves a key place in our research efforts. That is a characteristic of academic life we call autonomy, self-direction, or as discussed in Bill McKeachie's presentations at this conference, intrinsic motivation. For the most part, the interventions I have discussed treat faculty as relatively dependent learners. They do not maximize autonomy. (p. 84)

How specifically, can we help faculty in ways that would preserve their autonomy? Opponents of interventionism like McKeachie never quite say. They seem satisfied with the status quo. What if we looked for ways to intervene that enhance autonomy? Then, Menges concluded (in a note to me) that the interventionists might be accused of manipulating or coercing autonomy. I go even further in my conclusion: A fondness for autonomy amounts to one of our usual excuses for procrastination and inefficiency.

### Fourth Question: Are There Even More Reasons Why We Neglect Procrastination?

Yes; I hope you can tolerate a few more. One of these is simple. We typically know too little about procrastination to be helpful (as in the case of tacit knowledge about thriving in academe). Faculty developers, many of them without faculty, research, or even teaching backgrounds, may be particularly unable to help procrastinators past their inefficiencies. But why, other than the traditional prohibition of researching it, have we remained so uninformed about procrastination? There is a natural tendency for humans to suppose that each new failure is unique and unlike any other. Unless we are coached to do otherwise, we may learn little from our prior mistakes (Buehler, Griffin, and Ross, 1994). And when it comes to giving advice about procrastinating, we find that it, like other kinds of tacit knowledge, does not lend itself to easy description or specific correctives. At best, we imagine that correctives for teaching and learning can be learned but not taught (see Sternberg, Okagaki, and Jackson, 1990). As a result, usual wisdom about procrastination and inefficiency is superficial, conjectural, and incomplete (much like the literature on faculty development). So for example, popular books about time management say lots about scheduling, little about managing it when emergencies and surprises arise (e.g., Lakein, 1973). Blocked writers are counseled to put manuscripts in a drawer until inspiration arrives, not how to work effectively without it (e.g., Mack and Skjei, 1979). Popular books about teaching often dismiss research and claim the only kind of meaningful learning for teachers is self-learning of a sort that cannot be communicated between colleagues (e.g., Eble, 1985).

There is another reason why most of us know little about helping procrastinators. They resist help and they tend to make their well-intentioned helpers unusually angry, helpless, rejected (Birner, 1993; Turkington, 1983). Why are procrastinators so resistant to change, so resentful of those who offer it, even model it? They not only bring along their symptoms to treatment but they insist on maintaining a product (cf. process) orientation. That is, they concentrate more on the outcomes they think they need (e.g., at last losing twenty pounds and once doing it, losing it in a hurry) than on ways of learning to behave differently (Dweck, 1986). An example: Without a process orientation of working on what matters in the moment, writers and teachers readily stray from a planful, stepwise orientation to a stance of fear and anxiety where they come to dread loss of self-worth (autonomy?) even more than failure itself (Langer, 1989; Lay, 1986; Tremmel, 1993). What does it matter beyond the pain? Writers who could be working spend their time wishing for magical outcomes or resenting pressures to write (sometimes they even resent productive writers), instead of simply getting ideas onto paper or screen and revising them later (Boice, 1994). Faculty developers who could be directing ever-improving programs prefer to talk about relatively unmeasurable outcomes like autonomy and dignity. A product orientation wastes time and energy on misdirected rushing or passive waiting, on indignant ruminations about injustices and failures. A process orientation, in contrast, helps bring optimistic thoughts of what can be, of what needs to be accomplished, of what ongoing processes need changing to accomplish important goals (Ellis and Knaus, 1977). So, in the field of psychotherapy (where prejudice against research-practitioners is largely unknown); many therapists work hardest and most openly at intervening in a pessimistic, product orientation to replace it with an optimistic, process style of problem solving (e.g., Seligman, 1991; 1994). It occurs to neither them nor their patients that such a move is immoral or embarrassing. Why? It works and it proves far better than the alternative. Faculty developers, in contrast, are still locked into concerns about politeness.

Does this stance of faculty developers matter? As a result of their proudly autonomous, product-oriented styles, they cheerfully overlook the procrastinating professors who display the worst work habits. They fail to notice that procrastinators, including themselves, react most emotionally when things go badly and are most resistant to new opportunities for job enrichment (Boice, 1994; Jahoda, 1981). What might we notice if we paid more attention to this taboo topic? Procrastinating new faculty complain more than peers about unfair, unbearable pressures to publish while remaining most aloof from campus support programs for writers (Boice, 1992b). They tend to justify their nonparticipation in part by claiming busyness, in part by focusing on exceptions (i.e., they can readily cite folklore about colleagues who have procrastinated while apparently thriving— such as a fabled junior professor who apparently put off writing until a great binge of inspired work produced a brilliant, acclaimed manuscript in a single week). But what may make procrastinators most difficult to help is that they self-present as complainers too busy and proud to change and who do little to cope, a pattern that depletes sympathy in other people (Silver, Wortman, and Crofton, in press). Chronic procrastinators, far more than efficient colleagues, place high value on not appearing weak. And they suppose that giving up procrastination means sacrificing freedom and creativity, just as manics mistakenly resist taking lithium (Boice, 1994). Pride plays a large role in procrastination. So does the polite distancing from the topic and from research-practitioners commonly shown by faculty developers.

Procrastination is, I believe, so central to our discomfort with measured interventions and research-practitioners that we can profit in looking even more directly at the ways we dismiss and devalue it.

## TRADITIONAL DISDAIN FOR PROCRASTINATION

Academe displays a peculiar opposition to taking procrastination seriously. Academics (including faculty developers) who work with obvious discipline and organization are often disparaged. So too writers and other artists. Literary critics often dismiss writers (e.g., Dickens; Asimov) who write a lot and work hard as victims of their lower-middle class upbringing (Parini, 1989). Academics often suppose, erroneously, that writers who write prolifically suffer a loss of quality and creativity (Simonton, 1994). Clearly we disapprove of colleagues who act like "rate busters" and produce too much to appear genteel (Ellenberger, 1970). We conserve our highest approval for writers who seem to write without trying, whose finished, unrevised product supposedly flows, unrevised, in but a few sittings (e.g., Brown, 1981). And when we address procrastination as a problem, we do so lightly. There is no real tradition of research-practitioners working on procrastination.

### Usual Cures for Procrastination Are Romantic and Painless.

Kubie (1965) advised stymied writers to work in the evening, when tired. Then, presumably, our usual inhibitions are unalert and can be skirted by the precon-scious. Wiggers (1984) claimed that art therapies such as making a sculpture or painting of one's block would release inhibitions. Neither intervention has led to any proof of effectiveness (Boice, 1994). Why do they persist? They (like most tactics of noninterventionists including faculty developers) are amiably unthreat-ening and inefficient.

Even when we skip the myriad studies of procrastination with poor methodol-ogy and turn to exemplary accounts, similar problems persist. Investigations are incomplete and short-term, leaving readers wondering how well and how long the interventions work. One classic study is Barrios and Singer's (1981) account of experimentally unblocking a large sample of creative artists. They used classic dream induction procedures, for waking and sleeping dreamers, to try to implant expectations (and actions) of getting back to work in productive fashion. Some of their findings are fascinating: artists who were most stubborn about procrastinat-ing also showed the highest levels of guilty, dysphoric daydreaming. But some of their findings are frustrating. The induction procedures produced little or no new dreaming about creative work. Nor did the procedures work reliably to induce any more unblocking and timely work than in control subjects.

Even where studies were behavioral and used systematic programs of planned activities, they usually disappoint. In one, meetings with advisors for feedback about progress and strong incentives to stay on schedule helped thesis writers in measurable ways (Dillon, Kent, and Malott, 1980). All the writers showed clear progress in working in timely fashion and at making progress toward goals of fin-ishing stages of their projects. But we never find out if these students finished their theses or if they continued to work with lessened procrastinating thereafter. This, like most interventions for procrastination (or other student and faculty problems), only hints at what could have happened with serious, prolonged application.

## Usual Explanations Are Correlational (i.e., descriptive but not interventive)

The great bulk of contemporary research on procrastination is about its personal-ity correlates. Here too, tradition has cast procrastination in an amiable light. One of the most cited of these studies used the Myers-Briggs Type Indicator (MBTI) to explain kinds of procrastinators and supposed correctives for each (Jensen and DiTiberio, 1984). So, for example, extroverts may put off tasks like writing because they dislike its usual isolation. What they need to do, supposedly, is to make their writing sessions more extroverted by working amid more social con-tact and feedback. (But so might any writer.) The problem with this and similar studies is reminiscent of what kept phrenologists from credibility: These MBTI researchers picked out a few clear cases of personality types who behaved in expected ways and used them to prove the connection between personality types and writing problems. Nowhere was there evidence that "improving" personality patterns actually improved performance. The interventions were left politely unmentioned (perhaps politely undone). This is one of the few studies of blocking and procrastination cited by faculty developers.

There are more systematic correlational studies of procrastination, lots of them. Some are informative. Rothblum pioneered inquiries about why procrastination is more common and problematic for women. In so doing, she provided one of the first clear pictures of this problem, particularly its links to underappreciated causes such as aversions to work (i.e., laziness). Her factor analyses suggested an essential, two-part configuration for procrastination: fear of failure, and task aversiveness (Solomon and Rothblum, 1988). Examinations of her own self-report measure of procrastination amongst students helped specify essential procrastinative factors such as anxiety, emotionality, and self-esteem (Rothblum, Solomon, and Murakami, 1986). All these characteristics correlate with expected acts such as putting off self-paced quizzes and term papers, even irrational beliefs about the best ways to work (Beswick, Rothblum, and Mann, 1988). Accordingly, student procrastinators report more fears of failure (and fearing its consequences such as embarrassment more than the failure itself) and more avoidance of feedback (Rothblum, 1990).

Other researchers have added programmatic efforts to Rothblum's. Lay (e.g., 1992) finds that procrastinators tend to either over-or under-estimate times to complete tasks (depending if they are pessimists or optimists), to self-handicap by spending less adequate time on projects likely to succeed than on those likely to fail, to express remorse during experiences like exams (but only temporarily), and to suffer negative expectations. Milgram, another newcomer to the field, finds, among other things, that procrastinators are especially likely to self-describe in ways that protect self-esteem and that they are more inclined to put off and resent tasks seen as unpleasant or imposed (Milgram, Batori, and Mowrer, 1993). Ferrari (e.g., 1993), an aptly named, prolific new researcher in this area, links procrastination to abnormal concern with public images, low self-esteem (notably in women) that handicaps performance, impaired self-understanding, and a fondness for the arousal of working against deadlines.

Still, most of those findings about personality and procrastination have turned out to be suspect. Researchers have, as we saw much earlier, relied on procrastinators' self-descriptions to explain their problems (Lay and Schouwenberg, 1993), on commonly used measures confounded by socially prescribed ways of looking and acting (Flett, Blankenstein, Hewitt, and Koledin, 1992), and on artificial settings—with highly-structured tasks, short-term deadlines, and strong cues for self-management—that make poor management of time unlikely, even by students who normally display it (Lay and Schouwenberg, 1993). More important, correlational researchers tend to explain procrastination as characterological (i.e., inborn) and unmodifiable (as ingrained personality traits). What better way to keep procrastination distant and amiable? How better to placate anti-interventionists than to depict it as something tolerable and irreversible? This tradition of neglect has kept us from appreciating a problematic aspect of faculty behavior, one that demands interventions if most of our colleagues are to meet their potentials.

## The Most Widely Read Literature on Procrastination Is Popularized and Superficial

Another genre of literature on procrastination needs only a glance to reinforce what we have just considered. The best-received of popular books on the topic is Burka and Yuen's *Overcoming Procrastination* (1983). Its authors, predictably, display an amiable tone that will not offend readers, by reassuring us that they too are first-rate procrastinators: "We're still marveling that we finished this book only two years after the original deadline!" (p. ix). In a related vantage, on blocking, popular authors find particularly creative ways to make stalled, delayed efforts sound intellectually attractive. Leader (1991) defines blocking as somewhat akin to Twain's metaphor of "the tank running dry," as different from Keats' "delicious diligent indolence," as more than Thackeray's sitting unable to write or do anything else, as much a matter of misery as of silence and closer to an accumulated fatigue from fighting resistance for so long. Blocking, in Leader's lofty view, cannot be experienced by ordinary people, only by those who have already demonstrated talent. Elitism, again, is also a part of procrastination and of its excuses.

## Where Do Traditional Accounts of Procrastination Leave Us?

Still somewhat vague about what it is or if it is a serious problem. Even less informed about how to moderate it. Why? Its usually amiable portrayals make procrastination sound like a trait that embarrasses those in whom it is found—people who probably cannot change it in any case. Almost nowhere in these accounts is there a clear suggestion that procrastination is problem of skills deficits, a problematic style that can be learned and unlearned. What, apparently, has kept us from seeing procrastination as skills-related? Proprieties. Researchers and other experts on procrastinators rarely watch what procrastinators do that makes them different (much as many teaching consultants rely on teachers' descriptions of their classroom behavior, not on direct observations). We politely avoid noticing procrastinators procrastinating. Or the prices they really pay.

We already sense the problem of relying on self-reports for understanding unflattering behaviors. When, for example, faculty members are asked, retrospectively, to estimate their workweeks, they portray themselves as constantly busy and overworked. When, instead, they make these estimates on an ongoing basis during weeks (and when they know they will be unobtrusively observed and rated at unpredictable times), they provide a different picture. They spend far more time than they had realized on unnecessary things like memo writing or worrying, far less on priority projects like scholarly writing (Boice, 1987). What had first seemed a problem of too little time was finally seen as a failing of efficient time use. Eventually, with more and more success in moderating their procrastination, they come to see it as more a problem of learning how to work efficiently than of inborn personality styles.

There is hint of the same growing awareness in personality research. Silverman and Lay (in press) not only note that "trait" procrastination relates weakly to the qualities we already expect it to (fear of failure, perfectionism, self-handicapping). They also wonder if it isn't more a problem of poor habits, weak conscientiousness, and habitual escape from unpleasant cognitions. McCown, Johnson, and Petzel (1989) link it to poor time estimates and excessive time commitments, impulsivity, and poor task preparation. In other words, McCown et al. have helped raise awareness that procrastination may be mostly a problem of skills deficits. Clearly, a willingness to see procrastination and inefficiencies as problems of skill deficits helps open the door to meaningful combinations of research and practice.

## APPROXIMATIONS TO SKILLS DEFINITIONS OF PROCRASTINATION

These can be most readily found in literatures not immediately identified with procrastination (or with faculty development). Bond and Feather's (1988) Time Structure Questionnaire is a good example. It identifies five main factors of what we, here, might call nonprocrastinating, all of them more like skills than traditional personality types: 1) sense of purpose; 2) structured routine; 3) present-orientation (cf. ruminating about missed opportunities in the past); 4) effective organization; and 5) persistence. These positive qualities of time-use correlate significantly with self-esteem, healthy optimism, and efficient study habits. The TSQ correlates negatively with depression, distress, anxiety, physical symptoms of illness, and other undesirable, long-term outcomes of procrastination. (The positive factors of the TSQ such as organization also correspond to effective teaching skills; time structure shows how minimizing procrastination helps augment teaching.)

Real turning points in moving toward skills considerations have occurred in educational research that we tend to overlook in faculty development. In one, Zimmerman (1986) studied high achieving students to specify what he calls self-regulated strategies (what we, here, might label as the process-oriented, mindful and practiced styles typical of nonprocrastinators). Exemplary, efficacious students showed better strategies of a) self-evaluation, b) organization and transformation (e.g., use of outlines in preparing papers); c) goal-setting and planning and seeking information; d) keeping records and monitoring progress, e) restructuring their environments to facilitate work; f) rehearsing and summarizing; g) seeking social assistance; and h) reviewing records and notes. Ninety-one percent of Zimmerman's sample could be correctly identified as high achievers on the basis of their self-regulatory scores. And, the highest achievers proved least likely to use only one of the strategies just listed. Efficacy may have no singular skill; procrastination may have no one preventive.

In the second example of research in education, Fox (1985) combined personality measures and informal observations to identify what makes some of us especially productive writers: autonomy and self-direction, stamina, curiosity, playfulness with ideas (while putting off closure), and collegial communication. That is, they know how to work.

The third is Sternberg's research on how to provide useful but usually tacit knowledge to students who do not fare well in school. He aims to intervene to foster intelligences (i.e., learnable skills) essential to academic success, largely by modeling after what excellent students do: 1) They display good reading skills because they master time allocation (i.e., they waste little time on inappropriate responses; they use time more flexibly because they excel at time-sharing between subtasks). 2) They redefine the problem to make it soluble, by planning an efficient sequence of actions and steps. 3) They automatize some of the operations essential to problem solving (Sternberg, 1985). Said another way, excellent students know how to work, how to be efficacious.

Sternberg and his colleagues applied these discoveries in one of the first large-scale programs that related procrastination and efficacy to an educational system. Predictably, his interventions have been largely ignored; the essential results were published in an obscure journal (Sternberg, Okagaki, and Jackson, 1990).

His program began by identifying reasons why students lack practical knowledge for success in school (i.e., why they procrastinate). One explanation is that teachers rarely verbalize their expectations of students (e.g., of how they should allocate time in doing homework; of how to talk and not talk in class). Another is that poor students do not know how to manage their work (e.g., they do not understand ways of breaking bad habits, of getting organized, of finishing tasks on time). And a third reason is that unsophisticated students do not know how to cooperate (e.g., how social networks work; how to put themselves in someone else's place). By identifying the usually tacit, untaught, unappreciated rules of succeeding in school, Sternberg provided one of the first real-life pictures of what comprises academic procrastination. He has also provided clear suggestions of what kinds of skills-training (i.e., interventions) can counter it. (And, he offers hints of parallel skills that can be taught to novice teachers by research-practitioners.)

The final example comes from research on teaching composition. This richly descriptive tradition started most obviously with Perl's (1978) account of five unskilled college writers. They were most impaired by impatience, by rushing into composing tasks without first prewriting (e.g., planning before composing) and of delaying while editizing (e.g., checking too soon for perfect sentences). Put simply, these poor writers (who in many ways fit descriptions of procrastinators) showed skills deficits (not personality problems). They, like other procrastinators approached their work hurriedly and impulsively, with narrow and inflexible ways of beginning.

As is the case in areas where procrastination has become a polite topic of study, composition researchers have tended, more and more, to recast the problem in terms of what nonprocrastinators do. The best of these accountings is by Flower and Hayes (e.g., 1980) who use cognitive methods of inducing writers to talk aloud what they think as they write. The following ways of working distinguish the best student writers (Hayes and Flower, 1986): 1) They work planfully and construct better initial task representations (plots, story lines, outlines). 2) They follow subgoals, one step at a time, set up in hierarchical but flexible fashion. 3) They act as good problem solvers by generating elaborate networks with compelling, interconnected goals. 4) They revise by working less locally, by attending to the whole scope of their writing, not just to local sentences and paragraphs. In composition and revision they work more boldly, by, for example, proposing larger sentences and composing with larger units in mind.

So, in Hayes and Flower's view, efficacious writers work more fluently because they rely on a process orientation that encourages a wealth of planning, more playful exploration of their knowledge, readier identification of audience, and more revisions/drafts of what they write. There is also, in this research, a clear identification of where the most problematic kinds of procrastination and blocking usually occur: at the juncture between preparing and writing (unless planful prewriting activities and patience help ease this commonly painful transition).

When I reflect on this summary of research on procrastination, two related things stand out. First, closer, more objective examinations move depictions of procrastination nearer to problems of skills deficits, farther from notions of inborn, complex, and embarrassing problems. Second, a skills approach naturally shifts emphases toward efficacy (i.e., how people avoid excessive procrastination in confident, resilient fashion). There may be a message in this little-known literature for faculty developers, especially those who might consider serious interventionism and research-practice.

## HOW STUDIES OF EFFICACY—THE OPPOSITE OF PROCRASTINATION—HELP FACULTY

Here I refer most directly to my own research; there is little else available as yet in faculty development to support the study of efficacy. I undertook this positive direction in my own research-practice partly because studies of efficacy may tell us more about procrastination than examinations of failings. And partly to escape some of the negativity of reviewers who find interventions associated with procrastination offensive.

## Quick Starters as Models of Efficacy

This is how I got underway: I had, for over a decade, been tracking cohorts of new faculty though the daily activities of their academic workweeks. As a rule, I followed them closely for the first two to three years in the professoriate (Boice, 1992b). Only then, at long last, did I recognize the value of concentrating on new hires who succeed quickly (and who display the least procrastination).

This talented tenth clearly excels in at least three dimensions by their second or third semesters on campus: They are rated (by themselves, their peers, their senior colleagues, their students, and their editors/funding agencies) as performing well above average in domains of:

*a)* Self-management (exemplars less often complain of stress or busyness; they exhibit fewer mood swings; they miss fewer work days due to illness or trauma than do counterparts);

*b)* task management (they fare unusually well on standardized student ratings of teaching and on related indices of classroom performance; they write and publish more; they spend less time at teaching preparation—while doing much better at teaching); and,

*c)* social management (e.g., they arrange mentoring and other collegial/social supports in timely fashion, some of it before formal arrival on campus).

So, exemplary new faculty evidently arrive already skilled (or predisposed to quickly learn). Their skills mirror the three categories of competence for succeeding in school as found by Sternberg, Okagaki, and Jackson (1990). What Sternberg calls tacit knowledge (i.e., usually unstated, unaware knowledge of how to work) may be about the skills that promote nonprocrastinating. These skills are what I am calling efficacy (the management skills for efficient, successful work; and the self-efficacy of knowing where to find the confidence and support to proceed, resiliently—Bandura, 1986; 1990). Only when I had grown familiar with the usually tacit knowledge of efficacy and had seen its individual variations, did I begin to understand the opposite of efficacy—procrastination. Procrastination is a matter, in my opinion, of lacking the skills that make up efficacy.

Quick starters, not surprisingly, see themselves as frugal, careful indulgers of procrastination. They tend to allocate their time wisely (and, so, develop more awareness of time but less urgency about it). They commonly work at lecture preparation in brief daily sessions (and, so, get past the normal feelings of new faculty that they are too busy to attend, regularly, to important activities like socializing and scholarly writing). They balance time for teaching preparation with that spent on scholarly writing and, most important, spend only a modicum of time on both. They generally spend as much time socializing about writing as doing it. In the next three paragraphs, I expand these discoveries into the framework of management skills established by Sternberg:

## Professorial Efficacy Made Specific

*Task-management.*
What is most valued about efficaciousness by quick starters is their relative freedom from busyness (busyness is a close correlate of procrastination). They display more patience and readiness (cf. normal new faculty) to talk with undergraduate students about academic and research topics (the very involvement that is associated with the most student progress—Pascarella and Terenzini, 1991). They evidence more free time, more time spent socializing with colleagues, more time at hobbies and at exercising.

*Self-management*
Exemplars, again, fare better at managing their emotions while working. They rarely display prolonged depressions. They only occasionally depend on hypomania (a near relative of mania that induces rushing, euphoria, and decisiveness—in the short run) to find motivation for working. Why? Hypomania is inefficient to long-term productivity, creativity, and health. It is a common precursor of depression and of procrastination (Boice, 1994). Instead of working in great spurts or binges (and here is an example where task-and self-management blend), exemplars stand out for their moderation and stability. They usually work calmly, without rushing or anxiety. They work playfully, with mild happiness (e.g., with relaxed, open postures and occasional smiling) and joy (including spontaneous comments that are more often optimistic than pessimistic).

*Social-management*
Finally, quick starters display better skills of socializing. They are more likely to actively seek and accept the mentoring and collaboration that brings professional connections, productivity, and belonging. They more often let other people do some of the work (e.g., by enlisting undergraduates as research and teaching assistants). And they do all this in unhurried, timely fashion.

## Interventions with Colleagues Who Need Efficacy

Other new faculty who practice those three management skills eventually develop a kind of efficacy that clearly wards off procrastination. As they manage their time and their reactions to time pressures, they report paying mindful attention to the costs of procrastination. They come to realize that some of procrastination is inevitable (perhaps even desirable). They try, planfully but flexibly, to limit it to infrequent, inexpensive acts. When they do procrastinate and block, their delays and reluctances follow a predictable pattern that distinguishes them from the problem procrastinators they once were: a) Procrastination occurs in response to varied problems (cf. a repetition-compulsion to always put off and struggle with the same things). b) It occurs sporadically (cf. regularly, to the point where it interferes with everyday functioning). c) It occurs for specific reasons that are external and not taken personally (cf. things that seem to indicate a general trait of character weakness). This configuration of ways to moderate procrastination closely resembles the one described by Snyder and Higgins (1988) as the ideal attributional style for avoiding depression (the so-called EVS pattern: of external, variable, and specific explanations).

So, an intriguing discovery about exemplars and the faculty who learn to be more like them is that they display adaptive skills of managing procrastination. When they do procrastinate, they do it with little embarrassment, few excuses, and limited expense. Predictably but ironically, they object far less than do chronic procrastinators to participating in intervention programs that displace procrastination with efficacy.

With that sort of information in hand, my direct observational studies of new faculty took on a new depth and clarity (at least for me). In one such study, I followed 27 newcomers during their first two years on campus and I repeatedly watched and interviewed them about things that I had seen or inferred had happened to them (Boice, 1993a). At first, their reports were self-serving and superficial. With practice at "recollective-thinking-aloud" methods of accounting for what they thought and felt during important experiences, their reports grew simpler, more objective, more useful (Perkins, 1981). (I followed elaborate precautions against influencing interviewees and overvaluing the focal events that people typically emphasize during times of difficult transitions—Baumeister, 1991). From these extended recollectings, new faculty eventually assembled a short list, usually of three or four incidents, depicting the critical turning points in their early careers.

New faculty who evidenced chronic, problematic procrastination not only showed signs of probable career failure (e.g., levels of scholarly output and of student ratings clearly below departmental norms and stated expectations for retention/tenure). They also showed a remarkably uniform pattern of distinctive, usually successive turning points (what Clark, 1987, might call career fault lines). Here I portray them in terms of the specific patterns and events that commonly led up to the problems:

1. New faculty failed to arrange (or take advantage of) mentoring and other collegial supports by year two on campus;

2. they put off socializing and then reacted to colleagues (whose actions often seemed mysterious, even suspicious) as adversaries;

3. they often behaved as though too busy to interact with undergraduates, they were not well-received or civilly treated in classrooms, they found teaching unrewarding, they came to see both students and teaching as nuisances; and,

4. they behaved as though marginalized from and rejected by their campuses (e.g., spending minimal time in offices and rarely participating in campus activities).

In that list of turning points, it seems to me, lie clear hints about what kinds of interventions in faculty development could be particularly effective in helping new faculty make good starts. (The interventions would deal mainly with pro-crastination of efficiencies.) Other outcomes of that study reinforced my belief that this is a crucially important period to help our new hires. Points of no-return, all of them seemingly tied to procrastination, occur surprisingly soon in faculty careers. These oft-irreversible turning points happen with little warning; still, books of advice for new faculty amiably omit information about these perils. And, most worrisome, these missed opportunities to find efficacy occurred with much higher relative frequency among women and minorities as new hires.

This is why I felt justified in pursuing interventions that address procrastina-tion amongst faculty members: My experiences of getting to know the newcom-ers who typically keep a low profile as they make poor starts distressed me when I saw that they proceeded inefficaciously and with little help. They, particularly women as new faculty, suffered far more than colleagues and administrators seemed to realize. Their whole lives were often changed, indelibly, by this expe-rience of mysterious expectations, isolation, rejection, and failure.

These periods of heightened sensitivity spurred me to reconsider my tactics and appearance as a research-practitioner. Perhaps, I thought to myself, I can ease the way with my critics in faculty development by putting more emphasis on highlighting what exemplary colleagues do well and then by showing, stealthily, how easily other faculty can emulate these skills of excellence.

## ATTEMPTS TO MAKE INTERVENTIONS MORE POLITE

I had the good fortune of being able to model my research-practice after studies of the sort I mentioned earlier. We already know about the best of these, Sternberg's emphasis on uncovering the tacit skills of success and his quieter move of showing that poor students can be taught these management skills. Consider some of the outcomes that show the effectiveness of his interventions: After one semester, the experimental group had been taught enough skills at self-, task-, and social-man-agement so that their scores on the Survey of Study Habits and Attitudes (notably on scales of Delay Avoidance, Work Methods, Teacher Approval, and Education and Acceptance) increased significantly. Specifically, these at-risk-students learned better ways of managing attitudes and motivation, even of difficult skills like infor-mation processing (Sternberg, Okagaki, and Jackson, 1990).

### Efficacies Stated as Simple Principles for Intervention

In one of my own attempts to make interventions more polite, I began (as Sternberg had) by assembling more information about efficacy in early faculty careers and then I experimentally winnowed that usually tacit knowledge into simple, practical rules. In my case, the rules were selected not only for their distinctive association with exemplars. They also had to prove useful for transport to new faculty making slow, inefficient, procrastinative starts. Briefly, these are the rules; elsewhere I explain them in more detail (Boice, 1995a; 1995b; 1996b):

1. *Wait.* This rule helps teachers enhance motivation for working by tempering impatience and rushing. Its exercises include methods for calming, slowing, and noticing connections before and during starts. At first glance, the first rule conflicts with the second.

2. *Begin before feeling ready.* The second rule reflects how exemplars find imagination and confidence; they begin, well before feeling ready or competent, with regular practices of collecting, filing, rearranging, and outlining ideas while making sure they solve the right problem and have the necessary materials at hand. Neither efficacy nor its rewards (including happiness) just happen; its possessors must prepare for and cultivate it in these routine, preliminary ways (Csikszentmihalyi, 1990). Sometimes the second rule gets mastered before the first; there is no necessary separation or linearity in these rules.

3. *Work in brief, daily sessions.* This means working regularly at important tasks like prewriting, lecture writing, class preparations, and other things easily procrastinated. It also means a regular habit that is conducted with such economy and brevity that it does not supplant other important activities. (Exemplars do well at both teaching and writing and rarely let either get in the way of the other.) The methods of working in brief, daily bouts are initially aided by contingency management (i.e., performing the daily task in order to gain access to something more desirable, such as newspaper reading—but only in the short run, until a regular habit is established, because writers and teachers work better with intrinsic motivation). The most distinctive quality of exemplars, and of productive and creative people in general, is that they return to their desks every day. Why do they do this? They have established strong habits and their habitual activities have taken on rewarding qualities (Gardner, 1993).

4. *Stop.* Stopping in timely fashion is more difficult and important than learning to start; even exemplars struggle to master its use (e.g., pausing and stopping when breaks are needed, when enough has been done for the day). It means moving on from teaching to other things including rest. Its methods of practice include planned breaks, early stops (sometimes in the middle of tasks), and social cues about when pauses and stops are due.

5. *Balance preliminaries with writing and teaching.* We know about this sort

of balance from mentions of quick starters. Its mastery begins with open-mindedness to the possibility that it can be true ("You mean I don't need to spend more time preparing for classes than presenting them? That seems hard to believe"). Its essential practice consists of careful planning that includes scheduled times for preliminaries (in the case of writing, most preparatory sessions need to be made longer; in the case of teaching, shorter). Its seeming risks focus on getting enough writing done even while doing lots of prewriting (e.g., conceptual outlining) or teaching adequately without having prepared great amounts of detailed material.

6. *Supplant self-defeating thinking/habits.* The sixth rule aims to moderate the pessimistic, "self-downing" that leads to depression (and its inaction or overreaction—Seligman, 1991). It helps rescript habits that otherwise incline teachers to shyness, suspiciousness, and self-defeat (Baumeister and Scher, 1988). At its most complex, the sixth rule teaches ways of making private bets that discourage impulsiveness, by requiring too great a price for it. When these bets are made well, they make the immediately rewarding acts that tempt us to be disobedient and self-defeating too costly (Ainslee, 1975; Logue, 1994). Related exercises include a) habitual monitoring for negative self-talk and for maladaptive styles of working and socializing, and b) practice of Rational-Emotive self-therapies to defuse and redirect irrational thinking in and around working sessions.

7. *Manage emotions.* This rule is about the affective side of teaching. It means monitoring for excessive, counterproductive emotions, most often for the hypomania that rushes and superficializes work. It means working at a moderate pace punctuated by occasional bursts of excitement that do not prevent returning to unhurried gaits of working, that do not induce enduring depression and procrastination (Boice, 1994).

8. *Moderate attachments and reactions.* This rule reflects the venerable notion, amongst composition teachers that:
The worse the writer, the greater the attachment to the writing.
It means that successful writers tend to be less attached to their writing, especially in its form and experience. In my programs based around these rules, writers and teachers are coached to notice cues of overattachment: a reluctance to stop during sessions (i.e., a tendency to run overtime); an early tendency to suppose work is already brilliant and that its formal presentation must be brilliant; a reluctance to share early plans and approximations because they are not brilliant or because their ideas may be stolen.

9. *Let others, even critics, do some of the work.* All these rules are about letting go, none more than the ninth. It means delegating, collaborating. It prescribes regularly-scheduled sharing of writing and teaching by way of

soliciting constructive criticism. And its practice in my programs engages writers and teachers, via role-played approximations, to adopt socially skilled ways of soliciting, handling, and learning from criticism.

10. *Limit wasted effort.* This last rule comes toward the end of the usual year-long program, when teachers and writers are beginning to work on their own. So while some of its practices are idiosyncratic, some are necessarily similar. Its common theme relies on one of the most important findings of the program: wasted effort is the crux of resilience. So to limit inefficiencies (and increase resiliency), we practice monitoring for wasted efforts, notably those borne of impatience and intolerance. A typical example of the former is rushing until fatigue sets in; of the latter, overreacting to criticisms or interruptions.

## Outcomes of Applying These Exemplary Rules to Needy New Faculty (Boice, 1995b)

In one arrangement of interventions, volunteers (N = 16) practiced those ten rules as writers for a year. Contrasted to controls (matched new faculty members whose involvement was limited to periodic assessments of experiences and progress), participants met their expectations for outputs and successes. In year 1 they, cf. controls, evidenced: a) more completions of one scholarly manuscript per year (75% vs. 19%); b) more acceptances in refereed outlets (38% vs. 6%); c) higher scores on a campus-wide rating instrument of their teaching ($X$ = 2.4 vs. 2.0, where 4.0 was the maximum); and d) more explicit assurances from renewal/tenure committees of making adequate progress (38% vs. 13%). Clearly, the writing interventions (i.e., the ten rules for efficacy) made a significant difference in helping newcomers find good starts as scholarly writers. This advance was the apparent source of much relief and optimism for these new hires. Curiously, the rules for efficacy, even though explicitly aimed at writing, helped enhance teaching. Why? The general notions of how to work more economically, more happily, showed spontaneous transfer to struggles with teaching.

These same 16 new faculty stayed on for a second year of the program, this time with the rules and strategies adjusted, slightly, to focus on improving teaching. During this second year, the results were far better in teaching *and* in writing than for controls (who continued to be monitored in the second year)—and for participants who quit after year 1 (but who continued to be monitored for experiences and progress). Compared with controls who had never participated, second year participants evidenced: a) more completions of one scholarly manuscript per year (94% vs. 25%); b) more acceptances in refereed, departmentally condoned outlets (63% vs. 25%); c) higher teaching ratings by students( $X$ = 3.0 vs. 2.2); and d) far higher rates of assurances from retention committees.

New faculty (N = 16) who spent the first program year concentrating on teaching improvement, then year two on writing enhancement, showed similar but somewhat less impressive results (compared to their own controls and to the participants who began with the year-long writing program). Why was the reversed pattern somewhat less effective (though still a significant improvement over non-participation in either pattern)? Junior faculty in this second pattern were less enthusiastic about mastering teaching while still struggling with writing. On the study campuses where I obtained these data, teaching offers few rewards beyond self-satisfaction and student approval. Research, especially its writing and publishing, seemed to be the clear priority.

The better, more enjoyable, question is why the combined programs worked better than singular interventions (even for participants who continued the program, in just writing or teaching improvement, for two years). One reason was that transferring efficacies to another domain (either teaching or writing) evidently forced new faculty to express the rules and to conduct the strategies more economically, with more precision and accountability. That is, they were clearer about the point of each rule and more attentive to what parts of its application made the most difference. A second reason could be that acts of generalizing (what had been learned in the rules) quickly grew beyond the bounds of the combined program. The same rules for efficacy proved applicable to problems such as insomnia and delays at carrying out exercise programs; as they were applied with success elsewhere, they apparently became all the more successful with teaching and writing. The third reason is more mundane but no less important. A second year of participation meant more deliberate, coached practice; repeated trials made remastery easier and more thorough.

So here is one of the handful of studies of teaching improvement that demonstrates real changes during my observations of classroom behaviors (e.g., pacing/listening; discussing/answering; immediacy/approachability; checking for student comprehension) and outcomes that endure (e.g., improvements in student notetaking and in student ratings). And here is one of the first published studies to show how teaching and writing can be enhanced interactively in college faculty. Teaching can in fact be facilitated by certain kinds of improvement in working at writing, and vice-versa. Because I took the stance of a research-practitioner, I believe, I was better able to see this link and take advantage of it.

### Reactions of Traditional Critics

Did my tactic of emphasizing strategies based on exemplars (cf. just pointing out and correcting the failings of other new faculty) help ease the way past usual objections to assessed interventions? Perhaps partially. The paper was accepted for publication (after I agreed to make extensive apologies for its scientism) and one reviewer offered some bits of praise. We have already seen the reaction of the reviewer who wanted to keep it out of print ("Is there no room for the art in this?"). Research-practitioners who tilt, quixotically, with this taboo may have to settle for mixed results that permit even grudging publication.

I found something else more sustaining in this project. The new faculty who participated were particularly appreciative and informative. I enjoyed observing and learning from exemplars; they tended to be happy, uplifting colleagues with a lot to share. And I thrived on coaching other, more troubled, new faculty to find efficacious ways of working; they too had much to teach me about how to teach and about what universities typically fail to provide them that is essential (mostly social supports). Together, all these new faculty participated with me in stimulating meetings about what helped new faculty survive and thrive. And therein, I was helped to see that there is more to be learned about procrastination if colleagues are to be truly helped to excel as professors. One thing these groups did was to stimulate me to read more and more about the broad nature of their problems. Often they located and read the sources first.

An advantage of this adjunct literature is that it suggests directions researchers on procrastination can take. Another is that its already established credibility may help lend some legitimacy and tolerance for the subject of procrastination (and for its corrective, interventions carried out by research-practitioners) in faculty development.

## PROCRASTINATION SEEN IN CLOSE PARALLELS

The examples that follow could mention procrastination but usually do not. (That omission may contribute to their greater social acceptance.)

### Time Use

Some of this we already know: That reasonable organization and routine promote health, optimism, self-esteem, and productive study habits (Bond and Feather, 1988). That overinvestment of time in short-term relief sacrifices long-term benefits and underlies self-defeating patterns (Baumeister and Scher, 1988). That efficacious, intelligent people are more flexible and selective in allocating their time, better at time-sharing between tasks, and better at automatizing some operations as a way of saving effort and time (Sternberg, 1988). Presumably, deficits in the same skills cause procrastination.

These are related findings: Polychronic users of time (i.e., people who do more than one thing at a time) are better able to tolerate less precision and less rigid scheduling while working—although both remain important (Bluedorn, Kaufman, and Lee, 1992). So it is that polychronics are less concerned with promptness but more likely to achieve it than are monochronics. And so it is that polychronics work with less role overload and more sociability, even more toleration for unplanned interruptions. Procrastinators, in contrast, fail to manage such advantages because of poor timing: They delay use of problem solving strategies (i.e., interventions for themselves or for others) until too late for optimal results (Perkins, 1981). They do not know how to minimize fatigue and maximize the right kinds of practice (Ericsson and Charness, 1994). And, again, they busily insist on doing one thing, with as few interruptions as possible, at a time.

Procrastination is more than a kind of lazy delaying and avoiding. It is also a deficit in estimating time and a deficit in self-distraction skills. The result inclines people to act impulsively (Logue, 1994). Impulsivity, in turn, brings hostility, hurrying, overvalued goals, and more procrastination (Frese, Stewart, and Hanover, 1987). At its worst this pattern grows in oscillations of mood that interfere with work; at its best it means nervous tension, self-absorption, and oversensitivity (Wessman, 1973). Time-urgent people are hard on themselves and on coworkers (who get seen impatiently, as slow moving obstructions—Landy, Rastengary, Thayer, and Colvin, 1991). And even when these impatient, impulsive people do finish things, they complete them so quickly that they miss most of the rewards of setting them up (Ainslee, 1975).   Efficacious workers, in contrast, who develop a reasonable appreciation of time benefit in terms of:   orderliness and confidence (Wessman, 1973), and in reduced role overload and tensions (Macan, Shanani, Dipboye, and Phillips, 1990). They even manage more sleep (Ericsson and Charness, 1994). People skilled at time use report feeling more in charge of their time, better able to say no to people, better able to halt unprofitable routines and activities. Said another way, their use of time skills resembles self-efficacy (Britton and Tesser, 1991). Consider, in a glance back to the personality area we reviewed earlier, that only self-efficacy (measured as a seeming trait) predicts the frequency and reasons for putting off important activities (Ferrari, Parker, and Ware, 1992).

Some insights about time and timeliness come from sources foreign to higher education. Historians, for example, note that close consciousness of time is a recent occurrence; for over ninety-nine percent of human evolution we may have revelled in the primal laziness that allows recovery from battle, chase, or harvest. Regular work (and the occasional resentment it elicits) awaited two things: routine tillage and the organization of labor; the most excessive routines for work were first perfected in slavery and its kin (Durant, 1954). Only with industrial routines did employers appreciate the benefits of efficacy. The psychology of work funded by the industrial revolution established several empirical lessons that were never completely learned by academics (including faculty developers): That attentiveness (as required in most sorts of teaching and scholarly writing) is abnormal, transient, and exhausting. ("Primitives" knew far better than we how to use rhythms and resting to sustain it.) That the longer the work day, the greater the need for some unproductive work. That waste in work owes mostly to fatigue and that what most effectively reduces wasted effort (as indexed by error rates) is a slower pace and a proportional amount of rest. Or that the best way to reduce errors (including procrastination) is to work in shorter, more manageable segments (Rabinbach, 1990).

There is, in this old and forgotten literature, a surprising explanation for the taboo against treatments for procrastination. Early psychologists and sociologists noticed that wasted energy and poor use of time differentiated low socio-economic people from those of higher class. By the point where Marxists appropriated this discomfiting idea, it seemed even clearer that technology (i.e., interventions) could be used to increase the productivity of the lower classes. More important, in that view, technology could decrease the wasted energy of the have-nots and emancipate them from excessive competition, classism, and procrastination. But American scholars have expressed vitriolic condemnation of the psychology of work, supposing that any system that enhances efficiency must also be inhumane, coercive, paternalistic, and inherently evil (e.g., Banta, 1993). Why is something that worked, that in fact made most workers more efficient, less fatigued, more happy, so reflexively rejected? It violates a taboo. When we point out someone's inefficiency and suggest correctives, we may imply that person's lack of class. And, in an academic culture that allows only those with the right stuff to succeed, we perpetuate an impressive (albeit limited) means of demonstrating one's possession of class. We also display effective ways of maintaining the status quo. To offer effective help to people on the margins (usually individuals with questionable social class) violates one of our least discussed, least understood prohibitions (Kipnis, 1994).

Another way of drawing a parallel between procrastination and kindred literatures may seem more familiar.

## Distinctions Between Product and Process Orientations

Again, we know some of the basics. Monochronics, because they are excessively task-oriented and busy (i.e., product oriented), do not know how to combine tasks and flexibly modify priorities (Bluedorn et al., 1992). Effective organization and persistence depend on a present (i.e., process) orientation, on paying attention to what matters in the moment, not on worrying about past mistakes and injustices or future rejections (Bond and Feather, 1986). Expert writers, for instance, are better at developing their own knowledge, identifying audiences, and spotting problems. Why? They work from elaborate task representations and plans that keep them mindful of working with a broad view, but usually in the moment (Hayes and Flower, 1986). That is, experts are mainly process oriented, in a style of working that is the essence of mindfulness and competence (Langer, 1989). The same sorts of processes are important to teaching well (Boice, 1995a).

*Economies of mindfulness.* Process orientations, as we have seen, draw attention to what decisions and actions matter in the moment. They raise awareness of habits of thinking, feeling, and working and how they influence our efficacy (Tremmel, 1993). They encourage an unhurried pace, a sense of flow that makes the activity an enjoyable, intrinsically motivating end in itself (Amabile, 1983;

Csikszentmihalyi, 1990). They help rein-in a consciousness that may otherwise run towards fear, anxiety, and mindlessness, three of the factors behind procrastination (Field, 1934). They foster more patience and time spent, en route, for summarizing, questioning, and clarifying. Their slowed, more reflective and planful process generates the imaginativeness and confidence necessary to stimulate the social conversations and other involvements that impel decisive actions (Flower and Hayes, 1980).   And, process orientations are learning orientations that meet obstacles adaptively, by increasing effort selectively and by varying strategies (Dweck, 1980).

*Economies of effort and confidence.* Process orientations also enhance awareness of wasted time and effort. Skinner (1983), who constantly examined his work habits and outputs, came to the realization that he had been using his time inefficiently: "When I am not working, I must relax—not work on something else!" (p. 79). P.G. Wodehouse timed the entrances and exits of his characters so that there was no waste in his seemingly spontaneous writing (Jasen, 1981). But does this sort of planfulness constrain creativity? Studies of writers suggest just the opposite. Of Dickens it was said: "He had the architectural plans drawn up, as it were, but he needed to build freely and instinctively" (Ackroyd, 1990, p. 560). Expert problem solvers in general rehearse the whole process of important things they do, including the solution, beforehand. Then, as they work, they can concentrate on process matters that let them try alternatives, invent new concepts and schemata, even better understand what had already seemed a clear idea (Carey, 1986). A final advantage of process modes in building effort and confidence may be most important: They predispose us to improved self-efficacy. Why? The deeper the processing (e.g., ability to store and recall), the more calm and confident the mode of working (Meier, McCarthy, and Schmeck, 1984).

*Economies of motivation.* Process orientations promote the motivation and momentum that procrastinators often struggle to find. Motivation builds with habitual acts of collecting and formulating ideas that stimulate imagination, that push, almost imperceptibly, for action (Mills, 1959; Murray, 1978). Motivation builds as acts of formulating ideas turn into a high consciousness that controls attention, positively evaluates abilities, and sets a positive affect for proceeding (Glass and Arnkoff, 1982). Motivation, then, requires regular habits of paying attention *and* flexible styles of working. In this way, motivation gets a boost from long processing (e.g., matching/assimilating novel or complex information with established schemata). The calm success of figuring things out via long processing slows reactivity and overreaction while maintaining an emotional stance of interest and joy (Singer, 1988). Efficacy, in the end, is a matter of economy, one that includes calm arousal, lowered levels of perceived stress, and toleration (Bandura, 1990; Landino and Owen, 1988; Rosenbaum, 1980). Without this calm and confidence, the right risks are not taken, the right supports are not accessed, the right problems are not solved, and the right skills are not mastered (London, 1993). An example: Women new to the professoriate who are most harried by work react the most suspiciously and pessimistically to offers of mentoring (Boice, 1993a).

Overall, it seems, a process orientation promotes knowing how to work. But how does it actually promote efficacy?

### Problem-Solving

Information about problem-solving helps illuminate the cognitive, affective, and work components of procrastination. It is an enormous literature, one I can only sample as a prelude to the last section of this paper.

*Expertise.* We respond to the problems we pose (Flower, 1990). Without mindful planning, we risk procrastination. Writers, for instance, who lack clear demands, assignments, and resources will reserve their best efforts for other tasks (Hayes, 1988). What helps experts find optimal structures and permissions are things like these: re-seeing problems playfully (Stack, 1980); attentively noticing and planning while getting ready (cf. waiting passively); patiently finding the ideal pace that any task has (Perkins, 1981); concentrating deeply and taking risks (Amabile, 1983); and, practicing difficult, important tasks in deliberate, regular fashion (Ericsson and Charness, 1994). All these skills of expert problem-solvers are far less prominent in chronic, problematic procrastinators.

*Emotions.* Expert writers report experiencing more positive emotions while working, less boredom, anxiety, or confusion than do nonexperts (Brand, 1986). So do exemplary teachers (Boice, 1995a). Research on emotions makes the reason clear: a state of moderate happiness broadens awareness and flexibility in making decisions (Oatley and Jenkins, 1992). Other research indicates an even wider role for happiness. In Terman's famous longitudinal study of gifted subjects, those who turned out to be most successful showed more contentment, self-confidence, openness, and spontaneity by their 70s; they were largely free from pervasive hostility, irritability, and dissatisfaction (Schneidman, 1984). Efficacious faculty and their opposites, procrastinators, in my studies of writing and teaching display the same general pattern of differences (e.g., Boice, 1994; 1995b).

*Cognitions.* When we try to work with performance goals in minds (i.e., in a product mode, not a process mode), we make things more difficult than they need to be. To work effectively in a product mode, we must begin with already high estimates of our ability to master a challenging task. The usual result of trying to work in a product orientation is a combination of defensive strategies including withdrawal or debilitation in the face of obstacles and poorer learning (Dweck, 1986). So it is that product (cf. process) styles of working distinguish procrastinators.

These three dimensions of problem-solving (expertise, emotions, and cognitions) combine to make a singular point: Success at hard tasks depends on knowing how to work; procrastination is a lack of such skills. So, in overviewing this closely parallel literature, I hope to have reinforced the notions put forward more tentatively from the traditional scholarship on procrastination. Still, much more remains to be done to make procrastination (and its allied problems of interventions) clear and acceptable to arenas like faculty development. In the section that follows I use a few brief examples to show how procrastination can be seen more interconnectedly, in terms of phenomena that are not ordinarily linked to procrastination. In these even greater stretches, I think, we learn the most about the basic nature of procrastination. The more broadly we understand about it, the more likely we are to see the need for research-practitioners.

## PROCRASTINATION SEEN INTERCONNECTEDLY

### Binge Eating And Procrastination

Binge eaters are like procrastinators in suffering high standards and demanding expectations (Heatherton and Baumeister, 1991). They overrespond to the demands of others as threats to their self-esteem. To escape these discomforts, binge eaters narrow their attention away from broad, meaningful thought to self-focus and lowered levels of awareness (overall, to what we might label a product orientation). This narrowing fosters uncritical, mindless acceptance of irrational beliefs (most of them probably about outcomes, few about learning better ways of controlling food intake).

What does this have to do with procrastination? It identifies a point where we, as faculty developers, commit to procrastinating: the moment where we narrow our attention and logic in order to escape short-term discomforts. And it identifies a central weakness in procrastinators: They, like dieters, feel chronically restrained and anxious from overconcern with a product orientation (as evidenced in the busyness so common amongst faculty developers). Once they experience discomfort, they habitually turn to narrowing and the products of low-level thinking—the easy, the relieving, the immediately enjoyable. In that state we prefer guesses over data, magic over technology, art over science.

This literature offers different ways of combatting the perfectionism and overreaction that lead to bingeing and mindlessness, primarily by way of building efficacy: a) the process orientation of reflective awareness, of slowing and calming to find the ideal pace and the right problem to solve; b) the attribution of imperfections to external, variable, and sporadic things like lack of good strategy, effort, or interpretation (cf. inherent failings of character or self); and c) the habit of regular, deliberate practice at basic skills like waiting, planning, and building expertise. Experts on writing blocks even offer related insights about the moment where procrastinators lose control (Kellogg, 1994): While they remain fluent, writers work holistically, with broad phrases and meanings and intentions, and, so, coherently. But when they find a particular thought difficult, writers suddenly focus all their resources of short-term memory on a few words. This is when they lose track, misconnect, blunder, doubt, and block.

My point is this: When we, as faculty developers, take the stance of research-practitioners who face up to problems like procrastination, we will begin to look more expansively at scholarship on related subjects. Even binge eaters have something to teach us about why we procrastinate in dealing with the procrastination that debilitates our neediest colleagues. So, as we will see, does creative madness.

## Mental Health, Creativity, and Procrastination

Why would faculty developers want to look into such an odd domain? Ultimately, I argue, research-practice will take faculty development into concerns such as mental health. After all, practitioners in related fields such as social work have been admitted therapists for a long time. I begin this foreign venture into mental health with its best-known links to procrastination.

In this literature too there is a long and creative tradition of supporting the taboo against taking procrastination seriously. It does so by implying that healthy efficaciousness inhibits creative productivity, by linking creativity with mental illness and its disarray. Specifically, it focuses on mood disorders (depression and mania) as afflictions of successful writers and other creative sorts. This is the general proposition: manic-depressiveness occurs at uncommonly high rates amongst creatively productive people; thus, creativity must depend on its affective extremes. Holden (1987), for instance, lists writers who displayed unmistakable signs of manic-depressiveness and who committed suicide. The problem with these anecdotal accounts is that we cannot know how selective the samples are. Exponents of creative madness do not draw out comparable numbers for maladies in other stressful, oft-criticized kinds of occupations that presumably involve little creativity.

Jamison (1993) offers the most objective, systematic account of this fascinating topic. Yet, her presentation has its romantic side: "Who would *not* want an illness that has among its symptoms elevated and expansive mood, inflated self-esteem, abundance of energy, less need for sleep, intensified sexuality...and sharpened unusually creative thinking and increased productivity?" (p. 103). Specifically, Jamison supposes that the cycle of mania and depression, as it moves from its fiery side to its judgmental side, results in creativity of singular power. Manic-depressiveness, in her view, carries the divine (or at least biologically implanted) gift of multiple selves.

Consider the data Jamison calls up to support her enthusiastically received claims. She cites the studies of others such as Ludwig's (1992) computation that 18 percent of poets reviewed in the *New York Times* had committed suicide and that of all writers reviewed, the rate of hospitalization was 6-7 times that of non-artists. Jamison pays special tribute to the pioneering studies of Andreasen

(1987) who used modern diagnostic criteria to establish a relationship between mental illness and creativity: Of her 15 creative writers, 80 percent reported treatment for mood disorders. Jamison's own data are still more impressive: Of 47 eminent, award-winning British writers and artists, 38 percent reported treatment for mood disorder; one-third of those recalled histories of severe mood swings (often with extended elations prior to intensely creative moods).

But these and other reports of creative madness are confounded by methodological shortcomings (Rothenberg, 1990): Andreasen, for example, defined creativity arbitrarily. Both she and Jamison relied solely on writers' own self-reports to make judgments about frequency and severity of affective disorders. And, Rothenberg notes, writers may be better able to understand and communicate mental experiences than are most people. Ochse (1990) adds a related point. Eminent people often enjoy exaggerating their eccentricities.

But objective criticisms such as Rothenberg's have gone largely unnoticed amongst the proponents of creative madness. Why does it continue to grow in popularity despite its shortcomings? Notions of creative madness amiably excuse procrastinators their eccentricities and foibles, even their attacks on nonprocrastinators. Creative madness seemingly explains why so much important work comes in behind schedule and with impressive suffering. It even associates depression and mania, common outcomes of procrastination, with genius.

Simonton (1994) offers a more useful, less romantic view. While creative productivity seems to depend on "weirdness" (usually some mixture of psychoticism and mania), its level must be moderate enough to allow work. The somewhat odd individuals who achieve greatness, many of them from families with members whose mental illness is too excessive to work, are at risk of becoming unstable themselves when they lose their balance. What would move them past the usual habits and perseverance that permit successful working? What could impel them into affective and cognitive extremes that undermine creativity? Evidently, that unhealthy and unproductive shift occurs when they do not know how to work efficaciously under conditions of stress. And when they are prone to product orientations, bingeing, and mindlessness. (If this is true, it contradicts the traditional assumption of faculty developers that creative success at teaching relies solely on autonomy, not on learning how to work.)

The evidence for this maladaptive role of procrastination in creativity comes largely from my own direct observations of blocked writers and inhibited teachers (Boice, 1994; 1996a; 1996b). (Here too my reviewers have been anything but encouraging.) When teachers and writers work under an extended state of hypomania, they commonly produce more work, but only in the short run. Even then, the work tends to be rushed, unreflective, and underrevised. And soon after the binges have ended, writers and teachers show increased scores on the Beck Depression Inventory indicative of moderate or higher levels of dysphoria. In the longer run, these professors receive lower teaching ratings and produce fewer pages of prose than do colleagues who work without strong hypomania or extended binges. Teachers and writers who exacerbate their manic-depressive cycles by bingeing display a distinctive set of prices: more fatigue, insomnia, misery, social strife, and procrastination. And: writing adjudged by trained reviewers as of less quality and creativity, less self-rated satisfaction with writing, and fewer editorial acceptances. So, marked cycles of mania and depression in working actually lead to less of what the glamorists of creative madness claim. What psychiatry and other fields have assumed as a basis for creativity is more likely the symptom of working at it inefficaciously. What academics including higher educators and faculty developers have often assumed are the benefits of procrastinating is a misunderstanding.

Other, more traditionally objective views of problems with a relationship to procrastination will prove even more useful if we are likely to take procrastination and the need for research-practice seriously.

## Self-Defeating Behaviors

Here the core problems are well-established, without apology or embarrassment (Baumeister and Scher, 1988). Self-defeat is a problem of poor choices made under aversive states, in favor of short-term relief. It is irrational behavior (because it sacrifices larger, longer term rewards in favor of immediate gain) commonly seen as: self-handicapping (e.g., creating obstacles that carry the blame for anticipated failures); substance abuse (which replaces aversive short-term states with pleasant sensations and lowered self-awareness); face-work (where tangible rewards are sacrificed to save embarrassment); and, shyness (a protective, self-focused style of self-presentation that reduces the risk of social rejection by making no social impression at all). These impulsive, self-focused actions lead to predictable problems of perseveration beyond the point of diminishing returns, of choking under pressure, of learned helplessness, and of poor bargaining strategies with authority figures (e.g., ineffective ingratiation styles with editors and administrators). At their most basic, self-defeating behaviors show components that resemble those of procrastination; here, though, we can see the three basic themes more clearly: a) impatience in the face of constraining and perfectionistic pressures; b) impulsive relief in mindless, irrational activities with short-term rewards; and c) aftermaths of lowered efficacy (e.g., never completely processing the event to change the future behavior; never getting past the doubts raised by not having mastered long-term tasks). Do faculty who fail at their careers evidence self-defeating behaviors that could be treated with relatively simple interventions by research-practitioners? Undoubtedly.

What related problems dog many of our colleagues who struggle in the professoriate?

## Self-Control

The problem here, as in procrastination, is discounting events that are delayed. To get past this impulsivity requires learning how to wait and when to wait. It often means tolerating mild aversion, in the short-run, to eventually gain bigger rewards (Logue, 1994). Binge-eating, stealing, substance abuse, suicide attempts, and procrastination are impulsive acts and problems of self-control.

Far more research has been done on self-control than on procrastination; we know what helps rein in the impulsivity that undermines it: a) More deliberate practice at delaying rewards while carrying out more and more effortful tasks. b) Increased association of this industriousness with secondary rewards (e.g., satisfaction in doing good work—Eisenberger, 1992). And c) heightened mindfulness of noticing cues that portend troublesome impulses (Ainslee, 1975). Specifically, precommitments to not be impulsive must be precisely planned in terms of behaviors to be avoided or performed. There must be regular monitoring to notice whether precommitments work reliably. And precommitments need to be designed with loopholes for unusually strong impulses; i.e., there must be safety valves that exact a price for disobedience but still permit it (while still keeping exceptions exceptional).

Here, with problems of self-control, we at last have access to proven interventions. Why? Problems of self-control that inconvenience and endanger society with stealing and drug abuse demand action (Logue, 1994). So do problems of faculty acting out violently in a syndrome known as middle-age disillusionment (Boice, 1993b). When impulsivity, mindlessness, and lowered self-efficacy get to that level, we no longer call them procrastination or joke about them. Yet, most faculty developers, so far as I know, do not yet deal with such problems.

## Personality Disorders

The clearest view of procrastination comes in an understanding of its most pathological manifestations (far away from the things faculty developers usually discuss). Personality disorders occupy a dark corner of psychotherapy research; generally they are assumed to be highly inflexible, problematic, often irreversible styles of behaving (i.e., traits). Their nature is illustrated in a quick overview of the kinds of personality disorders with obvious roots in procrastination (American Psychiatric Association, 1994):   *Obsessive-compulsive types* display recurrent obsessions severe enough to be time-consuming and repetitive behaviors that do little more than relieve the anxiety of obsessiveness. Outcomes include poor allocation of time, missed deadlines, annoyed others (because OCPDers act out their frustrations passively, indirectly), and an intensity of working that makes relaxation and hobbies unlikely. *Dependent types* obviously act submissively and tend to cling. Less obviously, they have difficulties with everyday decisions, with initiating projects, and with self-confidence (largely because they equate disapproval with worthlessness). *Avoidant types* experience social inhibition, inadequacy, and hypersensitivity to negative evaluations; they see new people as critical and disapproving until proved otherwise. *Narcissistic types* are, by definition, grandiose but they are also impatient, ruminative about overdue success, and dismissive of advice. Narcissists are especially likely to procrastinate after hypomanic bursts of grandiosity. *Histrionic types* seek attention and crave excitement but they are impatient and cannot tolerate delayed gratification. So, for instance, they often initiate projects with great enthusiasm and then lose interest (procrastination includes problems of getting started and of getting finished).

There are other personality disorders with unmistakable links to procrastination (e.g., antisocial type; borderline type), but the five just summarized make my points adequately, I think. First, they suggest a rich but neglected pattern of procrastinating that runs through personality disorders. Second, while these components of procrastination are seen at their extreme in personality disorders, they may tell us something basic about the nature of procrastination in less pathological expressions. Third, when I examine the commonalities of procrastination in personality disorders (and take into account the other knowledge I reviewed here such as self-defeating behaviors), a simple pattern emerges. This is the triad of basic procrastination factors as I propose it:

1) First come problems of compulsions and impulsivity that owe largely to excessive perfectionism and impatience;

2) second comes a readiness or predisposition, once the narrowness and disinhibition are set up by step one, to move to easy, mindless acts (even though these tend to undermine progress toward important goals); and,

3) third comes the aftermath of disappointment, lowered self-confidence, disapproval by others, depression, and uncertainty about abilities. This outcome persists and causes the most observable aspects of procrastination (and of its close kin, blocking).

These factors suggest a working model of procrastination, one that may ease its understanding and acceptance. It could be a model for understanding the inefficiencies of the faculty we try to help, one that implies clear interventions. Faculty development is, after all, hindered by a lack of directive, testable theories to direct its research and practice (Menges and Mathis, 1988). I propose an approach to faculty development based on the problems of understanding and treating procrastination. I'll be brief.

## A MODEL OF PROCRASTINATION

The triad of procrastinative components just listed suggests links to many problems of our faculty colleagues. That is, difficulties of impatience, narrowing, and depressive attribution characterize almost all their imaginable psychopathologies and everyday problems. Examples: The excessive self-focus that accompanies depression and its many relatives (Ingram, 1990); the poor management that originates from vague goals, from lack of commitment to learning, and from weak feedback (Locke and Latham, 1990); the lack of sustained, deliberate practice (especially of difficult, delayable things) that keeps performers from finding success and expertise (Ericsson and Charness, 1994); the constricted social contacts that owe to pessimism and that undermine careers (Simonton, 1994).

My point isn't just about interrelatedness. It is also about simplicity. Presumably, the same three components that underlie most behavioral problems in the professoriate also comprise procrastination; knowing this makes procrastination far easier to conceptualize, understand, even treat. Something else emphasized in this review is reinforced by the content of these simple components: They essentially amount to problems of not knowing how to work efficaciously. Even professors need to learn how.

When I combine the triad above with Sternberg's notions of how students can best learn to manage themselves, their work, and their social supports, this is the model of procrastination that emerges (with each component I list a brief reminder of extant interventions that have been proven to help in my work as a research-practitioner):

1. *Impulsivity* is borne of self-imposed constraints and impatient demands for relief; it mirrors deficits in tacit knowledge about *self-management*. Already effective treatments for self-control aim at patience (via calming, slowing, active waiting while teaching) and at tolerance (e.g., by way of playful experience at handling criticism with less reactivity). Interventions begin at the simplest level, of building steady involvement in assignments such as self-monitoring of daily habits and of impulsive acts (as when procrastinators impatiently opt for easy tasks instead of sticking with plans for more difficult actions that carry delayed rewards).

2. *Mindlessness* emerges from a product (cf. process) orientation and is a problem of *task management*. Interventions reviewed earlier include coaching procrastinators to work in a process mode (e.g., by emulating the pauses for reflection and planning seen in exemplars—Boice, 1994): in small, regular, and timely bits of difficult chores; with clear learning goals and feedback (Locke and Latham, 1990); with the help of coaching and faded supports that promote self-instructions for coping with failures and for finding self-satisfaction (Meichenbaum, 1985).

3. The *pessimism and low self-efficacy* of procrastinating reflect problems of not knowing how to socialize, externalize, and attribute in optimistic, rewarding ways. Together they stimulate the essential deficit in *social management*. Treatments include teaching the social skills of a) cooperating (e.g., by accepting coaching), b) imaginarily taking the place of another (and, so, moving outward, away from self-focus and its narrowing), c)

finding ways to agree with and learn from disapproval, and d) treating one's own and others' failings tolerantly, by generally attributing them in a realistic EVS (external, variable, specific) pattern.

Here, then, is something unique in the fields of procrastination *and* faculty development: A general model that explains its causes in objective fashion, that lists proven interventions for alleviating them. Has it any usefulness for faculty developers and higher education researchers? It offers a clear definition of procrastination as a combined problem of impulsivity, mindlessness, and pessimism. It shows how procrastination and blocking are simply related parts of the same general process: procrastination is more the impulsivity of putting off the difficult in favor of relief; blocking is more the eventual result, seen as struggling, silence, and discouragement. (In everyday experience, procrastination and blocking are inseparable.) The model also suggests ways in which most mental disorders relate to procrastination; they share problems of impulsivity, narrowing, and pessimism. And, finally, the model suggests that interventions need be directed at all three components—self-, task-, and social management. How could procrastination, viewed this way, not apply to teaching improvement? Where else could we learn basics about procrastination?

Consider some of the research-practitioners in nearby fields from whom we could glean information about management skills: Bandura (1986), the expert on self-efficacy, offers specific strategies for self-management including ways of tempering the high arousal that usually debilitates performance. Sternberg (1988) prescribes task management strategies such as organizing knowledge into stored problem solutions and defining problems in ways that render them more soluble. Bruner (1990) practices methods of enhancing both task management and social management by exteriorizing (i.e., putting things outside our heads, moving away from excessive self-focus). So, for example, efficacious performers learn to store some of memory in notes and prompts, to rely for some information and help on published sources and colleagues. Scheier and Carver (1992) teach patients to reinterpret criticism and failure by shifting attributions away from self-blame and pessimism to the more external, EVS pattern we saw earlier. Seligman (1991) prescribes and practices strategies for acting towards others more openly, acceptingly, optimistically. Similarly, Meichenbaum (1993) teaches specific, positive modes of problem solving that help patients normalize reactions to social situations, by fostering new assumptive, attributional worlds. All these should apply to teaching problems.

## SUMMARY AND IMPLICATIONS FOR FACULTY DEVELOPMENT

What constructive, potentially helpful, points does this plea for more tolerance of research-practitioners in faculty development offer? It begins by pointing out a costly oversight: Our failure to pay much attention (or encouragement) to research-practitioners (particularly those who offer interventions as a means of ensuring credible, informative tactics that help improve teaching and other professorial activities). To substantiate the cost of this neglect, I reviewed some of the careful inquiries by Weimer and Lenze that show a surprising lack of progress in faculty development. To support my notion that research-practitioners are discouraged in faculty development, I cited examples of my own reviews and suggested that those for manuscripts with interventions were typically savaged.

Then I asked what makes interventions so objectionable. One insight comes from research on excuses: close examination of them is a social impropriety (even though some discomfort in facing up to it might be necessary for progress in improving teaching). Another comes in an examination of what kinds of excusable, ignorable acts are most embarrassing, least discussed: procrastination (and its interventions).

So, it seems, to understand why we have made interventions taboo in faculty development, we must look more closely at what about us would change if we put them into research-practice. The answer, again, is procrastination (the very thing we try to avoid researching, especially in higher education; the very topic that reminds us of our own inefficacies). To depict procrastination briefly but usefully, I began by showing why most of its literature is superficial and dismissable: The majority of its accounts are humorous and forgiving. Researchers have tended to accept procrastinators' own (socially acceptable) excuses/explanations (e.g., perfectionism). Most inquiries are one-shot and incomplete; as a rule we learn little what about ameliorates procrastination in lasting, healthy fashion.

To make better sense of procrastination (because it is the key to resisting research-practice), I reviewed recent movements towards skills explanations that not only account for its complexities but also offer ways of teaching procrastinators more efficient habits and attitudes (cf. traditional notions of procrastination as an immutable, thus forgivable, personality trait). So, for example, I depicted the precedent-breaking research-practice of Sternberg who identifies students' failures to succeed as not knowing how to work in school. When he teaches them the usually tacit knowledge of success, students learn self-, task-, and social management skills that help reduce procrastination and improve working habits. Then I described how I used the strengths of studies like Sternberg's to redirect my own intervention studies with new faculty members. I, as he, started by identifying the behaviors of exemplary performers (e.g., Sternberg found good students better at allocating their time; I found quick starters balancing their time between teaching preparation and presentation). And next, as he did, I used these skills as a basis for intervention programs with new faculty who were failing in the renewal/tenure process. I had hoped for two things. One was realized. These interventions (based around 10 simple economies of working) reliably and enduringly enhanced both the teaching and scholarly writing of participants on a variety of domains.    The other hope was not realized. I aimed to assuage the hostilities of reviewers towards my work as a research-practitioner; I imagined they might be more tolerant of interventions modeled entirely after what new faculty could do better (cf. what they were doing wrong). Once again, my naivete (in supposing my style as an interventionist would import from psychotherapeutic research-practice) tripped me up.

That reinstatement of objections to interventions provided the last and most important of my insights about this dilemma. I concluded that reactions to interventions are so irrationally personal and counterproductive because these kinds of research-practice are taboo. So I ended by showing how a variety of phenomena (e.g., self-defeating behaviors) that already possess credibility can help illuminate procrastination as a problem that deserves understanding and treatment in faculty development. And I used that broad review of kindred topics, even binge-eating and personality disorders, to suggest that procrastination has common roots in almost all psychopathologies, some serious and some not. Those commonalities suggest a skills explanation of procrastination, one as simple as this: 1) Procrastinators put off things that make them uncomfortable, particularly when they are unsure about how to do them efficaciously. With delays come anxiety, embarrassment, and inflated definitions of success (all in the absence of knowing how to work in a process mode and how to use waiting times to prepare). 2) Then, when there can be no more delays, actions are impulsively rushed (often in binges) and failure is risked compared with more reflective, informed ways of working at tasks with long-term rewards like research and writing. 3) Finally, the more procrastinators experience this vicious cycle, the lower their self-esteem and the less their inclination to find new ways of working (and the higher the value of socially acceptable ways of using time pressures to work).

This model could help promote more understanding, tolerance, and study of procrastination amongst faculty developers. It might even help us understand our own hesitancy to conduct interventions (consider that our usually inefficacious approach to interventions could easily fit the three stages just outlined). But what, on the other hand, might keep us tied to the status quo? The powerful forces of tradition and inertia. Perhaps even an understandable reserve towards research-practitioners who come from fields outside education.

I can, though, see promise for change on the horizon. Perry and his colleagues (e.g., Perry, Hechter, Menec, and Weinberg, 1993) are carrying out systematic, experimental studies of how attributional retraining for more optimistic stances facilitates student performance (possibly even that of the teachers who teach these orientations—Perry and Struthers, 1994). Lenze and Dinham (1994) are part of a large, long-term project to identify what new faculty know about teaching (e.g., these novices erroneously make assumptions about their students' knowledge based on recollections of their own experiences as students). And

Plax and Kearney (1992) are painstakingly identifying the negative classroom motivators that teachers use, unwittingly, as part of distancing themselves from students.

In these and in other such researches, measured interventions seem more and more inevitable. As that happens, I hope the path to interventionism in faculty development grows easier and more rewarding for hardier cojourneyers than it has for me.

## A Specific Example of How Simple Efficiencies Might Fit Higher Education Theories

One way to help convince higher education researchers to appreciate this view may be to show how efficiencies can inform contemporary theories and discussions. Consider our usual debates about what constitutes excellent teaching and whether excellence can be taught. The most sophisticated inferences derive from analyses of student ratings (Feldman, 1997). Researchers in that domain typically describe but do not attempt to change factors of teaching (e.g., enthusiasm). Moreover, they often depict the essential part of teaching excellence in terms of large, global factors (e.g., Abrami, d'Apollonia, and Rosenfield, 1996). So, they do little to discourage traditional notions (much as with procrastination) that good teaching relies largely on fixed personality traits. Why does that matter? Notions of personality traits deter interventions, even first-hand observations of what excellent teachers do.

Personality beliefs, if applied unthinkingly and indiscriminately, can hinder even our best interventive approaches. Murray (1991), for example, not only identifies teacher enthusiasm (along with secondary components of clarity and teacher-student interaction) as the most general factor from student evaluations. He also portrays it as a complex that can be represented behaviorally (e.g., movement and gestures) and taught to teachers. The result is an increase in expressiveness that leads to better student evaluations (Murray and Lawrence, 1980). But will practitioners readily and completely accept this model of change? Even the wisest and most venerable of experts on teaching, McKeachie (1997), expresses a conflict in embracing that seeming fact. In his experience (and in mine), some teachers simply prove incapable of displaying enthusiasm to an impressive degree. If you imagine other researchers and practitioners coming to the same conclusion and taking the next "logical" step—of supposing that the core of teaching is a trait-like essence that cannot be taught—then you can understand why we have procrastinated in following up Murray's lead as a research-practitioner.

But if, I argue, the label were not so strictly dependent on usual categories taken from student evaluation forms, the task of getting teachers to produce the same essential result might be more obviously realistic. Seen in terms of what actually distinguishes exemplary from struggling novice teachers, the more basic efficiency than enthusiasm may be nothing but "immediacies" (e.g., open postures, attentiveness to student responses, and positively motivating statements that induce students to perceive teachers as caring and approachable—Boice, 1996c). While teachers who come to display immediacies commonly teach with enthusiasm, not all do. With or without enthusiasm, the effect (including significantly enhanced student ratings of the usual sort) is essentially the same. Enthusiasm may be difficult to change in dramatic degrees, but immediacy is not because it is only a simple, easily learned efficiency.

How, in turn, would belief in the power of this efficiency affect our usual discussions? Consider the case of my friendly colleague Raymond Perry (Perry, 1991; Perry and Smart, 1997), the very person who solicited this chapter. Might he be induced to reconsider his claim that we cannot suppose the best teaching practices would improve the performance of helpless students? While he is undoubtedly right that helpless students will benefit from enhanced perceptions of personal control, he may be overlooking the role of teachers' potentially simple efficiencies in effecting that change. The mere addition of immediacies should, according to recent evidence, reduce the usual boredom and distraction displayed by otherwise helpless students (Boice, 1996c). It should also (according to that same study of efficiencies usually neglected and procrastinated by teachers) help ensure the high motivation and selective attention in students that Perry finds can compensate for inexpressive teachers. Why? Because immediacies involve students as active learners. Because immediacies apparently heighten student motivation and attention. Perhaps because immediacies enhance students' perception of personal control.

This, of course, is an empirical question. In an open, tolerant atmosphere, answers can be based on research practice. That general change in a willingness to reexamine our traditional practices might even, in turn, extend to the administrators who impact so much of what we do.

## What Faculty Developers and Their Administrators Might Glean from This Account

If faculty development is to make significant progress toward actually improving teaching and establishing respectability with the professoriate, several things must change. In particular, I think, practitioners need to do more to combine serious research and accountability with their programs. Just as important, the administrators who fund these programs need to place more value on their accountability. Most important, in my view, there needs to be an objective examination of the climate for research and interventions in faculty development. One way to initiate that change might lie in raising our awareness of counterproductive misbeliefs that have dominated the field for too long. I propose the following list of common myths among faculty developers as a beginning. Its content reflects my own experiences and those of other research-practitioners, many of whom have struggled much as I have.

**Common Myths About Research in Faculty Development:**

1. *That research is incompatible with good teaching or practice* (see, among other sources, my own article [Boice, 1995a] for one of the few clear disproofs of this belief; i.e., under reasonable circumstances, teaching and research can mutually facilitate each other);

2. *That research and quantification necessarily distort the teaching process* (the same, counterproductive notion held about psychotherapy until research-practitioners like Carl Rogers showed the advantages of analyzing the process into its learnable components);

3. *That research-practitioners who do interventions are inherently evil, manipulative people* (Carl Rogers, again, is one of many disproofs of this myth);

4. *That faculty developers, by dint of experience and conversation with other practitioners, know intuitively what works and what doesn't to facilitate teaching* (history is replete with examples of well-intentioned practitioners who mistakenly resisted scientifically-based changes from usual procedures; e.g., recall Ignaz Semmelweiss, famous for having been mercilessly persecuted by his colleagues for claiming that physicians should wash their hands after autopsies and before delivering babies);

5. *That faculty developers, because they are well-intentioned and experienced at helping teachers, need not be held accountable to their campuses or colleagues for the effectiveness of their programs* (without clear goals and ways of measuring how well we progress toward them, we risk procrastination and inefficiency and busyness);

6. *That research-based interventions are too difficult and time-consuming to become a part of everyday practice* (in fact such strategies help organize and redirect programs, usually toward more efficient efforts); and,

7. *That measured, effective interventions necessarily will be resisted by faculty and that most faculty do not need such formal help* (to accept this misbelief is to continue to condemn untraditional, underrepresented newcomers in the professoriate to marginal performances, even to perpetuate the inefficiencies of teaching that make it seem more generally difficult and unrewarding than it needs to be).

**REFERENCES**

Abrami, P.C., d'Apollonia, S., and Rosenfield, S. (1996). The dimensionality of student ratings of instruction: what we know and what we do not. In J.C. Smart (ed.), *Higher Education: Handbook of Theory and Research*, Vol. XI. Edison, NJ: Agathon Press. (Reprinted in Perry and Smart, 1997.)

Ackroyd, P. (1990). *Dickens*. New York: HarperCollins.

Ainslee, G. (1975). Specious reward: A behavioral theory of impulsiveness and impulse control. *Psychological Bulletin* 82: 463-496.

Amabile, T.M. (1983). *The Social Psychology of Creativity*. New York: Springer-Verlag.

American Psychiatric Association. (1994). *Diagnostic and Statistical Manual of Mental Disorders*. Fourth Edition. Washington, D.C.: American Psychiatric Association.

Andreasen, N.C. (1987). Creativity and mental illness. *American Journal of Psychiatry* 144: 1288-1292.

Astin, A.W. (1985). *Achieving Academic Excellence*. San Francisco: Jossey-Bass.

Bandura, A. (1986). *Social Foundations of Thought and Action*. Englewood Cliffs, NJ: Prentice-Hall.

Bandura, A. (1990). Conclusion: Reflections on nonability determinants of competence. In R.J. Sternberg and J. Kolligan (eds.), *Competence Considered* (pp.315-362). New Haven: Yale University Press.

Banta, M. (1993). *Taylored Lives*. Chicago: University of Chicago Press.

Barlow, D.H., Hayes, S.C., and Nelson, R. (1984). *The Scientist Practitioner*. New York: Pergamon.

Barrios, M.V., and Singer, J.L. (1981). The treatment of creative blocks: A comparison of waking imagery, hypnotic dream, and rational discussion techniques. *Imagination, Cognition, and Personality* 1: 89-101.

Baumeister, R.F. (1991). *Meanings of Life*. New York: Guilford.

Baumeister, R.F., and Scher, S.J. (1988). Self-defeating behavior patterns among normal individuals: Review and analysis of common self-destructive tendencies. *Psychological Bulletin* 104: 3-22.

Beswick, G., Rothblum, E.D., and Mann, L. (1988). Psychological antecedents of student procrastination. *Australian Psychologist* 1988: 207-217.

Birner, L. (1993). Procrastination: Its role in transference and countertransference. *Psychoanalytic Review* 80: 541-558.

Bluedorn, A.C., Kaufman, C.F., and Lane, P.M. (1992). How many things do you like to do at once? An introduction to monochronic and polychronic time. *Academy of Management Executive* 6: 17-26.

Boice, R. (1984). Reexamination of traditional emphases in faculty development. *Research in Higher Education* 21: 195- 209.

Boice, R. (1987). Is released time an effective device for faculty development? *Research in Higher Education* 26: 311- 326.

Boice, R. (1990). Mentoring new faculty: A program for implementation. *Journal of Staff, Program, & Organization Development* 143-160.

Boice, R. (1991). Quick starters. *New Directions for Teaching and Learning* 48: 111- 121.

Boice, R. (1992b). *The New Faculty Member*. San Francisco: Jossey-Bass.

Boice, R. (1993a). New faculty involvement of women and minorities. *Research in Higher Education* 34: 291-341.

Boice, R. (1993b). Primal origins and later correctives for midcareer disillusionment. *New Directions for Teaching and Learning* 55: 33-41.

Boice, R. (1993c). Writing blocks and tacit knowledge. *Journal of Higher Education* 64: 19-54.

Boice, R. (1994). *How Writers Journey to Comfort and Fluency: A Psychological Adventure*. Westport, CT: Praeger.

Boice, R. (1995a). Developing teaching, then writing amongst new faculty. *Research in Higher Education,* 36: 415-456.

Boice, R. (1995b). Writerly rules for teachers. *Journal of Higher Education* 66: 32-60.

Boice, R. (1996a). Classroom incivilities. *Research in Higher Education* 37: 453-486

Boice, R. (1996b). *First-Order Principles of College Teaching*. Bolton, CT: Anker.

Boice, R. (1996c) Immediacies enhance college teaching. Manuscript submitted for publication.

Bond, M.J, and Feather, N.T. (1988). Some coordinates of structure and purpose in the use of time. *Journal of Personality and Social Psychology* 55: 321-329.

Brand, A.G. (1986). *The Psychology of Writing: The Affective Experience*. Westport, CT: Greenwood.

Britton, B.K., and Tesser, A. (1991). Effects of time-management practices on college grades. *Journal of Educational Psychology* 83: 405-410.

Brown, R. (1981). This week's citation classic. *Current Contents* February 16, p. 16.

Bruner, J. (1990). *Acts of Meaning*. Cambridge: Harvard University Press.

Buehler, R., Griffin, D., and Ross M. (1944). Exploring the planning fallacy: why people underestimate task completion times. *Journal of Personality and Social Psychology* 67: 366-381.

Burka, J.B., and Yuen, L.M. *Procrastination*. Reading, MA: Addison-Wesley.

Carey, S. (1986). Cognitive science and science education. *American Psychologist* 41: 1123- 1130.

Carroll, J.G. (1977). Assessing the effectiveness of a training program for the university teaching assistant. *Teaching of Psychology* 4: 135-138.

Clark, B.R. (1987). *The Academic Life*. Princeton, NJ: Carnegie Foundation.

Csikszentmihalyi, M. (1990). *Flow: The Psychology of Optimal Experience*. New York: Harper and Row.

Dillon, M.J., Kent, H.M., and Malott, R.W. (1980). A supervisory system for accomplishing long-term projects. *Journal of Organizational Behavior Management* 2: 213-237.

Durant, W. (1954). *Our Oriental Heritage*. New York: Simon and Schuster.

Dweck, C. (1986). Motivational processes affecting learning. *American Psychologist* 41: 1040- 1048.

Eble, K.E. (1985). *The Aims of College Teaching*. San Francisco: Jossey-Bass.

Eble, K.E., and McKeachie, W.J. (1985). *Improving Undergraduate Education through Faculty Development*. San Francisco: Jossey-Bass.

Eisenberger, R. (1992). Learned industriousness. *Psychological Review* 99: 248-267.

Ellenberger, H. (1970). *The Discovery of the Unconscious*. New York: Basic Books.

Ellis, A., and Knaus, W.J. (1977). *Overcoming Procrastination*. New York: Institute for Rational Living.

Epel, N. (1993). *Writers Dreaming*. New York: Carol Southern Books.

Erickson, B.L., and Erickson, G.R. (1980). Working with faculty teaching behaviors. *New Directions for Teaching and Learning* 1: 57-67.

Ericsson, K.A., and Charness, N. (1994). Expert performance: Its structure and acquisition. *American Psychologist* 49: 725-747.

Feldman, K.A. (1997, forthcoming). Reflections on the study of effective college teaching and student ratings: one continuing quest and two unresolved issues. In J.C. Smart (ed.) *Higher Education: Handbook of Theory and Research,* Vol. XIII. Edison, NJ: Agathon Press.

Ferrari, J.R. (1991). A preference for a favorable public impression by procrastinators. *Personality and Individual Differences* 12: 1233-1237.

Ferrari, J.R. (1993). Christmas and procrastination: Explaining lack of diligence at a "real-world" task deadline. *Personality and Individual Differences* 14: 25-33.

Ferrari, J.R., Parker, J.T., and Ware, C.B. (1992). Academic procrastination: Personality correlates with Myers-Briggs types, self-efficacy, and academic locus of control. *Journal of Behavior and Personality* 7: 495-502.

Field, J. (1936, 1981) *A Life of One's Own*. Los Angeles: J.P. Tarcher.

Flett, G.L., Blankenstein, K.R., Hewitt, P.L., and Koledin, S. (1992). Components of perfectionism and procrastination in college students. *Journal of Social Behavior and Personality* 20: 85-94.

Flower, L. (1990). The role of task representation in reading-to-write. In L. Flower, V. Stein, J. Ackerman, M.J. Kantz, K. McCormick, and W.C. Peck. (eds.), *Reading-to-Write* (pp. 35-75). New York: Oxford University Press.

Flower, L.S., and Hayes, J.R. (1980). The cognition of discovery: Defining a rhetorical problem. *College Composition and Communication* 31: 21-32.

Fox, M.F. (1985). Publication, performance, and reward in science and scholarship. In J.C. Smart (ed.), *Higher Education: Handbook of Theory and Research,* Vol. 1. New York: Agathon Press.

Frese, M., Stewart, J., and Hanover, B. (1987). Goal orientation and planfulness: action styles as personality constructs. *Journal of Personality and Social Psychology.* 52: 1182-1194.

Gardner, H. (1993). *Creating Minds.* New York: Basic Books.

Gibson, G.W. (1992). *Good Start.* Bolton, MA: Anker.

Garth, R. (1992). Comment made at The Transition of Graduate Students to Teaching Faculty: The Lubin House Conference, Manhattan, September 25-27.

Glass, C.R., and Arnkoff, D.B. (1986). Think cognitively: Selected issues in cognitive assessment and therapy. *Advances in Cognitive Behavioral Research* 1: 35-71.

Hamada, R. (1986). In defense of procrastination. *University Magazine.* 8(1): 28-29.

Hayes, J.R. (1990). Individuals and environments in writing instruction. In B.F. Jones and I. Idol (eds.), *Dimensions of Thinking* (pp. 241-263). Hillsdale, NJ: Erlbaum.

Hayes, J.R., and Flower, L.S. (1986). Writing research and the writer. *American Psychologist* 41: 1106-1113.

Heatherton, T.F., and Baumeister, R.F. (1991). Binge eating as escape from self-awareness. *Psychological Bulletin* 110: 86-108.

Holden, C. (1987). Creativity and the troubled mind. *Psychology Today* 21(4): 9-10.

Ingram, R. (1990). Self-focused attention in clinical disorders: Review and conceptual model. *Psychological Bulletin* 107: 156-176.

Jahoda, M. (1981). Work, employment, and unemployment. *American Psychologist* 36: 184- 191.

Jamison, K.R. (1993). *Touched with Fire.* New York: Free Press.

Jasen, D.A. (1981). *P.G. Wodehouse: A Portrait of a master.* New York: Continuum.

Jensen, G.H., and DiTiberio, J.K. (1984). Personality and individual writing processes. *College Composition and Communication* 35: 285-300.

Kellogg, R. (1994). *The Psychology of Writing.* New York: Oxford University Press.

Kipnis, D. (1994). Accounting for the use of behavior technologies in social psychology. *American Psychologist* 49: 165-172.

Kraus. S.J. (1993). A new look at new faculty members. *Contemporary Psychology* 38: 543- 544.

Kubie, L.S. (1965). Blocks to creativity. *International Science and Creativity* 22: 69-78.

Lakein, A. (1974). *How to get control of your time and your life.* New York: Signet.

Landino, R.A., and Owen, S.V. (1988). Self-efficacy in university faculty. *Journal of Vocational Behavior* 33: 1-14.

Langer, E.J. (1989). *Mindfulness.* Reading, MA: Addison-Wesley.

Landy, F.J., Rastengary, H., Thayer, J., and Colvin, C. (1991). Time urgency: The construct and its measurement. *Journal of Applied Psychology* 1991: 644-657.

Lay, C.H. (1986). At last, my research article on procrastination. *Journal of Research on Personality* 20: 474-495.

Lay, C.H. (1992). Trait procrastination and the perception of person-task characteristics.

*Journal of Social Behavior and Personality* 7: 483-494.

Lay, C., and Schouwenberg, H.C. (1993) Trait procrastination, time management, and academic behavior. *Journal of Social Behavior and Personality* 8: 647-662.

Leader, Z. (1991). *Writer's Block.* Baltimore: Johns Hopkins University Press.

Levinson-Rose, J., and Menges, R.J. (1981). Improving college teaching: A critical review of research. *Review of Educational Research* 51: 403-434.

Lenze, L.F., and Dinham, S.M. (1994). Examining pedagogical knowledge of college faculty new to teaching. Paper presented at the American Educational Research Association, New Orleans, April.

Locke, E.A., and Latham, G.P. (1990). Work motivation and satisfaction: Light at the end of the tunnel. *Psychological Science* 1: 240-246.

Logue, A.W. (1994). *Self-Control.* Englewood-Cliffs, NJ: Prentice-Hall.

London, M. (1993). Relationships between career motivation, empowerment, and support for career development. *Journal of Occupational Development* 66: 55-69.

Ludwig, A.M. (1992). Creative achievement and psychopathology: Comparisons among professions. *American Journal of Psychotherapy* 46: 330-356.

Macan, T.H., Shahani, C., Dipboye, R.L., and Phillips, A.M. (1990). *Journal of Educational Psychology* 82: 760-768.

Mack, K., and Skjei, E. (1979). *Overcoming Writing Blocks.* Los Angeles: J.P. Tarcher.

Masters, W.H, and Johnson, V.E. (1970). *Human Sexual Inadequacy.* Boston: Little, Brown.

McCown, W., Johnson, J., and Petzel, T. (1989). Procrastination: Principal components analysis. *Personality and Individual Differences* 10: 197-202.

McKeachie, W.J. (1990). Research on college teaching: The historical background. *Journal of Educational Psychology* 82: 189-200.

McKeachie, W.J. (1997). Good teaching makes a difference—and we know what it is. In R.P. Perry and J.C. Smart (eds.), *Effective Teaching in Higher Education: Research and Practice.* Edison, NJ: Agathon Press.

Meier, S., McCarthy, P.R., and Schmeck, R.R. (1984). Validity of self-efficacy as a predictor of writing performance. *Cognitive Therapy and Research* 8: 107-120.

Meichenbaum, D. (1985). Teaching thinking: A cognitive-behavioral perspective. In S.F. Chipman and J.W. Segal (eds.), *Thinking and Learning Skills*, vol. 2 (pp. 407-426). Hillsdale, NJ: Erlbaum.

Meichenbaum, D. (1993). Changing conceptions of cognitive behavior modification: Retrospect and prospect. *Journal of Consulting and Clinical Psychology* 61: 202-204.

Menec, V.H., Perry, R.P., Struthers, C.W., Schonwetter, Hechter, F.J., and Eicholtz, B.L. (1994). Assessing at-risk college students with attributional retraining and effective teaching. *Journal of Applied Social Psychology* 24: 675-701.

Menges, R.J. (1991). Promising areas in faculty/staff development. Presented at the Improving University Conference, July 2-5, Glasgow.

Menges, R.J., and Mathis, B.C. (1988). *Key Resources on Teaching, Learning, Curriculum, and Faculty Development.* San Francisco: Jossey-Bass.

Milgram, N., Batori, G., and Mowrer, D. (1993). Correlates of academic procrastination. *Journal of School Psychology* 31: 487-500.

Mills, C.W. (1959). *The Sociological Imagination.* New York: Grove Press.

Murray, D.M. (1978). Write before writing. *College Composition and Communication* 29: 375-381.

Murray, H.G. (1991). Effective teaching behaviors in the college classroom. In J.C. Smart (ed.), *Higher Education: Handbook of Theory and Research,* Vol. VII. Edison, NJ: Agathon Press. (Reprinted in Perry and Smart, 1997.)

Murray, H.G., and Lawrence, C. (1980). Speech and drama training for lecturers as a means of improving university teaching. *Research in Higher Education* 13: 73-90.

Nelson, B. (1988). Deep-seated causes found for tendency to delay. *New York Times*, April 12, pp. c3 & C8.

Oatley, K., and Jenkins, J.M. (1992). Human emotions: Function and dysfunction. *Annual Review of Psychology* 43: 55-85.

Ochse, R. (1990). *Before the Gates of Excellence*. New York: Cambridge University Press.

Parini, J. (1989). The more they write, the more they write. *New York Times Book Review*, July 30, 10 & 24-25.

Pascarella, E.T., and Terenzini, P. (1991). *How College Affects Students*. San Francisco: Jossey-Bass.

Perkins, D.N. (1981). *The Mind's Best Work*. Cambridge: Harvard University Press.

Perl, S. (1978). *Five Writers Writing: Case Studies of the Composing Processes of Unskilled College Writers*. Ph.D. dissertation, New York University.

Perry, R.P. (1991). Perceived control in college students: implications for instruction in higher education. In J.C. Smart (ed.), *Higher Education: Handbook of Theory and Research*, Vol. VII. Edison, NJ: Agathon Press. (Reprinted in Perry and Smart, 1997.)

Perry, R.P. (1997). Teaching effectively: which students? what methods? In J.C. Smart (ed.) *Higher Education: Handbook of Theory and Research,* Vol. XIII. Edison, NJ: Agathon Press.

Perry, R.P., Hechter, F.J., Menec, V.H., and Weinberg, L.E. (1993). Enhancing achievement motivation and performance in college students: An attributional retraining perspective. *Research in Higher Education* 34: 687-723.

Perry, R.P., and Smart, J.C. (1997). *Effective Teaching in Higher Education: Research and Practice*. Edison, NJ: Agathon Press.

Perry, R.P., and Struthers, C.W. (1994). Attributional retraining in the college classroom: Some causes for optimism. Symposium paper presented the American Educational Research Association, New Orleans, April.

Plax, T.G., and Kearney, P.K. (1992). Teacher power in the classroom. In V.P. Richmond, and J.C. McCroskey (eds.), *Power in the Classroom* (pp. 67-84). Hillsdale, NJ: Erlbaum.

Rabinbach, A. (1990). *The Human Motor*. New York: Basic Books.

Rheingold, H.L. (1994). *The Psychologist's Guide to an Academic Career*. Washington, DC: American Psychological Association.

Rosenbaum, M. (1980). A schedule for assessing self-control behaviors. *Behavior Therapy*, 11, 109-121.

Ross, E.I. (1985). *How to Write While You Sleep*. Cincinnati: Writer's Digest Books.

Rothblum, E.D. (1990). The fear of failure: The psychodynamic, need achievement, fear of success, and procrastination models. In H. Leitenberg (ed.), *Handbook of Social and Evaluation Anxiety* (pp. 387-394). New York: Plenum.

Rothblum, E.D., Solomon, L.J., and Murakami, J. (1986). Affective, cognitive, and behavioral differences between high and low procrastinators. *Journal of Counseling Psychology* 33: 387-394.

Rothenberg, A. (1990). *Creativity and Madness*. Baltimore: Johns Hopkins Press.

Scheier, M.F., and Carver, S.C. (1992). Effects of optimism on psychological and physical well- being: Theoretical overview and empirical update. *Cognitive Therapy and Research* 16: 201-228.

Schneidman, E.S.(1984). Personality and "success" among a selected group of lawyers. *Journal of Personality Assessment* 48: 609-616.

Schouwenberg, H.C. (1992). Procrastinators and fear of failure: An exploration of reasons for procrastination. *European Journal of Personality* 6: 225-256.

Seligman, M.E.P. (1991). *Learned Optimism.* New York: A.A. Knopf.

Seligman, M.E.P. (1994). *What You Can change and What You Can't.* New York: Knopf.

Silver, R.C., Wortman, C.B., and Crofton, C. (in press). The role of coping in support provision: The self-presentational dilemma of victims of life crises. In I.G Sarason, B.R. Sarason and G.R. Pierce (eds.), *Social Support: An interactional view* (pp.??-??). New York: Wiley.

Silverman, R.J. (1977). Suffer in silence. *Journal of Higher Education* 48: 603-604.

Silverman, S., and Lay, C. (in press). The relations of agitation and dejection to trait procrastination and dilatory behavior over an academic exam period.

Simonton, D.K. (1994). *Greatness.* New York: Guilford.

Singer, J.L. (1988). Sampling ongoing unconsciousness and emotional implications for health. In M.J. Horowitz (ed.), *Psychodynamics and Cognition* (pp. 297-348). Chicago: University of Chicago Press.

Skinner, B.F. (1971). *Beyond Freedom and Dignity.* New York: Knopf.

Skinner, B.F. (1983). *A Matter of Consequences.* New York: Knopf.

Snyder, C.R., and Higgins, R.L. (1988). Excuses: Their effective role in the negotiation of reality. *Psychological Bulletin* 104: 23-35.

Solomon, L.J., and Rothblum, E.D. (1984). Academic procrastination: Frequency and cognitive-behavioral correlates. *Journal of Counseling Psychology* 31: 503-509.

Solomon, L.J., and Rothblum, E.D. (1988). Procrastination assessment scale—students. In M. Hersen and A.S. Bellak (eds.), *Dictionary of Behavioral Assessment Techniques* (pp. 358-360).

Solomon, R., and Solomon, J. (1993). *Up the University: Re-creating Higher Education in America.* Reading, MA: Addison-Wesley.

Stack, R. (1980). Writing as conversation. *Visible Language* 14: 376-382.

Sternberg, R.J. (1985). *Beyond IQ: A Triarchic Theory of Human Intelligence.* New York: Cambridge University Press.

Sternberg, R.J. (1988). *The Triarchic Mind: A New Theory of Human Intelligence.* New York: Penguin.

Sternberg, R.J., Okagaki, L., and Jackson, A.S. (1990). Practical intelligence for success in school. *Educational Leadership* 42: 35-39.

Tobias, S. (1990). *They're Not Dumb, They're Different.* Tucson, AZ: Research Corporation.

Tremmel, R. (1993). Zen and the art of reflective practice in teacher education. *Harvard Educational Review* 63: 434-468.

Turkington, C. (1983). Therapists must dodge procrastinator's traps. *APA Monitor*, December, p. 21.

Upper, D. (1974). An unsuccessful self-treatment of "writer's block." *Journal of Applied Behavior Analysis* 7: 497.

Wadsworth, E. (1994), Editor. *To Improve the Academy.* Stillwater, OK: New Forums Press.

Wagner, R.K., and Sternberg, R.J. (1986). Tacit knowledge and intelligence in the everyday world. In R.J. Sternberg and R.K. Wagner (eds.), *Practical Intelligence: Nature and Origin of Competence in the Everyday World.* New York: Cambridge University Press.

Weimer, M. (1992). Improving higher education: Issues and perspectives on teaching and learning. *To Improve the Academy* 11: 13-23.

Weimer, M., and Lenze, L.F. (1991). Instructional interventions: A review of the literature on efforts to improve instruction. In J.C. Smart (ed.), *Higher Education: Handbook of Theory and Research,* Vol. VII. Edison, NJ: Agathon Press. (Reprinted in Perry and Smart, 1997).

Wessman, A.E. (1993). Personality and the subjective experience of time. *Journal of Personality Assessment* 37: 103-114.

Wiggers, T.T. (1984). Dealing with the manana syndrome. Presented at the American Psychological Association, Aug. 24, Toronto.

Wright, W.A., and O'Neill, M.C. (1994). Teaching improvement practices: New perspectives. *To Improve the Academy* 13: 5-37.

Zimmerman, B.J. (1986). Development of a structured interview for assessing student use of self-regulated learning strategies. *American Educational Research Journal* 23: 614-628.

# McCarthyism and the Professoriate: A Historiographic Nightmare?

### Philo A. Hutcheson
*Georgia State University*

McCarthyism was a complex event stretching over several years from the late 1940s to the middle of the 1950s. Although exemplified by one United States Senator's attacks on intellectuals and government employees, investigations of the extent of the phenomenon indicate that Senator Joseph R. McCarthy (1908-1957) was a symbol—albeit startling—of repeated attacks from a variety of people. The attacks extended to curious proportions, as in the case of Robert J. Oppenheimer, father of the atomic bomb, who had his national security clearance revoked in 1953 (Sanders, 1979, pp. 127-128). This chapter examines those attacks specifically directed at professors, providing an analysis both of the attacks and of scholars' assessments of the period. Of particular interest is the support for McCarthy and McCarthyism outside and within higher education. Following a brief review of the nature of the historiographical problem, this work examines first the range of biographies of McCarthy, then scholars' investigations into McCarthyism, and then scholarly analyses of McCarthyism and the professoriate. The chapter concludes with a consideration of what we can know about the problem in historiographical terms and offers some substantial themes for possible future examinations of McCarthyism and the professoriate.

During McCarthyism the academic profession was often the subject of vituperative charges against its members' loyalty to the nation and the society. These attacks were as likely to focus on religious affiliations or apparently atypical allegiances as on political identity (Lazarsfeld and Thielens, 1958). Yet the attacks had a central theme: the "anti-American" characteristics and behaviors of individuals. In several cases the attacks destroyed professors' chances for successful careers. Despite these problems, higher education also continued its business at large. As Caplow and McGee point out in *The Academic Marketplace* (1958), higher education appointed new professors much as it had in the recent past, emphasizing their disciplinary distinction and institutional prestige. Although they found no evidence of political dismissals, they acknowledged that such dismissals had occurred.

Consequently two key historical questions arise. The first, given the repeated attacks on professors and the conduct of higher education at the time, is the historicity: "What happened?" This chapter offers some brief examinations of the events of the late 1940s and early 1950s.

The second question is fundamental to the nature of historical inquiry: "Can we know what happened?" The problem of examining Senator Joseph McCarthy and the era of McCarthyism strikes at the heart of the search for truth, the professoriate's twentieth-century mission. As Peter Novick argues in *That Noble Dream*, the objectivity question is the central problem for historians. McCarthyism inherently defines this problem because it is a history of attacks upon the academic profession; since that time professors writing about the events have typically positioned themselves in regard to who was right and who was wrong (Novick, 1988). The problem has further expression, since the attackers were generally unable to provide direct evidence of subversive activity. The professoriate is dependent not only upon argument but also direct evidence; as was remarkably clear in the McCarthy period, it is very difficult to develop responses to popular arguments that have no evidence. The historical issues of who did what when and where are immediately confounded by historiographical assumptions of how we know what we think we know. As Goodchild and Huk note, two issues arise in the consideration of historical study, method and theme (Goodchild and Huk, 1990, p. 208). The latter of these two is central to the investigation at hand.

Thus this essay examines scholarly views, the themes, of the attacks on professors during the McCarthy era, examining the differences among the interpretations. The views range from early arguments that McCarthyism was so powerful that professors could not halt the attacks to a tendency among later investigators to suggest that the failure to express opposition stemmed from timidity, if not cowardice. Has the powerlessness of the 1950s—when Hofstadter and Metzger (1955), Lazarsfeld and Thielens (1958), and MacIver (1955) wrote their examinations—given way to a deeper understanding of the frailties of professors and academe as voiced by Slaughter (1980) and Schrecker (1986)?

The historian of higher education must ask how vulnerable the professoriate was during the period, and whether it had substantial reason for timidity or reacted without sufficient cause. The historian must also ask how higher education was able to conduct much of its work as usual, and why the enterprise chose to act in that way. This essay re-asks the questions of power and the professoriate and offers a re-evaluation of the McCarthy era.

A key initial step in this examination is the identification of the actors. Senator Joseph McCarthy represents the epitome of the attacks, although he focused on other groups, particularly government officials. Those who agreed, in one way or another, with McCarthy and his arguments and methods, were more likely to attack professors and formed the era known as McCarthyism. Analyses of McCarthyism and the professoriate offer irregular reviews of the broader scholarly literature on McCarthyism, at best. This essay is therefore an attempt to frame discussions of McCarthyism and the professoriate in terms of the disciplinary literature as well as historiographical conceptions. Scholars examining McCarthyism and professoriate need to look at the broader literature, thereby establishing theoretical positions for their arguments about the period and the occupation. The following two sections examine Senator McCarthy and then McCarthyism.

## Senator Joseph P. McCarthy

The biographical literature on Joseph McCarthy is extensive, and it exhibits an extraordinary range of criticism. There are works that are unrepentant hagiographies, such as Roy Cohn's *McCarthy*. Cohn worked with the Senator and was a fervent supporter. For example, Cohn argues that McCarthy's use of figures, however inconsistent, had reason and purpose. In reference to McCarthy's infamous 1950 speech at Wheeling, West Virginia, when the Senator announced that there were 205 Communists working in the State Department (a figure he later revised to 57, then later again to 81), Cohn states that although the figures varied,

> let us never forget that the substance of his charges was true. There *were* persons working in the State Department whose activities and associations indicated that had pro-Communist leanings. Could any American rest easily, knowing pro-Communists may have been helping to shape our foreign policy? (Cohn, 1968, p. 277)

Cohn even recounts a story of a journalist's trip to Moscow in which the journalist maintains to a guide that there was a higher percentage of Communists on the faculty at City College of New York than on the faculty at Moscow University. Cohn declares, "Despite my respect for City College as an academic institution and despite the fact that my own father is a graduate of the school, I must admit that Lyons' story has an edge (though the statistics are of course figurative)" (1968, p. 4). From the point of view of supporters, Senator McCarthy spoke the truth regardless of the evidence.

Richard Rovere offers demonology in contrast to Cohn, introducing his subject as a "most gifted demagogue" whose "access to the dark places of the American mind" is unequaled (1959, p. 9). He continues by suggesting that McCarthy's followers were from "the world of the daft and the frenzied" before acknowledging his substantial support from "regular Republicans" (1959, p. 23) He also argues that it is difficult to examine McCarthyism because it "had no grit and substance as a doctrine and no organization" (1959, p. 22). Rovere concedes that regardless of the accuracy of McCarthy's charges, the Senator held the attention of the United States public and media, the Congress and two presidents of the country, and even the world. A contemporary biography of McCarthy, published in the early 1950s, also offers a critical perspective of the Senator. Jack Anderson and Ronald May (1952) conclude that McCarthy not only failed to catch any spies but aided the goals of Communism by violating precepts of democracy.

Thomas Reeves wrote the most extensive biography of Joseph McCarthy, "grounding the story on evidence and avoiding the caricatures posited over the years by both the Left and Right" (1982, p. xi). He indicates that McCarthy's intelligence combined with remarkable drive produced extraordinary educational results; he completed four years of high school in nine months. His drive sustained his first and succeeding electoral campaigns which he enlivened with "slashing attacks" on his opponents (1982, p. 23). Reeves agrees with Cohn and Rovere that Senator McCarthy did not heed the facts but was able to command great public and political attention.

Who, then, was Senator Joseph P. McCarthy? He appears to have been smart, unsophisticated, and hard-working; the accounts of McCarthy as a person are fairly uniform (Cohn, 1968; Fried, 1976; Reeves, 1982; Rovere, 1959). He was able to win his seat in the Senate because his opponent and Senate incumbent, Robert LaFollette (of the Wisconsin LaFollette family and Progressive tradition), lost the union vote of Milwaukee in the 1946 election (Rovere, 1959, p. 86). McCarthy was, to employ one scholar's colloquialism, "a master of bullshit," to the enjoyment of friends and at the substantial expense of foes (Reeves, 1982, p. 25). He had done little to command attention until his speech on February 9, 1950, to the Ohio County Women's Republican Club of Wheeling, West Virginia. McCarthy's charges of Communists in the federal government both excited the public and provided Republicans with a hammer and an anvil. His ability to act resulted from more than simply support from conservative quarters; for example, Cohn reports that McCarthy had good relationships with both Joseph and John Kennedy (Cohn, 1968). McCarthy eventually sharpened his attacks to the point of absurdity when he attacked the United States Army for promoting a dentist who had invoked the Fifth Amendment on his application for a commission (Fried, 1976, p. 279). That attack led to a fruitless series of confrontations with the United States Army and to his censure in December 1954 by the United States Senate (Ewald, 1984; Watkins, 1969).

Even Cohn, despite his fervent support of the Senator, had to admit that these attacks may have proved little (Cohn, 1968, pp. 93-109). Despite McCarthy's final level of absurdity, the biographies cannot escape the implication if not the direct statement that Joe McCarthy believed his charges. Fried argues that McCarthy was somewhat concerned about Communism and then came to realize that being a strongly vocal anti-Communist was a potent political stance (1976, pp. 40-43). In contrast, Rovere suggests that McCarthy was "flawed by his inability to believe what he was saying" (1959, p. 215); Rovere's own disbelief appears to have taken hold in this assessment. Other examinations of McCarthy indicate that he attacked those who he thought held Communist positions well before his 1950 Wheeling speech. As early as 1946 McCarthy was accusing opponents of being "'Communistically inclined'" (Oshinsky, 1976, p. 55). Reeves argues that McCarthy could be "swept away by a Cause," and that anti-Communism became just such an issue (1982; p. 185). As the following section indicates, followers of McCarthy formed a broad base of support and genuinely feared Communism.

## McCarthyism

The story of McCarthyism extends beyond the individual. Even in chronological terms, the bare and unconnected bones of history, McCarthy's opening attack on Communists in the government occurred well after other political figures had accused various organizations—including colleges and universities—of harboring Communists or former Communists. Public fear about the Soviet Union was already growing when McCarthy entered the Senate; from 1945 to 1947, Gallup polls recorded a substantial decrease, from 39 to 12 percent, of the proportion of United States citizens who considered the Soviet Union to be "peaceloving" (Fried, 1976, p. 3). While the period of McCarthyism was clearly virulent, the earlier attacks on Bolsheviks and Socialists in the post-World War I period may have evidenced more violations of civil liberties (Hutson, 1978). Richard Fried, author of two books on McCarthyism, captures the historical nature of anti-Communism in "The Red Perennial," the opening chapter of his book *Men Against McCarthy* (1990). The United States has a long and substantial history of anti-Communist activity.

McCarthyism also represents more than anti-Communism, as individuals attacked anyone who seemed to have questionable loyalties not only in political terms but also in broader social terms. What separates McCarthyism (and the period immediately before the Senator's efforts) from other anti-Communist periods is the level of sustained attacks on intellectuals—in entertainment and literature, the government, and indeed the academic profession (Buckley and Bozell, 1954; Fried, 1990). Generally, however, disciplinary examinations of McCarthyism do not address the professoriate but rather government officials and entertainers. Numbers might account for the differing levels of interest in government officials; one estimate suggests that several hundred federal employees lost their jobs because of "security risk" issues (McCormick, 1989, p. 66). Thus the following review offers a broad understanding of McCarthyism.

There is a literature treating McCarthyism in the same themes of hagiography and demonology as in the case of the biographies. Buckley and Bozell offer an intellectuals' apologia for McCarthyism (Buckley and Bozell, 1954). In contrast, Ford presents a highly critical examination of McCarthyism in an effort to "force the recall election" of McCarthy (1954, p. 7). In an attempt to warn readers in the early 1970s, Cook (1971) argued that McCarthyism showed potential for resurgence. This review, however, focuses on scholarly investigations.

In view of McCarthy's public position, as a politician, an initial step in examining McCarthyism would seem to be to raise political issues. To some degree, however, the literature on McCarthyism did not begin with political analyses. Robert Griffith argued in 1971 that it was not until Nelson Polsby's 1960 article on McCarthyism that the scholarly discussion of the topic shifted from sociological conceptions to political ones (Griffith, 1971).

The sociological conceptions of McCarthyism, however, eventually evidenced substantial theoretical and methodological problems. Perhaps the most enduring of conceptions to arise from early examinations of McCarthyism, status politics, failed to meet the empirical test. Seymour Lipset (1955) argued that cohorts whose status was apparently threatened in the rapid changes of the post-World War II period as well as working class ethnic groups were McCarthy supporters. Later, Martin Trow (1958) conducted an empirical investigation of that argument as applied to Vermont voters which called into question Lipset's work. Further empirical investigations—or in the case of Trow, a re-investigation of his work—showed that McCarthy's support (not only in Wisconsin but across the nation) did not necessarily come from groups whose status was threatened or from working class ethnic groups (Griffith, 1971, p. 25; Hixson, 1992; Rogin, 1967). Thus, despite the disciplinary chronology, this work examines first the political conditions of McCarthyism.

Michael Rogin (1967) found that voting support for McCarthy did not come from the populists (inheritors of the Populist traditions) or the progressives (inheritors of the Progressive traditions) or the ethnic working class. Subsequent analyses of voting behavior indicate that, in fact, such groups as the Polish-Americans of Milwaukee were the least likely to vote for McCarthy in his 1952 election. Analysis of his voting record and sources of support suggest that he was pro-business, anti-labor, and that his attacks on the establishment found favor among small business owners (Oshinsky, 1976). More generally, McCarthyism appeared to have its political support among Republicans, party affiliation consistently proving to be a better indicator of support than any other variable (Fried, 1990). Empirical investigations also suggest that Congressional distrust of domestic Communism provided support for McCarthyism. That distrust began in the 1930s, highlighted by the House's creation of the Special Committee on Un-American Activities in 1938, a committee that employed tactics that Senator McCarthy and his followers subsequently used (Hixson, 1992; Reeves, 1982).

Another important aspect of political support for McCarthyism is the role of liberals during this period. Their efforts, or in many cases, the lack thereof, reveal the extraordinary depth and breadth of McCarthyism as well as its historical extent. According to Richard Fried, "The names of John F. Kennedy, Paul Douglas, and other famous liberals do not often appear in the chronicle of opposition to McCarthy" (1990, p. 261). As an example, in 1954 Hubert Humphrey offered an amendment to the Communist Control Act (designed to outlaw the Communist Party) declaring that the Party was hostile and thus its members were not entitled to Constitutional rights. The Senate approved both the Act and the amendment (Griffith, 1971). The political context of McCarthyism is neatly summarized by Alan Wolfe, "Communism *was* outside the post-war consensus, the ideas of the radical right *were not*" (1981, p. 12). Robert Griffith argues that in investigating McCarthy and McCarthyism, he found "a thoroughly conventional politics rooted in political parties and interest groups" (1987, p. xi). Even during the New Deal, there was a liberal anti-Communist movement; the author of the Voorhis Act of 1940, which required organizations with foreign ties to register with the federal government, was a "devout liberal" (Fried, 1990, p. 52). Some scholars have identified Truman's policies as precedent for McCarthyism (Schrecker, 1994; Theoharis, 1971). The argument of New Deal political and legislative precedent, however, seems to obtain in historical terms. Liberals before and after World War II feared the presence of Communists in the federal government.

Earl Latham captures the extraordinary support for McCarthyism in documenting Communist infiltration of government-employee unions, the Department of Agriculture, and the National Labor Relations Board as well as Soviet espionage during World War II. He states that while the infiltration did not control Congress, Party members released information "which was valuable in agitational activity that might influence the course of policy" (1966, p. 123). Scholars as well as politicians were suspicious of Communist infiltration.

Richard Hofstadter appears to have been the first historian to address McCarthyism in extensive terms, formulating a historical model in his essay, "The Pseudo-Conservative Revolt," in *The New American Right*. Hofstadter discusses the anxieties of status politics, suggesting that both "old-family" and "new-family" Americans shared anger at "the Anglo-Saxon, Eastern, Ivy League intellectual gentlemen" so often attacked by McCarthy and his supporters (1955, pp. 45-50). In a key essay, C. Vann Woodward (1960) offered a revision of Hofstadter's arguments, suggesting that the theoretical model of status aspiration and status politics did not obtain in view of careful consideration of actual Populist sentiments and traditions. Woodward's thesis was eventually proven empirically by the political scientists, as noted in the earlier discussion of the work in that discipline.

William Hixson (1992) summarizes historians' examinations as well as those of other social scientists and offers a historiographical explanation for the changing explanations of McCarthyism. He suggests that during the 1960s the memories of such mass movements as Hitler and fascism receded and new memories of movements such as Martin Luther King's efforts took hold. Thus, he argues, the recent scholarship on McCarthy and McCarthyism has shifted away from mass movement theories. One recent mass movement theory, however, advanced by Wiebe, suggests that McCarthy used both national and local standards to sustain his attacks, establishing a mass movement. Attacks on Communism meant attacks on "atheism, sexual freedoms, strange accents, civil rights, or whatever most threatened a particular group's sense of security" (Wiebe, 1977, p. 1122).

There is also an important aspect to the historical narrative which bears review, if only for the strength of its historicity. During the McCarthy era, Mao Tse-tung gained control of China (making the world's most populated nation a Communist country), the Soviet Union tested its first nuclear weapon, and the North Korean army—with China as its ally—very nearly drove the South Korean army off the Korean peninsula. Only a few years before the start of the Korean War, the Allied forces had their ignominious retreat at Dunkirk. The Soviet Union and the United States were in the midst of building the Iron Curtain, and defeat was not far away in the memories of a recently embattled American public. Hofstadter noted in the mid-1950s, "All of us have reason to fear the power of international Communism, and all our lives are profoundly affected by it" (1955, p. 41). While he expressed far less public concern about domestic Communism than did the conservatives, he shared their general concern, and the extent of that sentiment cannot be ignored.

In the historical perspective, McCarthy's censure did not result in the end of McCarthyism as a political movement. The conservative magazine *The National Review*, with William F. Buckley (a supporter of McCarthy) as editor, began in 1955; in 1963 the Republican Party selected Barry Goldwater, one of McCarthy's "staunchest supporters," as its presidential candidate (Hixson, 1992, p. 46). As noted earlier, McCarthyism *per se* did not begin with McCarthy, except as an eponym.

McCarthyism, then, represents a conservative political position with liberal acquiescence or even acceptance, with appeals to the working class although its actual support derives from pro-business anti-labor groups. It occurred at a time when international political developments threatened the status of the United States. Its adherents "recklessly denigrated the loyalty" of countless United States citizens (Reeves, 1982, p. 207). In its broadest manifestation, beyond the political framework, McCarthyism represents attacks on those who were different— whether their differences were religious, ethnic, or sexual.

### Scholarly Examinations of McCarthyism and the Professoriate

McCarthy's own description of the Communist threat emphasized government officials much more heavily than the professoriate (McCarthy, 1952), and within the academic world he himself focused on only one professor, Owen Lattimore (1900-1989), director of the Page School of International Relations at the Johns Hopkins University and a sinologist (Lewis, 1992), although he questioned many more in his various roles on Senate committees and subcommittees and went to Boston to serve as a one-man investigation of a Harvard professor (Lewis, 1988).

McCarthy found Lattimore a convenient target shortly after the time when the Communists in China succeeded in ousting Chiang Kai-shek, when conservatives in the United States were convinced that the federal government—especially the executive branch—had "lost" China by refusing to aid Chiang Kai-shek. By and large, examinations of McCarthy's effect on the professoriate must encompass McCarthyism.

The examinations of McCarthyism and the professoriate tend to fall into two categories, each of which are reviewed in this section. The first category reviewed is composed of examinations that suggest the capacity of McCarthyism to influence if not control higher education. The second group is composed of investigations that typically conclude that the professoriate or higher education could have but failed to defend individual professors.

The earliest investigation is contemporary rather than historical. *The Year of the Oath* (Stewart, 1950) is a personal and comprehensive examination of the attempt by the regents of the University of California to require professors to sign a loyalty oath. The oath, amended by the regents in 1949, required professors to swear that they were not members of the Communist Party (1950, p. 20). Stewart suggests that a collective approach served the faculty well, as they were able to forestall the implementation of the oath.  He concludes, however, that the result of the opposition was a Pyrrhic victory at best given that the regents at the time of the book's publication had begun to dismiss professors. His call to resistance is admittedly ironic.

Another work on the California loyalty oath situation presents a detailed chronology of the events from 1949 to 1952. David Gardner's *The California Oath Controversy*, while designed to present the whole story, also admittedly treats "unfairly those whose regard for the university's welfare became essentially inconsequential" (1967, p. ix). Gardner concludes that the university only briefly but nevertheless deeply lost a measure of distinction as a result of the controversy. He also suggests that the faculty never attained the "effective and unhesitating use of power which the regents demonstrated" (1967, p. 246). Although Gardner's work focuses on the internal conditions of the situation, he argues that the regents' efforts resulted from a state legislative initiative as well as internal disagreements.

In 1955, Hofstadter and Metzger published the most comprehensive examination of academic freedom that has yet appeared in the study of United States higher education, *The Development of Academic Freedom in the United States*. The authors acknowledged, "Academic Freedom has become one of the central issues of our time," but cautioned readers that the work was "an analytical history, not a full-throated polemic" (p. ix). Nor did they address academic freedom in its current setting, in great part because the work was part of the larger American Academic Freedom Project which included Robert MacIver's *Academic Freedom in Our Time*. The reticence of one author, however, may have stemmed from deeper concerns. According to Peter Novick, Hofstadter

> did not feel that he could condemn the University of Washington for firing Communist professors: 'I dislike these Stalinists so—and I wonder what they would do for us or to us if they had control of things.' (Novick, 1988, p. 326)

Little wonder, then, that Hofstadter eschewed a polemic on academic freedom.

Co-author Walter Metzger saw little strength in the nature of academic freedom in the United States. He concluded that "one cannot but be appalled at the slender thread by which it hangs" (Hofstadter and Metzger, 1955, p. 506). The value of the work as analytical history, however, may be underestimated by scholars who have since investigated academic freedom issues. Metzger analyzed the nature of academic freedom cases reported in the *Bulletin* of the American Association of University Professors from 1915 to 1953. Of those 124 cases, 20 evidenced "ideological pressure" while in 57 cases the issues were "intramural and largely personal" (p. 492). Just as McCarthyism appears larger than its symbol, so too does academic freedom encompass more than the freedom of political expression.

The companion volume, *Academic Freedom in Our Time*, presents lengthy arguments as well as evidence—much of it from the American Association of University Professors—about the nature of academic freedom in broad terms as well as its current condition. Author Robert MacIver notes that such activities as censorship of books and loyalty oaths indicate the depth and breadth of the "new wave of intolerance" (1955, p. 34). He also points to the considerable lack of evidence in investigations by governmental and private agencies and the extraordinary number of such groups engaged in investigations. Yet he too reveals the ambiguity of the early 1950s, suggesting, "The problem of how to deal with the minute proportion of scholars who are Communists is only a minute part of the master problem of how to deal with Communism in the world, Communism as a world power" (1955, p. 52). His solution is reasoned defense rather than emotional outbursts. MacIver reminds his readers that it is essential for faculties as collectivities of professors to maintain a corporate identity, especially when times require the defense of colleagues. He documents the range of attacks, on Keynesians, atheists, nonconformists, and the sexually immoral as well as on those with supposed Communist affiliations.

Lazarsfeld and Thielens produced an extensive analysis in response to their question, "How did the general tension affect social science teaching?" in their work, *The Academic Mind* (1958, p. v). They were specifically interested in gauging the emotional reaction to McCarthyism. Their challenge, however, to use their work as a benchmark for further investigations, appears by and large ignored in subsequent efforts to understand McCarthyism and the professoriate; the literature review for this chapter revealed only a few empirical investigations of academic freedom cases (Ambrose, 1990; Metzger, 1978; Slaughter, 1980, 1981, 1987, 1994). From general measurements of self-esteem, "professors themselves are convinced that they are not accorded the prestige they deserve" (1958, p. 13) to their estimate of 990 incidents of attacks on academic freedom (ranging greatly in their intensity and substance) at 165 colleges and universities (1958, pp. 43-46), Lazarsfeld and Thielens document the depth and breadth of the impact of McCarthyism.

In terms of the emotional reaction to McCarthyism, just under half of the social science professors in their sample felt apprehensive but not paralyzed. Despite the attacks, however, only a small proportion of the sample felt that the professoriate had suffered degradation as a result of McCarthyism specifically. Lazarsfeld and Thielens also found that higher quality colleges faced more attacks on their faculties and were also more likely to protect their professors. Overall, the work documents "patterns of caution" among professors in their teaching, research, and professional obligations; these patterns were substantial if not fully empirical (1958, p. 192). Most troubling concerning the defense of colleagues or protesting administrative suppression of debate, Lazarsfeld and Thielens conclude: "The clear, if unconscious, implication is that the initiative would have to come from someone else" (1958, pp. 233-234). They found little in the academic mind to suggest it had the capacity or the means to resist McCarthyism.

The review of the Alex Novikoff case at the University of Vermont presents a biography within the political and institutional contexts of McCarthyism (Holmes, 1989). Professor Novikoff was, in his own words, a leader in the Communist Party in the 1930s, a time when he may also have experienced anti-Semitism while at Brooklyn College. Holmes offers a detailed examination of the activities of the Communist Party and its opponents in New York City as well as the institutional procedures at the University of Vermont (where Novikoff taught years after his Communist Party experience) which led to his dismissal. Holmes concludes his work by emphasizing the fragile nature of academic freedom.

Jane Sanders' account of events at the University of Washington, *Cold War on the Campus* (1979), is notable for being among the earliest of the institutional histories and for capturing the political nature—the conservative *and* liberal attacks on Communism—of McCarthyism. She also reviews the pre-World War II distaste for the "'radical' character of the university" (1979, p. 10). It is also the story of the enduring nature of McCarthyism, both before and after McCarthy himself, through the administration of different presidents and engaging different professors at different times. In many ways, Sanders' work is precedent for the ensuing works on McCarthyism and the professoriate. In reference to an initial investigation by a state legislative committee, the Canwell Committee, Sanders argues that "while the regents clearly expected dissent in the matter of the Canwell investigation, they expected [President] Allen to concur in its necessity" (1979, p. 26). The president responded by persuading the regents to use due process in the institutional examination of professors. Sanders develops a telling combination of argument and evidence to show that the president's use of due process furthered his objective of ridding the University of "subversive" professors. As a result of the institutional due process, the regents dismissed three professors and placed three others on probation.

The University of Washington faculty was divided on the issue of Communism; for example, a majority of those belonging to the local AAUP chapter supported a statement opposing the right of professors to belong to the Communist Party (1979, p. 29). Sanders makes clear the historical nature of McCarthyism and its effects in her examination of the shift of faculty policy regarding dismissal of those who invoked the Fifth Amendment. In 1948 the faculty declared that there was no necessary university action, and in 1953 the faculty supported examination of fitness to hold a faculty position. As concerns the administration, Sanders offers the valuable insight that different presidents at the University of Washington offered different interpretations of academic freedom. One president held that academic freedom protected thought but not action, at least not such action as membership in the Communist Party. For a later president, academic freedom did not include faculty choice of outside lecturers. The shifting interpretations of academic freedom and the external pressure resulted in problems which the University could not forestall, much less avoid.

Lionel Lewis focused on Owen Lattimore and the faculty, administration, and trustees at the Johns Hopkins University in *The Cold War and Academic Governance* (1993). The Lattimore case is an important if not significant case in McCarthyism and the professoriate. Lattimore was a sinologist with considerable influence in the federal government, and Senator McCarthy attacked him directly. The case was further complicated by Lattimore's strong responses to investigating committees which were far more accustomed to acquiescence or the Fifth Amendment. Despite considerable external pressure—as Lewis shows, both from federal political sources and the general public—the University did not dismiss Professor Lattimore during the McCarthy years. It did, however, arrange to place him on a paid leave of absence and eventually induced him to resign in 1962. While Lewis suggests that the case was a symbol for faculty, it appears to have been an ironic one; faculty solidarity failed to protect Lattimore in the long run. Lewis represents the Lattimore opponents as "moral entrepreneurs" who were successful in their attacks (p. 41).

Charles McCormick's examination of the dismissal of an art professor, Luella Mundel (1913- ), at Fairmont State College in West Virginia captures the historical and broad social conditions of McCarthyism (1989). He notes that a socially conservative local elite used red-baiting to arouse public animosity, that the university president was an anti-Communist liberal, and that there was never any direct evidence that the dismissed professor was in any way connected with Communism. The attacks appear to have centered on issues of "female nudity, nontraditional female behavior, and homosexuality" which were somewhat characteristic of recent doctoral recipients "affecting varied styles of intellectual searching—bohemianism or political dissent or avant garde cynicism," and ultimately on the issue of atheism (p. 33). His use of newspaper headlines from 1951 (such as "FANATIC REDS HALT ALLIED ADVANCE") effectively illustrates the fears of many in the United States during McCarthyism, a reminder that historical narrative is emotional as well as empirical (pp. 61-64). Both local and national forces pressured the university administration and faculty into the dismissal of Professor Mundel.

In contrast to the works that suggest the powerlessness of the professoriate and higher education, there are several examinations of McCarthyism and the professoriate that suggest that professors (and in some instances, administrators) could have defended themselves or colleagues against the attacks. Sheila Slaughter (1980) offers a critical view of the American Association of University Professors' general activity in defense of academic freedom and tenure principles, stating that the Association "sacrificed individuals and substantive principles in order to gain compliance for procedural safeguards from university officials for the profession as a whole" (p. 46). She calls the eventual AAUP report on academic freedom during the McCarthy era "a massive and pathetic equivocation" (p. 46). Slaughter softens her assessment in a more recent work, suggesting that "the degree of academic freedom varies with historical circumstance" (p. 84).

In *Cold War on Campus* (1988), Lionel Lewis analyzes attacks on professors at 58 campuses between 1947 and 1956, a period he identifies as one of "mass hysteria" (p. 8). He found little to characterize the attacks and investigations other than a focus on institutional and administrative concerns. The process emphasized administrative rather than professorial mechanisms, the administrations rarely had much evidence beyond the charges themselves, and there was "an element of capriciousness" (p. 235) in the tremendous variations of administrative processes. Lewis argues that academic administrators allowed the Cold War to have an effect on their institutions.

Seymour Lipset examines Harvard's experience in the 1950s, and concludes that the university did not maintain a consistent posture (Lipset, 1975). On the one hand, senior administrators defended Harvard professors in the case of external attacks; on the other hand, senior administrators refused appointments or reappointments because of *private* charges about Communist affiliations or activities. Lipset also notes the liberal intellectual opposition to Soviet aggression in Eastern Europe, such as the Berlin blockade of 1948. That sentiment was reflected among Harvard professors; a 1949 survey of the faculty indicated that a majority of its members was opposed to Communists on the faculty.

Sigmund Diamond (1992) provides an account which intertwines the personal and elite institutional effects of McCarthyism in *Compromised Campus*, a book resulting from his experience of being refused re-appointment at Harvard. Diamond makes clear that anti-Americanism extended beyond McCarthyism in his examination of the extensive collaboration between Harvard and Yale Universities and the FBI.

Schrecker's work, *No Ivory Tower* (1986), is the most direct and the most comprehensive of the examinations of McCarthyism and the professoriate as an issue. She argues that academe "came to adapt itself to the suppression of dissent" (p. 11). Acknowledging that the Communist Party was in fact "doctrinaire and secretive" (p. 25), the very arguments which liberal and conservative aca-demics used to decry membership, Schrecker suggests that professors were rarely doctrinaire and not necessarily secretive and that many had left the Party by the early 1940s. Nevertheless, colleges and universities chose to take action against these professors; Schrecker claims, in fact, that there were circulating lists of dis-missed professors, although she admits, however, that there is no documentation available about the lists (pp. 265-266). She concludes her examination with a chapter on the academic profession's response to McCarthyism, especially the AAUP. Criticizing the General Secretary of the Association, to whom she attributes a "strange pathology" (p. 336), Schrecker suggests that if professors had chosen to act, they could have stopped some of the dismissals. Consequently the nation's professors were at blame, evidencing liberal ambiguity and hence leaving colleagues to the mercy of the attacks.

The works on McCarthyism and the professoriate offer a variety of perspec-tives on the problems professors faced in the face of sustained and virulent attacks. In general, some note without condemnation the ambiguity of the period, as professors were reluctant to defend their colleagues because of their general sense of apprehension, in the words of Lazarsfeld and Thielens. Other observers are less patient with the profession, offering precise instances of professors and administrators acquiescing to demands of mass hysteria, as Lewis suggests, or even calling upon psychological disorders of pathology (see Schrecker) to explain the failure of professors to protect their own.

Of course, the division of investigations between the overwhelming power of McCarthyism and the timidity of the professoriate is to some degree an artifice. The two works by Lewis highlight the artifice, as one examines the failure of aca-demic administrations while the other lauds the defense of an attacked professor. Despite the artifice, however, the distinction is sufficient to lead to the historio-graphical question raised by this work.

## What Can We Know About McCarthyism and the Professoriate?

In terms of historicity—what happened?—advocates of McCarthyism used lack of evidence as a means to attack and as a means to sustain attacks and sanctions among professors. McCarthyism includes the widespread denial of appointment and promotion (or even the retention of position), with lists of the damned. McCarthyism includes the fear of professors and administrators, identifiable for example in their testimony when they identified their colleagues as Communist sympathizers in order to avoid incrimination. McCarthyism also includes attacks on marginal groups as in the case of Luella Mundel at Fairmont State College. Finally, it also consists of the variable use of institutional procedures to confirm external accusations.

In terms of historiography, two assumptions appear common to the literature on McCarthyism and the professoriate. First, scholars seem to understand the academy as a liberal institution. While there are problems with the shifting definitions of liberal and conservative over time, two scholars who examined the politics of professors provide some explanation: liberals are "critics *within* the system" while conservatives seek "to conserve the basic constitutional or constituent arrangements of American society and polity" (Ladd and Lipset, 1975, p. 123). The second assumption is that scholars seemingly invest the professoriate with power.

The assumption of the liberal academy has varying interpretations. For some scholars, the liberal nature of the institutions is apparently embedded in a Mertonian set of assumptions about the relationship between science and democratic society; the university advances democratic ideals through the pursuit of truth (Hofstadter and Metzger, 1955, pp. 365-366). For other scholars, the academy is seemingly *a priori* liberal and conservatives are, perhaps simply, exceptions. Schrecker (1986) raises the issue of anti-Marxist scholarship in the 1950s. While on the one hand she argues that the anxiety, as documented by Lazarsfeld and Thielens, helped to create such scholarship, on the other hand she does not consider that conservative scholars were in place in the academy by the time of McCarthyism. Their presence is noticeable even in McCarthy's own work; the foreword of his 1952 warning about the threat of Communism was written by a political science professor (McCarthy, 1952, pp. vii-viii).

In all interpretations, the assumption that the academy is a predominantly liberal institution escapes attention. Professors are not uniformly liberal, a historical fact clearly evidenced in the era of McCarthyism. While some professors refused to testify before state or federal committees investigating instances of anti-Americanism, others were willing to participate in such investigations (Sanders, 1979). Other cases suggest the deep-rooted political conservatism that justified charges without evidence (Benson, 1949). Probably the best known of the conservative professors is Sidney Hook, who presented an early argument that Communists should not be allowed to teach in the nation's colleges and universities (Hook; 1949).

Nor are administrators necessarily liberal. A startling example arises from the elite research universities—that very group which is very often accorded some semblance of defense against McCarthyism. In 1953 the presidents of the Association of American Universities issued a report on academic freedom which specifically stated that "invocation of the Fifth Amendment places upon a professor a heavy burden of proof of his fitness to hold a teaching position and lays upon his university an obligation to re-examine his qualifications for membership in its society." Membership in the Communist Party was even more damning, the presidents declaring that it "extinguishes the right to a university position, as does Communistic practice" (*Atlantic Monthly,* 1953, p. 46). Harold Taylor (1955) also presents evidence of some cases in which professors invoked the Fifth Amendment and their universities investigated the professors. As another example, Lazarsfeld and Thielens (1958) note that administrative committee and department head appointments most often went to middle-of-the-road professors. There should be no wonder as to why so seldom college and university administrators defended professors under attack.

More troubling for a rigorous historical perspective is the assumption of power. This problem is most evident in Schrecker's work; although she writes of the political characteristics of McCarthyism and the professoriate, she does not use power as an issue or an analytical concept. Nor does she discuss political civil liberties. Yet the historical narrative which develops from her work as well as the work of other authors affirms that professors do not hold much power, and what power they hold tends to be *de facto*. Sanders argues that the "adequacy" of academic freedom's defense "depends upon the consensus within the group of professional educators, which enables them to articulate the ideal to the society they serve" (1979, p. 173). Despite her emphasis on consensus, Sanders goes on to pinpoint the lack of legal standing for tenure until 1956 in the state of Washington (pp. 174-175). In legal terms, even as late as 1972 there was no specific legal standing for academic freedom (Van Alstyne, 1972). While state and federal officials have occasionally given support to professors and their academic freedom (the University of Wisconsin regents' declaration perhaps being the most notable), professors do not enjoy laws protecting their utterances or publications (Hofstadter and Metzger, 1955, pp. 427).

Wisconsin provides a substantial example of this problem as it existed in the 1950s. Michael O'Brien (1980) argues that University of Wisconsin president Edwin B. Fred withstood several attacks on the university, most of which occurred because of speakers (such as Owen Lattimore) being invited to campus (pp. 196-197). President Fred succeeded in his defense in great part because administrators "had carefully cultivated relations with government officials," many of whom were alumni (p. 197). O'Brien concludes, "Most important were the traditions, coordinated power, and constant vigilance of political forces in Wisconsin, ranging from Socialists to moderate Republicans" (p. 202). Political alliances rather than reasoned defense protected the University of Wisconsin.

Even in *de facto* terms, the boundaries of autonomy for the professoriate are weak. The professoriate does not enjoy economic or social defenses. Neither unions nor big business protect professors, and churches have contested professors and their ideas since the Board of Overseers dismissed the second master of Harvard College because of his opposition to infant baptism (Hofstadter and Metzger, 1955, p. 88). In essence, society grants the professoriate its autonomy and thus may choose to take away that condition. The historical political conditions of autonomy are extraordinarily problematic.

In this regard, accusations of timidity or equivocation tend to lose their accuracy; courage without power is unlikely to endure, resulting more often than not in martyrdom or sainthood—conditions often found in the works on McCarthyism and the professoriate. The academic profession apparently demands principled response as the method for the collectivity to use in the event of attacks on the occupation. It is not clear, however, that reasoned defense would suffice. Despite one suggestion that reasoned defense worked, the scholar's analysis of witnesses' styles of response focuses on successes in the post-McCarthy era, when the vehemence of attacks had declined greatly (Mulcahy, 1986). Nor is it clear how reasoned defense can provide a sustained effort against attacks that employ accusation and innuendo as evidence and argument (Lewis, 1993). McCarthy and McCarthyism highlight the professoriate's vulnerability in the face of both subtle and heavy-handed political maneuvering. Faculty solidarity and reasoned defense might slow the maneuvering, but there is no reason other than faith to suggest that a collectivity could halt the political power. The political context remains problematic.

What, then, is an appropriate historiographical framework for examinations of McCarthyism and the professoriate? In terms of external conditions, a thorough investigation needs to contain reviews of McCarthy, McCarthyism, and national conditions at that time. The last are seldom noted. Even when those conditions receive attention, scholars commonly write of them in dismissive tones, referring for example to the "Communist 'bogey'" (Holmes, 1989, p. 100), as if the social and political reality were nonexistent. Without indulging the Left or the Right about who was right or wrong during the Cold War, readers of this essay should remember that the *Bulletin of Atomic Scientists* repeatedly warned of the proximity of nuclear Armageddon. It is important to understand McCarthyism and the professoriate as a political history with substantive characteristics rather than as simply a story of the fallacies of the past. Furthermore, a political history includes the use of such tools of political science as analyses of power.

Institutional histories have been important to the history of higher education since the late nineteenth century, at times serving as "vehicles for describing changes in American intellectual life" (Goodchild and Huk, 1990, p. 202). Several institutional histories examining events during the McCarthy period have appeared, typically representing the public policy school, especially the public policy and organizational policy history approaches, which Goodchild and Huk (1990) identify in their analytical essay on institutional histories. One exception to this grouping is McCormick's *This Nest of Vipers*, which represents one aspect of the cultural history school. The questions which Goodchild and Huk raise about the limits of each school obtain in examining the histories and their relationship to McCarthyism and the professoriate. In the case of policy institutional histories, scholars have tended to identify causal characteristics between government activity and higher education institutions but have not necessarily interpreted the cultural nature of the events. The synthetic cultural approach addresses the interplay between external agencies and the institution, showing how each affected the other (Goodchild and Huk, 1990, pp. 265-268). A more comprehensive interpretation of the institutional examinations would suggest that what might have been internecine squabbles or wars in other times became, under the pressure of McCarthyism, vile affairs ending in sanctions or dismissals.

Thus in terms of internal conditions, it is important to understand McCarthyism and the professoriate as a historical issue of political conservatism, a long-standing issue among colleges and universities and one which engages an elite just as much as it engages any other group. Hofstadter and Metzger (1955) provide a set of important examples in their examination of the problems faced by anti-slavery professors (and administrators) in the North and the South prior to the Civil War. Whatever the political affiliations of administrators—which is not a fully troubling issue given the complicity if not direct action of liberals in the anti-Communist crusade—the Republican domination of governing boards clearly puts any investigation of McCarthyism and the professoriate into a political framework. Since McCarthyism was a national movement, questions about whether or not McCarthyism would appear on campus are moot. It is essential for scholars to understand that McCarthyism was part of higher education, it was indeed a popular and mass movement, and there is no evidence that colleges and universities—their faculties, their students, their administrations, their trustees— are some how miraculously immune from mass movements. Furthermore, McCarthyism is repeatedly a story of how vulnerable professors actually are, with little political power or any political civil liberties. Even in cases where the only evidence was the accusation, presidents and governing boards were able to sanction, even to the point of dismissal, the offending professor.

The current political historiography does not provide, however, sufficient grounds for analysis. While there is an apparent divide of the political historiography of McCarthyism into those who believe it an elite phenomenon of the Republicans or Democrats or those who see it as a mass phenomenon (Polsby, 1983), there is a more critical political issue in specifically considering McCarthyism and the professoriate. A rigorous analysis of the political base of McCarthy and McCarthyism indicates an anti-institutional characteristic as well as an anti-intellectual nature.

McCarthy's own imagery, Tailgunner Joe, is individually isolated rather than institutional. He pinpointed the intellectual—who rests within and upon institutions—by striking not just at the liberal identity but even more at the assumption of institution. His infamous Wheeling, West Virginia, speech was an attack on the United States Department of State, not on intellectuals *per se*. McCarthy and those who followed his goals and methods attacked not simply or solely intellectuals, but more fundamentally, institutions of United States society—including the United States Army. He was isolationist as an *individual* and not as a member of the polity or the polity's institutions. He knew that he could elicit support by attacking liberal intellectuals, playing on sentiments long extant in United States society as explained in Hofstadter's "personal" work on that topic (Hofstadter,

1962, p. vii). He was driven, however, by fundamentally radical conceptions that differ from conservative conceptions of this nation, which *protect* institutions. His anti-institutional conduct and the conservative protection of institutions is ultimately evident in the text of the censure by the United States Senate; the Senators condemned McCarthy for conduct unbecoming a member of that body, a body with complex rules and protocols. The Senate did not censure him for his anti-Communist efforts, and in fact earlier that year it passed the Communist Control Act (Oshinsky, 1976). McCarthy created, in the words of one author, "turmoil and confusion" (Griffith, 1971, p. 28). Both supporters and opponents of McCarthy (and McCarthyism) note his ability to create disorder. A psychological evaluation suggests that McCarthy had a personality type that led to such behavior (Landis, 1987). One book actually accuses McCarthy of being a threat to conservatism because of his disruptive tactics (Rorty and Decter, 1954). As William Hixson notes, "McCarthy may have distinguished himself in his exceptional disregard for truth" (1992, p. 3).

The variety of attacks, however, indicate that McCarthyism and the professoriate is not just a political story, and hence it is not simply a political historiography. McCormick's work illustrates the complexity of understanding social behavior, as the nest of vipers contained personal venom as well as political spite. Lionel Lewis, too, captures the personal nature of Lattimore's case in the midst of fervent anti-Communism. Examinations need to address the possibility of social as well as political problems.

The results which Lazarsfeld and Thielens report, that professors did not feel especially denigrated by McCarthyism, confirm the latter evaluations of McCarthyism as more rather than less characteristic of United States society. The attacks did not, ironically, really accentuate any critical social views of the professoriate. Higher education was able to continue business as usual because McCarthyism represented in great part struggles as old as higher education in this country— whether those struggles were the result of the accommodation of external political interference or internecine squabbles. As Carol Gruber concludes in *Mars and Minerva* (1975), professors have long been willing to compromise standards of truth for the service of the state. Those professors who attacked colleagues, those professors who failed to support colleagues, were inheritors of a long tradition. Nor has the academy been particularly hospitable to the eccentric. Laurence Veysey notes the general intolerance for the unusual in colleges and universities, highlighting Thorstein Veblen's career as an example (Veysey, 1965, pp. 422-424). In great part, then, examinations of McCarthyism and the professoriate represent the standard rather than the exception in the history of higher education.

## Conclusion

It appears that there is a method for relieving the historiographic nightmare. Novick argues that there has been a "collapse of professional historical study as an even minimally cohesive venture" in its broadest manifestation (1988, p. 579). The issue of McCarthyism and the professoriate appears narrow enough, however, to allow historical understanding, despite the development of apparently contrary perspectives in historical understanding of McCarthyism and the professoriate.

The primary problem of historical narrative in examination of McCarthyism and the professoriate is the very nature of McCarthy himself and more broadly McCarthyism. He was a fundamentally anti-institutional persona. McCarthyism, using the very methods of McCarthy—attacks without evidence as evidence, insinuation without apology—manifested the same anti-institutionalism. Thus, even more deeply disturbing than the lack of facts in cases of charges against academics, the anti-institutional character of the period denied professors. For they are indeed institutional, dependent on the university *qua* organization for survival. In fact, the credo of academic freedom, the 1940 Statement of Principles on Academic Freedom, is dependent upon the organizational action of individual colleges and universities. Determining the effect of McCarthy and McCarthyism on the professoriate is therefore dependent on determining the effect of an antithetical force.

A second disturbing feature of the historical narrative is the contradiction that effectiveness of the anti-institutionalism was dependent on institutional processes. In terms of McCarthyism and the professoriate, no better example exists than the 1953 statement by the Association of American Universities. The statement clearly identifies the university rather than any external process as responsible for investigating the professor. The AAU presidents were unambiguous in their desire to use institutional processes to investigate not only accused Communists but also those who exercised the Constitutional right of the Fifth Amendment, an essential defense against the attack without evidence as evidence (*Atlantic Monthly,* 1953). Anti-institutionalism found its meaning in the university as institution.

Nevertheless, there are substantial gaps in our understanding of McCarthyism and the professoriate. A variety of areas should command our further attention. There is a need to investigate further those cases at institutions such as Fairmont State College. Scholars need to learn more about those institutions with little or no declared interest in the protection of academic freedom and great interest in the service of the state. Alton Lee offers another example of an examination of a public institution serving the state in his examination of the University of South Dakota (1989). While counterpoints to the arguments that elite institutions generally protected their professors are instructive as to the enveloping nature of McCarthyism, colleges and universities more directly serving local constituencies may evidence more telling arguments about the force of McCarthyism inside as well as outside higher education. There are also instances of defenses at small liberal arts institutions such as Knox (*Journal of Higher Education,* 1953) and Colorado Colleges (Yaffe, 1986). Both of these institutions are located in states with strong conservative constituencies. To understand McCarthyism and the professoriate, the scholar needs to ask how such institutions fared, moving beyond issues at research universities to issues of national consequence; the institutional narratives, however, must acknowledge the national context as well as the disciplinary literature.

There is also the need to examine the role of the American Civil Liberties Union. A number of scholars allude to the ACLU but there is no full examination of that organization's role in McCarthyism and the professoriate. Despite the considerable treatment of the AAUP in many works, there also appears a need to investigate even further the actions of that organization. Its General Secretary, Ralph E. Himstead, is typically pictured, if not caricatured, as the villain in the years of Association inactivity (Holmes, 1989, pp. 163-167; Schrecker, 1986, p. 336). Important questions about the professorial leadership of the organization and the workload of the staff remain, however, largely unanswered. For example, Ralph Lutz wrote a letter urging the dismissal of Communist professors (Sanders, 1979, p. 98); Lutz was an AAUP leader. On the administrative burden, although Loya Metzger (1978) dismisses the problem as an issue of Himstead's personality, there may be serious questions about the rapid growth of the AAUP without concomitant staffing, especially during McCarthyism with its increased demand for the protection of professors. Finally, a year after Ralph Himstead's death, the Association's members approved a statement which was equivocal on the subject of professors' use of the Fifth Amendment (*AAUP Bulletin,* 1956).

There is a second stage of examination of McCarthy and McCarthyism in contextual terms of both analysis and issues of repression. One perspective could be the international. As Carl Kaestle has suggested, comparative historical studies have provided "generalizations...that reconciled previously contradictory generalizations" (1992, p. 365). It is time to begin comparative historical studies of academic freedom, despite the difficulties of comparing political events across national borders. One scholar has asked why indeed was there no McCarthy in England, a country with its own share of demagogues (Hixson, 1992, p. 6); the answer is not yet clear. Halsey and Trow (1971) offer one possible source of comparative historical understanding in their discussion of the strong relationship between the British government and professors in the late 1960s. In another supporting example, Byron Marshall (1992) offers evidence about the importance of the relationship between elites and the nature of academic freedom.

Other possible issues of comparative understanding (although not often framed that way) are the ones addressing ethnicity, gender, and sexuality. What about stories of those on the margin? While *This Nest of Vipers* begins the process of apprehending these stories, much more remains. In the disciplinary literature, scholars have suggested that McCarthyism linked accusations to differences. Richard Fried briefly examines the relationship between anti-Communism and racism in Senate races in the South (1976, pp. 95-101). Earl Latham points out that although the Communist Party highlighted the issue of race, there is little evidence of any African-American interest in the Communist Party (1966, pp. 23-27). Latham's comment highlights questions about any link between Communism and Blacks in the United States. Fried documents in another work, *Nightmare in Red*, state and federal officials' efforts to link integration and Communism and how American Indians' rights were subject to such attacks (1990, p. 169). Fried also notes links between anti-Communism and attacks on feminist reformers in the 1920s and the 1950s (pp. 43-44, 166-167). Finally, he documents the relationship between charges of Communism and homosexuals in the 1950s (pp. 167-168). Michael Miles also documents the relationship between such charges and homosexuals during the same period (1980, pp. 225-226).

The discussion of minorities is already evident in an examination of Catholics and McCarthyism; Crosby argues in *God, Church, and Flag* that "Catholics did in fact view themselves as an embattled minority" (1978, p. ix). There is now opportunity to expand the definition of minorities in McCarthyism, and hence our understanding of institutional protection or its absence, in the case of McCarthyism and the professoriate.

A final avenue of investigation, and perhaps one most disconcerting for the professoriate, would be an examination of McCarthyism and college students. Although not strictly an issue of the professoriate, it is of course difficult to separate professors and students. Despite an existing sentiment that college students were conservative or apathetic during the period, a number of anecdotal examples suggest that the sentiment is a facile interpretation. Even at Princeton, often described as an enclave of Republican wealth, students censured one of their own who vehemently attacked some students who were critical of McCarthy and McCarthyism (Meyer, 1952, pp. 316-318). Other examples include Hughes (1961, p. 474), Earnest (1953, pp. 337-338), Lipset (1975, pp. 189, 191, 197-204), and O'Brien—who notes that even Young Republicans at the University of Wisconsin were divided in their support for McCarthy (1980, pp. 195-196). MacIver reviewed students' defenses of professors, fellow students, and freedom of thought (1955, pp. 205-22). Finally, Sanders also briefly documents student political activity (1979, pp. 22, 130-131). While the anecdotes are perhaps thin, they are also clearly contrary to the conventional wisdom which suggests that college students in the 1950s were thoroughly and simply conservative. One author, in fact, argues that students in the late 1950s and early 1960s were more conservative than their predecessors in the early and middle 1950s (Evans, 1961).

In conclusion, what may be most troubling for the professor *qua* professor examining the issue of McCarthyism and the professoriate is the actual nature of the professoriate. While most scholars writing on the issue of McCarthyism and the professoriate acknowledge the tenuous nature of academic freedom, it is far less common in the literature to find expressions of concern about the acute vulnerability of the professoriate. It is apparent from the variety of examinations of

McCarthyism and the professoriate that academic freedom is ambiguous, subject to multiple definitions—even by those who supposedly subscribe to explicit statements such as the 1940 Statement of Principles on Academic Freedom and Tenure. The members of the Association of American Universities, elite research universities with *presumably* strong foundations for academic freedom, offered unanimous support for a document clearly violating policies and processes of the 1940 Statement. For an accurate historical point of view, the scholar must acknowledge that academic freedom has always been tenuous; such events as McCarthyism point to the ambiguous and tenuous nature of academic freedom, not that it is such only in times of crisis. This historiographical examination of McCarthyism and the professoriate notes as more important, however, professors' political condition: when those who can wield power choose to do so against professors, professors have little power to respond. It is not that McCarthyism or other popular movements critical of academe are ominous, but rather that the political condition of the professor is ominous. Politically vulnerable and organizationally dependent, the professoriate occupies a singular place in United States society, with autonomy granted but not secured.

## References

*AAUP Bulletin.* (1956). Academic freedom and tenure in the quest for national security, 42(1): 49-107.

Ambrose. C.M. (1990). Academic freedom in American public colleges and universities. *Review of Higher Education* 14(1): 5-32.

Anderson, J., and May, R.W. (1952). *McCarthy: The Man, the Senator, the "Ism".* Boston: Beacon Press.

*Atlantic Monthly.* (1953, June). The present danger: a report from the university presidents, pp. 44-46.

Benson, M.E. (1949, September 10). The right to demand scholars. *Saturday Review* 32: 34-35.

Buckley, W.F., Jr., and Bozell, L.B. (1954). *McCarthy and His Enemies: The Record and Its Meaning.* Chicago: H. Regnery Company.

Caplow, T., and McGee, R.J. (1958). *The Academic Marketplace.* Garden City, New York: Basic Books.

Cohn, R. (1968). *McCarthy.* New York: New American Library.

Cook, F.J. (1971). *The Nightmare Decade: The Life and Times of Senator Joe McCarthy.* New York: Random House.

Crosby, D.F., S.J. (1978). *God, Church, and Flag: Senator Joseph R. McCarthy and the Catholic Church 1950-1957.* Chapel Hill: University of North Carolina Press.

Diamond, S. (1992). *Compromised Campus: The Collaboration of Universities with the Intelligence Community, 1945-1955.* New York: Oxford University Press.

Earnest, E. *Academic Procession: An Informal History of the American College 1636 to 1953.* New York: Bobbs-Merrill Company, 1953.

Ewald, W.B., Jr. (1984). *Who Killed Joe McCarthy?.* New York: Simon and Schuster.

Evans, M.S. (1961). *Revolt on the Campus.* Chicago: Henry Regnery Company.

Ford Jr., S. (1954). *The McCarthy Menace: An Evaluation of the Facts and an Interpretation of the Evidence.* New York: William-Frederick Press.

Fried, R.M. (1976). *Men Against McCarthy*. New York: Columbia University Press.

Fried, R.M. (1990). *Nightmare in Red: The McCarthy Era in Perspective*. New York: Oxford University Press.

Gardner, D.P. (1967). *The California Oath Controversy*. Berkeley: University of California Press.

Goodchild, L.F., and Huk, I.P. (1990). The American college history: a survey of its historiographic schools and analytical approaches from the mid-nineteenth century to the present. In J.C. Smart (ed.), *Higher Education: Handbook of Theory and Practice* v. 6, New York: Agathon Press.

Griffith, R. (1971). The political context of McCarthyism. *The Review of Politics* 33: 24-35.

Griffith, R. (1987). *The Politics of Fear: Joseph R. McCarthy and the Senate*. Amherst: University of Massachusetts, 1987, second edition.

Gruber, C. (1975). *Mars and Minerva: World War I and the Uses of the Higher Learning in America*. Baton Rouge, Louisiana: Louisiana State University Press.

Halsey, A.H., and Trow, M.A. (1971). *The British Academics*. Cambridge, Massachusetts: Harvard University Press.

Hixson, W.B., Jr. (1992). *Search for the American Right Wing: An Analysis of the Social Science Record, 1955-1987*. Princeton: Princeton University Press.

Hofstadter, R. (1963). *Anti-intellectualism in American Life*. New York: Alfred A. Knopf.

Hofstadter, R. (1955). The pseudo-conservative revolt. In D. Bell (ed.), *The New American Right*. New York: Criterion Books.

Hofstadter, R., and Metzger, W.P. (1955). *The Development of Academic Freedom in the United States*. New York: Columbia University Press.

Holmes, D.R. (1989). *Stalking the Academic Communist: Intellectual Freedom and the Firing of Alex Novikoff*. Hanover, New Hampshire: University Press of New England.

Hook, S. (1949, February 27). Should Communists be permitted to teach? *New York Times Magazine*. pp. 7, 22-29.

Hughes, H.S. (1961). Why we had no Dreyfus case. *American Scholar* 30: 473-479.

Hutson, S.H. (ed.) (1978). *McCarthy and the Anti-Communist Crusade: A Selected Bibliography*. Los Angeles: Center for the Study of Armament and Disarmament, California State University Los Angeles.

*Journal of Higher Education* (1953). Editorial comments: Academic freedom versus intellectual freedom, 24(7): 442-443, 452.

Kaestle, C. (1992) Standards of evidence in historical research: How do we know when we know? *History of Education Quarterly* 32(3): 361-366.

Ladd, E.C., Jr., and Lipset, S.M. (1975). *The Divided Academy: Professors and Politics*. New York: McGraw-Hill Book Company.

Landis, M. (1987). *Joseph McCarthy: The Politics of Chaos*. Selinsgrove: Susquehanna University Press.

Latham, E. (1966). *The Communist Controversy in Washington: From the New Deal to McCarthy*. Cambridge: Harvard University Press.

Lazarsfeld, P.F., and Thielens, W., Jr. (1958). *The Academic Mind: Social Scientists in a Time of Crisis*. Glencoe, Illinois: The Free Press.

Lee, R.A. (1989). McCarthyism at the University of South Dakota, *South Dakota History* 19(3): 424-438.

Lewis, L.S. (1988). *Cold War on Campus: A Study of the Politics of Organizational Control*. New Brunswick, New Jersey: Transaction Books.

Lewis, L.S. (1993). *The Cold War and Academic Governance: The Lattimore Case at Johns Hopkins*. Albany: State University Press of New York.

Lipset, S.M. (1955). The sources of the "radical right." In D. Bell (ed.), *The New Ameri-*

*can Right* New York: Criterion Books.

Lipset, S.M. (1975). Political controversies at Harvard, 1636 to 1974. In S.M. Lipset and D. Riesman (eds.), *Education and Politics at Harvard.* New York: McGraw-Hill Book Company.

MacIver, R.M. (1955). *Academic Freedom in Our Time.* New York: Columbia University Press.

Marshall, B.K. (1992). *Academic Freedom and the Japanese Imperial University, 1860-1939.* Berkeley: University of California Press.

McCarthy, J.R. (1952). *McCarthyism: The Fight for America.* New York: Devin-Adair Company.

McCormick, C.H. (1989). *This Nest of Vipers: McCarthyism and Higher Education in the Mundel Affair, 1951-52.* Urbana: University of Illinois Press.

Meyer, K.E. (1952, April 5). McCarthy at Princeton. *Nation.* pp. 316-318.

Metzger, L. (1978). Professors in trouble: a quantitative analysis of academic freedom and tenure cases. Unpublished Ph.D. dissertation, Columbia University.

Miles, M. (1980). *The Odyssey of the American Right.* New York: Oxford University Press.

Mulcahy, R.P. (1986). Facing the American inquisition: responses to McCarthyism. *Maryland Historian* 17(2): 1-7.

Novick, P. (1988). *That Noble Dream: The "Objectivity Question" and the American Historical Profession.* New York: Cambridge University Press.

O'Brien, M. (1980). *McCarthy and McCarthyism in Wisconsin.* Columbia, Missouri: University of Missouri Press.

Oshinsky, D.M. (1976). *Senator Joseph McCarthy and the American Labor Movement.* Columbia, Missouri: University of Missouri Press.

Polsby, N.W. (1983). Down Memory Lane with Joe McCarthy. *Commentary* 75(2): 55-59.

Reeves, T.C. (1982). *The Life and Times of Joe McCarthy: A Biography.* New York: Stein and Day.

Rogin, M.P. (1967). *The Intellectuals and McCarthy: The Radical Specter.* Cambridge: M.I.T. Press.

Rorty, J., and Decter, M. (1954). *McCarthy and the Communists.* Boston: Beacon Press.

Rovere, R.H. (1959). *Senator Joe McCarthy.* London: Methuen & Co., Ltd.

Sanders, J. (1979). *Cold War on the Campus: Academic Freedom at the University of Washington, 1946-1964.* Seattle, University of Washington Press.

Schrecker, E. (1986). *No Ivory Tower: McCarthyism and the Universities.* New York: Oxford University Press.

Schrecker, E. (1994). *The Age of McCarthyism: A Brief History with Documents.* Boston: Bedford Books of St. Martin's Press.

Slaughter, S. (1980). The danger zone: Academic freedom and civil liberties. *Annals of the American Academy of Political and Social Science* 448: 46-61.

Slaughter, S. (1981). Political action, faculty autonomy and retrenchment: A decade of academic freedom, 1970-1980. In P. G. Altbach and R. O. Berdahl (eds.), *Higher Education in American Society* (1st ed.). Buffalo: Prometheus Books.

Slaughter, S. (1987). Academic freedom in the modern university. In P. G. Altbach and R. O. Berdahl (eds.), *Higher Education in American Society* (2nd ed.). Buffalo: Prometheus Books.

Slaughter, S. (1994). Academic freedom at the end of the century: Professional labor, gender, and professionalism. In P. G. Altbach, R. O. Berdahl, and P.J. Gumport (eds.), *Higher Education in American Society* (3rd ed.). Buffalo: Prometheus Books.

Stewart, G.R. (1950). *The Year of the Oath: The Fight for Academic Freedom at the University of California.* Garden City, New York: Doubleday & Company.

Taylor, H. (1955) The dismissal of Fifth Amendment professors. *The Annals of the American Academy of Political and Social Sciences* 300: 79-86.

Theoharis, A.G. (1971). *Seeds of Repression: Harry S Truman and the Origins of McCarthyism.* Chicago: Quadrangle Press.

Trow, M. (1958). Small businessmen, political tolerance, and support for McCarthy. *American Journal of Sociology* 44: 270-281.

Van Alstyne, W. (1972). The specific theory of academic freedom and the general issue of civil liberty. In E.L. Pincoffs (ed.), *The Concept of Academic Freedom.* Austin, Texas: University of Texas Press.

Veysey, L. (1965). *The Emergence of the American University.* Chicago: University of Chicago Press.

Watkins, A.V. (1969). *Enough Rope.* Englewood Cliffs, New Jersey: Prentice-Hall.

Wiebe, R.H. (1977). Modernizing the Republic. In B. Bailyn (ed.), *The Great Republic: A History of the American People* Lexington, Massachusetts: Heath Press.

Wolfe, A. (1981) Sociology, liberalism, and the radical right. *New Left Review* 128: 3-27.

Woodward, C.V. (1960) The Populist heritage and the intellectual. *American Scholar* 29: 55-72.

Yaffe, E. (1986, January). Days of suspicion—acts of courage. *Colorado College Bulletin*: 5-8.

# Author Index

# Subject Index

# Contents of Previous Volumes

**and Designs** John W. Creswell, *University of Nebraska-Lincoln*, Lester F. Goodchild, *University of Denver*, and Paul P. Turner, *University of Nebraska-Lincoln*
**Developments in State Funding for Higher Education** Daniel T. Layzell, *The University of Wisconsin System*
**Gender and Academic Publishing** Kathryn B. Ward, *Southern Illinois University*, and Linda Grant, *University of Georgia*
**The Dimensionality of Student Ratings of Instruction: What We Know and What We Do Not** Philip C. Abrami, Sylvia d'Apollonia, and Steven Rosenfield, *Concordia University*
**Organizational Effectiveness and Quality: The Second Generation** Kim S. Cameron and David Whetten, *Brigham Young University*
**Theory and Research in Administrative Leadership** Cameron Fincher, *University of Georgia*
**Governments, Governance, and Canadian Universities** Glen A. Jones, *Ontario Institute for Studies in Education*
**Doctoral Programs in American Higher Education** Jennifer Grant Haworth, *Loyola University Chicago*
**Author and Subject Indexes**
1996: 464 pages   ISBN 0-87586-115-6

*Order from:*
Agathon Press
100 Newfield Avenue
Edison, NJ 08837
TEL (908) 225-2727  FAX (908) 225-1552